NEW

FOUNDATION GCSE MATHEMATICS

Revision and Practice

Mark Bindley

OXFORD

OXFORD
UNIVERSITY PRESS
Great Clarendon Street, Oxford OX2 6DP

Oxford University Press is a department of the University of Oxford.
It furthers the University's objective of excellence in research, scholarship,
and education by publishing worldwide in

Oxford New York

Athens Auckland Bangkok Bogotá Buenos Aires Calcutta
Cape Town Chennai Dar es Salaam Delhi Florence Hong Kong Istanbul
Karachi Kuala Lumpur Madrid Melbourne Mexico City Mumbai
Nairobi Paris São Paulo Shanghai Singapore Taipei Tokyo Toronto Warsaw
with associated companies in Berlin Ibadan

Oxford is a registered trade mark of Oxford University Press
in the UK and in certain other countries

© Mark Bindley 2001

10 9 8 7 6 5 4 3 2 1

The moral rights of the authors have been asserted

Database right Oxford University Press (maker)

First published 2001

All rights reserved. No part of this publication may be reproduced,
stored in a retrieval system, or transmitted, in any form or by any means,
without the prior permission in writing of Oxford University Press,
or as expressly permitted by law, or under terms agreed with the appropriate
reprographics rights organisation. Enquiries concerning reproduction
outside the scope of the above should be sent to the Rights Department,
Oxford University Press, at the above address

You must not circulate this book in any other binding or cover
and you must impose this same condition on any acquirer

British Library Cataloguing in Publication Data

Data available

ISBN 0 19 914793 0 (School edition)
ISBN 0 19 914794 9 (Bookshop edition)

The photograph on page 176 is reproduced courtesy of Quadrant Picture Agency.
The Escher drawing on page 307 is reproduced courtesy of Cordon Art.

Cartoons by Martin Aston

Typeset by TechSet Ltd., Gateshead, Tyne and Wear
Printed and bound in Great Britain by Butler & Tanner Ltd. Frome and London

To the Teacher or Parent:

This book has been written for students working towards an entry at Foundation Level in GCSE Mathematics. The book prepares students for both non-calculator and calculator examination papers.

The book is divide into twenty units, each covering a range of mathematical skills. Each skill is introduced with explanations and worked examples. These are followed with carefully structured exercises to help students practice and gain confidence in their new mathematical skill.

At the beginning of each unit there is a short revision section to remind students of some skills they have already learned and will need in the unit. Each unit ends with a revision and self-test section followed by an extensive collection of past paper questions. These sections can be used immediately a unit is finished to check and consolidate a full understanding of the mathematics at examination level. The sections can also be used in the period before the final examination as an excellent resource for revision of the whole course.

The final unit provides advice and practice for coursework. This is divided into two sections, one for coursework based on general mathematical investigations, the other for coursework based on data handing tasks.

The book is designed to be used either as a course book over two or three years before the final examination or as a one year revision course. The author believes it a major advantage to have the whole course in one book. Students gain a clear picture of the work to be covered and, immediately prior to the examination, have access to a full revision guide for every topic that has been taught.

To the Student:

If you work hard and study all the sections in this book you will be well prepared to do your best in the final examination. It is especially important to work through all the end of unit revision sections again in the weeks just before the examination. Try to do as many of the past paper questions as you can because these will prepare you for the style of a GCSE examination.

Organise all the things that will make you feel comfortable in the examination. Make sure you have all the equipment you need plus spares for things like pens and calculators which can go wrong. What about a cushion and a mascot? If your school allows them, how about some mints to aid concentration?

If you are well prepared you will actually enjoy the examination because you will be demonstrating all the mathematical skills and knowledge you have worked hard to master.

Contents

1	**Number 1**	**1–33**
1.1	Place value in whole numbers	2
1.2	Writing numbers in figures and words	3
1.3	Approximation to the nearest 10	5
1.4	Approximation to the nearest 100	7
1.5	Approximation to the nearest 1000	8
1.6	Approximation to one significant figure	10
1.7	The addition table	11
1.8	Adding whole numbers 'in your head'	12
1.9	Subtracting whole numbers 'in your head'	14
1.10	Adding whole numbers with written calculations	17
1.11	Subtracting whole numbers with written calculations	19
1.12	Temperature	20
1.13	Temperature changes	21
1.14	Adding negative numbers	23
1.15	Subtracting negative numbers	24
1.16	Going overdrawn	25
1.17	Time	26
	Summary	27
	Revision exercise 1	29

2	**Shape and Space 1**	**34–55**
2.1	Turning	35
2.2	Turning through an angle	36
2.3	The protractor	37
2.4	Measuring angles, acute and obtuse angles	38
2.5	Drawing angles	40
2.6	Naming angles	41
2.7	Drawing triangles	43
2.8	Scale drawing	45
2.9	Bearings	48
	Summary	52
	Revision exercise 2	53

3	**Data Handling 1**	**56–69**
3.1	Designing a survey to collect data	57
3.2	Using tally marks and drawing bar charts	59
3.3	Pictograms	63
	Summary	65
	Revision exercise 3	65

4	**Number 2**	**70–102**
4.1	Multiplying numbers by 10	71
4.2	Multiplying numbers by 100	72
4.3	Multiplying numbers by 1000	73
4.4	Dividing numbers by 10	74
4.5	Dividing numbers by 100	75
4.6	Dividing numbers to 1000	76
4.7	The multiplication table	77
4.8	Multiplying numbers 'in your head'	78
4.9	Dividing numbers 'in your head'	79

4.10	Using division by 10, 100 or 1000 to divide numbers 'in your head'	81
4.11	Multiplying by single-digit numbers with written calculations	82
4.12	Multiplying by two-digit numbers with written calculations	83
4.13	Dividing by single-digit numbers with written calculations	84
4.14	Dividing by two-digit numbers with written calculations	86
4.15	Factors, even numbers, odd numbers, prime numbers and multiples	87
4.16	Highest common factor	88
4.17	Lowest common multiple (LCM)	89
4.18	Ratios	89
4.19	Scaling up or down from a ratio	91
4.20	Dividing quantities in a ratio	93
4.21	Squares and square roots	95
	Summary	96
	Revision exercise 4	98

5	**Algebra 1**	**103–124**
5.1	Using letters to represent quantities in addition and subtraction problems	104
5.2	Using letters to represent quantities in multiplication and division problems	105
5.3	Formulae	107
5.4	Substitution	109
5.5	Substitution involving BoDMAS	110
5.6	Substitution involving powers	112
5.7	Substitution with negative numbers	114
5.8	Substitution in formulae	115
5.9	Collecting like terms	117
5.10	Simplifying with different types of term	118
5.11	More simplification	119
	Summary	120
	Revision exercise 5	122

6	**Shape and Space 2**	**125–134**
6.1	Two- and three-dimensional shapes	126
6.2	Nets	127
6.3	Isometric drawings	129
6.4	Plans and elevations	131
	Summary	132
	Revision exercise 6	133

7	**Data Handling 2**	**135–154**
7.1	The mean and the range of a distribution	136
7.2	The median and the range of a distribution	138
7.3	Stem-and-leaf plots	140
7.4	The mode	141
7.5	Finding the mean, the median, the mode and the range	143
7.6	Data in tables	145
	Summary	148
	Revision exercise 7	150

8	**Number 3**	**155–175**
8.1	Place value in decimal numbers: Tenths	156
8.2	Ordering decimal numbers: Tenths	157
8.3	Place value in decimal numbers: Hundredths	158
8.4	Ordering decimal numbers: Hundredths	160
8.5	Place value in decimal numbers: Thousandths	161

8.6	Approximating decimal numbers: Nearest whole number	163
8.7	Approximating decimal numbers: Nearest tenth	164
8.8	Approximating decimal numbers: Nearest hundredth	165
8.9	Adding decimal numbers 'in your head'	166
8.10	Adding decimal numbers with written calculations	168
8.11	Subtracting decimal numbers 'in your head'	169
8.12	Subtracting decimal numbers with written calculations	170
	Summary	172
	Revision exercise 8	173

9	**Shape and Space 3**	**176–197**
9.1	Lines and angles	177
9.2	Opposite angles	179
9.3	Parallel lines and angles	180
9.4	Angles in triangles	181
9.5	Types of triangle	183
9.6	Quadrilaterals	184
9.7	Polygons	187
9.8	Angle sum of a polygon	189
	Summary	190
	Revision exercise 9	193

10	**Number 4**	**198–219**
10.1	Multiplying decimal numbers by 10	199
10.2	Multiplying decimal numbers by 100	200
10.3	Multiplying decimal numbers by 1000	201
10.4	Dividing decimal numbers by 10	202
10.5	Dividing decimal numbers by 100	203
10.6	Dividing decimal numbers by 1000	204
10.7	Multiplying decimal numbers 'in your head'	206
10.8	Multiplying decimal numbers with written calculations	207
10.9	Dividing decimal numbers without a calculator	109
10.10	Recurring decimals	210
10.11	Multiplying decimal numbers with a calculator	211
10.12	Dividing decimal numbers with a calculator	212
10.13	Metric and Imperial measure	213
	Summary	214
	Revision exercise 10	216

11	**Algebra 2**	**220–240**
11.1	Multiplying negative numbers	221
11.2	Dividing negative numbers	221
11.3	Multiplying letter terms by number terms	222
11.4	Multiplying letter terms by letter terms	223
11.5	Expanding brackets with a number term outside	223
11.6	Expanding and simplifying	224
11.7	Expanding brackets with a letter term outside	224
11.8	Expanding brackets with negative terms	225
11.9	Factorisation by extracting a number term outside a bracket	225
11.10	Factorisation by extracting a letter term outside a bracket	226
11.11	Solving equations by subtracting	226
11.12	Solving equations by adding	227
11.13	Solving equations by dividing	228
11.14	Solving equations by multiplying	229

11.15	Equations which require several operations to solve them	231
11.16	Equations with brackets	232
11.17	Equations with letter terms on both sides	233
11.18	Changing the subject of formulae	234
	Summary	235
	Revision exercise 11	237

12 Number 5   240–267

12.1	Understanding fractions	241
12.2	Improper fractions and mixed numbers	243
12.3	Equivalent fractions	243
12.4	Making pairs of equivalent fractions	245
12.5	Simplifying fractions	246
12.6	Adding fractions from the same family	247
12.7	Subtracting fractions with the same denominator	248
12.8	Adding and subtracting fractions with different denominations	249
12.9	Multiplying by fractions and fractions of a quantity	250
12.10	Percentages and fractions	252
12.11	Percentages of quantities	253
12.12	Fractions, percentages and decimals	255
12.13	Writing one number as a percentage of another	256
12.14	Increasing and decreasing an amount by a given percentage	258
	Summary	259
	Revision exercise 12	260

13 Algebra 3   268–306

13.1	Producing a sequence of numbers	269
13.2	Finding the next terms in a sequence	269
13.3	Using a formula for the nth term of a sequence	270
13.4	Using differences	271
13.5	Sequences based on patterns	273
13.6	Coordinates	276
13.7	Coordinates in four quadrants	280
13.8	Drawing a graph of a linear equation	282
13.9	Graphs of equations which produce curves	287
13.10	Using graphs to illustrate relationships	291
13.11	Distance and time graphs	295
	Summary	298
	Revision exercise 13	300

14 Shape and Space 4   307–331

14.1	Transformations	308
14.2	Reflections	311
14.3	Rotations	314
14.4	Reflectional symmetry	317
14.5	Rotational symmetry	318
14.6	Enlargements	321
14.7	Fractional enlargements	322
	Summary	325
	Revision exercise 14	327

15 Data Handling 3   332–354

15.1	Grouped data, bar charts and frequency polygons	333
15.2	Pie charts drawn with a protractor	337

15.3	Pie charts drawn with a pie chart scale	342
15.4	Reading information from pie charts	345
	Summary	347
	Revision exercise 15	351

16 Shape and Space 5 — 355–373
16.1	Perimeters	356
16.2	Area by counting squares	358
16.3	Area of a rectangle by calculation	360
16.4	Areas of shapes made from rectangles	362
16.5	Area of a parallelogram	363
16.6	Area of a triangle	365
16.7	Area of a compound shape	367
	Summary	369
	Revision exercise 16	371

17 Data Handling 4 — 374–385
17.1	Variables	375
17.2	Correlation	376
17.3	Scatter diagrams	377
17.4	Line of best fit	381
	Summary	382
	Revision exercise 17	383

18 Shape and Space 6 — 386–405
18.1	The radius and diameter of a circle	387
18.2	Finding the circumference if you know the diameter or radius	387
18.3	Finding the area if you know the radius	390
18.4	Finding the surface area of a cuboid	393
18.5	Finding volume by counting cubes	395
18.6	Finding the volume of a cuboid by using the formula	396
18.7	Finding the volume of a prism	398
	Summary	401
	Revision exercise 18	403

19 Data Handling 5 — 406–424
19.1	Simple probability	407
19.2	Probabilities of 0 and 1	410
19.3	Probability scales	412
19.4	Probabilities when two things happen	414
	Summary	419
	Revision exercise 19	420

20 Coursework advice — 425–434
20.1	Mathematical investigations	425
20.2	Data handling tasks	430

Answers — 435–486

Index — 487–488

1 Number 1

People use numbers everyday, particularly when spending money!

This unit is about:

- Place value in whole numbers
- Writing numbers in figures and words
- Approximating whole numbers
- Adding whole numbers
- Subtracting whole numbers
- Negative numbers
- Adding negative numbers
- Subtracting negative numbers

1.1 Place value in whole numbers

Dry Gulch had a population of 5 127 people.

The number	5 127 has four digits.
The **5** digit represents	**5 000** people
The **1** digit represents	**100** people
The **2** digit represents	**20** people
The **7** digit represents	**7** people

After the gold ran out, Dry Gulch became a ghost town and the sign had to be changed.

In	1 275:
The **1** digit represents	**1 000** people
The **2** digit represents	**200** people
The **7** digit represents	**70** people
The **5** digit represents	**5** people

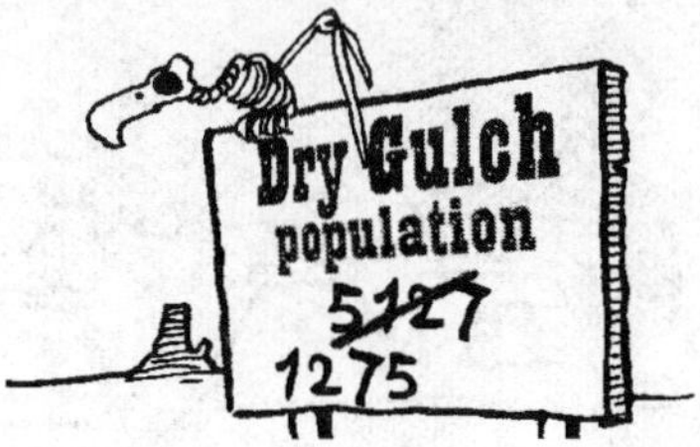

After oil was discovered the town sign was changed again.

In	7 512:
The **7** digit represents	**7 000** people
The **5** digit represents	**500** people
The **1** digit represents	**10** people
The **2** digit represents	**2** people

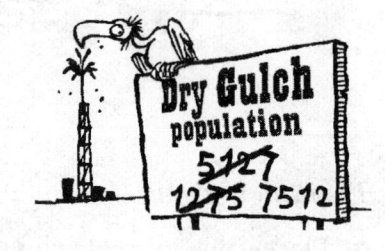

Exercise 1A

1. What does the underlined digit represent in each of these numbers?

   (a) 3<u>4</u>5 (b) 67<u>5</u> (c) <u>8</u>03 (d) 80<u>3</u> (e) 8<u>0</u>3
   (f) 1 <u>2</u>91 (g) <u>3</u> 905 (h) 2 2<u>2</u>2 (i) 7 38<u>4</u> (j) <u>6</u> 073
   (k) 3 <u>0</u>57 (l) 5 67<u>8</u> (m) 3 <u>3</u>75 (n) 9 1<u>7</u>9 (o) <u>2</u> 135
   (p) 6 22<u>1</u> (q) 5 6<u>6</u>4 (r) 1 <u>9</u>99 (s) <u>3</u> 212 (t) 8 21<u>0</u>

In Questions **2** to **9**, write down the value represented by each digit of the number.

2. 348 people saved as a boat sinks.

3. 903 pigeons lost after a race in stormy weather.

4. 2 658 students pass a new examination.

5. 7 190 cars cross to Calais in one day.

6. 3 527 dogs entered for a show.

7. 1 411 cats caught in a ruined building.

8. 8 006 fish stolen from a garden centre.

9. 12 467 people attend a home game.

10. Using the digits 5, 8 and 2, different three-digit numbers can be made like 528, 285 and 852.
    (a) Write down all the three-digit numbers you can make with 5, 8 and 2.
    (b) Write your numbers in order, from the smallest to the largest.

11. Using the digits 7, 3 and 9, different three-digit numbers can be made like 379, 739 and 937.
    (a) Write down all the three-digit numbers you can make with 7, 3 and 9.
    (b) Write your numbers in order, from the smallest to the largest.

12. Using the digits 1, 0, 6 and 4, different four-digit numbers can be made like 1 604, 6 041 and 4 160.
    (a) Write down all the four-digit numbers you can make with 1, 0, 6 and 4.
    (b) Write your numbers in order, from the smallest to the largest.

1.2 Writing numbers in figures and words

You need to know these numbers in words:

1	2	3	4	5	6	7	8	9
one	two	three	four	five	six	seven	eight	nine

11	12	13	14	15	16	17	18	19
eleven	twelve	thirteen	fourteen	fifteen	sixteen	seventeen	eighteen	nineteen

10	20	30	40	50	60	70	80	90
ten	twenty	thirty	forty	fifty	sixty	seventy	eighty	ninety

100	1 000	1 000 000
one hundred	one thousand	one million

You can use these numbers to write large numbers in words.

4 Number 1

Example

Write these numbers in words:

(a) 234   (b) 4 743   (c) 57 690

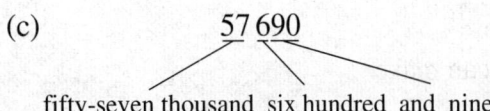

(a) 234 — two hundred and thirty-four

(b) 4 743 — four thousand seven hundred and forty-three

(c) 57 690 — fifty-seven thousand six hundred and ninety

Exercise 1B

1. Write each number in figures.
   (a) Three hundred and seventy-four.
   (b) Two hundred and eleven.
   (c) Five hundred and forty-eight.
   (d) Six hundred and nine.
   (e) Seven hundred and sixty.
   (f) One hundred and twenty-five.
   (g) Three thousand seven hundred and fifteen.
   (h) Six thousand four hundred and nineteen.
   (i) Fourteen thousand nine hundred and ninety.
   (j) Seventeen thousand eight hundred and fifty-four.
   (k) Twenty-four thousand five hundred and nineteen.
   (l) Forty-eight thousand six hundred and sixty.
   (m) Eighty-six thousand eight hundred and eighty-six.
   (n) Sixty-eight thousand and sixty-eight.
   (o) Ninety-two thousand and three.
   (p) Two hundred and twelve thousand one hundred and thirteen.
   (q) Three hundred and eighteen thousand seven hundred and sixteen.
   (r) Six hundred and eight thousand three hundred and thirty-nine.
   (s) Five hundred and eighty thousand two hundred and ninety-seven.
   (t) Six hundred thousand four hundred and four.

2. Write each number in words.
   (a) 358   (b) 217   (c) 677   (d) 469   (e) 111
   (f) 2 519   (g) 6 085   (h) 9 801   (i) 7 442   (j) 5 613
   (k) 15 723   (l) 18 459   (m) 34 098   (n) 67 112   (o) 10 111
   (p) 231 214   (q) 616 270   (r) 109 710   (s) 100 000   (t) 857 243

Approximation to the nearest 10 **5**

3. John is doing a project on trees' heights. He has collected this data.

Beech 161 ft
Sitka Spruce 216 ft
Giant Sequoia 272 ft
Ponderosa Pine 223 ft
Californian Redwood 366 ft
Black Cottonwood 147 ft

Douglas Fir 302 ft
Western Larch 177 ft
Noble Fir 278 ft
Hemlock 163 ft
Cedar 219 ft

John writes a list of trees in order of size. He writes the heights in words. Write out John's list, starting with:

Californian Redwood: Three hundred and sixty-six feet.

4. Zeelam has collected this data about the diameter of the Sun and the planets.

Sun 865 500 miles
Earth 7 962 miles
Saturn 74 600 miles
Neptune 30 800 miles
Mercury 3 032 miles

Mars 4 217 miles
Venus 7 521 miles
Jupiter 88 700 miles
Uranus 32 200 miles
Pluto 3 700 miles

Write Zeelam's list in order, starting with the smallest diameter. Write all the diameters in words.

|←— 7 962 miles —→|

1.3 Approximation to the nearest 10

There are 33 passengers on this bus

33 is nearer 30 than 40

There are 37 passengers on this bus

37 is nearer 40 than 30

There are 35 passengers on this bus

35 is exactly halfway between 30 and 40

To the nearest 10 ...

There are 30 people on the bus

There are 40 people on the bus

There are 40 people on the bus

Remember: If the number is halfway, you always round up.

The exact number of CDs could be either:

45, 46, 47, 48, 49, 50, 51, 52, 53 or 54.

If you had 55 CDs, you'd round the number up to 60.

Exercise 1C

1. Approximate each of these numbers to the nearest 10.

    (a) 13 (b) 17 (c) 11 (d) 28 (e) 26
    (f) 21 (g) 44 (h) 48 (i) 45 (j) 59
    (k) 53 (l) 55 (m) 75 (n) 72 (o) 76
    (p) 91 (q) 95 (r) 99 (s) 59 (t) 85

2. Approximate each of these numbers to the nearest 10.

    (a) 255 (b) 254 (c) 256 (d) 323 (e) 487
    (f) 136 (g) 135 (h) 134 (i) 797 (j) 973
    (k) 308 (l) 305 (m) 304 (n) 214 (o) 217
    (p) 594 (q) 595 (r) 793 (s) 898 (t) 996

3. A keen supporter says,
   'To the nearest 10, I have 60 players' autographs'.

   From this list, write down all the numbers which could not be the exact number of autographs.

   63, 57, 54, 65, 55, 64, 59, 69, 52, 60

4. Make a list of all the exact numbers that each statement could represent.

    (a) To the nearest 10, I own 80 videos.
    (b) To the nearest 10, there are 130 passengers on the boat.
    (c) To the nearest 10, I own 300 books.
    (d) To the nearest 10, there are 360 shopping days left before Christmas.
    (e) To the nearest 10, there are 1 000 students at this school.

1.4 Approximation to the nearest 100

Larger numbers can be rounded to the nearest 100.

828 is closer to 800 than 900

872 is closer to 900 than 800

Numbers in the middle are always rounded up

To the nearest 100 …

… 828 is 800   … 872 is 900   … 850 is 900

If a store manager said, 'To the nearest 100, we sold 700 Christmas Cards last week', then the exact number of cards sold could be any number between 650 and 749.

Exercise 1D

1. Approximate each of these numbers to the nearest 100.

   (a) 334   (b) 567   (c) 872   (d) 450   (e) 449
   (f) 451   (g) 752   (h) 725   (i) 750   (j) 619
   (k) 243   (l) 257   (m) 250   (n) 760   (o) 748
   (p) 683   (q) 545   (r) 554   (s) 913   (t) 950

2. Approximate each of these numbers to the nearest 100.

   (a) 999   (b) 1 356   (c) 1 365   (d) 1 342   (e) 1 309
   (f) 1 635   (g) 3 429   (h) 4 349   (i) 4 371   (j) 8 087
   (k) 5 031   (l) 5 099   (m) 5 050   (n) 3 789   (o) 3 923
   (p) 2 987   (q) 7 950   (r) 8 950   (s) 8 949   (t) 12 999

3. A bingo club manager says, 'To the nearest 100, there are 600 people here tonight'. From this list, write down the numbers which could not be the exact number of people.

   600, 611, 550, 660, 581, 518, 650, 549, 590, 649

8 Number 1

4. The statement, 'To the nearest 100, there are 1 500 people in the theatre', means that the exact number of people could be any number between 1 450 and 1 549. For each statement write down the two numbers that the approximation could be between.

(a) To the nearest 100, there are 200 nails in the packet.
(b) To the nearest 100, there are 500 tickets available.
(c) To the nearest 100, there are 800 students attending this school.
(d) To the nearest 100, there are 2 900 spectators watching the game.
(e) To the nearest 100, there are 55 600 voters in this constituency.

5. Alisha collected this data on the areas (in square miles) of the ten largest islands in the world:

Ellesmere (Canada) 81 930   Greenland 840 000
Great Britain 88 756   Borneo 286 967
Victoria (Canada) 82 119   Honshu (Japan) 88 930
New Guinea 316 856   Baffin (Canada) 183 810
Madagascar 227 000   Sumatra 182 866

Write out a list of the islands in order of size, starting with the largest. Write each island's area correct to the nearest 100 square miles.

1.5 Approximation to the nearest 1 000

Much larger numbers can be rounded to the nearest 1 000.

55 897 people attend a football match. A newspaper reports, '56 000 watch United beat Rangers'.
55 897 is closer to 56 000 than to 55 000.

If 55 223 people attend the match, the report would be, '55 000 watch United beat Rangers'.
55 223 is closer to 55 000 than to 56 000.

Remember that numbers in the middle are always rounded up.
If 55 500 people attend the match, the report would be, '56 000 watch United beat Rangers'.

If a magazine publisher says,
'To the nearest 1 000, we sell 65 000 copies every week', then the exact number of copies sold could be any number between 64 500 and 65 499.

Exercise 1E

1. Approximate each of these numbers to the nearest 1 000.
   (a) 3 860   (b) 2 113   (c) 1 925   (d) 1 213
   (e) 1 500   (f) 6 278   (g) 5 750   (h) 6 311
   (i) 4 591   (j) 7 500   (k) 8 490   (l) 6 499
   (m) 2 500   (n) 7 501   (o) 6 606   (p) 7 199
   (q) 9 483   (r) 9 500   (s) 9 678   (t) 9 999

2. Approximate each of these numbers to the nearest 1 000.
   (a) 10 678   (b) 18 390   (c) 19 500   (d) 12 399
   (e) 15 939   (f) 25 499   (g) 59 501   (h) 23 500
   (i) 32 259   (j) 21 529   (k) 45 188   (l) 25 678
   (m) 500 900   (n) 235 289   (o) 567 730   (p) 234 156
   (q) 349 500   (r) 499 500   (s) 999 500   (t) 949 678

3. The statement, 'To the nearest 1 000 square kilometres, the area of Lake Superior is 82 000 square kilometres', means that the exact area is between 81 500 square kilometres and 82 499 square kilometres.

   For each statement write down the two numbers that the approximation could be between.

   To the nearest 1 000:
   (a) there are 6 000 students in this University.
   (b) there are 5 000 secondary schools in England.
   (c) the distance from England to New Zealand is 19 000 miles.
   (d) there are 55 000 voters in this constituency.

4. Simon collected this data on the attendances at 10 football matches.

   Arsenal 38 098   Manchester United 55 216
   Everton 39 206   Wimbledon 10 106
   Middlesbrough 34 626   Coventry 23 098
   Southampton 15 253   Newcastle 36 783
   Blackburn 27 536   Sheffield Wednesday 33 513

   Write out a list of attendances in order of size, starting with the smallest. Round each attendance to the nearest 1 000 spectators.

1.6 Approximation to one significant figure

In the number 5 283, the digit 5 has the greatest value, 5 000.

5 is the most **significant figure**.

In the number 12 345, the digit 1 has the greatest value, 10 000.

1 is the most **significant figure**.

You can give any number approximated to one significant figure.

Examples

    23 is   20 to 1 s.f.
    65 is   70 to 1 s.f.
   268 is 300 to 1 s.f.
4 394 is 4 000 to 1 s.f.
55 897 is 60 000 to 1 s.f.

Hint:
s.f. is short for significant figure.

Remember:
If the second digit is 5 or more you round up.

Exercise 1F
Write each number correct to 1 significant figure:

1. 17
2. 24
3. 36
4. 43
5. 57
6. 75
7. 72
8. 85
9. 92
10. 99
11. 130
12. 183
13. 247
14. 283
15. 321
16. 389
17. 490
18. 409
19. 686
20. 668
21. 1 325
22. 2 341
23. 3 684
24. 5 099
25. 6 832
26. 7 500
27. 8 300
28. 5 628
29. 15 431
30. 14 531

1.7 The addition table

This table shows all the additions from $1 + 1$ to $10 + 10$.

+	1	2	3	4	5	6	7	8	9	10
1	2	3	4	5	6	7	8	9	10	11
2	3	4	5	6	7	8	9	10	11	12
3	4	5	6	7	8	9	10	11	12	13
4	5	6	7	8	9	10	11	12	13	14
5	6	7	8	9	10	11	12	13	14	15
6	7	8	9	10	11	12	13	14	15	16
7	8	9	10	11	12	13	14	15	16	17
8	9	10	11	12	13	14	15	16	17	18
9	10	11	12	13	14	15	16	17	18	19
10	11	12	13	14	15	16	17	18	19	20

For example: $5 + 9 = 14$

Exercise 1G

Answer all the questions without using a calculator or written calculations. Try to memorise the addition table but look up answers if you need to.

1. (a) $7 + 3$ (b) $6 + 2$ (c) $3 + 5$ (d) $9 + 6$ (e) $2 + 7$
   (f) $6 + 5$ (g) $4 + 3$ (h) $7 + 8$ (i) $9 + 1$ (j) $8 + 5$
   (k) $4 + 8$ (l) $5 + 7$ (m) $8 + 8$ (n) $4 + 9$ (o) $6 + 4$
   (p) $7 + 6$ (q) $9 + 9$ (r) $7 + 9$ (s) $8 + 9$ (t) $8 + 6$
   (u) $8 + 2$ (v) $6 + 6$ (w) $5 + 9$ (x) $7 + 4$ (y) $7 + 7$

2. (a) $10 + 3$ (b) $7 + 10$ (c) $10 + 5$ (d) $9 + 10$ (e) $4 + 10$
   (f) $10 + 8$ (g) $6 + 10$ (h) $10 + 10$ (i) $10 + 2$ (j) $3 + 2 + 10$
   (k) $6 + 3 + 10$ (l) $2 + 5 + 10$ (m) $10 + 4 + 5$ (n) $10 + 2 + 5$ (o) $10 + 4 + 4$
   (p) $3 + 10 + 3$ (q) $2 + 10 + 6$ (r) $1 + 10 + 7$ (s) $8 + 10 + 1$ (t) $5 + 5 + 10$
   (u) $10 + 4 + 1$ (v) $2 + 10 + 2$ (w) $1 + 10 + 2$ (x) $10 + 1 + 6$ (y) $10 + 1 + 3$

3. (a) $20 + 10$ (b) $30 + 10$ (c) $40 + 10$ (d) $60 + 10$ (e) $70 + 10$
   (f) $10 + 50$ (g) $20 + 30$ (h) $30 + 50$ (i) $30 + 60$ (j) $70 + 40$
   (k) $80 + 30$ (l) $90 + 50$ (m) $70 + 60$ (n) $50 + 80$ (o) $70 + 30$
   (p) $60 + 50$ (q) $80 + 70$ (r) $90 + 80$ (s) $80 + 60$ (t) $40 + 90$
   (u) $70 + 90$ (v) $70 + 50$ (w) $50 + 40$ (x) $60 + 90$ (y) $80 + 40$

4. (a) 20 + 30 + 7   (b) 40 + 10 + 5   (c) 20 + 20 + 8
   (d) 60 + 30 + 9   (e) 60 + 40 + 5   (f) 50 + 40 + 3
   (g) 50 + 70 + 1   (h) 20 + 80 + 6   (i) 60 + 90 + 8
   (j) 40 + 70 + 7   (k) 50 + 30 + 7   (l) 80 + 50 + 2
   (m) 90 + 40 + 6   (n) 70 + 30 + 6   (o) 80 + 80 + 5
   (p) 10 + 3 + 70   (q) 70 + 8 + 10   (r) 20 + 5 + 90
   (s) 50 + 6 + 60   (t) 60 + 3 + 60   (u) 60 + 9 + 50
   (v) 90 + 7 + 90   (w) 4 + 30 + 40   (x) 1 + 30 + 80

5. (a) 20 + 11   (b) 30 + 16   (c) 10 + 19   (d) 20 + 13   (e) 50 + 19
   (f) 40 + 12   (g) 30 + 17   (h) 80 + 15   (i) 60 + 16   (j) 70 + 19
   (k) 90 + 11   (l) 90 + 16   (m) 90 + 17   (n) 100 + 15 (o) 120 + 13
   (p) 120 + 18 (q) 150 + 12 (r) 110 + 14 (s) 110 + 11 (t) 180 + 18
   (u) 170 + 17 (v) 160 + 15 (w) 180 + 13 (x) 190 + 17 (y) 190 + 11

6. (a) 60 + 70 + 3 + 4   (b) 90 + 50 + 1 + 2   (c) 70 + 90 + 2 + 4
   (d) 40 + 80 + 3 + 3   (e) 80 + 90 + 5 + 2   (f) 90 + 30 + 4 + 4
   (g) 20 + 70 + 2 + 6   (h) 70 + 80 + 4 + 5   (i) 70 + 70 + 3 + 5
   (j) 80 + 7 + 50 + 2   (k) 90 + 6 + 40 + 3   (l) 60 + 4 + 40 + 4
   (m) 10 + 40 + 5 + 5   (n) 20 + 30 + 8 + 5   (o) 10 + 80 + 7 + 6
   (p) 20 + 40 + 8 + 7   (q) 30 + 30 + 6 + 5   (r) 30 + 50 + 8 + 9
   (s) 70 + 50 + 6 + 8   (t) 60 + 60 + 9 + 7   (u) 30 + 90 + 8 + 4
   (v) 90 + 60 + 9 + 5   (w) 30 + 80 + 8 + 9   (x) 90 + 90 + 9 + 9

1.8 Adding whole numbers 'in your head'

Anthony is playing darts. He has scored 67 with his first two darts and hits 18 with his third dart. What is his total score?

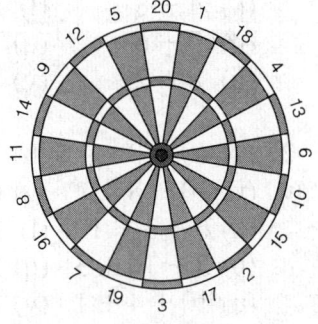

To find the total score without a calculator or a written calculation, think of a number line:

67 + 18:

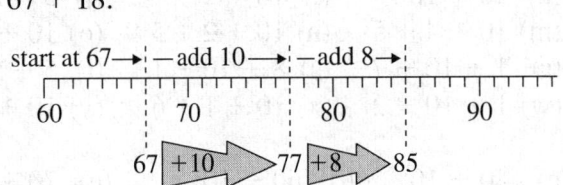

so 67 + 18 = 85.

You may need to note down some steps but try to do as much of the calculation as you can 'in your head'.

Example

John and Chantal are going on holiday. John has saved £83 and Chantal has saved £78. How much have they saved altogether?

83 + 78:

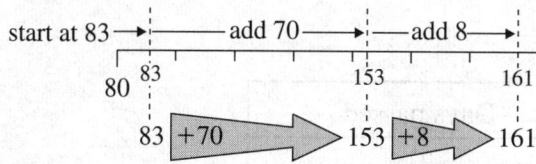

So 83 + 78 = 161.

They have saved £161 altogether.

Hint: Your number line doesn't have to be to scale.

Exercise 1H

Answer all the questions without using a calculator.

1. (a) 16 + 13   (b) 12 + 25   (c) 41 + 37   (d) 55 + 23   (e) 84 + 16
    (f) 29 + 34   (g) 56 + 17   (h) 45 + 37   (i) 19 + 37   (j) 26 + 38
    (k) 17 + 11   (l) 13 + 21   (m) 22 + 22   (n) 34 + 51   (o) 28 + 62
    (p) 55 + 27   (q) 19 + 19   (r) 17 + 17   (s) 8 + 55   (t) 48 + 27
    (u) 95 + 23   (v) 97 + 26   (w) 86 + 75   (x) 94 + 53   (y) 98 + 67

2. A seaside stall displays this sign.

    What is the total cost of:
    (a) A tea and a sandwich
    (b) A roll and a soft drink
    (c) A coffee and a roll
    (d) A hot dog and a soft drink
    (e) A coffee and a sandwich
    (f) A burger and a soft drink
    (g) A tea and a hot dog
    (h) Two teas
    (i) Two coffees
    (j) Two hot dogs
    (k) Two burgers and a soft drink
    (l) Two hot dogs and two teas
    (m) A roll, a sandwich and a tea
    (n) A tea, a coffee and a hot dog
    (o) Two soft drinks and a burger
    (p) Two teas and three hot dogs?

    Tea............ 45 p
    Coffee........ 55 p
    Sandwich... 87 p
    Roll............ 68 p
    Burger...... 125 p
    Hot Dog..... 110 p
    Soft Drink...35 p

3. Sonny is saving to buy a stereo which costs £215. He keeps a record of his weekly savings like this:

Saved this week	Total so far
£12	£12
£17	£29
£9	£38

    Copy and complete Sonny's record for the next ten weeks, when he saves: £22, £35, £5, £16, £17, £24, £18, £6, £11 and £23. If the final total is not £215, check for mistakes.

4. Maggie has collected this data on the number of days in each month:

January 31 February 28 March 31 April 30 May 31 June 30
July 31 August 31 September 30 October 31 November 30 December 31

Maggie starts a table like this.

By end of month	Days passed
January	31
February	59

Copy and complete Maggie's table. If the final total is not 365 days, check for mistakes.

1.9 Subtracting whole numbers 'in your head'

Most people work out subtractions by thinking about the addition table. If you want to work out $17 - 8$, you need to remember that $8 + 9 = 17$, so

$$17 - 8 = 9$$

Example

Melissa had 13 CDs but gave 7 to her brother. How many has she got left?

Remember that $7 + 6 = 13$
so $13 - 7 = 6$

Melissa has 6 CDs left.

To answer a more difficult question like $55 - 38$, you can think like this:

Start at 38 and find what to add on to get 55.

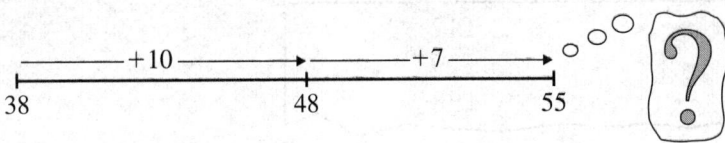

so the difference is 17 and

$$55 - 38 = 17$$

Exercise 1I

Do these subtraction questions in your head.

1. (a) 7 − 4   (b) 9 − 3   (c) 11 − 8   (d) 9 − 3   (e) 9 − 4
   (f) 12 − 3   (g) 16 − 7   (h) 14 − 6   (i) 11 − 5   (j) 10 − 3
   (k) 12 − 7   (l) 15 − 8   (m) 11 − 9   (n) 13 − 7   (o) 13 − 5
   (p) 18 − 9   (q) 16 − 8   (r) 15 − 7   (s) 13 − 6   (t) 16 − 9
   (u) 15 − 6   (v) 14 − 8   (w) 17 − 8   (x) 15 − 9   (y) 14 − 7

2. (a) 25 − 3   (b) 47 − 5   (c) 65 − 2   (d) 89 − 7   (e) 47 − 6
   (f) 46 − 6   (g) 27 − 5   (h) 88 − 4   (i) 34 − 3   (j) 55 − 1
   (k) 57 − 2   (l) 48 − 5   (m) 123 − 2   (n) 156 − 4   (o) 187 − 4
   (p) 239 − 6   (q) 67 − 7   (r) 88 − 5   (s) 83 − 3   (t) 29 − 8
   (u) 46 − 2   (v) 56 − 5   (w) 78 − 6   (x) 76 − 3   (y) 99 − 9

3. (a) 55 − 30   (b) 67 − 50   (c) 56 − 20   (d) 49 − 20   (e) 98 − 50
   (f) 76 − 40   (g) 83 − 30   (h) 72 − 60   (i) 34 − 20   (j) 85 − 40
   (k) 97 − 40   (l) 77 − 30   (m) 49 − 30   (n) 27 − 10   (o) 74 − 50
   (p) 83 − 60   (q) 97 − 70   (r) 55 − 40   (s) 55 − 10   (t) 85 − 70
   (u) 99 − 60   (v) 81 − 20   (w) 96 − 80   (x) 73 − 10   (y) 88 − 50

4. (a) 65 − 32   (b) 37 − 24   (c) 86 − 34   (d) 38 − 14   (e) 59 − 26
   (f) 54 − 33   (g) 68 − 27   (h) 59 − 37   (i) 43 − 12   (j) 82 − 21
   (k) 56 − 15   (l) 77 − 37   (m) 58 − 46   (n) 39 − 12   (o) 93 − 52
   (p) 58 − 38   (q) 47 − 16   (r) 85 − 74   (s) 67 − 33   (t) 68 − 22
   (u) 95 − 53   (v) 76 − 32   (w) 99 − 35   (x) 88 − 33   (y) 69 − 24

5. (a) 22 − 5   (b) 43 − 4   (c) 27 − 8   (d) 32 − 6   (e) 84 − 6
   (f) 65 − 7   (g) 82 − 4   (h) 73 − 5   (i) 54 − 7   (j) 46 − 7
   (k) 35 − 6   (l) 84 − 5   (m) 33 − 6   (n) 76 − 8   (o) 75 − 8
   (p) 37 − 9   (q) 48 − 9   (r) 31 − 4   (s) 51 − 5   (t) 62 − 7
   (u) 91 − 6   (v) 63 − 8   (w) 34 − 9   (x) 82 − 8   (y) 61 − 9

6. (a) 34 − 15   (b) 83 − 24   (c) 55 − 27   (d) 86 − 17   (e) 42 − 15
   (f) 54 − 26   (g) 72 − 43   (h) 84 − 37   (i) 93 − 15   (j) 24 − 18
   (k) 73 − 66   (l) 87 − 28   (m) 92 − 14   (n) 76 − 38   (o) 74 − 39
   (p) 43 − 18   (q) 55 − 26   (r) 76 − 39   (s) 95 − 28   (t) 46 − 19
   (u) 52 − 27   (v) 93 − 39   (w) 84 − 48   (x) 58 − 29   (y) 95 − 39

7. Paul needs to cook a large turkey for 240 minutes. He checks the oven and bastes the bird after these time gaps (in minutes):

    18, 25, 23, 31, 42, 17, 56 and 28.

    He keeps a record of how much cooking time is left every time he checks.

Time passed between checks	Time left
18 mins	222 mins
25 mins	197 mins

    Copy and complete Paul's table. If your final answer is not zero minutes, check for mistakes.

8. Nisha is conducting an experiment. She is measuring the temperature of wax as it cools.

    She records the temperature every 5 minutes for one hour. This is her data (in degrees centigrade):

    176, 155, 138, 124, 112, 98, 96, 95, 81, 64, 43, 31, 29

    She presents her results in this table:

Time (mins)	Temp (°C)	Temp fall (°C)
0	176	–
5	155	21
10	138	17

    Copy and complete Nisha's table.

1.10 Adding whole numbers with written calculations

If additions are too difficult to do in your head, you do them on paper.

Example

Find (a) 125 + 33   (b) 634 + 128   (c) 543 + 877

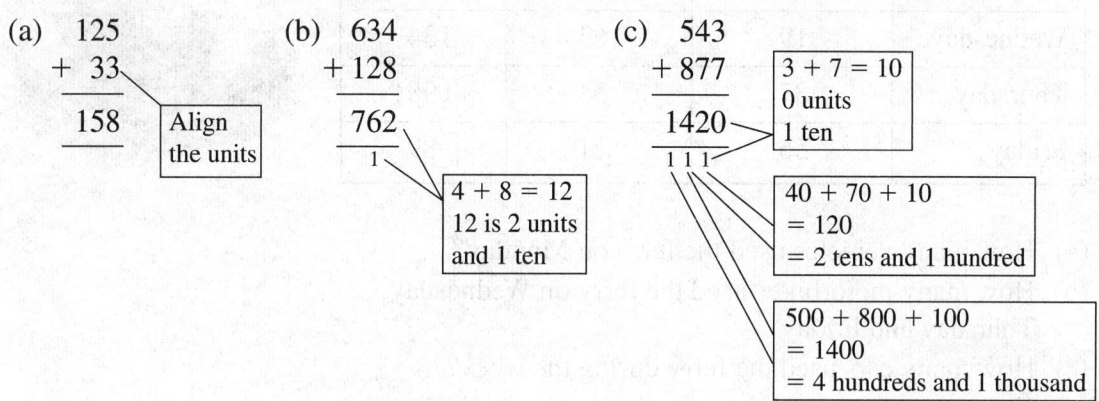

Exercise 1J

Answer all the questions without using a calculator.

1. (a) 27 + 52   (b) 45 + 54   (c) 87 + 12   (d) 62 + 35   (e) 182 + 14
   (f) 623 + 64   (g) 721 + 58   (h) 805 + 72   (i) 922 + 34   (j) 732 + 45
   (k) 426 + 123 (l) 130 + 209 (m) 321 + 567 (n) 203 + 86   (o) 921 + 17
   (p) 342 + 503 (q) 267 + 131 (r) 555 + 333 (s) 240 + 559 (t) 322 + 657
   (u) 703 + 196 (v) 750 + 239 (w) 57 + 102   (x) 84 + 304   (y) 39 + 150

2. (a) 23 + 47   (b) 56 + 38   (c) 27 + 38   (d) 19 + 35   (e) 13 + 67
   (f) 345 + 35   (g) 606 + 77   (h) 801 + 59   (i) 623 + 68   (j) 208 + 17
   (k) 245 + 83   (l) 415 + 92   (m) 365 + 84   (n) 423 + 87   (o) 278 + 191
   (p) 367 + 162 (q) 750 + 67   (r) 831 + 88   (s) 922 + 90   (t) 271 + 168
   (u) 237 + 128 (v) 481 + 395 (w) 506 + 149 (x) 422 + 17   (y) 645 + 274

3. (a) 45 + 67   (b) 27 + 95   (c) 56 + 44   (d) 31 + 89   (e) 89 + 34
   (f) 108 + 97   (g) 237 + 74   (h) 528 + 79   (i) 187 + 78   (j) 249 + 76
   (k) 347 + 875 (l) 238 + 194 (m) 375 + 96   (n) 231 + 99   (o) 346 + 185
   (p) 453 + 278 (q) 653 + 279 (r) 593 + 308 (s) 607 + 296 (t) 372 + 548
   (u) 456 + 789 (v) 487 + 798 (w) 689 + 987 (x) 567 + 583 (y) 234 + 766

4. This table shows the numbers of motorbikes, vans and cars which used a ferry during one week.

	Motorbikes	Vans	Cars
Monday	32	36	102
Tuesday	27	41	156
Wednesday	19	63	134
Thursday	37	54	98
Friday	56	21	89

(a) How many vehicles used the ferry on Monday?
(b) How many motorbikes used the ferry on Wednesday, Thursday and Friday?
(c) How many cars used the ferry during the week?
(d) How many vans used the ferry during the week?
(e) How many vehicles used the ferry during the week?

5. A group of students are saving each month for a school trip. The table shows their savings for the first four months.

	Month 1	Month 2	Month 3	Month 4
John	£25	£32	£21	£27
Hitesh	£38	£30	£26	£19
Ajay	£30	£27	£23	£28
Elizabeth	£35	£12	£33	£24
Amy	£50	£14	£17	£26
Deryn	£20	£26	£25	£37

(a) How much has John saved?
(b) How much has Hitesh saved?
(c) How much is saved in the first month?
(d) How much is saved in the third month?
(e) How much have Elizabeth and Deryn saved altogether?

1.11 Subtracting whole numbers with written calculations

If subtractions are too difficult to do in your head, you do them on paper.

Example

Find (a) $346 - 23$ (b) $852 - 38$ (c) $541 - 179$

(a)
$$\begin{array}{r} 346 \\ -\ 23 \\ \hline 323 \end{array}$$
Subtract from the units end

(b)
$$\begin{array}{r} 8\overset{4}{\cancel{5}}\overset{1}{2} \\ -\ 38 \\ \hline 814 \end{array}$$
Can't do $2 - 8$ so borrow a ten from 50: $12 - 8$ is 4

(c)
$$\begin{array}{r} \overset{4}{\cancel{5}}\overset{3}{\cancel{4}}\overset{1}{1} \\ -\ 179 \\ \hline 362 \end{array}$$
Can't do $1 - 9$ so borrow a 10 from 40: $11 - 9 = 2$

Can't do $30 - 70$ so borrow a 100: $130 - 70 = 60$

Exercise 1K

Answer all the questions without using a calculator.

1. (a) $87 - 56$ (b) $35 - 11$ (c) $56 - 32$ (d) $89 - 37$ (e) $58 - 14$
   (f) $123 - 12$ (g) $156 - 42$ (h) $245 - 23$ (i) $562 - 51$ (j) $347 - 25$
   (k) $340 - 120$ (l) $225 - 103$ (m) $453 - 142$ (n) $567 - 231$ (o) $698 - 377$
   (p) $452 - 132$ (q) $567 - 365$ (r) $777 - 234$ (s) $859 - 457$ (t) $750 - 430$
   (u) $806 - 701$ (v) $888 - 652$ (w) $999 - 457$ (x) $999 - 363$ (y) $789 - 678$

2. (a) $363 - 46$ (b) $271 - 35$ (c) $186 - 28$ (d) $137 - 18$ (e) $317 - 209$
   (f) $456 - 28$ (g) $362 - 29$ (h) $267 - 49$ (i) $583 - 69$ (j) $523 - 79$
   (k) $415 - 207$ (l) $367 - 249$ (m) $832 - 126$ (n) $555 - 247$ (o) $231 - 118$
   (p) $415 - 270$ (q) $367 - 294$ (r) $832 - 261$ (s) $555 - 274$ (t) $231 - 181$
   (u) $603 - 183$ (v) $207 - 196$ (w) $203 - 109$ (x) $305 - 127$ (y) $504 - 239$

3. (a) $234 - 79$ (b) $385 - 58$ (c) $271 - 92$ (d) $350 - 87$ (e) $321 - 58$
   (f) $621 - 156$ (g) $356 - 189$ (h) $450 - 195$ (i) $567 - 398$ (j) $278 - 189$
   (k) $452 - 177$ (l) $365 - 276$ (m) $680 - 543$ (n) $891 - 693$ (o) $673 - 285$
   (p) $451 - 252$ (q) $346 - 199$ (r) $670 - 191$ (s) $687 - 488$ (t) $713 - 615$
   (u) $708 - 89$ (v) $303 - 125$ (w) $502 - 163$ (x) $700 - 371$ (y) $800 - 259$

4 Thomas and Yasmin are timing the competitors in a marathon. These are the times (in minutes) of the first twenty runners:

175, 183, 189, 193, 195, 198, 200, 203, 206, 211, 214, 217, 221, 225, 232, 238, 245, 249, 251, 254

Yasmin starts to draw up a table like this:

Runner	Time behind winner
1st	–
2nd	+ 8 minutes
3rd	+ 14 minutes

Copy and complete Yasmin's table.

1.12 Temperature

Temperatures are measured in degrees Celsius (°C).

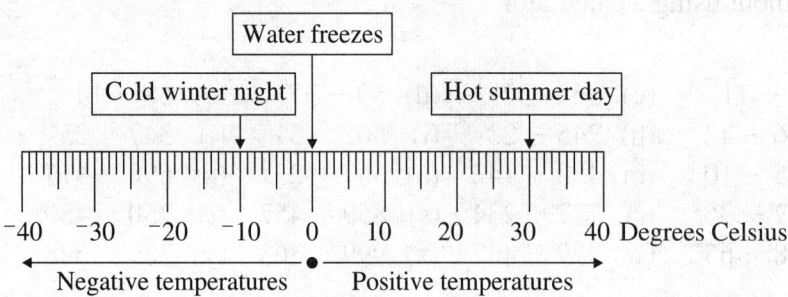

Example

A weather station records the lowest temperature each day.
These are the results for six days in December:

$^-5°C, 2°C, ^-1°C, 4°C, ^-3°C, 0°C$

Arrange the results into order, starting with the lowest.

Think of a number line:

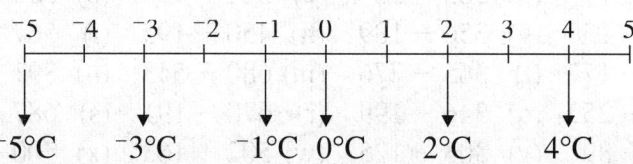

Exercise 1L

1. Arrange each list of temperatures into order, starting with the lowest.

   Hint: Use the number line to help you.

   (a) 7°C, ⁻6°C, ⁻8°C, 2°C, 5°C, ⁻7°C
   (b) 6°C, ⁻7°C, ⁻2°C, 0°C, 1°C, ⁻1°C, ⁻3°C, 5°C
   (c) 4°C, 7°C, 6°C, 8°C, 0°C, 9°C, 3°C, 4°C, 5°C, 9°C
   (d) 0°C, ⁻1°C, 2°C, 3°C, ⁻2°C, ⁻3°C, 1°C, ⁻4°C, 4°C, 5°C
   (e) ⁻20°C, 30°C, 40°C, ⁻30°C, ⁻40°C, ⁻50°C, 0°C, 10°C, 50°C, ⁻10°C
   (f) ⁻13°C, ⁻17°C, 11°C, 8°C, ⁻9°C, ⁻6°C, 11°C, ⁻20°C, ⁻7°C, ⁻19°C
   (g) 21°C, 43°C, ⁻17°C, ⁻29°C, 32°C, ⁻56°C, 81°C, ⁻73°C, 65°C, ⁻16°C
   (h) 65°C, 76°C, 82°C, 90°C, 34°C, 67°C, 0°C, 55°C, 39°C, 93°C

2. These are some of the highest and lowest temperatures recorded on the Earth. Write the list in order, starting with the highest temperature.

   ⁻45°C   The coldest temperature ever recorded in Europe (Finland)
   46°C   The hottest temperature recorded in Europe (Spain)
   53·1°C   The hottest temperature recorded in Australia (Cloncurry)
   ⁻68°C   The coldest temperature recorded in Siberia (Oymyakon)
   58°C   The hottest temperature recorded on Earth (Libya)
   ⁻88·3°C The coldest temperature recorded on Earth (Antarctica)
   ⁻58·3°C The coldest temperature recorded in Canada (Ellesmere Island)
   56·7°C   The hottest temperature recorded in the USA (Death Valley)

1.13 Temperature changes

The temperature is 5°C.

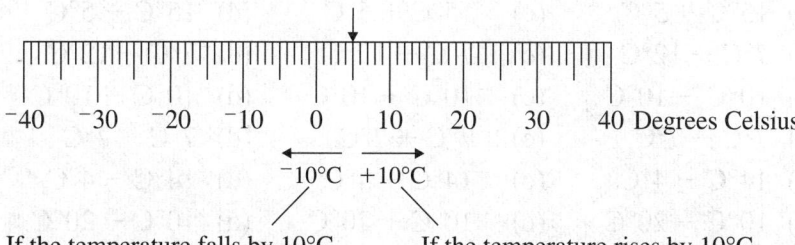

If the temperature falls by 10°C the new temperature will be ⁻5°C
5°C − 10°C = ⁻5°C

If the temperature rises by 10°C the new temperature will be 15°C
5°C + 10°C = 15°C

The temperature is ⁻5°C.

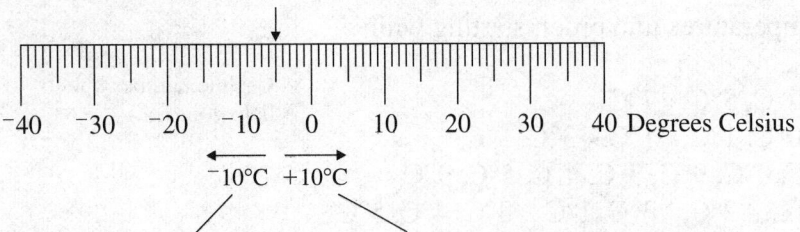

If the temperature falls by 10°C the new temperature will be ⁻15°C
⁻5°C − 10°C = ⁻15°C

If the temperature rises by 10°C the new temperature will be 5°C
⁻5°C + 10°C = 5°C

Examples

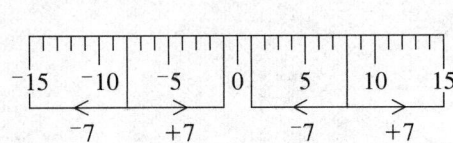

8°C + 7°C = 15°C
8°C − 7°C = 1°C
⁻8°C + 7°C = ⁻1°C
⁻8°C − 7°C = ⁻15°C

4°C + 6°C = 10°C
4°C − 6°C = ⁻2°C
⁻4°C + 6°C = 2°C
⁻4°C − 6°C = ⁻10°C

Exercise 1M

1. (a) 5°C + 8°C   (b) 5°C − 8°C   (c) ⁻5°C + 8°C   (d) ⁻5°C − 8°C
2. (a) 2°C + 3°C   (b) 2°C − 3°C   (c) ⁻2°C + 3°C   (d) ⁻2°C − 3°C
3. (a) 4°C + 7°C   (b) 4°C − 7°C   (c) ⁻4°C + 7°C   (d) ⁻4°C − 7°C
4. (a) 9°C + 2°C   (b) 9°C − 2°C   (c) ⁻9°C + 2°C   (d) ⁻9°C − 2°C
5. (a) 1°C + 10°C   (b) 1°C − 10°C   (c) ⁻1°C + 10°C   (d) ⁻1°C − 10°C
6. (a) 5°C + 6°C   (b) 5°C − 6°C   (c) ⁻5°C + 6°C   (d) ⁻5°C − 6°C
7. (a) 11°C + 6°C   (b) 11°C − 6°C   (c) ⁻11°C + 6°C   (d) ⁻11°C − 6°C
8. (a) 13°C + 8°C   (b) 13°C − 8°C   (c) ⁻13°C + 8°C   (d) ⁻13°C − 8°C
9. (a) 9°C + 3°C   (b) 9°C − 3°C   (c) ⁻9°C + 3°C   (d) ⁻9°C − 3°C
10. (a) 15°C + 5°C   (b) 15°C − 5°C   (c) ⁻15°C + 5°C   (d) ⁻15°C − 5°C
11. (a) 7°C + 12°C   (b) 7°C − 12°C   (c) ⁻7°C + 12°C   (d) ⁻7°C − 12°C
12. (a) 10°C + 10°C   (b) 10°C − 10°C   (c) ⁻10°C + 10°C   (d) ⁻10°C − 10°C
13. (a) 7°C + 7°C   (b) 7°C − 7°C   (c) ⁻7°C + 7°C   (d) ⁻7°C − 7°C
14. (a) 14°C + 4°C   (b) 14°C − 4°C   (c) ⁻14°C + 4°C   (d) ⁻14°C − 4°C
15. (a) 10°C + 20°C   (b) 10°C − 20°C   (c) ⁻10°C + 20°C   (d) ⁻10°C − 20°C
16. (a) 20°C + 10°C   (b) 20°C − 10°C   (c) ⁻20°C + 10°C   (d) ⁻20°C − 10°C
17. (a) 18°C + 9°C   (b) 18°C − 9°C   (c) ⁻18°C + 9°C   (d) ⁻18°C − 9°C

18. (a) 15°C + 25°C (b) 15°C − 25°C (c) ⁻15°C + 25°C (d) ⁻15°C − 25°C
19. (a) 13°C + 7°C (b) 13°C − 7°C (c) ⁻13°C + 7°C (d) ⁻13°C − 7°C
20. (a) 31°C + 23°C (b) 31°C − 23°C (c) ⁻31°C + 23°C (d) ⁻31°C − 23°C

1.14 Adding negative numbers

Adding a negative number is the same as subtracting.

Example 1
$$8 + {}^-7 = 8 - 7 = 1$$
$$3 + {}^-6 = 3 - 6 = {}^-3$$
$$^-5 + {}^-9 = {}^-5 - 9 = {}^-14$$
$$^-1 + {}^-5 = {}^-1 - 5 = {}^-6$$

With any two numbers, you can now make and solve six different problems.

Example 2
Starting with 7 and 2:
$$7 + 2 = 9$$
$$7 - 2 = 5$$
$$7 + {}^-2 = 5$$
$$^-7 + 2 = {}^-5$$
$$^-7 - 2 = {}^-9$$
$$^-7 + {}^-2 = {}^-9$$

Starting with 4 and 10:
$$4 + 10 = 14$$
$$4 - 10 = {}^-6$$
$$4 + {}^-10 = {}^-6$$
$$^-4 + 10 = 6$$
$$^-4 - 10 = {}^-14$$
$$^-4 + {}^-10 = {}^-14$$

Exercise 1N

Use a number line to help you work out these.

1. (a) 4 + 5 (b) 4 − 5 (c) 4 + ⁻5
   (d) ⁻4 + 5 (e) ⁻4 − 5 (f) ⁻4 + ⁻5
2. (a) 5 + 7 (b) 5 − 7 (c) 5 + ⁻7
   (d) ⁻5 + 7 (e) ⁻5 − 7 (f) ⁻5 + ⁻7
3. (a) 8 + 2 (b) 8 − 2 (c) 8 + ⁻2
   (d) ⁻8 + 2 (e) ⁻8 − 2 (f) ⁻8 + ⁻2
4. (a) 3 + 9 (b) 3 − 9 (c) 3 + ⁻9
   (d) ⁻3 + 9 (e) ⁻3 − 9 (f) ⁻3 + ⁻9
5. (a) 6 + 9 (b) 6 − 9 (c) 6 + ⁻9
   (d) ⁻6 + 9 (e) ⁻6 − 9 (f) ⁻6 + ⁻9
6. (a) 10 + 6 (b) 10 − 6 (c) 10 + ⁻6
   (d) ⁻10 + 6 (e) ⁻10 − 6 (f) ⁻10 + ⁻6
7. (a) 5 + 3 (b) 5 − 3 (c) 5 + ⁻3
   (d) ⁻5 + 3 (e) ⁻5 − 3 (f) ⁻5 + ⁻3

8. (a) $6 + 1$ (b) $6 - 1$ (c) $6 + {}^-1$
   (d) ${}^-6 + 1$ (e) ${}^-6 - 1$ (f) ${}^-6 + {}^-1$
9. (a) $7 + 10$ (b) $7 - 10$ (c) $7 + {}^-10$
   (d) ${}^-7 + 10$ (e) ${}^-7 - 10$ (f) ${}^-7 + {}^-10$
10. (a) $5 + 2$ (b) $5 - 2$ (c) $5 + {}^-2$
    (d) ${}^-5 + 2$ (e) ${}^-5 - 2$ (f) ${}^-5 + {}^-2$
11. (a) $11 + 3$ (b) $11 - 3$ (c) $11 + {}^-3$
    (d) ${}^-11 + 3$ (e) ${}^-11 - 3$ (f) ${}^-11 + {}^-3$
12. (a) $7 + 14$ (b) $7 - 14$ (c) $7 + {}^-14$
    (d) ${}^-7 + 14$ (e) ${}^-7 - 14$ (f) ${}^-7 + {}^-14$

1.15 Subtracting negative numbers

Subtracting a negative number is the same as adding.

Example 1

$8 - {}^-7 = 8 + 7 = 15$
$3 - {}^-6 = 3 + 6 = 9$
${}^-5 - {}^-9 = {}^-5 + 9 = 4$
${}^-1 - {}^-5 = {}^-1 + 5 = 4$

With any two numbers, you can now make and solve eight different problems.

Example 2

Starting with 6 and 3:
$6 + 3 = 9$
$6 - 3 = 3$
$6 + {}^-3 = 3$
$6 - {}^-3 = 6 + 3 = 9$
${}^-6 + 3 = {}^-3$
${}^-6 - 3 = {}^-9$
${}^-6 + {}^-3 = {}^-9$
${}^-6 - {}^-3 = {}^-6 + 3 = {}^-3$

Starting with 8 and 12:
$8 + 12 = 20$
$8 - 12 = {}^-4$
$8 + {}^-12 = {}^-4$
$8 - {}^-12 = 8 + 12 = 20$
${}^-8 + 12 = 4$
${}^-8 - 12 = {}^-20$
${}^-8 + {}^-12 = {}^-20$
${}^-8 - {}^-12 = {}^-8 + 12 = 4$

Hint:
For 8 and 12 the **difference** is 4, the **sum** is 20. There are only four possible answers: 4 or ${}^-4$, 20 or ${}^-20$.

Exercise 10

Use a number line to work out these.

1. (a) $10 + 5$ (b) $10 - 5$ (c) $10 + {}^-5$ (d) $10 - {}^-5$
   (e) ${}^-10 + 5$ (f) ${}^-10 - 5$ (g) ${}^-10 + {}^-5$ (h) ${}^-10 - {}^-5$
2. (a) $7 - 6$ (b) ${}^-7 + 6$ (c) $7 + {}^-6$ (d) ${}^-7 - {}^-6$
   (e) ${}^-7 + {}^-6$ (f) $7 + 6$ (g) $7 - {}^-6$ (h) ${}^-7 - 6$
3. (a) ${}^-4 - 3$ (b) $4 - {}^-3$ (c) $4 + 3$ (d) ${}^-4 + 3$
   (e) ${}^-4 - {}^-3$ (f) $4 + {}^-3$ (g) ${}^-4 + {}^-3$ (h) $4 - 3$

4. (a) $6 + 6$ (b) $^-6 + 6$ (c) $6 - 6$ (d) $^-6 - 6$
   (e) $6 + {}^-6$ (f) $^-6 + {}^-6$ (g) $6 - {}^-6$ (h) $^-6 - {}^-6$
5. (a) $10 + 2$ (b) $10 - 2$ (c) $10 + {}^-2$ (d) $10 - {}^-2$
   (e) $^-10 + 2$ (f) $^-10 - 2$ (g) $^-10 + {}^-2$ (h) $^-10 - {}^-2$
6. (a) $1 - 8$ (b) $^-1 + 8$ (c) $1 + {}^-8$ (d) $^-1 - {}^-8$
   (e) $^-1 + {}^-8$ (f) $1 + 8$ (g) $1 - {}^-8$ (h) $^-1 - 8$
7. (a) $^-7 - 3$ (b) $7 - {}^-3$ (c) $7 + 3$ (d) $^-7 + 3$
   (e) $^-7 - {}^-3$ (f) $7 + {}^-3$ (g) $^-7 + {}^-3$ (h) $7 - 3$
8. (a) $10 + 9$ (b) $^-10 + 9$ (c) $10 - 9$ (d) $^-10 - 9$
   (e) $10 + {}^-9$ (f) $^-10 + {}^-9$ (g) $10 - {}^-9$ (h) $^-10 - {}^-9$
9. (a) $9 + 4$ (b) $9 - 4$ (c) $9 + {}^-4$ (d) $9 - {}^-4$
   (e) $^-9 + 4$ (f) $^-9 - 4$ (g) $^-9 + {}^-4$ (h) $^-9 - {}^-4$
10. (a) $2 - 1$ (b) $^-2 + 1$ (c) $2 + {}^-1$ (d) $^-2 - {}^-1$
    (e) $^-2 + {}^-1$ (f) $2 + 1$ (g) $2 - {}^-1$ (h) $^-2 - 1$
11. (a) $^-16 - 3$ (b) $16 - {}^-3$ (c) $16 + 3$ (d) $^-16 + 3$
    (e) $^-16 - {}^-3$ (f) $16 + {}^-3$ (g) $^-16 + {}^-3$ (h) $16 - 3$
12. (a) $9 + 9$ (b) $^-9 + 9$ (c) $9 - 9$ (d) $^-9 - 9$
    (e) $9 + {}^-9$ (f) $^-9 + {}^-9$ (g) $9 - {}^-9$ (h) $^-9 - {}^-9$

1.16 Going overdrawn

The amount of money that is in your bank account is called the **balance**.

Taking money out of your account is called **making a withdrawal**.

Paying money into your account is called **making a deposit**.

Writing a cheque to pay for something is the same as making a withdrawal.

If you withdraw more money than is in your account, your account is **overdrawn** and you owe the bank money.

Example 1

(a) Ms Jones has a balance of £230 in her bank account.
    If she writes a cheque for £350, how much is she overdrawn?
    £350 is £120 more than £230, so Ms Jones has $^-$£120 in her account. She is £120 *overdrawn*.
(b) Mr Smith was £455 overdrawn but then made a deposit of £600.
    What is his new balance?
    Mr Smith's balance before he paid in the £600 was $^-$£455.
    £600 is £145 more than £455, so Mr Smith's new balance is £145.

Exercise 1P

Copy and complete this table.

	Balance	Change	New balance
1.	£340	deposit £400	
2.	£235	deposit £1 675	
3.	£389	withdraw £350	
4.	£1 745	withdraw £705	
5.	£3 450	cheque £2 775	
6.	£209	cheque £209	
7.	⁻£400	deposit £500	
8.	⁻£783	deposit £800	
9.	⁻£1 000	deposit £1 200	
10.	⁻£275	deposit £645	
11.	£500	withdraw £650	
12.	£456	withdraw £457	
13.	£371	withdraw £567	
14.	⁻£300	deposit £200	

1.17 Timetables

To travel by train or bus you need to be able to read a timetable.

Here is a train timetable:

London Kings Cross	Dep	10.00	10.30	11.30	12.00	12.30	13.00	13.30	14.00	14.30	15.00
Stevenage	..	..	..	..	12.01	..	..	..	14.01	..	..	..
Peterborough	Arr	11.15	11.45	12.47	13.15	13.44	14.14	14.47	15.15	15.44	16.14
	Dep	11.15	11.45	12.48	13.15	13.44	14.14	14.48	15.15	15.44	16.14
Grantham	..	..	..	12.14	13.15	..	14.11	..	15.15	..	16.11	..
Newark North Gate	..	..	..	12.26	13.27	..	14.23	..	15.27	..	16.23	..
Retford	..	..	..	..	13.54	..	..	..	15.54	..	..	..
Doncaster	Arr	12.47	13.22	14.29	14.47	15.19	15.44	16.29	16.47	17.19	17.44
	Dep	12.47	13.23	14.29	14.47	15.20	15.44	16.29	16.47	17.20	17.44
Wakefield Westgate	..	..	..	13.49	14.48	..	15.49	..	16.48	..	17.39	..
Leeds	Arr	..	14.13	15.13	..	16.13	..	17.13	..	18.13	..

Note:
Timetables are based on the 24-hour clock.

For example:
13.44 means 1.44 pm
17.39 means 5.39 pm.

You cannot use a calculator to work with times.

It is better to use a number line.

Example

A bus leaves Warwick at 13.05 and arrives in Birmingham at 14.23. How long was the journey? Draw a timeline:

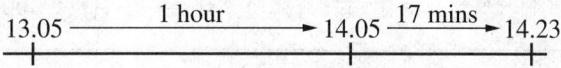

So the journey took 1 hour 17 minutes.

Exercise 1Q

Look at the timetable on page 26 and answer the questions (assume that all trains run to schedule).

1. Bethany wants to travel from London Kings Cross to Leeds. She needs to be in Leeds by 2.30 pm. What is the latest train that she could catch from London?

2. Colin is travelling from Peterborough to Wakefield Westgate, and gets on the same train as Bethany.
   (a) At what time does he leave Peterborough?
   (b) How long is Colin's journey? Give your answer in hours and minutes.

3. How much longer is Bethany's journey than Colin's journey?

4. Greg gets on the 14.00 train from London Kings Cross. He wants to travel to Newark North Gate but he will need to change at Peterborough.
   (a) How long must he wait on the platform at Peterborough?
   (b) What time does he arrive in Newark North Gate?

Summary

1. Each digit in a number has a place value.

2. Numbers can be written in words or figures.

3. Whole numbers can be approximated to the nearest 10, 100 or 1 000.

Checkout 1

1. What place value does each underlined digit have?
   (a) 4<u>7</u>8   (b) 2 <u>8</u>97

2. (a) Write three thousand nine hundred and ninety-four in figures.
   (b) Write 7 843 in words.

3. (a) Approximate to the nearest 10.
       (i) 78 (ii) 95 (iii) 231
   (b) Approximate to the nearest 100.
       (i) 710 (ii) 350 (iii) 2 483
   (c) Approximate to the nearest 1 000.
       (i) 3 500 (ii) 22 897 (iii) 45 123

28 Number 1

4. You can approximate a number to one significant figure (s.f. for short).

4. Give each number correct to 1 s.f.
(a) 37   (b) 42
(c) 321   (d) 584
(e) 1 731   (f) 2 399

5. You should work out simple calculations in your head.

5. (a) $5 + 9$ (b) $4 + 3 + 10$
(c) $50 + 60$ (d) $30 + 60 + 5$
(e) $40 + 16$ (f) $20 + 5 + 30 + 7$
(g) $12 + 26$ (h) $34 + 28$
(i) $14 - 8$ (j) $48 - 5$
(k) $55 - 40$ (l) $68 - 27$
(m) $35 - 7$ (n) $73 - 56$

6. Work out harder calculations on paper.

6. (a) $231 + 427$ (b) $178 + 219$
(c) $89 + 34$ (d) $234 + 766$
(e) $87 - 55$ (f) $453 - 142$
(g) $363 - 46$ (h) $832 - 261$
(i) $452 - 177$ (j) $687 - 488$

7. Negative temperatures are below 0°C.
You arrange temperatures using a number line:

$-10\ -9\ -8\ -7\ -6\ -5\ -4\ -3\ -2\ -1\ 0\ 1\ 2\ 3\ 4\ 5\ 6\ 7\ 8\ 9\ 10$ °C

← Getting colder   Getting warmer →

7. Arrange these temperatures in order, starting with the lowest.
$^-4°C, 7°C, 3°C, 2°C, ^-3°C,$
$4°C, 0°C, 1°C, ^-2°C, ^-1°C$

8. You can calculate temperature changes using a number line.

8. Work out:
(a) $15°C + 8°C$
(b) $15°C - 8°C$
(c) $^-15°C + 8°C$
(d) $^-15°C - 8°C$

9. Adding a negative number is the same as subtracting.

$8 + ^-7 = 8 - 7 = 1 \quad ^-5 + ^-9 = ^-5 - 9 = ^-14$

9. Find:
(a) $6 + 11$ (b) $6 - 11$
(c) $6 + ^-11$ (d) $^-6 + 11$
(e) $^-6 - 11$ (f) $^-6 + ^-11$

10. Subtracting a negative number is the same as adding.

$8 - ^-7 = 8 + 7 = 15 \quad ^-5 - ^-9 = ^-5 + 9 = 4$

10. Work out:
(a) $^-7 - 3$ (b) $7 - ^-3$
(c) $7 + 3$ (d) $^-7 + 3$
(e) $^-7 - ^-3$ (f) $7 + ^-3$
(g) $^-7 + ^-3$ (h) $7 - 3$

Revision exercise 1

1. (a) A year has 365 days.
     In this sentence the 3 means three hundreds.
     What does the 6 mean?
   (b) The match was watched by 7 651 people.
     What does the 7 in this sentence mean?
   (c) A zoo had 460 500 visitors in one year.
     Write this number in words. [AQA/NEAB]

2. Write this number in figures:

   two thousand and fourteen.
   [OCR]

3. The winning numbers in the National Lottery one week were:

   49   36   46   39   23   7

   Write the numbers in order of size. Put the smallest one first.
   [Edexcel]

4. (a) Write the number 807 in words.
   (b) Write the number one hundred thousand and fifty-seven in figures.
   (c) 5 342,   2 104,   483,   2 901,   712
     Write these numbers in order. Start with the smallest number.
     [Edexcel]

5. There are three cards with numbers on.
   The cards are placed to make the number 419.

   | 4 | 1 | 9 |

   (a) (i) Write the numbers 4, 1, 9 to give the highest possible number.
       (ii) Write the numbers 4, 1, 9 to give the lowest possible number.
   One extra card would be needed to make the number 419 ten times bigger.
   (b) Write down the extra number. [Edexcel]

6. (a) Write the number 'five thousand six hundred and seven' in figures.

   (b) Write 2 368 correct to the nearest ten. [OCR]

7. The number of people at a concert at Wembley was 36 098. Write down the number of people at the concert, rounding it to the nearest hundred. [WJEC]

8. Belgium has an area of 30 520 km^2.

   (a) Write 30 520 in words.

   (b) Write 30 520
      (i) to the nearest hundred
      (ii) to the nearest thousand [OCR]

9. Do not use a calculator in this question.
   You must show enough working to show that you did not use a calculator.

   In a cricket match, England's two scores were 326 runs and 397 runs.
   Australia's two scores were 425 runs and 292 runs.

   Which team had the higher total score?
   How many more runs did they score than the other team?
   [OCR]

10. Input ⟶ Subtract 4 ⟶ Output

    The diagram shows a 'Subtract 4' machine.

    Copy and complete the table.

Input	Output
6	2
9	
	14
	29

    [OCR]

11. Chris is 13 cm taller than Steven. Their heights add up to 307 cm.

    How tall is Steven? [AQA/SEG]

12. This table gives the height of **four** (4) mountains in North Wales.

Name of mountain	Height in metres
Moel Hebog	2 566
Carnedd Llywelyn	3 485
Tryfan	3 010
Y Glyder Fawr	3 280

(a) Write down, **in words**, the height of Tryfan.

(b) Find the **difference** in height between Carnedd Llwelyn and Y Glyder Fawr. [WJEC]

13. Browsers Bookshops has a shop in each of the five towns shown in the diagram below.
The diagram shows the distance in miles between the towns.

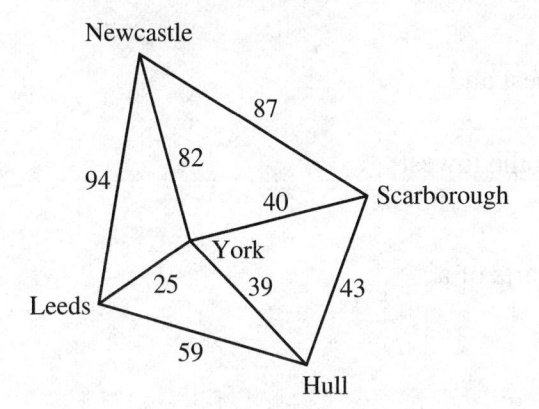

Shirley has to take books to each of the five towns.

She starts at York and finishes at York.

Write down the shortest route she can take. [Edexcel]

14. The table shows the midday and midnight temperatures recorded at Leeds one week last winter.

	Midday temperature (°C)	Midnight temperature (°C)
Monday	3	−3
Tuesday	−1	−4
Wednesday	0	−5
Thursday	−3	−7
Friday	2	−2

(a) Which day had the lowest midday temperature?

(b) Which day had the highest midnight temperature [OCR]

15. One of the supports on a pier is marked off in feet. It is used to measure the water level above or below the zero mark.

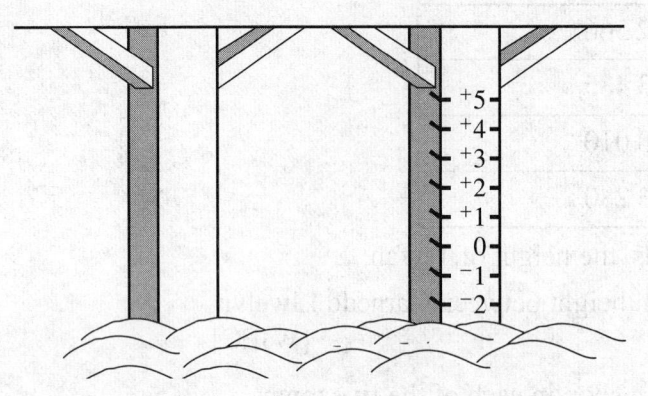

    During one Saturday, the reading was taken every 4 hours and the results were:

    $^-2$, $^+1$, $^+5$, 0, $^-1$, $^-4$

    (a) How many feet are there between the highest and lowest of these readings?

    (b) Write the readings in ascending order with the lowest first. [OCR]

16. This table shows the temperature in different parts of a fridge-freezer.

Fridge	4°C
Ice box	$^-6$°C

    (a) What is the difference in temperature between the fridge and the ice box?

    (b) The temperature in the freezer is 23 degrees lower than the temperature in the fridge.
    What is the temperature in the freezer? [OCR]

17. Joe and Melanie are on holiday in Death Valley National Park.
    The lowest point is 86 m **below** sea level.
    The highest point is 3 368 m **above** sea level.

    What is the difference in height between these two places? [OCR]

18. This is a map of Antarctica taken off the Internet.
It shows the temperatures in °C at nine weather stations round Antarctica.

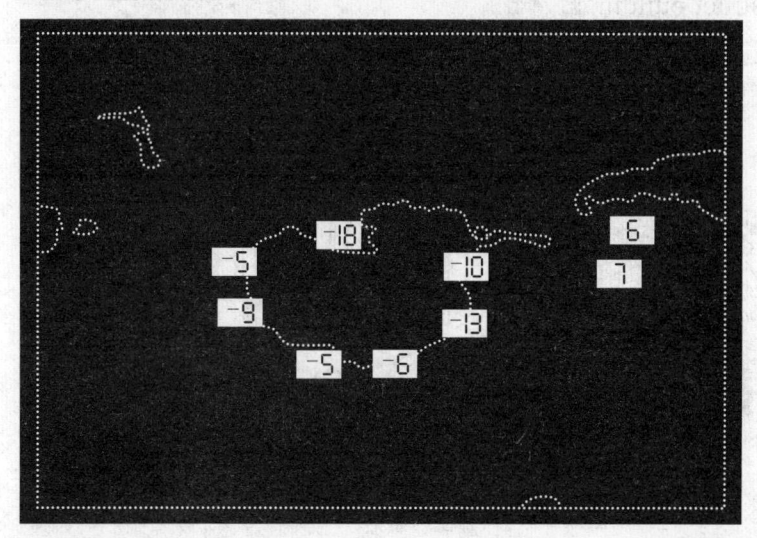

Temperatures shown on the map: −18, −5, −9, −5, −6, −10, −13, 6, 7

What is the difference in °C between the coldest and warmest temperatures shown on the map? [OCR]

19. The following is a weather page from CEEFAX.

Weather report for 14th December

	Daily hours of sunshine	Minimum night-time temperature (°C)	Maximum daytime temperature (°C)
Aberdeen	2·3	−15	−5
Aviemore	0	−18	−7
Belfast	1·3	−1	4
Birmingham	4·1	0	6
Bognor Regis	3·4	2	9
Bournemouth	5·4	4	11
Bristol	1·1	−3	2
Buxton	0	−7	−3
Cardiff	0·8	−2	−1

(a) Which place had the warmest daytime temperature?

(b) Which place had the coldest night-time temperature?

(c) What is the difference between the minimum night-time temperatures in Aberdeen and Cardiff?

(d) What is the difference between the maximum daytime temperatures in Bournemouth and Buxton? [WJEC]

2 SHAPE AND SPACE 1

Engineers use angles to construct buildings.

This unit is about:
- Turning through an angle
- The protractor
- Measuring angles, acute and obtuse angles
- Drawing triangles
- Scale drawing
- Bearings

You need to know:

Check in 2

- The fractions $\frac{1}{8}, \frac{1}{4}, \frac{3}{8}, \frac{1}{2}, \frac{5}{8}, \frac{3}{4}$ and $\frac{7}{8}$.

  1. Describe each of these turns using fractions. The first one is done for you.

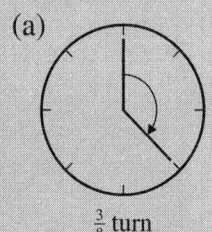

     (a) $\frac{3}{8}$ turn (b) (c) (d)

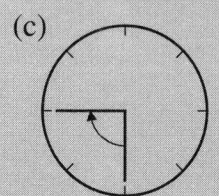

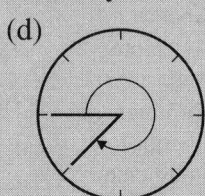

- The directions clockwise and anticlockwise.
  A clockwise turn follows the direction of hands of a clock.

  2. Describe the direction of these turns:

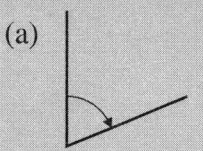

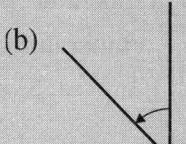

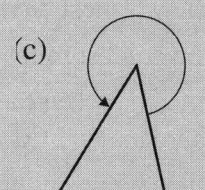

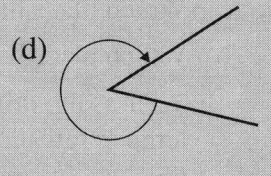

     (a) (b) (c) (d)

2.1 Turning

This is a bird's eye view of a telescope mounted on a stand.

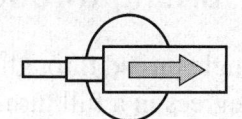

The telescope can be turned on its stand. These pictures show the telescope turned anticlockwise through $\frac{1}{4}$, $\frac{1}{2}$, $\frac{3}{4}$ and full turns.

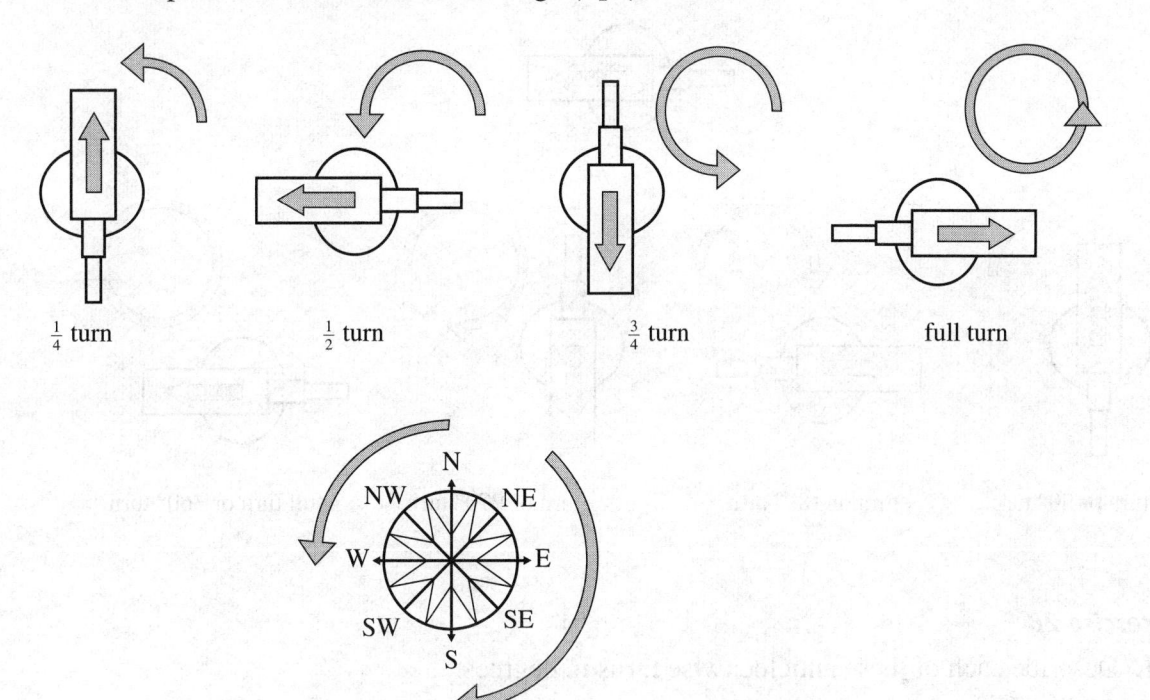

$\frac{1}{4}$ turn $\frac{1}{2}$ turn $\frac{3}{4}$ turn   full turn

Somebody looking North turns anticlockwise to look West. This is a $\frac{1}{4}$ turn.
Somebody looking NE turns clockwise to look South. This is a $\frac{3}{8}$ turn.

Exercise 2A

1. Describe each of these anticlockwise turns:
   - (a) North to South
   - (b) NE to SW
   - (c) West to South
   - (d) East to North
   - (e) SE to NW
   - (f) North to NW
   - (g) South to NE
   - (h) East to South
   - (i) SW to NW
   - (j) West to North
   - (k) SW to South
   - (l) SW to East
   - (m) SW to West
   - (n) North to SE
   - (o) NW to NE
   - (p) West to NE

2. Describe each of these clockwise turns:
   - (a) North to South
   - (b) NE to SW
   - (c) West to South
   - (d) East to North
   - (e) SE to NW
   - (f) North to NW
   - (g) South to NE
   - (h) East to South
   - (i) SW to NW
   - (j) West to North
   - (k) SW to South
   - (l) SW to East
   - (m) SW to West
   - (n) North to SE
   - (o) NW to NE
   - (p) West to NE

2.2 Turning through an angle

The angle turned through can be measured in degrees. There are 360 degrees in a full turn. The word degree is usually replaced with a small circle, so 360 degrees is written 360°.

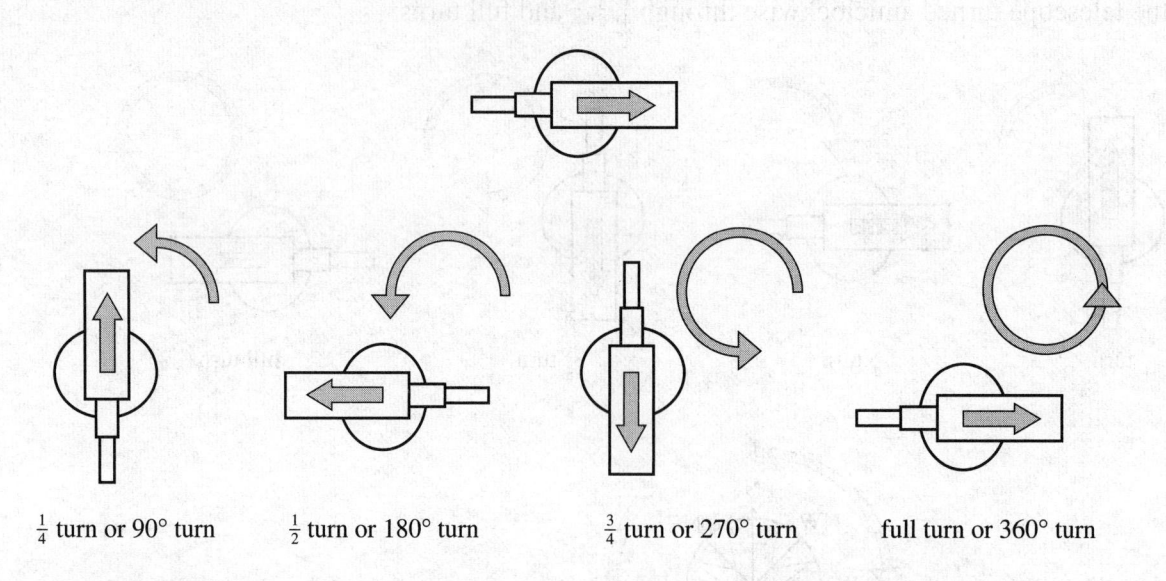

$\frac{1}{4}$ turn or 90° turn $\frac{1}{2}$ turn or 180° turn $\frac{3}{4}$ turn or 270° turn   full turn or 360° turn

Exercise 2B

1. Describe each of these anticlockwise turns in degrees:

   (a) West to South
   (b) NE to NW
   (c) East to West
   (d) East to South
   (e) SE to NW
   (f) East to North
   (g) South to West
   (h) NE to SW
   (i) West to North
   (j) NW to SW
   (k) West to East
   (l) NW to NE
   (m) North to NW
   (n) West to SW
   (o) SE to East
   (p) East to NE

2. Describe each of these clockwise turns in degrees:

   (a) West to South
   (b) NE to NW
   (c) East to West
   (d) East to South
   (e) SE to NW
   (f) East to North
   (g) South to West
   (h) NE to SW
   (i) West to North
   (j) NW to SW
   (k) West to East
   (l) NW to NE
   (m) North to NW
   (n) West to SW
   (o) SE to East
   (p) East to NE

2.3 The protractor

Angles are measured with a protractor.

To look at Boat A, the telescope must be turned anticlockwise through 30°.

To look at Boat B, the telescope must be turned anticlockwise through 145°.

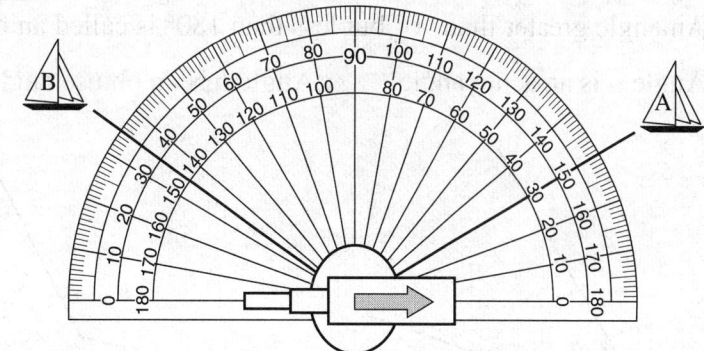

Exercise 2C

1. What anticlockwise angle must the telescope be turned through to look at each boat?

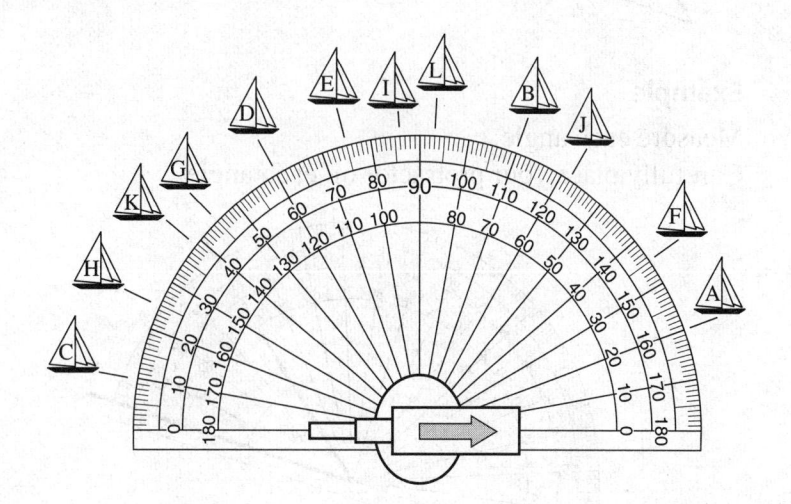

2. What clockwise angle must the telescope be turned through to look at each boat?

2.4 Measuring angles, acute and obtuse angles

An angle less than 90° is called an **acute** angle.
An angle greater than 90° but less than 180° is called an **obtuse** angle.

Angle *a* is an acute angle.   Angle *b* is an obtuse angle.

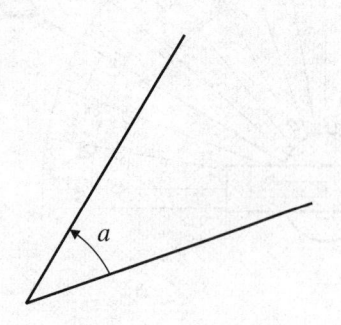

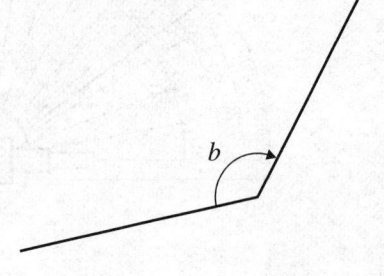

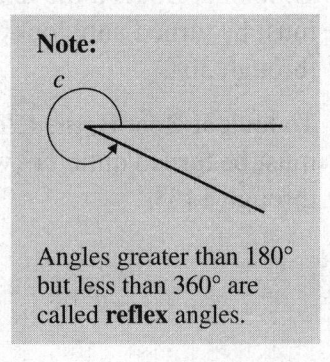

Note:

Angles greater than 180° but less than 360° are called **reflex** angles.

Example

Measure each angle.
Carefully place your protractor on each angle.

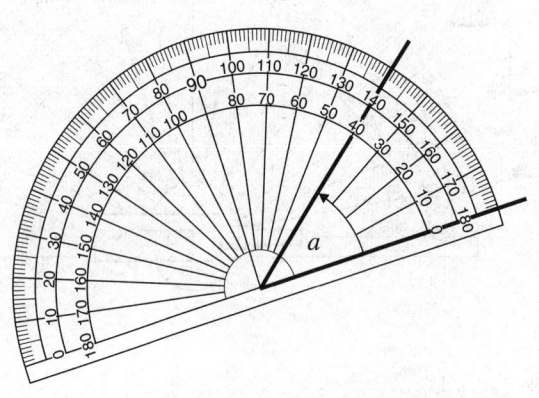

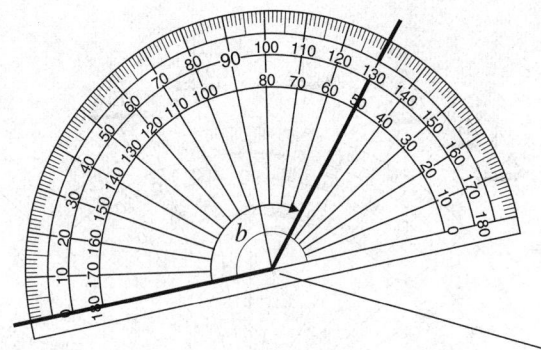

Read the size of the angle from the correct scale.
Angle *a* is acute so it is 40°.
Angle *b* is obtuse so it is 130°.

Hint:
Make sure the protractor is in place over the angle.

Exercise 2D

1. Measure each angle and state whether it is an acute angle or an obtuse angle.

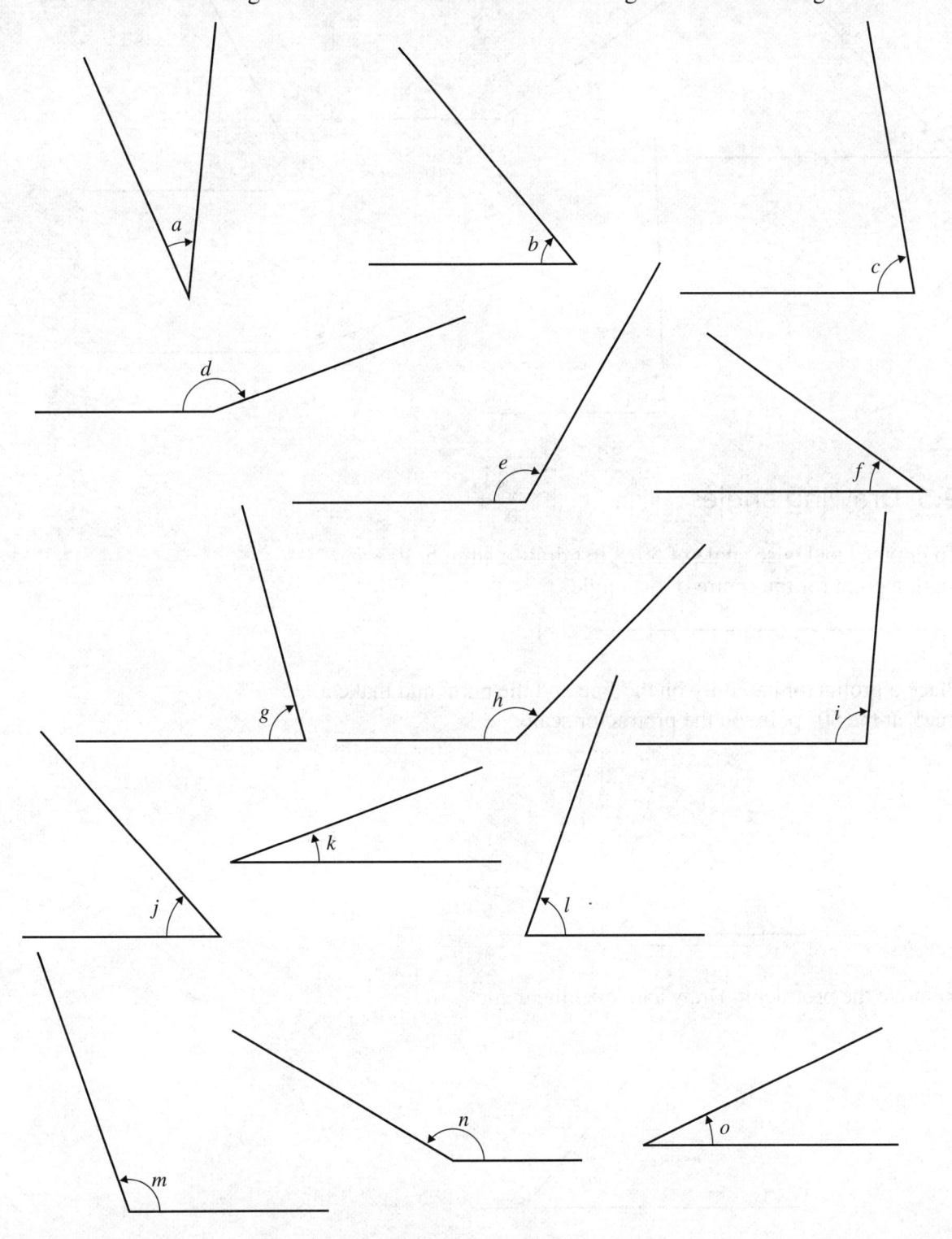

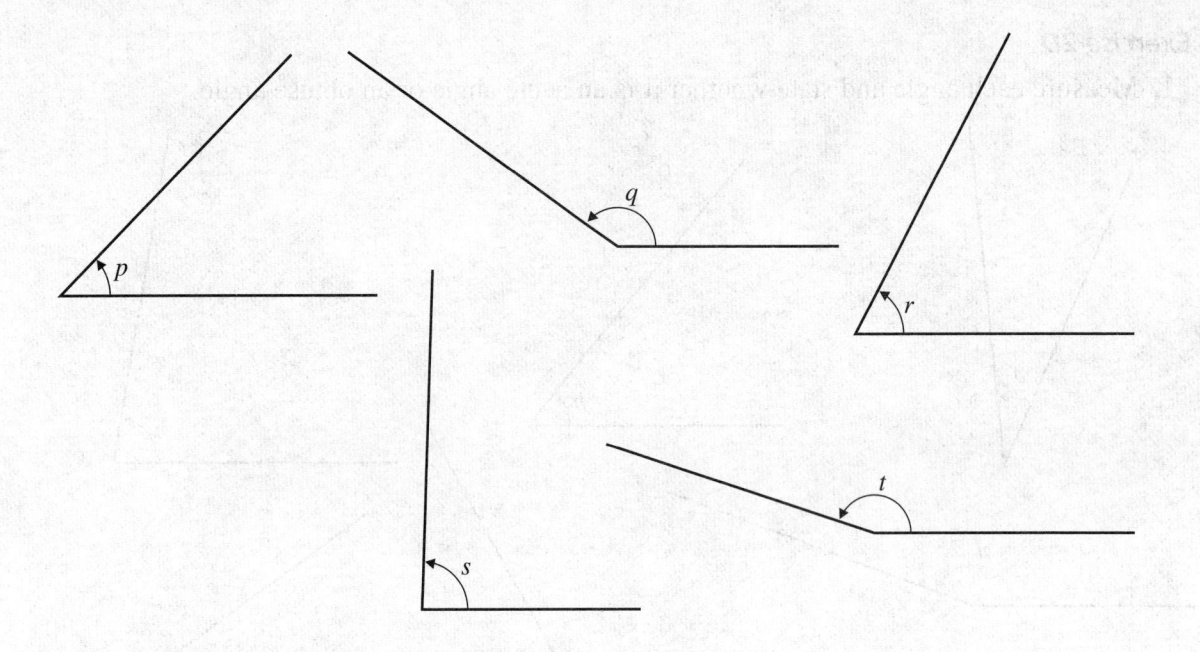

2.5 Drawing angles

To draw a clockwise angle of 50°, first draw a straight line and mark a point for the centre of the angle.

Place a protractor carefully on the line and the point and make a mark at the 50° point on the protractor scale.

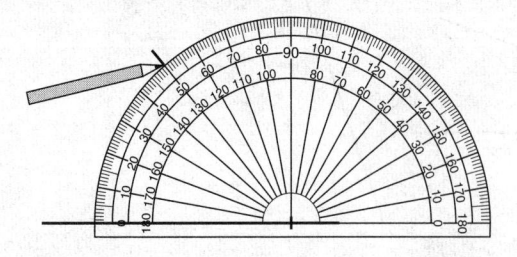

Remove the protractor. Draw and label the angle.

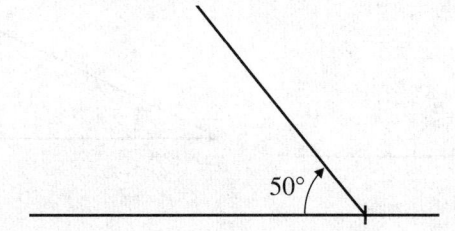

These diagrams show the stages in drawing an anticlockwise angle of 135°.

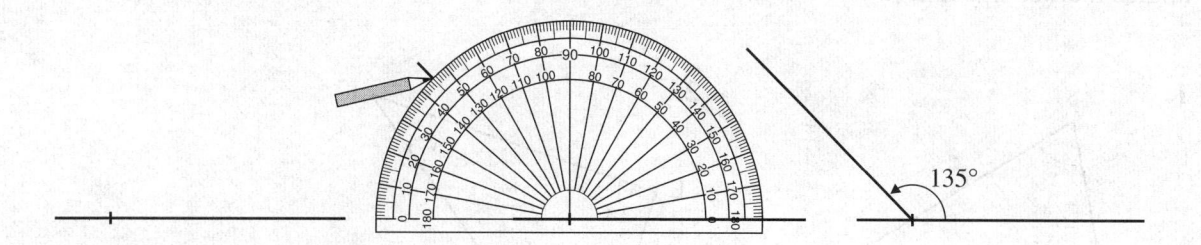

Exercise 2E

1. Draw and label each of the following clockwise angles.
   - (a) 20°
   - (b) 60°
   - (c) 80°
   - (d) 100°
   - (e) 120°
   - (f) 140°
   - (g) 160°
   - (h) 35°
   - (i) 75°
   - (j) 95°
   - (k) 115°
   - (l) 135°
   - (m) 155°
   - (n) 175°

2. Draw and label each of the following anticlockwise angles.
   - (a) 30°
   - (b) 50°
   - (c) 70°
   - (d) 110°
   - (e) 130°
   - (f) 150°
   - (g) 170°
   - (h) 45°
   - (i) 65°
   - (j) 85°
   - (k) 105°
   - (l) 125°
   - (m) 145°
   - (n) 165°

2.6 Naming angles

You will see angles named in different ways.

For example, in this triangle,

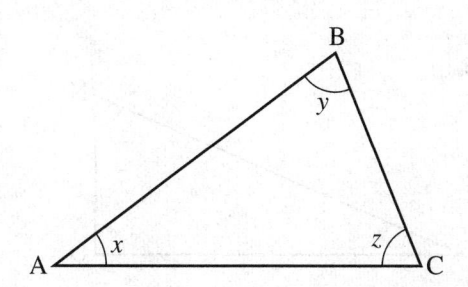

Angle x can also be called angle BAC or angle CAB.

Angle y can also be called angle ABC or angle CBA.

Angle z can also be called angle ACB or angle BCA.

Exercise 2F

In each triangle, write down two different ways to name the angles marked x, y and z.

1.

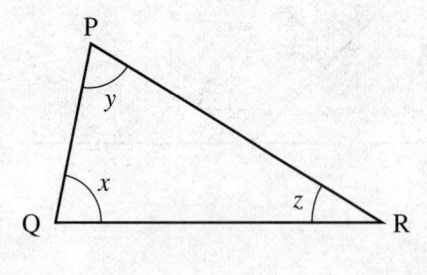

2.

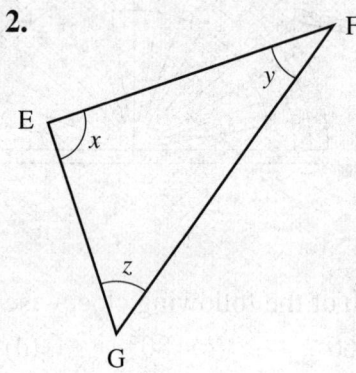

3.

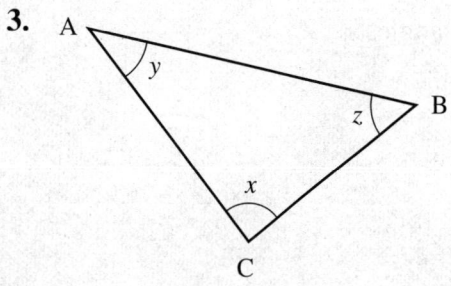

4.

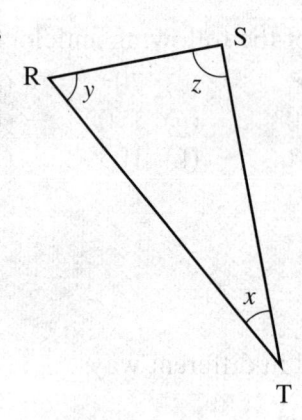

5.

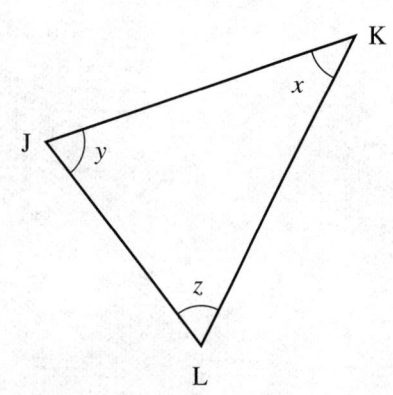

6.

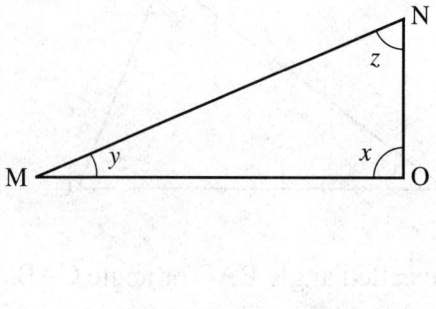

2.7 Drawing triangles

To draw accurate triangles you need to use geometrical equipment: ruler, protractor and compasses. Make sure your pencil is sharp!

Example 1
Draw the triangle ABC with AB = 10 cm, angle CAB = 30° and angle CBA = 60°.

First, draw a rough sketch.

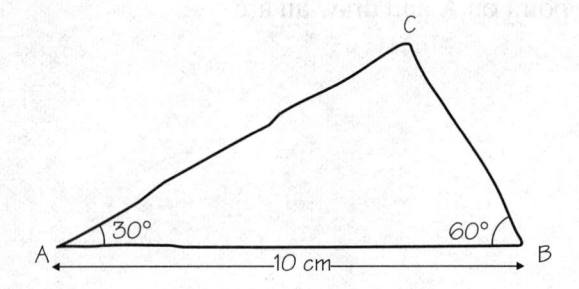

Then draw, using a ruler and protractor, an accurate triangle.

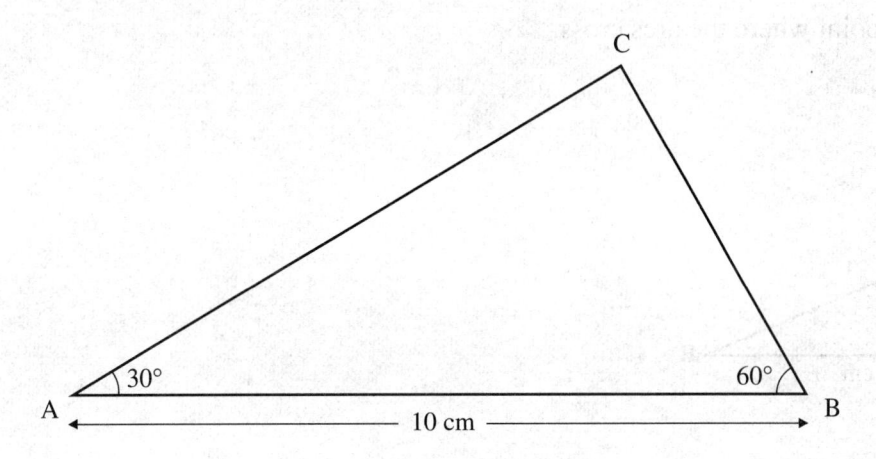

Example 2
Draw the triangle ABC with AB = 4 cm, BC = 5 cm and AC = 2 cm.

Draw the line AB, 4 cm long.

Open a pair of compasses to 5 cm. Put the point on B and draw an arc.

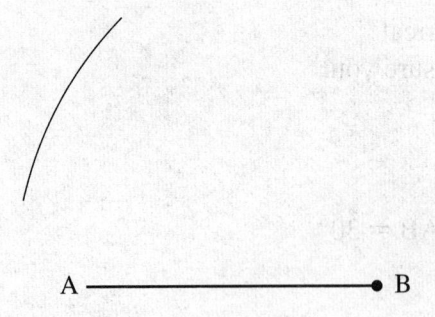

Open the compasses to 2 cm. Put the point on A and draw an arc.

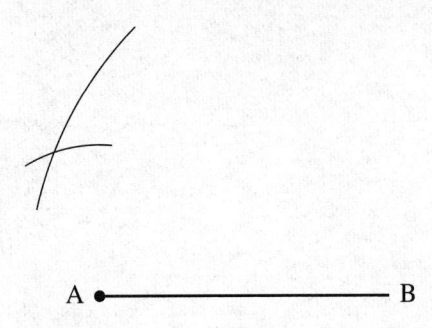

Connect A and B to the point where the arcs cross.

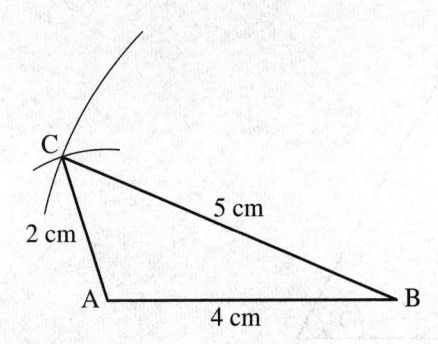

Exercise 2G

1. Draw the triangle XYZ with XY = 8 cm, angle ZXY = 40° and angle ZYX = 50°.

2. Draw the triangle PQR with PQ = 10 cm, angle RPQ = 60° and angle RQP = 60°.

3. Draw the triangle JKL with JK = 6 cm, angle LJK = 45° and angle LKJ = 45°.

4. Draw the triangle ABC with AB = 5 cm, angle CAB = 30° and angle CBA = 70°.

5. Draw the triangle CDE with CD = 12 cm, angle ECD = 20° and angle EDC = 90°.

6. Draw the triangle MNO with MN = 10 cm, MO = 8 cm and NO = 6 cm.

7. Draw the triangle RST with RS = 8 cm, ST = 8 cm and RT = 8 cm.

8. Draw the triangle ABC with AB = 9 cm, AC = 7 cm and BC = 6 cm.

9. Draw the triangle XYZ with XY = 10 cm, XZ = 8 cm and YZ = 8 cm.

10. Draw the triangle JKL with JK = 6 cm, JL = 9 cm and KL = 3 cm.

2.8 Scale drawing

If something is too big to draw full size, you can use a **scale**.

Example

Newquay is 15 km to the east and 20 km to the north of Camborne. Use a drawing with a scale of 1 cm = 5 km to find the direct distance from Newquay to Camborne.

Using a scale of 1 cm = 5 km, the distances become 3 cm and 4 cm. The scale drawing looks like this.

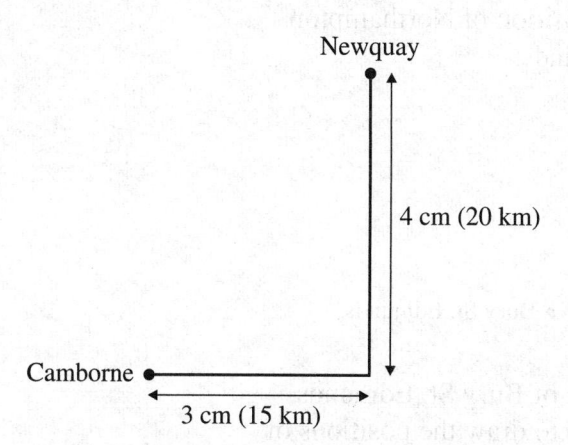

Hint:
If   5 km = 1 cm
then 15 km = 3 cm
and 20 km = 4 cm

Newquay

4 cm (20 km)

Camborne

3 cm (15 km)

The distance between Newquay and Camborne on the scale drawing is 5 cm.
The real distance between Newquay and Camborne is 25 km.

Hint:
If   1 cm = 5 km
then 5 cm = 25 km

Exercise 2H

1. This sketch shows three buildings in the village of Plumpton.

   • Church

   • Village hall   • Post office

   The church is 50 m due north of the village hall.
   (a) Use a scale of 1 cm = 10 m to draw the positions of the church and the village hall.
   (b) The post office is 70 m due east of the village hall. Add the post office to your drawing.
   (c) Use your drawing to find the direct distance between the church and the post office.

2. This sketch shows a ladder resting against a vertical wall. The ladder reaches 5 m up the wall and its base is 2 m from the wall.
   (a) Use a scale of 1 cm = 1 m to make an accurate drawing of the ladder.
   (b) Use your drawing to find the length of the ladder.

3. This sketch shows the relative position of Northampton, Peterborough and Bury St. Edmunds.

   • Peterborough

   • Northampton   • Bury St. Edmunds

   Northampton is 110 km due west of Bury St. Edmunds.
   (a) Use a scale of 1 cm = 10 km to draw the positions of Northampton and Bury St. Edmunds.
   (b) Peterborough is 55 km from Northampton and 75 km from Bury St. Edmunds. Use a pair of compasses to add the position of Peterborough to your drawing.

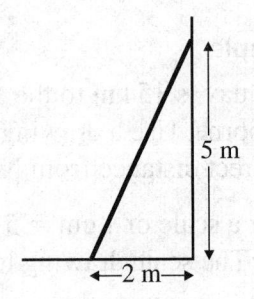

4. A tree has a shadow 20 m long when the Sun's rays are at an angle of 60° to the ground.
   (a) Use a scale of 1 cm = 4 m to make an accurate scale drawing of the tree.
   (b) Use your drawing to find the height of the tree.

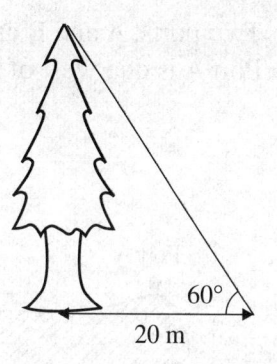

5. Thetford is 35 km to the east and 25 km to the south of Norwich.

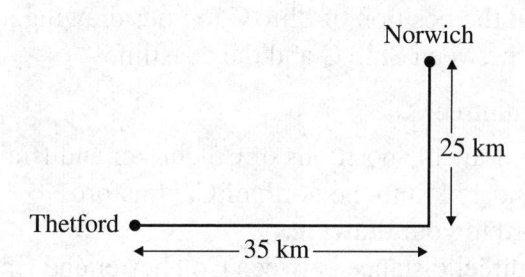

   (a) Use a scale of 1 cm = 5 km to draw the positions of Norwich and Thetford.
   (b) Use your drawing to find the direct distance from Norwich to Thetford.

6. Tiverton is 40 km to the east and 20 km to the south of Barnstaple.

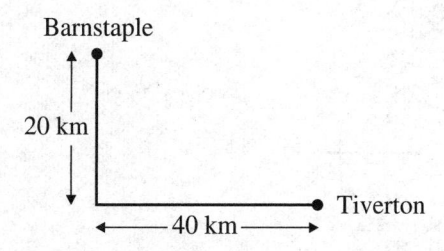

   (a) Use a scale of 1 cm = 5 km to draw the positions of Barnstaple and Tiverton.
   (b) Use your drawing to find the direct distance from Barnstaple to Tiverton.

7. Two ports, A and B are 140 km apart along a coastline.
   Port A is due west of Port B. A ship C is at sea off the coastline.

   • Ship C

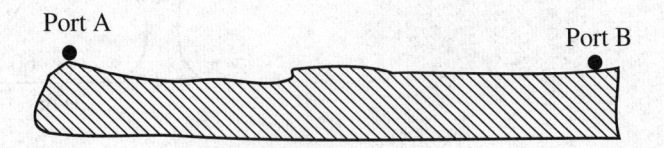

   Port A   Port B

   (a) Use a scale of 1 cm = 20 km to draw the positions of Port A and Port B.
   (b) Ship C is 80 km from Port A and 100 km from Port B.
       Use a pair of compasses to add the position of Ship C to your drawing.
   (c) Estimate the shortest distance between Ship C and the coastline.

8. Colchester is 24 km due east of Braintree.

   (a) Use a scale of 1 cm = 2 km to draw the positions of Colchester and Braintree.
   (b) Braintree is 6 km to the east and 15 km to the north of Chelmsford.
       Add the position of Chelmsford to your drawing.
   (c) Use your drawing to find the direct distance between Colchester and Chelmsford.

2.9 Bearings

A **bearing** is an angle giving a direction. All bearings are measured clockwise from North.

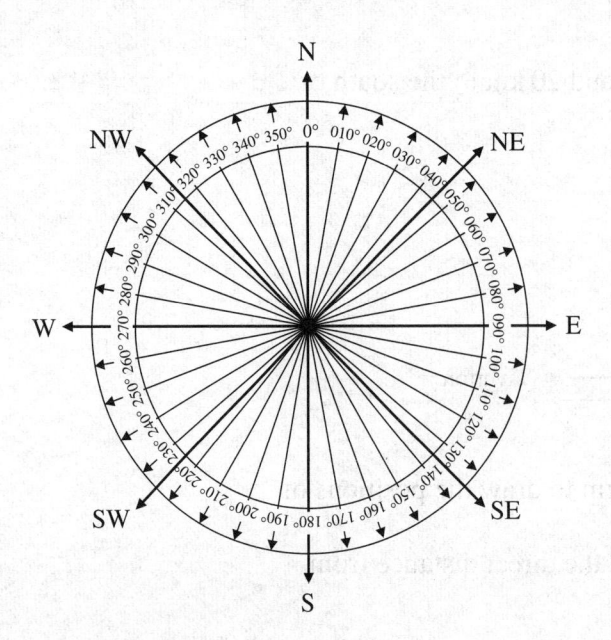

Bearings are always written with three digits. These diagrams show how bearings are used to describe directions.

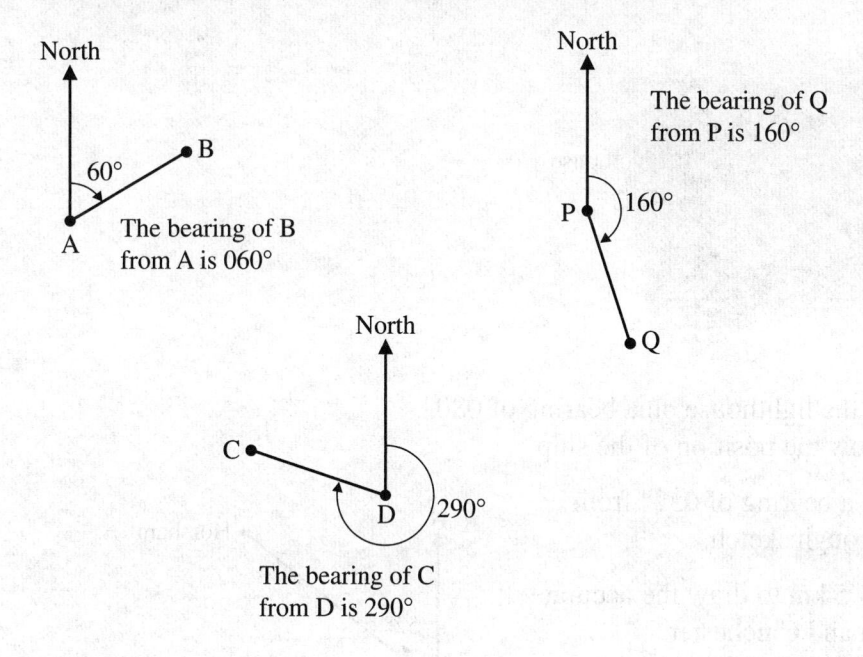

North

60°
A • ———— • B

The bearing of B from A is 060°

North

The bearing of Q from P is 160°

P • 160°

• Q

North

C •———• D) 290°

The bearing of C from D is 290°

Example

Royal Tunbridge Wells is 16 km on a bearing of 158° from Sevenoaks. Use a scale of 1 cm = 4 km to draw the positions of Royal Tunbridge Wells and Sevenoaks.

These are the stages in completing the drawing.

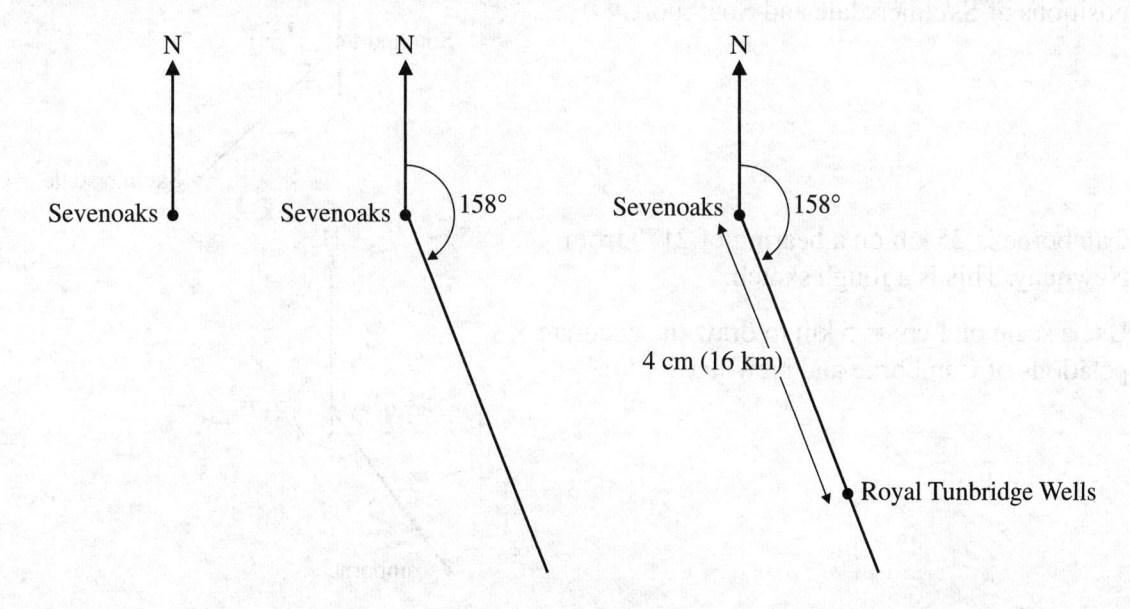

N

Sevenoaks •

N

Sevenoaks •) 158°

N

Sevenoaks •) 158°

4 cm (16 km)

• Royal Tunbridge Wells

50 Shape and Space 1

Exercise 2I

1. This map shows part of a coastline and a lighthouse. 1 cm on the map represents 2 km.

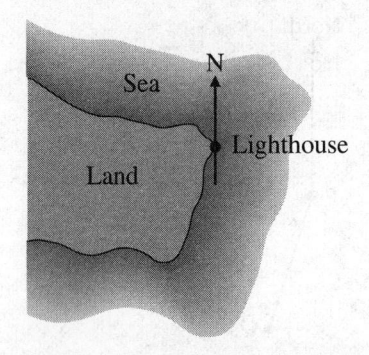

   A ship is 18 km from the lighthouse on a bearing of 080°. Copy the map and show the position of the ship.

2. Horsham is 40 km on a bearing of 052° from Chichester. This is a rough sketch.

   Use a scale of 1 cm = 5 km to draw the accurate positions of Horsham and Chichester.

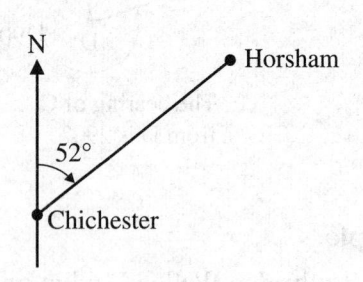

3. Skelmersdale is 18 km on a bearing of 133° from Southport. This is a rough sketch.

   Use a scale of 1 cm = 5 km to draw the accurate positions of Skelmersdale and Southport.

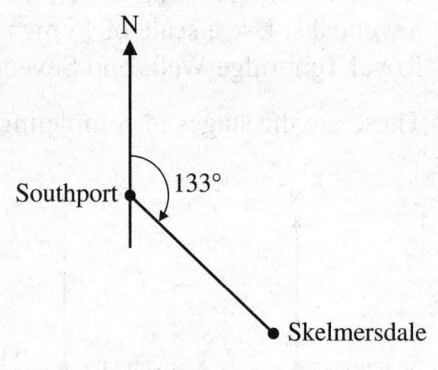

4. Camborne is 25 km on a bearing of 217° from Newquay. This is a rough sketch.

   Use a scale of 1 cm = 5 km to draw the accurate positions of Camborne and Newquay.

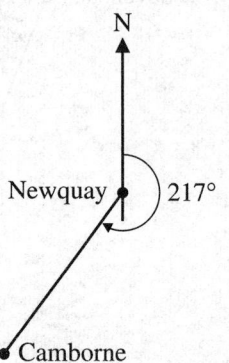

5. Taunton is 33 km on a bearing of 286° from Yeovil. This is a rough sketch.

   Use a scale of 1 cm = 5 km to draw the accurate positions of Taunton and Yeovil.

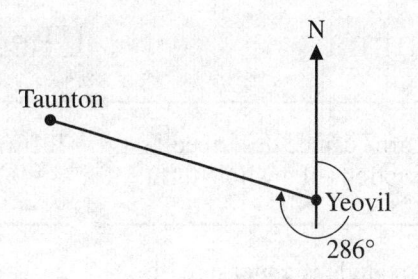

6. Melton Mowbray is 23 km on a bearing of 049° from Leicester. Nottingham is 35 km on a bearing of 355° from Leicester. This is a rough sketch.

   Use a scale of 1 cm = 5 km to draw the accurate positions of Leicester, Melton Mowbray and Nottingham.

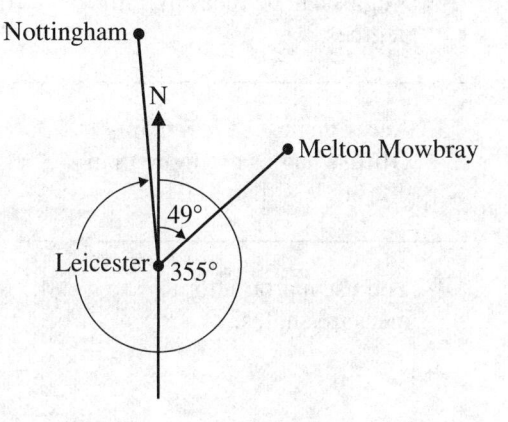

7. Milton Keynes is 35 km to the east and 35 km to the north of Oxford. This is a rough sketch.
   (a) Use a scale of 1 cm = 5 km to draw the accurate positions of Milton Keynes and Oxford.
   (b) Use your drawing to find the bearing of Milton Keynes from Oxford.

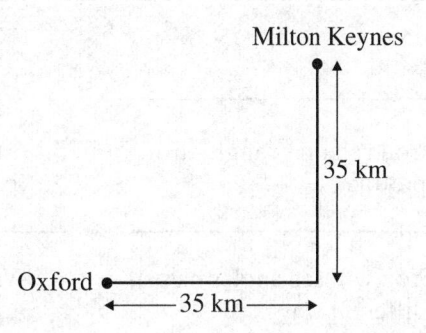

8. In the village of Rempham Vasey the village hall is 160 m north of the church.
   (a) Use a scale of 1 cm = 20 metres to draw the positions of the village hall and the church.
   (b) The local shop is on a bearing of 135° from the church. Add this bearing to your drawing.
   (c) The local shop is 240 m from the village hall. Use a pair of compasses to mark the position of the local shop on your drawing.
   (d) Use your drawing to find the bearing of the local shop from the village hall.

Summary

1. Turns can be described as fractions of a whole turn.

2. An angle is a measure of turn.
   Angles can be measured in degrees.

3. **Acute** angles are less than 90°.
   Obtuse angles are more than 90° but less than 180°.

4. You use a protractor to measure angles.

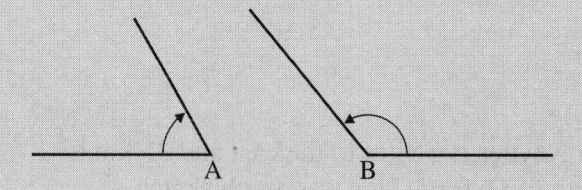

5. You can draw angles using a protractor.

6. You will see angles named in different ways.

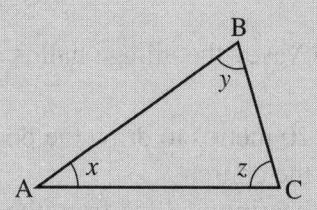

7. Triangles can be constructed with a ruler, protractor and pair of compasses.

Checkout 2

1. (a) Describe a clockwise turn from North to West.
   (b) Describe an anticlockwise turn from SE to West.

2. (a) How many degrees are there in a clockwise turn from West to NW?
   (b) How many degrees are there in an anticlockwise turn from NE to SE?

3. (a) Is angle A below an acute angle or an obtuse angle?
   (b) Is angle B below an acute angle or an obtuse angle?

4. Measure each of these angles.

5. (a) Draw a clockwise angle of 55°.
   (b) Draw an anticlockwise angle of 120°.

6. Write down two ways to name the angles marked x, y and z.

7. (a) Draw the triangle EFG with EF = 8 cm, angle GEF = 45° and angle GFE = 80°.
   (b) Draw the triangle ABC with AB = 7 cm, BC = 5 cm and AC = 10 cm.

8. Scale drawings are used if something is too big to draw full size.

8. In the village of Jessingham the church is 160 m due north of the pub. The local shop is due east of the pub and 200 m from the church.
   (a) Use a scale of 1 cm = 20 m to draw the positions of the church, pub and local shop.
   (b) How far is the local shop from the pub?

9. A **bearing** is an angle giving a direction. All bearings are measured clockwise from North. Bearings are always written with three digits.

9. Salisbury is 30 km on a bearing of 120° from Warminster. Use a scale of 1 cm = 5 km to draw the positions of Salisbury and Warminster.

Revision exercise 2

1. Helen is standing at H. She is facing North. She turns anticlockwise through 1 right angle.

   (a) In what direction is she now facing?

   Later Harry stands at H. He faces South. He turns clockwise through $1\frac{1}{2}$ right angles.

   (b) In what direction will he then be facing?

   [Edexcel]

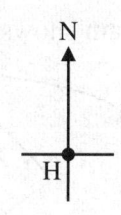

2. The diagram shows the position of some places in a village.

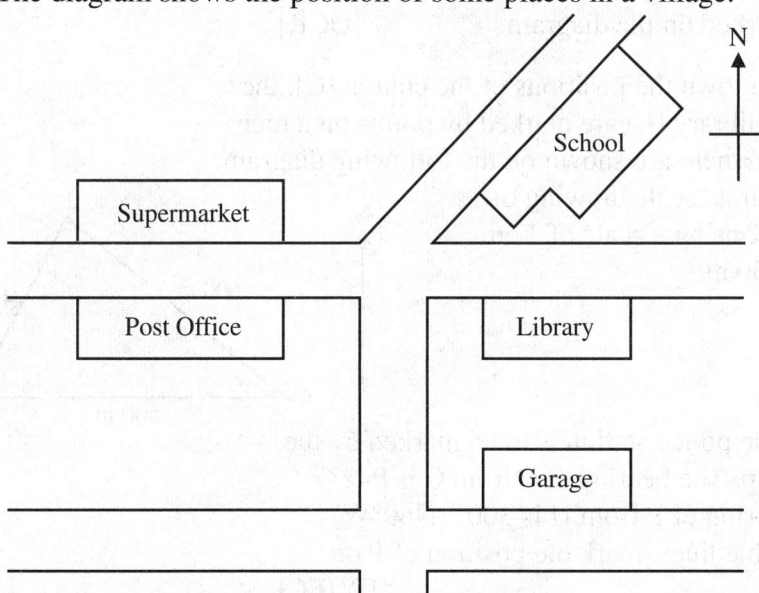

(a) Which place is South of the Library?

(b) Write down the compass direction of
    (i) the Library from the Post Office
    (ii) the Post Office from the School
    (iii) the Garage from the Supermarket.   [Edexcel]

3. (a) Measure and record the size of the angles marked x and y in the diagram.

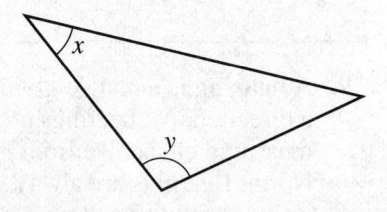

(b) Measure and record the length of the following line.

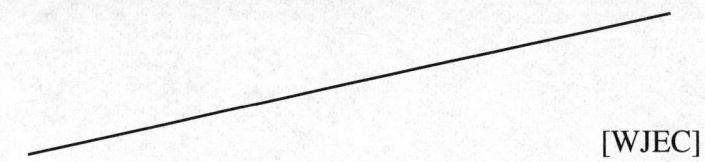

[WJEC]

4. This diagram shows the back window wiper on Sue's car.

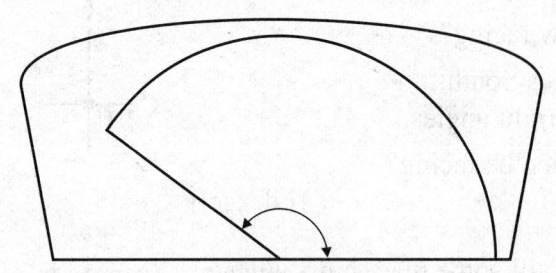

Measure the angle marked on the diagram.   [OCR]

5. During the survey of a town the positions of the church (C), the town hall (H) and the library (L) are marked by points on a map. The distances between them are shown on the following diagram.

    (a) Draw an accurate scale drawing of triangle CHL, using a scale of 1 cm to represent 50 m.

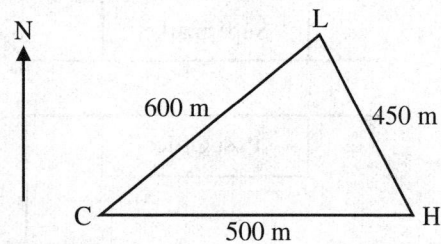

(b) The position of the police station is to be marked by the letter P on the map. The bearing of P from C is 042° (N42°E). The bearing of P from H is 300° (N60°W). By drawing suitable lines, mark the position of P on your diagram.   [WJEC]

6. San Fernando is on a bearing of 157° from Pasadena. Draw this bearing accurately on a diagram. [Edexcel]

7. The sketch map shows the positions of Poolbridge (P), Rosegrove (R) and Beacon Point (B).

   Beacon Point is 10 km due North of Poolbridge.

   Rosegrove is 7 km from Poolbridge on a bearing of 056°.

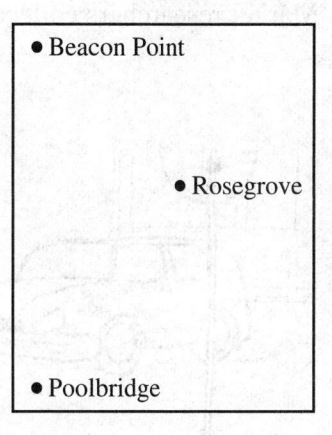

   (a) Construct triangle PBR using a scale of 1 cm to represent 1 km.
   (b) Use your diagram to find the distance of Rosegrove from Beacon Point.
   (c) Use your diagram to find the bearing of Rosegrove from Beacon Point. [OCR]

8. The diagram is part of a map showing the positions of several towns.

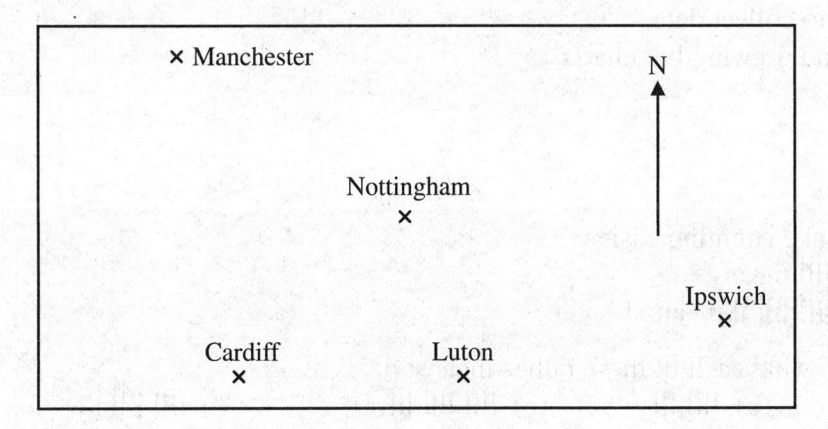

   (a) Which town is due West of Luton?
   (b) Write down the approximate compass direction of Nottingham from Cardiff.
   (c) Measure and write down the bearing of Manchester from Nottingham. [Edexcel]

3 Data Handling 1

Market researchers collect data that is used to shape future products.

- Designing a survey to collect data
- Using tally marks and drawing bar charts
- Using pictograms

You need to know:

> - Tally marks make counting easier.
>   For example: |||| means 5
> |||| |||| || means 12.
>
>   1. Write down what each of these tallies means:
>   (a) ||| (b) |||| ||| (c) |||| |||| |||| | (d) |||| |||| |||
>
>   2. Write these numbers using tally marks:
>   (a) 14   (b) 6   (c) 21   (d) 17

Data is another word for information.

One way to collect **data** is to use a survey or questionnaire.

3.1 Designing a survey to collect data

When you design a survey, try to provide tick boxes for as many answers as possible.

Don't use a question like:

What is your favourite type of TV programme? ....

Do use a question like:

- Which is your favourite type of TV programme?
  - ☐ Sport
  - ☐ Drama and films
  - ☐ Soap opera
  - ☐ Chat shows
  - ☐ Comedy
  - ☐ Wildlife and animals
  - ☐ News and documentaries

This will make it much easier to check the data you collect.

Example

Nathan is designing a survey on eye colours. He wants to find out:

- which is the most common eye colour
- whether eye colour distribution is different for men and women
- whether eye colour distribution depends on age.

Design a survey to provide the data he needs.

Tick one box for your eye colour.	Tick one box for your sex.	Tick one box for your age.
☐ Green	☐ Male	☐ 21–30
☐ Brown	☐ Female	☐ 31–40
☐ Blue		☐ 41–50
☐ Grey		☐ 51–60
☐ Other		☐ over 60

Exercise 3A

1. As part of a survey on healthy eating, John wants to find out:

   - How many students in his school consider their health when deciding what to eat for lunch.
   - Whether more boys than girls consider their health when deciding what to eat for lunch.
   - Whether more students in the older year groups consider their health when deciding what to eat for lunch.

   Design three questions which John should include in his survey.

2. As part of a survey on television viewing, Pria wants to find out:

   - How many hours of television people watch during an average day.
   - Whether women watch more television than men.
   - Whether different age groups have different viewing habits.

   Design three questions which Pria should include in her survey.

3. As part of a survey on pop music in her school, Toni wants to find out:

   - Which type of pop music is most popular with students.
   - Whether boys prefer different types of pop music to girls.
   - Whether younger students prefer different types of pop music to older students.

   Design three questions which Toni should include in her survey.

4. As part of a health questionnaire for young people, a Health Authority wants to find out:

   - How many young people smoke cigarettes.
   - If they smoke, how many cigarettes they smoke a day.
   - Whether young people are more likely to smoke cigarettes if one or more of their parents smokes cigarettes.

   Design three questions which the Health Authority should include in its survey.

3.2 Using tally marks and drawing bar charts

Twenty students are given a mark out of 5 for a short test. The results were:

   1, 2, 5, 4, 5, 4, 3, 3, 4, 5, 2, 2, 2, 4, 4, 2, 4, 5, 3, 4

This is the **raw data**. It has not been organised in any way.

Tally marks are often used to organise a list of results into a table. The marks for the twenty students can be organised into a table like this.

Mark	Tally	Frequency
0		0
1	|	1
2	|||||	5
3	|||	3
4	||||| ||	7
5	||||	4
Total		20

Remember:
The word **frequency** means the number of times something happens.

After the data has been organised, you can draw a **bar chart**.

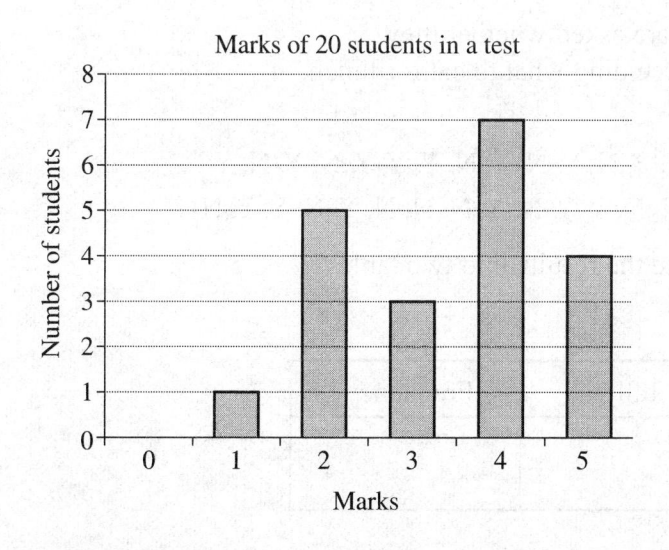

Marks of 20 students in a test

[Bar chart showing Number of students on y-axis (0 to 8) and Marks on x-axis (0 to 5). Bars: 0→0, 1→1, 2→5, 3→3, 4→7, 5→4]

Remember:
All bar charts should have a title and labels on each axis.

Exercise 3B

1. A gamekeeper checks the number of eggs in twenty-five nests. These are his results:

   3, 4, 0, 1, 3, 0, 2, 2, 3, 4, 4, 4, 5, 0, 1, 3, 4, 2, 2, 4, 2, 5, 0, 0, 2

   (a) Use tally marks to organise the results into a table like this:

Number of eggs	Tally	Frequency
0		
1		
2		
3		
4		
5		

   (b) Draw a bar chart using axes like these.

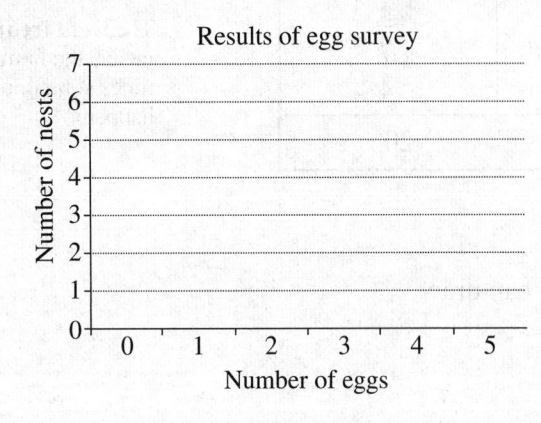

2. Twenty girls and twenty boys are asked whether they considered their health when deciding what to eat for lunch. These are the results:

   Girls: Y, Y, N, N, Y, Y, N, Y, N, Y, N, Y, N, Y, Y, Y, N, Y, N, Y

   Boys: Y, Y, Y, N, N, N, N, N, Y, Y, N, Y, N, N, N, Y, N, Y, Y, N

   (a) Use tally marks to organise the results into two tables with headings like this:

Girls	Tally	Frequency
Yes		
No		

(b) Draw two bar charts using axes like these.

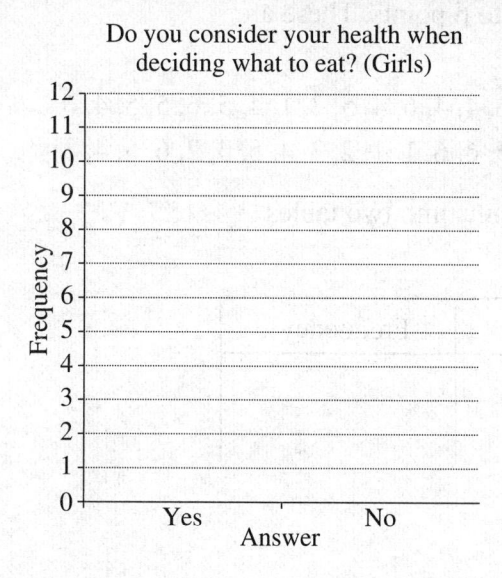

Do you consider your health when deciding what to eat? (Girls)

Frequency (0–12) vs *Answer* (Yes, No)

3. In a taste test, 30 people were asked to select their favourite sausage from four brands. The brands were Porkers (P), Sizzlers (S), Yumbos (Y) and Bangers (B). These are the results:

P, B, B, B, B, Y, P, Y, B, Y, P, P, S, B, B, B, S, Y, P, B, P, Y, P, S, P, Y, B, Y, B, P

(a) Use tally marks to organise the results into a table with headings like this:

Type of sausage	Tally	Frequency
Porkers		

(b) Draw a bar chart using axes like these.

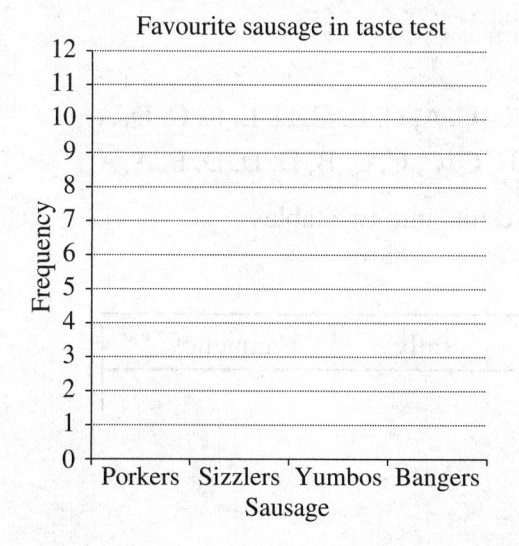

Favourite sausage in taste test

Frequency (0–12) vs *Sausage* (Porkers, Sizzlers, Yumbos, Bangers)

4. Kathy and Kyle both fire twenty-five shots at a target. The target has sections which score from 1 to 6 points. These are their scores:

   Kathy: 6, 4, 4, 3, 2, 6, 4, 1, 2, 5, 6, 4, 4, 6, 4, 5, 3, 1, 4, 5, 6, 5, 5, 4, 6
   Kyle: 5, 5, 4, 4, 4, 3, 4, 5, 6, 4, 5, 6, 6, 1, 1, 2, 3, 4, 5, 3, 2, 6, 5, 4, 3

   (a) Use tally marks to organise the results into two tables with headings like this:

Score	Tally	Frequency
1		
2		

   (b) Draw two bar charts.

5. Twenty men and twenty women answered this question:

   How many hours of television do you watch during an average day?

   ☐ A. less than one hour
   ☐ B. one to two hours
   ☐ C. two to three hours
   ☐ D. three to four hours
   ☐ E. more than four hours

   These are the results:

   Men: A, A, B, C, D, D, C, E, C, C, A, C, B, C, D, E, C, C, D, A
   Women: B, B, C, C, E, A, D, B, C, C, C, C, B, D, D, D, E, A, A

   (a) Use tally marks to organise the results into two tables with headings like this:

Numbers of hours watched	Tally	Frequency
Less than one hour		

   (b) Draw two bar charts.

3.3 Pictograms

Pictograms are sometimes used instead of bar charts. Pictures are used to replace the bars.

For example, the bar chart for student marks can be drawn as this pictogram.

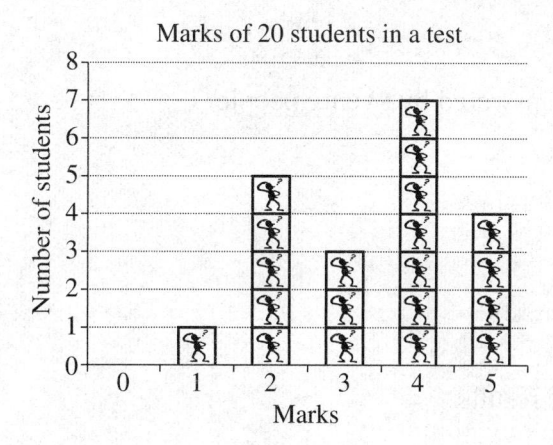

Marks of 20 students in a test

This is data on the number of lions living in a game reserve in six different years.

Year	1995	1996	1997	1998	1999	2000
Number of lions	150	165	172	190	218	205

To show this data with a pictogram, you need a scale because the numbers are large. If you use one lion symbol to represent 20 lions, the pictogram looks like this:

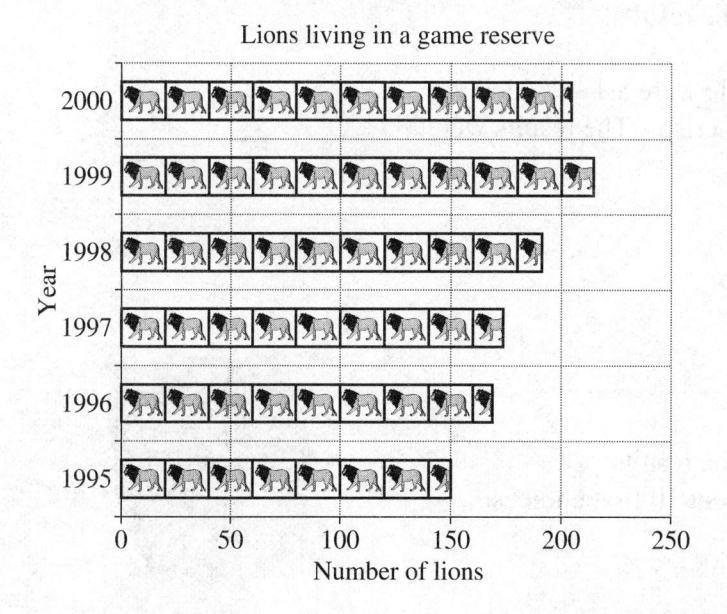

Lions living in a game reserve

Notice that if the number of lions does not divide exactly by 20, you need to draw part of a lion.

Drawing the same symbol many times can be very tedious. So, unless you are using a computer, always select very simple symbols for pictograms.

Exercise 3C

1. A question about eye colour was answered by twenty people in a survey. The results were:

    | Green | 4 |
    | Brown | 6 |
    | Blue | 8 |
    | Grey | 2 |
    | Other | 0 |

    Draw a pictogram to illustrate the results.

2. Thirty people answered a question about the type of house they live in. The results were:

    | Semi-detached house | 10 |
    | Detached house | 8 |
    | Bungalow | 3 |
    | Terraced house | 5 |
    | Flat | 4 |

    Draw a pictogram to illustrate the results.

3. In a survey, three hundred people were asked which was their favourite flavour of potato crisps. The results were:

    | Plain | 85 |
    | Cheese and Onion | 60 |
    | Salt and Vinegar | 74 |
    | Roast Chicken | 34 |
    | Prawn Cocktail | 22 |
    | Roast Beef | 15 |
    | Smoky Bacon | 10 |

    Draw a pictogram to illustrate the results.
    Use a symbol like this to represent 10 first choices.

Summary

1. When you design a survey, try to provide tick boxes for as many answers as possible.

2. **Tally marks** are often used to organise a list of results into a table. After the data has been organised a **bar chart** can be drawn.

3. Pictograms are sometimes sometimes used instead of bar charts. Pictures are used to replace the bars.

Checkout 3

1. As part of a survey on a local superstore, Sangita wants to find out:
   - How long it takes the person answering the survey to travel to the superstore.
   - Whether people who live closer visit the superstore more frequently.
   - Whether people who live closer spend less money per visit than people who live further away.

   Design three questions which Sangita should include in her survey. Each question should have at least four tick boxes for people to choose from.

2. Nina did a survey of the colours of cars passing the school. These are her results:

w	w	r	b	r	r	w	g	g	w
r	b	r	w	w	g	g	r	b	w
b	r	w	b	r	r	g	g	w	w

   Key: w = white
         b = blue
         r = red
         g = green

   (a) Use tally marks to organise Nina's results into a table.
   (b) Draw a bar chart for this data.

3. Draw a pictogram to illustrate Nina's results from Question 2 above.

Revision exercise 3

1. Fred is conducting a survey into television viewing habits. One of the questions in his survey is

   'How much television do you watch?'

   His friend Sheila tells him that it is not a very good question. Write down two ways in which Fred could improve his question. [Edexcel]

2. In a survey, Jason uses the following questionnaire to test the hypothesis 'more boys than girls like sport'.

> Which sex are you?   Male ☐   Female ☐
>
> Which ONE of these sports do you like best?
>
> Football ☐   Cricket ☐   Netball ☐   Basketball ☐   Hockey ☐   Rugby ☐   None of these ☐

(a) Explain why this questionnaire is not suitable for his survey.

(b) One evening he gives the questionnaire to all the people in the local gymnasium. Give **two** reasons why this is unlikely to be a suitable group of people to survey.

(c) In another survey, some 16-year-old pupils were asked:

'How long did you spend doing your homework last night?'

Design an observation sheet to collect this data.   [WJEC]

3. Karl's and Eleanor's school is near a busy main road.

They decide to carry out a survey of the different types of vehicles that travel on the main road.

Design a suitable data sheet so that they can collect their data easily.   [Edexcel]

4. Patrick carried out a survey of 45 pupils in Year 11.

He asked them how many books they had borrowed from the library in the last month.

These are Patrick's results.
 4, 6, 3, 9, 10, 5, 4, 7, 6, 3, 8, 3, 1, 9, 0,
12, 5, 6, 3, 3, 0, 7, 9, 4, 3, 8, 2, 1, 6, 1,
 3, 4, 6, 0, 7, 10, 4, 8, 1, 6, 7, 1, 2, 3, 1

Copy and complete this frequency table.

Number of books	Tally	Frequency
0 to 2		
3 to 5		
6 to 8		
more than 8		6

[Edexcel]

5. The bar chart shows the number of hours Jason spent watching television in one week.

   Hours spent watching television

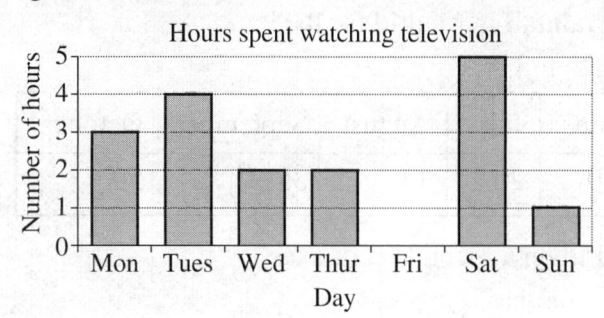

   (a) Write down the day on which he watched most television.
   (b) Work out the total number of hours he spent watching television during the week. [Edexcel]

6. The bar chart shows which day of the week shoppers went to a supermarket in 1994 and 1996.

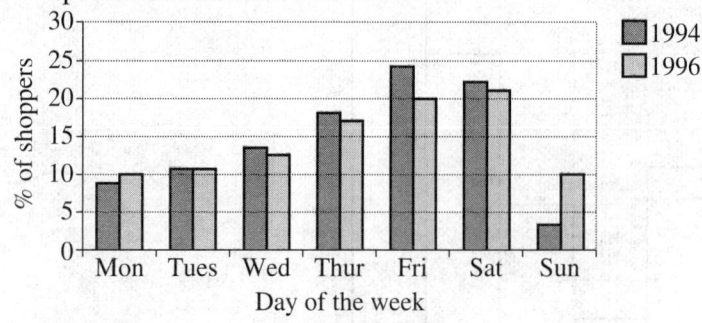

   (a) Which day of the week was the most popular day for shopping in 1994?
   (b) Did the shoppers choose different days to shop in 1996 compared with 1994? Give a reason for your answer.
   (c) 'In 1996, about half the shoppers did their shopping at the end of the week (Friday, Saturday and Sunday).'

   Is this statement true or false?
   Show all your working. [AQA/NEAB]

7. Zeeshan counts the number of vowels in a sentence. The results are shown in the table.

Vowel	a	e	i	o	u
Number	14	17	8	9	6

   Draw a bar chart to show this information. [Edexcel]

8. The bar chart below shows the monthly rainfall in Lisbon for six summer months.
   This table shows the monthly rainfall in Madrid for the same six months.

Month	May	June	July	August	September	October
Rainfall (mm)	40	40	20	15	35	50

   (a) Draw a bar chart for Madrid on a second set of axes.

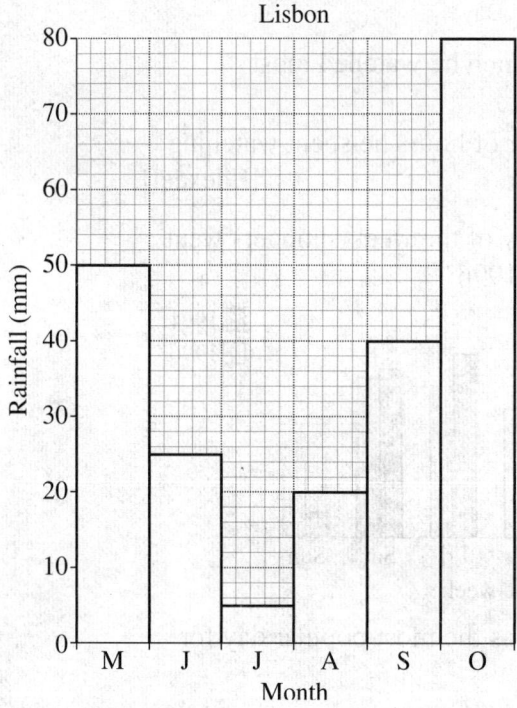

   (b) Compare the rainfall in the two cities.
       Give one way in which they are similar and one way in which they are different. [OCR]

9. Class 3P carry out a survey to find the number of lorries passing the school gates. The results are shown below.

Time	Number of lorries
10 a.m.–noon	35
noon–2 p.m.	20
2 p.m.–4 p.m.	30

   Draw a pictogram to represent the above data. [WJEC]

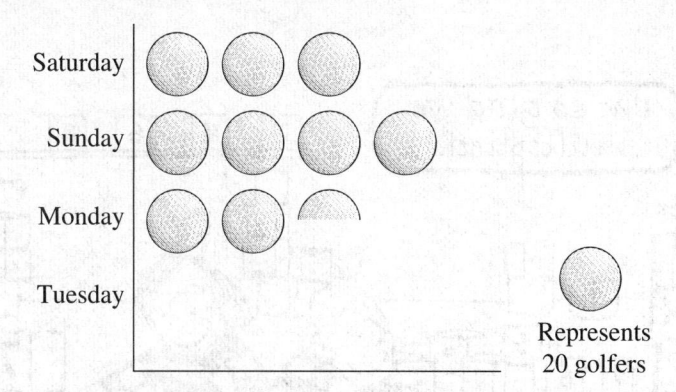

10. The pictogram shows the number of golfers who played at the local golf club last week.

(a) How many golfers played on Sunday?

(b) How many golfers played on Monday?

On Tuesday 35 golfers played.

(c) Copy and complete the pictogram to show this.

[Edexcel]

11. The diagram below is part of a pictogram.
The pictogram shows the number of lorries which crossed the North Sea by ferry during a week in 1996.

(a) How many lorries crossed the North Sea on the Tuesday?

On the Friday 300 lorries crossed the North Sea by ferry.

(b) Copy and complete the pictogram to show this information.   [Edexcel]

4 NUMBER 2

This unit is about:

- Multiplying numbers by 10, 100 or 1 000
- Dividing numbers by 10, 100 or 1 000
- Multiplying numbers 'in your head'
- Dividing numbers 'in your head'
- Multiplying or dividing without a calculator
- Factors, even numbers, odd numbers, prime numbers and multiples
- Ratio

You need to remember:

> ● Each digit in a number has place value (see Unit 1).
>
> 1. What is the value of the underlined digit in each number?
>   (a) 7<u>6</u>　　(b) <u>7</u>60　　(c) 7 <u>6</u>00　　(d) <u>7</u> 900　　(e) <u>7</u>90
>   (f) 7<u>9</u>　　(g) <u>4</u>5　　(h) <u>4</u>50　　(i) <u>4</u> 500　　(j) 1 0<u>1</u>1

Check in 4

4.1 Multiplying numbers by 10

To multiply a number by 10, move all the digits one place to the left and add a zero. A place value table will help.

Example

(a) 5 × 10 = 50

Th	H	T	U
		5	
	5	0	×10

(b) 30 × 10 = 300

Th	H	T	U
		3	0
	3	0	0	×10

(c) 75 × 10 = 750

Th	H	T	U
	7	5	
7	5	0	×10

(d) 356 × 10 = 3 560

Th	H	T	U
	3	5	6
3	5	6	0	×10

Exercise 4A

1. (a) 6 × 10 (b) 7 × 10 (c) 11 × 10 (d) 23 × 10
   (e) 32 × 10 (f) 45 × 10 (g) 80 × 10 (h) 61 × 10
   (i) 56 × 10 (j) 98 × 10 (k) 112 × 10 (l) 172 × 10
   (m) 451 × 10 (n) 390 × 10 (o) 916 × 10 (p) 206 × 10
   (q) 101 × 10 (r) 903 × 10 (s) 700 × 10 (t) 341 × 10

2. Pencils are sold in packs of 10. How many pencils are there in:
   (a) 8 packs
   (b) 24 packs
   (c) 33 packs
   (d) 72 packs
   (e) 100 packs
   (f) 144 packs?

3. There are 10 millimetres in a centimetre. How many millimetres are there in:
   (a) 5 centimetres
   (b) 13 centimetres
   (c) 22 centimetres
   (d) 35 centimetres
   (e) 70 centimetres
   (f) 100 centimetres?

4.2 Multiplying numbers by 100

To multiply a number by 100, move all the digits two places to the left and add two zeros.

Example
(a) 5 × 100 = 500

(b) 30 × 100 = 3 000

(c) 75 × 100 = 7 500

(d) 365 × 100 = 36 500

> **Hint:**
> TTh means Ten Thousands.

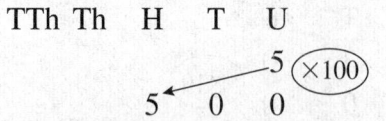

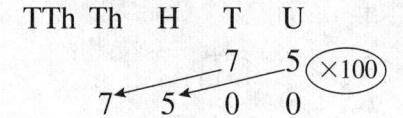

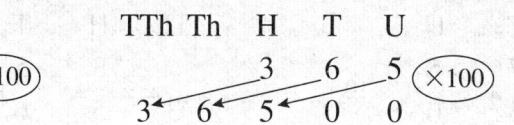

Exercise 4B

1. (a) 6 × 100
   (b) 7 × 100
   (c) 11 × 100
   (d) 23 × 100
   (e) 32 × 100
   (f) 45 × 100
   (g) 80 × 100
   (h) 61 × 100
   (i) 56 × 100
   (j) 98 × 100
   (k) 112 × 100
   (l) 172 × 100
   (m) 451 × 100
   (n) 390 × 100
   (o) 916 × 100
   (p) 206 × 100
   (q) 101 × 100
   (r) 903 × 100
   (s) 700 × 100
   (t) 341 × 100

2. There are 100 pennies in a pound.
   How many pennies are there in:
   (a) £3
   (b) £9
   (c) £20
   (d) £45
   (e) £600
   (f) £499?

3. There are 100 centimetres in a metre.
   How many centimetres are there in:
   (a) 2 metres
   (b) 38 metres
   (c) 27 metres
   (d) 80 metres
   (e) 76 metres
   (f) 100 metres?

4.3 Multiplying numbers by 1 000

To multiply a number by 1 000, move all the digits three places to the left and add three zeros.

Hint: HTh means Hundred Thousands.

Example
(a) 5 × 1 000 = 5 000

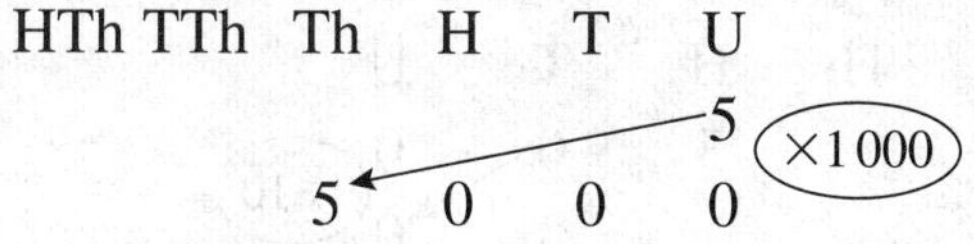

(b) 30 × 1 000 = 30 000

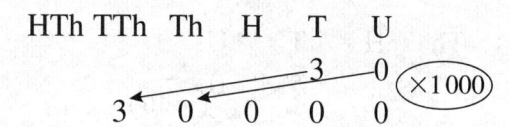

(c) 75 × 1 000 = 75 000

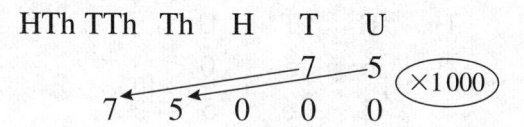

(d) 365 × 1 000 = 365 000

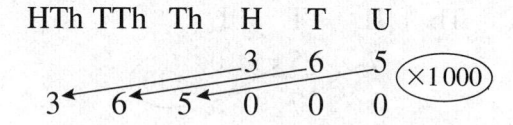

Exercise 4C

1. (a) 6 × 1 000
   (b) 7 × 1 000
   (c) 11 × 1 000
   (d) 23 × 1 000
   (e) 32 × 1 000
   (f) 45 × 1 000
   (g) 80 × 1 000
   (h) 61 × 1 000
   (i) 56 × 1 000
   (j) 98 × 1 000
   (k) 112 × 1 000
   (l) 172 × 1 000
   (m) 451 × 1 000
   (n) 390 × 1 000
   (o) 916 × 1 000
   (p) 206 × 1 000
   (q) 101 × 1 000
   (r) 903 × 1 000
   (s) 700 × 1 000
   (t) 341 × 1 000

2. There are 1 000 metres in a kilometre. How many metres are there in:
   (a) 4 kilometres
   (b) 19 kilometres
   (c) 27 kilometres
   (d) 83 kilometres
   (e) 100 kilometres
   (f) 153 kilometres?

3. There are 1 000 millilitres in a litre. How many millilitres are there in:
   (a) 5 litres
   (b) 13 litres
   (c) 22 litres
   (d) 35 litres
   (e) 70 litres
   (f) 100 litres?

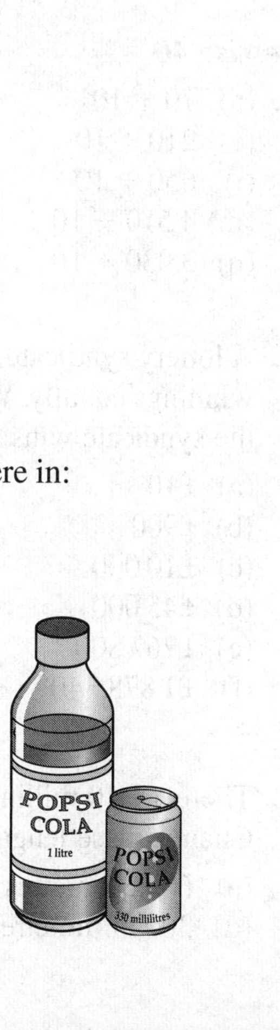

4.4 Dividing numbers by 10

To divide a number by 10, move all the digits one place to the right.

Example

(a) $50 \div 10 = 5$

Th	H	T	U
		5	0
			5

$\div 10$

(b) $300 \div 10 = 30$

Th	H	T	U
	3	0	0
		3	0

$\div 10$

(c) $750 \div 10 = 75$

Th	H	T	U
	7	5	0
		7	5

$\div 10$

(d) $3\,650 \div 10 = 365$

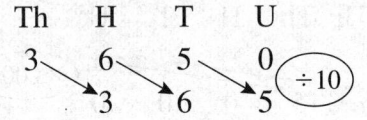

Th	H	T	U
3	6	5	0
	3	6	5

$\div 10$

Exercise 4D

1. (a) $70 \div 10$ (b) $80 \div 10$ (c) $120 \div 10$ (d) $320 \div 10$
   (e) $210 \div 10$ (f) $610 \div 10$ (g) $800 \div 10$ (h) $510 \div 10$
   (i) $650 \div 10$ (j) $890 \div 10$ (k) $1\,250 \div 10$ (l) $1\,270 \div 10$
   (m) $4\,510 \div 10$ (n) $2\,900 \div 10$ (o) $9\,030 \div 10$ (p) $1\,200 \div 10$
   (q) $3\,030 \div 10$ (r) $2\,000 \div 10$ (s) $5\,000 \div 10$ (t) $4\,100 \div 10$

2. A lottery syndicate has ten members. They share all winnings equally. What does each member receive if the syndicate wins a prize of:
   (a) £10
   (b) £900
   (c) £10 000
   (d) £45 000
   (e) £267 800
   (f) £1 878 340?

3. There are 10 millimetres in a centimetre.
   Change these lengths into centimetres.

   (a) 60 millimetres   (b) 170 millimetres   (c) 230 millimetres
   (d) 300 millimetres   (e) 500 millimetres   (f) 750 millimetres

4.5 Dividing numbers by 100

To divide a number by 100, move all the digits two places to the right.

Example

(a) 500 ÷ 100 = 5

(b) 3 000 ÷ 100 = 30

(c) 7 500 ÷ 100 = 75

(d) 36 500 ÷ 100 = 365

Exercise 4E

1. (a) 700 ÷ 100
    (b) 600 ÷ 100
    (c) 1 200 ÷ 100
    (d) 1 300 ÷ 100
    (e) 2 500 ÷ 100
    (f) 2 600 ÷ 100
    (g) 800 ÷ 100
    (h) 3 100 ÷ 100
    (i) 7 500 ÷ 100
    (j) 1 800 ÷ 100
    (k) 1 200 ÷ 100
    (l) 12 700 ÷ 100
    (m) 8 700 ÷ 100
    (n) 2 900 ÷ 100
    (o) 19 300 ÷ 100
    (p) 12 800 ÷ 100
    (q) 13 300 ÷ 100
    (r) 20 000 ÷ 100
    (s) 55 000 ÷ 100
    (t) 241 900 ÷ 100

2. There are 100 centimetres in a metre.
    Change these lengths into metres.
    (a) 300 centimetres
    (b) 900 centimetres
    (c) 600 centimetres
    (d) 4 500 centimetres
    (e) 7 800 centimetres
    (f) 6 700 centimetres

3. There are 100 pennies in a pound.
    Change these amounts into pounds.
    (a) 200 pennies
    (b) 400 pennies
    (c) 1 000 pennies
    (d) 3 000 pennies
    (e) 2 500 pennies
    (f) 8 700 pennies

4. Change these amounts into pence.
    (a) £4·66
    (b) £5·80
    (c) £1·66
    (d) £4·77
    (e) £5·84
    (f) £2·94
    (g) £1·91
    (h) £0·36
    (i) £3·06
    (j) £3·82
    (k) £3·62
    (l) £0·14

4.6 Dividing numbers by 1 000

To divide a number by 1 000, move all the digits three places to the right.

Example

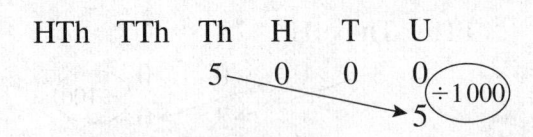

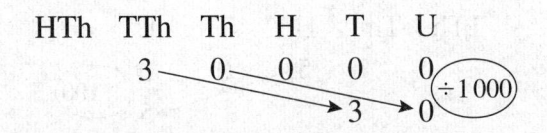

(a) 5 000 ÷ 1 000 = 5

(b) 30 000 ÷ 1 000 = 30

(c) 75 000 ÷ 1 000 = 75

(d) 365 000 ÷ 1 000 = 365

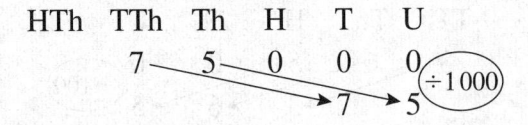

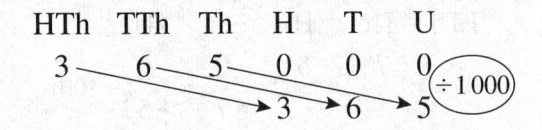

Exercise 4F

1. (a) 7 000 ÷ 1 000
   (b) 4 000 ÷ 1 000
   (c) 12 000 ÷ 1 000
   (d) 32 000 ÷ 1 000
   (e) 21 000 ÷ 1 000
   (f) 49 000 ÷ 1 000
   (g) 18 000 ÷ 1 000
   (h) 512 000 ÷ 1 000
   (i) 165 000 ÷ 1 000
   (j) 890 000 ÷ 1 000
   (k) 125 000 ÷ 1 000
   (l) 270 000 ÷ 1 000
   (m) 1 450 000 ÷ 1 000
   (n) 2 900 000 ÷ 1 000
   (o) 5 030 000 ÷ 1 000
   (p) 6 200 000 ÷ 1 000
   (q) 3 435 000 ÷ 1 000
   (r) 52 430 000 ÷ 1 000
   (s) 5 367 000 ÷ 1 000
   (t) 41 321 000 ÷ 1 000

2. There are 100 millilitres in a litre.
   Change these volumes into litres.

   (a) 1 000 millilitres
   (b) 9 000 millilitres
   (c) 10 000 millilitres
   (d) 5 000 millilitres
   (e) 27 000 millilitres
   (f) 78 000 millilitres

3. There are 1000 metres in a kilometre.
   Change these distances into kilometres.

   (a) 6 000 metres
   (b) 8 000 metres
   (c) 10 000 metres
   (d) 31 000 metres
   (e) 55 000 metres
   (f) 170 000 metres

4.7 The multiplication table

This table shows all the multiplications from 1×1 to 10×10.

×	1	2	3	4	5	6	7	8	9	10
1	1	2	3	4	5	6	7	8	9	10
2	2	4	6	8	10	12	14	16	18	20
3	3	6	9	12	15	18	21	24	27	30
4	4	8	12	16	20	24	28	32	36	40
5	5	10	15	20	25	30	35	40	(45)	50
6	6	12	18	24	30	36	42	48	54	60
7	7	14	21	28	35	42	49	56	63	70
8	8	16	24	32	40	48	56	64	72	80
9	9	18	27	36	45	54	63	72	81	90
10	10	20	30	40	50	60	70	80	90	100

For example:
$5 \times 9 = 45$

Exercise 4G

Answer all the questions without using a calculator or written calculations. Try to memorise the multiplication table but look up answers if you need to.

1. (a) 2×3 (b) 3×4 (c) 4×5 (d) 2×6 (e) 3×3
   (f) 4×4 (g) 5×3 (h) 2×5 (i) 6×4 (j) 3×7
   (k) 2×8 (l) 5×6 (m) 7×4 (n) 8×3 (o) 5×8
   (p) 4×8 (q) 7×2 (r) 4×2 (s) 10×3 (t) 2×10
   (u) 10×4 (v) 9×5 (w) 3×6 (x) 2×2 (y) 10×5

2. (a) 5×9 (b) 7×7 (c) 4×9 (d) 9×6 (e) 10×8
   (f) 9×7 (g) 8×8 (h) 9×9 (i) 7×10 (j) 10×10
   (k) 6×8 (l) 8×9 (m) 9×10 (n) 7×9 (o) 9×8
   (p) 10×6 (q) 8×7 (r) 7×6 (s) 9×2 (t) 3×9
   (u) 7×5 (v) 6×6 (w) 7×8 (x) 6×7 (y) 5×5

3. (a) $3 \times 5 \times 10$ (b) $4 \times 4 \times 10$ (c) $3 \times 6 \times 10$
   (d) $5 \times 4 \times 10$ (e) $2 \times 9 \times 10$ (f) $3 \times 8 \times 10$
   (g) $9 \times 3 \times 10$ (h) $6 \times 6 \times 10$ (i) $7 \times 3 \times 10$
   (j) $5 \times 5 \times 10$ (k) $3 \times 6 \times 10$ (l) $6 \times 8 \times 10$
   (m) $10 \times 6 \times 5$ (n) $10 \times 4 \times 8$ (o) $10 \times 8 \times 5$
   (p) $10 \times 2 \times 6$ (q) $4 \times 10 \times 6$ (r) $6 \times 10 \times 4$
   (s) $5 \times 10 \times 7$ (t) $7 \times 10 \times 7$ (u) $9 \times 10 \times 6$
   (v) $8 \times 10 \times 2$ (w) $3 \times 10 \times 3$ (x) $4 \times 10 \times 2$

78   Number 2

4. (a) $4 \times 9 \times 100$ (b) $6 \times 5 \times 100$ (c) $9 \times 4 \times 100$
   (d) $9 \times 5 \times 100$ (e) $6 \times 7 \times 100$ (f) $7 \times 2 \times 100$
   (g) $4 \times 3 \times 100$ (h) $5 \times 3 \times 100$ (i) $3 \times 7 \times 100$
   (j) $6 \times 3 \times 10 \times 10$ (k) $5 \times 2 \times 10 \times 10$ (l) $9 \times 3 \times 10 \times 10$
   (m) $7 \times 10 \times 4 \times 10$ (n) $8 \times 10 \times 6 \times 10$ (o) $8 \times 10 \times 4 \times 10$
   (p) $9 \times 10 \times 6 \times 10$ (q) $4 \times 10 \times 9 \times 10$ (r) $7 \times 10 \times 5 \times 10$
   (s) $9 \times 10 \times 7 \times 10$ (t) $8 \times 10 \times 8 \times 10$ (u) $9 \times 10 \times 8 \times 10$
   (v) $9 \times 10 \times 9 \times 10$ (w) $8 \times 10 \times 7 \times 10$ (x) $6 \times 10 \times 7 \times 10$
   (y) $2 \times 10 \times 9 \times 10$

5. (a) $3 \times 9 \times 1\,000$ (b) $4 \times 6 \times 1\,000$ (c) $4 \times 5 \times 1\,000$
   (d) $6 \times 3 \times 1\,000$ (e) $2 \times 4 \times 1\,000$ (f) $7 \times 5 \times 1\,000$
   (g) $6 \times 6 \times 10 \times 100$ (h) $7 \times 7 \times 10 \times 100$ (i) $8 \times 4 \times 10 \times 100$
   (j) $9 \times 5 \times 100 \times 10$ (k) $5 \times 5 \times 100 \times 10$ (l) $4 \times 9 \times 100 \times 10$
   (m) $7 \times 10 \times 8 \times 100$ (n) $5 \times 10 \times 7 \times 100$ (o) $6 \times 10 \times 9 \times 100$
   (p) $3 \times 10 \times 3 \times 100$ (q) $4 \times 10 \times 4 \times 100$ (r) $5 \times 10 \times 2 \times 100$
   (s) $9 \times 100 \times 7 \times 10$ (t) $7 \times 100 \times 6 \times 10$ (u) $8 \times 100 \times 5 \times 10$
   (v) $3 \times 100 \times 4 \times 10$ (w) $8 \times 100 \times 8 \times 10$ (x) $7 \times 100 \times 8 \times 10$
   (y) $8 \times 100 \times 9 \times 10$

6. (a) 30×40 (b) 80×20 (c) 50×60 (d) 40×70 (e) 30×80
   (f) 20×60 (g) 60×30 (h) 90×20 (i) 40×20 (j) 70×20
   (k) 50×60 (l) 70×40 (m) 60×70 (n) 80×50 (o) 60×80
   (p) 30×700 (q) 300×20 (r) 800×30 (s) 600×80 (t) 700×90
   (u) 50×400 (v) 30×500 (w) 90×400 (x) 40×900 (y) 90×800

4.8 Multiplying numbers 'in your head'

A baker fills trays with 36 loaves of bread. How many loaves does he need to fill 7 trays?

To answer this question without a calculator or written calculation, think of 36 as 3 tens and 6 units:

$$36 \text{ is } 30 + 6$$
$$30 \times 7 = 10 \times 3 \times 7$$
$$= 10 \times 21$$
$$= 210$$
$$6 \times 7 = 42$$
$$\text{so } 36 \times 7 = 210 + 42$$
$$= 252$$

You may need to write down some steps but try to do as much of the calculation as you can 'in your head'.

Example

Peter Ashworth orders wood screws in packets of 25. How many wood screws will he receive if he orders 8 packets?

> 20 x 8 = 160
> 5 x 8 = 40
> so 25 x 8 = 200

He will receive 200 wood screws.

Exercise 4H

Answer all the questions without using a calculator.

1. (a) 12×5 (b) 14×3 (c) 13×6 (d) 16×2 (e) 17×3
    (f) 4×14 (g) 8×12 (h) 4×18 (i) 4×16 (j) 5×15
    (k) 25×4 (l) 24×5 (m) 26×6 (n) 27×2 (o) 35×8
    (p) 7×16 (q) 9×31 (r) 8×42 (s) 7×42 (t) 6×44
    (u) 27×8 (v) 26×9 (w) 86×7 (x) 5×66 (y) 35×9

2. A driver earns £9 an hour. How much will he earn if he works:
    (a) 12 hours (b) 20 hours (c) 23 hours (d) 30 hours (e) 36 hours?

3. A farmer expects to harvest 200 kilograms of oil seeds from every acre of a crop she plants.

    How many kilograms of seed will she harvest if she plants:
    (a) 3 acres (b) 4 acres (c) 70 acres (d) 12 acres (e) 28 acres?

4. Jade Nichols decides to save £8 pounds every week from her wages to pay for her holiday. How much will she have saved after:
    (a) 10 weeks (b) 12 weeks (c) 20 weeks
    (d) 27 weeks (e) 51 weeks?

4.9 Dividing numbers 'in your head'

Most people work out divisions by thinking about the multiplication table. To work out $35 \div 7$, remember that $7 \times 5 = 35$ so $35 \div 7 = 5$

If there is not an exact answer from the multiplication tables you write a remainder.

Hint:
This triangle may help.

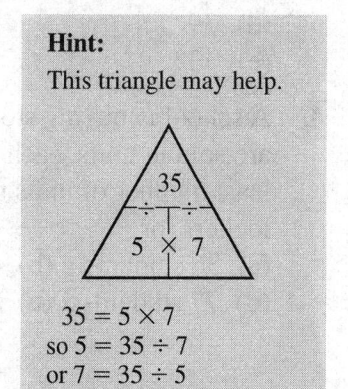

$35 = 5 \times 7$
so $5 = 35 \div 7$
or $7 = 35 \div 5$

Example

27 lollipops are shared by 4 children. How many lollipops does each child get and how many are left over?

Remembering that $4 \times 6 = 24$ gives you the answer:
$27 \div 4 = 6$ remainder 3

Exercise 4I

Answer all the questions without using a calculator or written calculations.

1. (a) $28 \div 4$ (b) $24 \div 6$ (c) $18 \div 3$ (d) $36 \div 4$
   (e) $14 \div 2$ (f) $15 \div 5$ (g) $24 \div 8$ (h) $18 \div 9$
   (i) $16 \div 4$ (j) $27 \div 3$ (k) $40 \div 4$ (l) $35 \div 5$
   (m) $42 \div 6$ (n) $63 \div 7$ (o) $40 \div 8$ (p) $18 \div 2$
   (q) $36 \div 6$ (r) $54 \div 9$ (s) $48 \div 8$ (t) $49 \div 7$
   (u) $56 \div 8$ (v) $72 \div 9$ (w) $30 \div 5$ (x) $45 \div 9$
   (y) $81 \div 9$

2. (a) $11 \div 2$ (b) $14 \div 3$ (c) $23 \div 4$ (d) $21 \div 5$
   (e) $33 \div 6$ (f) $36 \div 7$ (g) $38 \div 7$ (h) $21 \div 8$
   (i) $15 \div 9$ (j) $8 \div 6$ (k) $21 \div 2$ (l) $26 \div 3$
   (m) $50 \div 6$ (n) $43 \div 5$ (o) $37 \div 8$ (p) $83 \div 9$
   (q) $25 \div 7$ (r) $25 \div 3$ (s) $75 \div 8$ (t) $44 \div 7$
   (u) $42 \div 9$ (v) $57 \div 6$ (w) $48 \div 5$ (x) $67 \div 8$
   (y) $98 \div 9$

3. On a school trip, up to four students will share each bedroom. What is the least number of bedrooms needed if the number of students going on the trip is:
   (a) 36
   (b) 38
   (c) 29
   (d) 39
   (e) 43?

4. A school is buying storage lockers for students. The lockers are sold in units, each unit having 9 lockers. What is the least number of units the school needs to buy to provide lockers for:
   (a) 36 students (b) 47 students (c) 53 students
   (d) 77 students (e) 89 students?

4.10 Using division by 10, 100 or 1 000 to divide numbers 'in your head'

Example 1

$350 \div 70$

If you divide both numbers by 10, this division is the same as $35 \div 7 = 5$

Example 2

$72\,000 \div 900$

If you divide both numbers by 100, this division is the same as $720 \div 9$

$720 \div 9 = 10 \times 72 \div 9 = 10 \times 8 = 80$

Example 3

$180\,000 \div 2\,000$

If you divide both numbers by 1 000, this division is the same as
$180 \div 2 = 10 \times 18 \div 2 = 10 \times 9 = 90$

Exercise 4J

Answer all the questions without using a calculator or written calculations.

1. (a) $160 \div 20$ (b) $140 \div 70$ (c) $300 \div 50$ (d) $160 \div 40$ (e) $150 \div 50$
   (f) $200 \div 20$ (g) $60 \div 30$ (h) $180 \div 60$ (i) $400 \div 50$ (j) $200 \div 40$
   (k) $150 \div 30$ (l) $160 \div 80$ (m) $360 \div 60$ (n) $490 \div 70$ (o) $400 \div 80$
   (p) $360 \div 90$ (q) $100 \div 20$ (r) $630 \div 70$ (s) $210 \div 30$ (t) $240 \div 80$
   (u) $180 \div 90$ (v) $300 \div 60$ (w) $140 \div 20$ (x) $320 \div 40$ (y) $480 \div 80$

2. (a) $800 \div 400$ (b) $900 \div 300$ (c) $2\,400 \div 400$
   (d) $2\,500 \div 500$ (e) $3\,200 \div 800$ (f) $4\,500 \div 500$
   (g) $1\,600 \div 800$ (h) $2\,700 \div 900$ (i) $2\,800 \div 700$
   (j) $4\,800 \div 600$ (k) $5\,600 \div 700$ (l) $4\,200 \div 700$
   (m) $6\,400 \div 800$ (n) $2\,700 \div 900$ (o) $2\,400 \div 600$
   (p) $3\,500 \div 500$ (q) $4\,200 \div 600$ (r) $1\,200 \div 400$
   (s) $2\,800 \div 400$ (t) $5\,400 \div 600$ (u) $7\,200 \div 800$
   (v) $1\,800 \div 300$ (w) $3\,600 \div 400$ (x) $1\,800 \div 300$

3. (a) $45\,000 \div 9\,000$ (b) $12\,000 \div 3\,000$ (c) $12\,000 \div 2\,000$
   (d) $27\,000 \div 3\,000$ (e) $10\,000 \div 5\,000$ (f) $20\,000 \div 5\,000$
   (g) $24\,000 \div 3\,000$ (h) $56\,000 \div 7\,000$ (i) $54\,000 \div 9\,000$
   (j) $6\,000 \div 2\,000$ (k) $64\,000 \div 8\,000$ (l) $63\,000 \div 9\,000$
   (m) $4\,000 \div 2\,000$ (n) $81\,000 \div 9\,000$ (o) $42\,000 \div 6\,000$
   (p) $25\,000 \div 5\,000$ (q) $12\,000 \div 2\,000$ (r) $12\,000 \div 3\,000$
   (s) $36\,000 \div 4\,000$ (t) $20\,000 \div 4\,000$ (u) $42\,000 \div 7\,000$

4. (a) 600 ÷ 20   (b) 2 400 ÷ 40   (c) 35 000 ÷ 500
   (d) 2 400 ÷ 20   (e) 32 000 ÷ 800   (f) 72 000 ÷ 900
   (g) 48 000 ÷ 80   (h) 28 000 ÷ 40   (i) 28 000 ÷ 70
   (j) 320 000 ÷ 800   (k) 300 000 ÷ 600   (l) 350 000 ÷ 700
   (m) 24 000 ÷ 60   (n) 49 000 ÷ 70   (o) 27 000 ÷ 30
   (p) 20 000 ÷ 50   (q) 360 000 ÷ 60   (r) 54 000 ÷ 90
   (s) 630 000 ÷ 90   (t) 30 000 ÷ 600   (u) 720 000 ÷ 8 000
   (v) 810 000 ÷ 9 000   (w) 480 000 ÷ 6 000   (x) 480 000 ÷ 800
   (y) 560 000 ÷ 70

4.11 Multiplying by single-digit numbers with written calculations

If multiplications by single-digit numbers are too difficult to do in your head, you do them on paper.

Example

Find (a) 124×2 (b) 472×8 (c) 322×80

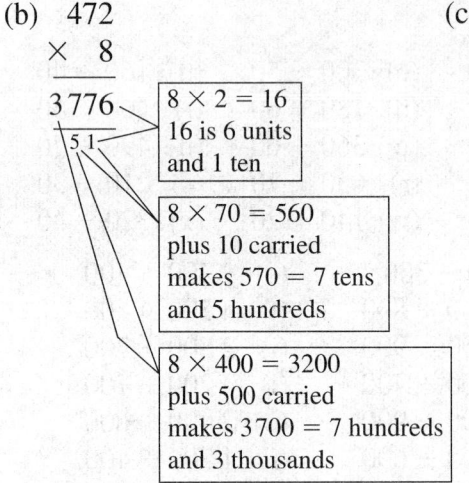

(a) 124
     × 2

     248

(b) 472
     × 8
    ----
    3 776
     5 1

$8 \times 2 = 16$
16 is 6 units and 1 ten

$8 \times 70 = 560$
plus 10 carried
makes 570 = 7 tens and 5 hundreds

$8 \times 400 = 3200$
plus 500 carried
makes 3 700 = 7 hundreds and 3 thousands

(c) 322
     × 80
    -----
    25 760

Put down a zero. This multiplies the answer by 10. Then multiply by 8.

Exercise 4K

Answer all the questions without using a calculator.

1. (a) 234 × 2   (b) 232 × 3   (c) 2 012 × 4   (d) 23 × 3   (e) 4 302 × 2
   (f) 45 × 5   (g) 36 × 4   (h) 62 × 5   (i) 47 × 3   (j) 56 × 6
   (k) 64 × 8   (l) 47 × 5   (m) 84 × 7   (n) 87 × 9   (o) 43 × 8
   (p) 242 × 3   (q) 341 × 5   (r) 207 × 6   (s) 308 × 3   (t) 509 × 9
   (u) 345 × 6   (v) 563 × 8   (w) 547 × 6   (x) 324 × 9   (y) 649 × 8

2. (a) 26×50 (b) 34×60 (c) 45×40 (d) 30×76 (e) 20×88
   (f) 40×72 (g) 67×30 (h) 73×50 (i) 80×88 (j) 39×40
   (k) 56×40 (l) 60×53 (m) 70×61 (n) 83×90 (o) 56×50
   (p) 30×57 (q) 231×40 (r) 567×50 (s) 344×60 (t) 202×90
   (u) 310×60 (v) 460×70 (w) 231×90 (x) 896×70 (y) 457×90

3. How many days are there in:
   (a) 12 weeks (b) 23 weeks (c) 40 weeks (d) 38 weeks (e) 52 weeks?

4. A politician has his office floors covered with hand-made ceramic tiles which cost £90 per square metre (m²).

   Find the cost of using the tiles to cover an office with a floor area of:
   (a) 17 m² (b) 23 m² (c) 38 m² (d) 72 m² (e) 98 m²

4.12 Multiplying by two-digit numbers with written calculations

If multiplications by two-digit numbers are too difficult to do in your head, you do them on paper.

Example
Find 463×85

```
      463
    ×  85
    -----
    2 315  ——— 463 × 5
  + 37 040 ——— 463 × 80
    ------
    39 355 ——— 463 × 85
```

Exercise 4L

1. (a) 26 × 34 (b) 64 × 45 (c) 53 × 24 (d) 47 × 32 (e) 56 × 43
   (f) 23 × 84 (g) 46 × 28 (h) 36 × 63 (i) 29 × 36 (j) 85 × 38
   (k) 59 × 23 (l) 76 × 22 (m) 34 × 56 (n) 85 × 55 (o) 78 × 39
   (p) 45 × 45 (q) 54 × 54 (r) 78 × 64 (s) 96 × 58 (t) 27 × 85
   (u) 67 × 39 (v) 38 × 54 (w) 85 × 58 (x) 96 × 75 (y) 58 × 65

2. (a) 234 × 41 (b) 563 × 22 (c) 781 × 51 (d) 607 × 45 (e) 730 × 36
   (f) 345 × 43 (g) 467 × 32 (h) 902 × 53 (i) 657 × 54 (j) 542 × 73
   (k) 709 × 85 (l) 560 × 74 (m) 355 × 67 (n) 902 × 55 (o) 983 × 24
   (p) 783 × 76 (q) 309 × 98 (r) 255 × 75 (s) 505 × 55 (t) 806 × 61
   (u) 788 × 61 (v) 592 × 47 (w) 775 × 84 (x) 957 × 86 (y) 692 × 78

3. The 123 students in Year 11 at Springfield High School are planning a leaving party. What will the total cost of the party be if each student pays:

   (a) £12 (b) £14 (c) £17 (d) £21 (e) £26?

4. A farmer expects to harvest 45 kilograms of apples from each tree he plants.
   How many kilograms will he harvest if he plants:

   (a) 45 trees (b) 80 trees (c) 144 trees
   (d) 586 trees (e) 855 trees?

4.13 Dividing by single-digit numbers with written calculations

If divisions by single-digit numbers are too difficult to do in your head, you do them on paper.

Example
Find 318 ÷ 7

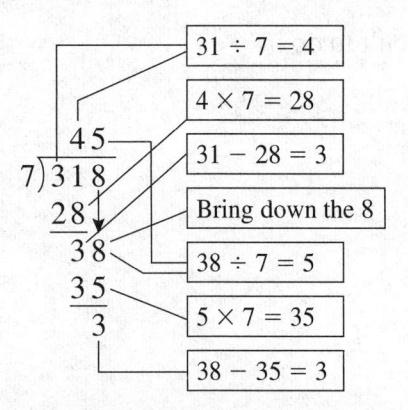

```
      4 5
    _____
 7 ) 3 1 8
     2 8
     ___
       3 8
       3 5
       ___
         3
```

- 31 ÷ 7 = 4
- 4 × 7 = 28
- 31 − 28 = 3
- Bring down the 8
- 38 ÷ 7 = 5
- 5 × 7 = 35
- 38 − 35 = 3

318 ÷ 7 = 45 remainder 3

Exercise 4M

1. (a) 255 ÷ 5 (b) 144 ÷ 2 (c) 138 ÷ 3
   (d) 208 ÷ 4 (e) 114 ÷ 2 (f) 365 ÷ 5
   (g) 352 ÷ 4 (h) 174 ÷ 3 (i) 240 ÷ 6
   (j) 192 ÷ 8 (k) 470 ÷ 5 (l) 198 ÷ 2
   (m) 294 ÷ 7 (n) 608 ÷ 8 (o) 396 ÷ 9
   (p) 522 ÷ 6 (q) 261 ÷ 3 (r) 384 ÷ 4
   (s) 455 ÷ 7 (t) 200 ÷ 8 (u) 261 ÷ 9
   (v) 492 ÷ 6 (w) 693 ÷ 9 (x) 520 ÷ 8
   (y) 576 ÷ 9

2. (a) 137 ÷ 2 (b) 200 ÷ 3 (c) 154 ÷ 5
   (d) 119 ÷ 4 (e) 306 ÷ 5 (f) 52 ÷ 3
   (g) 79 ÷ 2   (h) 114 ÷ 4 (i) 107 ÷ 6
   (j) 157 ÷ 8 (k) 140 ÷ 9 (l) 129 ÷ 7
   (m) 185 ÷ 9 (n) 227 ÷ 7 (o) 141 ÷ 6
   (p) 402 ÷ 8 (q) 195 ÷ 2 (r) 369 ÷ 4
   (s) 197 ÷ 5 (t) 242 ÷ 3 (u) 335 ÷ 6
   (v) 330 ÷ 8 (w) 232 ÷ 5 (x) 423 ÷ 7
   (y) 421 ÷ 9

3. Every day, from Monday to Friday, Michael puts a £1 coin in a jar in his bedroom. For how many weeks has Michael been saving when the amount in the jar is:
   (a) £65
   (b) £90
   (c) £125
   (d) £215
   (e) £260?

4. Each day, a farmer puts all the eggs his chickens have laid into boxes of six to sell.
   How many boxes can be filled and how many eggs will be left over if the chickens have laid:
   (a) 271 eggs
   (b) 440 eggs
   (c) 305 eggs
   (d) 475 eggs
   (e) 502 eggs?

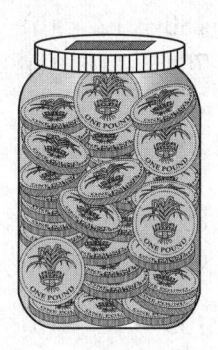

4.14 Dividing by two-digit numbers with written calculations

If divisions by two-digit numbers are too difficult to do in your head, you do them on paper.

Example

Find 500 ÷ 19

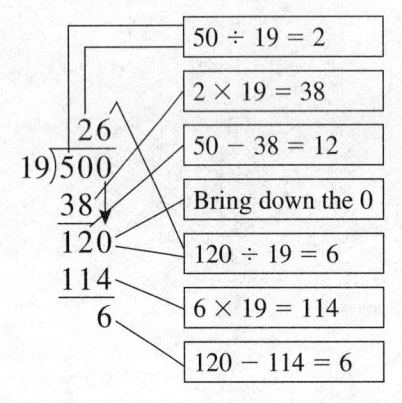

```
    26
19)500
    38
   120
   114
     6
```

- 50 ÷ 19 = 2
- 2 × 19 = 38
- 50 − 38 = 12
- Bring down the 0
- 120 ÷ 19 = 6
- 6 × 19 = 114
- 120 − 114 = 6

500 ÷ 19 = 26 remainder 6

Exercise 4N

1. (a) 180 ÷ 12 (b) 286 ÷ 11 (c) 195 ÷ 13 (d) 288 ÷ 12
   (e) 704 ÷ 11 (f) 350 ÷ 14 (g) 304 ÷ 19 (h) 270 ÷ 18
   (i) 256 ÷ 16 (j) 504 ÷ 12 (k) 374 ÷ 17 (l) 672 ÷ 21
   (m) 360 ÷ 18 (n) 225 ÷ 15 (o) 572 ÷ 22 (p) 609 ÷ 29
   (q) 744 ÷ 31 (r) 480 ÷ 32 (s) 490 ÷ 35 (t) 836 ÷ 38
   (u) 897 ÷ 39 (v) 492 ÷ 41 (w) 882 ÷ 42 (x) 900 ÷ 36
   (y) 663 ÷ 51

2. (a) 135 ÷ 12 (b) 187 ÷ 13 (c) 215 ÷ 14 (d) 270 ÷ 12
   (e) 222 ÷ 13 (f) 230 ÷ 19 (g) 317 ÷ 13 (h) 311 ÷ 14
   (i) 209 ÷ 13 (j) 245 ÷ 12 (k) 320 ÷ 19 (l) 311 ÷ 18
   (m) 320 ÷ 21 (n) 472 ÷ 21 (o) 600 ÷ 19 (p) 426 ÷ 35
   (q) 409 ÷ 25 (r) 923 ÷ 23 (s) 940 ÷ 31 (t) 579 ÷ 14
   (u) 680 ÷ 32 (v) 986 ÷ 42 (w) 946 ÷ 29 (x) 827 ÷ 19
   (y) 745 ÷ 51

3. A baker sells bags of 12 bread rolls.
   How many bags can she fill if she bakes:
   (a) 408 rolls (b) 396 rolls (c) 492 rolls
   (d) 876 rolls (e) 972 rolls?

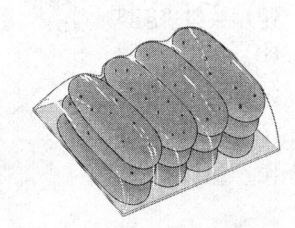

4. Wizzochoc bars cost 49p each. Pria spends all her money on Wizzochoc bars. How many bars can Pria buy and how much change will she get if she has:
   (a) £1·00
   (b) £2·50
   (c) £3·42
   (d) £4·50
   (e) £7·90?

4.15 Factors, even numbers, odd numbers, prime numbers and multiples

Any number which divides exactly into 24 is called a **factor** of 24.
The factors of 24 are 1, 2, 3, 4, 6, 8, 12 and 24.

The factors of 15 are 1, 3, 5 and 15.
The factors of 11 are 1 and 11.

An **even number** has 2 as a factor, so 24 is an even number.
The even numbers are 2, 4, 6, 8, 10, 12, 14, ...

An **odd number** does not have 2 as a factor, so 15 is an odd number.
The odd numbers are 1, 3, 5, 7, 9, 11, 13, ...

A **prime number** has only two factors, itself and 1, so 11 is a prime number.
The prime numbers are 2, 3, 5, 7, 11, 13, 17, ...

If any number divides exactly by 3, it is called a **multiple** of 3.

The first five multiples of 3 and 3, 6, 9, 12 and 15.
The first seven multiples of 9 are 9, 18, 27, 36, 45, 54 and 63.

Exercise 40

1. Write down all the factors of:
   (a) 8   (b) 18   (c) 10   (d) 12   (e) 27
   (f) 28   (g) 23   (h) 36   (i) 35   (j) 31
   (k) 40   (l) 48   (m) 50   (n) 51   (o) 64

2. Write down the next five even numbers after:
   (a) 14   (b) 22   (c) 36   (d) 108   (e) 200

3. Write down the next five odd numbers after:
   (a) 17   (b) 21   (c) 53   (d) 71   (e) 311

4. (a) Explain why 9 is not a prime number.
   (b) Explain why 15 is not a prime number.
   (c) Write down the first 15 prime numbers.

5. Write down the first six multiples of:
   (a) 4   (b) 5   (c) 6   (d) 7   (e) 8
   (f) 10   (g) 12   (h) 15   (i) 20   (j) 50

6. Look at this list of numbers: 9, 12, 15, 17, 18.
   Using each number only once, write down:
   (a) an even number (b) an odd number (c) a multiple of 5
   (d) a factor of 24 (e) a prime number

7. Look at this list of numbers: 1, 2, 5, 9, 14.
   Using each number only once, write down:
   (a) an even number (b) an odd number (c) a multiple of 3
   (d) a factor of 21 (e) a prime number

8. Look at this list of numbers: 3, 11, 20, 24, 25.
   Using each number only once, write down:
   (a) an even number (b) an odd number (c) a multiple of 5
   (d) a factor of 27 (e) a prime number

9. The factors of 12 are **1, 2**, 3, **4**, 6, 12.
   The factors of 8 are **1, 2, 4**, 8.

   The **common factors** of 8 and 12 are 1, 2, 4.

   Find all the common factors of:
   (a) 10 and 25   (b) 28 and 49   (c) 12 and 36
   (d) 18 and 24   (e) 35 and 45   (f) 16 and 40

4.16 Highest common factor (HCF)

The **highest common factor (HCF)** of two or more numbers is:

   the common factor with the highest value.

Example 1
Find the HCF of 18, 24 and 42.
- List all the factors of all the numbers: 18 factors: **1, 2, 3, 6**, 9, 18
                                             24 factors: **1, 2, 3**, 4, **6**, 8, 12, 24
                                             42 factors: **1, 2, 3, 6**, 7, 14, 21, 42
- List the common factors: common factors: 1, 2, 3, 6

The HCF of 18, 24 and 42 is: 6.

Exercise 4P
1. Find the HCF of:
   (a) 24 and 40   (b) 50 and 75   (c) 63 and 81
   (d) 49 and 91   (e) 45 and 60   (f) 132 and 55
   (g) 168 and 60   (h) 10 and 150   (i) 750 and 50
   (j) 240 and 150   (k) 242 and 176   (l) 144 and 360

2. Find the HCF of:
   (a) 24, 36 and 60
   (b) 45, 75 and 15
   (c) 49, 126 and 91
   (d) 26, 182 and 65
   (e) 126, 28 and 70
   (f) 60, 37 and 113
   (g) 175, 50 and 1 250
   (h) 99, 9 and 409
   (i) 154, 98 and 84
   (j) 234, 66 and 102
   (k) 104, 128 and 76
   (l) 72, 144 and 540

4.17 Lowest common multiple (LCM)

The **lowest common multiple (LCM** of two or more numbers is:

the smallest number into which they will all divide exactly.

Example 1

Find the LCM of 6, 8 and 12.

List the multiples: 6, 12, 18, **24**, …
                     8, 16, **24**, 32, …
                     12, **24**, 36, …

The LCM of 6, 8 and 12 is: **24**.

Exercise 4Q

1. Find the LCM of:
   (a) 2, 3 and 5
   (b) 3, 4 and 5
   (c) 5, 6 and 7
   (d) 4, 5 and 7
   (e) 5, 7 and 9
   (f) 2, 7 and 10
   (g) 2, 3, 5 and 7
   (h) 2, 6 and 10
   (i) 2, 5, 8 and 10

2. Find the LCM of:
   (a) 3, 5 and 8
   (b) 6, 7 and 9
   (c) 6, 7 and 8
   (d) 4, 5, 7 and 8
   (e) 4, 6, 7 and 12
   (f) 3, 5, 7 and 9
   (g) 2, 5, 7 and 11
   (h) 2, 6, 9 and 15
   (i) 3, 5, 8 and 12

4.18 Ratios

A **ratio** is used to compare numbers.

There are 12 patterned squares and 24 plain squares in this picture.

The ratio of patterned tiles to plain tiles is 12 to 24.
This is written as 12 : 24.

Ratios can be simplified by dividing both numbers by a common factor. 12 and 24 have 12 as a common factor so,

12 : 24 is the same as 1 : 2

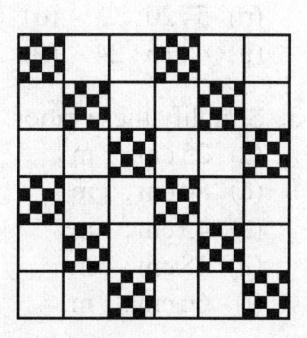

Example

Simplify these ratios:

(a) 6 : 4   (b) 25 : 40 : 60   (c) 64 centimetres : 1 metre

The simplified ratios are:

(a) 3 : 2   (b) 5 : 8 : 12   (c) 64 : 100 = 16 : 25

Exercise 4R

1. Write down the ratio of shaded tiles to white tiles in each picture.

   (a)   (b) 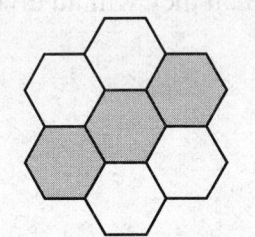   (c)

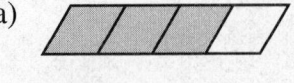

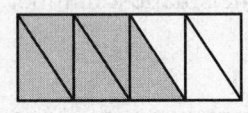

   (d) 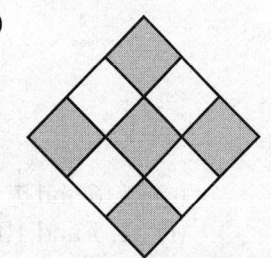   (e) 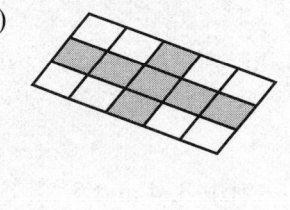   (f)

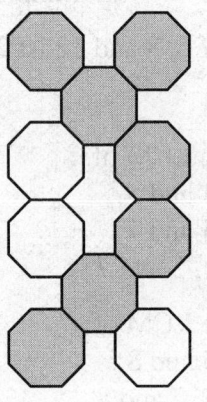

2. Simplify these ratios:

   (a) 2 : 10   (b) 8 : 12   (c) 5 : 35   (d) 9 : 15   (e) 2 : 18
   (f) 10 : 35   (g) 12 : 40   (h) 6 : 18   (i) 10 : 14   (j) 12 : 15
   (k) 7 : 42   (l) 15 : 27   (m) 12 : 14   (n) 6 : 16   (o) 6 : 15
   (p) 5 : 20   (q) 6 : 27   (r) 9 : 12   (s) 12 : 20   (t) 8 : 14
   (u) 4 : 16 : 24   (v) 25 : 30 : 35   (w) 30 : 48 : 12   (x) 70 : 80 : 50   (y) 12 : 18 : 24

3. Simplify these ratios:

   (a) 25 cm : 1 m   (b) 40 cm : 1 m
   (c) 80 cm : 1 m   (d) 5 cm : 1 m
   (e) 45 cm : 1 m   (f) 32 cm : 1 m
   (g) 18 cm : 1 m   (h) 75 cm : 1 m
   (i) 66 cm : 1 m   (j) 99 cm : 1 m

4. Simplify these ratios:
   (a) 50p : £1·00   (b) 65p : £1·00
   (c) 80p : £1·20   (d) £1·40 : £2·80
   (e) £1·40 : £2·10   (f) £1·40 : £3·50
   (g) £1·50 : £2·00   (h) £1·50 : £3·50
   (i) £5·00 : £25·00   (j) £1·60 : £4·00

5. A farmer has a herd of 80 cows. 16 of the cows have calves.
   Find the ratio of cows with calves to cows without calves.

6. In a bag of 24 beads, 3 are red and the rest are green.
   Find the ratio of red beads to green beads.

7. Wayne owns 75 CDs, of which 25 are single CDs and the rest are long play.
   Find the ratio of single CDs to long play CDs.

8. Jo and Jillian have picked 16 kilograms of strawberries. Jo picked 6 kilograms. Find the ratio of the weight picked by Jo to the weight picked by Jillian.

9. On a bus there are 45 passengers. 20 of the passengers are male. Find the ratio of male passengers to female passengers.

10. A double-decker bus has 74 seats. 40 of these seats are on the top deck.
    Find the ratio of top deck seats to bottom deck seats.

4.19 Scaling up or down from a ratio

You can use ratios to work out quantities.

Example 1

A recipe for the pastry for an apple tart for 4 people requires 200 g of flour, 50 g of butter and 50 g of lard. How much flour, butter and lard are required to make an apple tart for 12 people?

The recipe is for 4 people.

You divide each quantity by 4 to find the amount needed for each person.

   For one person: 50 g flour, 12·5 g butter, 12·5 g lard.

So for 12 people, you multiply these amounts by 12:

   600 g flour, 150 g butter, 150 g lard.

Example 2

Concrete is made by mixing sand, gravel and cement powder in the ratio 5 : 3 : 2. What quantities of sand and cement powder are needed to mix with 30 litres of gravel?

The gravel part of the ratio has been multiplied by 10. The quantities needed are:

      50 litres of sand and 20 litres of cement powder.

Exercise 4S

1. A recipe for a pizza for 2 people requires 200 g of tomato sauce, 150 g of ham and 160 g of cheese. Find the quantities of tomato sauce, ham and cheese required for a pizza for:
   (a) 4 people   (b) 6 people   (c) 8 people   (d) 1 person   (e) 3 people

2. To make a fruit punch, Sandra Mina mixes apple juice, orange juice and lemonade in the ratio 1 : 3 : 2. Find the quantities of orange juice and lemonade needed to mix with the following quantities of apple juice.
   (a) 2 litres   (b) 4 litres   (c) 5 litres   (d) 10 litres   (e) 7 litres

3. The ratio of students staying for school lunch to students going home for lunch is 4 : 5. How many students stay for lunch if the number going home is:
   (a) 250   (b) 300   (c) 125   (d) 475   (e) 335?

4. If Marco works for 5 hours, he earns £12. How much does Marco earn if he works for:
   (a) 10 hours   (b) 20 hours   (c) 15 hours   (d) 1 hour   (e) 3 hours?

5. A car travels 120 miles and uses 20 litres of petrol. How many miles can the car travel using:
   (a) 40 litres   (b) 60 litres   (c) 1 litre   (d) 15 litres   (e) 12 litres?

6. A pile of 24 books is 12 cm high. How high is a pile of:
   (a) 48 books   (b) 72 books   (c) 36 books   (d) 1 book   (e) 10 books?

7. A machine produces 800 plastic buckets in 5 hours. How many buckets are produced in:
   (a) 10 hours   (b) 15 hours   (c) 1 hour   (d) 3 hours   (e) 14 hours?

8. A recipe for 4 people requires 8 eggs, 12 peaches and 400 g of cream. Find the quantities of eggs, peaches and cream required for a recipe for:
   (a) 8 people   (b) 12 people   (c) 1 person   (d) 3 people   (e) 7 people

9. A recipe for 4 people requires 8 eggs, 12 peaches and 400 g of cream.
   Find the quantities of eggs and cream needed to mix with:
   (a) 48 peaches (b) 3 peaches (c) 6 peaches (d) 24 peaches (e) 18 peaches

10. If she works for 4 hours, Nisha earns £32 but pays £8 of this in tax. How much does Nisha earn and how much tax does she pay if she works for:
    (a) 12 hours (b) 1 hour (c) 3 hours (d) 6 hours (e) 9 hours?

4.20 Dividing quantities in a ratio

Example 1
Asaf and Afifa buy a packet of 24 sweets. Asaf pays 12p and Afifa pays 36p. How many sweets should each receive?

The ratio of the amounts paid is 12 : 36 or 1 : 3.

To share 24 in the ratio 1 : 3 means dividing 24 into 4 parts.
If 24 is divided into 4 parts, each part is 6.

Asaf receives 1 part or $1 \times 6 = 6$ sweets.
Afifa receives 3 parts or $3 \times 6 = 18$ sweets.
Check: $6 + 18 = 24$

Example 2
Share 42 in the ratio 5 : 1

To share 42 in the ratio 5 : 1 means dividing 42 into 6 parts.
If 42 is divided into 6 parts, each part is 7.
First share is $5 \times 7 = 35$
Second share is $1 \times 7 = 7$
Check: $35 + 7 = 42$

$5 + 1 = 6$

Example 3
Share 99 in the ratio 1 : 3 : 7

To share 99 in the ratio 1 : 3 : 7 means dividing 99 into 11 parts.
If 99 is split into 11 parts, each part is 9.
First share is $1 \times 9 = 9$
Second share is $3 \times 9 = 27$
Third share is $7 \times 9 = 63$
Check: $9 + 27 + 63 = 99$

$1 + 3 + 7 = 11$

Exercise 4T

1. Share 24 in the ratios:
   (a) 1 : 7   (b) 3 : 5   (c) 3 : 1   (d) 1 : 5   (e) 5 : 7

2. Share 72 in the ratios:
   (a) 2 : 1   (b) 1 : 3   (c) 5 : 3   (d) 7 : 2   (e) 4 : 5

3. Share 70 in the ratios:
   (a) 9 : 1   (b) 3 : 2   (c) 1 : 6   (d) 3 : 4   (e) 3 : 7

4. Share 120 in the ratios:
   (a) 2 : 1   (b) 3 : 2   (c) 1 : 5   (d) 7 : 3   (e) 9 : 1

5. Share 99 in the ratios:
   (a) 8 : 1   (b) 7 : 2   (c) 10 : 1   (d) 5 : 6   (e) 1 : 2

6. Share 42 in the ratios:
   (a) 5 : 1   (b) 6 : 1   (c) 3 : 1   (d) 5 : 2   (e) 4 : 3

7. Share 128 in the ratios:
   (a) 7 : 1   (b) 5 : 11   (c) 15 : 17   (d) 3 : 5   (e) 31 : 33

8. Share 40 in the ratios:
   (a) 1 : 2 : 5   (b) 1 : 2 : 2   (c) 2 : 3 : 5   (d) 1 : 2 : 7   (e) 1 : 1 : 2

9. Share 360 in the ratios:
   (a) 3 : 5 : 7   (b) 2 : 7 : 9   (c) 1 : 3 : 5   (d) 20 : 3 : 1   (e) 4 : 5 : 11

10. Share 630 in the ratios:
    (a) 2 : 5 : 8   (b) 1 : 8 : 9   (c) 1 : 2 : 18   (d) 7 : 8 : 15   (e) 15 : 12 : 8

11. Davinder and Marianna share the 120 g of cereal left in a packet in the ratio 3 : 2. How much cereal does Marianna receive?

12. A profit of £450 made on a market stall is shared between the stall holders in the ratio 4 : 5. How much does each receive?

13. William and Shafiq contribute £3 and £4 to buy orange squash which they sell at a school fair. They make £21 in total. If they share the £21 in the ratio of their contributions, how much will William receive?

14. A recipe for pastry mixes flour, butter and lard in the ratio 4 : 1 : 1. What weight of flour, butter and lard are required to make 900 g of the pastry?

15. Concrete can be made by mixing sand, gravel and cement powder in the ratio 5 : 3 : 2. What volume of sand, gravel and cement powder will be needed to make 300 litres of concrete?

4.21 Squares and square roots

To make a **square** number you multiply a number by itself.
The first square number is $1 \times 1 = 1$
The fifth square number is $5 \times 5 = 25$.

You write 7^2, 'seven squared', to mean 7×7.

Example 1
Find the value of 20^2.
$$20^2 = 20 \times 20 = 400$$

The area of this **square** is 2 cm $\times$ 2 cm = 4 cm^2

Exercise 4U
1. What is the value of 6^2?
2. Calculate the value of 'ten squared'.
3. Calculate the value of each of these:
   (a) 7^2 (b) 8^2 (c) 4^2 (d) 12^2 (e) 10^2

Finding a **square root** is the opposite of finding a **square**.

Example 2
Find the square root of 64.
$$64 = 8 \times 8 \quad \text{so } \mathbf{8} \text{ is the square root of 64.}$$
You write **the square root of 25** like this $\sqrt{25}$.

You can find the square root of a number in three different ways:

1. **by inspection** when you can see the answer
   Example Find $\sqrt{36}$ Answer = 6

   Hint:
   You should remember that $6 \times 6 = 36$.

2. **with a calculator**
   Example Find $\sqrt{3\,136}$
   Press ③ ① ③ ⑥ √ =
   so $\sqrt{3\,136} = 56$

3. **by trial and improvement**
   Example Find $\sqrt{256}$
   Try 10 $10 \times 10 = 100$ – too small
   Try 20 $20 \times 20 = 400$ – too large
   Try 15 $15 \times 15 = 225$ – a bit too small
   Try 16 $16 \times 16 = 256$ – just right   So $\sqrt{256} = 16$

Exercise 4V

1. Find each of these square roots by inspection.
   (a) $\sqrt{25}$ (b) $\sqrt{9}$ (c) $\sqrt{81}$ (d) $\sqrt{49}$ (e) $\sqrt{100}$
2. Use a calculator to find these square roots.
   (a) $\sqrt{289}$ (b) $\sqrt{1\,849}$ (c) $\sqrt{80\,656}$
3. Use trial and improvement to find $\sqrt{484}$.

Summary	Checkout 4
1. To multiply a number by 10, move all the digits one place to the left and add a zero.	1. Multiply these numbers by 10. (a) 23 (b) 36
2. To multiply a number by 100, move all the digits two places to the left and add two zeros.	2. Multiply these numbers by 100. (a) 17 (b) 30
3. To multiply a number by 1 000, move all the digits three places to the left and add three zeros.	3. Multiply these numbers by 1 000. (a) 7 (b) 49
4. To divide a number by 10, move all the digits one place to the right.	4. Divide these numbers by 10. (a) 50 (b) 560
5. To divide a number by 100, move all the digits two places to the right.	5. Divide these numbers by 100. (a) 400 (b) 3 500
6. To divide a number by 1 000, move all the digits three places to the right.	6. Divide these numbers by 1 000. (a) 3 000 (b) 78 000

7. You should work out simple calculations in your head.

7. Work out:
   (a) 6×7 (b) 8×9
   (c) 40×5 (d) 90×700
   (e) 23×5 (f) 42×8
   (g) $36 \div 6$ (h) $63 \div 9$

8. Work out harder calculations on paper.

8. Work out:
   (a) $41 \div 8$ (b) $47 \div 5$
   (c) $160 \div 20$ (d) $540 \div 60$
   (e) 125×6 (f) 18×50
   (g) 237×5 (h) 846×49
   (i) $375 \div 3$ (j) $407 \div 5$
   (k) $324 \div 12$ (l) $951 \div 21$

9. Any number which divides exactly into 24 is called a **factor** of 24.

9. Write down the factors of:
   (a) 32 (b) 60

10. An **even number** has 2 as a factor.

10. Write down the next five even numbers after:
    (a) 42 (b) 264

11. An **odd** number does not have 2 as a factor.

11. Write down the next five odd numbers after:
    (a) 51 (b) 377

12. A **prime** number has only two factors.

12. Write down all the prime numbers in this list: 6, 9, 7, 2, 15, 21, 23, 27, 31, 37, 50, 51, 53

13. If any number divides exactly by 3, it is called a **multiple** of 3.

13. Write down the first five multiples of:
    (a) 4 (b) 12

14. Ratios can be simplified by dividing both numbers by a common factor.

14. Simplify the ratios:
    (a) $4 : 16$ (b) $15 : 12 : 9$

15. You can scale up or down from a ratio.

15. If orange juice and water are mixed in the ratio of $2 : 7$, what quantity of water is needed to mix with 4 litres of orange juice?

16. You can divide in a ratio.

16. Divide £24 in the ratios:
    (a) $1 : 5$ (b) $5 : 6 : 1$

Revision exercise 4

1. (a) What is the value of the 4 in the number 3 648?
   (b) The number 2 539 is multiplied by 10.
       What is the value of the 5 in the answer?
   (c) The number 687 is divided by 10.
       What is the value of the 6 in the answer? [WJEC]

2. Paul has five numbered discs.

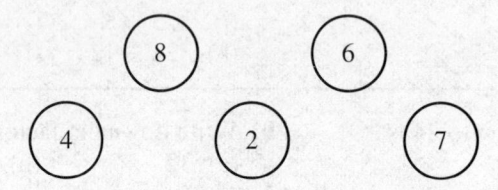

   (8) (6)
   (4) (2) (7)

   (a) (i) Which of Paul's numbers is a square number?
       (ii) Which of Paul's numbers is a multiple of 4, other than 4 itself?

   Paul uses some of the discs to make a four-figure number, 2 684, as shown.

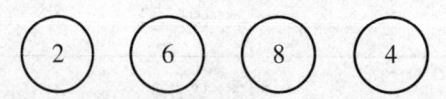

   (2) (6) (8) (4)

   (b) (i) What is the value of the 6 in Paul's number?
       (ii) Paul multiplies his number by 10.
            What is the value of the 6 in his new number?
                                                    [AQA/SEG]

3. Greyburn College has a team of 4 runners in the relay race.
   Each of the four runners runs 400 m.
   (a) What is the total distance of the race in metres?
   (b) Write your answer to (a) in kilometres. [OCR]

4. Tickets for a concert cost £3 each.
   Ramana has £17.
   Work out the greatest number of tickets that Ramana can buy. [Edexcel]

5. Joan saves 1p and 2p coins in a jar.
   She empties the jar and counts the coins.
   She writes down:

Coin	Number
1p	660
2p	767

   How much money does she have? [AQA/NEAB]

6. You may not use a calculator in this question.
   Show all your working.

   Hip Hop welcomes you Entry only £12

   On a busy Saturday, Hip Hop Amusement Park had 624 visitors.

   (a) How much money did they take that day?

   It costs £5 000 a day to run the park.

   (b) Work out the profit they made that day. [OCR]

7. (a) A coach will seat 46 pupils.
      (i) How many coaches are needed to take 197 pupils on a trip?
      (ii) The 197 pupils pay £2·60 each to cover the cost of the coaches.
          How much does it cost to hire each coach?
   (b) A coach took 3 hours to complete the journey of 132 miles.
       Calculate the average speed of the coach. [AQA/SEG]

8.

Ways of getting 192
12 × 16 = 192
24 × 8 = 192
48 × 4 = 192
96 × 2 = 192

Ways of getting 272
17 × 16 = 272
34 × ...... = 272
68 × ...... = 272
...... × ...... = 272

   Copy and complete the table for the number 272. [Edexcel]

9. Petrol costs 62p per litre.
   Work out the cost of 12 litres. [Edexcel]

10.

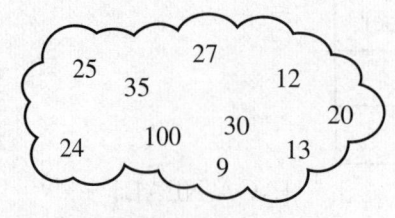

   Numbers in the cloud: 25, 27, 35, 12, 24, 100, 30, 20, 9, 13

   From the numbers in the cloud, write down
   (a) those numbers that 2 will divide into exactly
   (b) those numbers that 10 will divide into exactly
   (c) the number which is double one of the other numbers [Edexcel]

11. Write down two different pairs of numbers that multiply together to make 24. [Edexcel]

12. Members of the Swallow Club are going on a coach outing.

    The coach costs £448 to hire.
    There are 32 people going on the outing.
    They share the cost equally between them.

    How much do they each pay? [OCR]

13. Do not use a calculator when answering this question.
    All working must be shown.

    A company sells golf balls in packs of 36.
    How many packs can be filled using 775 golf balls and how many golf balls will be left over? [WJEC]

14. Do not use a calculator in this question.
    Show all your working clearly.

    Tony has a hot-dog stall.
    He uses sauce from a bottle which holds 224 ml.
    He puts about 7 ml of sauce on each hot-dog.
    (a) How many hot-dogs can he put sauce on from one bottle?
    (b) Tony buys the sauce in boxes of 24 bottles.
        One full bottle weighs 256 g.
        The empty box weighs 750 g.
        What is the total weight of a box full of sauce bottles? [AQA/NEAB]

15. Brian and Maggie took part in a sponsored walk.
They each walked 35 km.

  (a) Brian took 7 hours.
  Calculate his average speed.

  (b) Maggie walked at 4 km per hour.
  How long did she take?
  Write your answer in hours and minutes. [OCR]

16. Anthony has £10. He uses this money to buy as many roses as he can for his mother.
Each rose costs 65p.

  (a) How many roses does he buy?

  (b) How much money does he have left? [WJEC]

17. A school is taking all of its Year 11 students to a careers convention.
There are 248 students in the year.
The school hires a number of coaches to take the students.
Each coach can take 42 students.

  (a) What is the smallest number of coaches needed?

  (b) How many spare seats for students will there be? [OCR]

18. Write down

  (a) three different factors of 18

  (b) a factor of 18 which is a prime number [AQA/NEAB]

19. Write down the next two prime numbers greater than 13. [Edexcel]

20. Five numbers are shown below:

  23   26   56   73   74

  (a) Which two of these numbers have a total of 100?

  (b) Which two of these five numbers have a difference of 50?

  (c) What is the highest number you can make by multiplying two of these five numbers?

  (d) From these five numbers write down one which is a multiple of 7.

  (e) From these five numbers write down one which is prime. [AQA/NEAB]

21. Some of the very first coins were made from electrum.
Electrum is made from silver and gold.
These are mixed in the ratio 3 parts of silver to 7 parts of gold.

(a) How much gold should be mixed with 15 g of silver to make electrum?

(b) An electrum coin has a weight of 20 g.
What weight of gold does it contain? [OCR]

22. Malika's father won £128.

He shared the £128 between his three children in the ratio 6 : 3 : 1.
Malika was given the biggest share.

Work out how much money Malika received. [Edexcel]

23. This is a recipe for carrot salad.
It serves 4 people.

> 125 g brown rice
> 250 g carrots
> juice of $\frac{1}{2}$ orange
> 1 tablespoon olive oil
> 50 g walnuts

(a) Ann makes the salad for 4 people.
She opens a 1 kg bag of rice.

How much rice will be left?
State the units in your answer.

(b) David makes the salad for 12 people.
Copy and complete the list of ingredients that David needs.

> .... g brown rice
> .... g carrots
> juice of .... oranges
> .... tablespoons olive oil
> .... g walnuts [OCR]

5 Algebra 1

If you make x calls per quarter it will cost you 60 + 5x pounds. If you opt for Pay As You Go you can make a saving of 20xy per cent.

That much?

This unit is about:

- Using letters to represent quantities
- Formulae
- Substitution
- Substitution using BoDMAS
- Substitution using powers
- Substitution with negative numbers
- Substitution in formulae
- Collecting like terms

You need to remember:

- How to add and subtract negative numbers (see Unit 1).

  Calculate:
  1. $8 + 3$
  2. $8 + {}^-3$
  3. ${}^-8 + {}^-3$
  4. ${}^-8 + {}^-3$
  5. $8 - 3$
  6. ${}^-8 - 3$
  7. $8 - {}^-3$
  8. ${}^-8 - {}^-3$
  9. $7 + 11$
  10. $7 + {}^-11$
  11. ${}^-7 + 11$
  12. ${}^-7 + {}^-11$
  13. $7 - 11$
  14. ${}^-7 - 11$
  15. $7 - {}^-11$
  16. ${}^-7 - {}^-11$
  17. $5 + 5$
  18. $5 + {}^-5$
  19. ${}^-5 + 5$
  20. ${}^-5 + {}^-5$
  21. $5 - 5$
  22. ${}^-5 - 5$
  23. $5 - {}^-5$
  24. ${}^-5 - {}^-5$

5.1 Using letters to represent quantities in addition and subtraction problems

Wilma Flint is a fence erector. When working out the number of posts and panels she needs for a fence she uses this rule:

> The number of posts is always one more than the number of panels.

If the letter f represents the number of fence panels, the number of posts needed is $f + 1$.

Hmm...6 panels that means I need 7 posts.

Example

The letter g represents the number of computer games that Henry owns. Use the letter g to write the number of games owned by:

(a) Susan, who owns 5 games more than Henry
(b) Anton, who owns 8 games less than Henry.

(a) Susan owns $g + 5$ games.
(b) Anton owns $g - 8$ games.

Exercise 5A

1. The letter m represents Jarvinder's score in a mathematics test. Use the letter m to write the scores of:
   (a) Neal, who scored 15 marks less than Jarvinder
   (b) Ashley, who scored 2 marks more than Jarvinder
   (c) Claire, who scored 6 marks less than Jarvinder
   (d) Ruth, who scored 8 marks more than Jarvinder
   (e) Gurpal, who scored 1 mark more than Jarvinder
   (f) Stacey, who scored 10 marks less than Jarvinder.

2. The letter y represents Daniel's age in years. Use the letter y to write the ages of:
   (a) Kelly Marie, who is 2 years older than Daniel
   (b) Kimberly, who is 4 years younger than Daniel
   (c) Christopher, who is 7 years older than Daniel
   (d) Gary, who is 1 year older than Daniel
   (e) Robert, who is 9 years younger than Daniel
   (f) Carmen, who is 2 years younger than Daniel.

3. The letter *h* represents Sally's height in centimetres.
   Use the letter *h* to write the heights of:
   (a) John, who is 15 cm taller than Sally
   (b) Surbajit, who is 12 cm shorter than Sally
   (c) Penny, who is 10 cm taller than Sally
   (d) Jemma, who is 4 cm shorter than Sally
   (e) Duncan, who is 1 cm taller than Sally
   (f) Nathan, who is 11 cm shorter than Sally.

4. Seven friends buy a bag of cherries to share. The letter *c* represents the number of cherries that Chris ate.
   Use the letter *c* to write the number of cherries eaten by:
   (a) Sarah, who ate 5 more cherries than Chris
   (b) Emily, who ate 16 less cherries than Chris
   (c) Melissa, who ate 3 more cherries than Chris
   (d) Gavin, who ate 1 less cherry than Chris
   (e) Natalie, who ate 6 more cherries than Chris
   (f) Andrew, who ate 2 less cherries than Chris.

5.2 Using letters to represent quantities in multiplication and division problems

Billy Rubble is a builder. When he fits doors he knows that for each door he will need 3 hinges. If the letter *d* represents the number of doors he is installing in a house, he needs $d \times 3$ hinges.

The multiplication sign is not used in algebra and numbers are written before letters. So, you write:

The number of hinges needed is $3d$

If the letter *h* represents the number of hinges Billy has in stock, this is enough hinges to fit $h \div 3$ doors.

Division in algebra is shown by putting one quantity over the other. So, you write:

The number of doors that can be fitted is $\frac{h}{3}$.

Example

There are r bread rolls in a Family Pack. Use the letter r to write the number of bread rolls in:

(a) An Everyday Pack which has half as many rolls as a Family Pack.
(b) A Value Pack which has twice as many rolls as a Family Pack.

(a) An Everyday Pack has $\frac{r}{2}$ rolls.   (b) A Value Pack has $2r$ rolls.

Exercise 5B

1. The letter a represents John Brown's age in years.
   Use the letter a to write the ages of:
   (a) John's mother, who is twice as old as John
   (b) John's sister, whose age is John's age divided by 3
   (c) John's grandmother, who is 3 times as old as John
   (d) John's brother, whose age is John's age divided by 4
   (e) John's great-grandfather, who is 5 times as old as John
   (f) John's daughter, whose age is John's age divided by 20.

2. The letter m represents the number of marbles that Kevin owns.
   Use the letter m to write the number of marbles owned by:
   (a) Sandra, who owns 4 times as many marbles as Kevin
   (b) Gwen, who owns Kevin's number divided by 7
   (c) Nilha, who owns Kevin's number divided by 9
   (d) Sheila, who owns 3 times as many marbles as Kevin
   (e) Aaron, who owns 6 times as many marbles as Kevin
   (f) Vikram, who owns Kevin's number divided by 2.

3. Billy Rubble fits d doors in a new house.
   Use the letter d to write the number of:
   (a) Hinges needed, if he fits 4 to each door
   (b) Handles needed, if he fits 2 to each door
   (c) Screws needed, if he fits 16 to each door
   (d) Locks needed, if he fits 1 to each door
   (e) Wood framing needed, if he fits 5 metres to each door
   (f) Wood stain needed, if he uses $\frac{1}{2}$ litre on each door.

4. Betty Bun the baker has made b bread rolls.
   How many packets can she fill if:
   (a) There are 4 rolls in a packet
   (b) There are 6 rolls in a packet
   (c) There are 8 rolls in a packet
   (d) There are 12 rolls in a packet
   (e) There are 16 rolls in a packet
   (f) Each packet has the slogan '12 rolls plus 3 free'?

5.3 Formulae

Siloben is 3 years older than Gurpreet.

When Gurpreet is 12 years old, Siloben is 15 years old.
When Gurpreet is 14 years old, Siloben is 17 years old.
When Gurpreet is 16 years old, Siloben is 19 years old.

You can write a general rule like this:

Siloben's age = Gurpreet's age + 3

A general rule like this is called a **formula**. Formulae are usually written using letters to represent the quantities.

If you let S represent Siloben's age and G represent Gurpreet's age, the formula becomes:

$S = G + 3$

Example

A washing machine repairer calculates the cost of a repair like this:

Cost (c) = £45 + £20 × number of hours worked (h)

(a) Calculate the cost if the repair takes:
   (i) 2 hours   (ii) $1\frac{1}{2}$ hours

(b) Write a formula using the letters in brackets.

(a) (i) Cost = £45 + £20 × 2 = £45 + £40 = £85
   (ii) Cost = £45 + £20 × $1\frac{1}{2}$ = £45 + £30 = £75
(b) $c = 45 + 20h$

Exercise 5C

1. A plumber adds a call-out fee of £25 onto the cost of any repairs. He uses this formula to calculate his total bill.

   Total bill (b) = cost of repairs (r) + £25

   (a) Calculate the total bill if the cost of repairs is:
      (i) £30   (ii) £50   (iii) £80   (iv) £100
   (b) Write a formula using the letters in brackets.

2. Helen works in a fast food restaurant. She uses this formula to calculate her wages in pounds:

   Wages (w) = number of hours worked (n) × £4·50

   (a) Calculate Helen's wage if she works:
      (i) 5 hours
      (ii) 10 hours
      (iii) 20 hours
      (iv) 15 hours
   (b) Write a formula using the letters in brackets.

3. Anna Deal sells cars. She offers customers the option of credit using this formula:

   Total cost (T) = £1 000 + 24 × monthly payment (M)

   (a) Calculate the cost of buying a car if the monthly payments are:
      (i) £200   (ii) £100   (iii) £300   (iv) £150
   (b) Write a formula using the letters in brackets.

4. An approximate rule for changing temperatures in degrees Celsius (C) into temperatures in degrees Fahrenheit (F) is:

   Temperature in Fahrenheit (F) = 2 × temperature in Celsius (C) + 30

   (a) Change each of these temperatures to Fahrenheit:
      (i) 30°C   (ii) 40°C   (iii) 50°C   (iv) 100°C
   (b) Write a formula using the letters in brackets.

5. The cost, in pence, of an advertisement in a newspaper is calculated using this formula:

   Cost (C) = 25 × number of words (w) + 40

   (a) Work out the cost of placing an advertisement with:
      (i) 20 words   (ii) 30 words   (iii) 16 words   (iv) 50 words
   (b) Write a formula using the letters in brackets.

6. A school has a minibus which costs £20 each time it is used. A PE teacher uses this formula to calculate how much to charge her players when she uses the minibus:

   Cost per player (c) = 20 ÷ number of players travelling (p)

   (a) Calculate the cost per player if the number travelling is:
      (i) 5   (ii) 10   (iii) 8   (iv) 16
   (b) Write a formula using the letters in brackets.

7. This formula links foot length (L) measured in inches with shoe size (S):

   Shoe size (S) = 3 × length (L) − 25

   (a) What shoe sizes fit feet of length:
   - (i) 10 inches
   - (ii) 12 inches
   - (iii) 11 inches
   - (iv) 9 inches?

   (b) Write a formula using the letters in brackets.

8. A teacher hires a bus for £120 to take students to visit a theme park. The cost of a ticket to enter the park is £8. The teacher uses this formula to work out the cost per student:

   Cost per student (c) = 120 ÷ number of students travelling (n) + 8

   (a) Work out the cost per student if the number of students travelling is:
   - (i) 12   (ii) 24   (iii) 30   (iv) 40

   (b) Write a formula using the letters in brackets.

5.4 Substitution

An **expression** is a collection of letters and numbers.

For example: $3a + 2b$ is an expression.

If you know the values of the letter a and b, you can **substitute** them for the letters in the expression and find its value.

For example, if $a = 4$ and $b = 5$, then the value of the expression is:

$$3 \times 4 + 2 \times 5 = 12 + 10 = 22$$

Example

If $x = 5$ and $y = 7$, find the value of:
(a) $x + 9$ (b) $y - 5$ (c) $3x$ (d) $2y$ (e) $3x - 2y$

(a) $5 + 9 = 14$ (b) $7 - 5 = 2$ (c) $3 \times 5 = 15$ (d) $2 \times 7 = 14$ (e) $15 - 14 = 1$

Exercise 5D

1. If $m = 7$, find the value of:
   (a) $m + 3$ (b) $m + 4$ (c) $9 + m$ (d) $m - 3$ (e) $8 - m$
   (f) $3m$ (g) $3m + 5$ (h) $3m - 3$ (i) $2m + 1$ (j) $2m - 1$

2. If $s = 6$, find the value of:
   - (a) $s + 6$
   - (b) $15 + s$
   - (c) $s - 4$
   - (d) $12 - s$
   - (e) $s - 6$
   - (f) $3s$
   - (g) $3s - 4$
   - (h) $2s + 5$
   - (i) $4s - 20$
   - (j) $18 - 2s$

3. If $y = 5$, find the value of:
   - (a) $y + 10$
   - (b) $12 + y$
   - (c) $8 - y$
   - (d) $y - 3$
   - (e) $5 - y$
   - (f) $3y$
   - (g) $3y + 4$
   - (h) $2y - 5$
   - (i) $2y + 5$
   - (j) $25 - 4y$

4. If $x = 20$, find the value of:
   - (a) $x + 1$
   - (b) $11 + x$
   - (c) $x - 10$
   - (d) $30 - x$
   - (e) $x + x$
   - (f) $2x$
   - (g) $x + x + x$
   - (h) $3x$
   - (i) $x + x - 3$
   - (j) $2x - 3$

5. If $z = 16$, find the value of:
   - (a) $z + 16$
   - (b) $z + z$
   - (c) $2z$
   - (d) $18 - z$
   - (e) $z - 6$
   - (f) $3z$
   - (g) $z + z + z$
   - (h) $z + 16 + z$
   - (i) $3z - 40$
   - (j) $50 - 3z$

6. If $a = 3$ and $b = 4$, find the value of:
   - (a) $7 + a$
   - (b) $b + 16$
   - (c) $3a$
   - (d) $2b$
   - (e) $3a + 2b$
   - (f) $a + 2b$
   - (g) $3a - b$
   - (h) $2b - a$
   - (i) $a + b + 7$
   - (j) $2a + 3b + 1$

7. If $x = 4$ and $y = 1$, find the value of:
   - (a) $x + y$
   - (b) $x + x + y$
   - (c) $2x + y$
   - (d) $2x - y$
   - (e) $x - 2y$
   - (f) $3x + 4y$
   - (g) $x + 5y$
   - (h) $2x - 5y$
   - (i) $2x - 2$
   - (j) $2y - 2$

8. If $m = 7$ and $n = 4$, find the value of:
   - (a) $m + n$
   - (b) $m + n + n$
   - (c) $m + 2n$
   - (d) $2m + m$
   - (e) $3m$
   - (f) $n + 2n + n$
   - (g) $4n$
   - (h) $3m + 2n$
   - (i) $2m - 3n$
   - (j) $m + n - 10$

9. If $q = 10$ and $r = 15$, find the value of:
   - (a) $3q$
   - (b) $2r$
   - (c) $3q + 2r$
   - (d) $3q - 2r$
   - (e) $2q + 3r$
   - (f) $2q + 45$
   - (g) $30 - 2r$
   - (h) $60 - 3r$
   - (i) $6q - 60$
   - (j) $4r - 6q$

10. If $j = 18$ and $k = 12$, find the value of:
    - (a) $k + k$
    - (b) $k + k + k$
    - (c) $3k$
    - (d) $3k - 2j$
    - (e) $5k - 50$
    - (f) $j + k$
    - (g) $2j + 2k$
    - (h) $3j + 3k$
    - (i) $j - k$
    - (j) $2j - 2k$

5.5 Substitution involving BoDMAS

The expression xy means $x \times y$

The expression $\dfrac{x}{y}$ means $x \div y$

The expression $3xy$ means $3 \times x \times y$

The expression $3(x + y)$ means calculate $x + y$ and then multiply by 3

There should never be any doubt in which order multiplications, divisions, additions or subtractions are to be done.
The word **BoDMAS** will help you remember the order is always:

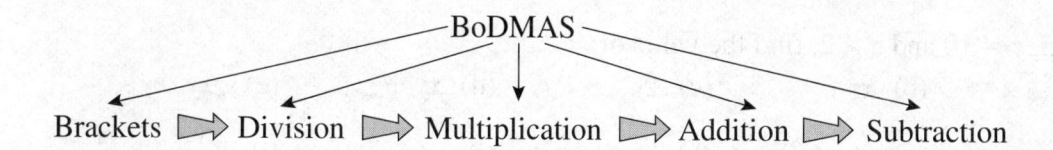

BoDMAS

Brackets ⇒ Division ⇒ Multiplication ⇒ Addition ⇒ Subtraction

Example
If $a = 4$ and $b = 2$, find the value of:
(a) ab (b) $3ab$ (c) $a + ab$ (d) $\dfrac{a}{b} - 1$ (e) $3(a + b)$

(a) $4 \times 2 = 8$
(b) $3 \times 4 \times 2 = 24$
(c) $4 + 4 \times 2 = 4 + 8 = 12$ (multiplication before addition)
(d) $4 \div 2 - 1 = 2 - 1 = 1$ (division before subtraction)
(e) $3 \times (4 + 2) = 3 \times 6 = 18$ (brackets before multiplication)

Exercise 5E

1. If $a = 3$ and $b = 4$, find the value of:
   (a) ab (b) $5ab$ (c) $b + ab$ (d) $a + ab$ (e) $ab + ba$
   (f) $2ab$ (g) $\dfrac{6b}{a}$ (h) $2(a + b)$ (i) $3(a + 4)$ (j) $5(b + 3)$

2. If $x = 2$ and $y = 1$, find the value of:
   (a) xy (b) $3xy$ (c) $x + xy$ (d) $\dfrac{x}{y} + y$ (e) $\dfrac{12}{x} + 3y$
   (f) $2x + 2y$ (g) $2(x + y)$ (h) $3(x + y)$ (i) $3x + 3y$ (j) $x(4y - 3)$

3. If $m = 4$ and $n = 5$, find the value of:
   (a) mn (b) $2mn$ (c) $2nm$ (d) $\dfrac{10m}{n}$ (e) $\dfrac{8n}{m}$
   (f) $3(n - m)$ (g) $3n - 3m$ (h) $5(m + n)$ (i) $5m + 5n$ (j) $n(m + n)$

4. If $p = 5$ and $q = 10$, find the value of:
   (a) pq (b) qp (c) $\dfrac{30}{p}$ (d) $\dfrac{30}{q}$ (e) $\dfrac{30}{(p + q)}$
   (f) $2p + 2q$ (g) $2(p + q)$ (h) $3(q - p)$ (i) $3q - 3p$ (j) $p(12 - q)$

5. If $e = 3$ and $f = 7$, find the value of:
   - (a) ef
   - (b) fe
   - (c) $\dfrac{30}{e}$
   - (d) $\dfrac{28}{f}$
   - (e) $\dfrac{40}{(e+f)}$
   - (f) $40(e+f)$
   - (g) $40e + 40f$
   - (h) $e + ef$
   - (i) $e(1+f)$
   - (j) $f(e+1)$

6. If $x = 5$, $y = 10$ and $z = 2$, find the value of:
   - (a) xy
   - (b) xz
   - (c) zy
   - (d) $xy + z$
   - (e) zxy
   - (f) $3(x+y)$
   - (g) $z(x+y)$
   - (h) $y(x-z)$
   - (i) $x(y-z)$
   - (j) $\dfrac{xy}{z}$

7. If $s = 3$, $t = 2$ and $u = 4$, find the value of:
   - (a) st
   - (b) ut
   - (c) us
   - (d) $2st$
   - (e) $20 - 2ut$
   - (f) $u + st$
   - (g) $u(s+t)$
   - (h) $us + ut$
   - (i) $\dfrac{us}{t}$
   - (j) $u + \dfrac{s}{t}$

8. If $p = 3$, $q = 1$ and $r = 2$, find the value of:
   - (a) $2pq$
   - (b) pqr
   - (c) $r(p+3)$
   - (d) $2pr$
   - (e) $q(r+2)$
   - (f) $qr + 3q$
   - (g) $3(pq+r)$
   - (h) $3pq + 3r$
   - (i) $p(q+r)$
   - (j) $pq + pr$

9. If $a = 3$, $b = 4$ and $c = 5$, find the value of:
   - (a) ab
   - (b) $a + cb$
   - (c) bc
   - (d) abc
   - (e) $a + bc$
   - (f) $ab + bc$
   - (g) $b(a+c)$
   - (h) $2(ab+ac)$
   - (i) $2a(b+c)$
   - (j) $c(ab+1)$

10. If $x = 9$, $y = 3$ and $z = 2$, find the value of:
    - (a) $2y - 7$
    - (b) $2x - yz$
    - (c) $6y - zx$
    - (d) $3(x-z)$
    - (e) $3x - 3z$
    - (f) $x(y+z)$
    - (g) $xy + xz$
    - (h) $x(y-z)$
    - (i) $xy - xz$
    - (j) $\dfrac{4x}{yz}$

5.6 Substitution involving powers

The expression x^2 means $x \times x$. x^2 is read as 'x squared'.

The expression y^3 means $y \times y \times y$. y^3 is read as 'y cubed'.

The expression x^5 means $x \times x \times x \times x \times x$. x^5 is read as 'x to the power 5'.

The expression $2x^3$ means $2 \times x \times x \times x$

The expression $2xy^2$ means $2 \times x \times y \times y$

The expression $2x^2y$ means $2 \times x \times x \times y$

The expression $(x + y^2)$ means $(x+y) \times (x+y)$

The expression $\sqrt{x}$ means find a number which, when you square it, gives you x. $\sqrt{x}$ is read as 'the square root of x'.

Example

If $a = 3$ and $b = 4$, find the value of:
(a) a^2 (b) b^3 (c) a^5 (d) $2a^3$ (e) $2ab^2$ (f) $2a^2b$ (g) $(a+b)^2$
(h) $\sqrt{b}$ (i) $\sqrt{a}$

(a) $3 \times 3 = 9$
(b) $4 \times 4 \times 4 = 64$
(c) $3 \times 3 \times 3 \times 3 \times 3 = 243$
(d) $2 \times 3 \times 3 \times 3 = 54$
(e) $2 \times 3 \times 4 \times 4 = 96$
(f) $2 \times 3 \times 3 \times 4 = 72$
(g) $(3+4)^2 = 7^2 = 7 \times 7 = 49$
(h) $\sqrt{b} = \sqrt{4} = 2$ (because $2 \times 2 = 4$)
(i) $\sqrt{a} = \sqrt{3} = 1.7$ (using $\sqrt{}$ key on a calculator)

Exercise 5F

You will need a calculator to complete this exercise.

1. If $e = 1, f = 2$ and $g = 3$, find the value of:
   (a) e^2 (b) f^2 (c) g^2 (d) e^3 (e) f^3 (f) g^3
   (g) e^4 (h) f^4 (i) g^4 (j) e^5 (k) $\sqrt{e}$

2. If $a = 5, b = 6$ and $c = 7$, find the value of:
   (a) a^2 (b) b^2 (c) c^2 (d) a^3 (e) b^3 (f) c^3
   (g) a^4 (h) b^4 (i) c^4 (j) a^5 (k) $\sqrt{a}$

3. If $x = 8, y = 9$ and $z = 10$, find the value of:
   (a) x^2 (b) y^2 (c) z^2 (d) x^3 (e) y^3 (f) z^3
   (g) x^4 (h) y^4 (i) z^4 (j) x^5 (k) $\sqrt{y}$ (l) $\sqrt{z}$

4. If $e = 5, f = 6$ and $g = 7$, find the value of:
   (a) $2e^2$ (b) $2f^2$ (c) $2g^2$ (d) ef^2 (e) e^2f (f) fg^2
   (g) f^2g (h) eg^2 (i) e^2g (j) $(e+f)^2$ (k) $\sqrt{(2e+f)}$

5. If $x = 2$ and $y = 3$, find the value of:
   (a) $2x^2$ (b) $2y^3$ (c) $3x^4$ (d) $2y^2$ (e) x^5
   (f) x^6 (g) xy (h) x^2y (i) xy^2 (j) $x^2 + y^2$

6. If $a = 1$ and $b = 2$, find the value of:
   (a) a^2 (b) b^3 (c) $a^3 + b^2$ (d) a^4 (e) a^7
   (f) ab (g) a^2b (h) ab^2 (i) $2ab^2$ (j) $(2a+b)^2$

7. If $m = 4$ and $n = 5$, find the value of:
   (a) m^2 (b) $n^2 + m^2$ (c) $n^3 + m^3$ (d) $2n^2$ (e) $2m^2$
   (f) $2n^2 + 2m^2$ (g) $2(n^2 + m^2)$ (h) $n^2 - m^2$ (i) $(n-m)(m+n)$ (j) $3m^2$

8. If $a = 3, s = 4$ and $u = 6$, find the value of:
   (a) as (b) u^2 (c) $2as$ (d) $u^2 - 2as$ (e) u^3
   (f) $(a+s)^2$ (g) $u^2 + us$ (h) $u(u+s)$ (i) $s(u-a)$ (j) $su - sa$

9. If $x = 3$, $y = 4$ and $z = 8$, find the value of:
   (a) $x + 2$
   (b) $12 - 2y$
   (c) $5z - 11$
   (d) $3(2x + y)$
   (e) xy
   (f) $x(y + z)$
   (g) z^3
   (h) zy^2
   (i) z^2y
   (j) $(x + y)^3$

10. If $a = 10$, $b = 5$ and $c = 1$, find the value of:
    (a) $a + b$
    (b) $a - b$
    (c) $5b - 7$
    (d) abc
    (e) $2ab + c$
    (f) $\dfrac{ac}{b}$
    (g) a^3b
    (h) ab^3
    (i) $a^3 + b^3$
    (j) $(a + b)^2$

5.7 Substitution with negative numbers

A negative number multiplied by a positive number gives a negative answer.

Examples
(a) $4 \times {}^-3 = {}^-12$ (b) ${}^-5 \times 5 = {}^-25$
(c) If $p = {}^-2$, $q = 4$ and $r = {}^-3$, then:
$p + q = {}^-2 + 4 = 2$
$q - p = 4 - {}^-2 = 4 + 2 = 6$
$3r = 3 \times {}^-3 = {}^-9$
$p - q = {}^-2 - 4 = {}^-6$
$4p = 4 \times {}^-2 = {}^-8$
$4p + 3r = 4 \times {}^-2 + 3 \times {}^-3 = {}^-8 + {}^-9 = {}^-17$
$3r - 2q = 3 \times {}^-3 - 2 \times 4 = {}^-9 - 8 = {}^-17$
$4r - 5p = 4 \times {}^-3 - 5 \times {}^-2 = {}^-12 - {}^-10 = {}^-12 + 10 = {}^-2$

Exercise 5G

1. If $m = {}^-7$, find the value of:
   (a) $m + 3$
   (b) $m + 4$
   (c) $9 + m$
   (d) $m - 3$
   (e) $8 - m$
   (f) $3m$
   (g) $3m + 5$
   (h) $3m - 3$
   (i) $2m + 1$
   (j) $2m - 1$

2. If $s = {}^-6$, find the value of:
   (a) $s + 6$
   (b) $15 + s$
   (c) $s - 4$
   (d) $12 - s$
   (e) $s - 6$
   (f) $3s$
   (g) $3s - 4$
   (h) $2s + 5$
   (i) $4s - 20$
   (j) $18 - 2s$

3. If $y = {}^-5$, find the value of:
   (a) $y + 10$
   (b) $12 + y$
   (c) $8 - y$
   (d) $y - 3$
   (e) $5 - y$
   (f) $3y$
   (g) $3y + 4$
   (h) $2y - 5$
   (i) $2y + 5$
   (j) $25 - 4y$

4. If $x = {}^-20$, find the value of:
   (a) $x + 1$
   (b) $11 + x$
   (c) $x - 10$
   (d) $30 - x$
   (e) $x + x$
   (f) $2x$
   (g) $x + x + x$
   (h) $3x$
   (i) $x + x - 3$
   (j) $2x - 3$

5. If $z = {}^-16$, find the value of:
   (a) $z + 16$ (b) $z + z$ (c) $2z$ (d) $18 - z$ (e) $z - 6$
   (f) $3z$ (g) $z + z + z$ (h) $z + 16 + z$ (i) $3z - 40$ (j) $50 - 3z$

6. If $a = 2$ and $b = {}^-4$, find the value of:
   (a) $7 + a$ (b) $b + 16$ (c) $3a$ (d) $2b$ (e) $3a + 2b$
   (f) $a + 2b$ (g) $3a - b$ (h) $2b - a$ (i) $a + b + 7$ (j) $2a + 3b + 1$

7. If $x = {}^-4$ and $y = 4$, find the value of:
   (a) $x + y$ (b) $x + x + y$ (c) $2x + y$ (d) $2x - y$ (e) $x - 2y$
   (f) $3x + 4y$ (g) $x + 5y$ (h) $2x - 5y$ (i) $2x - 2$ (j) $2y - 2$

8. If $m = 5$ and $n = {}^-4$, find the value of:
   (a) $m + n$ (b) $m + n + n$ (c) $m + 2n$ (d) $2m + m$ (e) $3m$
   (f) $n + 2n + n$ (g) $4n$ (h) $3m + 2n$ (i) $2m - 3n$ (j) $m + n - 10$

9. If $q = {}^-10$ and $r = 5$, find the value of:
   (a) $3q$ (b) $2r$ (c) $3q + 2r$ (d) $3q - 2r$ (e) $2q + 3r$
   (f) $2q + 45$ (g) $30 - 2r$ (h) $60 - 3r$ (i) $6q - 60$ (j) $4r - 6q$

10. If $j = {}^-18$ and $k = {}^-12$, find the value of:
    (a) $k + k$ (b) $k + k + k$ (c) $3k$ (d) $3k - 2j$ (e) $5k - 50$
    (f) $j + k$ (g) $2j + 2k$ (h) $3j + 3k$ (i) $j - k$ (j) $2j - 2k$

5.8 Substitution in formulae

A formula is a rule to calculate a value.

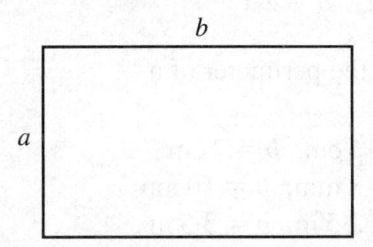

For example, the formula $P = 2a + 2b$ can be used to calculate the perimeter (P) of a rectangle if you know the side lengths a and b.

Example 1

$S = 180n - 360$. Find the value of S when $n = 10$

$\qquad n = 10$

so $\qquad S = 180 \times 10 - 360 = 1\,800 - 360 = 1\,440$

Example 2

The cost C pence, of a newspaper advertisement of n words is given by the formula
$$C = 30n + 40$$

Find the cost of an advertisement of 20 words.

$n = 20$

so $\quad C = 30 \times 20 + 40 = 600 + 40 = 640$ pence $= £6\cdot40$

Example 3

When a stone is dropped over a cliff, the distance d metres it has fallen after t seconds is given by the formula
$$d = 5t^2$$

How far will a stone fall in 3 seconds?

$t = 3$

so $\quad d = 5 \times 3 \times 3 = 45$ metres.

Exercise 5H

1. Use the formula $p = f + 1$ to calculate the value of p when:
   - (a) $f = 3$
   - (b) $f = 5$
   - (c) $f = 8$
   - (d) $f = 25$
   - (e) $f = 50$
   - (f) $f = 31$

2. Use the formula $C = 3d$ to calculate the value of C when:
   - (a) $d = 4$
   - (b) $d = 3$
   - (c) $d = 2$
   - (d) $d = 1$
   - (e) $d = 1\cdot5$
   - (f) $d = 2\cdot1$

3. Use the formula $P = 2a + 2b$ to calculate the perimeter of a rectangle when:
   - (a) $a = 3$ cm, $b = 5$ cm
   - (b) $a = 6$ cm, $b = 7$ cm
   - (c) $a = 2$ m, $b = 1$ m
   - (d) $a = 8$ mm, $b = 10$ mm
   - (e) $a = 3\cdot5$ cm, $b = 4$ cm
   - (f) $a = 2\cdot5$ m, $b = 3\cdot5$ m

4. Use the formula $V = RI$ to calculate the value of V when:
   - (a) $R = 100$, $I = 2$
   - (b) $R = 50$, $I = 3$
   - (c) $R = 240$, $I = 1$
   - (d) $R = 100$, $I = 2\cdot5$
   - (e) $R = 40$, $I = 6$
   - (f) $R = 50$, $I = 3\cdot5$

5. Use the formula $T = 4f - 5g$ to calculate the value of T when:
   - (a) $f = 6$, $g = 4$
   - (b) $f = 10$, $g = 6$
   - (c) $f = 2\cdot5$, $g = 1$
   - (d) $f = 5$, $g = 4$
   - (e) $f = 4\cdot5$, $g = 1\cdot5$
   - (f) $f = 2$, $g = 2$

6. Use the formula $v = u + at$ to calculate the value of v when:
   (a) $u = 0, a = 2, t = 3$
   (b) $u = 1, a = 3, t = 5$
   (c) $u = 6, a = 4, t = 1$
   (d) $u = 0, a = 5, t = 4$
   (e) $u = 4, a = 4, t = 4$
   (f) $u = 3, a = 0, t = 5$

7. Use the formula $s = 2t + 32$ to calculate the value of s when:
   (a) $t = 1$
   (b) $t = 2$
   (c) $t = 3$
   (d) $t = 0$
   (e) $t = {}^-1$
   (f) $t = {}^-2$

8. Use the formula $d = \dfrac{C}{3}$ to calculate the value of d when:
   (a) $C = 9$
   (b) $C = 12$
   (c) $C = 21$
   (d) $C = 30$
   (e) $C = 72$
   (f) $C = 4 \cdot 5$

9. Use the formula $A = 3r^2$ to calculate the value of A when:
   (a) $r = 2$
   (b) $r = 3$
   (c) $r = 1$
   (d) $r = 4$
   (e) $r = 5$
   (f) $r = 1 \cdot 5$

10. Use the formula $A = \dfrac{(a + b)h}{2}$ to calculate the value of A when:
    (a) $a = 2, b = 3, h = 4$
    (b) $a = 1, b = 1, h = 2$
    (c) $a = 8, b = 5, h = 3$
    (d) $a = 1 \cdot 5, b = 2 \cdot 5, h = 4$
    (e) $a = 2, b = 2 \cdot 5, h = 2$
    (f) $a = 3, b = 2, h = 7$

5.9 Collecting like terms

Remember: an **expression** is a collection of letters and numbers.
For example:

$3ab + 2b + 7$ is an **expression**.

These are the **terms** of the expression.

Terms with the same letter part are called **like terms**.

   $3a$ and $2a$ are like terms.

   $7y$, $2y$ and y are like terms.

An expression can be **simplified** by **collecting like terms**.

Example
(a) $3a + 2a = 5a$ (b) $7y + 2y + y = 10y$ (c) $5x - 4x = x$

Hint:
x is $1x$ – you don't need to write the 1!

Exercise 5I
Simplify each expression by collecting like terms.

1. $5a + 6a$
2. $7y + 3y$
3. $2w + w$
4. $x + 5x$
5. $8m + 5m$
6. $2q + 2q$
7. $v + v$
8. $4r + 7r$
9. $3b + 17b$
10. $5g + 5g$
11. $8w - 3w$
12. $4x - x$
13. $5t - 4t$
14. $9e - 6e$
15. $7u - u$
16. $6u - 5u$
17. $5y - 2y$
18. $8i - 2i$
19. $9r - 8r$
20. $2x - x$
21. $3x + 5x + 6x$
22. $6y + 5y + y$
23. $5t + t + 3t$
24. $8a + 5a + 6a$
25. $7b + b + b$
26. $x + x + x + x$
27. $2w + w + 5w$
28. $d + 2d + 3d$
29. $7e + 3e + e$
30. $5r + 6r + 7r$
31. $4x + 7x - 3x$
32. $5a + a - 3a$
33. $2q + 3q - q$
34. $b + 3b - 2b$
35. $x + 5x - 5x$
36. $3x - 6x + 4x$
37. $x - 4x + 6x$
38. $4z - 7z + 4z$
39. $3e - 8e + 7e$
40. $5a - 7a + 9a$
41. $9x - 5x - x$
42. $7y - 2y - 3y$
43. $8m - m - 3m$
44. $9u - 4u - 2u$
45. $6y - 2y - 3y$
46. $8z - z - z$
47. $9b - 5b - 3b$
48. $11d - 5d - 3d$
49. $6h - h - 2h$
50. $10a - 5a - a$

5.10 Simplifying with different types of term

Example
Simplify:
(a) $3a + 2b + a + 3b$
(b) $5x + 3y - x + y$
(c) $5r + 8 - 2r + 2$
(d) $4x - 5y - 2x + 4y$

Remember: The sign in front of the number goes with the number.

(a) $\quad 3a + 2b + a + 3b$
$= 3a + a + 2b + 3b$
$= 4a + 5b$

(b) $\quad 5x + 3y - x + y$
$= 5x - x + 3y + y$
$= 4x + 4y$

(c) $\quad 5r + 8 - 2r + 2$
$= 5r - 2r + 8 + 2$
$= 3r + 10$

(d) $\quad 4x - 5y - 2x + 4y$
$= 4x - 2x - 5y + 4y$
$= 2x - y$

Exercise 5J
Simplify each expression by collecting like terms.

1. $4x + y + 3x + 2y$
2. $5t + 3s + 4t + 3s$
3. $4m + 2n + 5m + n$
4. $3a + b + a + 3b$
5. $4y + 5y + 2z + z$
6. $5r + 6r + 3s + 2s$

7. $7y + 2 + 3y + 2$
8. $6u + 3v + v + u$
9. $8 + n + 3 + 5n$
10. $3e + 2e + 5f + f$
11. $5x + 2y - x + y$
12. $6a + 5b - 5a + 3b$
13. $x + 3y + x - 2y$
14. $2 + 3f + 2f - 1$
15. $3m + 2n - 2m + n$
16. $5x - 3x + y + y$
17. $7 - 2 + 3v + v$
18. $2p + 3q + p - q$
19. $5r + 2s - 3r + s$
20. $6a + 3b + b - 5a$
21. $4x + 5y - x - y$
22. $4a + 7 - 3a - 6$
23. $8e - 7e + 4f - 2f$
24. $5s + 6 - 4s - 5$
25. $6x + 4y - 3x - 2y$
26. $4r - 2s - r + 4s$
27. $6x - 5y - x + 6y$
28. $8u - 8 - 4u + 10$
29. $5a + 3b - 2a - 2b$
30. $6y + 4z - 5y - 3z$
31. $3a + 2b + a - 4b$
32. $5x + 7y + 2x - 9y$
33. $6e + 5f + e - 8f$
34. $7u + 5t + 8u - 10t$
35. $6y + 3z + 2y - 4z$
36. $6a + 2b - 4a - 5b$
37. $4m - 2n - 2m + n$
38. $4a + 7 - 2a - 8$
39. $6y - 9 + y - 11$
40. $7x - 3y - 4x - 2y$

5.11 More simplification

The perimeter of a rectangle is the total distance round the outside.

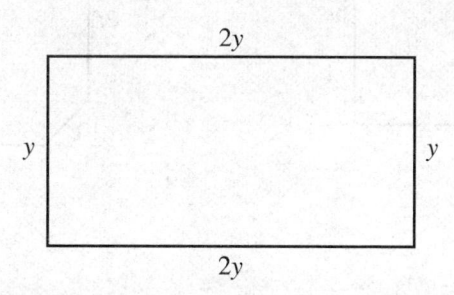

The perimeter of this rectangle is $2y + y + 2y + y = 6y$

Exercise 5K

Find an expression for the perimeter of each shape.

1. Rectangle with sides $2a$, a, $2a$, a.

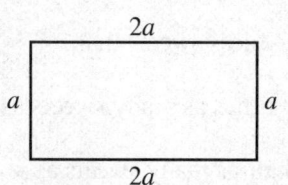

2. Triangle with sides b, b, b.

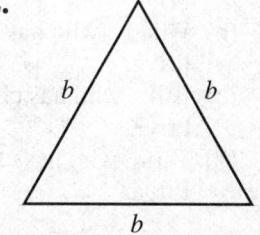

3. Hexagon with sides y, x, x, y, x, x.

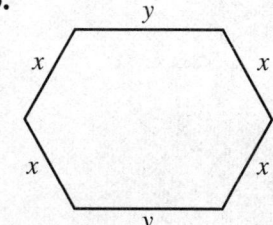

4. Triangle with sides $3a$, $5a$, $4a$.

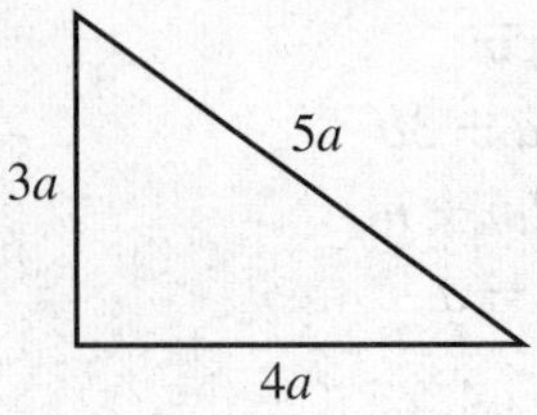

5. Trapezium with sides $3x$ (top), $2y$, $2y$, $2x$ (bottom).

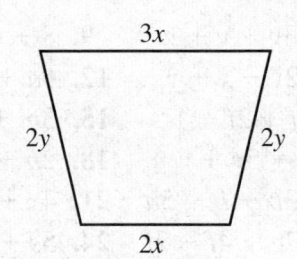

6. Rhombus with all sides $2m$.

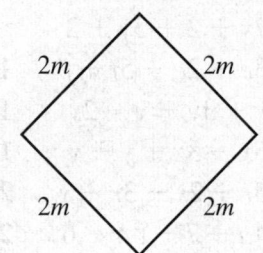

7. Pentagon with all sides $3a$.

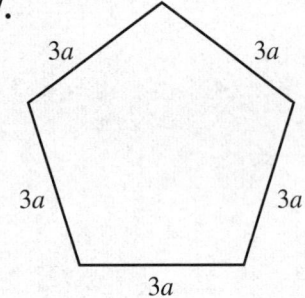

8. Octagon with alternating sides a and 2.

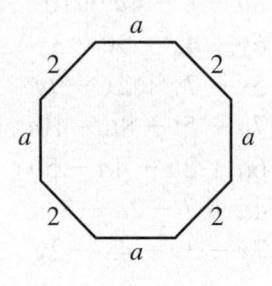

9. Cross shape with sides labelled x, y.

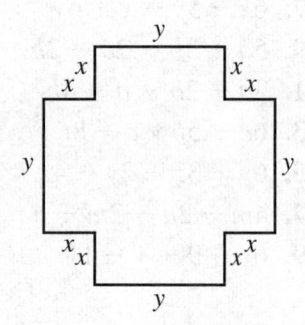

10. Parallelogram with sides $2m$ and $3n$.

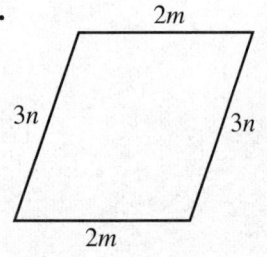

11. Rectangle with sides 5 and $6e$.

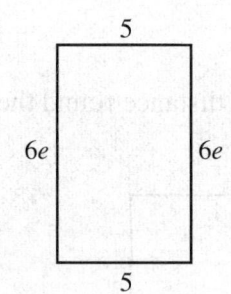

12. Octagon with alternating sides e and $2f$.

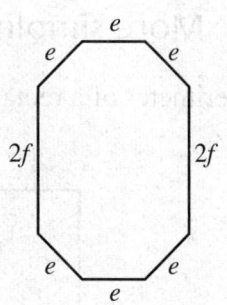

Summary

1. Letters can be used to represent quantities.

Checkout 5

1. The letter s represents the number of 'pic-n-mix' sweets that Priya has chosen. Use the letter s to write the number of sweets chosen by:
   (a) Kimberly, who has chosen 3 more sweets than Priya.
   (b) Wendy, who has chosen 3 less sweets than Priya.
   (c) Billy, who has chosen 3 times as many sweets as Priya.
   (d) Tariq, who has chosen half as many sweets as Priya.

2. Formulae can be used to solve problems.

2. A mechanic uses this formula to calculate the cost in pounds of repair:
Total cost (C) = cost of parts (P)
　　　　　　　　+ hours worked $(H) \times 20$
   (a) Calculate the cost of repairs if:
       (i) Parts cost £50 and 3 hours are worked
       (ii) Parts cost £85 and 5 hours are worked.
   (b) Write the formula using the letters in brackets.

3. You can substitute numbers for letters to find the value of an expression.

3. If $x = 2$, $y = 3$ and $z = 4$, find the value of:
   (a) $x + 1$　　(b) $z - 2$　　(c) $4y$
   (d) $18 - x$　　(e) $y + 2z$　　(f) $4x - 2y$
   (g) xy　　(h) $5yz$　　(i) $x + yz$
   (j) $4(x + y)$　　(k) $\dfrac{3z}{(x+z)}$　　(l) $xy + 3xz$
   (m) x^2　　(n) z^3　　(o) xy^2

4. A negative number × a positive number = a negative number.

4. If $a = 2$ and $b = {}^-3$, find the value of:
   (a) $a + b$　　(b) $a - b$　　(c) $3a$
   (d) $4b$　　(e) $5a + 2b$　　(f) $3a - 5b$
   (g) $14 + 3b$　　(h) $3a - 10$　　(i) $a + b + 1$
   (j) $3a + 2b + 6$　　(k) $3(a + b)$　　(l) $ab + b$

5. You can substitute in formulae.

5. (a) Use the formula $p = 3t + 7$ to find the value of p when:
       (i) $t = 5$　　(ii) $t = 1$　　(iii) $t = {}^-1$
   (b) Use the formula $y = mx + c$ to find the value of y when:
       (i) $m = 3$, $x = 2$ and $c = 1$
       (ii) $m = 2$, $x = {}^-2$ and $c = 5$

6. You can simplify an expression by collecting like terms.

6. (a) Simplify each expression by collecting like terms:
       (i) $5t + 7t$　　　　　(ii) $7y + 4y + y$
       (iii) $9a - 3a$　　　　(iv) $3a + 2b + 3a + 5b$
       (v) $6x + 7y - 4x + y$　　(vi) $3d + 2e + 2d - e$
       (vii) $6x + 3y + x - 4y$　　(viii) $7a - 3b - 2a + b$
       (ix) $9p - 3q - 2p - 3q$　　(x) $7u + 3v - 8v - 4u$
   (b) Write an expression for the perimeter of this shape.

Revision exercise 5

1. Cheryl was working out the cost of hiring a van for a day.
   First of all she worked out the mileage cost.
   She used the formula:

   > Mileage cost = mileage rate × number of miles travelled

   The mileage rate was 8 pence per mile.
   Cheryl travelled 240 miles.

   (a) Work out the mileage cost.

   Cheryl worked out the total hire cost by using the formula:

   > Total hire cost = basic hire cost + mileage cost

   The basic hire cost was £35.

   (b) Work out the total hire cost. [Edexcel]

2. An approximate rule to convert feet into metres is

   > Multiply by 3 then divide by 10

   (a) Use this approximate rule to convert 12 feet into metres.
   (b) Write down an approximate rule that could be used to convert metres into feet. [AQA/NEAB]

3. Solent Garden Centre sells Christmas trees in pots.
   The price of a tree is £4 per metre plus £6 for the pot.
   (a) What is the cost of a 2 metre tree in a pot?
   (b) A tree of height h metres in a pot costs C pounds.
       Write a formula connecting C and h.
   (c) Mrs Dukes wants a tree in a pot for the school hall.
       She has £26 to spend.
       What is the height of the tallest tree in a pot that she can buy? [OCR]

4. (a) Write, in symbols, the rule

   'To find y, multiply k by 3 and then subtract 1'.

   (b) Work out the value of k when $y = 14$. [Edexcel]

5. John uses this rule to change a temperature from °C into °F.

> Multiply the temperature in °C by two and add thirty to the answer.

Use this rule to change
(a) 19°C into °F
(b) ⁻3°C into °F [OCR]

6. Jay tells Shaun a rule to change temperatures in °C to °F.

Multiply by 1.8 then add 32

(a) Use Jay's rule to complete the table.

°C	30	10	⁻5
°F	86		

(b) Write Jay's rule in symbols.
c is the temperature in °C.
f is the temperature in °F. [OCR]

7. A coach has x passengers upstairs and y passengers downstairs.
   (a) Write down an expression, in terms of x and y, for the total number of passengers on the coach.

   Tickets for the journey on the coach cost £5 each.

   (b) Write down an expression, in terms of x and y, for the total amount of money paid by the passengers on the coach. [Edexcel]

8. David makes a certain type of shirt with 8 buttons on each shirt.
   In one week, David makes x of these shirts.

   (a) Write down, in terms of x, the total number of buttons on these x shirts.

   (b) David also makes blouses. Each week he makes twice as many blouses as shirts. Write down, in terms of x, the total number of blouses that he makes in a week.

   (c) Each blouse has 6 buttons. Write down, in terms of x, the total number of buttons on the blouses that he makes each week.

   (d) Write down, in terms of x, the total number of buttons on the shirts and the blouses that he makes each week. Simplify your answer as far as possible. [WJEC]

9. Use the formula
   $$v = u + at$$
   to calculate v when $u = 2$, $a = 3$ and $t = 6$. [OCR]

10. (a) Simplify the algebraic expression
    $$6x + 7 - 2x + 4$$

    (b) Using the formula
    $$a = 5b - \frac{c}{4}$$
    find the value of a when $b = 12$ and $c = 24$. [AQA/SEG]

11. Peter, Jennifer and Ruchi go to their school's Summer Fayre.
    They visit the Bran Tub.
    Peter has seven goes.
    He has 40p change from £2·50.

    (a) How much does the Bran Tub cost per go?

    (b) Ruchi decides to try the Hoopla stall.
        She gives the stallholder £2 for 4 goes and receives change.
        The cost of each go is C pence.
        Which of these expressions gives the change in pence?

        A $4C - 2$ B $4C - 200$ C $2 - 4C$ D $200 - 4C$

        [AQA/NEAB]

6 SHAPE AND SPACE 2

It doesn't look like this in the diagram.

This unit is about:

- Two- and three-dimensional shapes
- Nets
- Isometric drawings
- Plans and elevations

You need to remember:

- How to construct triangles using a ruler, a protractor and a pair of compasses (see Unit 2).

  Make an accurate drawing of each triangle.

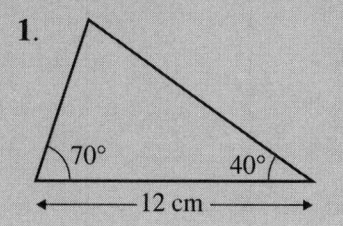

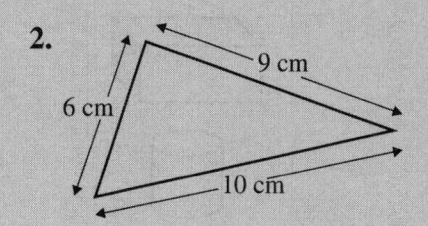

  1. Triangle with base 12 cm, angles 70° and 40°.
  2. Triangle with sides 6 cm, 9 cm, 10 cm.

6.1 Two- and three-dimensional shapes

When a two-dimensional shape is extended into three dimensions it makes a 3-D shape.

For example, a square can become a cube or a cuboid.

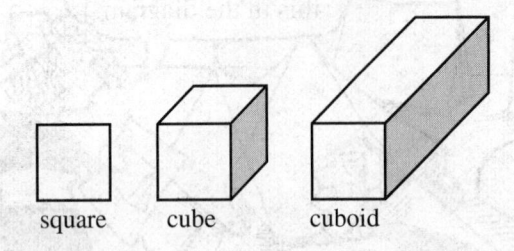

square   cube   cuboid

These are some of the words used to describe 3-D shapes.

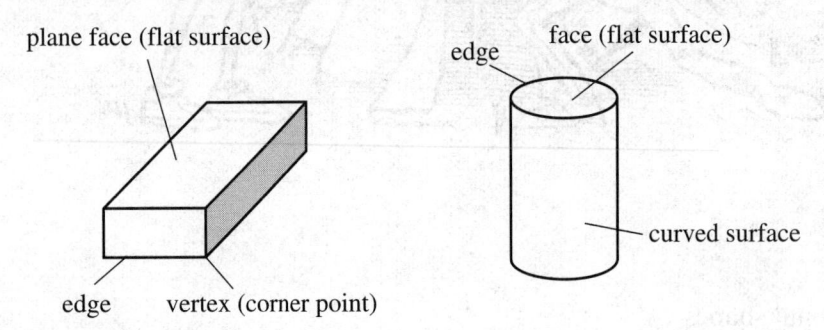

plane face (flat surface)
edge
face (flat surface)
curved surface
edge   vertex (corner point)

Exercise 6A

Copy and complete this table which continues on page 127.

Name	3-D shape	Plane faces	Curved surfaces	Vertices	Edges
Cube		6	0	8	12
Cuboid					
Cylinder					
Triangular prism					

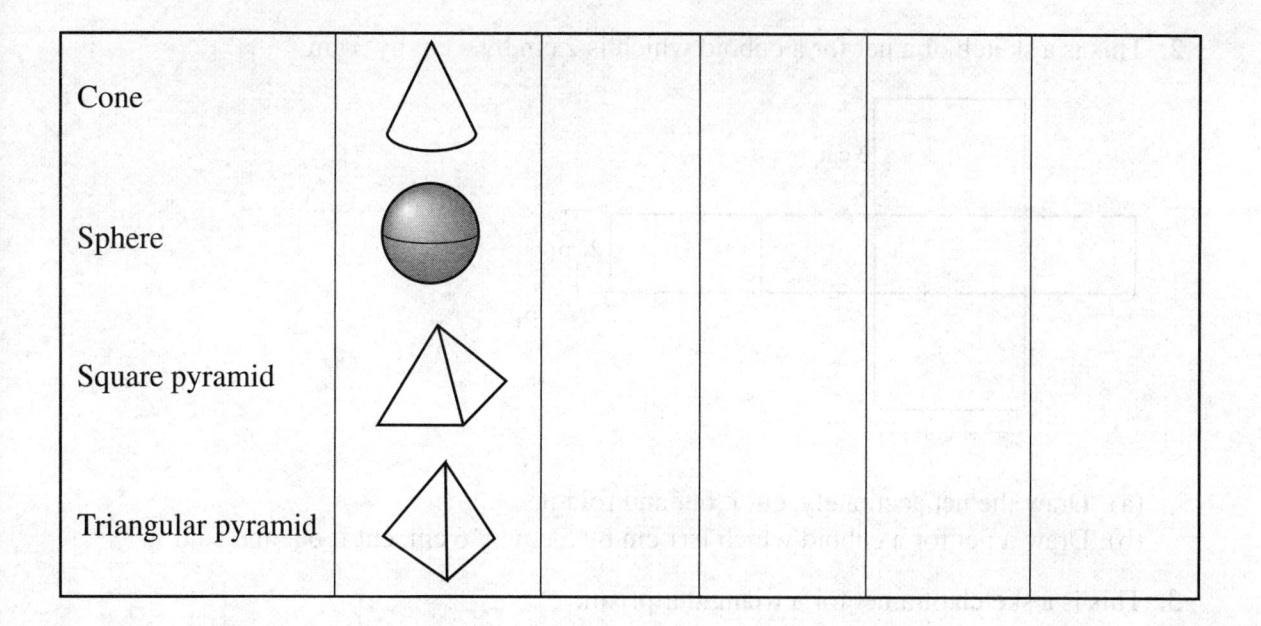

Cone					
Sphere					
Square pyramid					
Triangular pyramid					

6.2 Nets

A **net** is a flat shape which can be folded into a 3-D shape.

This net can be folded to make a cube.

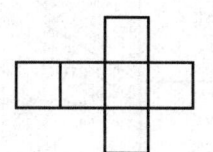

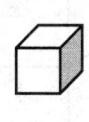

Exercise 6B

1. Copy these shapes on squared paper. Cut them out and fold them. Which shapes are nets for a cube?

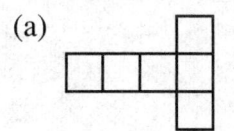

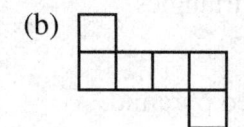

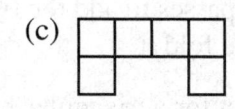

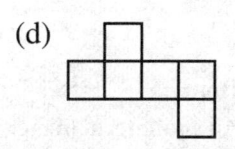

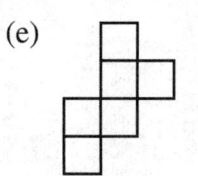

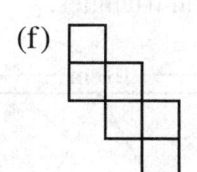

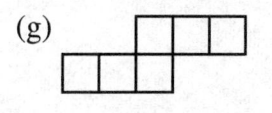

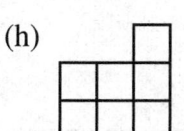

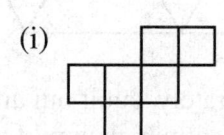

   (a)   (b)   (c)

   (d)   (e)   (f)

   (g)   (h)   (i)

2. This is a sketch of a net for a cuboid which is 2 cm by 4 cm by 3 cm.

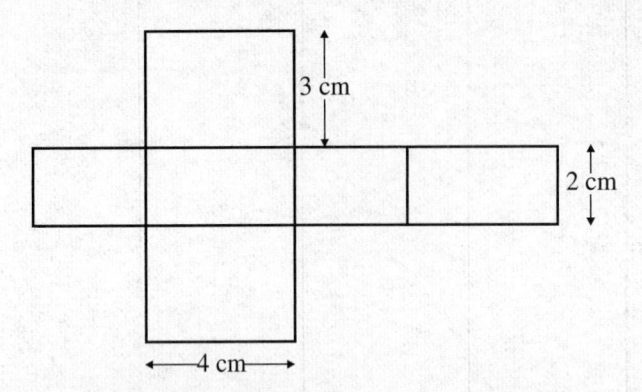

   3 cm

   2 cm

   4 cm

   (a) Draw the net accurately, cut it out and fold it.
   (b) Draw a net for a cuboid which is 1 cm by 5 cm by 6 cm, cut it out and fold it.

3. This is a sketch of a net for a triangular prism.

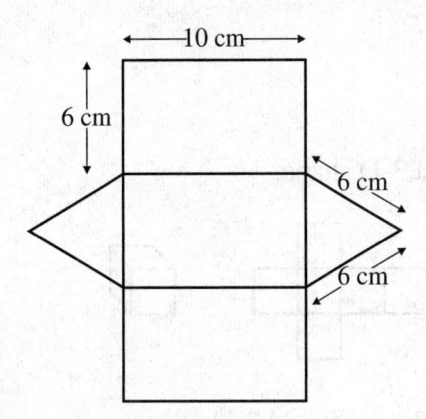

   10 cm

   6 cm

   6 cm

   6 cm

   (a) Draw the three rectangles accurately on squared paper.
   (b) Use a pair of compasses to add the two triangles.
   (c) Cut out the net and fold it.

4. This is a sketch of a net for a triangular-based pyramid, made from four equilateral triangles.

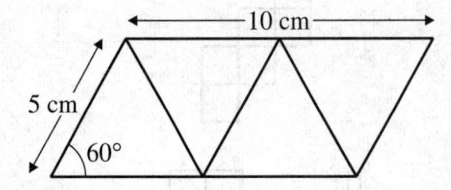

   10 cm

   5 cm

   60°

   Hint:

   An **equilateral** triangle has 3 equal angles. All three angles are 60°.

   (a) Draw the net accurately, cut it out and fold it.
   (b) Sketch a different net which would make the same pyramid.

5. This is a sketch of a net of a 3-D shape.

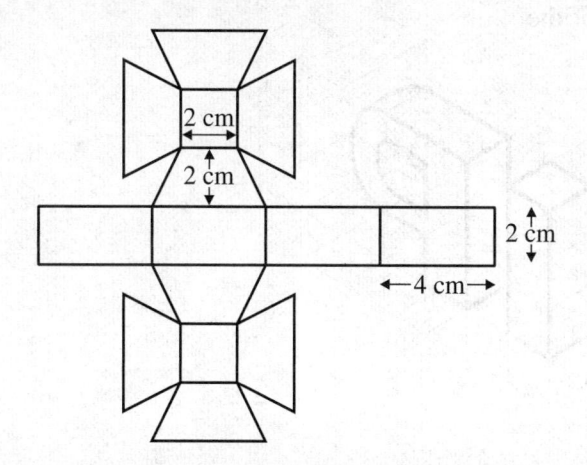

(a) Describe the 3-D shape you think the net will make.
(b) Draw the net accurately on squared paper, adding glue flaps where you think they are needed.
(c) Cut out the net and glue it together.
(d) How many plane faces does the 3-D shape have?
(e) How many edges does the 3-D shape have?
(f) How many vertices does the 3-D shape have?

6.3 Isometric drawings

You can use isometric paper to draw 3-D shapes.

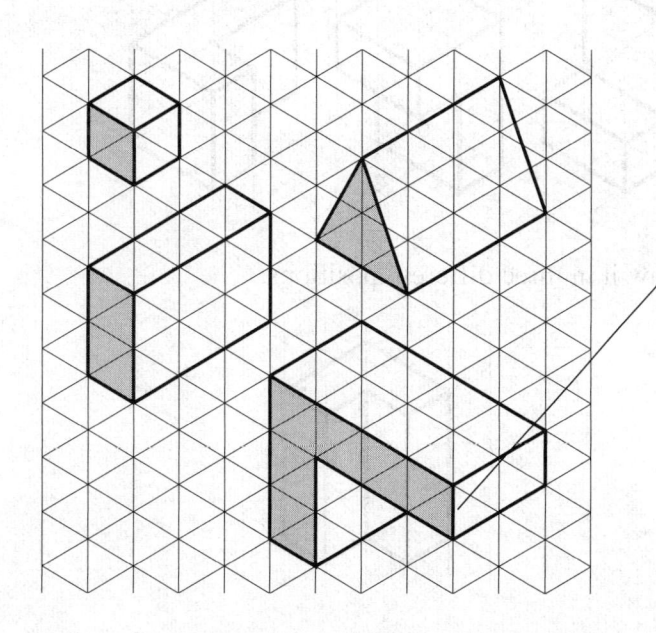

Hint:
You can use vertical lines in an isometric drawing.
Do not use horizontal lines!

Exercise 6C

1. These are isometric drawings of the 3-D letters, T, R, I and P.

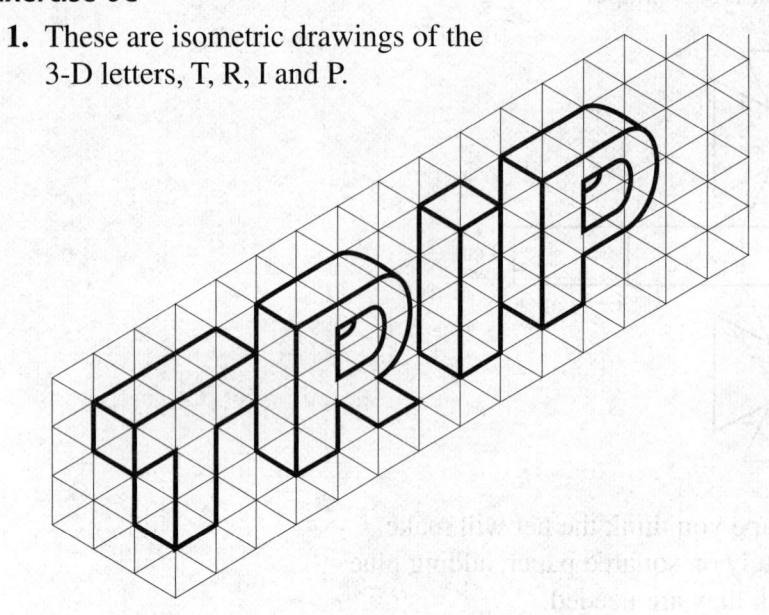

   (a) Copy the drawings.
   (b) Make an isometric drawing of a 3-D letter H.
   (c) Make an isometric drawing of a 3-D letter K.
   (d) Make an isometric drawing of a complete name.

2. These isometric drawings show the same 3-D shape in four different positions.

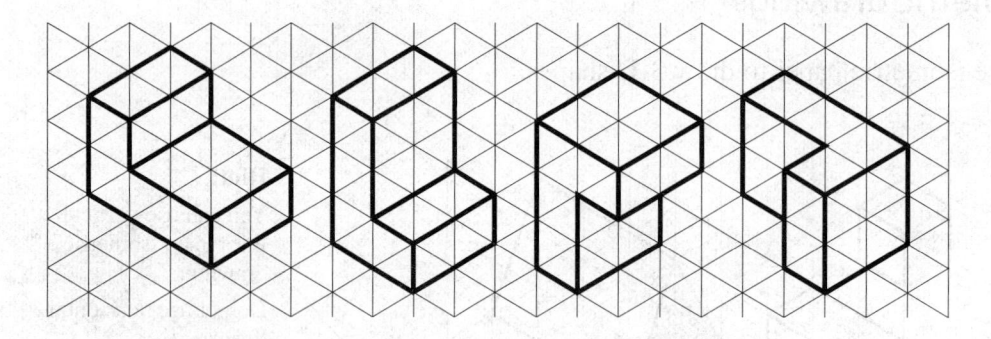

   Copy this 3-D shape and draw it in three different positions.

6.4 Plans and elevations

Plans and elevations can also be used to draw 3-D shapes.

This is a 3-D cross with a plan and two elevations.

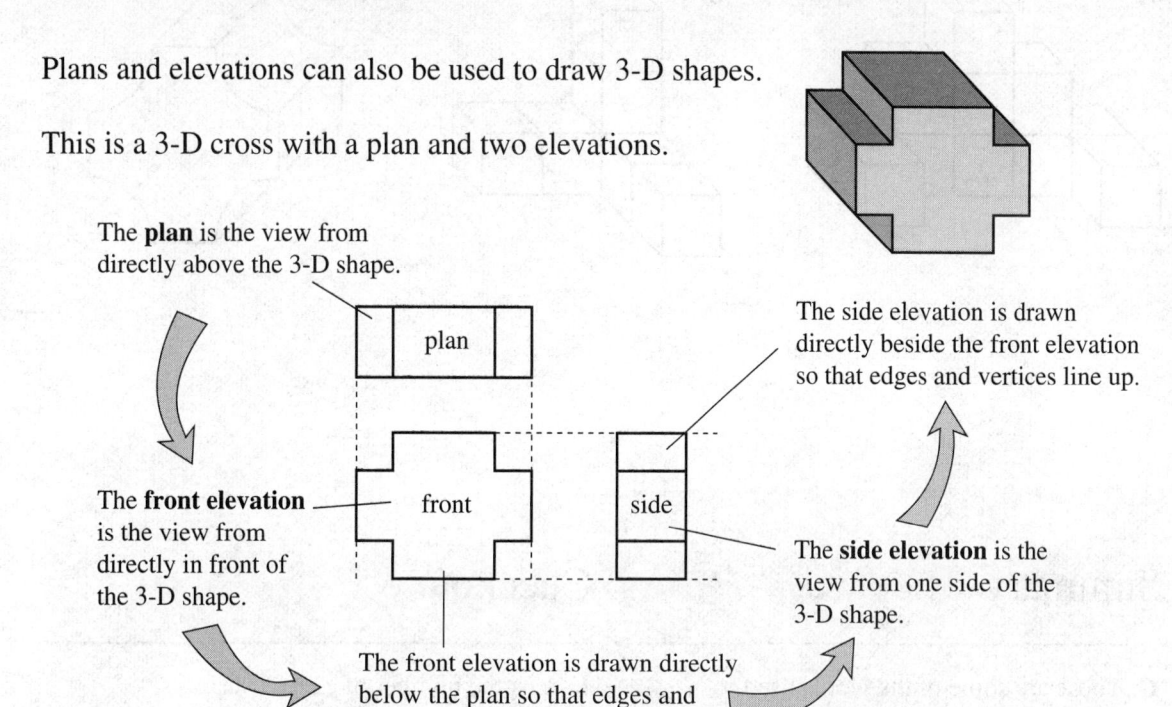

The **plan** is the view from directly above the 3-D shape.

The **front elevation** is the view from directly in front of the 3-D shape.

The side elevation is drawn directly beside the front elevation so that edges and vertices line up.

The **side elevation** is the view from one side of the 3-D shape.

The front elevation is drawn directly below the plan so that edges and vertices line up.

Exercise 6D

Draw a plan, front elevation and side elevation for each 3-D shape. Line your drawings up carefully.

1.
2.
3.
4.
5.
6.

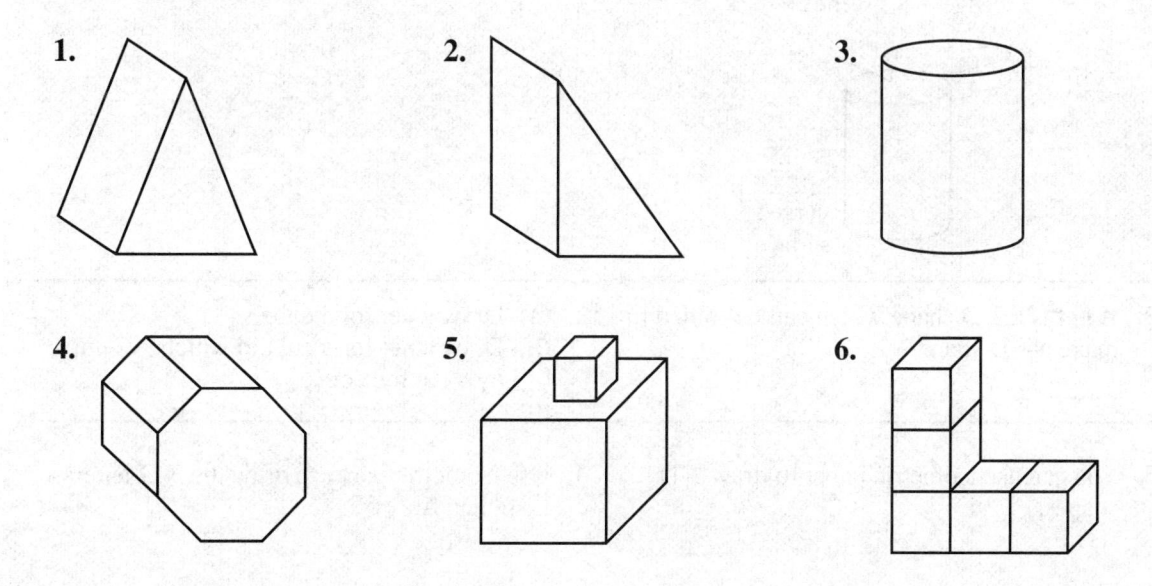

132 Shape and Space 2

7.

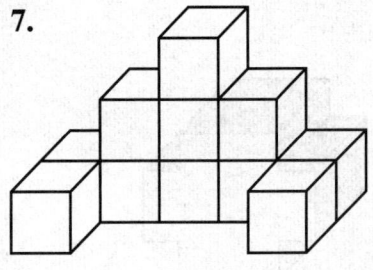

8.

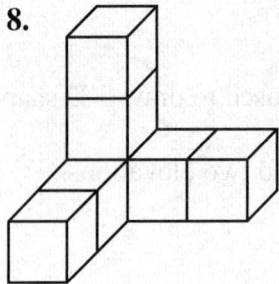

9.

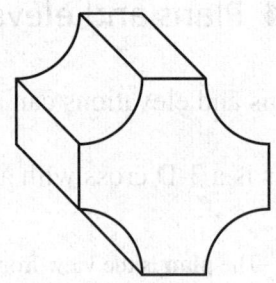

Summary

1. These are some of the words used to describe 3-D shapes.

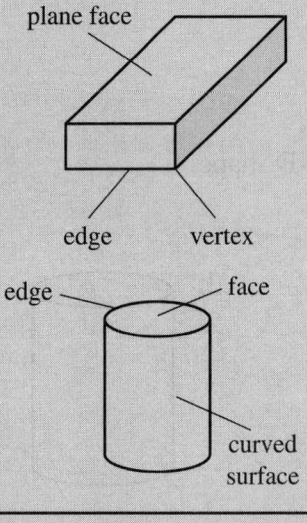

   plane face

   edge   vertex

   edge   face

   curved surface

2. A **net** is a 2-D shape which can be folded to make a 3-D shape.

3. You can use isometric paper to draw 3-D shapes.

Checkout 6

1. List the number of curved surfaces, plane faces, edges and vertices for each 3-D shape.
   (a) a cuboid   (b) a cylinder

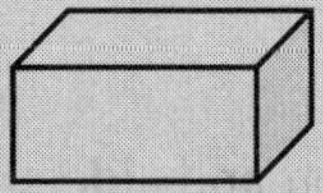

2. (a) Draw a net for a cube.
   (b) Draw a net for a cuboid which is 3 cm by 4 cm by 5 cm.

3. Use isometric paper to draw the 3-D letters, L, W and A.

4. The **plan** is the view from directly above the 3-D shape.

   The **front elevation** is the view from directly in front of the 3-D shape.

   The **side elevation** is the view from one side of the 3-D shape.

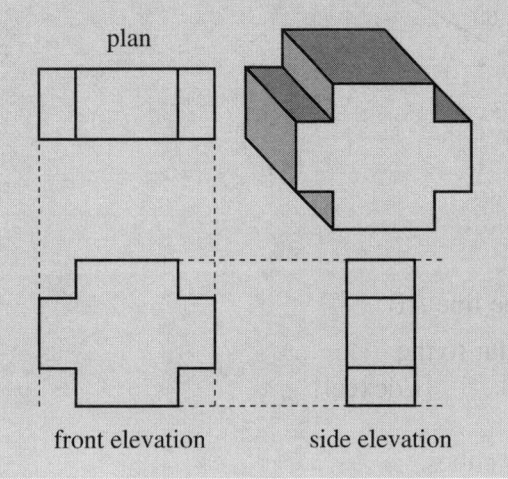

4. Draw a plan, front view and side elevation for this 3-D shape. Line your drawing up carefully.

Revision exercise 6

1. Below are four diagrams showing some three-dimensional objects.

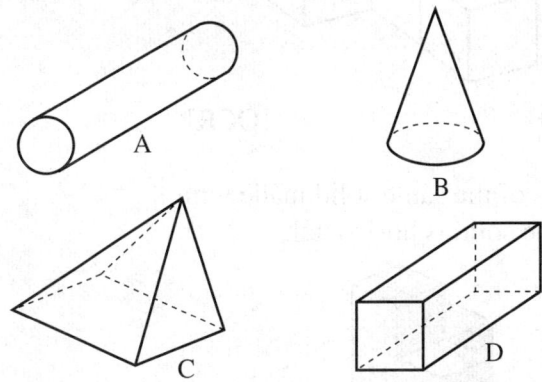

   (a) Give the mathematical name for
   - (i) object A
   - (ii) object B
   (b) How many edges has object C?
   (c) How many faces has object D?
   (d) Sketch a triangular prism. [OCR]

2. Here is a net of a prism.

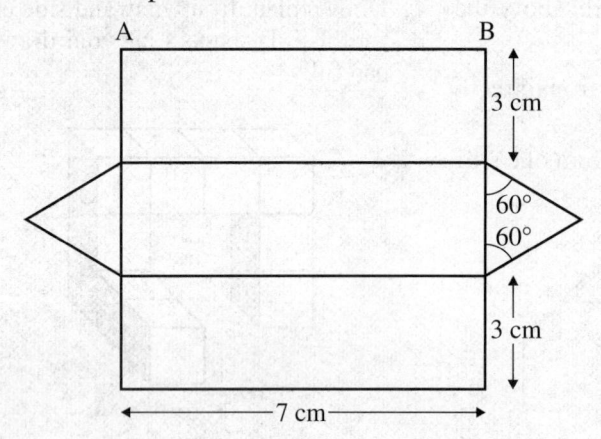

   (a) Make an accurate drawing of the net.
   (b) Mark, with a P, a line that is parallel to the line AB.
   (c) Mark with an X, a line that is perpendicular to the line AB. [Edexcel]

3. Here is a plan view of a solid made from four cubes.

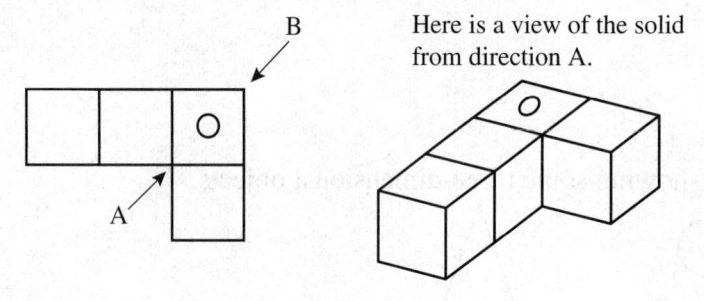

   Here is a view of the solid from direction A.

   Draw the view from direction B. [OCR]

4. These drawings show two views of the same solid made with centimetre cubes. The base of the solid is horizontal.

   (a) How many centimetre cubes are there in the solid?
   (b) Draw an accurate full size plan view of the solid. [OCR]

7 DATA HANDLING 2

Speech bubble: I don't know why you find the place strange, it has always seemed pretty average to us.

This unit is about:

- The mean and the range of a distribution
- The median and the range of a distribution
- The mode
- Finding the mean, the median, the mode and the range
- Data in tables

You need to remember:

Check in 7

- How to add whole numbers in your head (see Unit 1).
  1. Calculate:
     (a) 4 + 5 + 6 + 7   (b) 12 + 13 + 15   (c) 8 + 8 + 9 + 9 + 9
     (d) 15 + 16 + 17   (e) 23 + 27 + 31   (f) 34 + 45 + 61
     (g) 32 + 33 + 34 + 35 + 36 + 36 + 32 + 31

- How to multiply and divide numbers.
  2. Calculate:
     (a) 6 × 5   (b) 7 × 3   (c) 9 × 8   (d) 6 × 7   (e) 18 × 5
     (f) 60 ÷ 5   (g) 49 ÷ 7   (h) 120 ÷ 3   (i) 210 ÷ 7   (j) 216 ÷ 9

- How to order numbers:
  3. Order these numbers, starting with the smallest.
     (a) 6, 9, 23, 7, 2, 5
     (b) 121, 63, 47, 105, 89
     (c) 6, 2, 7, 1, 9, 5, 6, 2, 7
     (d) 17, 12, 15, 12, 19, 21, 9, 17

7.1 The mean and the range of a distribution

Gurpal threw tens sets of three darts at a board. His scores were:
    34, 45, 20, 41, 60, 83, 70, 30, 26, 61

A set of values like this is called a **distribution**.

The **range** of a distribution = greatest value − least value
The range of Gurpal's scores = 83 − 20 = 63

The **mean** of a distribution = total of the distribution ÷ number of values
This distribution has 10 values which add up to 470
The mean of Gurpal's scores = 470 ÷ 10 = 47

You can use the mean and the range to compare two distributions.
These are Gurpreet's scores when he also threw ten sets of three darts:
    45, 44, 52, 40, 43, 45, 49, 54, 60, 48

The range of Gurpreet's scores = 60 − 40 = 20
The mean of Gurpreet's scores = 480 ÷ 10 = 48

The players are quite evenly matched in terms of their mean scores. The ranges however show that Gurpreet is the more consistent player because the range of his scores is much lower.

Exercise 7A

1. Calculate the range and the mean of each distribution.
   - (a) 4, 5, 6, 7, 8
   - (b) 5, 5, 6, 6, 6, 7, 7
   - (c) 3, 4, 1, 2, 3, 5, 6, 4, 8
   - (d) 3, 3, 3, 2, 4, 1, 5
   - (e) 6, 7, 8, 8, 8, 9, 10
   - (f) 4, 5, 3, 2, 4, 5, 3, 2
   - (g) 2, 2, 2, 3, 3, 4, 4, 5, 5, 5
   - (h) 2, 2, 3, 4, 5, 5, 5, 6, 7, 8, 8, 8
   - (i) 10, 10, 11, 10, 9, 11, 10, 12, 14, 10
   - (j) 16, 15, 13, 17, 14
   - (k) 22, 20, 25, 24, 28, 20, 22
   - (l) 102, 102, 102, 103, 103, 103
   - (m) 6, 7, 7, 8, 8, 8, 8, 8, 9, 9, 9, 9
   - (n) 15, 16, 17, 14, 15, 17, 18
   - (o) 32, 32, 33, 34, 35, 36, 36, 37, 36, 32

2. In a book sale, Professor Higgins bought:

   six books at £5 each
   three books at £3 each
   one book at £2

   (a) What was the total cost of the books?
   (b) What was the mean cost of the books?

3. Lisa and Lucy have both completed 10 French homeworks.
   These are their marks out of 10.

   Lisa   7, 8, 7, 8, 7, 8, 8, 7, 7, 8
   Lucy   3, 9, 10, 4, 5, 9, 10, 3, 10, 10

   (a) Calculate the range for each person.
   (b) Calculate the mean mark for each person.
   (c) Say who you think is better at French. Give reasons for
       your answer.

4. A scientist weighs two samples of potatoes. The weights in
   grams of the samples are:

   Sample One   260, 234, 245, 270, 256, 275, 234, 244, 249, 252
   Sample Two   270, 230, 295, 218, 280, 278, 211, 276, 284, 254

   (a) Calculate the range of each sample.
   (b) Calculate the mean of each sample.
   (c) Explain how the two samples differ.

5. Sally and Greg are saving to go on holiday. These are the
   savings each made over an eight-week period:

   Sally   £12   £10   £5   £10   £15   £12   £10   £10
   Greg   £2   £20   £18   £0   £5   £4   £20   £15

   (a) Calculate the range for each person.
   (b) Calculate the mean savings per week for each person.
   (c) Is there a difference between the ways that Greg and
       Sally are saving?

6. Alexandra and Emmanuel play an 18-hole round of golf.
   These are their scores.

   Alexandra   7, 8, 6, 5, 5, 7, 8, 9, 7, 5, 10, 9, 9, 12, 8, 8, 15, 6
   Emmanuel   9, 9, 9, 9, 10, 10, 8, 8, 9, 9, 8, 10, 9, 8, 10, 5, 5, 8

   (a) Calculate the range for each person.
   (b) Calculate the mean shots per hole for each person.
   (c) Who do you think is the best player? Give a reason for
       your answer.

7.2 The median and the range of a distribution

Kelly sometimes travels to school by bus. These are the number of times she has used the bus in the last 9 weeks:

3, 4, 2, 3, 3, 2, 1, 0, 3

The **median** of a distribution is the value in the middle **when the values are arranged in order**.

If this distribution is arranged in order it becomes:

0, 1, 2, 2, *3*, 3, 3, 3, 4

The middle value is 3. The median number of times Kelly uses the bus is 3.
The range of the distribution = 4 − 0 = 4

You can use the median and the range to compare two distributions.
These are the number of times Gavin has used the bus in the last 9 weeks:

4, 4, 5, 1, 2, 4, 3, 5, 4

If this distribution is arranged in order it becomes:

1, 2, 3, 4, *4*, 4, 4, 5, 5

The middle value is 4. The median number of times Gavin uses the bus is 4.
The range of the distribution = 5 − 1 = 4

You can say that, on average, Gavin uses the bus more often than Kelly.

These are the number of times Nisha has used the bus in the last ten weeks:

5, 1, 1, 4, 4, 3, 2, 3, 5, 4

There are an even number of values in this distribution, so there is no exact middle value. The median is found like this:

1, 1, 2, 3, *3*, *4*, 4, 4, 5, 5

Median = (3 + 4) ÷ 2 = 3·5

Exercise 7B

1. Calculate the median of each distribution.

   (a) 4 5 6 7 8
   (b) 5 5 6 6 6 7 7
   (c) 3 4 1 2 3 5 6 4 8
   (d) 3 3 3 2 4 1 5
   (e) 6 7 8 8 8 9 10
   (f) 4 5 3 2 4 5 3 2
   (g) 2 2 2 3 3 4 4 5 5 5
   (h) 2 2 3 4 5 5 5 6 7 8 8 8
   (i) 10 10 11 10 9 11 10 12 14 10
   (j) 16 15 13 17 14
   (k) 22 20 25 24 28 20 22
   (l) 102 102 102 103 103 103
   (m) 6 7 7 8 8 8 8 8 9 9 9 9
   (n) 15 16 17 14 15 17 18
   (o) 32 32 33 34 35 36 36 37 36 32

2. During one week, two country vets each buy petrol every day. These are the number of litres that each buys.

Day	Vet 1	Vet 2
Monday	40	22
Tuesday	10	24
Wednesday	35	23
Thursday	12	20
Friday	36	26

   (a) Find the range for each vet.
   (b) Find the median for each vet.
   (c) Describe the differences between the two distributions.

3. A netball team wins a tournament after playing five matches. These are the scores in their matches.

   24 12   34 5   15 14   20 17   18 14

   (a) Find the median number of goals the team scores.
   (b) Find the range of the goals the team scores.
   (c) Find the median number of goals scored against the team.
   (d) Find the range of the goals scored against the team.

4. The midday temperatures in two different seaside resorts for a week during July were:

Skegness   22°C 21°C 23°C 24°C 26°C 24°C 24°C
Eastbourne   28°C 30°C 24°C 20°C 19°C 26°C 30°C

(a) Find the median midday temperature and the range for Skegness.
(b) Find the median midday temperature and the range for Eastbourne.
(c) Describe the differences between the midday temperatures in the two resorts.

5. The scores of the players in two cricket teams during a game were:

Team 1   64, 32, 85, 52, 30, 0, 10, 24, 0, 24, 31
Team 2   29, 45, 26, 43, 42, 35, 40, 14, 28, 28, 26

(a) Find the median score and the range for Team 1.
(b) Find the median score and the range for Team 2.
(c) Which team won the match?

6. A shop prices researcher buys half a kilogram of tomatoes in eight different supermarkets in two different areas. These are her results.

North West   54p, 64p, 58p, 45p, 53p, 62p, 48p, 50p
South West   64p, 60p, 62p, 48p, 67p, 54p, 56p, 65p

(a) Find the median price and the range for the North West.
(b) Find the median price and the range for the South West.
(c) Compare the price of tomatoes in the two areas.

7.3 Stem-and-leaf plots

A stem-and-leaf plot is a frequency diagram that can help you to find the median value easily.

A stem-and-leaf plot may be called a stem plot.

Example

This data shows the number of words in sentences taken from two newspapers. Show the data as a stem-and-leaf plot and find the median for The Recorder.

The Chronicle
37, 44, 21, 18, 34, 25, 30, 19, 22, 31
40, 38, 27, 34, 18, 19, 33, 41, 32, 27
35, 28, 22, 26, 33, 36, 41, 35, 23, 19

The Recorder
16, 23, 5, 22, 24, 31, 18, 22, 17, 25
28, 24, 29, 31, 19, 25, 30, 8, 21, 19
24, 18, 26, 33, 38, 28, 30, 22, 4, 21

Stem-and-leaf plot to show the number of words in a sentence

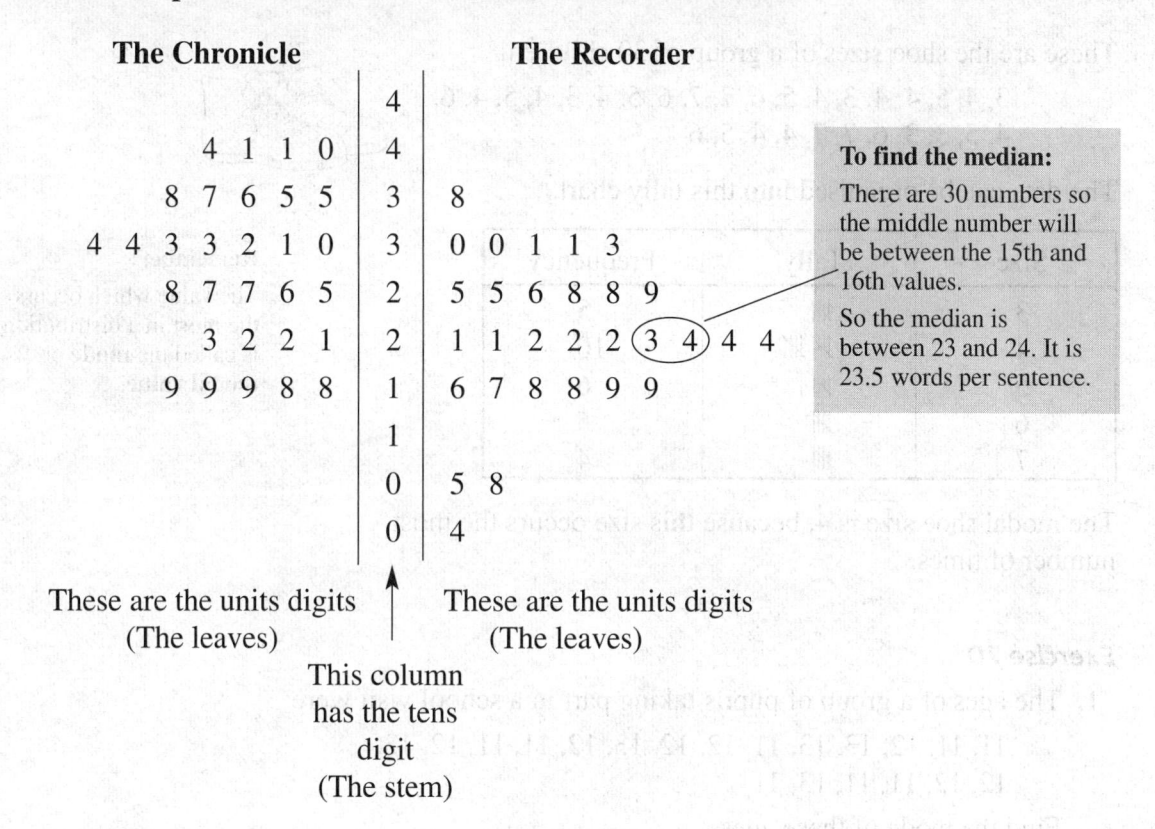

```
        The Chronicle                The Recorder
                           4 |
              4  1  1  0 | 4 |
              8  7  6  5  5 | 3 | 8
        4  4  3  3  2  1  0 | 3 | 0  0  1  1  3
              8  7  7  6  5 | 2 | 5  5  6  8  8  9
                    3  2  2  1 | 2 | 1  1  2  2  2 (3  4) 4  4
                    9  9  9  8  8 | 1 | 6  7  8  8  9  9
                           1 |
                           0 | 5  8
                           0 | 4
```

These are the units digits   These are the units digits
(The leaves)   (The leaves)

This column has the tens digit (The stem)

To find the median:
There are 30 numbers so the middle number will be between the 15th and 16th values.

So the median is between 23 and 24. It is 23.5 words per sentence.

Exercise 7C

1. Use the stem-and-leaf plot above to find the median number of words used in a sentence for The Chronicle.

2. This data gives the number of sandwiches sold each day by two shops.

Kwik Bite
36, 42, 28, 21, 51, 43, 29, 35, 41, 40
27, 44, 35, 29, 44, 31, 35, 56, 38, 43
26, 37, 46, 38, 29, 28, 29, 41, 37, 33

Lunch Box
55, 39, 44, 48, 42, 39, 38, 32, 47, 56
49, 56, 48, 46, 49, 38, 44, 41, 52, 53
56, 42, 47, 45, 37, 30, 49, 54, 51, 46

(a) Show the two sets of data on a stem-and-leaf plot.

(b) For each shop find the median value for the data.

(c) Which shop seems to have the better sandwich trade? Explain your answer.

7.4 The mode

These are the shoe sizes of a group of 30 children:

3, 4, 5, 4, 4, 3, 4, 5, 6, 7, 7, 6, 5, 4, 3, 4, 5, 4, 6,
4, 5, 3, 3, 6, 7, 7, 4, 4, 5, 6

The data can be organised into this tally chart.

Size	Tally	Frequency
3							5
4												10
5								6
6							5
7						4

Remember:
The value which occurs the most in a distribution is called the **mode** or **modal value**.

The modal shoe size is 4, because this size occurs the most number of times.

Exercise 7D

1. The ages of a group of pupils taking part in a school visit were:

   11, 11, 12, 13, 13, 11, 12, 12, 13, 12, 11, 11, 12, 13,
   12, 12, 11, 11, 13, 11

   Find the mode of these ages.

2. The number of goals scored in eleven Premier League matches one Saturday was:

   1, 0, 0, 2, 3, 5, 2, 4, 5, 2, 3

   Find the modal number of goals scored.

3. Chantal and Lindsey have both completed ten homeworks for their GCSE Drama course. These are their marks.

   Chantal   6, 8, 8, 9, 7, 9, 8, 9, 10, 10
   Lindsey   7, 7, 7, 6, 6, 8, 6, 8, 7, 8

   (a) Find the mode and the range for Chantal's marks.
   (b) Find the mode and the range for Lindsey's marks.

4. Adam and Josef both shoot at a target 15 times. These are their scores.

   Adam   3, 4, 5, 4, 5, 6, 5, 7, 8, 5, 3, 5, 6, 8, 7
   Josef   4, 6, 5, 6, 5, 4, 6, 4, 7, 8, 8, 5, 6, 6, 6

   (a) Find the mode and the range for Adam's scores.
   (b) Find the mode and the range for Josef's scores.

5. This table shows the number of people (in thousands) visiting a museum during each season of a year.
   (a) How many people visited the museum during the year?
   (b) Which was the modal season?

Season	Visitors (thousands)
Spring	8
Summer	15
Autumn	10
Winter	3

6. Thirty people take part in a taste test. They are asked to select their favourite flavour ice-cream from a choice of Strawberry (S), Vanilla (V), Chocolate (C), Pistachio (P) and Mint Choc-Chip (M). These are the results:

   V, V, V, P, M, S, C, C, V, V, C, P, S, S, M, P, M, S, M,
   V, M, V, V, M, S, P, S, S, M, P

   Find the modal choice for favourite flavour.

7.5 Finding the mean, the median, the mode and the range

You need to remember which average is which. This might help you:

- The mean is mean because you have to work it out.
- The median is the middle.
- The mode is the most fashionable item.

Exercise 7E

1. Find the mean, median, mode and range of each distribution.
   (a) 2, 4, 5, 3, 8, 10, 3
   (b) 28, 28, 27, 25, 23, 23, 24, 26, 23, 25, 23
   (c) 2, 4, 5, 3, 3, 2, 2, 3, 3
   (d) 8, 8, 8, 0, 7, 6, 6, 7, 9, 9, 7, 22, 7

2. Philip keeps a check on eleven students at his driving school. This is the number of attempts each student needs before they pass the test:

   0, 0, 1, 1, 2, 2, 4, 5, 6, 6, 6

   (a) Find the mean number of attempts before passing.
   (b) Find the median number of attempts before passing.
   (c) Find the modal number of attempts before passing.
   (d) Find the range of the number of attempts before passing.

3. The midday temperature is recorded each day during a week in January. These are the results:

   ⁻4°C, ⁻3°C, ⁻3°C, 0°C, 1°C, 1°C, 1°C,

   (a) Find the mean midday temperature during the week.
   (b) Find the median midday temperature during the week.
   (c) Find the modal midday temperature during the week.
   (d) Find the range of the midday temperatures during the week.

4. Roberta and Robert saved some of their pocket money each week to go on holiday. This is a list of how much they saved each week.

   Roberta   £2, £2.50, £3, £1, £2, £3.50, £2, £1, £3, £2.50
   Robert   £1, £5, £0.50, £6, £0.25, £0.75, £5, £1, £1, £4

   (a) Find the mean, median, mode and range of the amounts which Roberta saved each week.
   (b) Find the mean, median, mode and range of the amounts which Robert saved each week.

5. Eunice works in a zoo. One of her jobs is to look after a group of 10 baby snakes. She measures the snakes each week to check their growth. These are the results for two successive weeks.

   Week One   125 mm, 134 mm, 128 mm, 120 mm, 125 mm,
              125 mm, 128 mm, 125 mm, 120 mm, 130 mm
   Week Two   137 mm, 144 mm, 142 mm, 145 mm, 145 mm,
              145 mm, 148 mm, 145 mm, 143 mm, 144 mm

   (a) Find the mean, median, mode and range of the distribution of lengths for week one.
   (b) Find the mean, median, mode and range of the distribution of lengths for week two.

6. Tommy is testing two makes of oven for a consumer magazine. He sets the temperature control to 200°C and then measures the actual temperature inside the ovens every five minutes for one hour. These are his results.

   Oven One
   Temperature (°C)   189, 191, 195, 195, 195, 195, 199, 200, 200, 200, 202, 203

   Oven Two
   Temperature (°C)   198, 200, 200, 202, 202, 203, 204, 205, 205, 205, 206, 206

   (a) Find the mean, median, mode and range of the distribution of temperatures for oven one.
   (b) Find the mean, median, mode and range of the distribution of temperatures for oven two.

7.6 Data in tables

Ricky fired 40 shots at a target. This table shows his results.

Score	Frequency
1	6
2	4
3	12
4	15
5	3

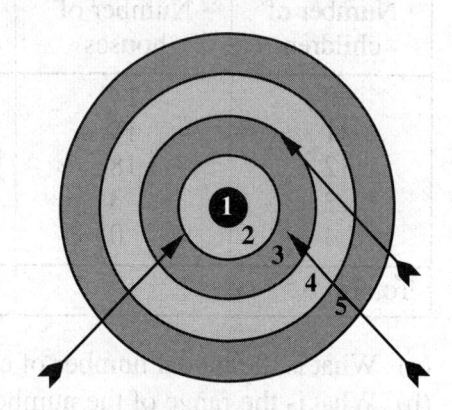

The **range** of Ricky's scores = 5 − 1 = 4

Ricky's **modal** score was 4, because this is his most frequent score.

With forty values, the median is between the 20th and 21st values. Imagine the table written out as a long list, starting 1, 1, 1, 1, 1, 1, 2, 2, 2, 2, 3, …. You will see that the 20th and 21st scores are both 3. Ricky's **median** score is 3.

To find the mean score from the table you need to add an extra column for the score multiplied by the frequency.

Score	Frequency	Score × Frequency
1	6	1 × 6 = 6
2	4	2 × 4 = 8
3	12	3 × 12 = 36
4	15	4 × 15 = 60
6	3	6 × 3 = 18
Totals	40	128

The table shows that Ricky scored a total of 128 points with his 40 shots.
Ricky's mean score = 128 ÷ 40 = 3·2

Exercise 7F

1. The table below shows the distribution of children per family on an estate of 50 houses.

Number of children	Number of houses	Number of children × Number of houses
0	14	
1	15	
2	18	
3	3	
4	0	
Totals		

   (a) What is the modal number of children per house?
   (b) What is the range of the number of children per house?
   (c) In a distribution of 50 values, where is the median value?
   (d) What is the median number of children per house?
   (e) Copy and complete the table.
   (f) Calculate the mean number of children per house.

2. Amy collects eggs each morning from her pet hens. This table shows the number of eggs she collected each day during April.

Number of eggs	Frequency	Number of eggs × Frequency
0	4	
1	1	
2	7	
3	4	
4	4	
5	4	
6	3	
7	1	
8	1	
9	1	
Totals		

   (a) What was the modal number of eggs that Amy collected?
   (b) What was the range of the number of eggs that Amy collected?
   (c) In a distribution of 30 values, where is the median value?
   (d) What is the median number of eggs that Amy collected?
   (e) Copy and complete the table.
   (f) Calculate the mean number of eggs that Amy collected.

3. A spelling test has ten words. These are the results for a class of 20 pupils.

Number correct	Frequency	Number correct × Frequency
0	0	
1	0	
2	0	
3	1	
4	1	
5	2	
6	3	
7	4	
8	5	
9	3	
10	1	
Totals		

(a) What is the modal number of correct answers?
(b) What is the range of the number of correct answers?
(c) In a distribution of 20 values, where is the median value?
(d) What is the median number of correct answers?
(e) Copy and complete the table.
(f) Calculate the mean number of correct answers.

4. This table shows the number of tests taken by 100 driving school students before passing.

Number of tests taken	Frequency	Number of tests taken × Frequency
1	43	
2	31	
3	17	
4	6	
5	2	
6	1	
Totals		

(a) What is the modal number of tests taken?
(b) What is the range of the number of tests taken?

(c) In a distribution of 100 values, where is the median value?
(d) What is the median number of tests taken?
(e) Copy and complete the table.
(f) Calculate the mean number of tests taken.

5. Zippo Mints come in a packet with a label saying, 'Average contents 34 sweets'. The number of sweets in 25 packets is checked by a trading standards officer. These are her results:

Number of sweets	Number of packets	Number of sweets × Number of packets
30	4	
31	1	
32	2	
33	4	
34	8	
35	3	
36	3	
Totals		

(a) What is the modal number of sweets per packet?
(b) What is the range of the number of sweets per packet?
(c) In a distribution of 25 values, where is the median value?
(d) What is the median number of sweets per packet?
(e) Copy and complete the table.
(f) Calculate the mean number of sweets per packet.
(g) Are Zippo Mints entitled to claim, 'Average contents 34 sweets'?

Summary

1. A set of values is called a **distribution**.
   The **range** of a distribution
   = greatest value − least value
   The **mean** of a distribution
   = total of the distribution
   ÷ number of values

Checkout 7

1. Find the mean and the range of each set of numbers.
   (a) 3   3   6   5   3
   (b) 1   2   1   1   1   3   3   6
   (c) 10   11   11   15   11   10   10   10
   (d) 14   14   13   16   16   16   12   14   15   16

2. The **median** of a distribution is the value in the middle **when the values are arranged in order**.

2. Find the median of each set of numbers in Question 1.

3. The value which occurs the most in a distribution is called the **mode** or **modal value**.

3. Find the mode of each set of numbers in Question 1.

4. An examination question may ask you to work out the mean, the median, the mode and the range.

4. A doctor keeps a check on eleven patients at her surgery. This is the number of times each patient visits her during one month:

 0 0 0 1 2 2 3 4 5 7 9

(a) Find the mean number of visits.
(b) Find the median number of visits.
(c) Find the modal number of visits.
(d) Find the range of the number of visits.

5. An examination question may ask you to work out the mean, the median, the mode and the range for data arranged in a table.

5. The table below shows the distribution of children per family on an estate of 50 houses.

Number of children	Number of houses	Number of children × Number of houses
0	1	
1	23	
2	19	
3	6	
4	1	
Totals		

(a) What is the modal number of children per house?
(b) What is the range of the number of children per house?
(c) In a distribution of 50 values, where is the median value?
(d) What is the median number of children per house?
(e) Copy and complete the table.
(f) Calculate the mean number of children per house.

Revision exercise 7

1. Ten teams took part in a quiz.
   Their scores are shown below.

   15, 13, 17, 11, 14, 15, 16, 15, 16, 8

   Work out the mean score. [Edexcel]

2. Ben recorded the number of minutes that it took him to get to work on each of 6 days. The results were:

   25, 19, 27, 23, 28, 22

   Calculate the mean of these times. [OCR]

3. The handspans of some children were measured.
   The measurements, in centimetres, are shown.

   15 13 16 15 14 14 15 12
   12 14 13 15 13 15 13

   (a) (i) What is the range of the children's handspans?
       (ii) Calculate the mean handspan.

   A second group of children have handspans with the same mean as the first group. The range of their handspans is 7 cm.

   (b) Describe **one** difference between the handspans of the two groups. [AQA/SEG]

4. Boxes of eggs containing broken eggs cannot be sold in shops.
   The table shows how many boxes of Grade A eggs and Grade B eggs could not be sold in a week at one shop.

Grade	Mon	Tue	Wed	Thur	Fri
A	14	16	16	14	16
B	14	12	9	11	15

   (a) For the Grade A eggs, calculate:
       (i) the range
       (ii) the mean
   (b) For the Grade B eggs, the range is 6 boxes and the mean is 12·2 boxes.
       Use this information to compare the two grades.
       Which grade would you recommend the shopkeeper to stock?
       Give a reason. [AQA/NEAB]

5. A student measures the amount of rain which falls each day.
   His results, in millimetres, for 10 days are shown below.

   1 0 0 2 8 10 6 1 0 0

   (a) What is the range of these amounts of rain?
   (b) What is the mode?
   (c) Find the median.
   (d) Calculate the mean of these 10 amounts of rain.
   (e) Which average gives the best idea of the amount of rainfall over the 10 days?
       Give a reason for your answer. [OCR]

6. William is a member of a quiz team.
   Here are William's scores in the last nine quizzes.

   67 52 59 43 49 65 68 48 53

   (a) Calculate his mean score.
   (b) Find his median score.
   (c) Find the range of his scores. [OCR]

7. (a) The following diagram shows the number of pupils who were absent from Aberglas Primary School each day for one week in April.

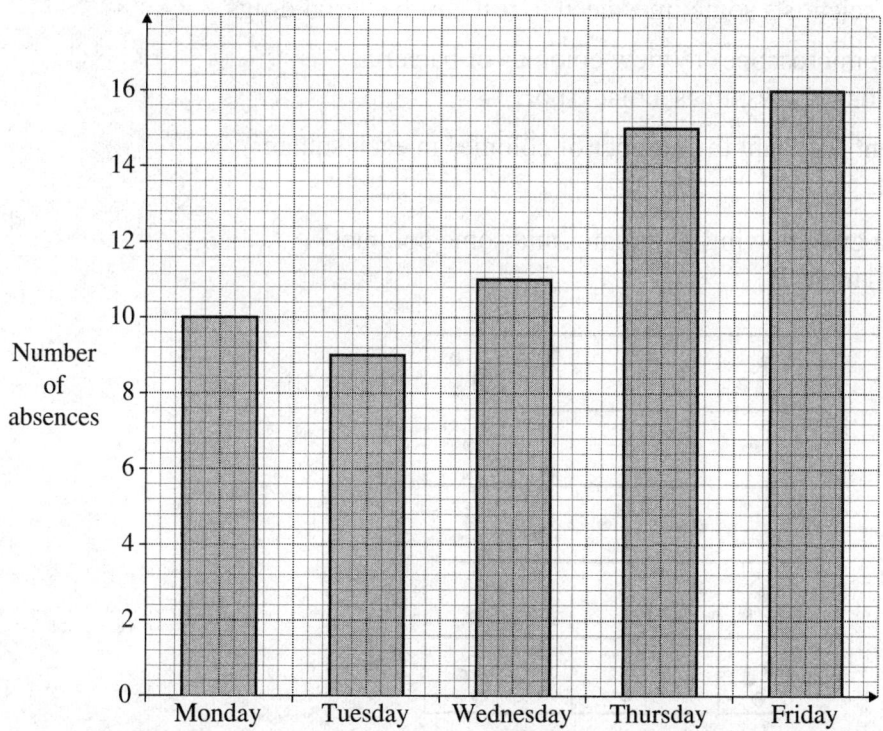

(i) On which day was the least number of pupils absent?
(ii) How many pupils were absent on Thursday?
(iii) How many more pupils were absent on Friday than on Monday?

(b) Calculate the mean of the numbers of daily absences for the week in April.

(c) The daily absences during a week in June are shown in the following table.

Monday	Tuesday	Wednesday	Thursday	Friday
12	14	8	18	23

(i) Draw a bar chart for this data.
(ii) Write down the range of daily absences for this week in June.
(iii) The mean of the numbers of daily abscences for the week in June is 15.
Which of the two weeks given above had the better attendance rate?
Give a reason for your answer.   [WJEC]

8. Medical scientists sometimes need to test anti-bacterial drugs.

They use microscopes to view colonies of bacteria.
Each colony shows up as a blackspot.

The scientists count the number of colonies in each square of a grid.

Here is a grid showing 25 squares and some colonies.
This is Sample 1.

(a) Copy and complete this frequency table to show the number of colonies per square.

Number of colonies per square	Tally	Frequency
0		
1		
2		
3		
4		

(b) Calculate the mean number of colonies per square.
Show your working.
(c) What is the modal number of colonies per square?
(d) Some modern microscopes count the colonies automatically.
The print-out shows the results as a bar chart.
It also shows the mean, mode, median and range.
Here is the print-out for Sample 2.

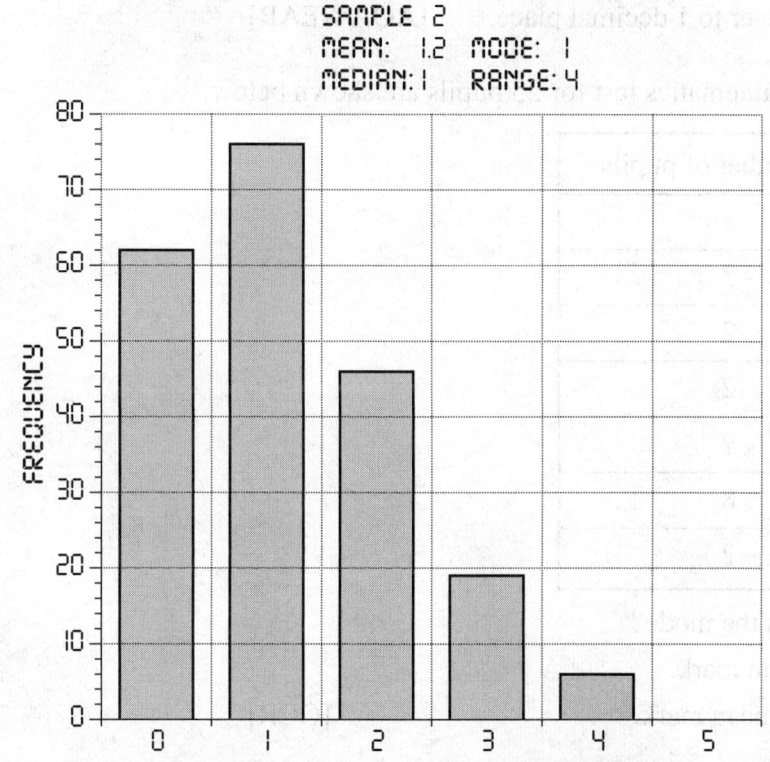

SAMPLE 2
MEAN: 1.2   MODE: 1
MEDIAN: 1   RANGE: 4

(i) State one similarity between the two samples.
(ii) State one difference between the two samples. [OCR]

9. A teacher asks all his class,

   'How many children are there in your family?'

   Here are their replies.

Number of children in the family	Number of replies
1	7
2	12
3	5
4	2
5	0

   (a) How many children are in the class?
   (b) What is the most common number of children in the family for this class?
   (c) Calculate the mean number of children per family in this class.
   Give your answer to 1 decimal place. [AQA/NEAB]

10. The results of a Mathematics test for 25 pupils are shown below.

Mark	Number of pupils
4	1
5	3
6	2
7	2
8	7
9	8
10	2

    (a) Which mark is the mode?
    (b) Find the median mark.
    (c) Calculate the mean mark. [OCR]

8 NUMBER 3

This unit is about:

- Place value in decimal numbers
- Ordering decimal numbers
- Approximating decimal numbers
- Adding decimal numbers
- Subtracting decimal numbers

You need to remember:

- How to add whole numbers with written calculations (see Unit 1).
  1. 47 + 85
  2. 235 + 97
  3. 567 + 45
  4. 267 + 389
  5. 307 + 58
- How to subtract whole numbers with written calculations.
  6. 56 − 15
  7. 143 − 162
  8. 153 − 29
  9. 456 − 289
  10. 1 234 − 505

8.1 Place value in decimal numbers: Tenths

The number 3·8 has a **decimal point**.
The first digit which follows a decimal point is the **tenths** digit.
The number 3·8 means 3 and $\frac{8}{10}$.

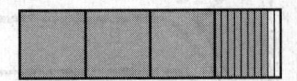

Example
Write the number represented by this picture as a decimal.

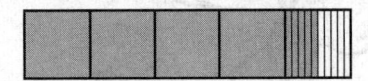

The number is 4·5.

Exercise 8A
You will need 2 millimetre graph paper for this exercise.

1. Write each number represented by a picture as a decimal.

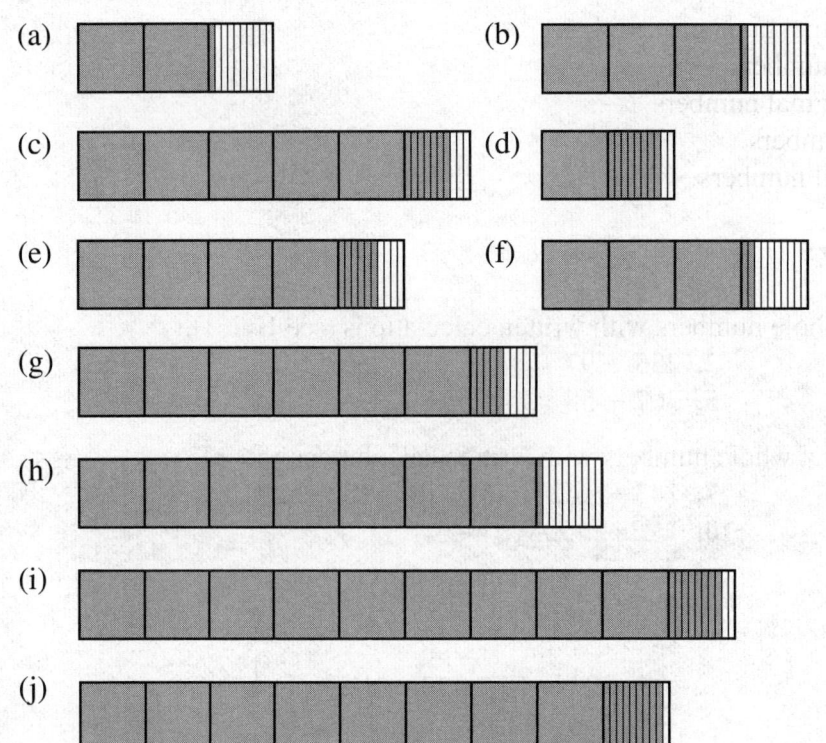

   (a)
   (b)
   (c)
   (d)
   (e)
   (f)
   (g)
   (h)
   (i)
   (j)

2. Draw pictures to represent these decimals.
   (a) 2·7   (b) 6·1   (c) 4·9   (d) 1·2   (e) 7·6
   (f) 6·7   (g) 5·5   (h) 9·3   (i) 3·4   (j) 8·7

3. Anita is measuring the length of a worm. This picture shows her ruler.

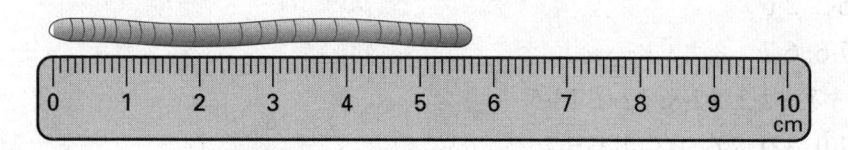

   Anita can write down the length of the worm like this:
   5 cm 7 mm

   Or, Anita can use a decimal point and write the length like this:
   5·7 cm

   Write each of these worm lengths with a decimal point.
   (a) 5 cm 8 mm   (b) 6 cm 3 mm   (c) 2 cm 9 mm   (d) 4 cm 4 mm   (e) 8 cm 1 mm
   (f) 9 cm 7 mm   (g) 7 cm 9 mm   (h) 5 cm 2 mm   (i) 10 cm 5 mm   (j) 12 cm 6 mm

   Write each of these worm lengths in centimetres and millimetres.
   (k) 4·9 cm   (l) 9·5 cm   (m) 10·3 cm   (n) 8·3 cm   (o) 9·1 cm
   (p) 1·9 cm   (q) 3·8 cm   (r) 8·6 cm   (s) 12·4 cm (t) 13·3 cm

8.2 Ordering decimal numbers: Tenths

Nadia works on a farm which sells 'pick your own' fruit. One of her jobs is to weigh the boxes of strawberries that people have picked. She records these weights for ten boxes.

4·1 kg, 2·3 kg, 0·9 kg, 1·2 kg, 3·2 kg,
1·7 kg, 0·8 kg, 3·5 kg, 2·6 kg, 1·5 kg

These weights can be sorted into order, starting with the smallest, like this. Order the whole number part first:

   0·9 kg   0·8 kg   1·2 kg   1·7 kg   1·5 kg   2·3 kg   2·6 kg   3·2 kg   3·5 kg

Now order the decimal part:
   0·8 kg   0·9 kg   1·2 kg   1·5 kg   1·7 kg   2·3 kg   2·6 kg   3·2 kg   3·5 kg

Exercise 8B

Write a list of these numbers sorted into order, starting with the smallest.

1. 1·1, 2·3, 1·7, 2·4, 1·9
2. 3·1, 4·3, 3·8, 4·0, 2·7
3. 6·8, 8·6, 4·5, 5·4, 6·2, 2·6
4. 3·5, 5·3, 1·9, 9·1, 7·6, 6·7
5. 12·4, 13·3, 12·0, 13·7, 12·2, 12·8, 12·0, 13·5
6. 2·5, 3·6, 1·7, 4·3, 2·9, 3·0, 2·6, 1·1, 4·4, 6·2
7. 8·1, 5·6, 7·3, 2·6, 4·9, 4·6, 8·2, 8·0, 7·3, 9·1
8. 3·5, 3·4, 2·6, 0·7, 0·9, 2·1, 1·5, 3·0, 1·7, 2·2
9. 6·7, 7·6, 8·3, 3·8, 9·2, 2·9, 3·0, 0·3, 5·1, 1·5
10. 15·6, 14·3, 18·2, 14·6, 15·0, 13·3, 13·0, 14·5, 19·4, 18·0, 15·1, 13·2
11. 22·4, 23·6, 22·8, 23·6, 22·0, 23·0, 22·5, 22·9, 23·8, 23·0, 22·1, 23·8
12. 45·3, 43·5, 42·6, 46·2, 41·0, 40·1, 43·8, 48·3, 44·7, 47·4, 44·3, 43·4

8.3 Place value in decimal numbers: Hundredths

The number 3·87 has two digits after the decimal point.

The second digit which follows a decimal point is the **hundredths** digit.

The number 3·87 means 3 and $\frac{8}{10}$ and $\frac{7}{100}$.

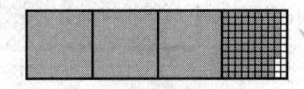

Example

Write the number represented by this picture as a decimal.

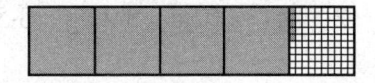

The number is 4·05.

Exercise 8C

You will need 2 millimetre graph paper for this exercise.

1. Write each number represented by a picture as a decimal.

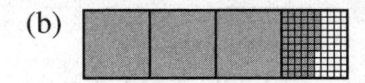

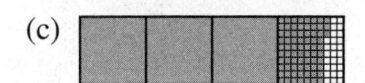

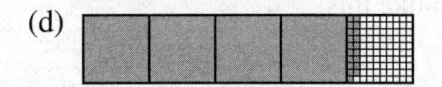

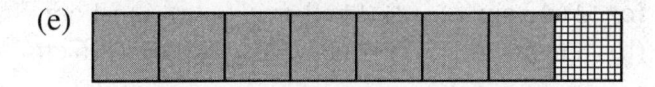

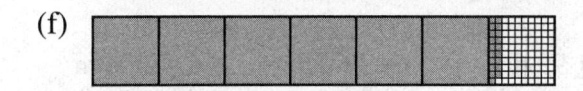

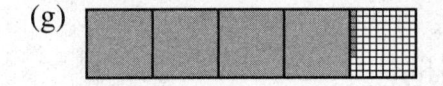

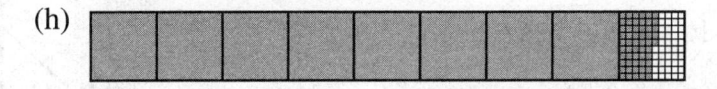

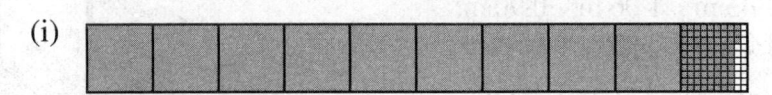

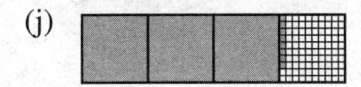

   (a)

   (b)

   (c)

   (d)

   (e)

   (f)

   (g)

   (h)

   (i)

   (j)

2. Draw pictures to represent these decimals.
   - (a) 2·74
   - (b) 6·13
   - (c) 4·99
   - (d) 1·02
   - (e) 7·62
   - (f) 7·26
   - (g) 5·05
   - (h) 9·37
   - (i) 3·04
   - (j) 8·76

3. Thomas is measuring the long jump on Sports Day. He is using a ruler marked in metres, tenths of a metre and centimetres. This picture shows him measuring a jump of 4 metres and 47 centimetres.

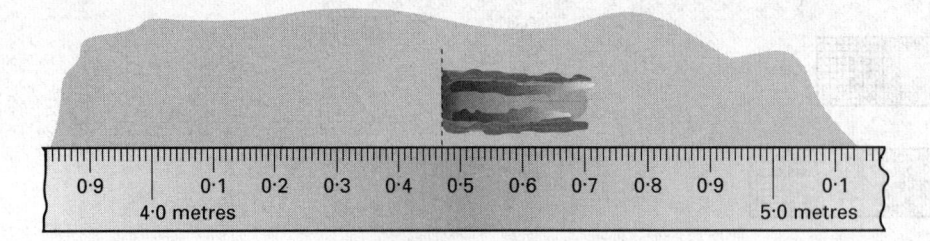

Thomas can write down the length of the jump like this:
   4 m 47 cm

Or, he can use a decimal point and write the length like this:
   4·47 m

Remember:
100 cm = 1 m

Write each of these jump lengths with a decimal point.
(a) 3 m 38 cm   (b) 2 m 30 cm   (c) 2 m 3 cm   (d) 2 m 9 cm   (e) 4 m 1 cm
(f) 4 m 87 cm   (g) 5 m 6 cm   (h) 3 m 50 cm (i) 1 m 5 cm   (j) 4 m 96 cm

Write each of these jumps lengths in metres and centimetres.
(k) 4·92 m   (l) 3·51 m   (m) 1·99 m   (n) 2·60 m   (o) 2·06 m
(p) 2·45 m   (q) 4·09 m   (r) 3·10 m   (s) 3·01 m   (t) 2·11 m

8.4 Ordering decimal numbers: Hundredths

These are the heights jumped by 10 students in a school high jump competition:

   1·32 m, 0·89 m, 1·45 m, 1·06 m, 0·90 m,
   1·22 m, 1·02 m, 1·20 m, 0·95 m, 1·34 m

These heights can be sorted into order, starting with the smallest.

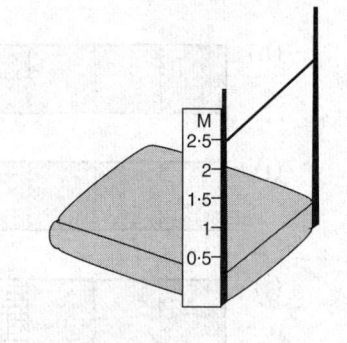

You order the whole number part first:

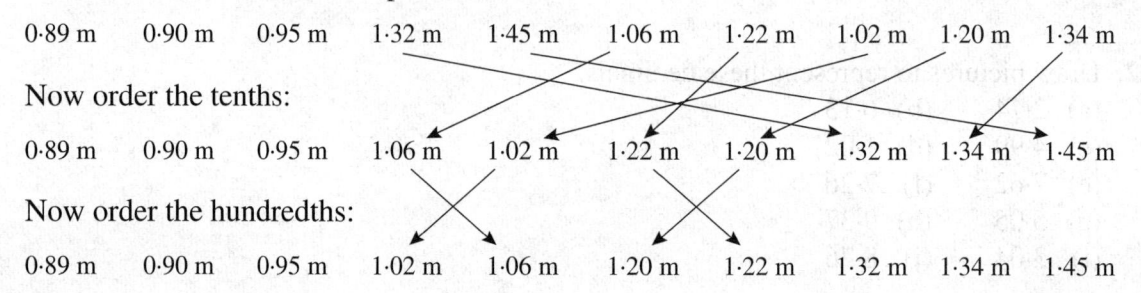

0·89 m   0·90 m   0·95 m   1·32 m   1·45 m   1·06 m   1·22 m   1·02 m   1·20 m   1·34 m

Now order the tenths:

0·89 m   0·90 m   0·95 m   1·06 m   1·02 m   1·22 m   1·20 m   1·32 m   1·34 m   1·45 m

Now order the hundredths:

0·89 m   0·90 m   0·95 m   1·02 m   1·06 m   1·20 m   1·22 m   1·32 m   1·34 m   1·45 m

To sort decimals with a mixture of decimal places it can help to add zeros.

Hint:
If the hundredths column is empty, put a zero in it to help you compare the number.

Example
Sort these numbers into order, starting with the smallest.

2·31, 2·3, 2·6, 2·06, 2·53, 2·1

First make the number of decimal places the same by adding zeros:

2·31   2·30   2·60   2·06   2·51   2·10

The whole number parts are all 2, so sort using the tenths:

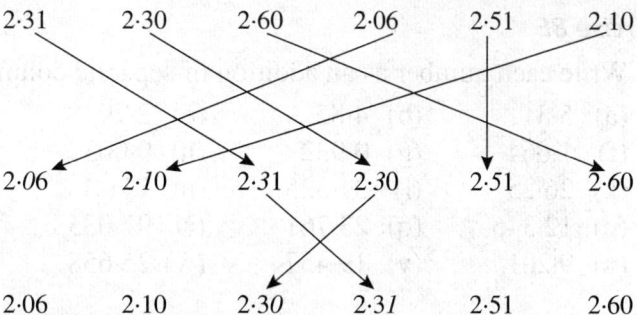

2·06   2·10   2·31   2·30   2·51   2·60

Now sort using the hundredths:

2·06   2·10   2·30   2·31   2·51   2·60

So the order is: 2·06, 2·1, 2·3, 2·31, 2·51, 2·6

Exercise 8D
Write a list of these numbers sorted into order, starting with the smallest.

1. 2·32, 2·23, 3·41, 3·14, 3·20, 3·02
2. 1·55, 1·21, 1·34, 1·43, 1·91, 1·84
3. 4·22, 4·12, 4·31, 4·13, 4·44, 4·04
4. 5·06, 5·63, 5·82, 5·02, 5·12, 5·21
5. 6·03, 7·25, 4·52, 4·02, 5·50, 6·21
6. 9·03, 9·01, 9·10, 9·04, 9·03, 9·33
7. 12·21, 12·35, 11·99, 10·68, 12·34, 13·52, 10·99, 10·09
8. 3·05, 4·5, 6·7, 6·34, 5·16, 5·2
9. 0·13, 0·3, 0·1, 0·09, 0·9, 0·01
10. 9·0, 9·3, 9·29, 9·03, 9·2, 9·19
11. 12·4, 12·37, 12·98, 12·89, 12·8, 12·9, 12·45, 12·4, 12·5, 12·37
12. 32·27, 32·72, 32·7, 32·2, 32·56, 32·65, 32·6, 32·06, 32·5, 32·05

8.5 Place value in decimal numbers: Thousandths

The number 3·875 has three digits after the decimal point.

The third digit which follows a decimal point is the **thousandths** digit.

The number 3·875 means 3 and $\frac{8}{10}$ and $\frac{7}{100}$ and $\frac{5}{1000}$.

Example

Write each number as an addition of separate column values.

(a) 5·31   (b) 14·235

(a) $5·31 = 5 + \frac{3}{10} + \frac{1}{100}$ (b) $14·235 = 10 + 4 + \frac{2}{10} + \frac{3}{100} + \frac{5}{1000}$

Exercise 8E

1. Write each number as an addition of separate column values.

    (a) 5·3   (b) 4·85   (c) 2·79   (d) 6·61   (e) 6·16
    (f) 1·664   (g) 0·932   (h) 9·003   (i) 8·072   (j) 5·302
    (k) 26·25   (l) 31·325   (m) 231·4   (n) 345·67   (o) 34·075
    (p) 12·346   (q) 23·761   (r) 97·035   (s) 39·012   (t) 9·002
    (u) 9·201   (v) 19·457   (w) 25·658   (x) 67·054   (y) 33·333

2. Write the decimal number represented by each addition.

    (a) $3 + \frac{7}{10}$ (b) $7 + \frac{3}{10}$ (c) $6 + \frac{3}{10} + \frac{5}{100}$ (d) $7 + \frac{6}{100}$

    (e) $20 + 7 + \frac{3}{10} + \frac{1}{100} + \frac{6}{1000}$ (f) $30 + 1 + \frac{5}{10} + \frac{1}{1000}$

    (g) $40 + \frac{3}{10} + \frac{6}{100} + \frac{8}{1000}$ (h) $40 + 5 + \frac{7}{100} + \frac{9}{1000}$

    (i) $60 + \frac{7}{1000}$ (j) $70 + 5 + \frac{4}{10} + \frac{3}{1000}$

    (k) $100 + 40 + 8 + \frac{6}{10} + \frac{5}{100} + \frac{7}{1000}$ (l) $300 + 5 + \frac{7}{100}$

    (m) $500 + 80 + \frac{5}{10} + \frac{1}{1000}$ (n) $100 + 10 + 1 + \frac{1}{10} + \frac{1}{100} + \frac{1}{1000}$

    (o) $30 + 7 + \frac{2}{10} + \frac{3}{1000}$ (p) $600 + 50 + 7 + \frac{3}{100} + \frac{6}{1000}$

    (q) $7000 + 200 + 50 + 7 + \frac{8}{10} + \frac{6}{100} + \frac{3}{1000}$ (r) $5000 + 200 + 3 + \frac{5}{10} + \frac{6}{1000}$

    (s) $6000 + \frac{6}{1000}$ (t) $\frac{3}{10} + \frac{2}{1000} + 500$

    (u) $80 + 9 + \frac{6}{100} + 100 + \frac{7}{1000}$

    (v) $20 + \frac{2}{10} + 2000 + 200 + \frac{2}{100} + \frac{2}{1000}$

    (w) $\frac{6}{100} + 3000 + \frac{2}{1000} + 100 + 5$

    (x) $\frac{5}{1000} + 6 + 200 + \frac{7}{10} + 7000 + \frac{5}{100}$

8.6 Approximating decimal numbers: Nearest whole number

Susan weighs her dog Benji and finds she is 19·7 kg.
Susan might approximate and say Benji is about 20 kg.
This is because 19·7 is closer to 20 than to 19.

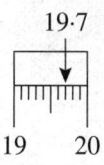

If Benji weighed 19·3 kg, Susan would say Benji is about 19 kg.

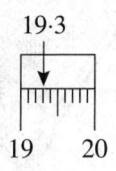

The number 19·5 is exactly half way between 19 and 20. When a number is in the middle we always round up. If Benji weighed 19·5 kg, Susan would say Benji is about 20 kg.

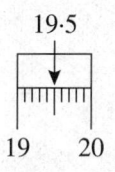

The word **correct** describes approximations. Susan would say she had given Benji's weight **correct to the nearest kilogram**.

Example

In a maths lesson, Elia measured the hand spread of six friends. These are her results:

15·4 cm, 16·8 cm, 17·2 cm, 17·5 cm, 18·2 cm and 18·5 cm

Write Elia's measurements correct to the nearest centimetre.

The results are: 15 cm, 17 cm, 17 cm, 18 cm, 18 cm and 19 cm.

Exercise 8F

1. Write the numbers in these lists correct to the nearest whole number.
   (a) 1·1, 2·3, 1·7, 2·4, 1·9
   (b) 3·1, 4·3, 3·8, 4·0, 2·7
   (c) 6·8, 8·6, 4·5, 5·4, 6·2, 2·6
   (d) 3·5, 5·3, 1·9, 9·1, 7·6, 6·7
   (e) 12·4, 13·3, 12·0, 13·7, 12·2, 12·8, 12·0, 13·5
   (f) 15·6, 14·3, 18·2, 14·6, 15·0, 13·3, 13·0, 14·5, 19·4, 18·0, 15·1, 13·2
   (g) 22·4, 23·6, 22·8, 23·6, 22·0, 23·0, 22·5, 22·9, 23·8, 23·0, 22·1, 23·8
   (h) 45·3, 43·5, 42·6, 46·2, 41·0, 40·1, 43·8, 48·3, 44·7, 47·4, 44·3, 43·4

2. Billy is measuring the height of some seedlings and writing the results down to the nearest centimetre. He records the height of one seedling as 9 cm. Which of these lengths could be Billy's accurate measurement:

A 9·0 cm   B 9·7 cm
C 9·5 cm   D 8·6 cm
E 8·4 cm   F 9·4 cm
G 8·5 cm   H 9·1 cm
I 9·8 cm   J 8·9 cm?

8.7 Approximating decimal numbers: Nearest tenth

Tariq jumped 4·37 m in the school long jump competition. Tariq approximates his jump and says, 'I jumped about 4·4 m.' This is because 4·37 is closer to 4·4 than to 4·3.

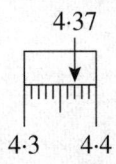

If Tariq had jumped 4·32 m he would say 'I jumped about 4·3 m.'

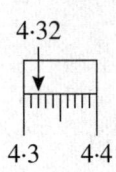

The number 4·35 is exactly in the middle between 4·3 and 4·4. When a number is in the middle you always round up. If Tariq had jumped 4·35 m, he would say, 'I jumped about 4·4 m.'

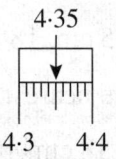

When you correct to the nearest tenth, you have written the number **correct to one decimal place**.

Example

Write these measurements correct to one decimal place.

(a) 15·24 cm (b) 16·38 cm (c) 17·25 cm
(d) 17·53 cm (e) 18·29 cm (f) 18·95 cm

The corrected measurements are:

(a) 15·2 cm (b) 16·4 cm (c) 17·3 cm
(d) 17·5 cm (e) 18·3 cm (f) 19·0 cm

Exercise 8G

1. Write out each list, giving each number correct to one decimal place.
   (a) 2·32, 2·28, 3·41, 3·14, 3·25, 3·09
   (b) 1·55, 1·20, 1·34, 1·43, 1·98, 1·85
   (c) 4·20, 4·95, 4·36, 4·13, 4·44, 4·08
   (d) 5·06, 5·63, 5·82, 5·97, 5·19, 5·21
   (e) 6·08, 7·25, 4·52, 4·19, 5·56, 6·98
   (f) 9·03, 9·75, 9·10, 9·06, 9·07, 9·35
   (g) 12·21, 12·35, 11·99, 10·68, 12·34, 13·52, 10·99, 10·09
   (h) 3·05, 4·50, 6·73, 6·34, 5·17, 5·95

2. Jody has calculated the average amount he spends each day on his school dinner. He writes down:

   'I spend £1·40, correct to the nearest 10p, on my school dinner each day.'

   Which of these amounts could be the exact answer to Jody's calculation:
   A £1·42   B £1·45   C £1·37   D £1·44
   E £1·34   F £1·39   G £1·36   H £1·35
   I £1·43   J £1·40?

8.8 Approximating decimal numbers: Nearest hundredth

Samantha and three friends decide to share the £13·79 cost of a taxi ride home from a disco. She uses a calculator to work out 13·79 ÷ 4 and gets the answer 3·4475. Samantha knows that £3·4475 is not an actual amount of money so she rounds the answer to £3·45. This is because 3·4475 is closer to 3·45 than to 3·44.

If the fare had been £13·77, Samantha's answer would have been £3·4425. Samantha would round this to £3·44.

If the fare had been £13·78, Samantha's answer would have been £3·445. When a number is in the middle we always round up. Samantha would round this to £3·45.

When we correct to the nearest hundredth, we say we have written the number **correct to two decimal places**.

Example

Write these measurements correct to two decimal places.

(a) 15·246 m (b) 16·381 m (c) 17·255 m
(d) 17·532 m (e) 18·996 m (f) 18·550 m

The corrected numbers are:

(a) 15·25 m (b) 16·38 m (c) 17·26 m
(d) 17·53 m (e) 19·00 m (f) 18·55 m

Exercise 8H

1. Write out each list, giving each number correct to two decimal places.
   (a) 2·325, 2·237, 3·401, 3·104, 3·236, 3·502
   (b) 1·505, 1·281, 1·334, 1·493, 1·916, 1·845
   (c) 4·225, 4·128, 4·371, 4·153, 4·349, 4·404
   (d) 5·016, 5·163, 5·196, 5·105, 5·997, 5·121
   (e) 6·403, 7·525, 4·659, 4·602, 5·550, 6·528
   (f) 9·935, 9·395, 9·104, 9·996, 9·308, 9·138
   (g) 12·005, 12·315, 11·904, 10·607, 12·314, 13·059, 10·926, 10·394
   (h) 3·056, 4·523, 6·995, 6·994, 5·106, 5·218, 7·999, 4·456

2. Arup and some friends shared the cost of a meal in an Indian restaurant. Arup used a calculator to work out that each person needed to pay £8·78, correct to the nearest penny. Which of these amounts could be the exact answer to Arup's calculation:

   A £8·784   B £8·776   C £8·774   D £8·784
   E £8·785   F £8·7866 G £8·7845 H £8·7891
   I £8·78   J £8·78333?

8.9 Adding decimal numbers 'in your head'

Simple decimal additions can be completed without a calculator or written calculations.

Examples

(a) 0·4 + 0·5 = 0·9
(b) 0·7 + 0·6 = 1·3
(c) 3·1 + 4·5 = 3 + 4 + 0·1 + 0·5 = 7·6
(d) 8·2 + 2·9 = 8 + 2 + 0·2 + 0·9 = 10 + 1·1 = 11·1
(e) 7·25 + 1·3 = 7 + 1 + 0·2 + 0·3 + 0·05 = 8·55

Exercise 8I

Do these in your head.

1. (a) 0·4 + 0·3 (b) 0·3 + 0·5 (c) 0·8 + 0·1 (d) 0·4 + 0·4
   (e) 0·5 + 0·2 (f) 0·3 + 0·3 (g) 0·4 + 0·2 (h) 0·5 + 0·1
   (i) 0·2 + 0·2 (j) 0·5 + 0·4 (k) 0·6 + 0·3 (l) 0·7 + 0·1
   (m) 0·8 + 0·2 (n) 0·9 + 0·1 (o) 0·6 + 0·2 (p) 1·2 + 0·1
   (q) 1·3 + 0·2 (r) 2·4 + 0·1 (s) 2·1 + 0·3 (t) 3·2 + 0·7
   (u) 2·1 + 0·6 (v) 3·3 + 0·7 (w) 1·5 + 0·5 (x) 5·4 + 0·6
   (y) 3·1 + 0·1

2. (a) 0·5 + 0·6 (b) 0·7 + 0·6 (c) 0·8 + 0·8 (d) 0·8 + 0·5
   (e) 0·9 + 0·2 (f) 0·3 + 0·9 (g) 0·4 + 0·8 (h) 0·9 + 0·5
   (i) 0·8 + 0·3 (j) 0·7 + 0·4 (k) 0·9 + 0·4 (l) 0·8 + 0·8
   (m) 0·9 + 0·9 (n) 0·6 + 0·9 (o) 0·9 + 0·7 (p) 1·5 + 0·7
   (q) 2·6 + 0·8 (r) 1·6 + 0·6 (s) 3·7 + 0·7 (t) 4·8 + 0·9
   (u) 2·2 + 0·8 (v) 6·5 + 0·5 (w) 2·4 + 0·7 (x) 3·8 + 0·9
   (y) 4·7 + 0·5

3. (a) 3·1 + 5·1 (b) 4·2 + 6·4 (c) 1·6 + 2·3 (d) 7·2 + 6·3
   (e) 1·3 + 2·3 (f) 5·2 + 1·7 (g) 1·6 + 2·2 (h) 1·5 + 3·3
   (i) 7·2 + 3·2 (j) 6·5 + 6·1 (k) 7·6 + 2·4 (l) 8·6 + 1·1
   (m) 4·4 + 3·3 (n) 6·3 + 8·1 (o) 7·4 + 6·1 (p) 5·4 + 7·1
   (q) 1·1 + 5·2 (r) 8·1 + 8·1 (s) 2·9 + 3·1 (t) 5·8 + 2·2
   (u) 6·5 + 9·4 (v) 5·2 + 6·5 (w) 3·4 + 5·4 (x) 9·7 + 8·3
   (y) 6·8 + 9·1

4. (a) 7·5 + 3·5 (b) 7·9 + 6·3 (c) 5·4 + 2·9 (d) 6·7 + 2·4
   (e) 2·6 + 3·6 (f) 1·8 + 1·5 (g) 3·9 + 7·2 (h) 1·7 + 1·8
   (i) 3·7 + 2·6 (j) 1·8 + 5·4 (k) 1·9 + 3·6 (l) 3·8 + 2·3
   (m) 4·6 + 3·5 (n) 4·9 + 3·5 (o) 3·8 + 1·9 (p) 1·8 + 4·6
   (q) 3·7 + 2·3 (r) 4·9 + 5·7 (s) 4·8 + 4·8 (t) 6·9 + 7·9
   (u) 3·7 + 5·7 (v) 8·6 + 6·8 (w) 7·7 + 3·9 (x) 8·3 + 9·8
   (y) 7·2 + 9·9

5. (a) 0·3 + 0·04 (b) 2·05 + 0·6 (c) 1·06 + 0·7 (d) 0·9 + 1·04
   (e) 2·8 + 1·02 (f) 0·6 + 0·34 (g) 1·7 + 0·15 (h) 2·45 + 3·4
   (i) 6·56 + 1·2 (j) 1·3 + 2·64 (k) 1·62 + 0·03 (l) 0·51 + 2·08
   (m) 1·85 + 0·04 (n) 0·73 + 3·06 (o) 1·05 + 1·94 (p) 1·43 + 0·08
   (q) 3·56 + 0·08 (r) 0·76 + 5·08 (s) 2·06 + 2·76 (t) 3·07 + 5·89
   (u) 0·78 + 0·6 (v) 1·84 + 0·2 (w) 0·8 + 3·76 (x) 2·95 + 6·05
   (y) 3·99 + 1·09

8.10 Adding decimal numbers with written calculations

If decimal additions are too difficult to do in your head, you do them on paper.

Example

(a) 3·4 + 7·8 + 2·6   (b) 13·75 + 14·86   (c) 4·45 + 7 + 6·3

(a)   3·4
        7·8
      + 2·6
      ─────
       13·8
        1↑

Line up the decimal points.

(b)   13·75
     + 14·86
     ───────
       28·61
         1↑1

Line up the decimal points.

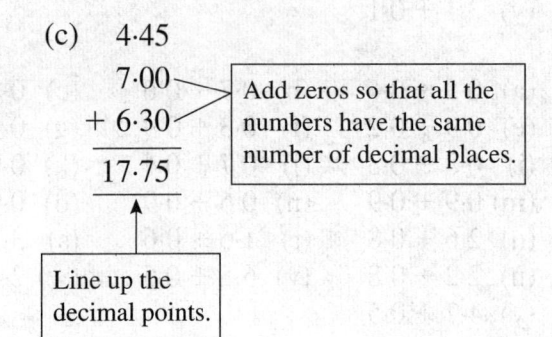

(c)   4·45
        7·00
      + 6·30
      ──────
       17·75
          ↑

Add zeros so that all the numbers have the same number of decimal places.

Line up the decimal points.

Exercise 8J

Do these on paper.

1. (a) 3·6 + 2·7 + 4·6
   (b) 5·3 + 6·7 + 8·1
   (c) 6·6 + 7·6 + 0·9
   (d) 3·7 + 8·4 + 9·2
   (e) 8·6 + 6·4 + 2·5
   (f) 5·7 + 8·7 + 9·7
   (g) 2·2 + 6·1 + 9·0
   (h) 7·8 + 0·6 + 1·9
   (i) 2·5 + 3·5 + 6·5
   (j) 6·4 + 4·6 + 7·8
   (k) 15·3 + 6·4 + 0·8
   (l) 0·7 + 6·5 + 2·3
   (m) 7·8 + 5·4 + 0·1
   (n) 6·7 + 8·4 + 9·3
   (o) 0·6 + 3·8 + 5·9
   (p) 9·6 + 0·9 + 0·7
   (q) 9·0 + 0·7 + 1·8
   (r) 4·5 + 6·0 + 0·8
   (s) 5·5 + 6·6 + 7·7
   (t) 6·3 + 0·9 + 0·5
   (u) 0·7 + 1·7 + 9·6
   (v) 0·8 + 0·6 + 9·1
   (w) 8·9 + 13·2 + 34·0
   (x) 19·7 + 0·9 + 8·6
   (y) 11·5 + 15·8 + 0·9

2. (a) 3·67 + 4·32
   (b) 7·22 + 6·35
   (c) 9·05 + 8·74
   (d) 4·75 + 0·24
   (e) 8·62 + 9·27
   (f) 7·66 + 3·25
   (g) 8·07 + 6·66
   (h) 3·56 + 5·29
   (i) 7·09 + 3·76
   (j) 6·43 + 5·39
   (k) 7·45 + 6·62
   (l) 8·73 + 0·95
   (m) 10·56 + 7·51
   (n) 9·81 + 11·27
   (o) 15·93 + 7·25
   (p) 1·24 + 1·86
   (q) 5·65 + 1·58
   (r) 3·67 + 2·89
   (s) 5·76 + 0·84
   (t) 9·98 + 0·09
   (u) 13·45 + 6·87
   (v) 7·89 + 18·11
   (w) 16·87 + 9·63
   (x) 56·45 + 34·66
   (y) 89·56 + 76·27

3. (a) $5 + 6 \cdot 3 + 0 \cdot 2$ (b) $7 \cdot 3 + 15 + 2 \cdot 8$ (c) $9 \cdot 7 + 6 \cdot 3 + 9$
   (d) $17 \cdot 5 + 8 + 2 \cdot 3$ (e) $6 \cdot 7 + 6 \cdot 5 + 18$ (f) $20 + 7 \cdot 6 + 9 \cdot 4$
   (g) $7 \cdot 5 + 9 + 11 \cdot 2$ (h) $8 + 4 \cdot 6 + 6$ (i) $4 + 2 \cdot 5 + 4 \cdot 09$
   (j) $9 + 1 \cdot 23 + 4 \cdot 45$ (k) $4 \cdot 65 + 7 + 0 \cdot 9$ (l) $17 + 1 \cdot 7 + 0 \cdot 17$
   (m) $10 \cdot 05 + 5 \cdot 63 + 2 \cdot 1$ (n) $5 \cdot 04 + 4 \cdot 5 + 5$ (o) $9 \cdot 9 + 8 + 6 \cdot 74$
   (p) $34 \cdot 4 + 76 \cdot 015$ (q) $54 \cdot 8 + 9 \cdot 237$ (r) $8 \cdot 999 + 0 \cdot 001$
   (s) $34 + 3 \cdot 4 + 0 \cdot 34$ (t) $56 \cdot 71 + 8 \cdot 34 + 5$ (u) $0 \cdot 99 + 9 \cdot 9 + 19$
   (v) $78 \cdot 6 + 7 \cdot 86 + 0 \cdot 786$ (w) $67 \cdot 45 + 8 \cdot 9 + 0 \cdot 51 + 13$
   (x) $34 \cdot 506 + 4 \cdot 891 + 6 \cdot 05$ (y) $54 \cdot 5 + 67 \cdot 32 + 17 + 0 \cdot 992$

4. A group of 8 friends want to buy a CD which costs £9·50. When they check their pockets, these are the amounts of money each has:

     £2·38, £3·75, £2·73, £2·60,
     £2·89, £3·09, £2·86, £2·65

Which three of these amounts add up to exactly £9·50?

8.11 Subtracting decimal numbers 'in your head'

You need to be able to do simple decimal subtractions without a calculator or written calculations.

Examples
(a) $0 \cdot 8 - 0 \cdot 3 = 0 \cdot 5$
(b) $7 \cdot 6 - 1 \cdot 4 = 6 \cdot 2$
(c) $1 \cdot 6 - 0 \cdot 9 = 0 \cdot 7$
(d) $8 \cdot 2 - 2 \cdot 9 = 8 \cdot 2 - 2 - 0 \cdot 9 = 6 \cdot 2 - 0 \cdot 9 = 5 \cdot 3$

Exercise 8K
Do these in your head.

1. (a) $0 \cdot 9 - 0 \cdot 2$ (b) $0 \cdot 8 - 0 \cdot 1$ (c) $0 \cdot 5 - 0 \cdot 4$ (d) $0 \cdot 7 - 0 \cdot 7$ (e) $0 \cdot 5 - 0 \cdot 3$
   (f) $0 \cdot 8 - 0 \cdot 4$ (g) $0 \cdot 3 - 0 \cdot 2$ (h) $0 \cdot 2 - 0 \cdot 1$ (i) $0 \cdot 7 - 0 \cdot 4$ (j) $0 \cdot 9 - 0 \cdot 5$
   (k) $2 \cdot 9 - 0 \cdot 4$ (l) $4 \cdot 8 - 0 \cdot 7$ (m) $3 \cdot 6 - 0 \cdot 4$ (n) $2 \cdot 8 - 0 \cdot 5$ (o) $5 \cdot 7 - 0 \cdot 3$
   (p) $2 \cdot 6 - 1 \cdot 4$ (q) $5 \cdot 6 - 2 \cdot 2$ (r) $6 \cdot 9 - 2 \cdot 7$ (s) $5 \cdot 6 - 1 \cdot 6$ (t) $7 \cdot 9 - 2 \cdot 7$
   (u) $8 \cdot 7 - 3 \cdot 4$ (v) $7 \cdot 8 - 4 \cdot 6$ (w) $9 \cdot 9 - 6 \cdot 3$ (x) $2 \cdot 8 - 0 \cdot 8$ (y) $9 \cdot 9 - 5 \cdot 1$

2. (a) $1 \cdot 7 - 0 \cdot 8$ (b) $1 \cdot 4 - 0 \cdot 6$ (c) $1 \cdot 3 - 0 \cdot 5$ (d) $1 \cdot 2 - 0 \cdot 4$ (e) $1 \cdot 6 - 0 \cdot 8$
   (f) $1 \cdot 7 - 0 \cdot 9$ (g) $1 \cdot 3 - 0 \cdot 6$ (h) $1 \cdot 5 - 0 \cdot 8$ (i) $1 \cdot 1 - 0 \cdot 4$ (j) $1 \cdot 2 - 0 \cdot 6$
   (k) $1 \cdot 1 - 0 \cdot 5$ (l) $1 \cdot 3 - 0 \cdot 8$ (m) $1 \cdot 2 - 0 \cdot 3$ (n) $1 \cdot 1 - 0 \cdot 6$ (o) $1 \cdot 2 - 0 \cdot 5$
   (p) $1 \cdot 5 - 0 \cdot 6$ (q) $1 \cdot 6 - 0 \cdot 9$ (r) $1 \cdot 3 - 0 \cdot 7$ (s) $1 \cdot 1 - 0 \cdot 8$ (t) $1 \cdot 4 - 0 \cdot 7$
   (u) $1 \cdot 3 - 0 \cdot 9$ (v) $1 \cdot 4 - 0 \cdot 8$ (w) $1 \cdot 1 - 0 \cdot 9$ (x) $1 \cdot 3 - 0 \cdot 9$ (y) $1 \cdot 5 - 0 \cdot 7$

3. (a) 8·2 − 1·6   (b) 7·3 − 2·7   (c) 6·4 − 5·9
    (d) 7·2 − 1·8   (e) 4·5 − 6·7   (f) 6·7 − 2·7
    (g) 9·3 − 2·9   (h) 9·4 − 8·6   (i) 6·7 − 4·6
    (j) 9·3 − 5·7   (k) 7·5 − 3·8   (l) 5·6 − 3·7
    (m) 6·1 − 4·6   (n) 3·4 − 1·7   (o) 4·5 − 2·8
    (p) 6·7 − 2·8   (q) 4·5 − 2·9   (r) 7·3 − 4·9
    (s) 9·3 − 7·4   (t) 8·7 − 3·9   (u) 6·5 − 3·8
    (v) 7·6 − 5·8   (w) 3·2 − 1·8   (x) 2·8 − 1·9
    (y) 5·6 − 4·8

8.12 Subtracting decimal numbers with written calculations

If decimal subtractions are too difficult to do in your head, you do them on paper.

Example

(a) 35·7 − 24·9   (b) 65·47 − 28·23   (c) 124·5 − 6·38

(a) $\overset{4\,1}{3\cancel{5}}\cdot 7$
     − 24·9
     ─────
      10·8
     ↑
     Line up the decimal points.

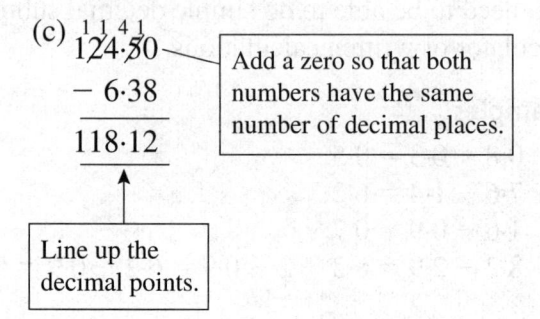

(b) $\overset{5\,1}{\cancel{6}5}\cdot 47$
     − 28·23
     ──────
       37·24
     ↑
     Line up the decimal points.

(c) $\overset{1\,1\,4\,1}{124\cdot \cancel{5}0}$
     − 6·38
     ──────
      118·12
     ↑
     Line up the decimal points.

Add a zero so that both numbers have the same number of decimal places.

Exercise 8L

Do these on paper.

1. (a) 23·8 − 12·7   (b) 34·6 − 11·5   (c) 48·9 − 26·2
    (d) 56·3 − 32·1   (e) 29·5 − 15·5   (f) 32·8 − 11·9
    (g) 67·3 − 24·6   (h) 56·8 − 21·9   (i) 35·7 − 24·9
    (j) 87·3 − 24·7   (k) 64·9 − 35·7   (l) 43·7 − 28·2
    (m) 81·6 − 45·4   (n) 93·4 − 58·3   (o) 26·7 − 18·5
    (p) 12·5 − 8·6   (q) 34·6 − 7·8   (r) 58·4 − 9·5
    (s) 67·5 − 9·9   (t) 27·4 − 8·6   (u) 45·6 − 18·7
    (v) 93·7 − 28·9   (w) 84·5 − 17·8   (x) 56·2 − 28·4
    (y) 95·1 − 45·3

2. (a) 45·34 − 24·12 (b) 56·77 − 11·35 (c) 67·45 − 32·21
   (d) 89·07 − 56·05 (e) 34·56 − 12·34 (f) 45·64 − 22·47
   (g) 78·23 − 67·18 (h) 43·62 − 31·35 (i) 67·54 − 16·49
   (j) 43·26 − 31·08 (k) 56·35 − 43·84 (l) 89·32 − 46·51
   (m) 78·19 − 31·91 (n) 45·67 − 24·76 (o) 85·02 − 12·51
   (p) 34·56 − 29·21 (q) 67·94 − 59·22 (r) 83·65 − 78·43
   (s) 43·55 − 27·24 (t) 84·27 − 78·03 (u) 80·16 − 31·54
   (v) 70·35 − 67·52 (w) 50·22 − 17·56 (x) 50·03 − 21·78
   (y) 60·04 − 11·57

3. (a) 67·32 − 4·7   (b) 70·45 − 12·7   (c) 56·39 − 31·6
   (d) 74·21 − 7·4   (e) 87·31 − 45·4   (f) 16·7 − 3·45
   (g) 36·9 − 11·36 (h) 56·3 − 22·25   (i) 89·2 − 17·07
   (j) 16·4 − 5·27   (k) 4·5 − 3·72   (l) 7·6 − 0·85
   (m) 13·6 − 2·77   (n) 78·2 − 31·93   (o) 56·7 − 42·82
   (p) 42·7 − 6·85   (q) 34·2 − 8·56   (r) 27·3 − 18·92
   (s) 67·3 − 28·54 (t) 34·31 − 18·55 (u) 27 − 19·53
   (v) 34 − 25·81   (w) 67 − 0·56   (x) 89 − 3·67
   (y) 78 − 49·47

4. Sammy-Jo works in a clothes shop. She is preparing this poster for display in a sale.

SUPER DRESS SALE

OLD PRICE	SALE PRICE	SAVING
£56·99	£35·50	£21·49
£45·50	£32·80	
£58·00	£25·99	
£62·55	£49·89	
£56·30	£45·79	
£69·00	£45·99	
£56·20	£45·59	
£37·90	£23·99	
£60·00	£39·99	
£80·00	£65·69	

Copy and complete the poster for Sammy-Jo.

Summary

1. The first digit after a decimal point is the **tenths** digit.

2. The second digit after a decimal point is the **hundredths** digit.

3. It will help to add a zero in the hundredths column when sorting numbers with two decimal places.

4. The third digit after a decimal point is the **thousandths** digit.

5. It will help to add a zero in the thousandths column when sorting numbers with three decimal places.

Checkout 8

1. (a) What place value does the underlined digit have?
   (i) 3·7   (ii) 14·8   (iii) 67·3
   (b) Write these lengths with a decimal point:
   (i) 3 cm 5 mm   (ii) 6 cm 8 mm
   (c) Write these lengths in millimetres and centimetres:
   (i) 4·3 cm   (ii) 6·9 cm
   (d) Write this list in order, starting with the smallest number:
   3·4, 3·2, 3·0, 4·2, 2·4, 2·9, 3·8, 3·5

2. (a) What place value does the underlined digit have?
   (i) 3·79   (ii) 14·86   (iii) 67·37
   (b) Write these lengths with a decimal point:
   (i) 3 m 54 cm   (ii) 6 m 83 cm
   (c) Write these lengths in metres and centimetres:
   (i) 4·78 m   (ii) 13·65 m

3. Write the list in order, starting with the smallest number:
   (a) 6·42, 6·28, 6·09, 6·31, 6·25, 6·30, 6·80, 6·08
   (b) 5·7, 5·65, 5·04, 5·6, 5·55, 5·5, 5·05, 5·4

4. (a) What place value does the underlined digit have?
   (i) 3·792   (ii) 14·806   (iii) 67·375
   (b) Write as a decimal:
   (i) $3 + \frac{2}{10} + \frac{3}{100} + \frac{7}{1\,000}$

   (ii) $20 + \frac{7}{10} + \frac{6}{1\,000} + 5 + \frac{3}{100}$

5. Write the list in order, starting with the smallest number:
   (a) 7·427, 7·423, 7·401, 7·435, 7·048, 7·421
   (b) 8·76, 8·653, 8·049, 8·63, 8·55, 8·5, 8·059, 8·488

6. Correct to the nearest whole number, 17·3, 18·5 and 9·7 are 17, 19 and 10.

6. Write correct to the nearest whole number:
   (a) 12·7   (b) 13·5   (c) 4·3

7. Correct to one decimal places, 12·25, 3·42 and 5·78 are 12·3, 3·4 and 5·8.

7. Write correct to one decimal place:
   (a) 5·63   (b) 8·79   (c) 6·95

8. Correct to two decimal places, 3·456, 8·795 and 4·064 are 3·46, 8·80 and 4·06.

8. Write correct to two decimal places:
   (a) 6·783   (b) 7·049   (c) 12·996

9. Simple decimal numbers can be added or subtracted in your head.

9. Do these in your head.
   (a) 0·6 + 0·5   (b) 1·6 + 2·3
   (c) 0·75 + 0·4   (d) 0·75 + 0·04
   (e) 5 + 2·9   (f) 3·25 + 1·13
   (g) 0·9 − 0·3   (h) 1·7 − 0·6
   (i) 6·7 − 2·2   (j) 4·6 − 3·8

10. For more difficult calculations, add zeros so that all numbers have the same number of decimal places. Then line up the decimal points and use normal written methods for addition or subtraction. Don't forget to carry the point down into the answer.

10. Do these on paper.
    (a) 4·7 + 5·6 + 2·1   (b) 3·4 + 17 + 2·96
    (c) 34·78 + 49·56   (d) 13·7 + 34·56 + 4·9
    (e) 23·9 − 12·7   (f) 56·2 − 27·4
    (g) 70·45 − 4·8   (h) 67 − 13·45

Revision exercise 8

1. Fiona has four cards with numbers on.

   [3] [7] [1] [5]

   (a) Write down the largest number she can make.
       She must use all four cards.
   (b) Write down the smallest number she can make.
       She must use all four cards.

   She is given another card.
   It has a decimal point on it.

   [·]

   (c) Write down the smallest number she can make now.
       She must use all five cards.   [OCR]

2.

The diagram shows some potatoes on a set of scales.
Write down the weight of the potatoes. [Edexcel]

3.

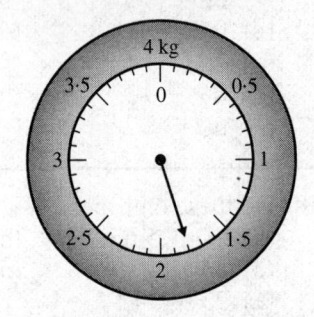

The diagram shows the dial on a weighing machine.
It shows weights up to 4 kilograms.

(a) To what weight is the arrow pointing?
Give your answer in
(i) kilograms
(ii) grams

(b) A further 1·3 kilograms is put on the weighing machine.
What is the new position of the arrow on the dial?
[OCR]

4. Sali and Marc are decorating their house.

(a) They buy two tins of paint. One tin costs £8·98 and the other costs £9·87.
(i) Find the total cost of the paint.
(ii) They pay for the paint using a £20 note.
How much change should they be given?

(b) Marc buys 18 packets of patterned tiles.
(i) Each packet contains 6 tiles.
How many tiles does Marc buy?
(ii) Marc paid £234 for the tiles.
What is the cost of one packet of tiles? [WJEC]

5.

PAT'S PLACE

Cod	£1·20
Plaice	£1·35
Sausage	90p
Chicken	£1·80
Meat pie	70p
Portion of chips	50p
Mushy peas	25p

Dean was sent to buy the supper for the family.
He made this list.

Mum	Plaice and chips	£ ....
Dad	Cod, chips and peas	£ ....
Sharon	Meat pie and chips	£ ....
Me	Sausage, chips and peas	£ ....
	Total	£ ....

Copy and complete the costs on Dean's list. [AQA/NEAB]

9 SHAPE AND SPACE 3

Geometric shapes are used in design and architecture.

This unit is about:

- Lines and angles
- Opposite angles
- Parallel lines and angles
- Angles in triangles
- Types of triangle
- Quadrilaterals
- Polygons
- Angle sum of a polygon

You need to remember:

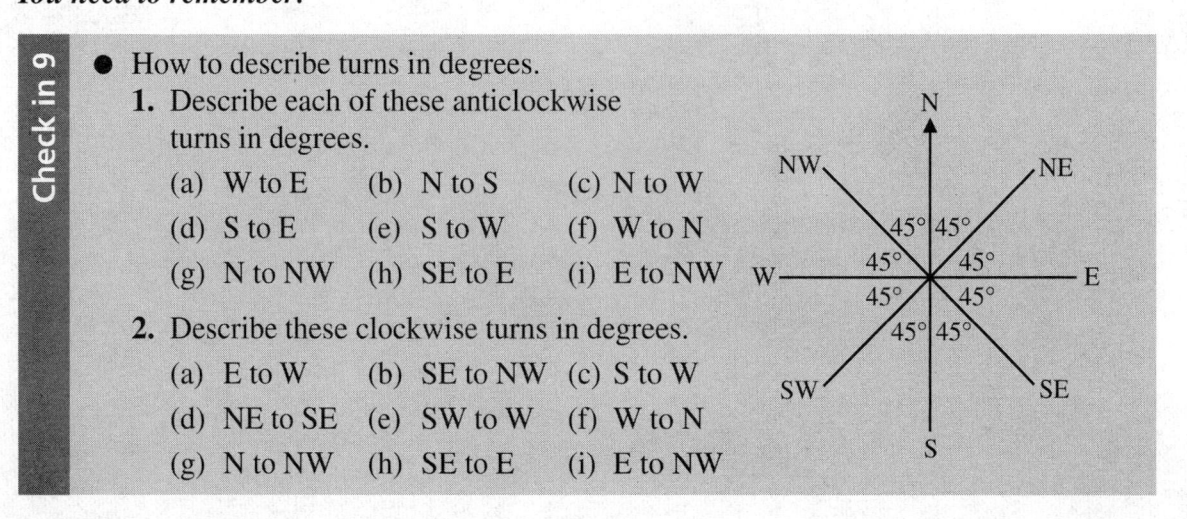

Check in 9

- How to describe turns in degrees.
  1. Describe each of these anticlockwise turns in degrees.
     - (a) W to E
     - (b) N to S
     - (c) N to W
     - (d) S to E
     - (e) S to W
     - (f) W to N
     - (g) N to NW
     - (h) SE to E
     - (i) E to NW
  2. Describe these clockwise turns in degrees.
     - (a) E to W
     - (b) SE to NW
     - (c) S to W
     - (d) NE to SE
     - (e) SW to W
     - (f) W to N
     - (g) N to NW
     - (h) SE to E
     - (i) E to NW

9.1 Lines and angles

Remember:

There are 90° in a quarter turn.

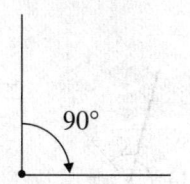

90°

There are 180° in a half turn.

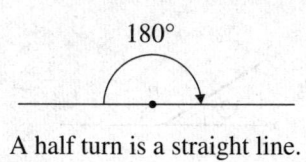

180°

A half turn is a straight line.

There are 360° in a full turn.

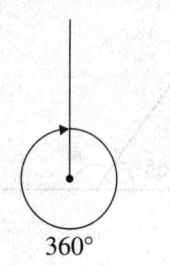

360°

Look back to page 35 if you need more help.

Examples

Find the angles a, b and c in these diagrams.

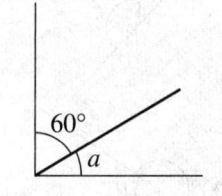

60°, a

125°, b

280°, c

$a = 90° - 60° = 30°$ 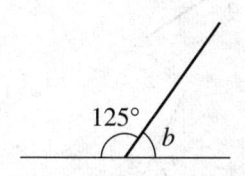 $b = 180° - 125° = 55°$ 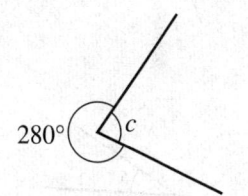 $c = 360° - 280° = 80°$

Exercise 9A

Find each angle marked with a letter in these diagrams.

1. 40°, a

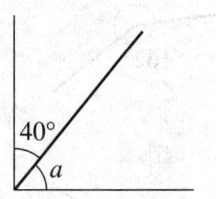

2. 80°, b

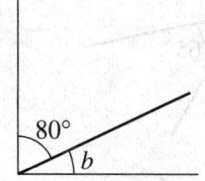

3. c, 45°

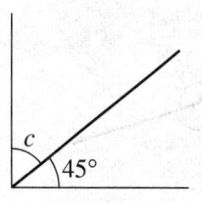

4. d, 25°

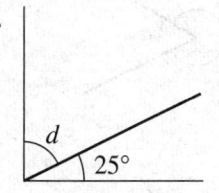

5. 5°, e

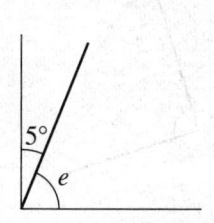

6. f, 62°

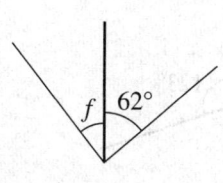

7. 34°, g

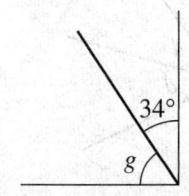

8. h, 57°

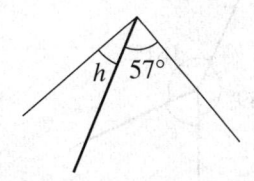

9. 23°, 32°, i

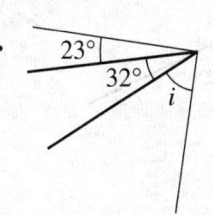

10. 20°, j, j

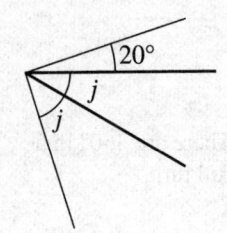

11. 135°, k

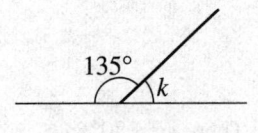

12. 140°, l

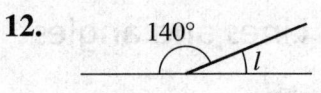

13. 65°, m

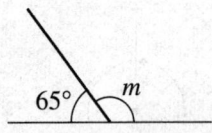

14. 32°, n

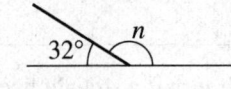

15. 111°, o

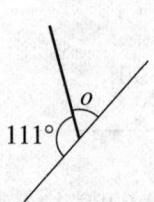

16. 84°, p

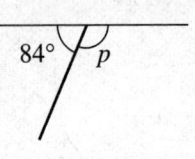

17. 133°, q

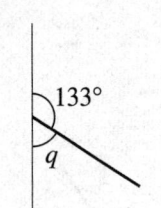

18. 28°, r

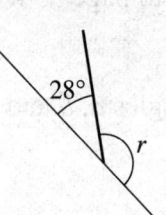

19. s, 42°, 103°

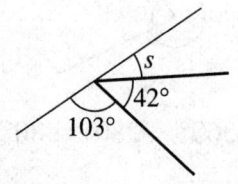

20. t, t, 80°

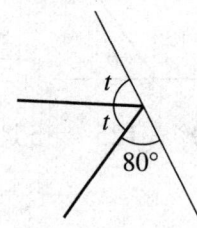

21. 300°, u

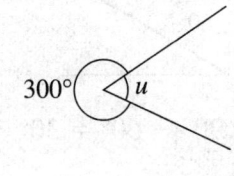

22. v, 200°

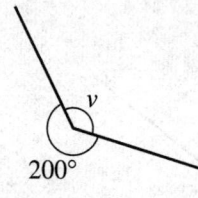

23. w, 65°

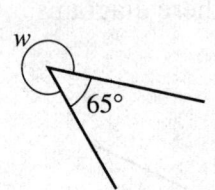

24. x, 162°

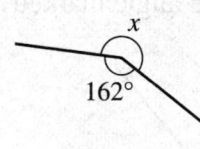

25. 123°, y

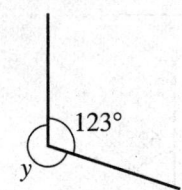

26. 270°, z

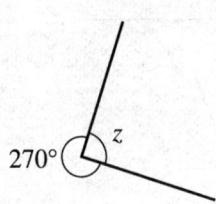

27. 315°, a

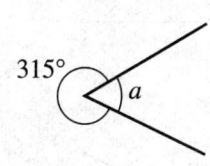

28. b, 74°

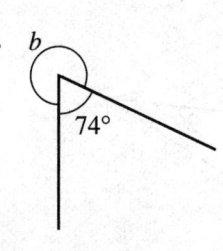

29. 161°, 149°, c

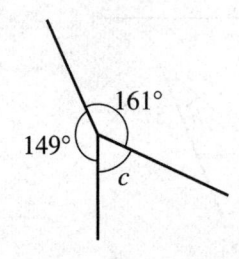

30. d, d, 280°

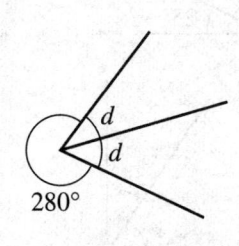

9.2 Opposite angles

Two pairs of opposite angles are created when straight lines cross.
Opposite angles are always equal.

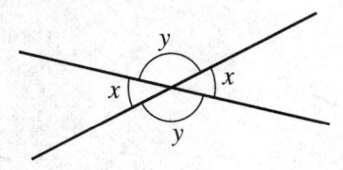

Example
Find the angles e, f and g.

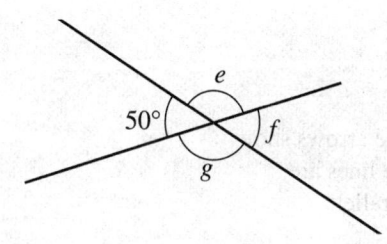

angle $f = 50°$ (because angle f and $50°$ are opposite angles)
angle $e = 130°$ (because angle e and $50°$ make a straight line)
angle $g = 130°$ (because angle g and angle e are opposite angles)

Exercise 9B
Find each angle marked with a letter in these diagrams.

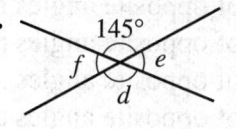

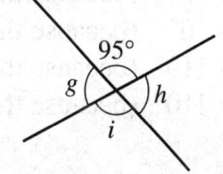

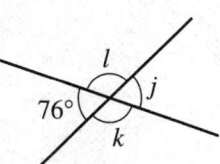

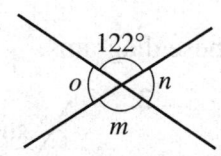

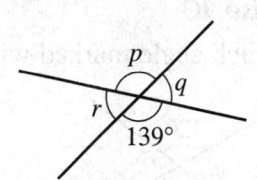

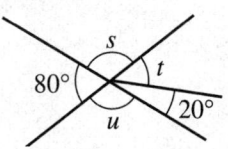

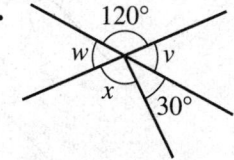

1. $80°$, a, b, c
2. $145°$, f, e, d
3. $95°$, g, h, i
4. $76°$, l, j, k
5. $122°$, o, n, m
6. $139°$, p, q, r
7. $80°$, s, t, u, $20°$
8. $120°$, w, v, x, $30°$
9. z, y, a, $50°$, $80°$

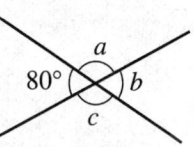

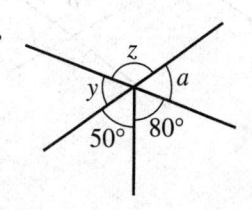

9.3 Parallel lines and angles

When a line crosses a pair of parallel lines, two sets of identical opposite angles are formed.

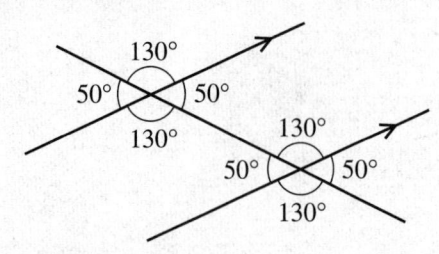

Remember:
Parallel lines never meet, like train tracks.

Example
Find the angles e, f, g, h, i, j and k.

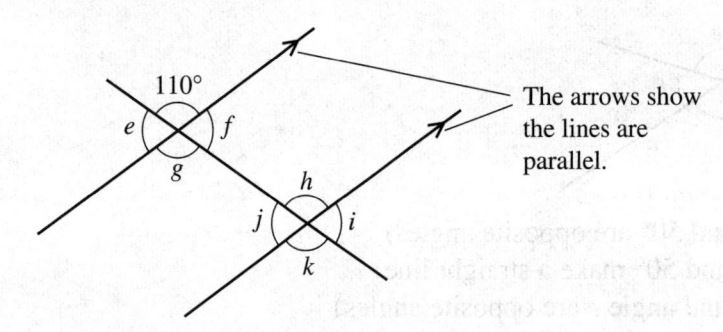

The arrows show the lines are parallel.

angle $g = 110°$ (because angle g and $110°$ are opposite angles)
angle $e = 70°$ (because angle e and $110°$ make a straight line)
angle $f = 70°$ (because angle e and angle f are opposite angles)
angle $j = 70°$ (because the two pairs of opposite angles are identical)
angle $i = 70°$ (because the two pairs of opposite angles are identical)
angle $h = 110°$ (because the two pairs of opposite angles are identical)
angle $k = 110°$ (because the two pairs of opposite angles are identical)

Exercise 9C
Find each angle marked with a letter in these diagrams.

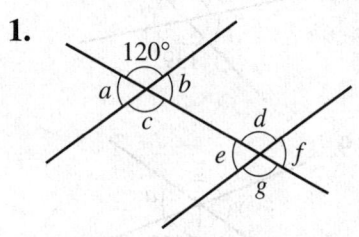

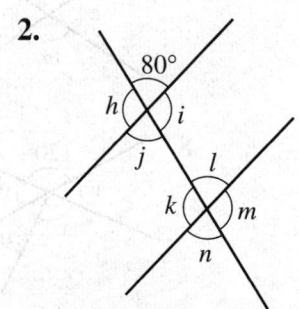

1.

2.

3.

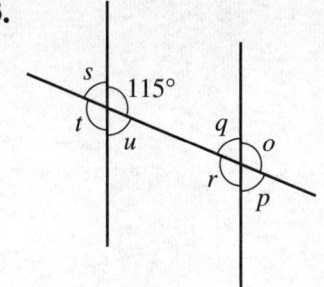

4.

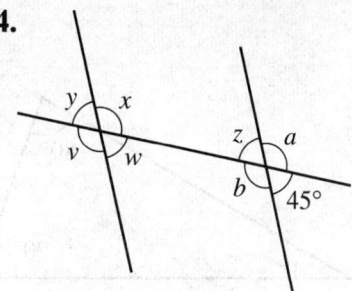

5. Macclesfield to Matlock, 108°, angle c at Matlock.

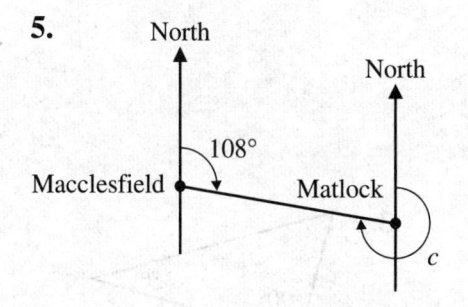

6. Llanelli to Porthcawl, angle e, angle d, 305° at Porthcawl.

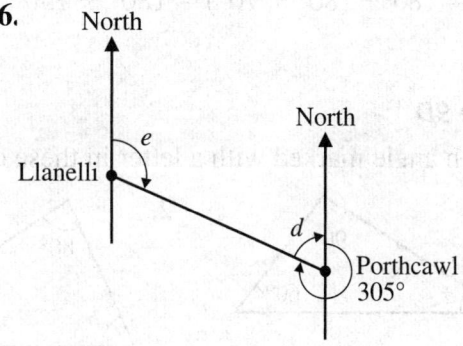

7. Hexagon with angles 240°, 60°, f, g, h, i, j, k.

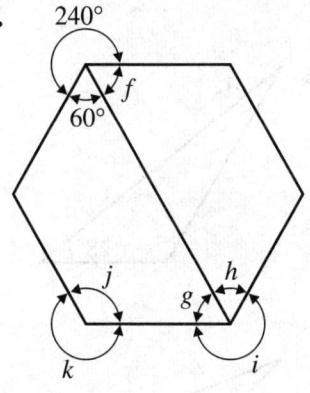

8. Thetford to Norwich, 55°, angles l and m.

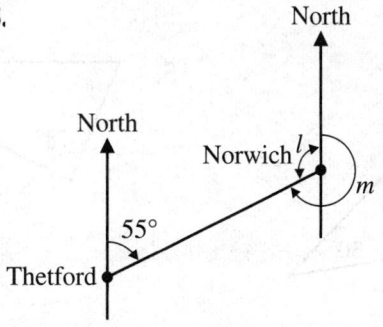

9.4 Angles in triangles

The three angles in any triangle add up to 180°.

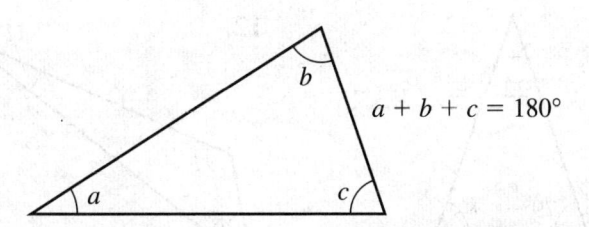

$a + b + c = 180°$

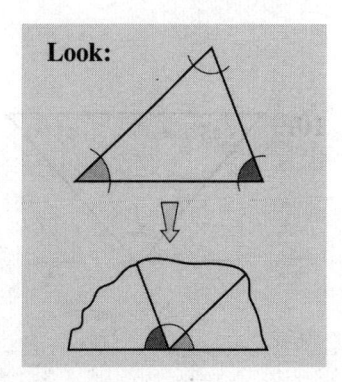

If you know two angles, you can find the third angle.

Look:

182 Shape and Space 3

Example

Find angle a.

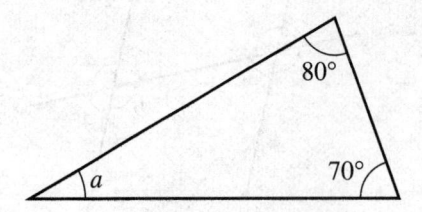

angle $a = 180° - (80° + 70°) = 180° - 150° = 30°$

Exercise 9D

Find each angle marked with a letter in these diagrams.

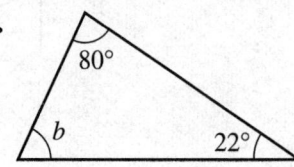

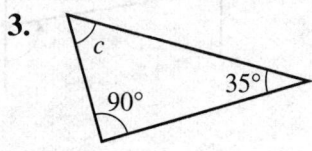

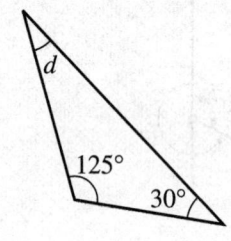

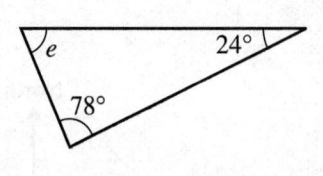

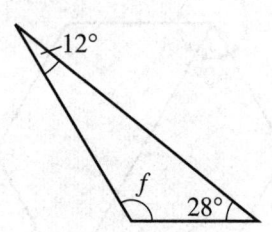

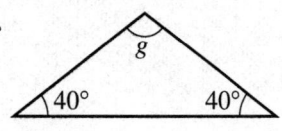

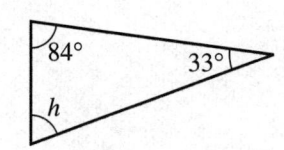

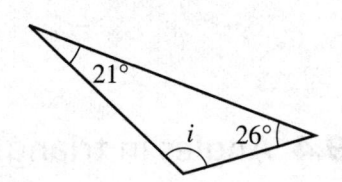

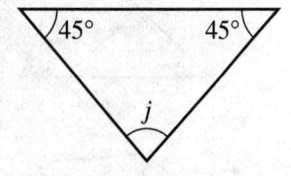

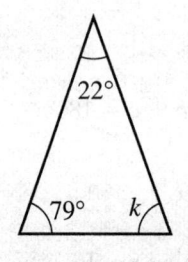

1. (triangle with 90°, 60°, a)
2. (triangle with 80°, 22°, b)
3. (triangle with 90°, 35°, c)
4. (triangle with 125°, 30°, d)
5. (triangle with 78°, 24°, e)
6. (triangle with 12°, 28°, f)
7. (triangle with 40°, 40°, g)
8. (triangle with 84°, 33°, h)
9. (triangle with 21°, 26°, i)
10. (triangle with 45°, 45°, j)
11. (triangle with 22°, 79°, k)
12. (triangle with 11°, 58°, l)

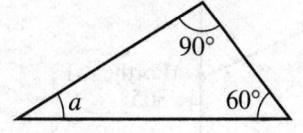

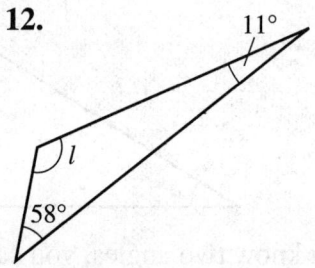

9.5 Types of triangle

An **isosceles** triangle has two equal sides and two equal angles.

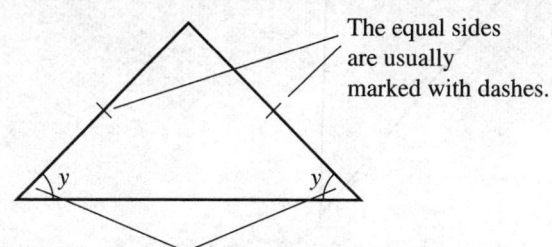

The equal sides are usually marked with dashes.

The equal angles are formed between the equal sides and the third side.

An **equilateral** triangle has three equal sides and three equal angles of 60°.

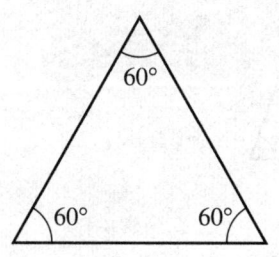

Example

Find each angle marked with a letter in these diagrams.

(a)

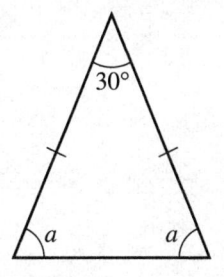

(b)

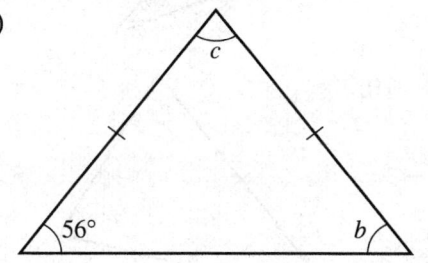

The triangle is isosceles.
$a + a = 180° - 30° = 150°$
$a = 150° \div 2 = 75°$

The triangle is isosceles.
$b = 56°$ (because it is the other equal angle)
$c = 180° - (56° + 56°) = 68°$

Exercise 9E

Find each angle marked with a letter in these diagrams.

1.

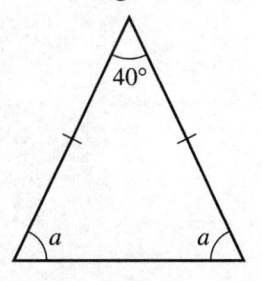

2.

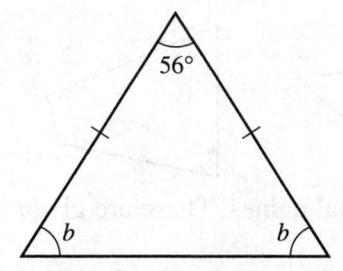

184 Shape and Space 3

3.

4.

5.

6.

7.

8.

9.

10.

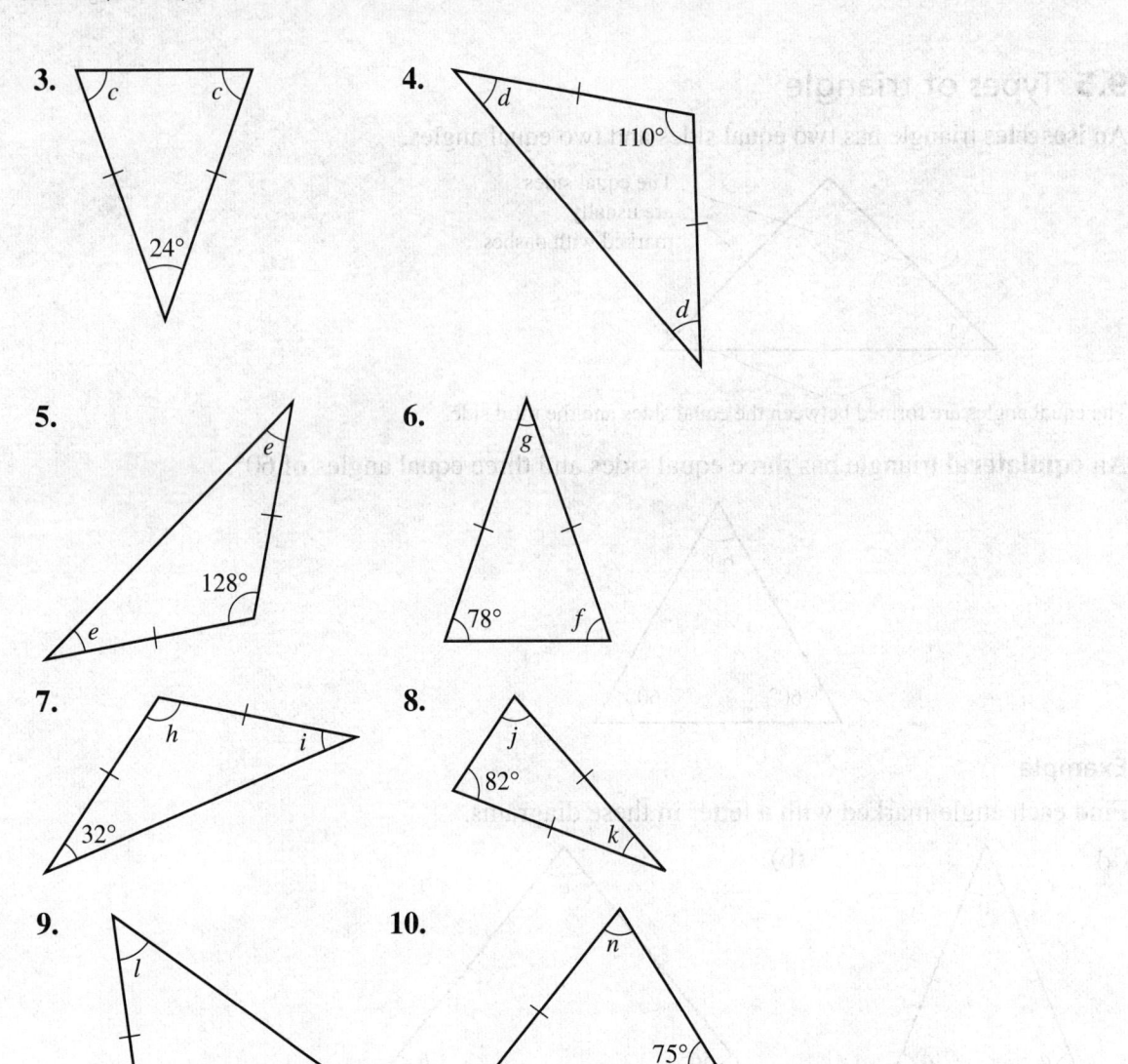

9.6 Quadrilaterals

A quadrilateral is a shape with four straight sides.
These shapes are all quadrilaterals.

Some quadrilaterals have special names. These are given in the next exercise.

Exercise 9F

Use centimetre squared paper for this exercise.

1. A quadrilateral with one pair of parallel sides is called a **trapezium**.

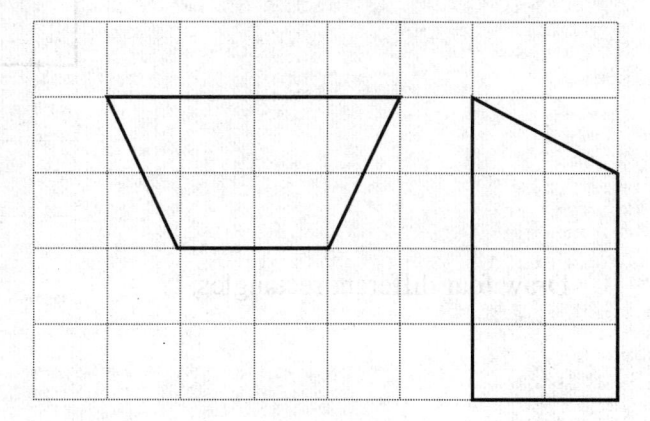

   Draw four different trapeziums.

2. A quadrilateral with two pairs of parallel sides is called a **parallelogram**.

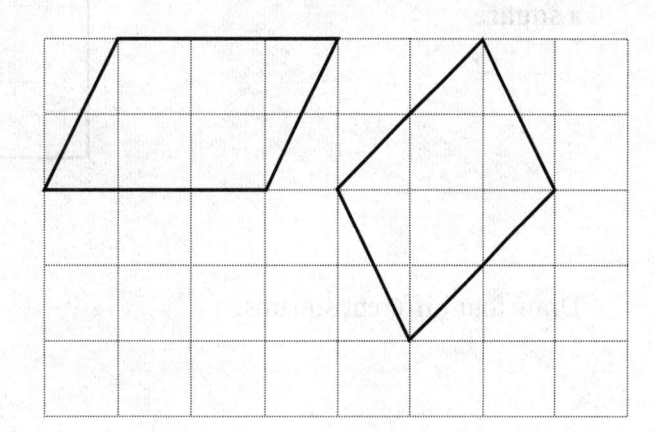

   Draw four different parallelograms.

3. A quadrilateral with four equal sides is called a **rhombus**.

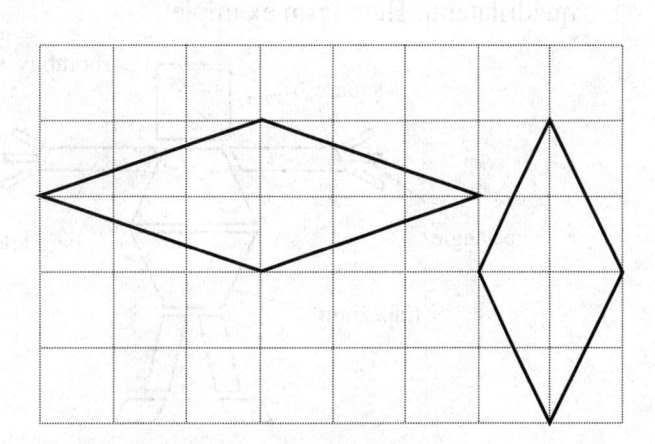

   Draw four different rhombuses.

186 Shape and Space 3

4. A quadrilateral with internal angles of 90° is called **rectangle**.

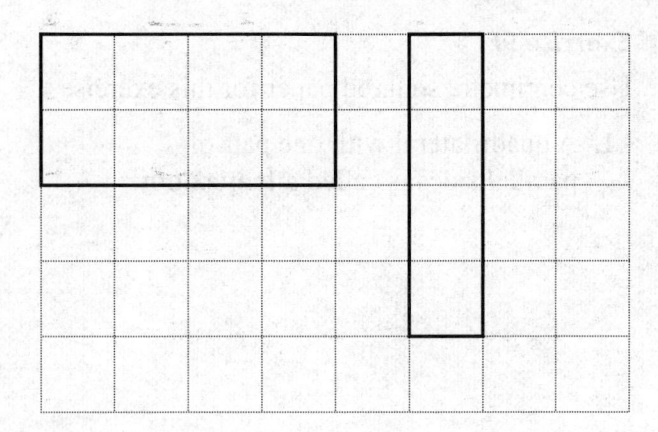

   Draw four different rectangles.

5. A quadrilateral with four equal sides **and** internal angles of 90° is called a **square**.

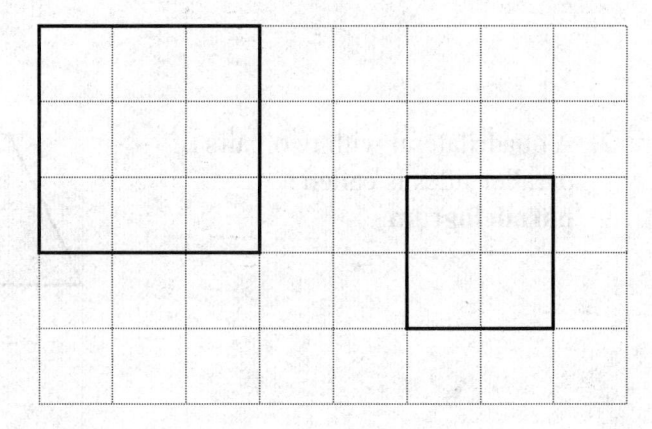

   Draw four different squares.

6. Draw a robot made up only from quadrilaterals. Use each type of quadrilateral at least once. Label one of each type of quadrilateral. Here is an example:

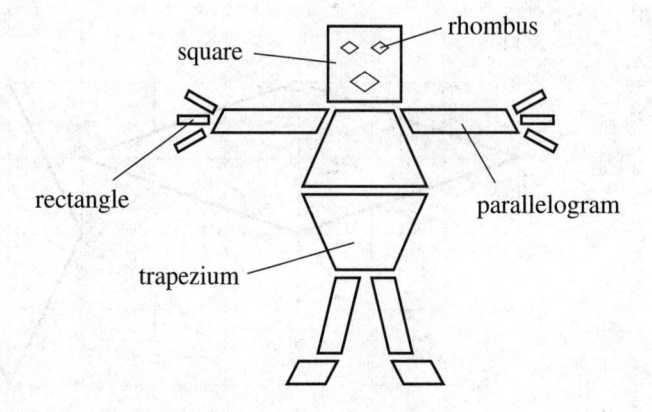

   square — rhombus — rectangle — parallelogram — trapezium

9.7 Polygons

A **polygon** is a shape with straight sides.

A triangle is a polygon with three sides.

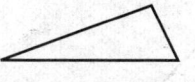

A quadrilateral is a polygon with four sides.

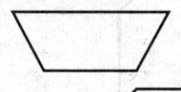

This is a polygon with six sides, called a **hexagon**.

A **regular** polygon has all its sides and angles equal. This is a regular polygon with five sides, called a **pentagon**.

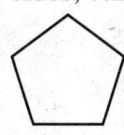

The angles inside a polygon are called interior angles. It also has exterior angles.

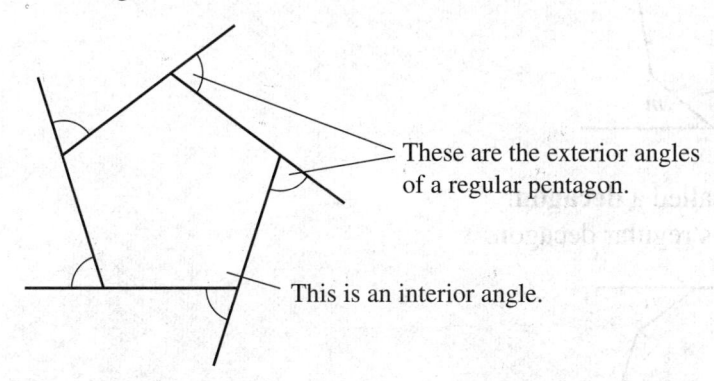

These are the exterior angles of a regular pentagon.

This is an interior angle.

The **exterior** angles of any polygon add up to 360°.
Each exterior angle of a regular pentagon is 360° ÷ 5 = 72°.
Each interior angle of the pentagon makes an angle of 180° with an exterior angle.
Each interior angle of a regular pentagon = 180° − 72° = 108°.

Example
Find the angles p and q in this regular hexagon.

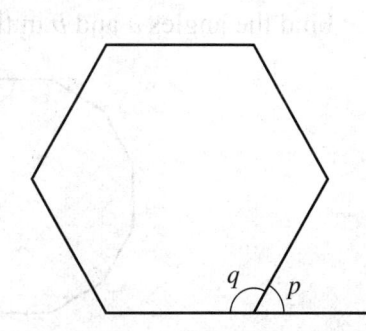

The exterior angles add up to 360°.
$p = 360 ÷ 6 = 60°$
Each interior angle makes an angle of 180° with an exterior angle.
$q = 180° − 60° = 120°$

Exercise 9G

1. A polygon with eight sides is called an **octagon**.
   Find the angles p and q in this regular octagon.

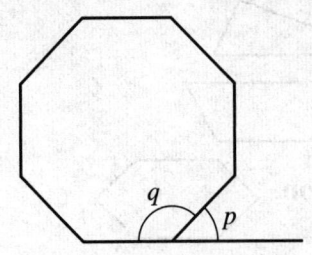

2. A polygon with nine sides is called a **nonagon**.
   Find the angles m and n in this regular nonagon.

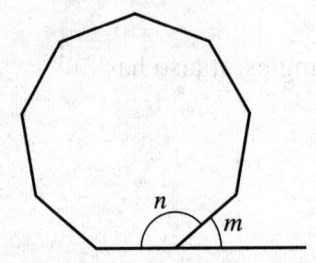

3. A polygon with ten sides is called a **decagon**.
   Find the angles c and d in this regular decagon.

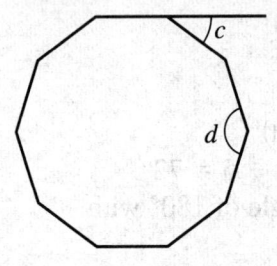

4. A polygon with twelve sides is called a **dodecagon**.
   Find the angles a and b in this regular dodecagon.

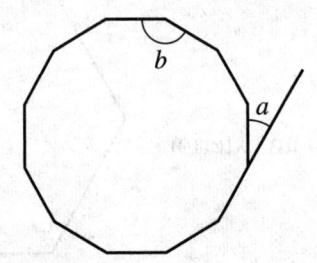

9.8 Angle sum of a polygon

The interior angles of any triangle add up to 180°.
There is a similar fixed sum for the interior angles of any other type of polygon.
You can find the sum by dividing the polygon into triangles.

Example

Find the sum of the interior angles in a pentagon.

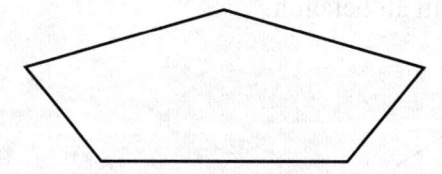

First, divide the pentagon into triangles.

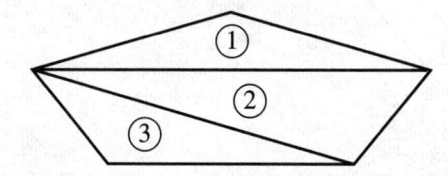

The interior angles in each triangle add up to 180°.
The interior angles in a pentagon add up to 3 × 180° = 540°.

Exercise 9H

1. Find the angle x in this pentagon.

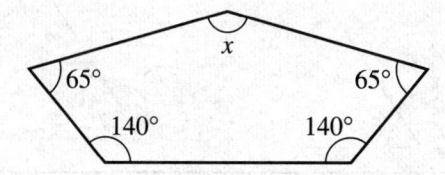

2. (a) Find the sum of the interior angles in a quadrilateral.
   (b) Find the angle a in this diagram.

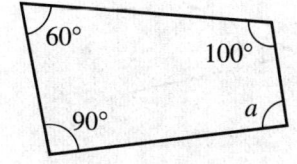

3. (a) Find the sum of the interior angles in a hexagon.
   (b) Find the angle z in this diagram.

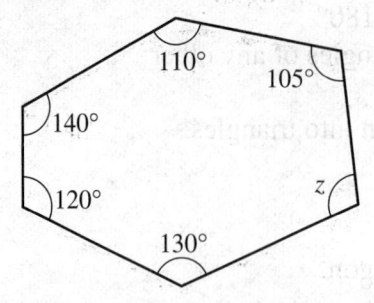

4. (a) Find the sum of the interior angles in an octagon.
   (b) Find the angle y in this diagram.

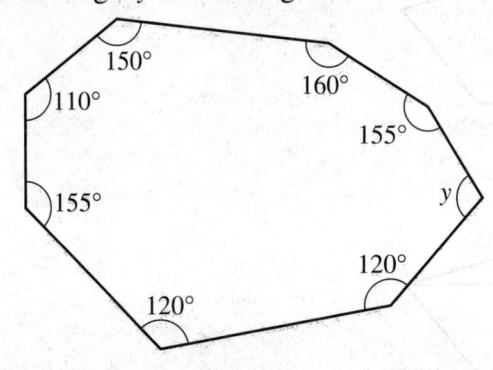

Summary and Checkout 9

- A right angle is 90°. A straight line is 180°. A circle is 360°. Missing angles can be found in right angles, straight lines and circles.

   1. Find the angles marked with letters.

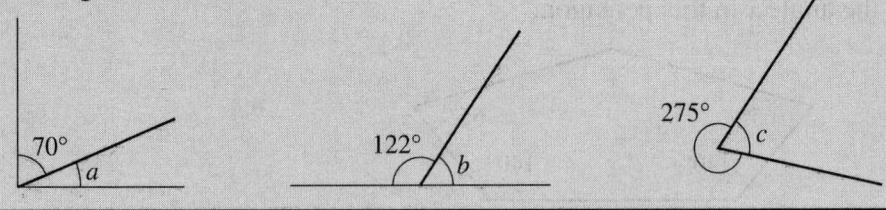

- Two pairs of opposite angles are created when straight lines cross. Pairs of opposite angles are always equal.

   2. Find the angles e, f and g.

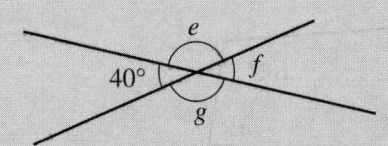

- When a pair of parallel lines is crossed by a third line, two sets of identical opposite angles are formed.

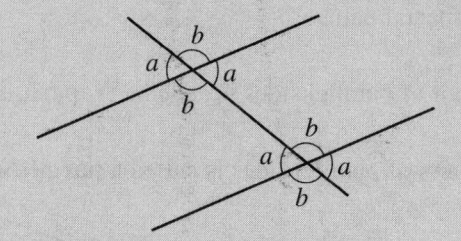

3. Find the angles marked with letters.

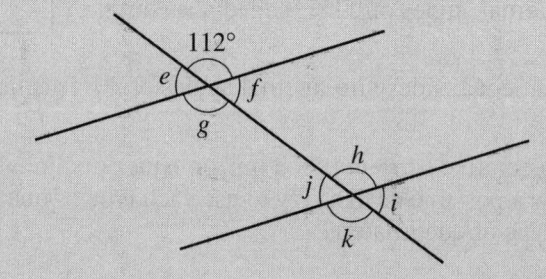

- The three angles in any triangle add up to 180°. If two angles are known, the third angle can be calculated.

   4. Find angle *a*.

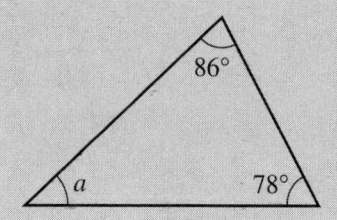

- An **isosceles** triangle has two equal sides and two equal angles. The equal angles are formed between the equal sides and the third side. The equal sides are usually marked with dashes. An **equilateral** triangle has three equal sides and three equal angles of 60°.

   5. Find each angle marked with a letter in these diagrams.

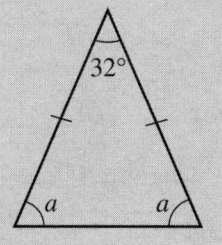

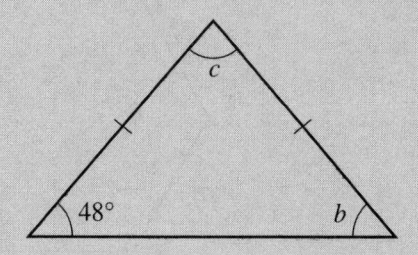

- A quadrilateral is a shape with four straight sides.

  Some quadrilaterals have special names.

  A quadrilateral with one pair of parallel sides is called a **trapezium**.

  A quadrilateral with two pairs of parallel sides is called a **parallelogram**.

  A quadrilateral with four equal sides is called a **rhombus**.

  A quadrilateral with internal angles of 90° is called a **rectangle**.

  A quadrilateral with four equal sides **and** internal angles of 90° is called a **square**.

  6. Lucy is making a decorative surround for a mirror using small mosaic tiles in the shape of quadrilaterals. Draw a possible design. Try to use each type of quadrilateral at least once. Label one of each type of quadrilateral.

- A **polygon** is a shape with straight sides.
  A **triangle** has three sides.
  A **quadrilateral** has four sides.
  A **pentagon** has five sides.
  A **hexagon** has six sides.
  A **heptagon** has seven sides.
  An **octagon** has eight sides.
  A **nonagon** has nine sides.
  A **decagon** has ten sides.
  A **dodecagon** has twelve sides.

  The exterior angles of any polygon add up to 360°.

  7. Find the angles p and q in this regular hexagon.

- There is a fixed sum for the interior angles of any polygon.
  You can calculate the sum by dividing the polygon into triangles.

  8. (a) Find the sum of the interior angles in a hexagon.
     (b) Find the angle z in this diagram.

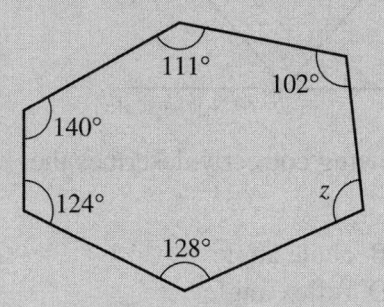

Revision exercise 9

1. Work out the sizes of the angles, p, q, r, s and t in the diagrams below.

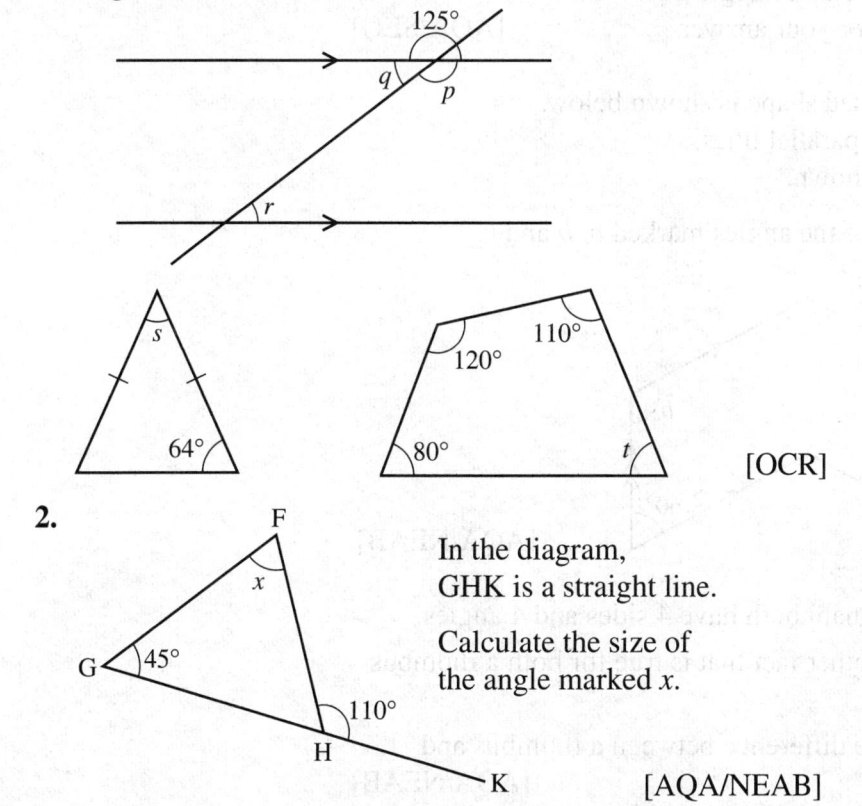

   [OCR]

2. In the diagram, GHK is a straight line.

   Calculate the size of the angle marked x.

   [AQA/NEAB]

3. AB is parallel to CD.
   CP = DP. Angle CPD = 110°.

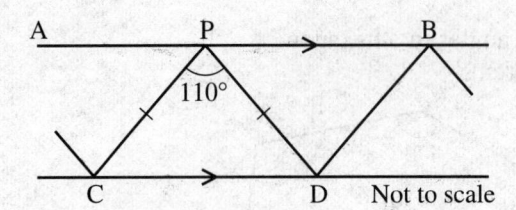

   (a) (i) Which of the following correctly describes the angle CPD?

   A right angle   B acute angle
   C obtuse angle D reflex angle

   (ii) Which of the following correctly describes the triangle CPD?

   A right angled B isosceles
   C equilateral   D scalene

   (b) Work out the size of angle CDP.

   (c) Write down the size of angle BPD.
   Give a reason for your answer.   [AQA/SEG]

4. A sketch of a six-sided shape is shown below.
   It has three pairs of parallel lines.
   An angle of 60° is shown.

   Work out the sizes of the angles marked a, b and c.

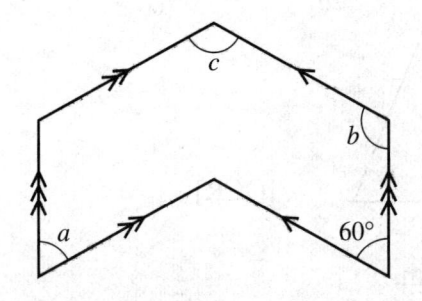

   [AQA/NEAB]

5. A rhombus and a square both have 4 sides and 4 angles.
   (a) Write down another fact that is true for both a rhombus and a square.
   (b) Write down one difference between a rhombus and a square.   [AQA/NEAB]

6. (a) The diagram shows a quadrilateral.

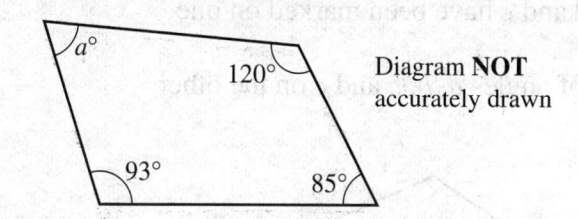

   Diagram **NOT** accurately drawn

   Work out the size of the angle marked $a°$.

   (b) The diagram shows a regular hexagon.

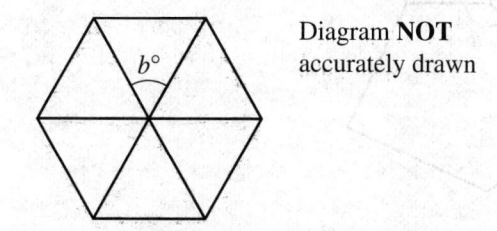

   Diagram **NOT** accurately drawn

   Work out the size of the angle marked $b°$.

   (c) The diagram shows a regular octagon.

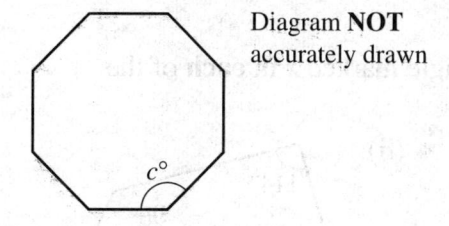

   Diagram **NOT** accurately drawn

   Work out the size of the angle marked $c°$.

   [Edexcel]

7. (a) This diagram shows a shape with 5 sides.

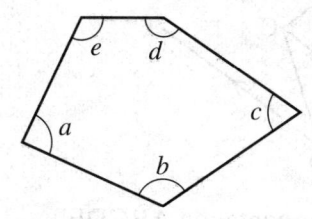

   (i) What is the mathematical name given to a shape with 5 sides?
   (ii) Explain why the shape in the diagram is **not** regular.

(b) Three of the shapes are fitted together.

(i) The angles a, b, c, d and e have been marked on one of the shapes.
Mark the positions of angles a, b, c and e on the other two shapes.

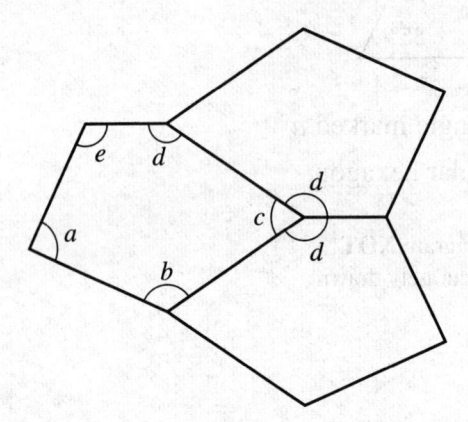

(ii) The three angles c, d and d fit together exactly.
Angle c is 66°.
Calculate the size of angle d.   [AQA/NEAB]

8. (a) Write down the size of the angle marked x in **each** of the following diagrams.

(i) 57°, x

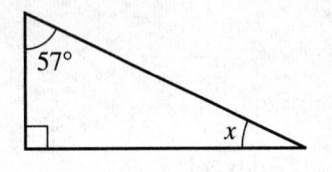

(ii) 114°, 96°, 65°, x

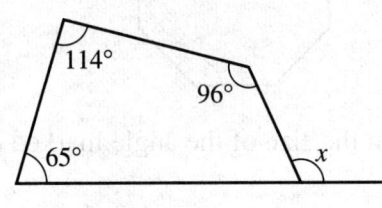

(b) 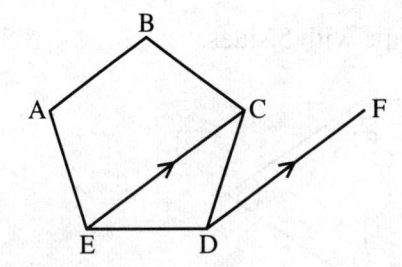 The above diagram shows a regular pentagon ABCDE, a diagonal EC and a line DF which is parallel to EC.
Each interior angle of the regular pentagon is 108°.
(i) Calculate the size of $\widehat{ECD}$.
(ii) Calculate the size $\widehat{CDF}$.   [WJEC]

9.

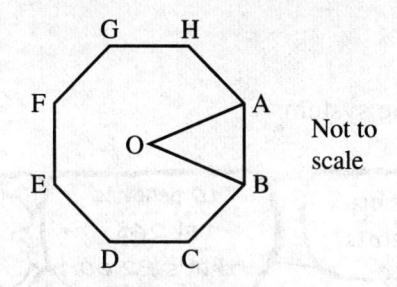

ABCDEFGH is a regular octagon with centre O.

(a) Calculate angle AOB. Show your working clearly.

(b) Calculate angle ABC. Show your working clearly. [OCR]

10. This is sketch of a regular pentagon with centre O.

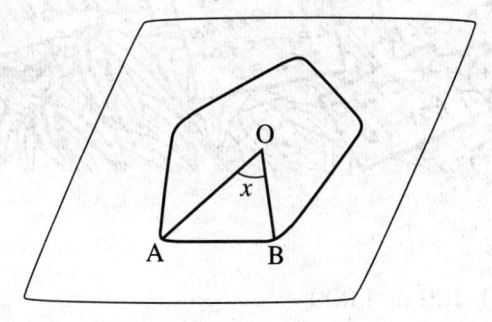

(a) Work out the size of angle x.

(b) What type of triangle is OAB? [OCR]

10 Number 4

Money, length and weight all use the metric system.

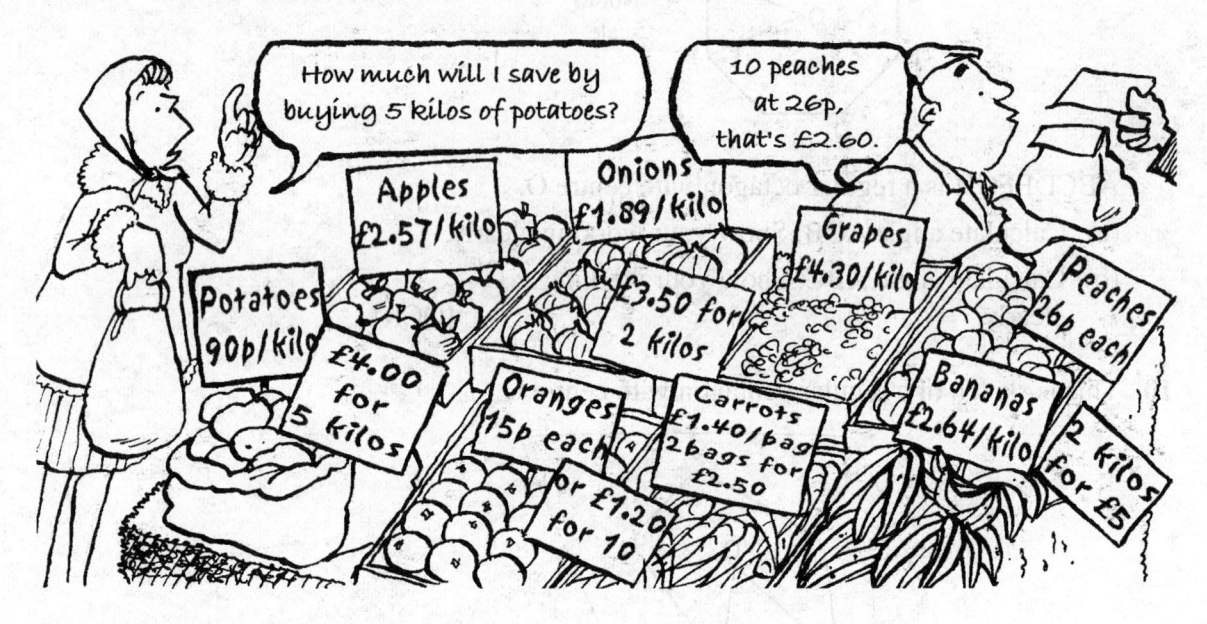

This unit is about:

- Multiplying decimal numbers by 10, 100 or 1 000
- Dividing decimal numbers by 10, 100 or 1 000
- Multiplying decimal numbers without a calculator
- Dividing decimal numbers without a calculator
- Recurring decimals
- Multiplying decimal numbers with a calculator
- Dividing decimal numbers with a calculator

You need to remember:

- How to multiply numbers
  1. Work out:
     (a) 34×7 (b) 23×5 (c) 48×17 (d) 234×26 (e) 345×72
- How to divide numbers
  2. Work out:
     (a) $120 \div 5$ (b) $261 \div 3$ (c) $576 \div 8$ (d) $450 \div 18$ (e) $714 \div 14$

10.1 Multiplying decimal numbers by 10

When a decimal number is multiplied by 10, all the digits move one place to the left, while the decimal point remains fixed.

Example

(a) $35 \times 10 = 350$

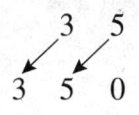

(b) $3.5 \times 10 = 35$

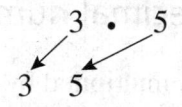

(c) $0.35 \times 10 = 3.5$

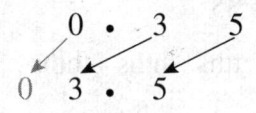

(d) $0.035 \times 10 = 0.35$

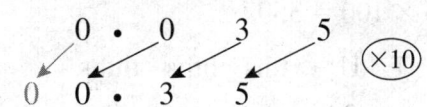

There are 10 millimetres (mm) in one centimetre (cm). To convert a length in centimetres to a length in millimetres, you multiply by 10.

Example

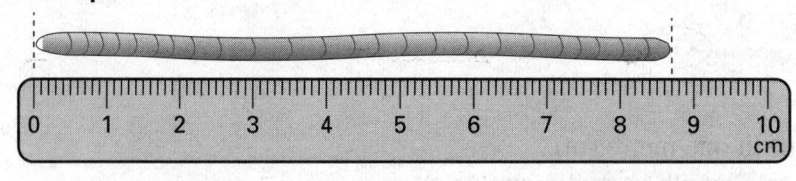

The length of the worm is 8·7 cm.

The length of the worm is also $8.7 \times 10 = 87$ mm.

Exercise 10A

1. Multiply each number by 10.
   - (a) 56
   - (b) 453
   - (c) 273
   - (d) 703
   - (e) 102
   - (f) 4·5
   - (g) 8·7
   - (h) 19·3
   - (i) 54·1
   - (j) 78·9
   - (k) 7·23
   - (l) 5·27
   - (m) 23·21
   - (n) 30·56
   - (o) 21·67
   - (p) 0·67
   - (q) 0·345
   - (r) 0·205
   - (s) 0·528
   - (t) 0·223
   - (u) 0·02
   - (v) 0·034 5
   - (w) 0·052
   - (x) 0·067 4
   - (y) 0·005 42

2. Change each length into millimetres.
   (a) 2 cm   (b) 6 cm   (c) 8 cm   (d) 1 cm   (e) 2·0 cm
   (f) 2·6 cm (g) 7·4 cm (h) 5·9 cm (i) 4·3 cm (j) 3·5 cm
   (k) 15·8 cm (l) 24·9 cm (m) 35·5 cm (n) 89·6 cm (o) 28·9 cm
   (p) 2·56 cm (q) 5·37 cm (r) 7·05 cm (s) 9·08 cm (t) 6·75 cm
   (u) 0·9 cm (v) 0·7 cm (w) 0·1 cm (x) 0·2 cm (y) 0·35 cm

10.2 Multiplying decimal numbers by 100

When a decimal number is multiplied by 100, all the digits move two places to the left, while the decimal point remains fixed.

Example
(a) $3·5 \times 100 = 350$

H T U • tths hths thths
    3 • 5
3 5 0   ×100

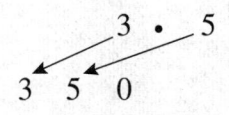

(b) $0·35 \times 100 = 35$

H T U • tths hths thths
    0 • 3 5
0 3 5   ×100

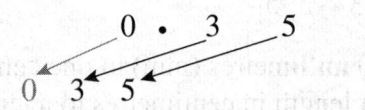

(c) $0·035 \times 100 = 3·5$

H T U • tths hths thths
    0 • 0 3 5
0 0 3 • 5   ×100

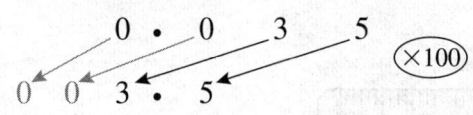

There are 100 centimetres (cm) in one metre (m).
To convert a length in metres to a length in centimetres, you multiply by 100.

Example

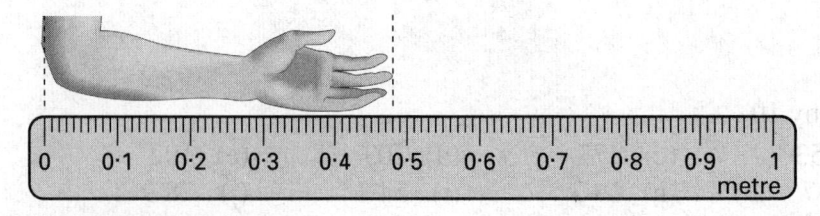

The length of the arm is 0·48 m.

The length of the arm is also $0·48 \times 100 = 48$ cm.

Exercise 10B

1. Multiply each number by 100.
   - (a) 7
   - (b) 6
   - (c) 57
   - (d) 123
   - (e) 347
   - (f) 4·5
   - (g) 7·8
   - (h) 3·4
   - (i) 18·7
   - (j) 27·3
   - (k) 5·67
   - (l) 7·31
   - (m) 19·56
   - (n) 0·83
   - (o) 34·51
   - (p) 0·537
   - (q) 0·347
   - (r) 0·524
   - (s) 0·564
   - (t) 0·231
   - (u) 0·032
   - (v) 0·076 1
   - (w) 0·093 2
   - (x) 0·072 5
   - (y) 0·001 5

2. Change all these lengths into centimetres.
   - (a) 2 m
   - (b) 5 m
   - (c) 3 m
   - (d) 4 m
   - (e) 1·0 m
   - (f) 1·5 m
   - (g) 1·7 m
   - (h) 2·5 m
   - (i) 8·9 m
   - (j) 7·6 m
   - (k) 15·3 m
   - (l) 29·5 m
   - (m) 32·8 m
   - (n) 27·5 m
   - (o) 34·1 m
   - (p) 5·64 m
   - (q) 9·25 m
   - (r) 8·63 m
   - (s) 9·34 m
   - (t) 7·31 m
   - (u) 0·25 m
   - (v) 0·37 m
   - (w) 0·83 m
   - (x) 0·62 m
   - (y) 0·77 m

10.3 Multiplying decimal numbers by 1 000

When a decimal number is multiplied by 1 000, all the digits move three places to the left, while the decimal point remains fixed.

Examples
(a) 358 × 1 000 = 358 000
(b) 35·8 × 1 000 = 35 800
(c) 3·58 × 1 000 = 3 580
(d) 0·358 × 1 000 = 358

Hint:
Use a place value table like this one:

TTh   Th   H   T   U   •   tths   hths   thths

There are 1 000 millilitres (ml) in one litre (ℓ).
To convert a volume in litres to a volume in millilitres, you multiply by 1 000.

Example

The volume of the cola is 0·330 ℓ.
The volume of the cola is also 0·330 × 1 000 = 330 ml.

Exercise 10C

1. Multiply each number by 1 000.
   - (a) 5
   - (b) 9
   - (c) 67
   - (d) 453
   - (e) 217·0
   - (f) 3·5
   - (g) 9·8
   - (h) 5·4
   - (i) 17·7
   - (j) 47·3
   - (k) 5·68
   - (l) 7·51
   - (m) 19·76
   - (n) 0·93
   - (o) 38·51
   - (p) 0·437
   - (q) 0·347
   - (r) 0·724
   - (s) 0·594
   - (t) 0·271
   - (u) 0·052 3
   - (v) 0·096 1
   - (w) 0·097 2
   - (x) 0·081 5
   - (y) 0·000 5

2. Change all these volumes into millilitres.
   - (a) 4 ℓ
   - (b) 1·5 ℓ
   - (c) 1·7 ℓ
   - (d) 15·3 ℓ
   - (e) 27·5 ℓ
   - (f) 9·34 ℓ
   - (g) 7·31 ℓ
   - (h) 0·250 ℓ
   - (i) 0·373 ℓ
   - (j) 6·258 ℓ

3. There are 1 000 metres (m) in one kilometre (km).
   Change all these lengths into metres.
   - (a) 5 km
   - (b) 2·4 km
   - (c) 4·5 km
   - (d) 12·5 km
   - (e) 18·4 km
   - (f) 45·9 km
   - (g) 7·45 km
   - (h) 0·526 km
   - (i) 0·573 km
   - (j) 9·456 km

4. There are 1 000 grams (g) in one kilogram (kg).
   Change all these weights into grams.
   - (a) 9 kg
   - (b) 6·4 kg
   - (c) 3·2 kg
   - (d) 14·7 kg
   - (e) 14·8 kg
   - (f) 32·8 kg
   - (g) 6·33 kg
   - (h) 0·585 kg
   - (i) 0·843 kg
   - (j) 7·540 kg

10.4 Dividing decimal numbers by 10

When a decimal number is divided by 10, all the digits move one place to the right, while the decimal point remains fixed.

Examples
(a) 3 580 ÷ 10 = 358
(b) 358 ÷ 10 = 35·8
(c) 35·8 ÷ 10 = 3·58
(d) 3·58 ÷ 10 = 0·358

Hint:
Use a place value table like this one:

Th H T U • tths hths thths
       3 5 •   8
       3 • 5   8   ÷10

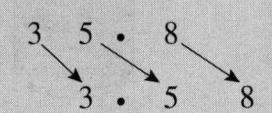

There are 10 millimetres (mm) in one centimetre (cm).
To convert a length in millimetres to a length in centimetres, you divide by 10.

Example

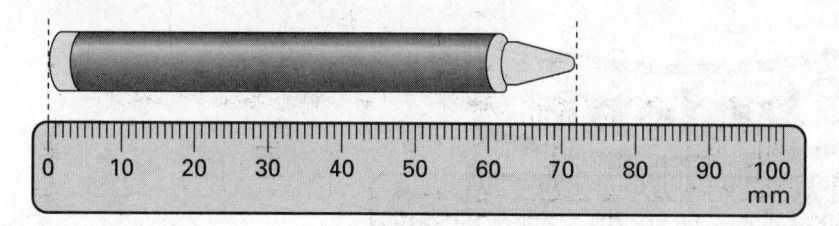

The length of the crayon is 72 mm.
The length of the crayon is also 72 ÷ 10 = 7·2 cm.

Exercise 10D

1. Divide each number by 10.
   - (a) 70
   - (b) 250
   - (c) 340
   - (d) 250
   - (e) 4 560
   - (f) 23
   - (g) 67
   - (h) 123
   - (i) 456
   - (j) 271
   - (k) 45·6
   - (l) 34·7
   - (m) 65·9
   - (n) 99·9
   - (o) 56·2
   - (p) 4·7
   - (q) 9·03
   - (r) 6·17
   - (s) 8·1
   - (t) 7·6
   - (u) 0·32
   - (v) 0·9
   - (w) 0·09
   - (x) 0·53
   - (y) 0·053

2. Change all these lengths into centimetres.
   - (a) 200 mm
   - (b) 600 mm
   - (c) 500 mm
   - (d) 100 mm
   - (e) 60 mm
   - (f) 260 mm
   - (g) 740 mm
   - (h) 590 mm
   - (i) 430 mm
   - (j) 350 mm
   - (k) 158 mm
   - (l) 249 mm
   - (m) 355 mm
   - (n) 896 mm
   - (o) 289 mm
   - (p) 25·6 mm
   - (q) 53·7 mm
   - (r) 70·5 mm
   - (s) 90·8 mm
   - (t) 67·5 mm

10.5 Dividing decimal numbers by 100

When a decimal number is divided by 100, all the digits move two places to the right, while the decimal point remains fixed.

Examples

(a) 3 580 ÷ 100 = 35·8
(b) 358 ÷ 100 = 3·58
(c) 35·8 ÷ 100 = 0·358

Hint:

H T U • tths hths thths
3 5 • 8   ÷100
      0 • 3 5 8

There are 100 centimetres (cm) in one metre (m).
To convert a length in centimetres to a length in metres, you divide by 100.

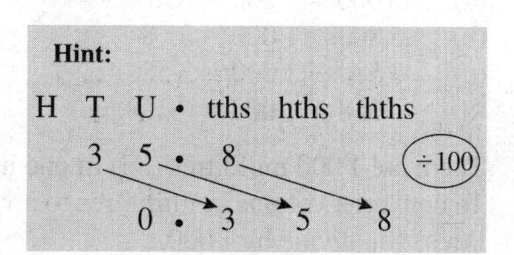

Example

The length of the banner is 89 cm.
The length of the banner is also 89 ÷ 100 = 0·89 m.

Exercise 10E

1. Divide each number by 100.
   (a) 700   (b) 2 500   (c) 3 400   (d) 2 500   (e) 45 600
   (f) 230   (g) 670   (h) 1 230   (i) 4 560   (j) 2 710
   (k) 456   (l) 347   (m) 659   (n) 999   (o) 562
   (p) 24·7   (q) 19·3   (r) 26·17   (s) 8·1   (t) 7·6
   (u) 0·32   (v) 0·9   (w) 0·09   (x) 0·53   (y) 0·053

2. Change all these lengths into metres.
   (a) 200 cm   (b) 600 cm   (c) 500 cm   (d) 100 cm   (e) 60 cm
   (f) 260 cm   (g) 740 cm   (h) 590 cm   (i) 430 cm   (j) 350 cm
   (k) 158 cm   (l) 249 cm   (m) 355 cm   (n) 896 cm   (o) 289 cm
   (p) 25·6 cm   (q) 53·7 cm   (r) 70·5 cm   (s) 90·8 cm   (t) 67·5 cm

10.6 Dividing decimal numbers by 1 000

When a decimal number is divided by 1 000, all the digits move three places to the right, while the decimal point remains fixed.

Examples

(a) 358 000 ÷ 1 000 = 358
(b) 35 800 ÷ 1 000 = 35·8
(c) 3 580 ÷ 1 000 = 3·58
(d) 358 ÷ 1 000 = 0·358

There are 1 000 millilitres (ml) in one litre (ℓ).
To convert a volume in millilitres to a volume in litres, you divide by 1 000.

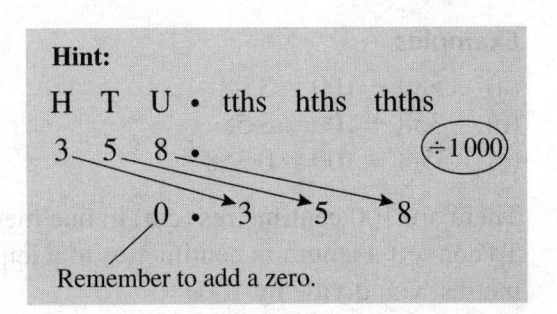

Hint:
H T U • tths hths thths
3 5 8 •   ÷ 1000
      0 • 3 5 8
Remember to add a zero.

Example

The volume of the cough medicine is 1 300 ml.

The volume of the cough medicine is also $1\,300 \div 1\,000 = 1·3\,\ell$.

Exercise 10F

1. Divide each number by 1 000.
   - (a) 5 000
   - (b) 9 000
   - (c) 3 500
   - (d) 9 800
   - (e) 5 400
   - (f) 17 700
   - (g) 47 300
   - (h) 5 680
   - (i) 7 550
   - (j) 9 374
   - (k) 3 856
   - (l) 437
   - (m) 271
   - (n) 52·3
   - (o) 96·1
   - (p) 9·72
   - (q) 8·1
   - (r) 5·7
   - (s) 9
   - (t) 11
   - (u) 0·5
   - (v) 1·9
   - (w) 0·17
   - (x) 0·05
   - (y) 3·142

2. Change all these volumes into litres.
   - (a) 400 ml
   - (b) 150 ml
   - (c) 170 ml
   - (d) 53 ml
   - (e) 25 ml
   - (f) 75 ml
   - (g) 750 ml
   - (h) 250 ml
   - (i) 500 ml
   - (j) 1 250 ml

3. There are 1 000 metres (m) in one kilometre (km).
   Change all these lengths into kilometres.
   - (a) 500 m
   - (b) 240 m
   - (c) 3 500 m
   - (d) 12 700 m
   - (e) 18 450 m
   - (f) 45 900 m
   - (g) 7 457 m
   - (h) 5 269 m
   - (i) 573·5 m
   - (j) 1 456·8 m

4. There are 1 000 grams (g) in one kilogram (kg).
   Change all these weights into kilograms.
   - (a) 900 g
   - (b) 640 g
   - (c) 320 g
   - (d) 147 g
   - (e) 148 g
   - (f) 1 328 g
   - (g) 1 633 g
   - (h) 2 585 g
   - (i) 3 843 g
   - (j) 7 500 g

10.7 Multiplying decimal numbers 'in your head'

Look at this calculation:

$$0.3 \times 4$$

You can use these rules to find the answer:

- Ignore any decimal points and multiply normally. → $3 \times 4 = 12$
- Count the number of digits after the decimal point(s) in the calculation. → There is 1 d.p. in 0.3
- Put the same number of digits after the decimal point in the answer. → $12 \rightarrow 1.2$

$$0.3 \times 4 = 1.2$$

One digit after the decimal point (for both 0.3 and 1.2)

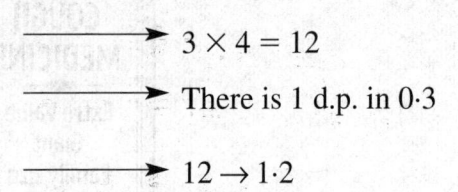

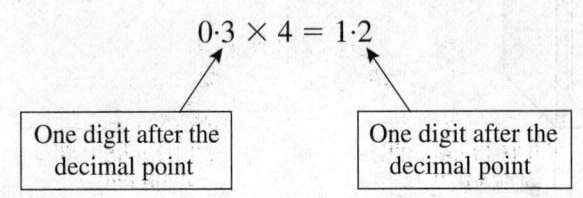

In the same way:

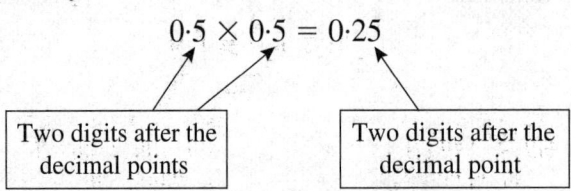

$$0.5 \times 0.5 = 0.25$$

Two digits after the decimal points (for both sides)

Examples

(a) $0.8 \times 2 = 1.6$ (b) $0.4 \times 0.5 = 0.20$ (c) $0.03 \times 7 = 0.21$
(d) $0.03 \times 0.7 = 0.021$ (e) $2.3 \times 2 = 4.6$ (f) $1.2 \times 0.4 = 0.48$

Exercise 10G

Do these in your head.

1. (a) 0.5×2 (b) 0.8×1 (c) 0.3×3 (d) 5×0.6 (e) 7×0.2
(f) 8×0.5 (g) 0.9×2 (h) 0.6×2 (i) 0.2×5 (j) 0.1×6
(k) 8×0.4 (l) 4×0.4 (m) 9×0.5 (n) 8×0.6 (o) 6×0.4
(p) 0.7×9 (q) 0.4×2 (r) 0.1×1 (s) 0.1×9 (t) 0.5×3

2. (a) 0.6×0.3 (b) 0.5×0.1 (c) 0.7×0.6 (d) 0.8×0.3 (e) 0.9×0.4
(f) 0.7×0.5 (g) 0.3×0.9 (h) 0.8×0.8 (i) 0.7×0.7 (j) 0.4×0.1
(k) 0.1×0.3 (l) 0.6×0.6 (m) 0.9×0.8 (n) 0.4×0.7 (o) 0.7×0.8
(p) 0.9×0.9 (q) 0.2×0.1 (r) 0.3×0.2 (s) 0.9×0.6 (t) 0.1×0.7

3. (a) 0.05×5 (b) 0.04×3 (c) 0.06×4 (d) 0.08×2 (e) 0.09×2
(f) 3×0.09 (g) 7×0.04 (h) 5×0.08 (i) 2×0.07 (j) 5×0.03
(k) 0.02×6 (l) 0.03×3 (m) 0.02×2 (n) 0.01×5 (o) 0.03×2
(p) 5×0.06 (q) 7×0.01 (r) 4×0.02 (s) 8×0.01 (t) 5×0.04

4. (a) 0.04×0.4 (b) 0.06×0.3 (c) 0.04×0.1 (d) 0.08×0.4 (e) 0.06×0.6
   (f) 0.03×0.1 (g) 0.6×0.01 (h) 0.7×0.6 (i) 0.8×0.08 (j) 0.9×0.06
   (k) 0.8×0.07 (l) 0.1×0.09 (m) 0.08×0.6 (n) 0.05×0.2 (o) 0.09×0.5
   (p) 0.07×0.9 (q) 0.08×0.9 (r) 0.07×0.7 (s) 0.7×0.03 (t) 0.8×0.03

5. (a) 1.2×3 (b) 1.1×4 (c) 2.2×2 (d) 1.5×3 (e) 1.3×3
   (f) 1.2×0.2 (g) 1.1×0.5 (h) 3.2×0.2 (i) 2.1×0.3 (j) 4.1×0.2
   (k) 0.32×2 (l) 0.22×4 (m) 5×0.11 (n) 2×0.42 (o) 3×0.33
   (p) 0.12×0.2 (q) 0.11×0.5 (r) 0.31×0.6 (s) 0.42×0.4 (t) 0.15×0.4

6. This board shows the prices at Runnigan's travelling fair.

   Find the cost of:
   (a) 3 rides on the Dodgems
   (b) 4 rides on the Big Wheel
   (c) 6 rides on the Tea Cups
   (d) 4 rides on the Waltzer
   (e) 8 rides on the Swing Boats
   (f) 5 rides on the Rockets

   RUNNIGAN'S FAIR
   Dodgems £1.20
   Big Wheel £1.50
   Tea Cups £0.60
   Waltzer £1.20
   Swing Boats £1.10
   Rockets £0.75

10.8 Multiplying decimal numbers with written calculations

If written calculations are needed, the same rules are used to place the point in the answer.

Examples

(a) 12.4×2

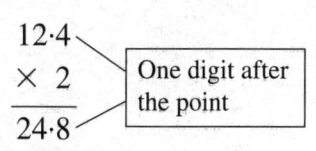

```
  12.4
×    2
  ────
  24.8
```
One digit after the point

(b) 4.72×8

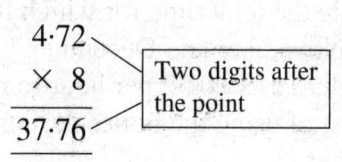

```
  4.72
×    8
  ────
 37.76
```
Two digits after the point

(c) 3.22×80

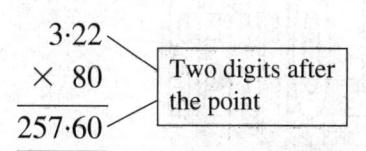

```
   3.22
×    80
  ─────
 257.60
```
Two digits after the point

(d) 4.63×8.5

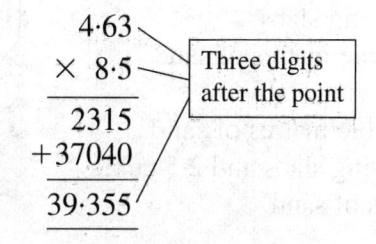

```
   4.63
×   8.5
  ─────
   2315
 +37040
  ─────
 39.355
```
Three digits after the point

Exercise 10H

Do these on paper.

1. (a) 4.5×7 (b) 5.6×8 (c) 3.9×5 (d) 8.2×5 (e) 4.7×6
   (f) 16.5×6 (g) 16.3×4 (h) 29.1×7 (i) 34.5×6 (j) 32.6×6

2. (a) 3.25×8 (b) 7.03×5 (c) 9.06×7 (d) 4.25×6 (e) 5.36×8
   (f) 7.08×6 (g) 6.24×5 (h) 8.77×3 (i) 4.65×9 (j) 2.45×6

3. (a) 5.7×40 (b) 7.2×80 (c) 5.4×90 (d) 2.7×50 (e) 3.8×90
   (f) 7.22×20 (g) 6.45×40 (h) 9.34×30 (i) 8.64×70 (j) 7.31×50

4. (a) 1.6×1.7 (b) 1.5×1.5 (c) 1.8×2.2 (d) 1.3×4.5 (e) 2.5×3.8
   (f) 4.51×7.6 (g) 6.03×1.4 (h) 8.25×1.7 (i) 1.25×1.8 (j) 4.26×7.2

5. A carpet used for hallways costs £8·56 per metre.
   Find the cost of carpeting hallways of length:
   (a) 3 m (b) 5 m (c) 20 m (d) 7·8 m (e) 14·2 m

6.
   ASSISTANT COOK
   £4·65 per hour
   To work 28 hours per week at
   John Mansfield School, Peterborough

   (a) How much will the assistant cook earn each week?
   (b) How much will the assistant cook earn if she works 38 weeks each year?

7. During November, a central heating boiler was used for 4·6 hours each day. During December, the same boiler was used for 5·4 hours each day.
   (a) Calculate the total time for which the boiler was used during November and December.
   (b) The boiler costs £0.52 per hour to run. Calculate the total cost of using the boiler during November and December.

8. Find the total cost of:
   (a) 24 paving slabs
   (b) 1·5 cubic metres of sand
   (c) 144 paving slabs
   (d) 3·2 cubic metres of sand
   (e) 30 paving slabs and 2·5 cubic metres of sand

   SPECIAL OFFER
   PAVING SLABS £1·45 each
   SAND £5·68 per cubic metre

10.9 Dividing decimal numbers without a calculator

In this example, the number you are dividing into has a decimal point.

Example

$3.15 \div 7$

$$\begin{array}{r} 0.45 \\ 7\overline{)3.15} \\ 2\ 8 \\ \overline{35} \\ 35 \\ \overline{0} \end{array}$$

The decimal point is directly above the decimal point in the calculation.

In this example, the number you are dividing into has no decimal point.

Example

$17 \div 4$

$$\begin{array}{r} 4.25 \\ 4\overline{)17.00} \\ 16 \\ \overline{1\ 0} \\ 8 \\ \overline{20} \\ 20 \\ \overline{0} \end{array}$$

A decimal point and zeros are added to the 17 so that division can continue past the decimal point. The decimal point is directly above the decimal point in the calculation.

Exercise 10I

Do these on paper.

1. (a) $19.2 \div 6$ (b) $6.5 \div 5$ (c) $10.8 \div 4$ (d) $24.3 \div 3$ (e) $12.8 \div 8$
   (f) $13.5 \div 5$ (g) $23.2 \div 4$ (h) $10.6 \div 2$ (i) $17.1 \div 3$ (j) $28.8 \div 6$
   (k) $2.24 \div 4$ (l) $1.74 \div 3$ (m) $7.44 \div 6$ (n) $0.45 \div 3$ (o) $5.04 \div 6$
   (p) $3.75 \div 3$ (q) $21.64 \div 4$ (r) $21.35 \div 7$ (s) $20.16 \div 9$ (t) $6.85 \div 5$

2. (a) $7 \div 2$ (b) $15 \div 4$ (c) $13 \div 4$ (d) $22 \div 5$ (e) $21 \div 2$
   (f) $67 \div 4$ (g) $18 \div 5$ (h) $37 \div 2$ (i) $33 \div 4$ (j) $18 \div 4$
   (k) $69 \div 2$ (l) $126 \div 5$ (m) $226 \div 4$ (n) $3 \div 4$ (o) $4 \div 5$
   (p) $1 \div 2$ (q) $1 \div 4$ (r) $9 \div 8$ (s) $7 \div 8$ (t) $13 \div 8$

3. A syndicate wins a lottery prize of £12 367. How much will each person get, correct to the nearest penny, if the number in the syndicate is:
   (a) 4 people (b) 8 people (c) 5 people (d) 2 people (e) 10 people?

10.10 Recurring decimals

Sometimes, no matter how many zeros you add, the answer repeats the same pattern over and over again. This is called a **recurring decimal**. The answer is written with dots over the recurring digits.

Examples

(a) $10.3 \div 3$

$$\begin{array}{r} 3.33 \\ 3\overline{)10.00} \\ \underline{9}\downarrow \\ 10 \\ \underline{9}\downarrow \\ 10 \end{array}$$

$10 \div 3 = 3.\dot{3}$

(b) $13.6 \div 6$

$$\begin{array}{r} 2.266 \\ 6\overline{)13.6000} \\ \underline{12}\downarrow \\ 16 \\ \underline{12}\downarrow \\ 40 \\ \underline{36}\downarrow \\ 40 \\ \underline{36}\downarrow \\ 40 \end{array}$$

$13.6 \div 6 = 2.2\dot{6}$

Exercise 10J

1. Do these on paper.
   (a) $16 \div 3$ (b) $14 \div 6$ (c) $25 \div 9$ (d) $136 \div 3$ (e) $137 \div 3$
   (f) $23 \div 6$ (g) $25 \div 6$ (h) $41 \div 3$ (i) $12 \div 9$ (j) $31 \div 9$
   (k) $4.9 \div 9$ (l) $7.1 \div 9$ (m) $12.5 \div 3$ (n) $6.2 \div 6$ (o) $1.21 \div 3$
   (p) $0.7 \div 6$ (q) $0.22 \div 3$ (r) $0.28 \div 9$ (s) $0.4 \div 6$ (t) $0.4 \div 3$

2. Chantal, Jo and Laura always share equally the taxi fare home on Friday night. How much does each pay, correct to the nearest penny, if the fare is:
   (a) £14 (b) £17 (c) £18·50 (d) £15·40 (e) £14·80?

10.11 Multiplying decimal numbers with a calculator

To complete the calculation 3·56 × 1·2, you press the keys:

| 3 | · | 5 | 6 | × | 1 | · | 2 | = |

The answer is 4·272

You often need to round the answer given by a calculator.

Suppose the calculation was to solve the problem,
'Find the cost of 1·2 kg of cheese at £3·56 a kg'.
The answer will be £4·27 to the nearest penny.

Exercise 10K

Use a calculator to solve these.

1. Give the full answer to each calculation and also the answer correct to one decimal place.
   - (a) 1·5 × 3·7
   - (b) 56·1 × 24·3
   - (c) 17·3 × 5·7
   - (d) 1·85 × 0·7
   - (e) 26·5 × 9·6
   - (f) 7·5 × 9·1
   - (g) 67·3 × 24·2
   - (h) 3·14 × 13·1
   - (i) 34·7 × 6·4
   - (j) 74·5 × 16·3
   - (k) 9·2 × 30·7
   - (l) 45·3 × 9·8
   - (m) 12·9 × 8·4
   - (n) 3·14 × 8·32
   - (o) 51·6 × 8·67
   - (p) 3·14 × 13·6
   - (q) 7·5 × 56·33
   - (r) 67·8 × 19·1
   - (s) 85·4 × 40·3
   - (t) 56·7 × 89·39

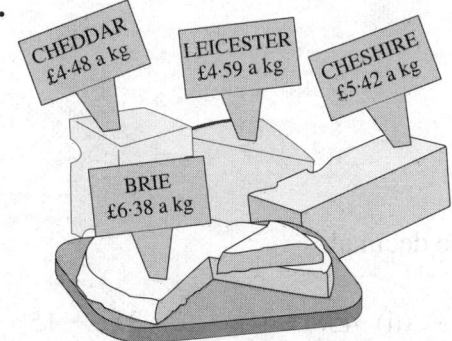

2.
   CHEDDAR £4·48 a kg
   LEICESTER £4·59 a kg
   CHESHIRE £5·42 a kg
   BRIE £6·38 a kg

   Find the cost, to the nearest penny, of:
   - (a) 1·3 kg of Cheddar
   - (b) 0·8 kg of Leicester
   - (c) 0·5 kg of Cheshire
   - (d) 1·1 kg of Brie
   - (e) 0·7 kg of Cheddar
   - (f) 0·25 kg of Cheshire
   - (g) 0·3 kg of Brie
   - (h) 1·25 kg of Leicester
   - (i) 0·45 kg of Cheshire
   - (j) 0·36 kg of Brie
   - (k) 0·28 kg of Cheddar
   - (l) 0·54 kg of Leicester

3. A television can be bought for £234 cash or with a £23·40 deposit and 12 monthly payments of £22·80.
   (a) How much does it cost to buy the television by monthly payments?
   (b) How much cheaper is it to pay cash for the television?

4. A roll of cloth is sold at £4·58 per metre. Find the cost of the following lengths of the cloth:
   (a) 5 m   (b) 3·8 m   (c) 2·5 m   (d) 0·9 m   (e) 4·7 m

10.12 Dividing decimal numbers with a calculator

To complete the calculation 3·56 ÷ 1·2, you press the keys:

| 3 | . | 5 | 6 | ÷ | 1 | . | 2 | = |

The answer is 2·9666667 (on an eight-digit calculator).

You often need to round the answer given by a calculator.

Suppose the calculation was to solve the problem,

'A piece of cheese weighing 1·2 kg costs £3·56, find the cost per kg'.

The answer will be £2·97 to the nearest penny.

Exercise 10L
Solve these using a calculator.

1. Give the answer to each calculation correct to one decimal place.
   (a) 35 ÷ 11   (b) 45 ÷ 8   (c) 137 ÷ 9   (d) 458 ÷ 12   (e) 311 ÷ 15
   (f) 13·5 ÷ 7   (g) 8·9 ÷ 17   (h) 56·7 ÷ 16   (i) 68·9 ÷ 46   (j) 234·56 ÷ 53
   (k) 15 ÷ 0·9   (l) 64 ÷ 1·1   (m) 125 ÷ 4·6   (n) 364 ÷ 5·8   (o) 100 ÷ 1·3
   (p) 16·7 ÷ 8·6 (q) 1·23 ÷ 6·7 (r) 8·19 ÷ 1·13 (s) 33·28 ÷ 3·1 (t) 0·452 ÷ 1·9

2. The total cost of a school trip to London will be £463·80. Find the cost per student (to the nearest penny) if the number going on the trip is:
   (a) 32   (b) 38   (c) 43   (d) 41   (e) 47

3. A teacher buys a box of 60 sweatshirts for £280.
   (a) How much does each sweatshirt cost?
   (b) How much must the teacher sell each sweatshirt for if she wants to make a £200 profit for the school?

4. A car is travelling at 95 kilometres per hour.
   (a) How many metres will the car travel in one hour at this speed?
   (b) How many metres will the car travel in one minute at this speed?
   (c) How many metres will the car travel in one second at this speed?

10.13 Metric and Imperial measure

Most of the measurements we use are metric, that is they are based on the decimal system.
There are still some imperial measures in use such as miles, feet and pints.
You need to know approximate conversions between metric and imperial units.
This table shows the conversions you need to know.

	Approximate conversions
Length	1 inch ≈ 2·54 cm 1 mile ≈ 1·61 km
Mass	1 pound ≈ 454 g 1 kilogram ≈ 2·21 pounds
Capacity	1 gallon ≈ 4·55 litres 1 litre ≈ 1·76 pints

The symbol ≈ stands for 'is approximately equal to'. The measurement given is a good working estimate.

Example
Natalie drives a distance of 12 miles.
Roughly how many kilometres (km) has she driven?
Give your answer to 1 decimal place.

   1 mile ≈ 1·61 km
   12 × 1·61 = 19·32
   Natalie has driven roughly 19·3 km.

Exercise 10M
1. Convert these distances to kilometres. Give your answer to 1 dp.
   (a) 10 miles   (b) 4 miles   (c) 25 miles   (d) 8·5 miles

2. A jam making plant uses 420 lb of sugar an hour.
   Roughly how many kilograms is this?

3. A watering can holds 3 Imperial gallons.
   Approximately how many litres of water will the watering can hold?

4. The length of a carpet is measured as 4′ 8″.
   (a) Roughly what is this in centimetres?
   (b) Roughly how long is the carpet in metres?

   > 4′ stands for 4 feet and 8″ stands for 8 inches.
   > 12 inches = 1 foot

5. For a flight an aircraft has 3 850 litres of fuel.
   (a) Roughly how many gallons is this?
   (b) Jim estimates that the aircraft has about 2 200 pints of fuel.
       Is this a good estimate? Explain your answer.

6. A man gives his weight as 168 lb.
   What is his weight in kilograms?

Summary

1. When a decimal number is multiplied by 10, all the digits move one place to the left, while the decimal point remains fixed.

2. There are 10 millimetres (mm) in one centimetre (cm).

3. When a decimal number is multiplied by 100, all the digits move two places to the left, while the decimal point remains fixed.

4. There are 100 centimetres (cm) in one metre (m).

5. When a decimal number is multiplied by 1 000, all the digits move three places to the left, while the decimal point remains fixed.

6. There are 1 000 millilitres (ml) in one litre (ℓ).

Checkout 10

1. Multiply each number by 10:
   (a) 13·45   (b) 0·25
   (c) 1·034

2. Change each length into millimetres:
   (a) 3·4 cm   (b) 13·8 cm
   (c) 9·6 cm

3. Multiply each number by 100:
   (a) 13·45   (b) 0·253
   (c) 1·034

4. Change each length into centimetres:
   (a) 3·42 m   (b) 13·08 m
   (c) 9·67 m

5. Multiply each number by 1 000:
   (a) 13·45   (b) 0·253
   (c) 1·532 4

6. Change each volume into millilitres:
   (a) 3·42 ℓ (b) 3·108 ℓ
   (c) 0·35 ℓ

7. When a decimal number is divided by 10, all the digits move one place to the right, while the decimal point remains fixed.

7. (a) Divide each number by 10:
   (i) 13·4 (ii) 25 (iii) 1·34
   (b) Change each length into centimetres:
   (i) 45 mm (ii) 127 mm (iii) 6 mm

8. When a decimal number is divided by 100, all the digits move two places to the right, while the decimal point remains fixed.

8. (a) Divide each number by 100:
   (i) 134·8 (ii) 25·3 (iii) 1·4
   (b) Change each length into metres:
   (i) 342 cm (ii) 35 cm
   (iii) 196 cm

9. When a decimal number is divided by 1 000, all the digits move three places to the right, while the decimal point remains fixed.

9. (a) Divide each number by 1 000:
   (i) 1 345 (ii) 253 (iii) 1.5
   (b) Change each volume into litres:
   (i) 1 342 ml (ii) 310 ml
   (iii) 35 ml

10. To find the answer to a decimal multiplication:
    - Ignore any decimal points and multiply normally.
    - Count the number of digits after the decimal point(s) in the calculation.
    - Put the same number of digits after the decimal point in the answer.

10. (a) Do these in your head.
    (i) $0·5 \times 3$
    (ii) $6 \times 0·2$
    (iii) $0·3 \times 0·4$
    (iv) $0·6 \times 0·05$
    (v) $1·2 \times 4$
    (vi) $0·9 \times 11$
    (vii) $1·2 \times 0·3$
    (viii) $2·4 \times 0·04$
    (b) Do these on paper.
    (i) $4·8 \times 7$
    (ii) $2·35 \times 9$
    (iii) $1·25 \times 1·8$
    (iv) $4·26 \times 3·2$

11. When dividing decimals, zeros are added so that division can continue past the decimal point. The decimal point in the answer is directly above the decimal point in the calculation.

11. Do these on paper.
    (a) $4·5 \div 5$ (b) $5·04 \div 6$
    (c) $21·42 \div 7$ (d) $0·48 \div 3$
    (e) $23 \div 4$ (f) $15 \div 8$

12. A **recurring decimal** repeats the same pattern over and over again. The answer is written with dots over the recurring digits.

12. Do these on paper.
    (a) $17 \div 3$ (b) $0·4 \div 6$
    (c) $12·5 \div 9$ (d) $1·21 \div 6$

13. Calculator answers often need to be rounded.

13. (a) Calculate correct to 1 decimal place:
    (i) 13×16.89
    (ii) 2.7×1.05
    (iii) 85.3×17.4
    (iv) 4.58×16
    (v) $13 \div 16.89$
    (vi) $2.7 \div 1.05$
    (vii) $85.3 \div 17.4$
    (viii) $4.58 \div 16$
   (b) Calculate correct to 2 decimal places:
    (i) 3.45×1.31
    (ii) 3.207×17
    (iii) 6.83×1.2
    (iv) 3.5×3.08
    (v) $3.45 \div 1.31$
    (vi) $3.207 \div 17$
    (vii) $6.83 \div 1.2$
    (viii) $3.5 \div 3.08$

Revision exercise 10

1. Tickets for a football match cost £4·70 each.

   (a) How much will 100 tickets cost?

   Children can buy tickets at half price.
   Mr and Mrs Smith and their two children buy tickets.

   (b) Work out the total cost of the tickets. [Edexcel]

2. Jim is making a cake.
   He opens a new 1·5 kg bag of flour.
   He uses 250 g of flour.
   How many grams of flour does he have left? [OCR]

3. John measured his father's height.
   It was 187.
   Is the 187 in metres or in centimetres or in millimetres?
   [WJEC]

4. Human hair grows approximately 1 cm per month.
   Donna wants to grow her hair to waist length.
   It will have to grow another 0·3 metre.
   How many years will it take for Donna's hair to grow to waist length? [AQA/NEAB]

5. The usual price of a film is £2·98.
   Winston bought a special offer pack of 4 for £8·95.
   (a) How much did each film actually cost him?
       Give your answer to the nearest penny.
   (b) How much did Winston save on the usual price of each
       film? [OCR]

6. Tom went on a day trip to France.
   (a) On the ferry he changed £120 into francs.
       The exchange rate was £1 = 7·80 francs.
       How many francs did he get for his £120?
   (b) On his return he had 200 francs left.
       He changed them back into pounds at the rate of 7·95 francs.
       How much did he get to the nearest penny? [OCR]

7. Chocolate bars cost 35p each.
   (a) Jason buys 5 bars.
       How much change does Jason get from £5?
   (b) How many bars of chocolate can Jason buy with £5?
   (c) A bag contains 1·1 kg of chocolate bars. Each bar weighs 55 g.
       How many chocolate bars are in the bag? [AQA/SEG]

8. Louise and Colin go to Portugal for their holiday.
   Louise changes £250 into escudos and Colin changes £200 into escudos.
   The exchange rate is £1 = 300 escudos.
   (a) How many escudos do they each get?
   (b) At the end of their holiday Louise has 1 500 escudos left
       and Colin has 1 100 escudos left.
       They put their escudos together and go to the bank to
       change them into pounds.
       The bank changes escudos into pounds at the rate 325 escudos = £1.
       How many pounds do they get? [WJEC]

9. (a) A calculator display gives the value of π as 3·141 592 7.
       Write down this value of π correct to four decimal places.
   (b) A two kilogram bar of Chocco costs £5·72.
       A one pound bar of Chocco costs £1·45.
       Which bar of Chocco gives the better value for money?
       You must show your working.
   (c) You are asked to find the capacity of a teacup.
       State the units in which you would give your answer. [OCR]

10. Three sizes of cola are sold in a garage shop.
The volume in millilitres and the cost in pence are shown under each one.

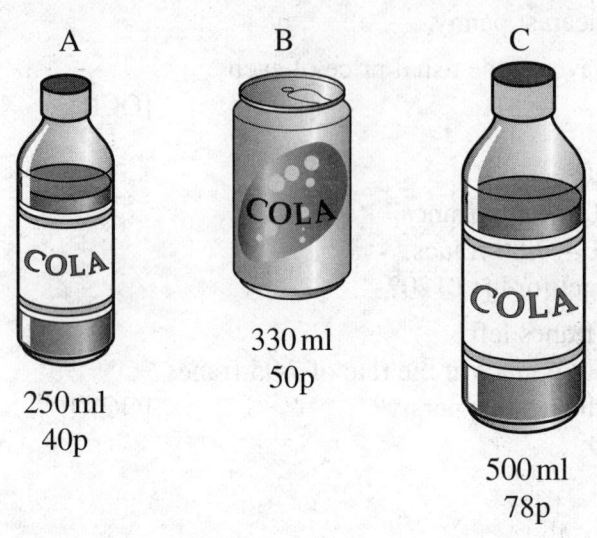

A — 250 ml, 40p
B — 330 ml, 50p
C — 500 ml, 78p

(a) Work out how many millitres of cola you get for 1p in bottle A.

(b) Which size gives you best value?
Show your working clearly. [OCR]

11. Sian shops at a supermarket and is given the following bill.

Item	Cost
1 jar of honey	£ 1·76
2·5 kilograms of new potatoes at 36p/kg	
2 jars of tea at £1·98 per jar	£ 3·96
Topside of beef	£11·45
3 packets of Weetabix at £1·54 per packet	
Total	£

(a) Copy the bill and complete the spaces.

(b) The supermarket gives 1 saver point for every complete £5 spent.
How many saver points does Sian get with the above bill? [WJEC]

12. This is a supermarket bill.

COSTCUT		22/5/98
2 litres of milk	52p per litre	£1·04
30 eggs	12p per egg	£36·00
3 jars of coffee	£4·20 per jar	£12·60
	Total	£49·64

   The bill is incorrect.
   (a) Which values in the right-hand column are wrong?
   (b) Calculate the correct total of the bill. [OCR]

13. Copy and complete the following bill.

    2 shirts costing £14·99 each   £........·........
    2 ties costing £8·49 each   £........·........
                           Total   £........·........
    [WJEC]

14. Pam, Margaret, Howard and John had a meal together.
    This was the menu.

    Menu

Chef's pate	£1·80
Soup	£1·30
Roast beef	£6·75
Salmon	£5·95
Lentil crumble	£4·75
Fresh strawberries	£1·75
Chocolate gateau	£1·95
Ice cream	£1·05

    They had 4 soups;
              2 roast beef, 1 salmon and 1 lentil crumble;
              3 fresh strawberries and 1 ice cream.
    They also had a bottle of wine costing £6·50.
    They agreed to share the bill equally among them.
    How much did each one pay? [OCR]

11 Algebra 2

Equations in algebra are all about balancing.

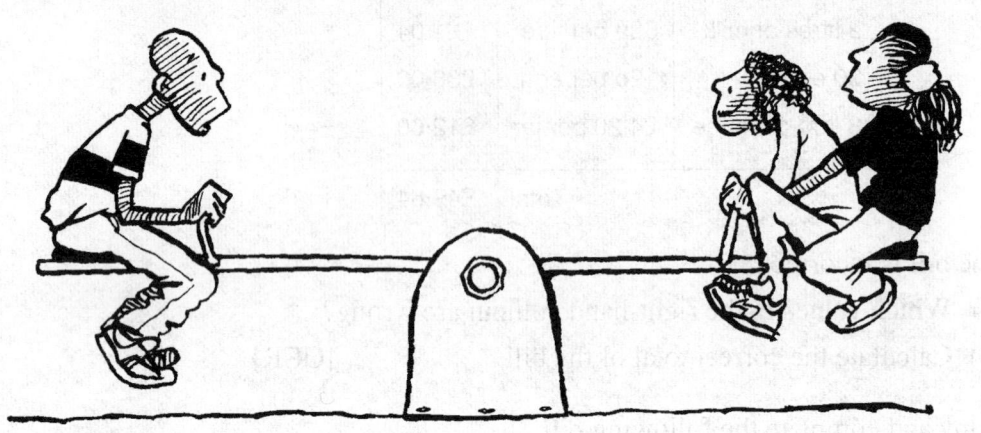

This unit is about:

- Multiplying and dividing negative numbers
- Multiplying terms
- Expanding brackets
- Factorisation
- Solving equations

You need to remember:

- How to add and subtract negative numbers (see Unit 1).
  1. Write down the answers to:

     (a) $7 + 4$ (b) $7 + {}^-4$ (c) ${}^-7 + 4$ (d) ${}^-7 + {}^-4$
     (e) $7 - 4$ (f) ${}^-7 - 4$ (g) $7 - {}^-4$ (h) ${}^-7 - {}^-4$
     (i) $3 + 12$ (j) $3 + -12$ (k) ${}^-3 + 12$ (l) ${}^-3 + {}^-12$
     (m) $3 - 12$ (n) ${}^-3 - 12$ (o) $3 - {}^-12$ (p) ${}^-3 - {}^-12$

- Some rules of algebra (see Unit 5).

  $3a$ means $3 \times a$ xy means $x \times y$ $2ab$ means $2 \times a \times b$

  $\dfrac{x}{y}$ means $x \div y$ x^2 means $x \times x$ y^3 means $y \times y \times y$

  2. If $x = 4$, $y = 5$, and $z = {}^-2$, find the value of:

     (a) $x + y$ (b) $3x$ (c) $5y$ (d) $7z$ (e) $7x + 3y$
     (f) $4x + 2z$ (g) xy (h) $4xy$ (i) x^2 (j) y^3

11.1 Multiplying negative numbers

A multiplication with one negative and one positive number gives a negative answer.

Example
(a) $4 \times {}^-3 = {}^-12$ (b) ${}^-5 \times 5 = {}^-25$

A multiplication with two negative numbers gives a positive answer.

Example
(a) ${}^-4 \times {}^-3 = 12$ (b) ${}^-5 \times {}^-5 = 25$

Exercise 11A

1. $4 \times {}^-2$
2. $5 \times {}^-3$
3. $2 \times {}^-3$
4. ${}^-3 \times 2$
5. $4 \times {}^-4$
6. $6 \times {}^-3$
7. $8 \times {}^-2$
8. $9 \times {}^-3$
9. $5 \times {}^-4$
10. $6 \times {}^-1$
11. ${}^-3 \times 8$
12. ${}^-2 \times 6$
13. ${}^-7 \times 4$
14. ${}^-8 \times 5$
15. ${}^-9 \times 1$
16. ${}^-7 \times 3$
17. ${}^-8 \times 4$
18. ${}^-7 \times 5$
19. ${}^-9 \times 2$
20. ${}^-10 \times 3$
21. ${}^-3 \times {}^-3$
22. ${}^-3 \times {}^-1$
23. ${}^-1 \times {}^-7$
24. ${}^-8 \times {}^-6$
25. ${}^-9 \times {}^-5$
26. ${}^-9 \times {}^-7$
27. ${}^-4 \times {}^-9$
28. ${}^-5 \times {}^-6$
29. ${}^-5 \times {}^-1$
30. ${}^-7 \times {}^-2$
31. ${}^-9 \times {}^-6$
32. ${}^-6 \times {}^-7$
33. ${}^-8 \times 8$
34. $9 \times {}^-9$
35. ${}^-9 \times 8$
36. ${}^-1 \times {}^-8$
37. $4 \times {}^-6$
38. ${}^-6 \times 6$
39. $2 \times {}^-2$
40. ${}^-7 \times {}^-7$

11.2 Dividing negative numbers

A division with one negative and one positive number gives a negative answer.

Example
(a) ${}^-12 \div 3 = {}^-4$ (b) $24 \div {}^-6 = {}^-4$

A division with two negative numbers gives a positive answer.

Example
(a) ${}^-12 \div {}^-3 = 4$ (b) ${}^-24 \div {}^-6 = 4$

Exercise 11B

1. $^-16 \div 4$
2. $^-12 \div 6$
3. $^-32 \div 8$
4. $^-42 \div 6$
5. $^-15 \div 3$
6. $^-56 \div 8$
7. $^-24 \div 6$
8. $^-9 \div 3$
9. $^-27 \div 9$
10. $^-45 \div 5$
11. $24 \div ^-3$
12. $63 \div ^-9$
13. $35 \div ^-7$
14. $4 \div ^-2$
15. $81 \div ^-9$
16. $21 \div ^-7$
17. $20 \div ^-5$
18. $18 \div ^-2$
19. $18 \div ^-9$
20. $14 \div ^-7$
21. $^-14 \div ^-7$
22. $^-30 \div ^-6$
23. $^-40 \div ^-8$
24. $^-48 \div ^-6$
25. $^-49 \div ^-7$
26. $^-6 \div ^-3$
27. $^-10 \div ^-5$
28. $^-18 \div ^-6$
29. $^-8 \div ^-4$
30. $^-4 \div ^-1$
31. $^-5 \div 1$
32. $5 \div ^-1$
33. $^-5 \div ^-1$
34. $16 \div ^-8$
35. $^-16 \div 8$
36. $^-16 \div ^-8$
37. $^-36 \div 9$
38. $28 \div ^-7$
39. $^-54 \div ^-9$
40. $^-64 \div ^-8$

11.3 Multiplying letter terms by number terms

To multiply a letter term by a number term, write out in full what the multiplication means and then simplify.

Example 1
$3 \times 2a = 3 \times 2 \times a = 6 \times a = 6a$

Remember, a multiplication with one negative and one positive number gives a negative answer.

Example 2
(a) $4 \times ^-3b = 4 \times ^-3 \times b = ^-12 \times b = ^-12b$

(b) $^-5 \times 6z = ^-5 \times 6 \times z = ^-30 \times z = ^-30z$

Remember, a multiplication with two negative numbers gives a positive answer.

Example 3
$^-4 \times ^-3x = ^-4 \times ^-3 \times x = 12 \times x = 12x$

Exercise 11C

1. $4 \times 2x$
2. $6y \times 3$
3. $7 \times 2p$
4. $5 \times 5a$
5. $6z \times 6$
6. $8u \times 3$
7. $5 \times 4m$
8. $3b \times 7$
9. $7q \times 3$
10. $6 \times 6w$
11. $4 \times ^-3e$
12. $5 \times ^-6t$
13. $3 \times ^-2x$
14. $3 \times ^-y$
15. $4 \times ^-u$
16. $5 \times ^-x$
17. $1 \times ^-a$
18. $9 \times ^-2d$
19. $10 \times ^-4r$
20. $6 \times ^-6y$
21. $^-3 \times 2x$
22. $^-4 \times 5c$
23. $^-7p \times 6$
24. $^-3 \times x$
25. $^-4 \times y$
26. $^-z \times 2$
27. $^-3 \times 5t$
28. $^-1 \times t$
29. $^-1 \times x$
30. $^-4z \times 4$
31. $^-2 \times ^-2x$
32. $^-3 \times ^-5m$
33. $^-2 \times ^-6p$
34. $^-4x \times ^-2$
35. $^-2y \times ^-5$
36. $^-1 \times ^-2t$
37. $^-1 \times ^-t$
38. $^-e \times ^-3$
39. $^-e \times ^-1$
40. $^-4 \times ^-4x$

11.4 Multiplying letter terms by letter terms

To multiply a letter term by a letter term, write out in full what the multiplication means and then simplify.

Examples
(a) $3x \times 4y = 3 \times x \times 4 \times y = 3 \times 4 \times x \times y = 12 \times x \times y = 12xy$
(b) $8m \times m = 8 \times m \times m = 8 \times m^2 = 8m^2$
(c) $^-3e \times 2f = ^-3 \times e \times 2 \times f = ^-3 \times 2 \times e \times f = ^-6 \times e \times f = ^-6ef$
(d) $^-6x \times ^-x = ^-6 \times x \times ^-1 \times x = ^-6 \times ^-1 \times x \times x = 6 \times x \times x = 6x^2$

Exercise 11D

1. $2a \times 2b$
2. $5s \times 3t$
3. $4a \times b$
4. $7u \times 7v$
5. $2c \times 8d$
6. $a \times 6b$
7. $7y \times x$
8. $5r \times 6s$
9. $6x \times 4y$
10. $7p \times 5q$
11. $6z \times z$
12. $7u \times u$
13. $x \times 5x$
14. $3a \times 2a$
15. $2x \times 2x$
16. $3y \times 3y$
17. $4r \times 2r$
18. $6e \times 2e$
19. $5t \times 5t$
20. $3w \times 7w$
21. $^-3a \times 2b$
22. $5m \times ^-2n$
23. $3a \times ^-b$
24. $^-x \times 2y$
25. $y \times ^-2x$
26. $^-3z \times 2z$
27. $^-3a \times 2a$
28. $^-4r \times r$
29. $x \times ^-3x$
30. $4b \times ^-3b$
31. $^-3e \times ^-2f$
32. $^-2x \times ^-4y$
33. $^-e \times ^-f$
34. $^-r \times ^-s$
35. $^-4m \times ^-3n$
36. $^-x \times ^-2x$
37. $^-3y \times ^-2y$
38. $^-3a \times ^-4a$
39. $^-x \times ^-x$
40. $^-y \times ^-y \times ^-y$

11.5 Expanding brackets with a number term outside

To **expand** a bracket means to multiply each term in the bracket by the term outside the bracket.

Examples
(a) $3(a + 5) = 3 \times a + 3 \times 5 = 3a + 15$
(b) $5(2x - 3) = 5 \times 2x - 5 \times 3 = 10x - 15$
(c) $6(2w - 3x) = 6 \times 2w - 6 \times 3x = 12w - 18x$

Exercise 11E

Expand each bracket.

1. $3(x + 2)$
2. $5(y + 1)$
3. $8(w + 3)$
4. $7(3 + e)$
5. $6(a + 4)$
6. $4(x - 1)$
7. $5(t - 3)$
8. $9(e - 5)$
9. $3(4 - w)$
10. $5(x - 4)$
11. $3(2a + 4)$
12. $4(5b + 3)$
13. $6(5e + 3)$
14. $2(3x + 2)$
15. $5(6t + 4)$
16. $7(3r - 4)$
17. $8(2x - 3)$
18. $2(4 - 3m)$
19. $5(1 - w)$
20. $6(4 - 2w)$
21. $5(2a + 3b)$
22. $6(a + 4b)$
23. $7(2x + 2y)$
24. $6(3e + 4f)$
25. $4(6t + 5u)$
26. $3(4x - 5y)$
27. $5(2a - 3b)$
28. $5(3b - 2a)$
29. $6(2w - 4x)$
30. $5(5m - 5n)$

11.6 Expanding and simplifying

Examples

(a) $2(s + 1) + 3(2s + 5) = 2s + 2 + 6s + 15 = 8s + 17$

(b) $2(3 + y) + 4(2y - 1) = 6 + 2y + 8y - 4 = 10y + 2$

Exercise 11F

Expand each bracket and simplify.

1. $3(x + 2) + 4(x + 3)$
2. $4(y + 3) + 5(y + 1)$
3. $5(2a + 3) + 4(a + 3)$
4. $2(2z + 1) + 5(3 + 4z)$
5. $6(4q + 3) + 3(2q + 2)$
6. $3(x + 3) + 2(2x + 5)$
7. $4(2w + 1) + 3(2w + 1)$
8. $2(2w + 4) + 3(4 + 3w)$
9. $5(2w + 3) + 4(w - 2)$
10. $6(x + 3) + 3(x - 6)$
11. $5(x + 3) + 2(x - 5)$
12. $4(a + 3) + 2(a - 5)$
13. $5(2w + 1) + 4(2w - 2)$
14. $4(3e + 2) + 3(e - 3)$
15. $2(2x - 1) + 3(x + 1)$
16. $2(2x - 1) + 3(x - 1)$
17. $4(2y - 3) + (3y + 5)$
18. $3(2x - 4) + 2(x + 1)$
19. $5(2w - 2) + 3(w - 2)$
20. $4(2z - 3) + 5(3z - 2)$

11.7 Expanding brackets with a letter term outside

Examples

(a) $m(8 + 3n) = m \times 8 + m \times 3n = 8m + 3mn$

(b) $a(a - 5) = a \times a - a \times 5 = a^2 - 5a$

(c) $2x(3x + 2y) = 2x \times 3x + 2x \times 2y = 6x^2 + 4xy$

Exercise 11G

Expand each bracket.

1. $b(3 + 5a)$
2. $a(5 - 3b)$
3. $y(2 - 5x)$
4. $x(x + 2)$
5. $y(y + 7)$
6. $z(2z + 1)$
7. $m(2m - 1)$
8. $d(3 + 2d)$
9. $a(5a - 3)$
10. $2b(b - 1)$
11. $b(2b - 2)$
12. $3s(s - 1)$
13. $5r(2r + 3)$
14. $a(1 + b)$
15. $x(2 - y)$
16. $a(a + b)$
17. $d(d + 2e)$
18. $m(3 - 2n)$
19. $2a(3a + 4b)$
20. $2x(4y + 6x)$
21. $3u(2v + 3u)$
22. $4r(4r + 2s)$
23. $r(16r - 8s)$
24. $2x(5x - 3y)$
25. $4p(3q - 2p)$

11.8 Expanding brackets with negative terms

Take extra care when there is a negative term outside a bracket.

Examples
(a) $^-2(2x + 7) = ^-2 \times 2x + ^-2 \times 7 = ^-4x - 14$
(b) $^-4(2a - 7) = ^-4 \times 2a - ^-4 \times 7 = ^-8a - ^-28 = ^-8a + 28 = 28 - 8a$
(c) $^-(3a + 2b) = ^-1 \times (3a + 2b) = ^-1 \times 3a + ^-1 \times 2b = ^-3a - 2b$
(d) $^-m(2m - 3n) = ^-m \times 2m - ^-m \times 3n = ^-2m^2 - ^-3mn = ^-2m^2 + 3mn = 3mn - 2m^2$

Exercise 11H
Expand each bracket.

1. $^-2(a + 3)$
2. $^-4(x + 1)$
3. $^-2(2b + 3)$
4. $^-2(3 + 2z)$
5. $^-5(4 + 6t)$
6. $^-9(2w + 1)$
7. $^-2(5 + 5r)$
8. $^-6(2b + 2)$
9. $^-3(x + 5)$
10. $^-7(1 + x)$
11. $^-2(x - 1)$
12. $^-2(1 - x)$
13. $^-4(s - 1)$
14. $^-4(1 - s)$
15. $^-3(2w - 1)$
16. $^-4(1 - 2w)$
17. $^-5(3x - 5)$
18. $^-5(5 - 3x)$
19. $^-4(2p - 3)$
20. $^-4(3 - 2p)$
21. $^-(x + 2)$
22. $^-(y + 3)$
23. $^-(a + b)$
24. $^-(2a + 3b)$
25. $^-(2x + y)$
26. $^-(x - 1)$
27. $^-(y - 2x)$
28. $^-(2a - 3b)$
29. $^-(3x - 2y)$
30. $^-(3p - 5q)$
31. $^-a(a + b)$
32. $^-x(2x + y)$
33. $^-d(3 + 2d)$
34. $^-v(4v + 2)$
35. $^-s(2s + t)$
36. $^-t(t - s)$
37. $^-2w(2w - 3)$
38. $^-4x(2x - 2y)$
39. $^-2a(3a - 3b)$
40. $^-5m(2n - 4m)$

11.9 Factorisation by extracting a number term outside a bracket

Look at the expression $4x + 6$.

The terms $4x$ and 6 have 2 as a common factor. This means you can write the expression using a bracket:

$$4x + 6 = 2(2x + 3)$$

This is called **factorising** the expression. You can test each answer by expanding the bracket again.

Examples
(a) $6y + 12 = 6(y + 2)$ Test: $6(y + 2) = 6y + 12$
(b) $10a - 15 = 5(2a - 3)$ Test: $5(2a - 3) = 10a - 15$

Exercise 11I

Factorise each expression.

1. $3x + 9$
2. $5x + 15$
3. $6a + 18$
4. $4m + 12$
5. $7b + 14$
6. $4r - 16$
7. $5t - 20$
8. $9w - 18$
9. $3w - 15$
10. $4y - 24$
11. $3w + 21$
12. $6m - 36$
13. $7y + 21$
14. $11a - 22$
15. $12w + 24$
16. $6e + 9$
17. $8u + 12$
18. $15a + 20$
19. $12b + 18$
20. $12w + 15$
21. $12y - 16$
22. $20v - 25$
23. $18c - 24$
24. $6t - 15$
25. $14m - 21$
26. $15x + 18$
27. $16t - 24$
28. $30r + 35$
29. $30p - 12$
30. $28z + 21$

11.10 Factorisation by extracting a letter term outside a bracket

Examples

(a) $x + 2xy = x(1 + 2y)$ Test: $x(1 + 2y) = x + 2xy$

(b) $9x + 6xy = x(9 + 6y) = 3x(3 + 2y)$ Test: $3x(3 + 2y) = 9x + 6xy$

(c) $a^2 + ab = a(a + b)$ Test: $a(a + b) = a^2 + ab$

Exercise 11J

Factorise each expression.

1. $a + ab$
2. $2x + xy$
3. $3p + 5pq$
4. $3t + 2st$
5. $5a + 7ab$
6. $6xy + x$
7. $4st + 3t$
8. $5e - 4ef$
9. $7u - 5uv$
10. $3ab - 5b$
11. $6ab + 9a$
12. $8u + 12uv$
13. $15e + 20ef$
14. $9x + 12xy$
15. $12r + 16rs$
16. $20xy - 25y$
17. $18ab - 12b$
18. $4yz - 6y$
19. $15e - 12ef$
20. $20pq - 30q$
21. $x^2 + xy$
22. $x^3 + xy$
23. $2ab + a^2$
24. $5st + t^2$
25. $5st + 10t^2$
26. $x^2 + 2xy$
27. $2x^2 + 2xy$
28. $2x^2 + 4xy$
29. $7a^3 + 14ab$
30. $2ab + 3a^2b$

11.11 Solving equations by subtracting

An **equation** is a statement about the value of a letter.
For example this equation:

$$x + 5 = 20$$

means that if you add 5 to the value of the letter x you will get the answer 20.

You **solve** an equation by working out the value of the letter.

To help solve an equation, you can **subtract any number from both sides of the equation**.

Example 1

Solve the equation: $x + 5 = 20$

Subtract 5 from both sides: $x + 5 - 5 = 20 - 5$

This gives the solution: $x = 15$

Example 2

Solve the equation: $a + 30 = 20$

Subtract 30 from both sides: $a + 30 - 30 = 20 - 30$

This gives the solution: $a = {}^-10$

Exercise 11K

Solve the equations.

1. $x + 7 = 11$
2. $y + 9 = 12$
3. $a + 7 = 14$
4. $s + 8 = 9$
5. $x + 7 = 8$
6. $y + 4 = 4$
7. $c + 15 = 23$
8. $z + 11 = 23$
9. $f + 5 = 50$
10. $m + 6 = 14$
11. $x + 3 = 2$
12. $y + 7 = 3$
13. $a + 5 = 0$
14. $e + 9 = 3$
15. $t + 8 = 3$
16. $x + 7 = 1$
17. $d + 2 = {}^-2$
18. $z + 3 = {}^-4$
19. $y + 4 = 0$
20. $d + 7 = {}^-1$

11.12 Solving equations by adding

To help solve an equation, you can **add any number to both sides of the equation**.

Example 1

Solve the equation: $x - 5 = 20$

Add 5 to both sides: $x - 5 + 5 = 20 + 5$

This gives the solution: $x = 25$

Example 2

Solve the equation: $a - 30 = {}^-20$

Add 30 to both sides: $a - 30 + 30 = {}^-20 + 30$

This gives the solution: $a = 10$

Exercise 11L
Solve the equations.

1. $x - 5 = 15$
2. $e - 7 = 10$
3. $a - 8 = 3$
4. $z - 5 = 0$
5. $t - 9 = 1$
6. $u - 5 = 5$
7. $d - 5 = 3$
8. $r - 20 = 1$
9. $x - 7 = 0$
10. $d - 6 = 16$
11. $d - 5 = {}^-1$
12. $x - 6 = {}^-2$
13. $t - 5 = {}^-3$
14. $y - 7 = {}^-7$
15. $u - 9 = {}^-3$
16. $x - 2 = {}^-2$
17. $b - 4 = {}^-10$
18. $z - 3 = {}^-4$
19. $p - 1 = {}^-6$
20. $g - 3 = {}^-6$

11.13 Solving equations by dividing

To help solve an equation, you can **divide both sides of the equation by any number.**

Remember, a division with one negative and one positive number gives a negative answer.

Example 1
(a) ${}^-12 \div 3 = {}^-4$ (b) $24 \div {}^-6 = {}^-4$

Remember, a division with two negative numbers gives a positive answer.

Example 2
(a) ${}^-12 \div {}^-3 = 4$ (b) ${}^-24 \div {}^-6 = 4$

Example 3
Solve the equation: $\qquad 3x = 15$

Divide both sides by 3: $\qquad \dfrac{3x}{3} = \dfrac{15}{3}$

This gives the solution: $\qquad x = 5$

Example 4
Solve the equation: $\qquad {}^-2x = 14$

Divide both sides by ${}^-2$: $\qquad \dfrac{{}^-2x}{{}^-2} = \dfrac{14}{{}^-2}$

This gives the solution: $\qquad x = {}^-7$

Example 5

Solve the equation: $\quad -x = -8$

Divide both sides by -1: $\quad \dfrac{-x}{-1} = \dfrac{-8}{-1}$

This gives the solution: $\quad x = 8$

Exercise 11M

Solve the equations.

1. $4x = 16$
2. $5r = 25$
3. $2w = 18$
4. $6y = 36$
5. $5m = 30$
6. $2a = 16$
7. $7u = 21$
8. $8y = 24$
9. $5t = 40$
10. $4c = 12$
11. $-4y = 20$
12. $-9x = 27$
13. $-6t = 30$
14. $-2x = 18$
15. $-7u = 28$
16. $6y = -18$
17. $4r = -32$
18. $3y = -15$
19. $2z = -20$
20. $6t = -6$
21. $-4x = -8$
22. $-3x = -27$
23. $-5f = -40$
24. $-8v = -16$
25. $-9x = -36$
26. $-x = -7$
27. $-a = -21$
28. $-s = 7$
29. $-3r = 30$
30. $-2m = -40$

11.14 Solving equations by multiplying

To help solve an equation, you can **multiply both sides of the equation by any number.**

Remember, a multiplication with one negative and one positive number gives a negative answer.

Example 1

(a) $-4 \times 3 = -12$ 　　(b) $6 \times -4 = -24$

Remember, a multiplication with two negative numbers gives a positive answer.

Example 2

(a) $-4 \times -3 = 12$ 　　(b) $-6 \times -4 = 24$

Example 3

Solve the equation: $\quad \dfrac{x}{3} = 4$

Multiply both sides by 3: $\quad \dfrac{x}{3} \times 3 = 4 \times 3$

This gives the solution: $\quad x = 12$

Example 4
Solve the equation: $\dfrac{x}{-2} = 5$

Multiply both sides by -2: $\dfrac{x}{-2} \times -2 = 5 \times -2$

This gives the solution: $x = -10$

Example 5
Solve the equation: $\dfrac{w}{-3} = -5$

Multiply both sides by -3: $\dfrac{w}{-3} \times -3 = -5 \times -3$

This gives the solution: $w = 15$

Exercise 11N
Solve the equations.

1. $\dfrac{x}{4} = 4$
2. $\dfrac{c}{5} = 3$
3. $\dfrac{a}{6} = 2$
4. $\dfrac{t}{7} = 1$

5. $\dfrac{y}{3} = 3$
6. $\dfrac{m}{7} = 5$
7. $\dfrac{x}{6} = 8$
8. $\dfrac{z}{2} = 5$

9. $\dfrac{t}{4} = 6$
10. $\dfrac{h}{9} = 5$
11. $\dfrac{j}{5} = -4$
12. $\dfrac{y}{3} = -5$

13. $\dfrac{z}{6} = -7$
14. $\dfrac{d}{3} = -1$
15. $\dfrac{r}{2} = -9$
16. $\dfrac{d}{8} = -1$

17. $\dfrac{y}{-5} = 6$
18. $\dfrac{u}{-2} = 15$
19. $\dfrac{x}{-3} = 10$
20. $\dfrac{t}{-1} = 12$

21. $\dfrac{x}{-2} = -9$
22. $\dfrac{z}{-3} = -8$
23. $\dfrac{r}{-5} = -9$
24. $\dfrac{m}{-9} = -5$

25. $\dfrac{s}{-2} = -10$
26. $\dfrac{e}{8} = 7$
27. $\dfrac{e}{-8} = 7$
28. $\dfrac{e}{8} = -7$

29. $\dfrac{e}{-8} = -7$
30. $\dfrac{a}{6} = -8$

11.15 Equations which require several operations to solve them

Example 1

Solve the equation: $2x + 7 = 29$

Subtract 7 from both sides: $2x + 7 - 7 = 29 - 7$

This gives: $2x = 22$

Divide both sides by 2: $\dfrac{2x}{2} = \dfrac{22}{2}$

This gives the solution: $x = 11$

Example 2

Solve the equation: $30 - 5x = 5$

Subtract 30 from both sides: $30 - 5x - 30 = 5 - 30$

This gives: $^{-}5x = {^{-}}25$

Divide both sides by $^{-}5$: $\dfrac{^{-}5x}{^{-}5} = \dfrac{^{-}25}{^{-}5}$

This gives the solution: $x = 5$

Example 3

Solve the equation: $\dfrac{x}{5} - 7 = 1$

Add 7 to both sides: $\dfrac{x}{5} - 7 + 7 = 1 + 7$

This gives: $\dfrac{x}{5} = 8$

Multiply both sides by 5: $\dfrac{x}{5} \times 5 = 8 \times 5$

This gives the solution: $x = 40$

Exercise 11O

Solve the equations.

1. $2x + 3 = 15$
2. $3x + 1 = 13$
3. $5a + 7 = 42$
4. $3e + 2 = 8$
5. $4m + 5 = 9$
6. $7s + 4 = 18$
7. $3p + 5 = 23$
8. $3x + 3 = 12$
9. $5s + 2 = 42$

10. $6y + 7 = 13$
11. $8y - 1 = 31$
12. $2x - 4 = 2$
13. $3a - 8 = 4$
14. $5z - 3 = 27$
15. $8x - 6 = 10$
16. $2x - 7 = 13$
17. $5p - 3 = 27$
18. $3m - 12 = 3$
19. $3t - 6 = {}^-3$
20. $4x - 10 = {}^-2$
21. $17 - 2x = 1$
22. $12 - 4x = 4$
23. $20 - 3a = 2$
24. $18 - 5x = 8$
25. $15 - 9z = 6$
26. $7 - 2q = 9$
27. $11 - 3y = 17$
28. $15 - 3z = 6$
29. $24 - 2m = 0$
30. $6 - 4y = 18$
31. $\frac{a}{4} + 1 = 3$
32. $\frac{z}{3} - 2 = 1$
33. $\frac{p}{4} + 5 = 10$
34. $\frac{q}{6} - 1 = 1$
35. $\frac{x}{5} + 7 = 8$
36. $\frac{y}{3} - 2 = 3$
37. $\frac{a}{4} + 3 = 2$
38. $\frac{x}{7} + 4 = 2$
39. $\frac{2x}{3} + 4 = 10$
40. $\frac{5x}{4} - 7 = 8$

11.16 Equations with brackets

Example

Solve the equation: $\qquad 3(2x + 5) = 21$

Expand the bracket: $\qquad 6x + 15 = 21$

Subtract 15 from both sides: $6x + 15 - 15 = 21 - 15$

This gives: $\qquad 6x = 6$

Divide both sides by 6: $\qquad \frac{6x}{6} = \frac{6}{6}$

This gives the solution: $\qquad x = 1$

Exercise 11P

Solve the equations.

1. $2(x + 1) = 12$
2. $2(a + 3) = 14$
3. $5(z + 4) = 25$
4. $6(3 + m) = 30$
5. $7(2 + p) = 14$
6. $3(z - 2) = 18$
7. $5(t - 3) = 20$
8. $2(x - 5) = 0$
9. $4(t - 1) = 16$
10. $7(q - 2) = 14$
11. $5(2x - 1) = 35$
12. $4(2a + 2) = 32$
13. $5(3z + 4) = 35$
14. $6(2 + 3s) = 48$
15. $3(3 + 2x) = 33$
16. $4(2x - 1) = 44$
17. $2(3x - 7) = 4$
18. $4(5a - 9) = 24$

19. $2(4y - 5) = {}^-2$
20. $3(5z - 8) = 6$
21. $4(3 - x) = 4$
22. $5(6 - x) = 10$
23. $7(8 - y) = 14$
24. $4(9 - y) = 20$
25. $2(8 - y) = 12$
26. $2(8 - y) = 20$
27. $3(4 - 2x) = 6$
28. $4(15 - 3a) = 12$
29. $3(8 - 2y) = 30$
30. $4(2 - 3y) = 44$

11.17 Equations with letter terms on both sides

Sometimes there are letter terms on both sides of an equation.
The first step is to get all the letter terms on one side.

Example 1

Solve the equation: $\qquad\qquad\qquad\qquad 11a - 5 = a + 25$

Subtract a from both sides: $\qquad\qquad 11a - 5 - a = a + 25 - a$

This gives: $\qquad\qquad\qquad\qquad\quad 10a - 5 = 25$

Adding 5 to both sides gives: $\qquad\qquad\quad 10a = 30$

Dividing both sides by 10 gives: $\qquad\qquad a = 3$

Example 2

Solve the equation: $\qquad\qquad\qquad\qquad 3p + 2 = 18 - 5p$

Add $5p$ to both sides: $\qquad\qquad 3p + 2 + 5p = 18 - 5p + 5p$

This gives: $\qquad\qquad\qquad\qquad\quad 8p + 2 = 18$

Subtracting 2 from both sides gives: $\qquad\quad 8p = 16$

Dividing both sides by 8 gives: $\qquad\qquad\quad p = 2$

Exercise 11Q

Solve the equations.

1. $7p - 11 = 2p + 4$
2. $5a + 3 = a + 11$
3. $12w - 7 = 10w - 1$
4. $5t = 8 - 3t$
5. $2w - 7 = 8 - 3w$
6. $12x + 4 = 32 - 2x$
7. $x - 13 = 8 - 3x$
8. $c + 7 = 70 - 8c$
9. $3a - 5 = 2a + 8$
10. $8 - 2w = 38 - 7w$
11. $4 - s = 15 - 2s$
12. $3e = 8 - 5e$
13. $x = 28 - 6x$
14. $3x + 28 = 4 - 9x$

15. $5b - 18 = 4 - 2b$
16. $x + 7 = 2x + 8$
17. $x + 8 = 2x + 7$
18. $2z - 5 = 3z + 9$
19. $4q - 5 = 5q - 9$
20. $7t - 18 = 10t - 3$
21. $8 - 3b = 5b - 7$
22. $2 - x = 4x + 12$
23. $13 - 5m = 2m - 1$
24. $18 - 7q = 3q + 19$
25. $14 - 2k = k - 1$
26. $3(x + 5) = 4x + 3$
27. $5(2s - 1) = 8s + 1$
28. $3(2w - 1) = 5(w + 1)$
29. $7(3y - 5) = 2(5y - 1)$
30. $5(6y - 4) = 2(3y + 4)$

11.18 Changing the subject of formulae

In the formula $P = 2(l + w)$ the subject is P.

You can change the subject of any formula, but you must use the rules of algebra.

Example 1
Make w the subject of the formula $\longrightarrow$ $P = 2(l + w)$

- **Step 1** Deal with any fractions or brackets. $\quad P = 2l + 2w$
- **Step 2** Get the term with the new subject on its own on one side of the formula. $\quad P - 2l = 2w$
- **Step 3** Divide both sides by 2 to get the subject. $\quad \dfrac{P - 2l}{2} = w$

w is now the subject of the formula.

Example 2
Make g the subject of the formula $\longrightarrow$ $t = 2\pi\sqrt{\dfrac{l}{g}}$

- **Step 1** Deal with the $\sqrt{}$ by squaring both sides. $\quad t^2 = \dfrac{4\pi^2 l}{g}$
- **Step 2** Deal with the fraction by $\times$ both sides by g. $\quad gt^2 = 4\pi^2 l$
- **Step 3** Divide both sides by t^2 to get the subject. $\quad g = \dfrac{4\pi^2 l}{t^2}$

g is now the subject of the formula.

(The subject of the formula can be written on the LHS or the RHS.)

Exercise 11R
1. Make y the subject of each of these formulas.
   - (a) $3x = y - 5$
   - (b) $3y = 3x - 2$
   - (c) $2 = 3x + y$
   - (d) $2x - 3y = 5$
   - (e) $2x = 3 + 2y$
   - (f) $2a = b(2y + 1)$

2. A formula used to calculate velocity is:
$$v = u + ft$$

Give all answers correct to 2 dp.

(a) Make t the subject of the formula.
(b) Find a value for t when: $v = 34.5$, $u = 6.75$ and $f = 2.62$
(c) Calculate a value for u when: $v = 175.4$, $f = 28.6$ and $t = 4.5$

3. Velocity can be calculated with this formula:
$$v^2 = u^2 + 2fs$$

(a) Make s the subject of the formula.
(b) Calculate a value for s when: $v = 11.6$, $u = 0.8$ and $f = 4.65$
(c) Make v the subject of the formula.
(d) Calculate a value for v when: $u = 0.88$, $f = 16.5$ and $s = 100.8$
(e) Make u the subject of the formula.
(f) Calculate a value for u when: $v = 15.65$, $f = 3.4$ and $s = 7.3$

Summary

Checkout 11

1. A multiplication or division with one negative number gives a negative answer. A multiplication or division with two negative numbers gives a positive answer.

1. Calculate.
   (a) 5×4
   (b) $^-5 \times 3$
   (c) $4 \times ^-2$
   (d) $^-3 \times ^-8$
   (e) $9 \times ^-2$
   (f) $^-4 \times 4$
   (g) $^-6 \times ^-6$
   (h) 7×2
   (i) $18 \div ^-2$
   (j) $12 \div 3$
   (k) $^-15 \div 5$
   (l) $^-21 \div ^-7$
   (m) $^-30 \div 10$
   (n) $^-25 \div ^-5$
   (o) $8 \times ^-2$
   (p) $32 \div 4$

2. You can multiply letter terms by number terms.

2. Calculate.
   (a) $3 \times 4d$
   (b) $5x \times 6$
   (c) $2 \times 9w$
   (d) $4 \times 5y$
   (e) $^-2 \times 3e$
   (f) $6y \times ^-1$
   (g) $^-4r \times 5$
   (h) $^-3 \times ^-2x$

3. You can multiply letter terms by letter terms.

3. Calculate.
   (a) $2x \times 3y$
   (b) $4r \times 5s$
   (c) $2w \times 3y$
   (d) $a \times 5b$
   (e) $^-2e \times 3f$
   (f) $3x \times ^-2y$
   (g) $^-5t \times ^-3s$
   (h) $4r \times r$
   (i) $3x \times 2x$
   (j) $^-2y \times y$
   (k) $^-5t \times ^-3t$
   (l) $x \times ^-7x$

4. You can expand brackets.

4. Expand these brackets.
   (a) $4(x + 2)$
   (b) $3(x - 1)$
   (c) $6(2x + 3)$
   (d) $2(5t - 1)$
   (e) $6(3 - 5j)$
   (f) $5(2a + 3c)$
   (g) $6(2x + y)$
   (h) $3(3u - 2v)$
   (i) $x(x + 1)$
   (j) $d(d + e)$
   (k) $z(2z + 5)$
   (l) $x(x + y)$
   (m) $s(2s + 3t)$
   (n) $p(2q - 3p)$
   (o) $3c(c + 2d)$
   (p) $4y(2x - 3y)$

5. You can expand brackets with a negative term outside.

5. Expand these brackets.
   (a) ⁻2(x + 1)
   (b) ⁻3(z + 4)
   (c) ⁻4(2x + 3)
   (d) ⁻7(x + 2)
   (e) ⁻3(x − 1)
   (f) ⁻2(2x − 4)
   (g) ⁻5(4 − x)
   (h) ⁻6(2 − 5x)
   (i) ⁻(y + 4)
   (j) ⁻(2x − 6)
   (k) ⁻(a + b)
   (l) ⁻(a − b)
   (m) ⁻x(x + 3)
   (n) ⁻y(y − 2)
   (o) ⁻2s(1 − s)
   (p) ⁻4t(2p − 3t)

6. You can factorise by extracting a number term outside a bracket.

6. Factorise.
   (a) $3x + 9$
   (b) $5t + 15$
   (c) $4m - 20$
   (d) $7t - 14$
   (e) $15x + 40$
   (f) $9r + 24$
   (g) $12x - 15$
   (h) $20p - 30$

7. You can factorise by extracting a letter term outside a bracket.

7. Factorise.
   (a) $x + xy$
   (b) $cd + 2d$
   (c) $3ab - 2b$
   (d) $4f - 2ef$
   (e) $2x^2 + x$
   (f) $3x^2 + 2x$
   (g) $2ab - a^2$
   (h) $5x - 10xy$

8. You can solve equations by subtracting.

8. Solve.
   (a) $x + 5 = 30$
   (b) $r + 7 = 7$
   (c) $y + 13 = {}^-13$

9. You can solve equations by adding.

9. Solve.
   (a) $c - 7 = 3$
   (b) $u - 5 = 2$
   (c) $m - 5 = {}^-1$

10. You can solve equations by dividing.

10. Solve.
    (a) $3m = 30$
    (b) $8t = 16$
    (c) $5x = {}^-40$

11. You can solve equations by multiplying.

11. Solve.
    (a) $\frac{x}{3} = 4$
    (b) $\frac{n}{5} = 2$
    (c) $\frac{v}{4} = {}^-5$

12. You can solve equations which require several operations.

12. Solve.
    (a) $2x + 5 = 11$
    (b) $3e - 8 = 22$
    (c) $7 - 2e = 1$
    (d) $\frac{x}{5} + 1 = 4$
    (e) $\frac{m}{3} - 1 = 9$
    (f) $\frac{2c}{3} + 3 = 7$

13. You can solve equations with brackets.

13. Solve.
    (a) $3(x + 1) = 18$
    (b) $5(2x - 3) = 25$
    (c) $3(10 - 2y) = 6$
    (d) $4(2 - 2e) = 16$

14. You can solve equations with letter terms on both sides.

14. Solve.
    (a) $2x + 1 = x + 4$
    (b) $3y + 2 = y + 8$
    (c) $5t - 4 = 2t + 8$
    (d) $5(x + 1) = 6x + 1$

Revision exercise 11

1. (a) Write each of the following expressions in its simplest form.
   (i) $f + g + f + f + g$
   (ii) $y \times t \times 3$
   (iii) $r \times r$
   (b) Multiply out the following expression by removing the brackets.
   $$3(2t + 5)$$ [OCR]

2. Multiply out these brackets.
   (a) $3(5x + 4)$
   (b) $9(7 - 2x)$ [OCR]

3. Lindi thought of a number.
   She multiplied the number by 5.
   Her answer was 30.
   What number did Lindi think of? [Edexcel]

4. Maureen thought of a number.
   She divided this number by 4.
   She then added 3.
   Her answer was 9.
   What number did Maureen think of? [Edexcel]

5. Find the numbers which make these two equations correct.
   (a) $A \times 9 = 54$
   (b) $5 \times B = 35$ [OCR]

6. All lengths in this diagram are in centimetres.

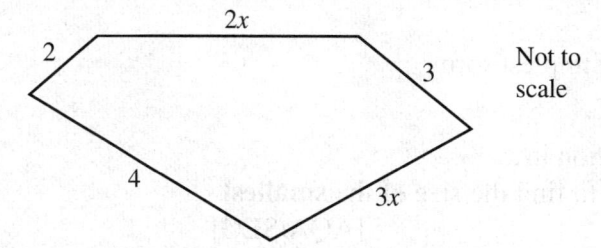

   Not to scale

   (a) Write down an expression for the perimeter of this pentagon, in terms of x.
       Simplify your answer.

   The perimeter is 34 cm.

   (b) (i) Use this to form an equation.
       (ii) Solve the equation to find x. [OCR]

7.

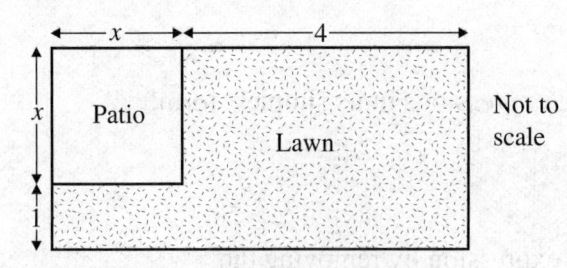

All lengths in this question are in metres.

A rectangular garden has a square patio of side x metres in one corner.
The remainder of the garden is lawn.

(a) Write down an expression, in terms of x, for the longest side of the lawn.

(b) Find an expression, in terms of x, for the perimeter of the lawn.

(c) The perimeter of the lawn is 34 metres.
Find the value of x. [OCR]

8. The angles of a triangle are $(2x - 3)°$, $(x + 4)°$ and $(x + 19)°$.

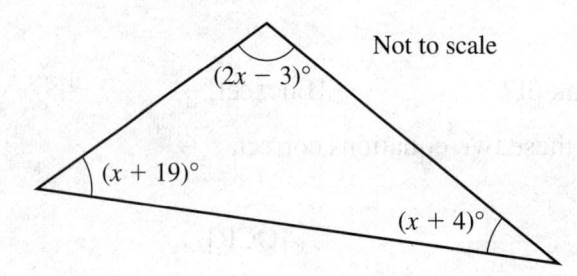

(a) Write an expression, in terms of x, for the sum of the angles.
Write your answer in its simplest form.

The sum of the angles is 180°.

(b) (i) Write down an equation in x.
(ii) Solve your equation to find the size of the **smallest** angle in the triangle. [AQA/SEG]

9. P and k are connected by the formula $P = 20 + 4k$
(a) Find the value of P when
(i) $k = 2$
(ii) $k = {}^-3$
(b) Find the value of k when $P = 72$. [OCR]

10. James works in a factory making sheds.
    His weekly wage depends on how many sheds he makes.
    This formula is used to calculate his weekly wage:
    $$w = 6x + 50$$
    x is the number of sheds he makes. w is his weekly wage in pounds.
    (a) Work out his weekly wage when he makes 40 sheds.
    (b) His wage for one week was £236.
        How many sheds did he make? [OCR]

11. Solve the equations:
    (a) $5x - 3 = 7$
    (b) $5x + 5 = 7 + x$ [AQA/NEAB]

12. (a) The perimeter of a rectangle is given by
        $$P = 2(L + B)$$
        where L and B are the lengths of the sides.
        Find P when $L = 17$ and $B = 13$.
    (b) Solve $4x - 5 = x + 1$ [AQA/NEAB]

13. Solve the equations:
    (a) $t + 4 = 7$
    (b) $7y = 4$
    (c) $\dfrac{x}{2} = 30$
    (d) $3p - 4 = 11$ [OCR]

14. (a) Solve $3x = 24$
    (b) Solve $18 + 3y = 6 - y$ [Edexcel]

15. (a) Solve $3x - 2 = 10$
    (b) Solve $5x + 2 = 3x + 3$ [OCR]

16. Solve the equations:
    (a) $3w = {}^-18$
    (b) $3(x - 4) = 12$
    (c) $3y + 7 = 13 - y$ [OCR]

17. Solve the following equations:
    (a) $3x - 4 = 11$
    (b) $5x + 17 = 3(x + 6)$ [WJEC]

18. Solve the following equations:
    (a) $4x - 7 = 20$
    (b) $3(y + 5) = 42$ [Edexcel]

12 NUMBER 5

This unit is about:

- Fractions
- Decimals
- Percentages

You need to remember:

- Your multiplication tables.
  1. Write down the answers to:

     (a) 2×3 (b) 4×5 (c) 3×3 (d) 4×4
     (e) 4×8 (f) 5×6 (g) 8×3 (h) 9×5
     (i) 3×6 (j) 7×7 (k) 9×6 (l) 7×9
     (m) 8×7 (n) 9×9 (o) 7×6 (p) 5×7

- How to divide with multiplication tables.
  2. Write down the answers to:

     (a) $28 \div 4$ (b) $18 \div 3$ (c) $14 \div 2$ (d) $24 \div 8$
     (e) $42 \div 6$ (f) $40 \div 8$ (g) $36 \div 6$ (h) $48 \div 8$
     (i) $30 \div 5$ (j) $56 \div 7$ (k) $24 \div 4$ (l) $15 \div 5$
     (m) $63 \div 7$ (n) $54 \div 9$ (o) $72 \div 9$ (p) $45 \div 9$

12.1 Understanding fractions

This pie chart shows the pets owned by the student in a class.
You can use **fractions** to describe the chart. The chart shows that:

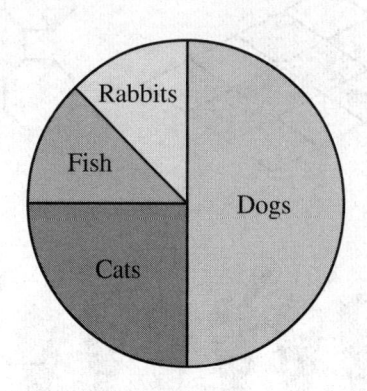

- $\frac{1}{2}$ of the students own dogs
- $\frac{1}{4}$ of the students own cats
- $\frac{1}{8}$ of the students own fish
- $\frac{1}{8}$ of the students own rabbits.

You can use fractions to describe the ways things are divided.

$\frac{4}{5}$ of this shape is coloured. $\frac{2}{3}$ of the faces are smiling.

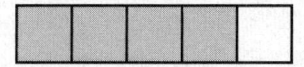

Exercise 12A

1. What fraction of each shape is coloured?

   (a)

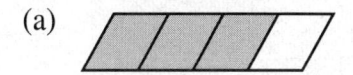

   (b)

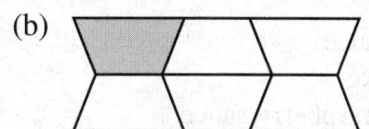

   (c)

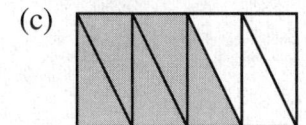

   (d)

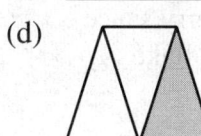

   (e)

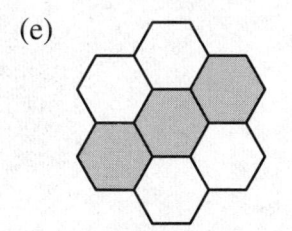

   (f)

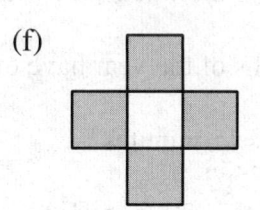

   (g)

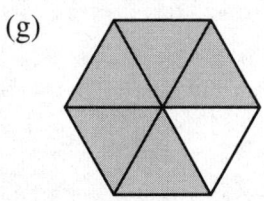

   (h)

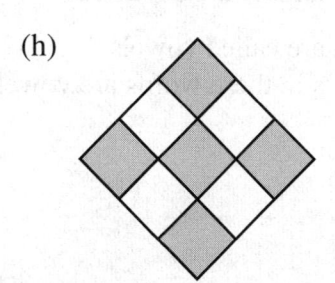

(i) (j)

2.

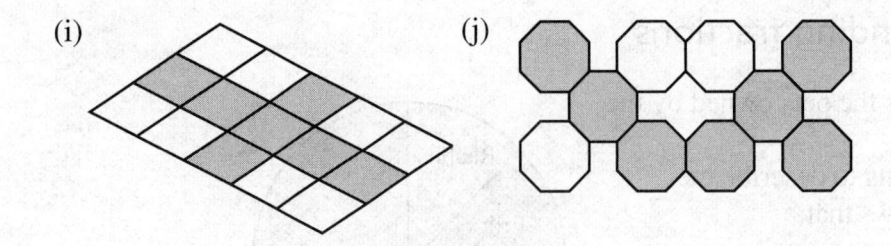

What fraction of these ice-creams:
(a) have a flake
(b) have raspberry sauce
(c) do not have a flake
(d) have a flake and raspberry sauce
(e) have neither a flake nor raspberry sauce
(f) have raspberry sauce but not a flake
(g) do not have raspberry sauce?

3. (a) What fraction of the days of the week start with the letter T?
   (b) What fraction of the months of the year have exactly 30 days?
   (c) What fraction of an hour is 15 minutes?
   (d) What fraction of £1·00 is 75p?
   (e) What fraction of one minute is 30 seconds?

4. The letters a, e, i, o and u are called vowels.
   What fraction of the letters in these words are vowels?
   (a) Manchester
   (b) apple
   (c) piglets
   (d) umbrella
   (e) octopus

12.2 Improper fractions and mixed numbers

A fraction like $\frac{12}{7}$ is called an **improper** fraction because it is greater than one. $\frac{12}{7}$ can be written as $1\frac{5}{7}$.

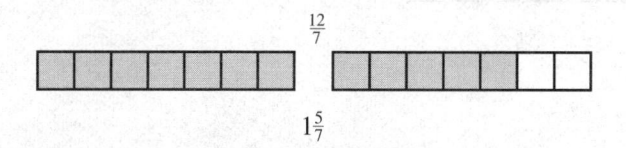

A quantity like $1\frac{5}{7}$ is called a **mixed number**.

Examples

(a) $\frac{3}{2} = 1\frac{1}{2}$ (b) $\frac{13}{4} = 3\frac{1}{4}$ (c) $\frac{8}{3} = 2\frac{2}{3}$

Exercise 12B

1. Change each improper fraction into a mixed number.
   - (a) $\frac{12}{5}$
   - (b) $\frac{7}{4}$
   - (c) $\frac{9}{5}$
   - (d) $\frac{4}{3}$
   - (e) $\frac{5}{2}$
   - (f) $\frac{6}{3}$
   - (g) $\frac{7}{6}$
   - (h) $\frac{8}{7}$
   - (i) $\frac{5}{3}$
   - (j) $\frac{9}{7}$
   - (k) $\frac{13}{12}$
   - (l) $\frac{19}{3}$
   - (m) $\frac{18}{6}$
   - (n) $\frac{29}{4}$
   - (o) $\frac{9}{1}$
   - (p) $\frac{33}{5}$
   - (q) $\frac{11}{2}$
   - (r) $\frac{9}{4}$
   - (s) $\frac{15}{13}$
   - (t) $\frac{100}{99}$
   - (u) $\frac{6}{5}$
   - (v) $\frac{21}{17}$
   - (w) $\frac{11}{4}$
   - (x) $\frac{19}{2}$
   - (y) $\frac{17}{4}$

2. Change each mixed number into an improper fraction.
   - (a) $1\frac{1}{2}$
   - (b) $2\frac{1}{3}$
   - (c) $1\frac{1}{4}$
   - (d) $1\frac{2}{5}$
   - (e) $2\frac{1}{6}$
   - (f) $1\frac{4}{7}$
   - (g) $1\frac{1}{8}$
   - (h) $1\frac{5}{12}$
   - (i) $1\frac{5}{13}$
   - (j) $7\frac{1}{4}$
   - (k) $6\frac{1}{2}$
   - (l) $3\frac{2}{3}$
   - (m) $2\frac{3}{4}$
   - (n) $2\frac{1}{5}$
   - (o) $2\frac{5}{6}$
   - (p) $2\frac{1}{7}$
   - (q) $1\frac{5}{8}$
   - (r) $3\frac{7}{12}$
   - (s) $2\frac{1}{17}$
   - (t) $3\frac{5}{7}$
   - (u) $9\frac{1}{2}$
   - (v) $7\frac{1}{3}$
   - (w) $6\frac{3}{4}$
   - (x) $1\frac{4}{5}$
   - (y) $3\frac{5}{6}$

12.3 Equivalent fractions

$\frac{1}{2}$ and $\frac{2}{4}$ are different ways of writing the same fraction.

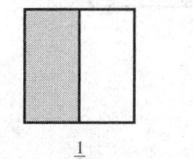

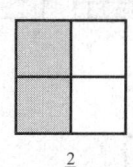

$\frac{1}{2}$ and $\frac{2}{4}$ are **equivalent** fractions.

$\frac{2}{3}$ and $\frac{6}{9}$ are also equivalent fractions.

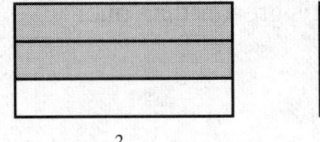

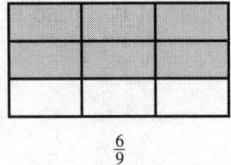

$\frac{2}{3}$ $\frac{6}{9}$

Exercise 12C

What equivalent fractions are shown in these diagrams?

1. 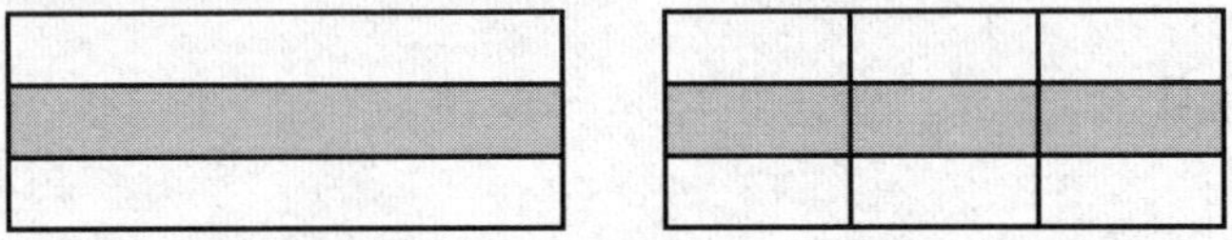
2. 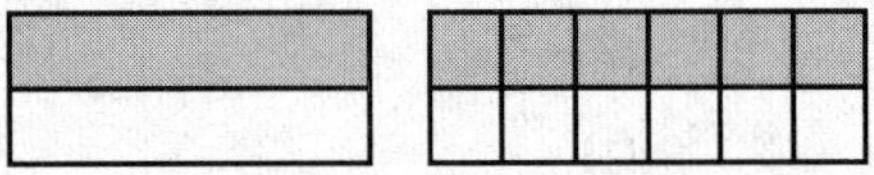
3. 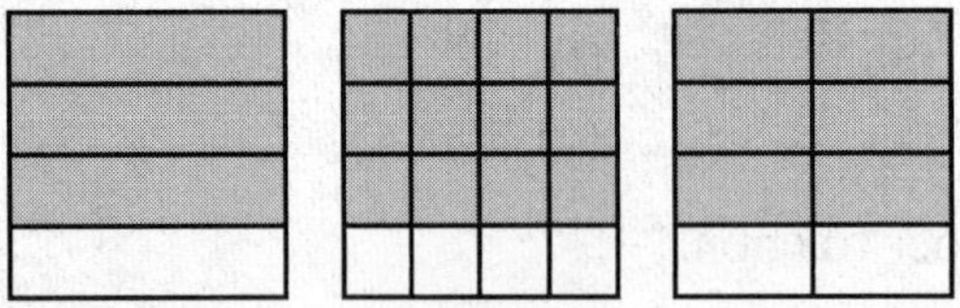
4. 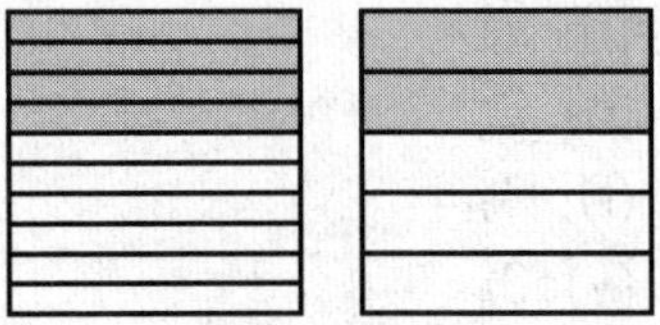
5. 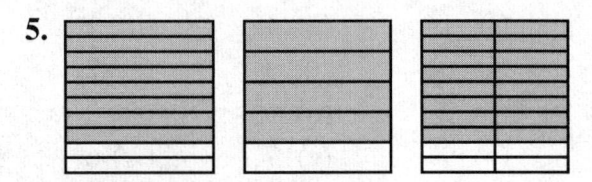
6. 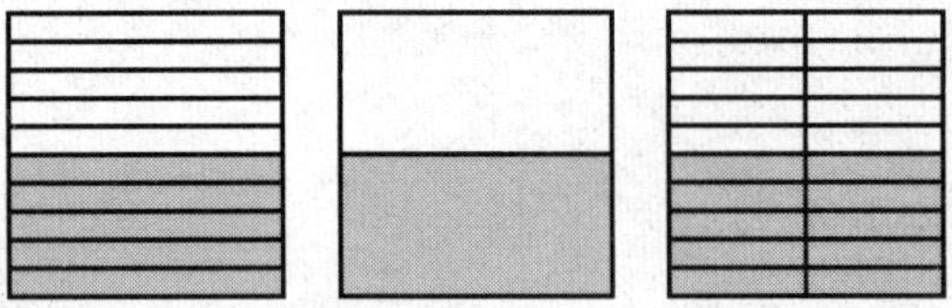
7. 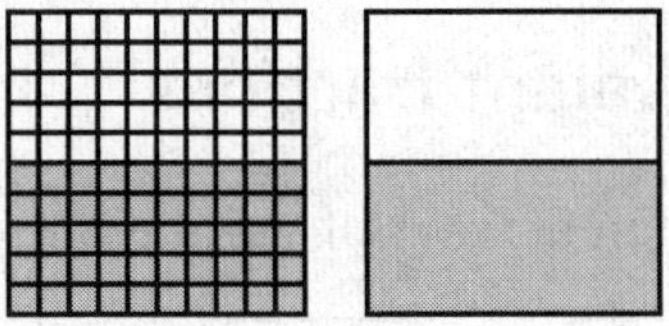
8.

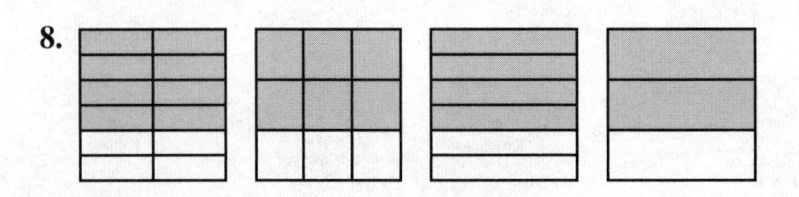

12.4 Making pairs of equivalent fractions

Look at this pair of equivalent fractions:

$$\frac{2}{3} \quad \frac{8}{12}$$

$\frac{2}{3}$ can be turned into $\frac{8}{12}$ by multiplying both the 2 and the 3 by 4.

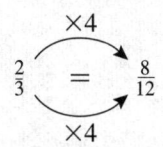

$$\frac{2}{3} \xrightarrow{\times 4} \frac{8}{12}$$

A similar multiplication exists for all pairs of equivalent fractions.

Example
Complete the missing number in this pair of equivalent fractions.

$$\frac{3}{4} = \frac{}{20}$$

The 4 has been multiplied by 5. The 3 must also be multiplied by 5 to fill in the missing number.

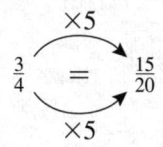

$$\frac{3}{4} \xrightarrow{\times 5} \frac{15}{20}$$

Exercise 12D
Copy and complete the following pairs of equivalent fractions.

1. $\frac{3}{4} = \frac{}{12}$
2. $\frac{2}{3} = \frac{}{6}$
3. $\frac{4}{5} = \frac{}{25}$
4. $\frac{1}{2} = \frac{}{8}$
5. $\frac{1}{2} = \frac{}{12}$
6. $\frac{2}{3} = \frac{}{15}$
7. $\frac{3}{5} = \frac{}{15}$
8. $\frac{3}{4} = \frac{}{20}$
9. $\frac{4}{5} = \frac{}{20}$
10. $\frac{1}{6} = \frac{}{42}$
11. $\frac{3}{7} = \frac{}{42}$
12. $\frac{1}{2} = \frac{}{14}$
13. $\frac{4}{7} = \frac{}{14}$
14. $\frac{3}{8} = \frac{}{40}$
15. $\frac{7}{10} = \frac{}{40}$
16. $\frac{1}{4} = \frac{}{12}$
17. $\frac{2}{3} = \frac{}{12}$
18. $\frac{3}{5} = \frac{}{35}$
19. $\frac{6}{7} = \frac{}{35}$
20. $\frac{7}{12} = \frac{}{24}$
21. $\frac{5}{8} = \frac{}{24}$
22. $\frac{5}{9} = \frac{}{90}$
23. $\frac{3}{5} = \frac{}{30}$
24. $\frac{2}{5} = \frac{}{45}$
25. $\frac{3}{8} = \frac{}{24}$

12.5 Simplifying fractions

Look at this fraction:

$$\frac{6}{15}$$

Both 6 and 15 can be divided by 3, so this fraction can be simplified.

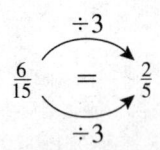

$$\frac{6}{15} \xrightarrow{\div 3} \frac{2}{5}$$

Example
Simplify the fractions:
(a) $\frac{4}{16}$ (b) $\frac{27}{30}$ (c) $\frac{40}{25}$

The simplified fractions are:

(a) $\frac{4}{16} \xrightarrow{\div 4} \frac{1}{4}$ (b) $\frac{27}{30} \xrightarrow{\div 3} \frac{9}{10}$ (c) $\frac{40}{25} \xrightarrow{\div 5} \frac{8}{5} = 1\frac{3}{5}$

Exercise 12E

1. Simplify each of the following fractions.
   (a) $\frac{2}{4}$ (b) $\frac{8}{32}$ (c) $\frac{9}{12}$ (d) $\frac{4}{6}$ (e) $\frac{20}{25}$
   (f) $\frac{15}{25}$ (g) $\frac{50}{70}$ (h) $\frac{24}{27}$ (i) $\frac{54}{60}$ (j) $\frac{70}{110}$
   (k) $\frac{9}{27}$ (l) $\frac{12}{14}$ (m) $\frac{3}{6}$ (n) $\frac{16}{4}$ (o) $\frac{20}{15}$
   (p) $\frac{20}{30}$ (q) $\frac{40}{32}$ (r) $\frac{18}{30}$ (s) $\frac{105}{75}$ (t) $\frac{18}{18}$
   (u) $\frac{45}{50}$ (v) $\frac{3}{9}$ (w) $\frac{54}{63}$ (x) $\frac{22}{33}$ (y) $\frac{44}{50}$

2. What fraction of 1 hour is:
   (a) 30 minutes   (b) 10 minutes   (c) 15 minutes
   (d) 20 minutes   (e) 5 minutes?

3. What fraction of 1 minute is:
   (a) 25 seconds   (b) 40 seconds   (c) 36 seconds
   (d) 55 seconds   (e) 24 seconds?

4. What fraction of £1·00 is:
   (a) 25p   (b) 50p   (c) 75p   (d) 80p   (e) 45p?

Remember:
There are
- 60 minutes in 1 hour
- 60 seconds in 1 minute

12.6 Adding fractions from the same family

$\frac{3}{4}$ means 3 out of 4 parts.

$\frac{3}{4}$ of this shape is shaded.

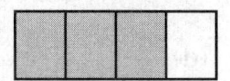

3 parts are shaded — 3 — 3 is the **numerator**
There are 4 parts in total — 4 — 4 is the **denominator**

The **denominator** of a fraction is the family it belongs to.

$\frac{3}{4}$ belongs to 'quarters'. $\quad \frac{1}{5}$ belongs to 'fifths'.

You can add fractions from the same family.
You just add the numerators.

Example

(a) $\frac{2}{7} + \frac{1}{7} = \frac{3}{7}$ \qquad (b) $\frac{3}{5} + \frac{3}{5} = \frac{6}{5} = 1\frac{1}{5}$

(c) $1\frac{3}{4} + \frac{3}{4} = 1\frac{6}{4} = 2\frac{2}{4} = 2\frac{1}{2}$ \qquad (d) $2\frac{3}{8} + 3\frac{7}{8} = 5\frac{10}{8} = 6\frac{2}{8} = 6\frac{1}{4}$

Exercise 12F

1. Add $\frac{3}{5}$ to:
  (a) $\frac{1}{5}$ \quad (b) $\frac{2}{5}$ \quad (c) $\frac{3}{5}$ \quad (d) $\frac{4}{5}$ \quad (e) $1\frac{4}{5}$

2. Add $\frac{3}{4}$ to:
  (a) $\frac{1}{4}$ \quad (b) $\frac{3}{4}$ \quad (c) $1\frac{1}{4}$ \quad (d) $2\frac{3}{4}$ \quad (e) $5\frac{1}{4}$

3. Add $\frac{2}{7}$ to:
  (a) $\frac{1}{7}$ \quad (b) $\frac{3}{7}$ \quad (c) $\frac{5}{7}$ \quad (d) $\frac{6}{7}$ \quad (e) $1\frac{5}{7}$

4. Add $1\frac{2}{3}$ to:
  (a) $\frac{1}{3}$ \quad (b) $\frac{2}{3}$ \quad (c) $1\frac{1}{3}$ \quad (d) $2\frac{2}{3}$ \quad (e) $3\frac{1}{3}$

5. Add $1\frac{3}{4}$ to:
  (a) $\frac{3}{4}$ \quad (b) $2\frac{1}{4}$ \quad (c) $5\frac{3}{4}$ \quad (d) $1\frac{1}{2}$ \quad (e) $5\frac{1}{2}$

6. Add $\frac{3}{11}$ to:
  (a) $\frac{3}{11}$ \quad (b) $\frac{5}{11}$ \quad (c) $\frac{7}{11}$ \quad (d) $11\frac{5}{11}$ \quad (e) $4\frac{10}{11}$

7. Add $1\frac{5}{6}$ to:
  (a) $\frac{5}{6}$ \quad (b) $\frac{1}{6}$ \quad (c) $1\frac{5}{6}$ \quad (d) $5\frac{1}{6}$ \quad (e) $11\frac{5}{6}$

8. Add $3\frac{8}{9}$ to:
  (a) $\frac{7}{9}$ \quad (b) $\frac{1}{9}$ \quad (c) $\frac{5}{9}$ \quad (d) $7\frac{1}{9}$ \quad (e) $\frac{4}{9}$

9. Add $1\frac{5}{8}$ to:
   (a) $\frac{5}{8}$ (b) $\frac{7}{8}$ (c) $1\frac{3}{8}$ (d) $4\frac{7}{8}$ (e) $5\frac{1}{8}$

10. Add $3\frac{5}{12}$ to:
    (a) $\frac{3}{12}$ (b) $\frac{7}{12}$ (c) $\frac{5}{12}$ (d) $\frac{11}{12}$ (e) $3\frac{7}{12}$

12.7 Subtracting fractions with the same denominator

Example
(a) $\frac{7}{8} - \frac{3}{8} = \frac{4}{8} = \frac{1}{2}$
(b) $1\frac{6}{7} - \frac{2}{7} = 1\frac{4}{7}$
(c) $8\frac{4}{11} - \frac{7}{11} = 8 - \frac{3}{11} = 7\frac{8}{11}$
(d) $6\frac{4}{7} - 3\frac{3}{7} = 3\frac{4}{7} - \frac{3}{7} = 3\frac{1}{7}$

Exercise 12G

1. Subtract $\frac{2}{5}$ from:
   (a) $\frac{4}{5}$ (b) $\frac{3}{5}$ (c) $3\frac{4}{5}$ (d) $6\frac{2}{5}$ (e) $1\frac{3}{5}$

2. Subtract $\frac{1}{4}$ from:
   (a) $\frac{3}{4}$ (b) $\frac{1}{2}$ (c) $3\frac{3}{4}$ (d) $8\frac{1}{4}$ (e) $9\frac{1}{2}$

3. Subtract $\frac{3}{7}$ from:
   (a) $\frac{4}{7}$ (b) $\frac{5}{7}$ (c) $1\frac{4}{7}$ (d) $4\frac{6}{7}$ (e) $7\frac{3}{7}$

4. Subtract $5\frac{2}{9}$ from:
   (a) $8\frac{4}{9}$ (b) $6\frac{7}{9}$ (c) $5\frac{5}{9}$ (d) $9\frac{8}{9}$ (e) $5\frac{1}{3}$

5. Subtract $2\frac{1}{4}$ from:
   (a) $3\frac{3}{4}$ (b) $5\frac{1}{4}$ (c) $7\frac{3}{4}$ (d) $3\frac{1}{2}$ (e) $2\frac{1}{2}$

6. Subtract $2\frac{3}{11}$ from:
   (a) $3\frac{4}{11}$ (b) $2\frac{8}{11}$ (c) $5\frac{9}{11}$ (d) $7\frac{7}{11}$ (e) 3

7. Subtract $\frac{4}{9}$ from:
   (a) $6\frac{5}{9}$ (b) $1\frac{4}{9}$ (c) $1\frac{3}{9}$ (d) $1\frac{2}{9}$ (e) 1

8. Subtract $\frac{5}{8}$ from:
   (a) $4\frac{7}{8}$ (b) $4\frac{5}{8}$ (c) $4\frac{3}{8}$ (d) $4\frac{1}{8}$ (e) 4

9. Subtract $3\frac{3}{4}$ from:
   (a) $5\frac{1}{4}$ (b) $6\frac{1}{4}$ (c) $7\frac{1}{2}$ (d) 14 (e) $2\frac{1}{4}$

10. Subtract $2\frac{5}{8}$ from:
    (a) 5 (b) $4\frac{3}{8}$ (c) $6\frac{1}{8}$ (d) 7 (e) $7\frac{1}{2}$

12.8 Adding and subtracting fractions with different denominators

Look at this addition problem:

$$\frac{2}{3} + \frac{1}{2}$$

The denominators of both fractions are turned into 6. The addition becomes:

$$\frac{4}{6} + \frac{3}{6} = \frac{7}{6} = 1\frac{1}{6}$$

> To do a sum like this, the fractions must be from the same family so you must make the denominators the same.

The denominator of 6 was chosen because both 2 and 3 divide exactly into 6. 2 and 3 are factors of 6. (See page 86.)

Example

(a) $\frac{3}{4} + \frac{2}{3} = \frac{9}{12} + \frac{8}{12} = \frac{17}{12} = 1\frac{5}{12}$

(b) $\frac{7}{8} - \frac{3}{4} = \frac{7}{8} - \frac{6}{8} = \frac{1}{8}$

(c) $1\frac{2}{3} + 2\frac{4}{7} = 3\frac{14}{21} + \frac{12}{21} = 3\frac{26}{21} = 4\frac{5}{21}$

(d) $2\frac{1}{2} - 1\frac{4}{5} = 1\frac{5}{10} - \frac{8}{10} = 1 - \frac{3}{10} = \frac{7}{10}$

Exercise 12H

1. (a) $\frac{3}{4} + \frac{1}{5}$ (b) $\frac{3}{4} + \frac{1}{2}$ (c) $\frac{1}{5} + \frac{2}{3}$
   (d) $\frac{1}{2} + \frac{2}{3}$ (e) $\frac{1}{2} + \frac{5}{7}$ (f) $\frac{4}{5} + \frac{2}{3}$
   (g) $\frac{3}{4} + \frac{5}{7}$ (h) $\frac{7}{10} + \frac{5}{7}$ (i) $\frac{5}{6} + \frac{3}{5}$
   (j) $\frac{5}{12} + \frac{5}{6}$ (k) $2\frac{1}{2} + \frac{1}{3}$ (l) $3\frac{1}{4} + \frac{2}{5}$
   (m) $1\frac{1}{2} + \frac{5}{6}$ (n) $2\frac{3}{10} + \frac{4}{5}$ (o) $3\frac{1}{2} + \frac{3}{10}$
   (p) $2\frac{3}{4} + 1\frac{5}{6}$ (q) $1\frac{4}{5} + 2\frac{2}{3}$ (r) $3\frac{3}{4} + 2\frac{3}{5}$
   (s) $1\frac{4}{5} + 3\frac{3}{4}$ (t) $1\frac{5}{6} + 3\frac{2}{9}$ (u) $3\frac{2}{3} + 1\frac{4}{9}$
   (v) $2\frac{5}{8} + 5\frac{3}{4}$ (w) $4\frac{1}{2} + 3\frac{5}{11}$ (x) $2\frac{5}{12} + 3\frac{1}{3}$
   (y) $2\frac{5}{12} + 3\frac{3}{4}$

2. (a) $\frac{3}{5} - \frac{1}{2}$ (b) $\frac{5}{8} - \frac{1}{2}$ (c) $\frac{11}{12} - \frac{2}{3}$
   (d) $\frac{7}{9} - \frac{2}{3}$ (e) $\frac{11}{16} - \frac{5}{8}$ (f) $\frac{13}{24} - \frac{3}{8}$
   (g) $\frac{11}{15} - \frac{2}{5}$ (h) $\frac{3}{4} - \frac{2}{5}$ (i) $\frac{4}{5} - \frac{3}{4}$
   (j) $\frac{11}{12} - \frac{1}{4}$ (k) $3\frac{3}{4} - \frac{5}{12}$ (l) $2\frac{1}{2} - \frac{1}{3}$
   (m) $3\frac{3}{5} - \frac{1}{4}$ (n) $2\frac{2}{3} - \frac{1}{5}$ (o) $3\frac{3}{4} - \frac{3}{5}$
   (p) $2\frac{1}{2} - 1\frac{2}{5}$ (q) $6\frac{4}{5} - 2\frac{2}{15}$ (r) $5\frac{6}{7} - 1\frac{1}{3}$
   (s) $4\frac{2}{3} - 1\frac{5}{12}$ (t) $2\frac{5}{6} - 1\frac{4}{9}$ (u) $3\frac{1}{3} - \frac{3}{4}$
   (v) $4\frac{1}{2} - \frac{7}{12}$ (w) $6\frac{1}{4} - \frac{7}{8}$ (x) $3\frac{2}{3} - 1\frac{4}{5}$
   (y) $2\frac{1}{3} - 1\frac{5}{6}$

12.9 Multiplying by fractions and fractions of a quantity

One quarter of the spectators at a local football match support the away team. If there are 240 supporters at the match, how many are away team supporters?

To calculate $\frac{1}{4}$ of a quantity, you divide by 4.
So, the number of away team
supporters $= \frac{1}{4}$ of $240 = 240 \div 4 = 60$

The number of home team
supporters $= \frac{3}{4}$ of $240 = (240 \div 4) \times 3 = 60 \times 3 = 180$

Example 1
(a) $\frac{1}{5}$ of $155 = 155 \div 5 = 31$
(b) $\frac{4}{5}$ of $155 = (155 \div 5) \times 4 = 31 \times 4 = 124$
(c) $\frac{1}{3}$ of $69 = 69 \div 3 = 23$
(d) $\frac{2}{3}$ of $69 = (69 \div 3) \times 2 = 46$

The word 'of' can be replaced with a multiplication sign.

Example 2
(a) $\frac{3}{4}$ of $48 = \frac{3}{4} \times 48 = (48 \div 4) \times 3 = 12 \times 3 = 36$
(b) $\frac{5}{8}$ of $64 = \frac{5}{8} \times 64 = (64 \div 8) \times 5 = 8 \times 5 = 40$

Exercise 12I

1. Calculate $\frac{1}{5}$ of:
   (a) 10   (b) 25   (c) 125   (d) 250   (e) 1 000

2. Find $\frac{1}{4}$ of:
   (a) 20   (b) 44   (c) 64   (d) 100   (e) 600

3. Calculate $\frac{1}{3}$ of:
   (a) 18   (b) 6   (c) 3   (d) 36   (e) 300

4. Multiply by $\frac{1}{2}$:
   (a) 50   (b) 18   (c) 44   (d) 72   (e) 96

5. Calculate $\frac{1}{8}$ of:
   (a) 16   (b) 8   (c) 80   (d) 800   (e) 1 600

6. Multiply by $\frac{1}{6}$:
   (a) 42   (b) 54   (c) 48   (d) 66   (e) 72

7. Multiply by $\frac{1}{7}$:
   (a) 14 (b) 21 (c) 56 (d) 63 (e) 700

8. Calculate $\frac{1}{10}$ of:
   (a) 50 (b) 70 (c) 210 (d) 450 (e) 600

9. Find $\frac{3}{5}$ of:
   (a) 20 (b) 45 (c) 25 (d) 150 (e) 2 000

10. Calculate $\frac{3}{4}$ of:
    (a) 24 (b) 40 (c) 20 (d) 88 (e) 500

11. Calculate $\frac{2}{3}$ of:
    (a) 12 (b) 21 (c) 30 (d) 48 (e) 150

12. Multiply by $\frac{2}{5}$:
    (a) 60 (b) 15 (c) 45 (d) 70 (e) 100

13. Calculate $\frac{3}{8}$ of:
    (a) 8 (b) 24 (c) 640 (d) 248 (e) 360

14. Multiply by $\frac{5}{6}$:
    (a) 36 (b) 66 (c) 48 (d) 240 (e) 180

15. Multiply by $\frac{4}{7}$:
    (a) 28 (b) 35 (c) 70 (d) 84 (e) 840

16. Calculate $\frac{7}{10}$ of:
    (a) 20 (b) 40 (c) 350 (d) 500 (e) 1 000

17. Of the 120 apples in a box, $\frac{2}{5}$ are damaged when the box is dropped. How many are not damaged?

18. Police estimate that $\frac{5}{8}$ of the 24 000 spectators at a football match support the home team. How many support the away team?

19.

SUPER SALE $\frac{1}{3}$ OFF

FOR EXAMPLE
Coat £90 reduced by £30 to £60

Find the amount the following items will be reduced by and their new cost:

(a) A dress costing £60
(b) A pair of trousers costing £45
(c) A top costing £30
(d) A pair of shoes costing £36
(e) A shirt costing £18
(f) A jacket costing £48
(g) A belt costing £12
(h) A pair of socks costing £2·40

20. There are 240 marks available in an examination. Marianna scores $\frac{7}{8}$ of the marks and Barry scores $\frac{4}{5}$ of the marks. How many marks do Marianna and Barry score each?

12.10 Percentages and fractions

Percentages are fractions with a denominator of 100.
% means 'out of 100'.

10% is the same as $\frac{10}{100} = \frac{1}{10}$
50% is the same as $\frac{50}{100} = \frac{1}{2}$
40% is the same as $\frac{40}{100} = \frac{2}{5}$

Example
Change these percentages into fractions.
(a) 11%   (b) 25%   (c) 64%

(a) $11\% = \frac{11}{100}$
(b) $25\% = \frac{25}{100} = \frac{1}{4}$
(c) $64\% = \frac{64}{100} = \frac{16}{25}$

Exercise 12J
Change these percentages into fractions.

1. 30%
2. 20%
3. 75%
4. 90%
5. 80%
6. 5%
7. 45%
8. 4%
9. 12%
10. 24%
11. 60%
12. 2%
13. 22%
14. 98%
15. 35%
16. 72%
17. 95%
18. 65%
19. 17%
20. 42%
21. 12%
22. 14%
23. 16%
24. 99%
25. 15%

12.11 Percentages of quantities

If calculations are simple they can be done in your head or on paper. With more difficult numbers use a calculator.

How much can you save if you book this holiday before the end of June?

14 nights in Ibiza
Half board, two-star hotel.
Flight to and from Gatwick.
£340 per person
Save <u>20%</u> if you book by the end of June

The saving will be 20% of £340.

10% of £340 is £34
so 20% of £340 is £68.

Example 1

Calculate 45% of 80

$$45\% \text{ of } 80 = \frac{45}{100} \times 80 = 80 \div 100 \times 45 = 36$$

Example 2

A plumber charges £62·40 for a repair but adds 17·5% V.A.T. to the bill. Find the total charge.

17·5% of 62·40 = 62·4 ÷ 100 × 17·5 = 10·92
Total charge = £62·40 + £10·92 = £73·32

Exercise 12K

1. Calculate.
   - (a) 10% of 700
   - (b) 25% of 800
   - (c) 50% of 600
   - (d) 75% of 400
   - (e) 20% of 80
   - (f) 15% of 120
   - (g) 40% of 95
   - (h) 4% of 125
   - (i) 80% of 150
   - (j) 30% of 60
   - (k) 60% of 45
   - (l) 70% of 200
   - (m) 45% of 400
   - (n) 12% of 150
   - (o) 34% of 300
   - (p) 65% of 240
   - (q) 16% of 25
   - (r) 25% of 16
   - (s) 8% of 250
   - (t) 90% of 90
   - (u) 24% of 75
   - (v) 64% of 275
   - (w) 78% of 350
   - (x) 55% of 60
   - (y) 60% of 55

2. Calculate.
   (a) 5% of 62
   (b) 17% of 80
   (c) 11% of 92
   (d) 56% of 127
   (e) 23% of 267
   (f) 42% of 384
   (g) 3% of 1 200
   (h) 7% of 95
   (i) 45% of 508
   (j) 98% of 580
   (k) 18% of 670
   (l) 9% of 15
   (m) 17·5% of 80
   (n) 17·5% of 240
   (o) 17·5% of 140
   (p) 17·5% of 99
   (q) 12·5% of 56
   (r) 3·1% of 250
   (s) 24% of 67·8
   (t) 50% of 34·8
   (u) 75% of 44·8
   (v) 7·5% of 160
   (w) 7·5% of 48
   (x) 12·5% of 16·8
   (y) 14·3% of 34·2

3. **15% Off GRAND SALE**

   FOR EXAMPLE
   Coat £98 reduced by £14·70 to £83·30

   Find the amount the following items will be reduced by and the new cost:
   (a) A dress costing £80
   (b) A pair of trousers costing £60
   (c) A top costing £30
   (d) A pair of shoes costing £70
   (e) A shirt costing £45
   (f) A jacket costing £48
   (g) A belt costing £18
   (h) A pair of socks costing £4·80

4. **CLASSIC COMPUTERS**

   Computer systems from £400 to £4 000

   Example. Home System 3 000

   £550 + 17·5% V.A.T.

   £550 + £96·25 = **£646·25**

   These are the prices of computer systems before V.A.T. is added. Calculate the amount of V.A.T. to add and the full price.
   (a) Home System 4 000, £640
   (b) Office System 2 000, £800
   (c) Game Player 5 000, £1 200
   (d) Home Office 4 000, £500
   (e) Game Player 2 000, £750
   (f) Home System 1 000, £320
   (g) Office System 5 000, £3 250
   (h) Home Office 2 000, £390

12.12 Fractions, percentages and decimals

To change a fraction to a decimal, you divide the top number by the bottom number.
To change a decimal to a percentage, you multiply by 100.

Example

Change $\frac{3}{4}$ to a decimal and a percentage.

$$\begin{array}{r} 0.75 \\ 4\overline{)3.00} \\ \underline{2\ 8} \\ 20 \\ \underline{20} \\ 0 \end{array}$$

$\frac{3}{4} = 0.75 = 75\%$

When the numbers are more difficult, use a calculator.

Example

Change $\frac{23}{25}$ to a decimal and a percentage.

$\frac{23}{25} = 23 \div 25 = 0.92 = 92\%$

Exercise 12L

1. Change each fraction to a decimal and a percentage.
   (a) $\frac{1}{2}$ (b) $\frac{1}{4}$ (c) $\frac{3}{4}$ (d) $\frac{3}{5}$ (e) $\frac{7}{10}$ (f) $\frac{11}{20}$ (g) $\frac{3}{25}$
   (h) $\frac{27}{50}$ (i) $\frac{1}{5}$ (j) $\frac{9}{10}$ (k) $\frac{3}{20}$ (l) $\frac{18}{25}$ (m) $\frac{1}{50}$ (n) $\frac{2}{5}$
   (o) $\frac{1}{10}$ (p) $\frac{9}{20}$ (q) $\frac{17}{25}$ (r) $\frac{43}{50}$ (s) $\frac{7}{20}$ (t) $\frac{21}{25}$ (u) $\frac{11}{50}$
   (v) $\frac{13}{20}$ (w) $\frac{11}{25}$ (x) $\frac{49}{50}$ (y) $\frac{24}{25}$

2.

HEEL'S SHOES	SOLE'S SHOES	SHOO'S SHOES
SPECIAL OFFER	*SPECIAL OFFER*	*SPECIAL OFFER*
LE BOC TRAINERS	**LE BOC TRAINERS**	**LE BOC TRAINERS**
Normal price £120	Normal price £120	Normal price £120
$\frac{1}{3}$ OFF	30% OFF	$\frac{5}{12}$ OFF

(a) What is the cash reduction in Heel's shop?
(b) What is the cash reduction in Sole's shop?
(c) What is the cash reduction in Shoo's shop?
(d) What is the percentage reduction in Heel's shop?
(e) What is the percentage reduction in Shoo's shop?

12.13 Writing one number as a percentage of another

To write one number as a percentage of another:

- form a fraction with the two numbers
- convert the fraction to a decimal
- convert the decimal to a percentage.

Example 1

Write 48 as a percentage of 64.

48 as a fraction of 64 = $\frac{48}{64}$

48 as a percentage of 64 = 48 ÷ 64 × 100 = 75%

Example 2

Siloben scores 126 out of 144 in an English test.
What is her percentage mark?

Siloben's mark as a fraction = $\frac{126}{144}$

Siloben's mark as a percentage = 126 ÷ 144 × 100 = 87·5%

Example 3

A coat is reduced from £76 to £57 in a sale.
What is the percentage reduction?

Cash reduction = £76 − £57 = £19

Reduction as a fraction = $\frac{19}{76}$

Reduction as a percentage = 19 ÷ 76 × 100 = 25%

Exercise 12M

1. Write:
   (a) 40 as a percentage of 80
   (b) 36 as a percentage of 48
   (c) 6 as a percentage of 24
   (d) 10 as a percentage of 25
   (e) 27 as a percentage of 45
   (f) 9 as a percentage of 60
   (g) 35 as a percentage of 125
   (h) 64 as a percentage of 80
   (i) 78 as a percentage of 156
   (j) 15 as a percentage of 50
   (k) 56 as a percentage of 80
   (l) 300 as a percentage of 400
   (m) 39 as a percentage of 156
   (n) 132 as a percentage of 240
   (o) 484 as a percentage of 605
   (p) 221 as a percentage of 425
   (q) 39 as a percentage of 65
   (r) 63 as a percentage of 90
   (s) 76 as a percentage of 80
   (t) 51 as a percentage of 150
   (u) 360 as a percentage of 800
   (v) 35 as a percentage of 500
   (w) 44 as a percentage of 275
   (x) 126 as a percentage of 150
   (y) 412 as a percentage of 515

2.

```
HISTORY TEST (marks out of 80)
Janice      12
Jo          24
Rob         48
Elizabeth   60
Mike        32
Fozia       56
Kaleek      40
Nicky       50
Ruth        70
Yvette      76
```

This list was pinned up after a History test. Copy out the list, giving each mark as a percentage of 80.

3. Write each of these times as a percentage of one hour:
   (a) 15 minutes (b) 30 minutes (c) 12 minutes (d) 27 minutes (e) 36 minutes
   (f) 45 minutes (g) 48 minutes (h) 51 minutes (i) 39 minutes (j) 57 minutes

4. Andrew is the manager of a record shop. He decides to hold a sale of Abba items. Before the sale he starts to prepare this list for the staff.

Sale items only	Old price	Sale price	Cash saving	% saving
CDs	£12·50	£10·00	£2·50	20%
Single CDs	£3·60	£3·06	£0·54	
Tapes	£11·60	£8·70		
Posters	£4·80	£4·20		
Books	£5·40	£2·97		

Copy and complete Andrew's list.

5. Oranges can be bought for 12p each or £1·62 for a bag of 15.
   (a) How much does it cost to buy 15 oranges at 12p each?
   (b) What is the saving by buying a bag of 15 oranges?
   (c) What is the percentage saving by buying a bag of 15 oranges?
   (d) Special offer bags of the oranges are marked '20% extra free'. How many oranges do these bags contain?
   (e) What fraction of the oranges in special offer bags are free?

12.14 Increasing and decreasing an amount by a given percentage

Example 1
If an Inter City season ticket costs £2 632 now, how much will it cost after a 21% rise?

Method 1
To find the new cost of a ticket you find 21% of £2 632 and then add this to the original:

$$21\% \text{ of } £2\,632 = \frac{21}{100} \times £2\,632$$

Increase in fare = £552·72
New cost of fare = £2 632 + £552·72
= £3 184·72

Method 2
Consider the original amount of £2 632 as 100%. Increasing it by 21% is the same as finding 121% of the original cost.

$$121\% = \frac{121}{100} = 1·21$$

Therefore the quickest way of increasing the original fare by 21% is to multiply it by 1·21.

121% of £2 632 = 1·21 × £2 632
New cost of fare = £3 184·72

Example 2
The marked price of a sweater is £24·90. What is its sale price?

Method 1
The reduction = 20% of £24·90

$$= \frac{20}{100} \times £24·90$$

= £4·98
The sale price = £24·90 − £4·98
= £19·92

Method 2
£24·90 is the equivalent of 100% and so decreasing the price by 20% is equivalent to finding 80% of the original price.

$$\frac{80}{100} \times £24·90 \quad = 0·80 \times £24·90$$

Sale price = £19·92

Exercise 12N
Give all answers to the nearest 1p.

1. Increase the following rail fares by 10%.
   (a) £9·20   (b) £3·70   (c) £5·00   (d) £9·81   (e) £9·13

2. Increase the given amount by the required percentage:
   (a) £72·12 by 50%   (b) 95p by 10%   (c) £360 by 120%
   (d) £220 by 30%   (e) £124·80 by 25%   (f) £19·99 by 90%

3. Reduce the following marked prices by 20% to find the sale prices:
   (a) £30·00   (b) £10·50   (c) £17·60   (d) 45p   (e) £12·99

4. Increase the given amount by the required percentage:
   (a) £54·10 by 8%   (b) 84p by 30%   (c) £128 by 60%
   (d) £27·15 by $17\frac{1}{2}$%   (e) £99·05 by 40%   (f) £1·62 by 33%

Summary

1. You can use fractions to describe the way things are divided.

2. $\frac{12}{5}$ is an **improper fraction** and can be written as a **mixed number** like this: $2\frac{2}{5}$
   The mixed number $4\frac{2}{3}$ can be written as the improper fraction $\frac{14}{3}$.

3. **Equivalent** fractions are different ways of writing the same fraction. $\frac{3}{4}$ and $\frac{6}{8}$ are equivalent fractions.

4. Fractions can be simplified by dividing the top and bottom by the same number.

5. Fractions can be added and subtracted by making the denominators the same.
   $$\frac{3}{4} + \frac{2}{3} = \frac{9}{12} + \frac{8}{12} = \frac{17}{12} = 1\frac{5}{12}$$
   $$2\frac{1}{2} - 1\frac{4}{5} = 1\frac{5}{10} - \frac{8}{10} = 1 - \frac{3}{10} = \frac{7}{10}$$

Checkout 12

1. What fraction of each shape is coloured?
   (a)
   (b)

2. (a) Write as mixed numbers:
       (i) $\frac{17}{2}$ (ii) $\frac{16}{3}$ (iii) $\frac{9}{4}$
   (b) Write as improper fractions:
       (i) $3\frac{1}{2}$ (ii) $2\frac{3}{4}$ (iii) $7\frac{2}{3}$

3. Complete these pairs of equivalent fractions:
   (a) $\frac{3}{4} = \frac{}{12}$ (b) $\frac{1}{2} = \frac{}{24}$
   (c) $\frac{3}{8} = \frac{}{16}$ (d) $\frac{4}{5} = \frac{}{25}$

4. Simplify:
   (a) $\frac{6}{8}$ (b) $\frac{14}{35}$
   (c) $\frac{10}{16}$ (d) $\frac{15}{45}$

5. (a) $\frac{3}{4} + \frac{3}{4}$ (b) $\frac{4}{5} + \frac{3}{5}$
   (c) $\frac{5}{11} + \frac{9}{11}$ (d) $3\frac{2}{3} + \frac{2}{3}$
   (e) $\frac{3}{4} - \frac{1}{4}$ (f) $\frac{5}{6} - \frac{1}{6}$
   (g) $\frac{7}{9} - \frac{4}{9}$ (h) $\frac{1}{3} - \frac{2}{3}$
   (i) $\frac{2}{3} + \frac{4}{5}$ (j) $\frac{3}{4} + \frac{5}{6}$
   (k) $1\frac{2}{3} + \frac{2}{9}$ (l) $4\frac{3}{5} + \frac{7}{10}$
   (m) $\frac{4}{5} - \frac{2}{3}$ (n) $\frac{7}{8} - \frac{3}{4}$
   (o) $1\frac{4}{5} - \frac{3}{10}$ (p) $3\frac{1}{3} - \frac{8}{9}$

6. To calculate $\frac{1}{4}$ of a quantity, you divide by 4.
$\frac{1}{4}$ of 240 = 240 ÷ 4 = 60

6. Calculate $\frac{1}{5}$ of:
   (a) 25 (b) 40
   (c) 250 (d) 600

7. The word 'of' can be replaced with a multiplication sign.
$\frac{2}{5}$ of 45 = $\frac{2}{5}$ × 45 = (2 × 45) ÷ 5 = 90 ÷ 5 = 18

7. Calculate $\frac{3}{4}$ of:
   (a) 16 (b) 64
   (c) 100 (d) 300

8. Percentages are fractions with 100 as their bottom number.
$64\% = \frac{64}{100} = \frac{16}{25}$

8. Change these percentages to fractions:
   (a) 20% (b) 75% (c) 36%

9. To work out a percentage of a quantity, change the percentage to a fraction.
45% of 80 = $\frac{45}{100}$ × 80 = 80 ÷ 100 × 45 = 36

9. Calculate:
   (a) 50% of 400 (b) 25% of 16
   (c) 12% of 175 (d) 85% of 260
   (e) 17·5% of £20 (f) 17·5% of £36

10. To change a fraction to a decimal, divide the top number by the bottom number.
To change a decimal to a percentage, multiply by 100

10. Change each fraction to a decimal and a percentage.
    (a) $\frac{3}{4}$ (b) $\frac{4}{5}$ (c) $\frac{3}{20}$ (d) $\frac{23}{25}$

11. To write one number as a percentage of another:
    • form a fraction with the two numbers
    • convert the fraction to a decimal
    • convert the decimal to a percentage.

11. (a) Write:
    (i) 60 as a percentage of 120
    (ii) 24 as a percentage of 50
    (iii) 150 as a percentage of 250
    (b) A coat is reduced from £80 to £56. Find the percentage reduction.

Revision exercise 12

1. Calculate the height of this piece of card. Give your answer as a fraction.

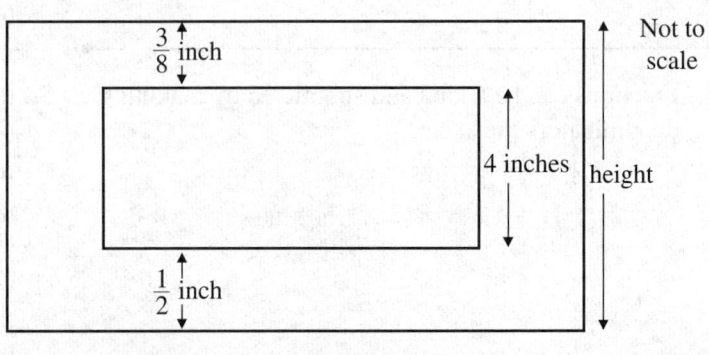

$\frac{3}{8}$ inch

4 inches

height

$\frac{1}{2}$ inch

Not to scale

[OCR]

2. This is a drawing of a bolt. It is not drawn to scale.

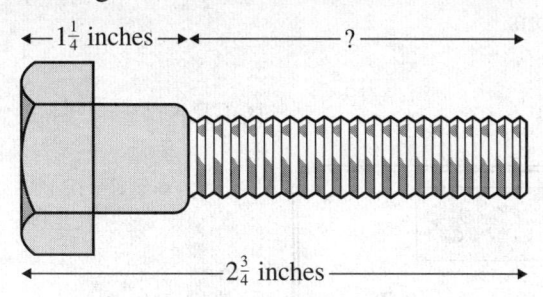

   Calculate the length marked '?'. [OCR]

3. This signpost was seen on a country road.
   The road passes through the three villages Ayton, Beeby and Ceegrave.

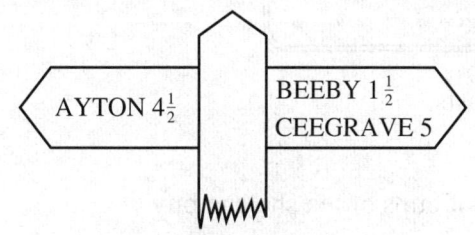

   How many miles is it along this road
   (a) from Ayton to Beeby
   (b) from Beeby to Ceegrave? [OCR]

4. At 08:50 Mr Khan drove onto a motorway.
   He left the motorway $1\frac{1}{2}$ hours later.

   (a) At what time did he leave the motorway?

   On the motorway Mr Khan drove at a steady speed of 60 miles per hour.

   (b) How far did he travel along the motorway? [OCR]

5. Boxes of Bobs Biscuits used to contain 650 grams of biscuits.
   New boxes contain one fifth more.
   How much does a new box contain? [OCR]

6. Anil earns £800 each month.
   Each month, one quarter of his monthly income is used to pay the rent on his flat. One fifth of the income that he has left after paying the rent is put into a savings account in a building society.
   What **fraction** of his monthly income is left after the above amounts have been taken away? [WJEC]

7. Work out these sums.
   Give your answers using fractions.
   (a) $1\frac{1}{4} + 3\frac{1}{2}$
   (b) $2\frac{1}{8} - 1\frac{1}{16}$ [OCR]

8.

Sam's Cafe

Cup of Tea	80p
Cup of Coffee	90p
Breakfast	£2·95
Today's Special	£4·00

   (a) Work out the cost of 5 Breakfasts.

   Dara buys some cups of tea.

   (b) Work out the greatest number of cups of tea she can buy with £5.

   A child's meal costs $\frac{7}{10}$ of the price of Today's Special.

   (c) Work out the cost of a child's meal. [Edexcel]

9. In Year 11 of a school, $\frac{1}{4}$ of the students support City and $\frac{3}{8}$ of them support Rovers.
   There are 160 students in Year 11.
   (a) (i) How many of them support City?
       (ii) How many of them support Rovers?
   (b) Work out $\frac{1}{4} + \frac{3}{8}$
   (c) Write $\frac{1}{4}$ as a percentage.
   (d) Change $\frac{3}{8}$ to a decimal. [OCR]

10. (a) (i) Write $\frac{1}{4}$ as a decimal.
        (ii) Write 0·2 as a fraction.
        (iii) Write 30% as a decimal.
        (iv) Write $\frac{1}{4}$, 0·2 and 30% in order of size, starting with the smallest.
    (b) David earned £12 000 last year. His wage is increased by 4%.
        Calculate the increase in his yearly wage.
    (c) Share £140 in the ratio 5 : 2. [WJEC]

11. (a) Find $\frac{4}{7}$ of £56.

(b)

SALE sale SALE sale
Prices DOWN by 15%

Mary buys a television set in this sale.
The usual price of the television was £480.
Calculate the sale price of the television. [WJEC]

12.

(a) What percentage of this whole shape is shaded?

(b) Copy the diagram and shade some more squares so that altogether $\frac{1}{3}$ of the whole shape is now shaded. [OCR]

13.

Portable TV

CASH PRICE
£361·50

CREDIT PRICE
Pay $\frac{1}{3}$ of the Cash Price
Plus 8 payments of £33·75

(a) How much is saved by paying the cash price instead of the credit price?

(b) Another television set costs £550.
In a sale the price is reduced by 12%.
Calculate the new price of this television set.
[AQA/SEG]

14. The cost of each television is shown on the price tag.

A £199 — 25% off marked price

B £185 — $\frac{1}{5}$ off marked price

Which television set is cheaper?
Show all your working. [OCR]

15. Work out the sale price of this dress.

PRICE £45
SALE All prices reduced by **20%**

[OCR]

16. In 1997 Mrs Patel earned £16 640 for a 52-week year.
At the start of 1998 she was given a rise of 3%.
Calculate how much she will earn **per week** in 1998.
[OCR]

17. Kitty invests £1 500 in an account for 3 years at 8% per annum simple interest.
Calculate the total amount in the account at the end of the 3 years. [WJEC]

18. Christopher has received his gas bill for the period June to August.
The details of the bill are as follows.

   Number of units of gas used is 7 939.
   The cost of one unit of gas is 1·52 pence.
   Number of days in this period is 92.
   The standing charge is 10·39 pence per day.

(a) Find, in pounds, the cost of the gas, including the standing charge, for the June to August period.
Show your working.

(b) V.A.T. at 5% is charged on gas bills.
How much is Christopher's gas bill including V.A.T.?
Give your answer in pounds, correct to the nearest penny. [WJEC]

19. In a normal week. Jane works $41\frac{1}{2}$ hours.
She is paid £3·75 an hour.

(a) How much does she earn?

Last week she worked 4 hours overtime on Sunday.
Her overtime rate is $1\frac{1}{2}$ times her normal hourly rate.

(b) How much did she earn last week?

One week she earned £175.
20% of this was deducted.

(c) How much money did she have left? [OCR]

20. *Computers-by-post* advertises a printer for £200 + V.A.T.
V.A.T. is charged at $17\frac{1}{2}$%.
What is the total cost? [OCR]

21. Emma buys a garden spade from a store.
The spade is advertised as costing £24 plus V.A.T. at 17·5%.

(a) Work out 17·5% of £24.

(b) What is the full price of the spade?

The store offers to take 15% off the full price of the spade because it is scratched.

(c) Work out 15% of the full price of the spade.

(d) The salesman tells Emma she has a bargain because the 15% discount is the same as not paying V.A.T.
Is this true? [AQA/NEAB]

22. A teacher is organising a trip to Pleasureland.
There are 560 pupils going on the trip.
The pupils will go by coach.
Each coach can carry 52 pupils.

(a) Work out how many coaches are needed.

45% of the pupils are boys.

(b) Work out the number of boys going on the trip.

The number of teachers needed on the trip is found by using this formula:

> Number of teachers on the trip equals 'the number of pupils divided by 25 and rounded down to the next whole number'.

(c) How many teachers are needed on the trip?

Do NOT use your calculator for part (d) of this question. Show all your working.

Each pupil pays £14 to go on the trip.

(d) Work out the total amount paid by the pupils.

[Edexcel]

23. In a test Suzanne scored 39 out of 60.
    What is this as a percentage? [OCR]

24. The population of the UK is about fifty-five million. Doctors think that about 1 in 5 of the population suffers from eczema.
    (a) How many million people suffer from eczema?
    (b) What percentage of the whole population suffers from eczema? [OCR]

25. In a maternity hospital, 200 babies were born during May. 100 of them were girls.
    (a) What percentage of the babies were girls?
    (b) What is the ratio   Boy babies : Girl babies?
        Give your answer in its lowest terms.
    (c) In June, the number of babies born in the hospital increased by 5%.
        Calculate the total number of babies born in June.
        [OCR]

26. In a hockey tournament, the Gladiators team was awarded 40 corners.
    It scored from 30 of them.
    (a) What percentage is this?
    (b) The Allstars team scored 35 out of 50 corners.
        Which is the better team at scoring from corners?
        Give a reason for your answer. [OCR]

27. Bestbuys Supermarket is cutting many of its prices.

> Doughnuts were 76p
> NOW 25% OFF

(a) Doughnuts have been reduced in price by 25%. Calculate the cost of the doughnuts now.

(b) Bestbuys are selling apples for 25p per pound.
Quickways, a rival supermarket, charge £1·20 for 3 kilograms of the same variety of apples.
1 kilogram is just over 2 pounds.
In which supermarket are the apples cheaper?

(c) Two of Bestbuys special offers are shown below.

> RUMP STEAK
> ~~£3 per pound~~
> £2 per pound

> LAMB CHOPS
> ~~£2·50 per pound~~
> £1·50 per pound

Anne says 'There is £1 off steak and lamb. Those are good offers'.
Bill says 'The offer on lamb is better'.
Explain why Bill thinks that.

(d) The Bestbuys offer with the greatest percentage reduction is on grapefruit.

> GRAPEFRUIT
> WAS 29p
> NOW 17p

Calculate the percentage reduction in the price of grapefruit. [AQA/NEAB]

13 ALGEBRA 3

Algebra is useful because you can understand it whatever language you speak.

Algebra in the Middle ages.

5 in A quad -7 in A plano + 9 aequatur 0. A simple equation me thinks...

This unit is about:

- Sequences of numbers
- Finding a formula for the *n*th term of a sequence
- Coordinates
- Drawing a graph of a linear equation
- Graphs of equations which produce curves
- Using graphs to illustrate relationships
- Distance and time graphs

You need to remember:

- How to use a formula (see Unit 5).
    1. If $x = 4$, $y = 2$ and $z = {}^-3$, find the value of t if:
        (a) $t = x + y$
        (b) $t = 2y$
        (c) $t = 3z$
        (d) $t = 5x + 1$
        (e) $t = 3x - 2y$
        (f) $t = y^2$
        (g) $t = 8 - 2y$
        (h) $t = 8 - 2z$
        (i) $t = xy - z$
        (j) $t = x^2 + z$

- How to solve equations (see Unit 11).
    2. Solve:
        (a) $3x = 12$
        (b) $4 + y = 7$
        (c) $\dfrac{y}{5} = 4$
        (d) $t - 7 = 1$
        (e) $2t + 1 = 31$
        (f) $4r - 3 = 25$
        (g) $5x + 1 = 26$
        (h) $8 - 2m = 0$
        (i) $2e + 5 = 10$
        (j) $3n + 1 = 43$

Check in 13

13.1 Producing a sequence of numbers

If you start with the number 1 and keep adding 2, you get the numbers:

1, 3, 5, 7, 9, 11, 13, 15, 17, 19, 21 ...

A set of numbers like this is called a **sequence**. Each number is called a **term** of the sequence. The way each new number is found is called the **rule** for the sequence.

Example

The first number in a sequence is 2, the rule for forming new numbers is to multiply by 2. Write down the first 5 terms of the sequence.

The first 5 terms are: 2, 4, 8, 16, 32

Exercise 13A

Write down the first 5 terms of each sequence.

1. The first number is 2, the rule is to add 3.
2. The first number is 1, the rule is to multiply by 3.
3. The first number is 5, the rule is to add 4.
4. The first number is 2, the rule is to add 4.
5. The first number is 100, the rule is to subtract 3.
6. The first number is 6, the rule is to add 5.
7. The first number is 1, the rule is to multiply by 4.
8. The first number is 2, the rule is to add 5.
9. The first number is 3, the rule is to add 6.
10. The first number is 1, the rule is to add 7.
11. The first number is 100, the rule is to subtract 10.
12. The first two numbers are 1 and 1, the rule is to add the two previous terms.

13.2 Finding the next terms in a sequence

You may be asked to write down the next terms in a sequence. Look carefully at the terms you are given to discover the rule. Use the rule to produce the number of new terms required.

Examples

Find the next two terms in each sequence.
(a) 2, 9, 16, 23, 30 ...

The rule is to add 7. The next two terms are 37 and 44.

(b) 3, 6, 12, 24, 48 …

The rule is to multiply by 2. The next two terms are 96 and 192.

(c) 100, 95, 90, 85, 80 …

The rule is to subtract 5. The next two terms are 75 and 70.

Exercise 13B

Write down the next two terms in each sequence.

1. 7, 12, 17, 22, 27 …
2. 110, 100, 90, 80, 70 …
3. 1, 5, 25, 125, 625 …
4. 5, 9, 13, 17, 21 …
5. 3, 4, 7, 11, 18 …
6. 9, 11, 13, 15, 17 …
7. 1 024, 512, 256, 128, 64 …
8. 1, 2, 4, 7, 11 …
9. 1, 3, 9, 27, 81 …
10. 8, 11, 14, 17, 20 …
11. 60, 56, 52, 48, 44 …
12. 3, 18, 33, 48, 63 …
13. 1 000, 100, 10, 1, 0.1 …
14. 7, 19, 31, 43, 55 …
15. 13, 19, 25, 31, 37 …
16. 1, 2, 3, 5, 8 …
17. 1, 3, 6, 10, 15 …
18. 1, 12, 23, 34, 45 …
19. 0.002, 0.02, 0.2, 2, 20 …
20. 8, 4, 2, 1, 0.5 …

13.3 Using a formula for the nth term of a sequence

The sequence 1, 2, 3, 4, 5, 6, 7 … is called the sequence of natural numbers. The natural numbers can be used to number the terms of any other sequence. For example, the terms of the sequence 1, 4, 7, 10, 13 … can be numbered like this:

1st	2nd	3rd	4th	5th
1	4	7	10	13

The sequence 1, 4, 7, 10, 13 … can be formed from the natural numbers by multiplying each natural number by 3 and then subtracting 2.

1st term $= 3 \times 1 - 2 = 1$
2nd term $= 3 \times 2 - 2 = 4$
3rd term $= 3 \times 3 - 2 = 7$
4th term $= 3 \times 4 - 2 = 10$
5th term $= 3 \times 5 - 2 = 13$

A formula for the sequence can be written like this:

nth term $= 3 \times n - 2$
$= 3n - 2$

Example

Write down the first 5 terms of a sequence if the formula for the *n*th term is:

nth term $= 2n + 3$

1st term $= 2 \times 1 + 3 = 5$
2nd term $= 2 \times 2 + 3 = 7$
3rd term $= 2 \times 3 + 3 = 9$
4th term $= 2 \times 4 + 3 = 11$
5th term $= 2 \times 5 + 3 = 13$

Exercise 13C

Write down the first five terms of the sequences produced by these formulae.

1. nth term $= 2n$
2. nth term $= 3n$
3. nth term $= 4n$
4. nth term $= 5n$
5. nth term $= 6n$
6. nth term $= 7n$
7. nth term $= 8n$
8. nth term $= 9n$
9. nth term $= 10n$
10. nth term $= n + 1$
11. nth term $= n + 3$
12. nth term $= n + 4$
13. nth term $= 2n + 1$
14. nth term $= 3n + 1$
15. nth term $= 4n + 1$
16. nth term $= 2n - 1$
17. nth term $= 3n - 1$
18. nth term $= 4n - 1$
19. nth term $= 5n + 2$
20. nth term $= 3n + 4$
21. nth term $= 4n - 3$
22. nth term $= 2n + 5$
23. nth term $= 5n - 4$
24. nth term $= 6n - 3$
25. nth term $= 2n + 7$
26. nth term $= 3n - 3$
27. nth term $= 4n + 5$
28. nth term $= 5n + 4$
29. nth term $= 3n + 8$
30. nth term $= 10n - 7$

13.4 Using differences

In the sequence 5, 8, 11, 14, 17 ... there is a constant difference between each pair of terms. To find a formula for the *n*th term of a sequence, first find the constant difference between each pair of terms. In this case, the constant difference is 3.

1st		2nd		3rd		4th		5th
5	+3	8	+3	11	+3	14	+3	17

The constant difference of 3 means this sequence is based on the sequence with the formula: nth term $= 3n$.

Write this sequence in above the given sequence.

n	1st	2nd	3rd	4th	5th
$3n$	3	6	9	12	15
	5	8	11	14	17

Look carefully at the two sequences. You will see that the second sequence is formed from the first by adding 2. The formula for the nth term of the sequence is: nth term $= 3n + 2$.

Example 1

Find a formula for the nth term of the sequence: 4, 6, 8, 10, 12 ...

The constant difference is 2. The sequence is based on the sequence with the formula nth term $= 2n$

n	1st	2nd	3rd	4th	5th
$2n$	2	4	6	8	10
	4	6	8	10	12

The formula is: nth term $= 2n + 2$

Example 2

Find a formula for the nth term of the sequence: 2, 7, 12, 17, 22 ... and the 50th term of the sequence

The constant difference is 5. The sequence is based on the sequence with the formula: nth term $= 5n$

n	1st	2nd	3rd	4th	5th
$5n$	5	10	15	20	25
	2	7	12	17	22

The formula is: nth term $= 5n - 3$.
The 50th term $= 5 \times 50 - 3 = 247$

Exercise 13D

Find a formula for the nth term and the 50th term of each sequence.

1. 5, 7, 9, 11, 13 ...
2. 6, 9, 12, 15, 18 ...
3. 7, 11, 15, 19, 23 ...
4. 3, 8, 13, 18, 23 ...
5. 8, 14, 20, 26, 32 ...
6. $^-$1, 1, 3, 5, 7 ...
7. 1, 4, 7, 10, 13 ...
8. 2, 6, 10, 14, 18 ...
9. 4, 9, 14, 19, 24 ...
10. 4, 11, 18, 25, 32 ...
11. 7, 9, 11, 13, 15 ...
12. 9, 12, 15, 18, 21 ...
13. 11, 15, 19, 23, 27 ...
14. 8, 13, 18, 23, 28 ...
15. 14, 24, 34, 44, 54 ...
16. 0, 2, 4, 6, 8 ...
17. 5, 8, 11, 14, 17 ...
18. 8, 12, 16, 20, 24 ...
19. 13, 18, 23, 28, 33 ...
20. 9, 19, 29, 39, 49 ...

13.5 Sequences based on patterns

Look at this sequence of patterns based on a hexagon with a side length of 1 unit.

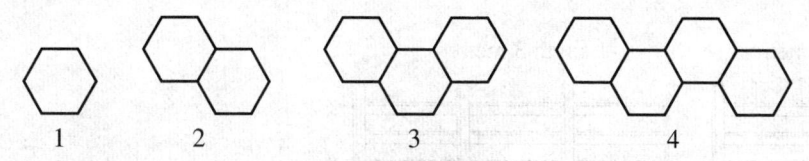

1   2   3   4

The perimeters of the hexagons form the sequence 6, 10, 14, 18 …

This sequence has a constant difference of 4.

n	1st	2nd	3rd	4th
$4n$	4	8	12	16
	6	10	14	18

The formula for the perimeter of the nth pattern is: nth perimeter $= 4n + 2$

Example

Matchsticks are placed to form this sequence of patterns.

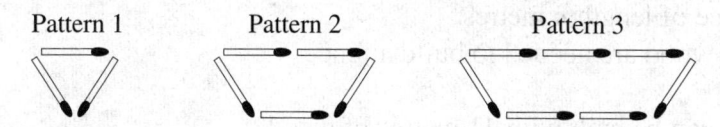

Pattern 1   Pattern 2   Pattern 3

(a) Find a formula for the number of matchsticks needed to form the nth pattern.
(b) How many matchsticks are in the 100th pattern?
(c) Which pattern uses 51 matches?

(a) The sequence of matchsticks is:

n	1st	2nd	3rd
	3	5	7

The constant difference is 2.

n	1st	2nd	3rd
$2n$	2	4	6
	3	5	7

The formula is: number of matchsticks needed to make the nth pattern $= 2n + 1$

(b) The number of matchsticks in the 100th pattern $= 2 \times 100 + 1 = 201$

(c) We have to find n when $2n + 1 = 51$
Subtracting 1 from both sides gives $2n = 50$
Dividing both sides by 2 gives $n = 25$
Pattern number 25 uses 51 matches.

Exercise 13E

1. Wilma Flint builds ranch fences using 1 metre lengths of wood. She builds fences of different length like this:

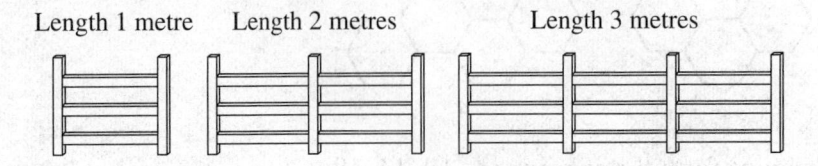

   Length 1 metre   Length 2 metres   Length 3 metres

   (a) How many metres of wood are used to build a fence of length 1 metre?
   (b) Copy and complete this table.

Fences length in metres	1	2	3	4
Metres of wood needed		9	13	

   (c) Find a formula for the number of metres of wood needed to build a fence of length n metres.
   (d) How many metres of wood are needed to build a fence of length 25 metres?
   (e) What length of fence can be built with 41 metres of wood?

2. A restaurant has tables which can seat 4 people. The tables are put together like this to make seating for larger parties of guests.

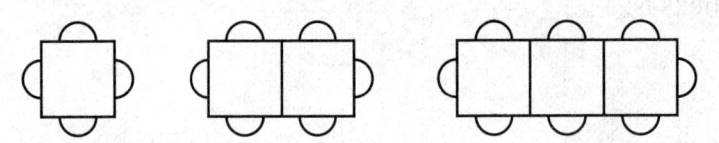

   (a) Copy and complete this table.

Number of tables	1	2	3	4
Number of seats	4	6		

   (b) Find a formula for the number of seats provided if n tables are put together.
   (c) How many seats are provided if 20 tables are put together?
   (d) How many tables are needed to provide 32 seats?

3. This sequence of patterns is made from octagons with a side length of 1 centimetre.

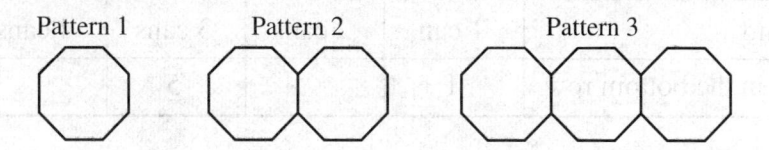

Pattern 1   Pattern 2   Pattern 3

(a) What is the perimeter of pattern 2?
(b) Copy and complete this table.

Pattern number	1	2	3	4
Perimeter	8 cm		20 cm	

(c) Find a formula for the perimeter of the nth pattern.
(d) Find the perimeter of the 60th pattern.
(e) Which pattern has a perimeter of 62 centimetres?

4. Matchsticks are placed to form this sequence of patterns.

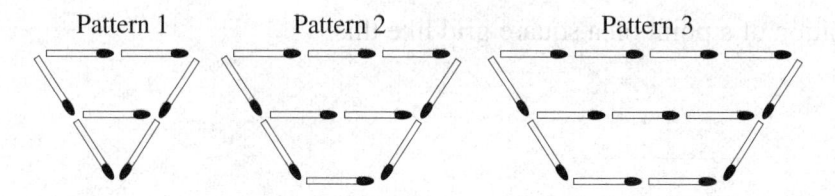

Pattern 1   Pattern 2   Pattern 3

(a) Find a formula for the number of matchsticks needed to form the nth pattern.
(b) Find the number of matchsticks in the 100th pattern.
(c) Which pattern requires 40 matchsticks?

5. A supermarket displays cans of beans by building them into pyramids like this:

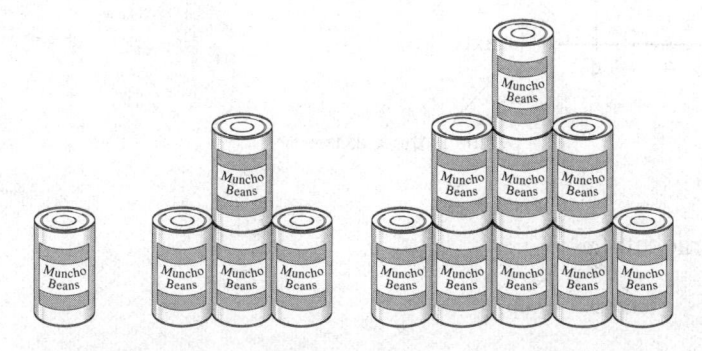

(a) Copy and complete this table.

Height of pyramid	1 can	2 cans	3 cans	4 cans
Number of cans in the bottom row	1		5	

(b) Find a formula for the number of cans in the bottom row of a pyramid n cans high.

(c) How many cans will be in the bottom row of a pyramid 25 cans high?

(d) How high is the pyramid with 29 cans in its bottom row?

13.6 Coordinates

Coordinates fix the position of a point on a square grid like this:

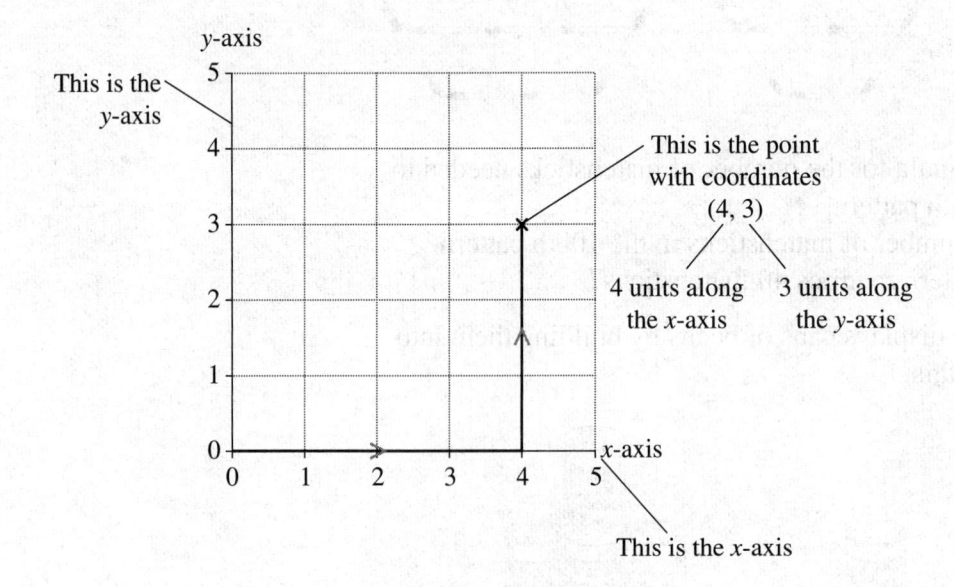

This is the y-axis

This is the point with coordinates (4, 3)

4 units along the x-axis *3 units along the y-axis*

This is the x-axis

Coordinates are written in a bracket: (x, y)

(across) (up)

Look at the grid below.

> A is the point with coordinates (1,4)
> B is the point with coordinates (4,1)
> C is the point with coordinates (1,0)
> D is the point with coordinates (3,3)
> E is the point with coordinates (0,2)

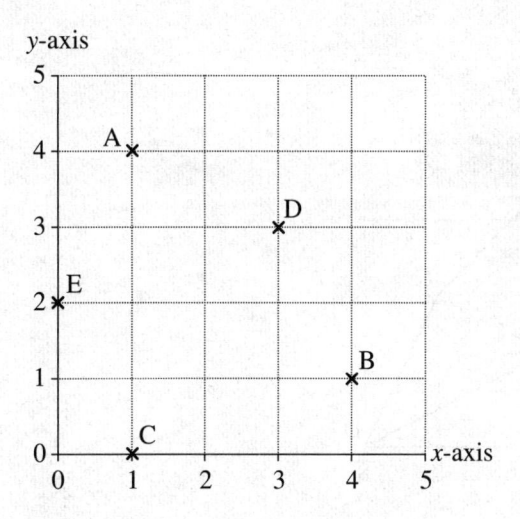

Exercise 13F

1. Write down the coordinates of the points A to J on this grid.

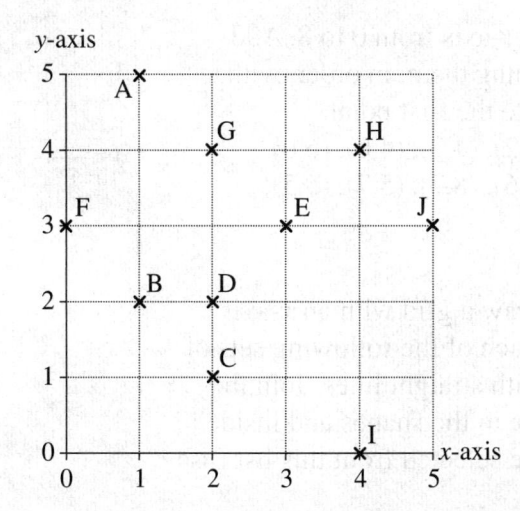

278 Algebra 3

2. The outline of a jet has been drawn on this grid.
   Write down the coordinates of the corner points A to M.

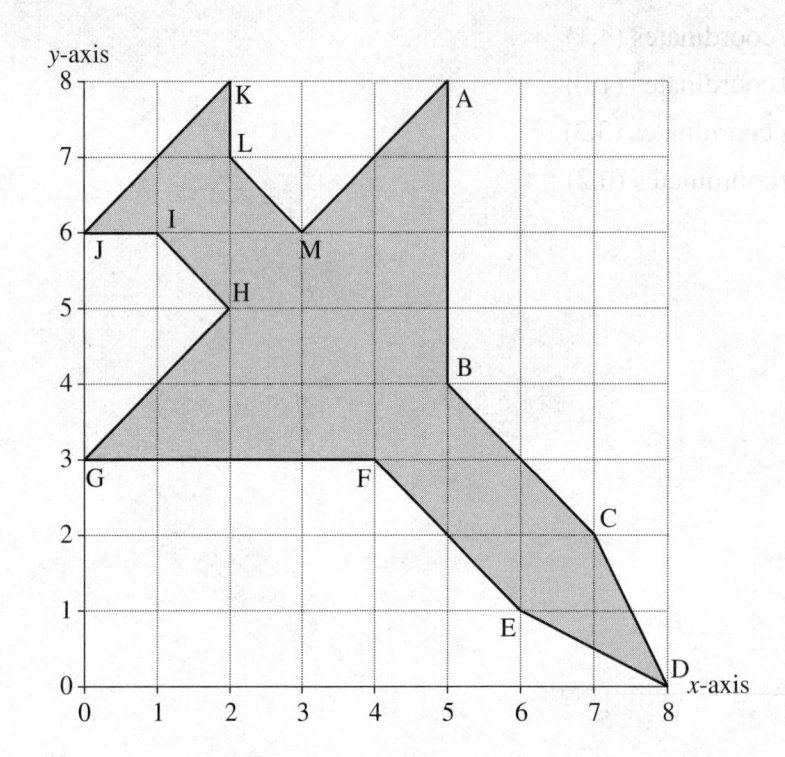

3. Draw a grid with an *x*-axis and a *y*-axis from 0 to 8. Add each of the following points, joining them, in order, with straight lines. Join the last point to the first point.
   (2,4), (4,2), (6,2), (8,4), (8,8), (6,6), (4,6), (2,8)

   You can copy this grid:

4. Draw a grid with an *x*-axis and a *y*-axis from 0 to 8. Add each of the following points, joining them, in order, with straight lines. Join the last point to the first point.
   (0,5), (0,2), (1,2), (1,0), (3,0), (3,2), (4,2), (4,0), (6,0), (6,2), (8,2), (8,3), (6,3), (6,6), (8,6), (8,7), (5,7), (5,5), (2,5), (2,7), (1,7), (1,5)

5. For each part of this question, draw a grid with an *x*-axis and a *y*-axis from 0 to 10. Add each of the following sets of points, joining them, in order, with straight lines. Join the last point to the first point. Shade in the shapes and inside each shape write its correct name selected from this list (use each name once only).

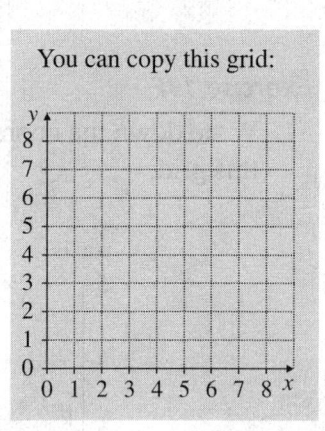

Isosceles triangle, Rectangle, Pentagon, Quadrilateral, Rhombus, Trapezium, Square, Hexagon, Right-angled triangle, Parallelogram, Kite.

Hint: Look back at Unit 9 to find out what these words mean.

(a) (0,8), (0,10), (3,9)
(b) (0,7), (1,8), (2,8), (1,6)
(c) (5,8), (5,9), (6,10), (7,9), (7,8)
(d) (0,1), (1,2), (3,2), (2,1)
(e) (4,3), (4,4), (5,4), (5,3)
(f) (2,3), (1,5), (2,6), (3,5)
(g) (2,0), (4,1), (5,1), (7,0)
(h) (8,10), (10,10), (10,7)
(i) (5,2), (7,3), (9,2), (7,1)
(j) (4,6), (4,7), (7,7), (7,6)
(k) (6,4), (6,5), (8,6), (10,5), (10,4), (8,3)

6. The treasure map below has a key which starts like this:

Place	Location
Caves	(9,5)
Dead Person's Point	$(8\frac{1}{2}, 7\frac{1}{2})$

Copy and complete the key.

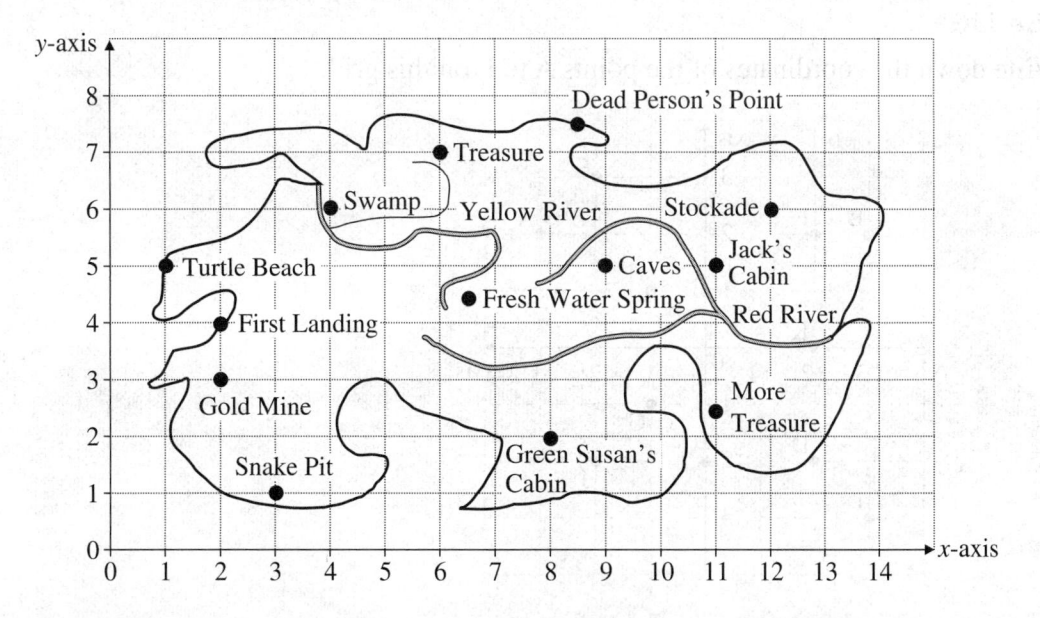

13.7 Coordinates in four quadrants

Coordinates can be extended to fix the position of a point on a square grid like this:

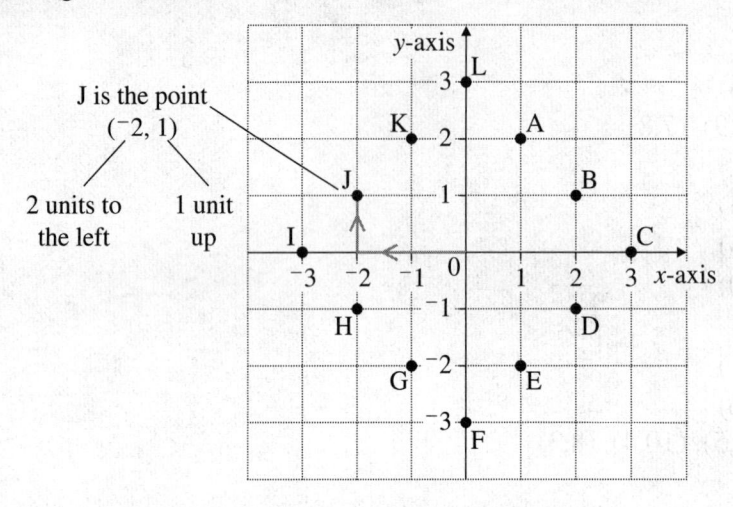

J is the point (⁻2, 1)
2 units to the left
1 unit up

Look at the grid.

A is the point with coordinates (1,2)
C is the point with coordinates (3,0)
E is the point with coordinates (1,⁻2)
G is the point with coordinates (⁻1,⁻2)
I is the point with coordinates (⁻3,0)
K is the point with coordinates (⁻1,2)

B is the point with coordinates (2,1)
D is the point with coordinates (2,⁻1)
F is the point with coordinates (0, ⁻3)
H is the point with coordinates (⁻2,⁻1)
J is the point with coordinates (⁻2,1)
L is the point with coordinates (0,3)

Exercise 13G

1. Write down the coordinates of the points A to L on this grid.

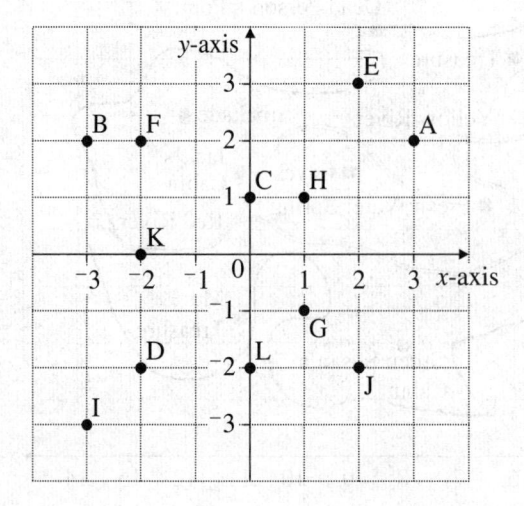

2. The outline of a cat has been drawn on this grid. Write down the coordinates of the corner points A to O.

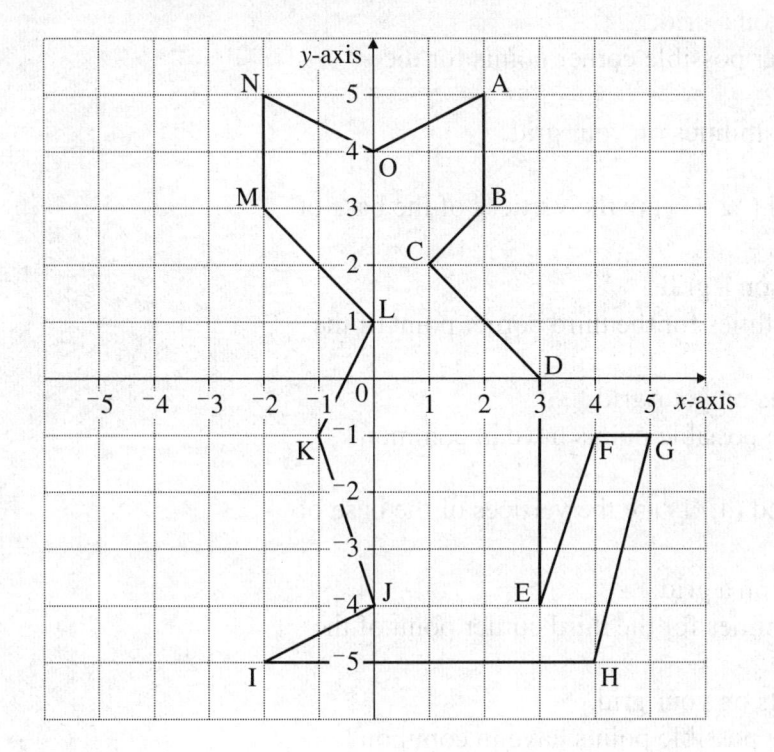

3. For each part of this question, draw a grid with an x-axis and a y-axis from ⁻4 to 4. Add each of the following sets of points, joining them, in order, with straight lines. Join the last point to the first point.

   You can copy this grid:

   (a) (3,0), (0,3), (⁻3,0), (0,⁻3)
   (b) (4,0), (3,4), (⁻4,0), (⁻3,⁻4)
   (c) (⁻3,⁻3), (⁻1,⁻2), (0,4), (1,⁻2), (3,⁻3)
   (d) (⁻2,4), (2,4), (3,⁻1), (2,⁻4), (⁻2,⁻4), (⁻3,⁻1)
   (e) (4,⁻1), (1,⁻1), (1,0), (4,0), (0,3), (⁻4,0), (⁻1,0), (⁻1,⁻1), (⁻4,⁻1), (⁻4,⁻3), (4,⁻3)
   (f) (2,0), (2½,0), (1½,1), (2,1), (1,2), (1½,2), (½,3), (1,3), (0,4), (⁻1,3), (⁻½,3), (⁻1½,2), (½,⁻3), (⁻1,2), (⁻2,1), (⁻1½,1), (⁻2½,0), (⁻2,0), (⁻3,⁻1), (⁻½,⁻1), (-½,-2), (-1,-2), (⁻½,⁻3), (1,⁻2), (½,⁻2), (½,⁻1), (3,⁻1)

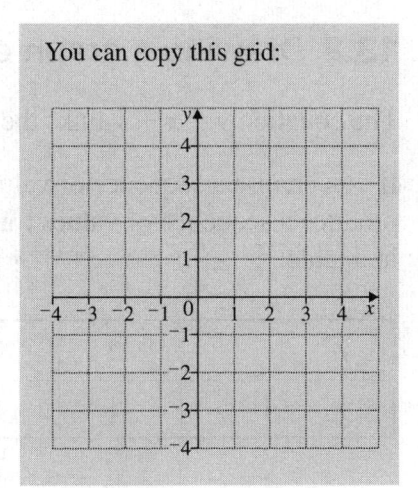

282 Algebra 3

4. The points (⁻2,1) and (4,1) are two of the corner points of a square.
   (a) Plot these points on a grid.
   (b) What are the other possible corner points for the square?
   (c) Show all the possibilities on your grid.

5. The points (⁻2,3) and (⁻2,⁻1) are the vertices of the base of an isosceles triangle.
   (a) Plot these points on a grid.
   (b) List some possibilities for the third corner point of the isosceles triangle.
   (c) Show these points on your grid.
   (d) What do all these possible points have in common?

6. The points (⁻2,⁻1) and (4,⁻1) are the vertices of the base of an isosceles triangle.
   (a) Plot these points on a grid.
   (b) List some possibilities for the third corner point of the isosceles triangle.
   (c) Show these points on your grid.
   (d) What do all these possible points have in common?

13.8 Drawing a graph of a linear equation

The equation $y = x + 1$ links the values of x and y.

If you choose a sequence of values for x, the equation will produce a sequence of values for y. You can show the results in a table.

x	⁻2	⁻1	0	1	2
$y = x + 1$	⁻1	0	1	2	3

The table gives coordinates to plot: (⁻2,⁻1) (⁻1,0) (0,1) (1,2) (2,3)

Plot the points and join them together.

The completed diagram is **the graph of $y = x + 1$**

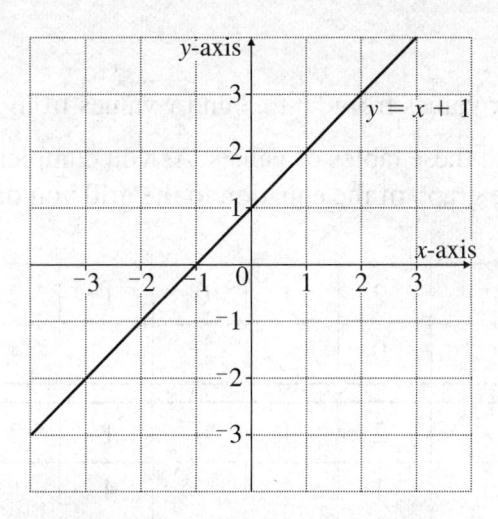

Example

Using x values from $^-2$ to 2, draw the graph of $y = 2x - 1$.

First complete a table of values for x and y.

x	$^-2$	$^-1$	0	1	2
$y = 2x - 1$	$^-5$	$^-3$	$^-1$	1	3

$(^-2, ^-5)$ $(^-1, ^-3)$ $(0, ^-1)$ $(1, 1)$ $(2, 3)$

Then, draw a grid and plot the points.

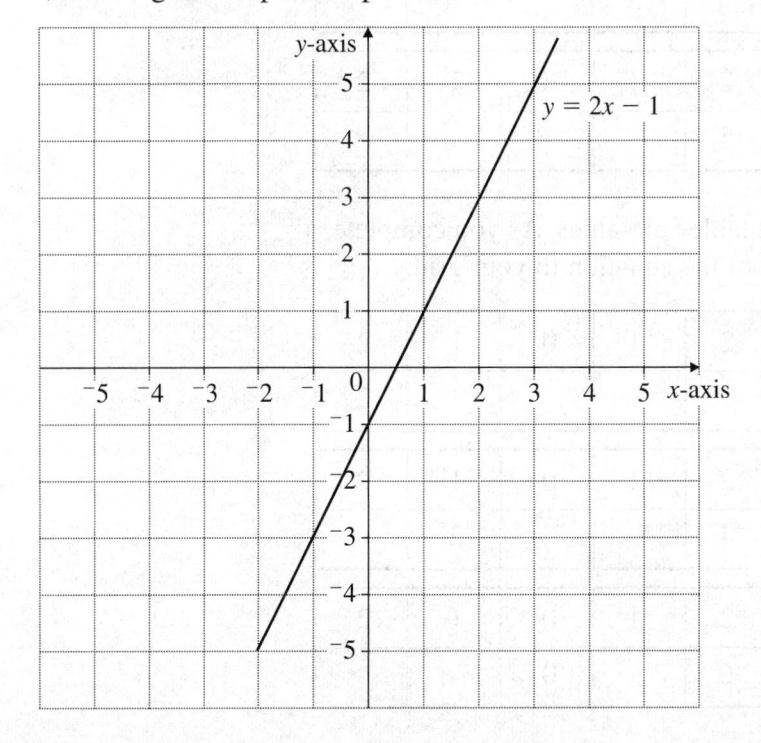

Exercise 13H

1. Draw a grid with x values from $^-3$ to 3 and y values from $^-6$ to 6.

2. Copy and complete these tables of values. As you complete each table, add the graph of the equation to the grid you drew for Question **1**.

   (a)

x	$^-2$	$^-1$	0	1	2
$y = x + 2$	0				4

   (b)

x	$^-2$	$^-1$	0	1	2
$y = x + 3$	1			4	

   (c)

x	$^-2$	$^-1$	0	1	2
$y = x + 4$	2		4		

   (d)

x	$^-2$	$^-1$	0	1	2
$y = x - 1$	$^-3$		$^-1$		

   (e)

x	$^-2$	$^-1$	0	1	2
$y = x - 2$		$^-3$		$^-1$	

   (f)

x	$^-2$	$^-1$	0	1	2
$y = x - 3$	$^-5$		$^-3$		

3. Copy and complete these tables of values. As you complete each table, add the graph of the equation to your grid.

   (a)

x	$^-2$	$^-1$	0	1	2
$y = x$	$^-2$				2

   (b)

x	$^-2$	$^-1$	0	1	2
$y = 2x$	$^-4$			2	

   (c)

x	$^-2$	$^-1$	0	1	2
$y = 3x$	$^-6$		0		

(d)

x	$^-2$	$^-1$	0	1	2
$y = {^-2x}$	4		0		$^-4$

(e)

x	$^-2$	$^-1$	0	1	2
$y = {^-3x}$	6			$^-3$	$^-6$

(f)

x	$^-2$	$^-1$	0	1	2
$y = {^-x}$	2		0	$^-1$	

4. Draw a grid with x values from $^-3$ to 3 and y values from $^-1$ to 12.

   Copy and complete these tables of values. As you complete each table, add the graph of the equation to your grid.

(a)

x	$^-2$	$^-1$	0	1	2
$y = 3 - x$	5				1

(b)

x	$^-2$	$^-1$	0	1	2
$y = 2 - x$	4			1	

(c)

x	$^-2$	$^-1$	0	1	2
$y = 1 - x$	3		1		

(d)

x	$^-2$	$^-1$	0	1	2
$y = 4 - x$	6	5	4		

(e)

x	$^-2$	$^-1$	0	1	2
$y = 8 - 2x$	12		8		4

5. Draw a grid with x values from $^-4$ to 4 and y values from $^-2$ to 2.

286 Algebra 3

6. Copy and complete these tables of values. As you complete each table, add the graph of the equation to the grid you drew for Question **5**.

(a)

x	-2	-1	0	1	2
$y = \dfrac{x}{2}$	-1		0	$\tfrac{1}{2}$	

(b)

x	-3	-1	0	1	3
$y = \dfrac{x}{3}$	-1	$-\tfrac{1}{3}$	0		

(c)

x	-4	-1	0	1	4
$y = \dfrac{x}{4}$	-1		0		

(d)

x	-2	-1	0	1	2
$y = \dfrac{-x}{2}$	1		0		-1

(e)

x	-3	-1	0	1	3
$y = \dfrac{-x}{3}$	1				

(f)

x	-4	-1	0	1	4
$y = \dfrac{-x}{4}$	1		0	$-\tfrac{1}{4}$	

7. Copy and complete these tables of values and draw the graph of the equation on a suitable grid.

(a)

x	-2	-1	0	1	2
$y = 2x + 1$	-3				5

(b)

x	$^-2$	$^-1$	0	1	2
$y = 3x - 1$	$^-7$			2	

(c)

x	$^-2$	$^-1$	0	1	2
$y = 2x - 3$	$^-7$		$^-3$		

(d)

x	$^-2$	$^-1$	0	1	2
$y = \dfrac{x}{2} + 3$	2		3	$3\tfrac{1}{2}$	

(e)

x	$^-2$	$^-1$	0	1	2
$y = 3 - 2x$	7			1	$^-1$

(f)

x	$^-2$	$^-1$	0	1	2
$y = 3x - 4$	$^-10$		$^-4$	$^-1$	

13.9 Graphs of equations which produce curves

Some equations will produce curves when plotted on a graph.

For example, this table shows a sequence of y values given by the equation $y = x^2$.

x	$^-3$	$^-2$	$^-1$	0	1	2	3
$y = x^2$	9	4	1	0	1	4	9

⇩ ⇩ ⇩ ⇩ ⇩ ⇩ ⇩

($^-3$,9) ($^-2$,4) ($^-1$,1) (0,0) (1,1) (2,4) (3,9)

When these values are plotted on a grid, it is quite clear that they cannot be connected with a straight line. The points are connected with a smooth curve to draw the graph of $y = x^2$.

Algebra 3

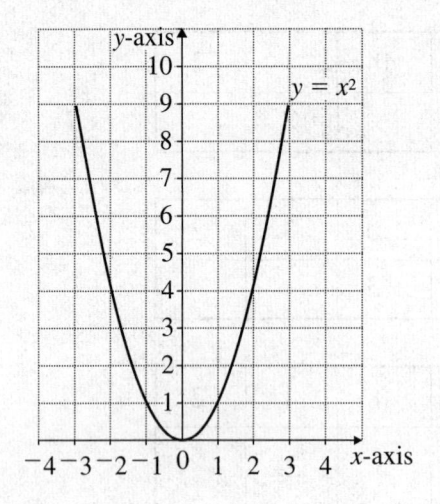

Example

Using x values from 1 to 8, draw the graph of $y = \dfrac{8}{x}$.

This is the table of values.

x	1	2	3	4	5	6	7	8
$y = \dfrac{8}{x}$	8	4	2·7	2	1·6	1·3	1·1	1

(1,8) (2,4) (3,2·7) (4,2) (5,1·6) (6,1·3) (7,1·1) (8,1)

This is the graph.

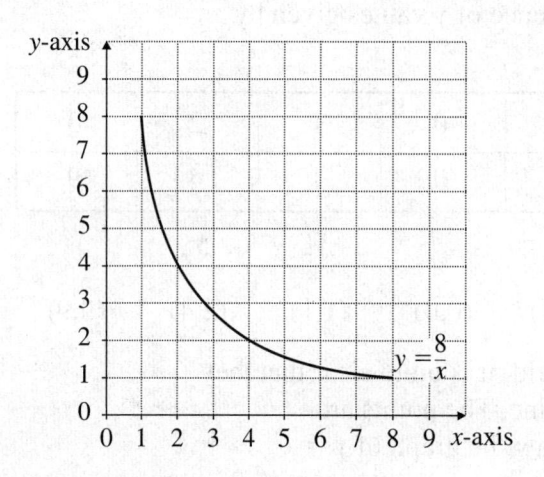

Exercise 131

1. Draw a graph with x values from $^-4$ to 4 and y values from $^-4$ to 16.

2. Copy and complete these tables of values. As you complete each table, add the graph of the equation to the grid you drew for Question **1**.

   (a)
x	$^-3$	$^-2$	$^-1$	0	1	2	3
$y = x^2 + 2$	11			2			11

   (b)
x	$^-3$	$^-2$	$^-1$	0	1	2	3
$y = x^2 + 4$	13				5		

   (c)
x	$^-3$	$^-2$	$^-1$	0	1	2	3
$y = x^2 + 6$		10				10	

   (d)
x	$^-3$	$^-2$	$^-1$	0	1	2	3
$y = x^2 - 2$	7		$^-1$	$^-2$			

   (e)
x	$^-3$	$^-2$	$^-1$	0	1	2	3
$y = x^2 - 4$	5	0		$^-4$	$^-3$		

3. Draw a grid with x and y values from 0 to 12.

   Copy and complete these tables of values. As you complete each table, add the graph of the equation to your grid.

   (a)
x	1	2	3	4	5	6	7	8	9	10	11	12
$y = \dfrac{12}{x}$	12				2·4		1·7	1·5	1·3		1·1	1

   (b)
x	1	2	3	4
$y = \dfrac{4}{x}$			1·3	

   (c)
x	1	2	3	4	5	6
$y = \dfrac{6}{x}$				1·5	1·2	

4. (a) Copy and complete this table of values.

x	−3	−2	−1	0	1	2	3
x^2	9	4		0	1		
$2x$	−6	−4			2		6
$y = x^2 + 2x$	3		−1	0		8	

(b) Draw the graph of $y = x^2 + 2x$ with values of x from −3 to 3.

5. (a) Copy and complete this table of values.

x	−3	−2	−1	0	1	2	3
x^2	9	4		0	1		
x	−3	−2			1		3
$y = x^2 - x$	12		2	0	0	2	

(b) Draw the graph of $y = x^2 - x$ with values of x from −3 to 3.

6. (a) Copy and complete this table of values.

x	−3	−2	−1	0	1	2	3
8	8	8	8	8	8	8	8
x^2	9	4		0	1		
$y = 8 - x^2$	−1	4	7		7		−1

(b) Draw the graph of $y = 8 - x^2$ with values of x from −3 to 3.

7. (a) Copy and complete this table of values.

x	−3	−2	−1	0	1	2
x^2	9	4		0	1	
$3x$	−9	−6	−3		3	
5	5	5	5		5	
$y = x^2 + 3x + 5$	5	3		5		15

(b) Draw the graph of $y = x^2 + 3x + 5$ with values of x from −3 to 2.

13.10 Using graphs to illustrate relationships

Graphs are often used to illustrate real-life relationships.
This graph shows the relationship between the distance that a car travels and the petrol it uses.

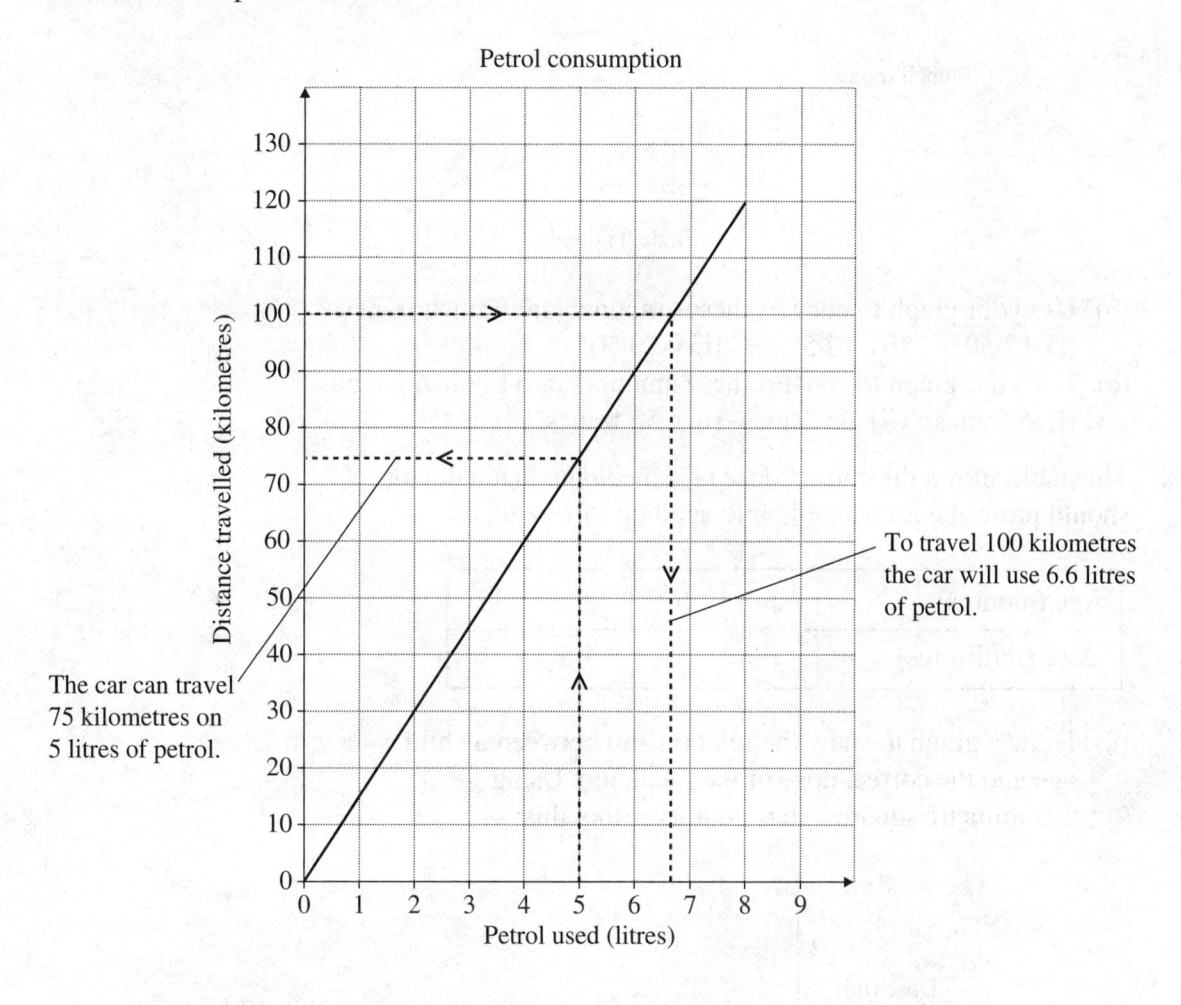

Petrol consumption

The car can travel 75 kilometres on 5 litres of petrol.

To travel 100 kilometres the car will use 6.6 litres of petrol.

The arrows added to the graph show how you can use it to estimate.

Exercise 13J

1. On a particular day, this table gave the conversion rate from English pounds into French francs.

English pounds	0	2	4	6	8	10
French francs	0	20	40	60	80	100

(a) Draw a graph to show the relationship between English pounds and French francs. Using 1 centimetre squares, start your axes like this.

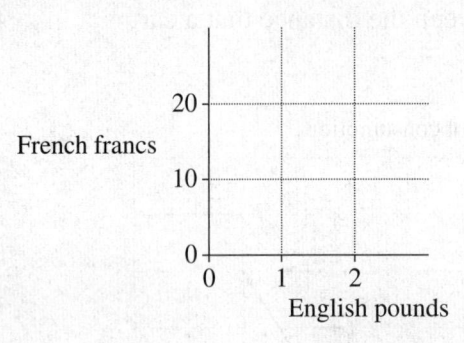

French francs

(b) Use your graph to convert these amounts into French francs.
(i) £2·50   (ii) £7·50   (iii) £9·50
(c) Use your graph to convert these amounts into English pounds.
(i) 5 francs   (ii) 35 francs   (iii) 55 francs

2. This table shows the correct dose of a medicine that a doctor should prescribe for a small child aged up to 1 year.

Age (months)	3	6	9	12
Dose (millilitres)	1·5	3	4·5	6

(a) Draw a graph to show the relationship between a child's age and the correct dose of the medicine. Using 1 centimetre squares, start your axes like this:

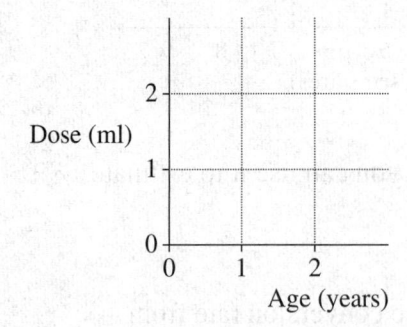

Dose (ml)

(b) Use your graph to estimate the correct dose for a child of age:
(i) 1 month   (ii) 8 months   (iii) 11 months
(c) Use your graph to estimate the age of a child who is given a dose of:
(i) 2 ml   (ii) 10 ml   (iii) 5 ml

3. This table shows the relationship between weight and cost for the 'pick-and-mix' sweets sold in a cinema.

Weight (grams)	0	250	500
Cost (pence)	0	200	400

   (a) Draw a graph to show the relationship between weight and cost for the sweets. Using 1 centimetre squares, start your axes like this:

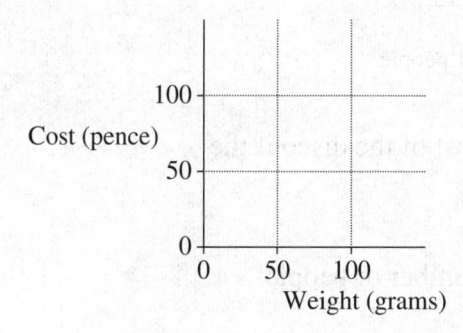

   (b) Use your graph to estimate the cost of sweets which weigh:
       (i) 100 grams   (ii) 300 grams   (iii) 450 grams
   (c) Use your graph to estimate the weight of sweets which cost:
       (i) £0·40   (ii) £2·80   (iii) £3·20

4. Melissa wants to hire a disco for her birthday. She has seen this advertisement for the 'Five High Disco'.

   FIVE HIGH DISCO
   £20 plus 50p per person

   (a) Copy and complete this table for the charges made by the 'Five High Disco'.

Number of people	10	30	50	70	90
Cost of disco (£)	25	35			

(b) Draw a graph to show the relationship between the number of people and the cost. Using 1 centimetre squares, start your axes like this:

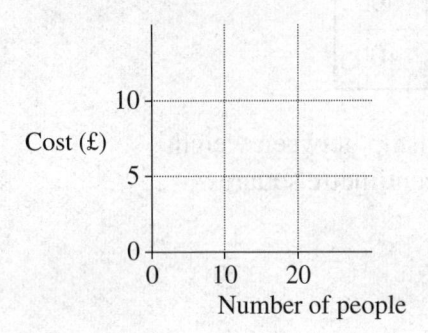

Cost (£)

Number of people

(c) Use your graph to estimate the cost of the disco if the number of people attending is:
(i) 20 (ii) 35 (iii) 65

(d) Use your graph to estimate the number of people attending if the cost is:
(i) £60 (ii) £40 (iii) £50

5. The relationship between the height of a birthday candle and the time for which it has been burning is described by this formula:

'The candle loses 1 cm in height for every minute it burns.'

(a) Draw a graph to show the change in height of a 5 centimetre birthday candle as it burns for 5 minutes. Using 1 centimetre squares, start your axes like this:

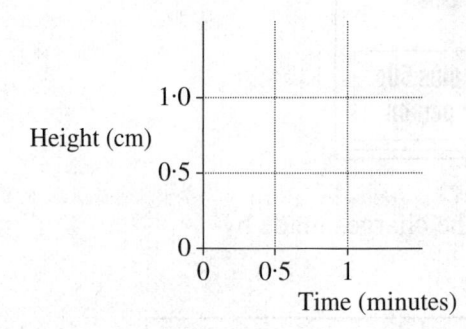

Height (cm)

Time (minutes)

(b) Make up two questions that you could use your graph to answer. Write down your questions and their answers.

13.11 Distance and time graphs

A journey of 5 kilometres from home to school takes 20 minutes. The journey starts with a 500 metre walk to the bus stop. This takes 5 minutes. There is then a 5 minute wait for a bus. The bus takes 10 minutes to complete the journey to school.

You can use this graph to show the journey.

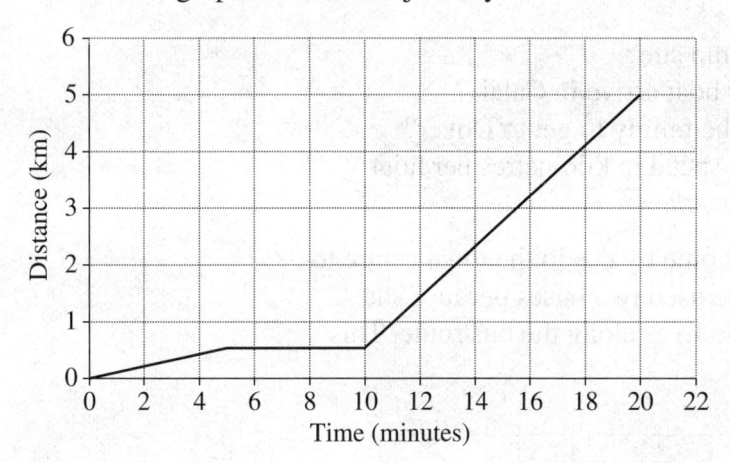

Exercise 13K

1. A family travel from their home in England to the car ferry at Dover and cross to Calais in France. They then travel to a camp site in northern France to spend the night. Their journey is shown on this graph.

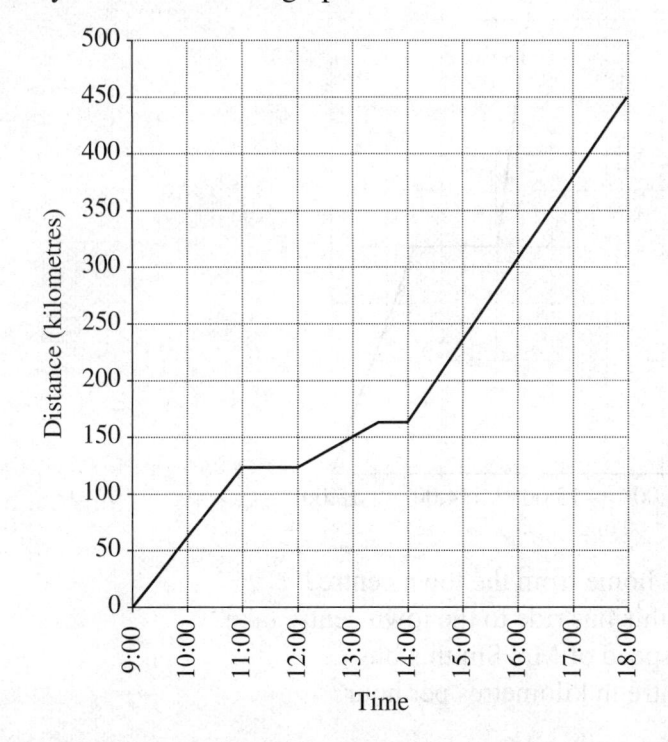

(a) At what time did they leave home?
(b) Where were they at 11:30?
(c) How long did they wait for the ferry to leave?
(d) How far from home were they at 16:00?
(e) How far was it from:
   (i) their home to Dover
   (ii) Dover to Calais
   (iii) Calais to their camp site?
(f) At what time did their boat arrive in Calais?
(g) How long did it take the family to get to Dover?
(h) What was the average speed in kilometres per hour from their home to Dover?

2. Mrs Smith travelled from home by bus to the town centre to shop. On the way home she used two buses because she wished to visit a friend who lives along the bus route. This graph shows her journey.

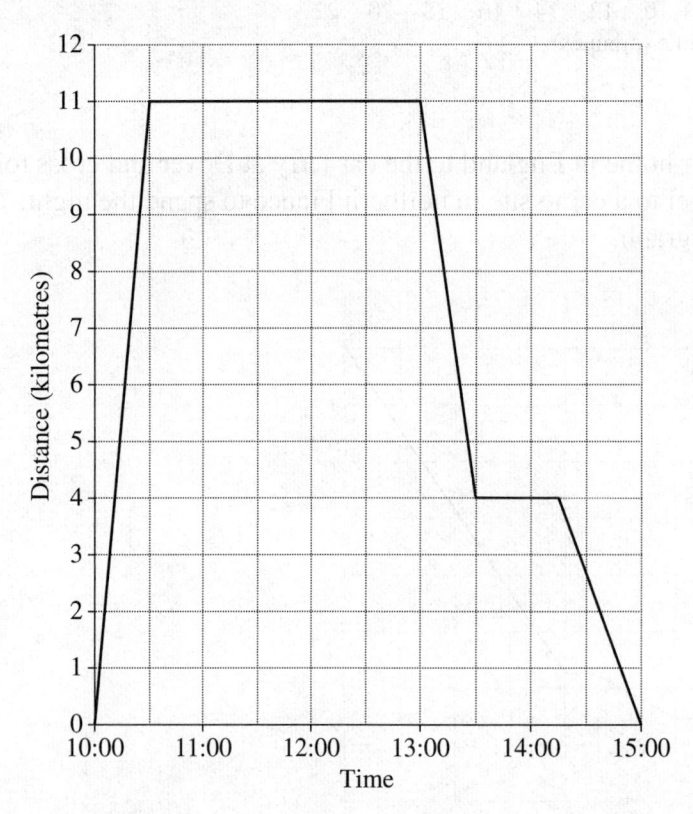

(a) How far is Mrs Smith's home from the town centre?
(b) How long did Mrs Smith's bus ride to the town centre take?
(c) What was the average speed of Mrs Smith's bus journey to the town centre in kilometres per hour?

(d) How long did Mrs Smith stay in the town centre?
(e) How long did Mrs Smith's bus ride to her friend's house take?
(f) How far is the friend's house from the town centre?
(g) What was the average speed of Mrs Smith's bus journey to her friend's house in kilometres per hour?
(h) How long did Mrs Smith stay at her friend's house?
(i) How long did the journey home from Mrs Smith's friend's house take?
(j) What was the average speed of Mrs Smith's bus journey from her friend's house to her home in kilometres per hour?

3. A slow train leaves Peterborough for London. Twenty minutes later a fast train leaves London for Peterborough. The journeys of both trains are shown on this graph.

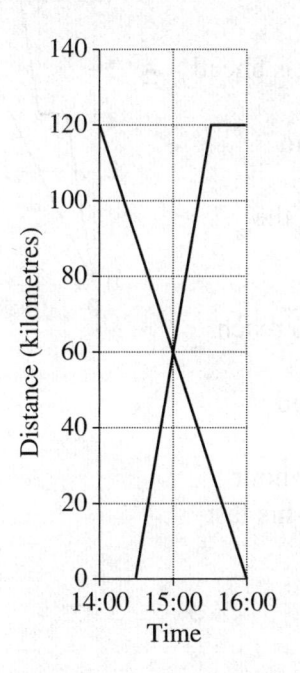

(a) At what time did the slow train leave Peterborough?
(b) At what time did the fast train leave London?
(c) At what time did the slow train arrive in London?
(d) At what time did the fast train arrive in Peterborough?
(e) How far is it from London to Peterborough?
(f) How far from Peterborough were the two trains when they passed each other?
(g) At what time did the two trains pass each other?

(h) What was the average speed in kilometres per hour of the slow train?
(i) What was the average speed in kilometres per hour of the fast train?
(j) How many minutes after the fast train arrived in Peterborough did the slow train arrive in London?

4. Two boys take part in a 10 kilometre cycle race. One cycles at a steady speed, the other cycles in spurts and then stops to rest. The steady cyclist is called Alim, the other cyclist is called Farath. This graph shows the race.
   (a) How long does Farath rest for when he stops for the second time?
   (b) How far has Farath cycled when he stops for the second time?
   (c) How far is Farath ahead of Alim after 5 minutes?
   (d) What is the greatest distance that Farath is ahead of Alim during the race?
   (e) At what distance from the start does Alim overtake Farath?
   (f) For what time during the race is Alim in the lead?
   (g) By what distance does Alim beat Farath?
   (h) How much slower than Farath is Alim to reach the 6 kilometre point in the race?
   (i) At what speed, in kilometres per hour, did Farath cycle after his third rest?
   (j) At what average speed in kilometres per hour would Farath have needed to cycle after his last rest to tie the race?

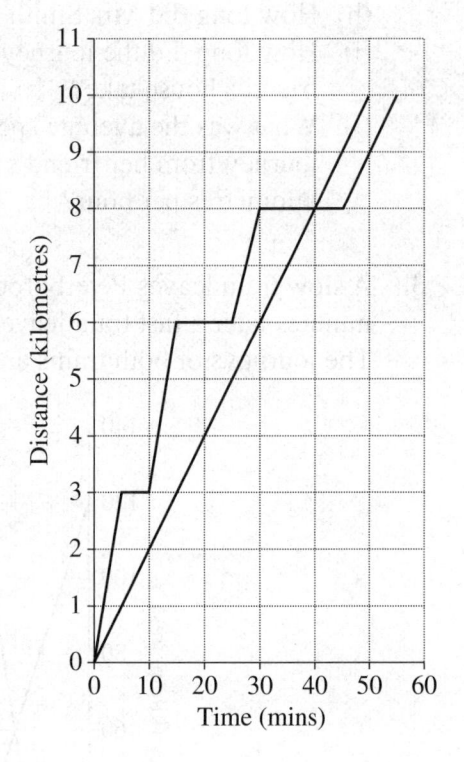

Summary

1. A **sequence** is a set of numbers produced using a fixed rule.

Checkout 13

1. What are the next two numbers in each sequence?
   (a) 3, 6, 9, 12 …   (b) 18, 16, 14, 12 …
   (c) 2, 4, 8, 16 …   (d) 400, 200, 100, 50 …

2. A formula for the nth term can be used to produce a sequence.

2. Write down the first 5 terms of the sequence produced by the formula:
   (a) nth term = $5n$
   (b) nth term = $n + 5$
   (c) nth term = $n - 1$
   (d) nth term = $3n + 5$

3. To find a formula for the nth term of a sequence, find the common difference between the terms. The formula will be based on the sequence produced by multiplying by this number.

3. Find a formula for the nth term of each sequence.
   (a) 4, 9, 14, 19, 24 ...
   (b) 11, 14, 17, 20, 23 ...
   (c) 9, 11, 13, 15, 17 ...
   (d) 7, 11, 15, 19, 23 ...

4. You can fix positions and plot points using coordinates.

4. The points (1,1) and (1,⁻1), are the corner points of a square.
   (a) Plot these points on a grid.
   (b) What are the other possible corner points for the square?
   (c) Show all the possibilities on your grid.

5. You can draw the graph of an equation from a table of values.

5. Using x values from ⁻2 to 2, draw the graphs of:
   (a) $y = x + 5$
   (b) $y = x - 5$
   (c) $y = 3x + 1$
   (d) $y = 2x - 4$

6. Some equations produce curved graphs.

6. Using x values from ⁻3 to 3, draw the graphs of:
   (a) $y = x^2 + 3$
   (b) $y = x^2 - 5$
   (c) $y = 9 - x^2$

7. Real-life relationships can be illustrated with a graph.

7. This table shows the relationship between the time a plumber works and his bill.

Hours worked	1	5	10
Cost (£)	40	120	220

   (a) Draw a graph from the values in the table. Use 1 cm to represent 1 hour on the x-axis and 1 cm to represent £20 on the y-axis.
   (b) How much will repairs cost that take:
       (i) 3 hours
       (ii) 6 hours?
   (c) How long did repairs take which cost:
       (i) £160
       (ii) £100?

8. Problems involving distance and time can be solved with graphs.

8. Mr Williams lives near a motorway junction, 100 kilometres from London. At 9.00 a.m. he leaves home and travels up the motorway at a steady speed of 60 kilometres per hour towards London. Ten minutes later, his daughter Chantal also travels on the motorway towards London at 75 kilometres per hour.
   (a) Draw a distance–time graph using 1 cm to represent 15 minutes on the time axis and 1 cm to represent 10 kilometres on the distance axis.
   (b) Estimate:
      (i) The time at which Mr Williams arrives in London.
      (ii) The time at which Chantal Williams arrives in London.
      (iii) The time at which Chantal Williams overtakes Mr Williams.
      (iv) The distance from London at which Chantal Williams overtakes Mr Williams.

Revision exercise 13

1. Write down the next number in this number pattern.

   4, 13, 22, 31, ...

   How did you find the number? [WJEC]

2. (a) Write down the next two numbers in this number sequence.

   1, 7, 13, 19, 25, ...

   (b) Write down a number in the sequence that divides exactly by 5. [Edexcel]

3. The first four numbers in a sequence are:

   47, 39, 31, 23, ...

   (a) What is the rule for this sequence?
   (b) How many positive numbers are there in the full sequence?
   (c) 47 is the first number in the sequence.
       What is the eighth number? [AQA/NEAB]

4. Here are the first five numbers in a simple number sequence.

   1, 3, 7, 13, 21, ...

   (a) Write down the next two numbers in the sequence.
   (b) Describe, in words, the rule to continue this sequence.
       [Edexcel]

5. Here is a number pattern.
Two numbers are missing.

    6,   12,   18,   ...,   ...,   36

(a) Write down the missing numbers.

(b) Describe, in words, the rule that you used to find the missing numbers in the pattern. [Edexcel]

6. A sequence begins 1, 3, 7, 15, ...
The rule for continuing the sequence is shown.

> Multiply the last number by 2 and add 1

(a) What is the next number in the sequence?

(b) This sequence uses the same rule.

    $^-2$, $^-3$, $^-5$, $^-9$, ...

What is the next number in this sequence? [AQA/SEG]

7. The first 5 terms of a sequence are

    4,   7,   10,   13,   16, ...

(a) Write down the next 2 terms.

(b) Explain how you worked out your answers to part (a).

(c) Find the 20th term of the sequence.

(d) Find the formula for the nth term of the sequence. [OCR]

8. (a) Input → add 5 → multiply by 2 → Output

Use the above instructions to complete this table.

Input	Output
3	
$^-2$	

(b) Write down the next number in the following sequence.

    3, 7, 11, 15, ...

Write down the nth term in this sequence. [WJEC]

9. A fence is made from posts and rails.

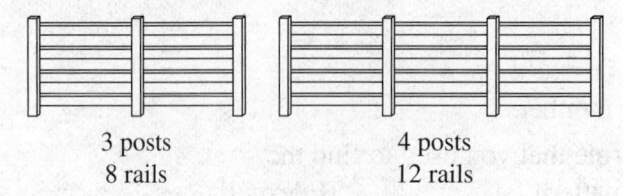

   3 posts
   8 rails

   4 posts
   12 rails

   (a) Complete the table below.

Posts	2	3	4	5	6
Rails		8	12		

   (b) How many rails are there for 15 posts?
   Explain how you can work this out without drawing a diagram. [OCR]

10. The hexagons here are made from matches.

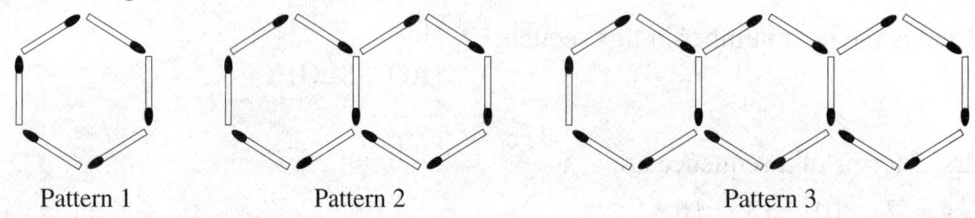

    Pattern 1   Pattern 2   Pattern 3

    (a) (i) How many matches would there be in pattern 6?
        (ii) Explain how you got your answer.

    A rule to find the number of matches (m) from the pattern number (p) is

Multiply by 5 and add 1

    (b) Write this rule using algebra.
    (c) Write down a rule to find the pattern number from the number of matches. [OCR]

11. A, B, C and D are the corners of a rectangle.
    (a) A is the point (2,1), B is the point (5,2) and C is the point (3,8).
        Plot and label the points A, B and C.
    (b) Draw the complete rectangle and label the fourth corner D.
    (c) Write down the coordinates of D. [OCR]

12. (a) On a grid, plot the following points.

    A (2,5)   B (5,7)   C (11,5)   D (5,3)

    Join them up to form a quadrilateral ABCD.

    (b) How many lines of symmetry has quadrilateral ABCD?

    (c) What is the mathematical name for the shape of quadrilateral ABCD?

    (d) Find the area of quadrilateral ABCD.   [AQA/NEAB]

13. A rhombus ABCD is drawn on the grid below. The diagonals AC and BD are also shown.

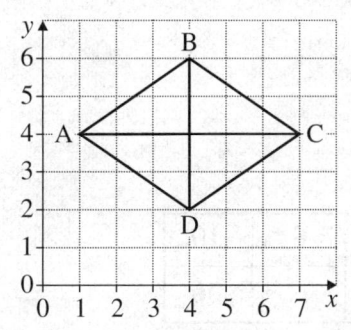

    (a) Write down the coordinates of
        (i) C
        (ii) the mid-point of AC
    (b) Write down the lengths of the two diagonals AC and BD.
    (c) A formula to find the area of a rhombus is

    Area = $pq \div 2$

    where p and q are the lengths of the diagonals.
    Use this formula to calculate the area of the rhombus drawn on the grid above.
    Show all your working.   [AQA/NEAB]

14. (a) In the table opposite, $y = 4x + 3$.
        Copy and complete the table.
    (b) Plot the points from the table on a grid.
        Use a scale of 2 cm = 1 unit on the x-axis and 2 cm = 5 units on the y-axis.
    (c) Use your graph to find the value of x when

    $4x + 3 = 13$

x	y
0	3
1	7
2	
3	15
4	

    [OCR]

15. (a) Complete this table of values for $y = 3x - 1$.

x	$^-2$	$^-1$	0	1	2	3
y			$^-1$			8

(b) Draw the graph of $y = 3x - 1$.
Use a scale of 1 cm = 1 unit on both axes.

(c) Use your graph to find
  (i) the value of x when $y = 3·5$
  (ii) the value of y when $x = {}^-1·5$ [Edexcel]

16. A spring stretches when objects are hung from it.
The formula for its length is
$$l = 2w + 16$$
w is the weight in kg.
l is the length of the spring in cm.

(a) Copy and complete this table.

w	0	2	4	6	8	10
l	16			28		36

(b) Draw the graph on a grid.
Use a scale of 1 cm = 1 unit on the w-axis and
1 cm = 5 units on the l-axis.

(c) Jane hangs an object on the spring.
She measures the length of the spring. It is 29 cm.
Use your graph to find the weight of the object. [OCR]

17. (a) Complete this table of values for $y = x^2 - 1$.

x	$^-2$	$^-1$	0	1	2
$y = x^2 - 1$	3			0	

(b) Draw the graph of $y = x^2 - 1$.
(c) Find the value of y when $x = 1·5$. [AQA/SEG]

18. (a) Complete the following table, which gives values of $x^2 + 2$ for values of x from $^-2$ to 4.

x	$^-2$	$^-1$	0	1	2	3	4
$x^2 + 2$	6		2	3	6		18

(b) On graph paper, draw the graph of $y = x^2 + 2$ for values of x from $^-2$ to 4. [WJEC]

19. (a) Complete the table of values for the equation
$y = x^2 - 5$

x	−3	−2	−1	0	1	2	3
x^2	9						
$y = x^2 - 5$	4						

(b) Draw the graph of $y = x^2 - 5$, for values of x from −3 to 3. [OCR]

20. The diagram shows a conversion graph between Pounds (£) and German Deutschmarks (DM).

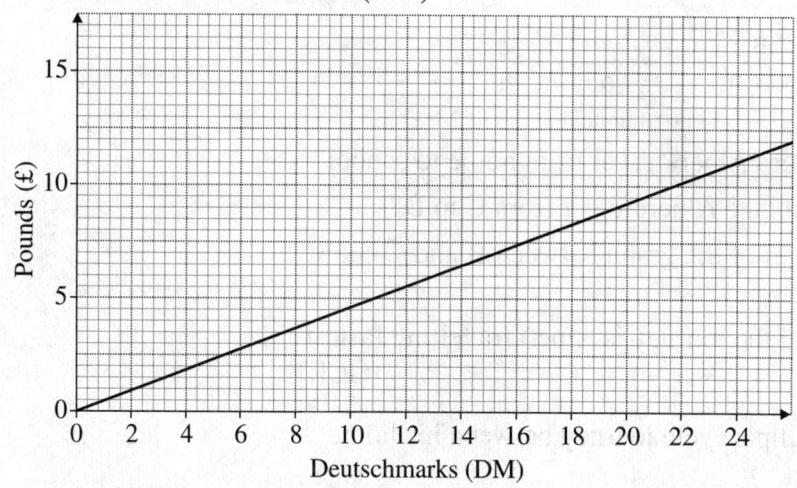

Use the graph to write down how many
(a) Deutschmarks can be exchanged for £10
(b) Pounds can be exchanged for 8 Deutschmarks.
[Edexcel]

21. David's school has a weather station.
One day David took readings of the temperature every hour.
Here are his results.

Time	09:00	10:00	11:00	12:00	13:00	14:00	15:00
Temperature (°C)	10	12	16	20	22	21	17

(a) Plot these points and join them with straight lines.
Use a scale of 2 cm = 1 hour on the time axis and 2 cm = 5°C on the temperature axis.
(b) Use your graph to estimate
  (i) the temperature at 14:30
  (ii) the time when the temperature was 15°C. [OCR]

22. This is a distance–time graph of Albert's journey from home (A) to school (E).

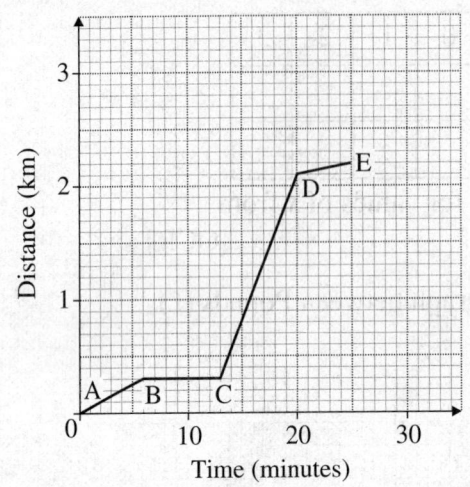

   (a) What distance does Albert travel from home to school?
   (b) How long does it take Albert to get from C to D?
   (c) What does the part of the graph between B and C show about Albert's journey?
   (d) For which part of the journey is Albert travelling fastest?
   [OCR]

23. The graph shows Philip's cycle journey between his home and the sports centre.

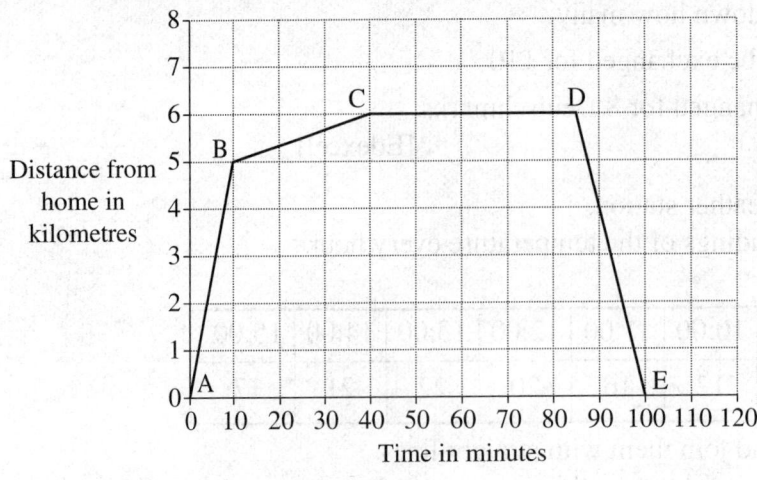

   (a) Explain what happened between C and D.
   (b) Explain what changed at B.
   (c) Explain what happened at E.
   (d) Work out the total distance that Philip travelled. [OCR]

14 SHAPE AND SPACE 4

Transformations describe how shapes change.

This unit is about:

- Translations
- Reflections
- Rotations
- Symmetry
- Enlargements
- Fractional enlargements

You need to remember:

- A position on a grid is described using coordinates.
  1. Write down the coordinates of each point on the grid.

14.1 Translations

A **translation** slides a shape from one position to another without turning it.

Translations are usually shown on a square grid.

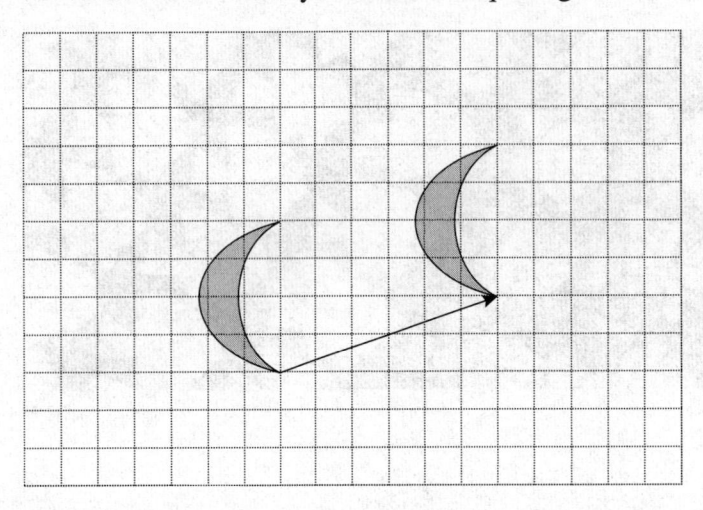

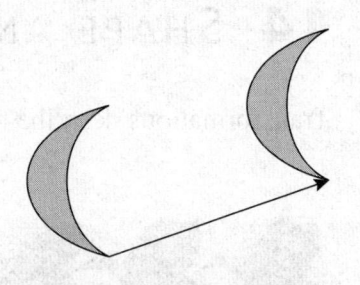

Note:
These shapes are **congruent** because they are exactly the same shape and size.

The translation of the moon shape is 6 squares to the right and 2 squares up.

Translations are often written in a vertical bracket like this: $\binom{+6}{+2}$

The horizontal movement is always put at the top of the bracket.

Plus signs show that the movement is to the **right** or **up**.

Minus signs show that the movement is to the **left** or **down**.

Here are some more translations applied to the moon shape.

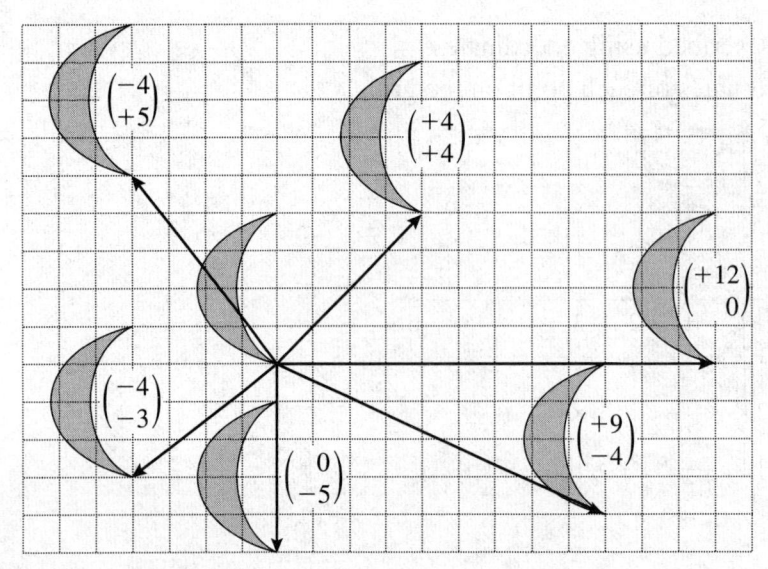

Exercise 14A

1. The diagram shows a shaded triangle moved to ten new positions.

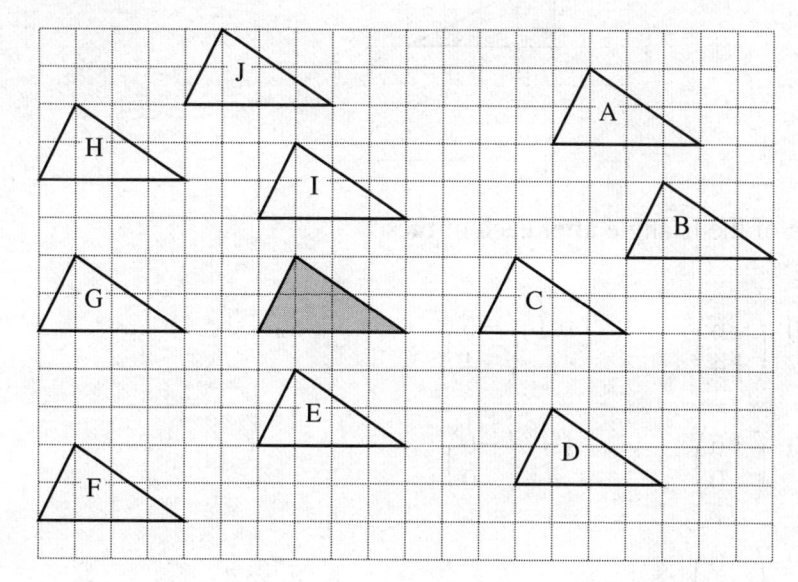

   Note:
   All these shapes are **congruent** to each other.

   Use vertical brackets to write down the translations which move the shaded triangle to each new position.

2. The diagram shows a shaded diamond moved to ten new positions.

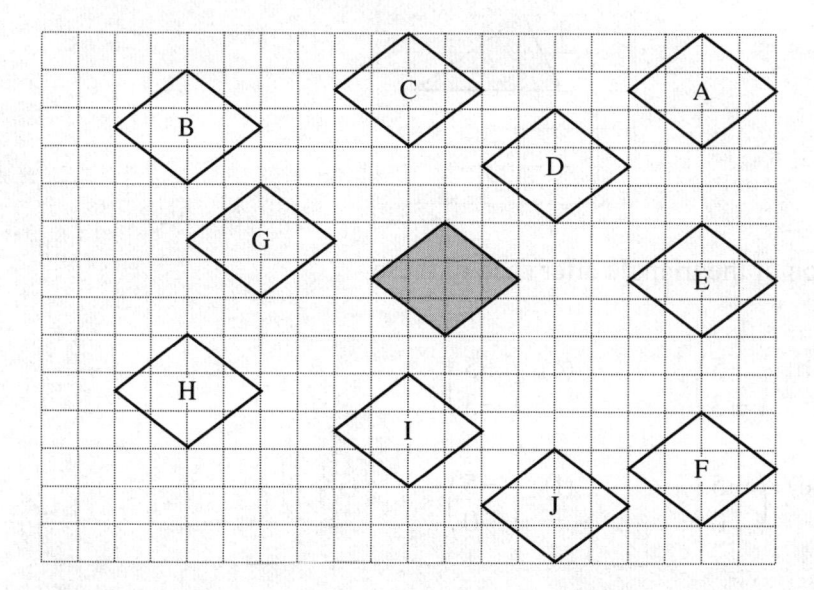

   Use vertical brackets to write down the translations which move the shaded diamond to each new position.

3. Copy this triangle onto squared paper.

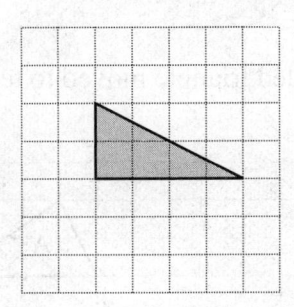

   Show the new position of the triangle after each of these translations.

   (a) $\begin{pmatrix} +6 \\ +4 \end{pmatrix}$ (b) $\begin{pmatrix} -6 \\ +4 \end{pmatrix}$ (c) $\begin{pmatrix} +6 \\ -4 \end{pmatrix}$

   (d) $\begin{pmatrix} -6 \\ -4 \end{pmatrix}$ (e) $\begin{pmatrix} +6 \\ 0 \end{pmatrix}$ (f) $\begin{pmatrix} -6 \\ 0 \end{pmatrix}$

   (g) $\begin{pmatrix} 0 \\ +4 \end{pmatrix}$ (h) $\begin{pmatrix} 0 \\ -4 \end{pmatrix}$

4. Copy this triangle onto squared paper.

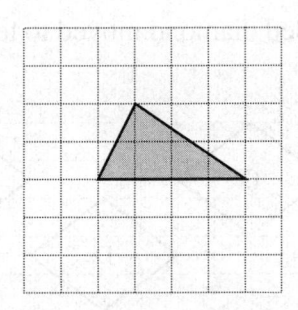

   Show the new position of the triangle after each of these translations.

   (a) $\begin{pmatrix} +5 \\ +3 \end{pmatrix}$ (b) $\begin{pmatrix} -5 \\ +3 \end{pmatrix}$ (c) $\begin{pmatrix} +5 \\ -3 \end{pmatrix}$

   (d) $\begin{pmatrix} -5 \\ -3 \end{pmatrix}$ (e) $\begin{pmatrix} +5 \\ 0 \end{pmatrix}$ (f) $\begin{pmatrix} -5 \\ 0 \end{pmatrix}$

   (g) $\begin{pmatrix} 0 \\ +3 \end{pmatrix}$ (h) $\begin{pmatrix} 0 \\ -3 \end{pmatrix}$

5.

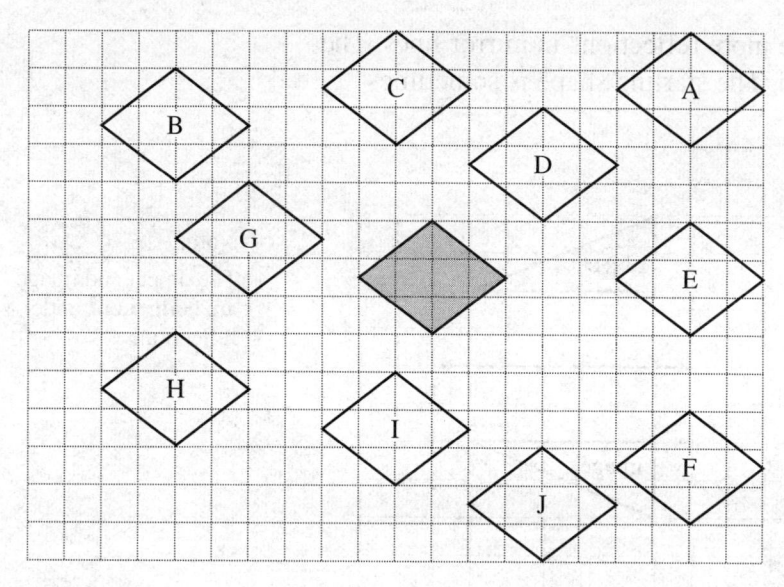

Use vertical brackets to write down the translations that move:

(a) A to B
(b) A to C
(c) A to D
(d) A to E
(e) A to F
(f) B to A
(g) B to D
(h) B to E
(i) B to I
(j) B to J
(k) C to G
(l) C to A
(m) C to E
(n) C to H
(o) C to I
(p) I to H
(q) H to I
(r) J to F
(s) G to A
(t) F to B

Which of the shapes are congruent to each other?

14.2 Reflections

A **reflection** makes an image of a shape in a mirror line.

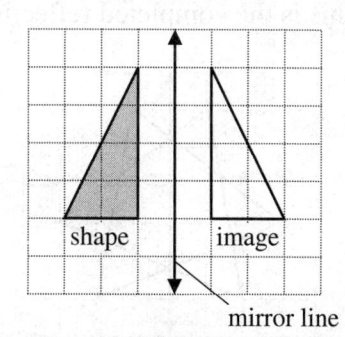

Shape and Space 4

This diagram shows some more reflections in mirror lines. The starting shapes are shaded. The starting shape is sometimes called the object.

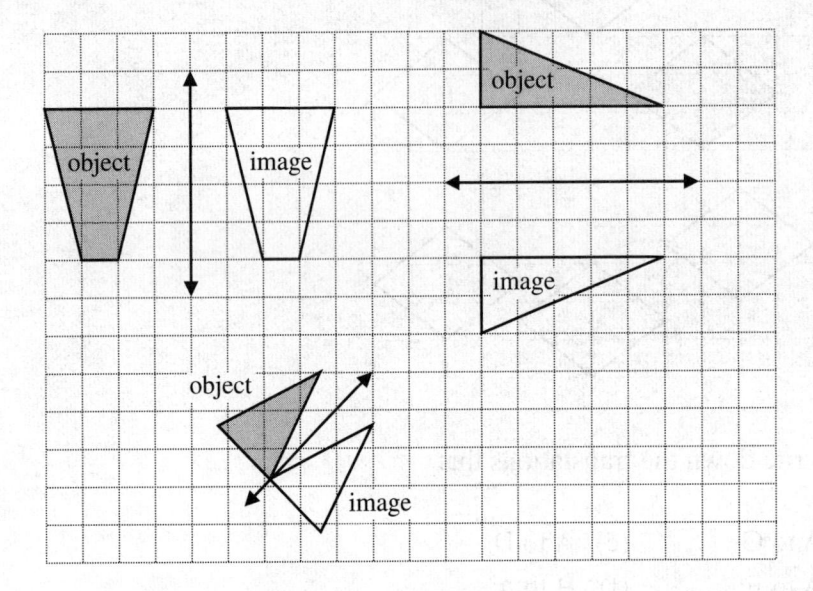

Note:
The object and image are **congruent** under a reflection.

To reflect a shape, imagine the object is drawn with wet ink. The image is the shape printed by the wet ink if the paper is folded along the mirror line.

To complete a reflection with a diagonal mirror line, turn the page to make the mirror line vertical or horizontal.

If a shape crosses the mirror line the image will also cross the mirror line.

Example
Reflect this shape in the mirror line.   This is the completed reflection.

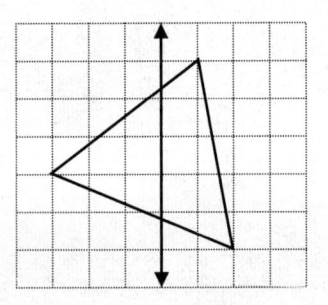

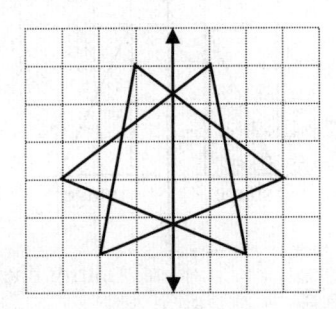

Exercise 14B

Copy these diagrams onto squared paper. Reflect each shape in the mirror line.

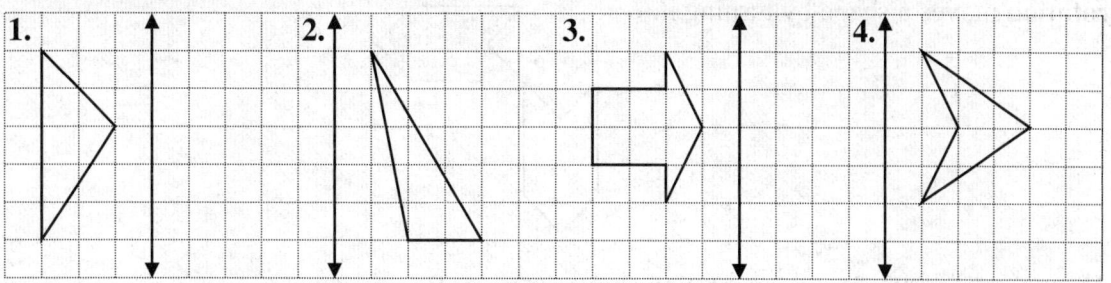

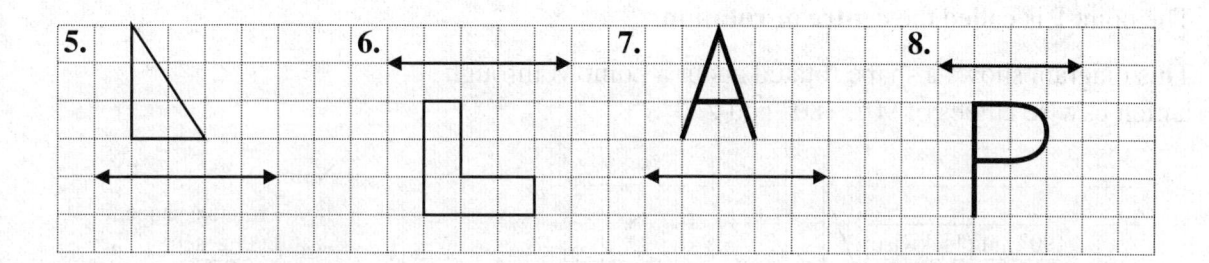

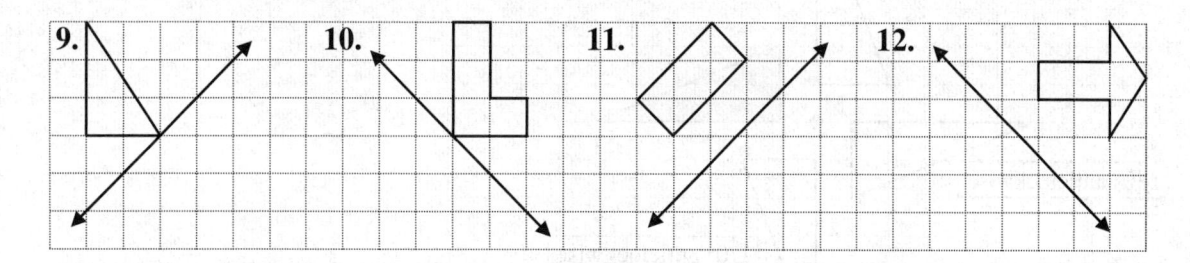

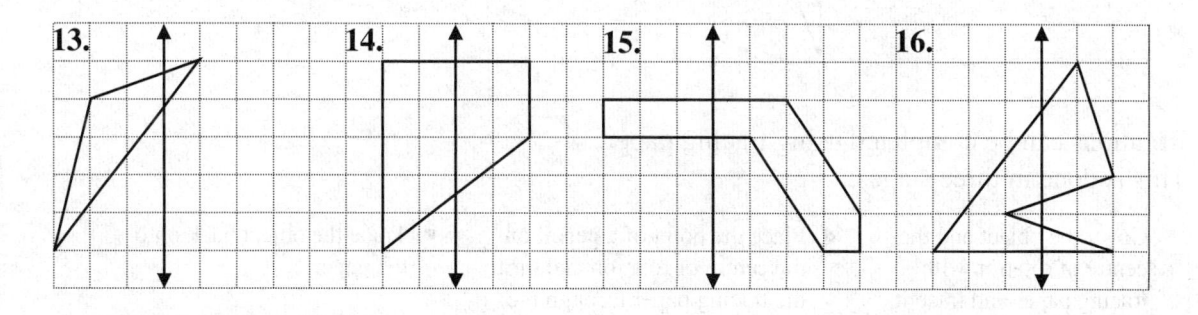

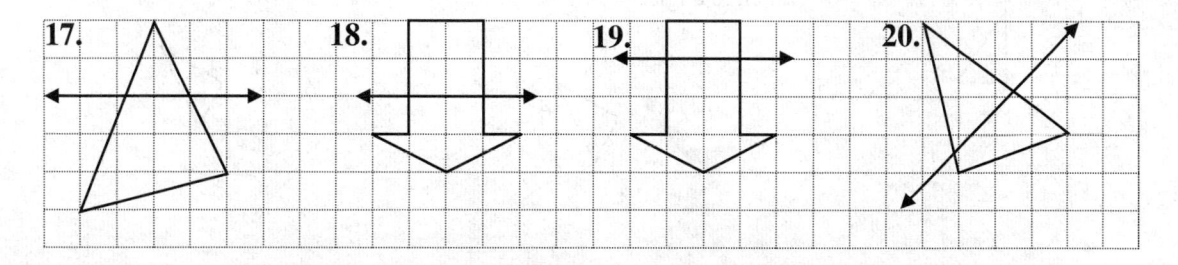

14.3 Rotations

A **rotation** moves a shape by turning it.

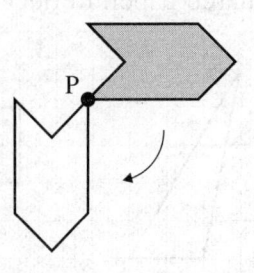

This rotation is a 90° clockwise rotation about the point P.

The point P is called the **centre of rotation**.

This diagram shows a shape rotated about a point M through anticlockwise angles of 90°, 180° and 270°.

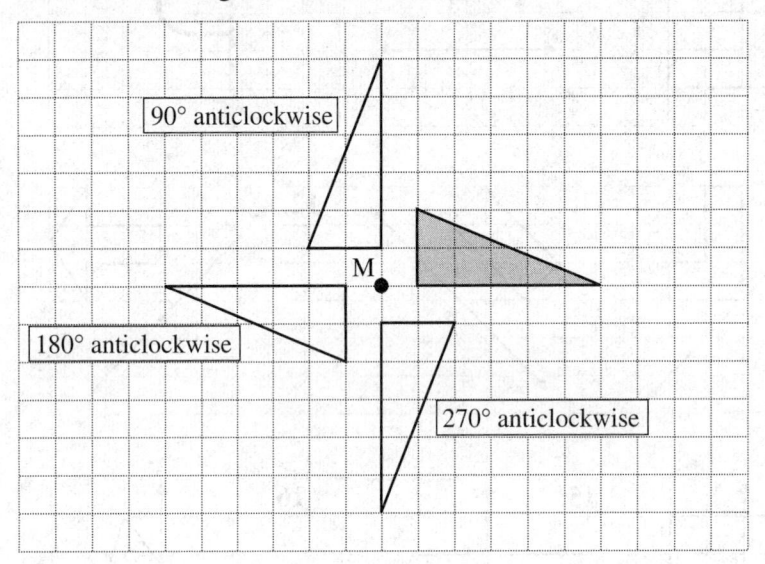

Note:
If you rotate a shape, it is still congruent to the original shape.

Rotations can be completed using tracing paper.
This is done in three stages:

- Cover the object and the centre of rotation with tracing paper and trace it. 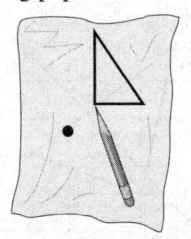
- Place the point of a pencil on the centre of rotation and turn the tracing paper through the required angle. 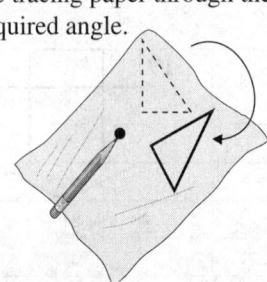
- Trace the object back onto the paper.

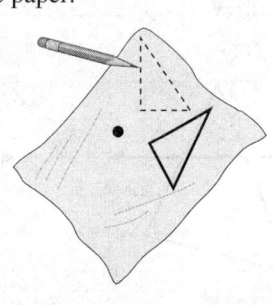

Exercise 14C

1. Copy each diagram onto squared paper and use tracing paper to complete the given rotation.

   (a) 90° clockwise about P

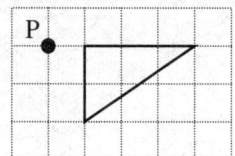

   (b) 180° clockwise about M

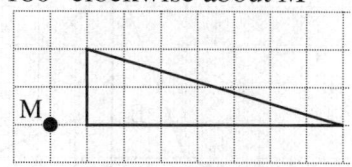

   (c) 90° clockwise about A

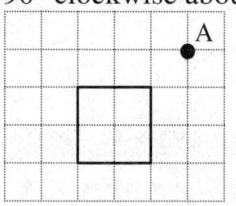

   (d) 90° anticlockwise about B

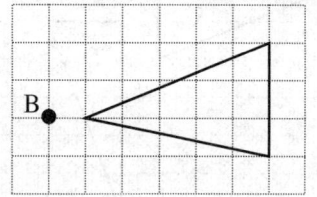

   (e) 180° anticlockwise about P

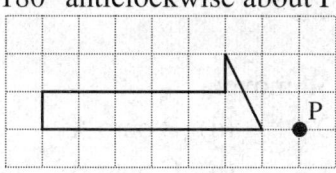

   (f) 90° anticlockwise about Q

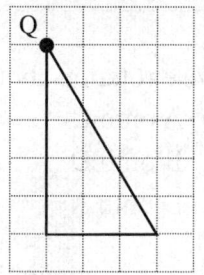

   (g) 270° clockwise about O

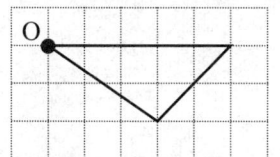

   (h) 270° anticlockwise about T

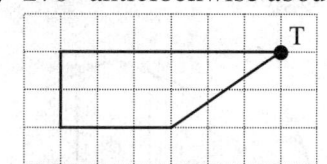

   (i) 90° clockwise about M

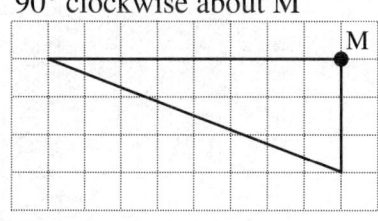

   (j) 90° anticlockwise about M

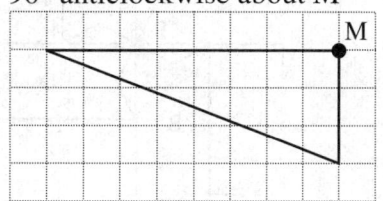

   (k) 90° clockwise about P

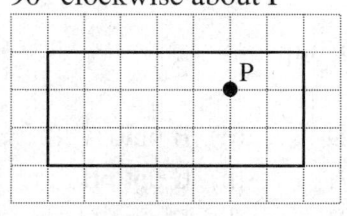

   (l) 90° anticlockwise about P

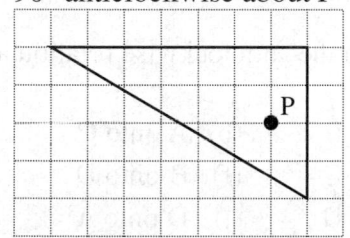

2. Look at this diagram.

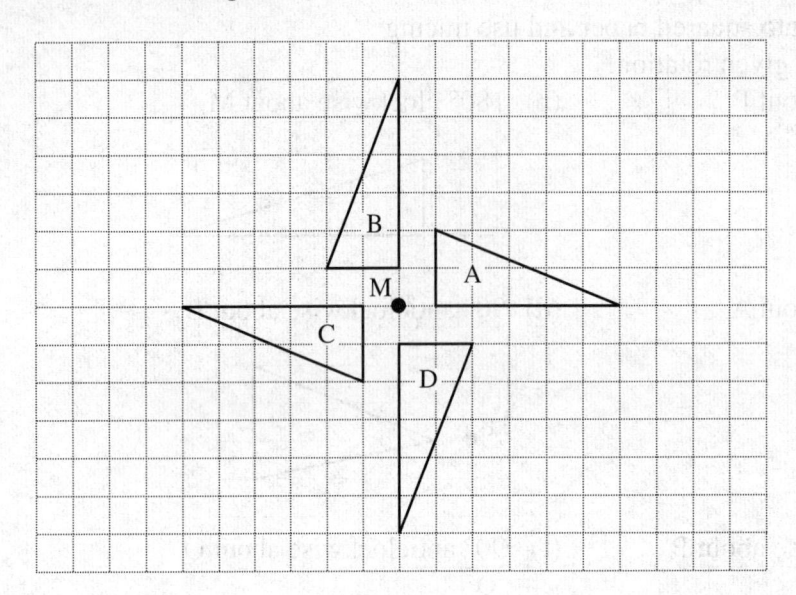

Write down the clockwise rotation about M which will move:
(a) A onto B (b) A onto C (c) A onto D (d) B onto A
(e) B onto C (f) B onto D (g) C onto A (h) C onto B
(i) C onto D (j) D onto A (k) D onto B (l) D onto C

3. Look at this diagram.

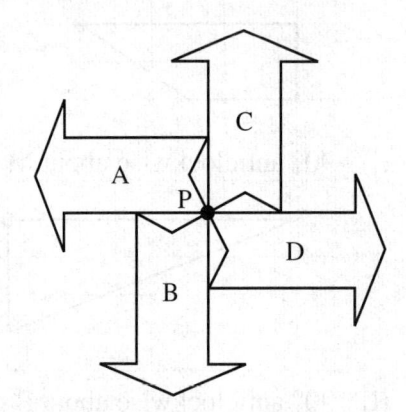

Write down the anticlockwise rotation about P which will move:
(a) A onto B (b) A onto C (c) A onto D (d) B onto A
(e) B onto C (f) B onto D (g) C onto A (h) C onto B
(i) C onto D (j) D onto A (k) D onto B (l) D onto C

14.4 Reflectional symmetry

A shape has **reflectional symmetry** if one half of the shape reflects onto the other.

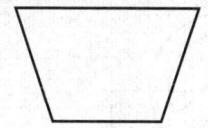

This shape has reflectional symmetry because this mirror line can be drawn on it.

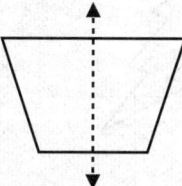

The mirror line is called a **line of symmetry**.

Some shapes have several lines of symmetry. This square has four lines of symmetry.

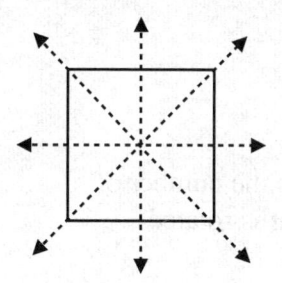

Exercise 14D

Trace each diagram onto squared paper and mark all the lines of symmetry on each shape.

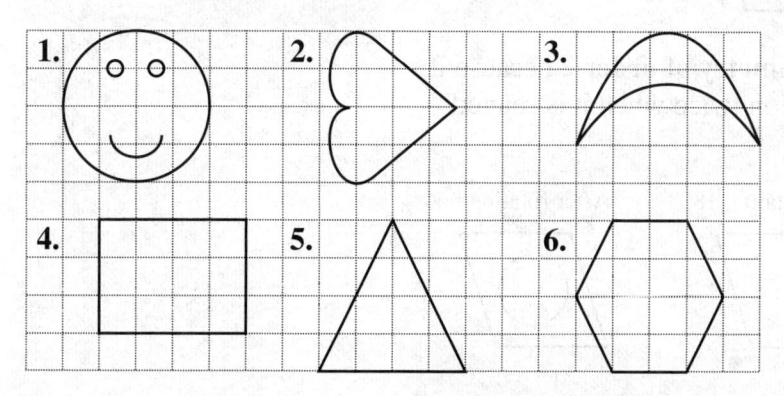

1.
2.
3.
4.
5.
6.

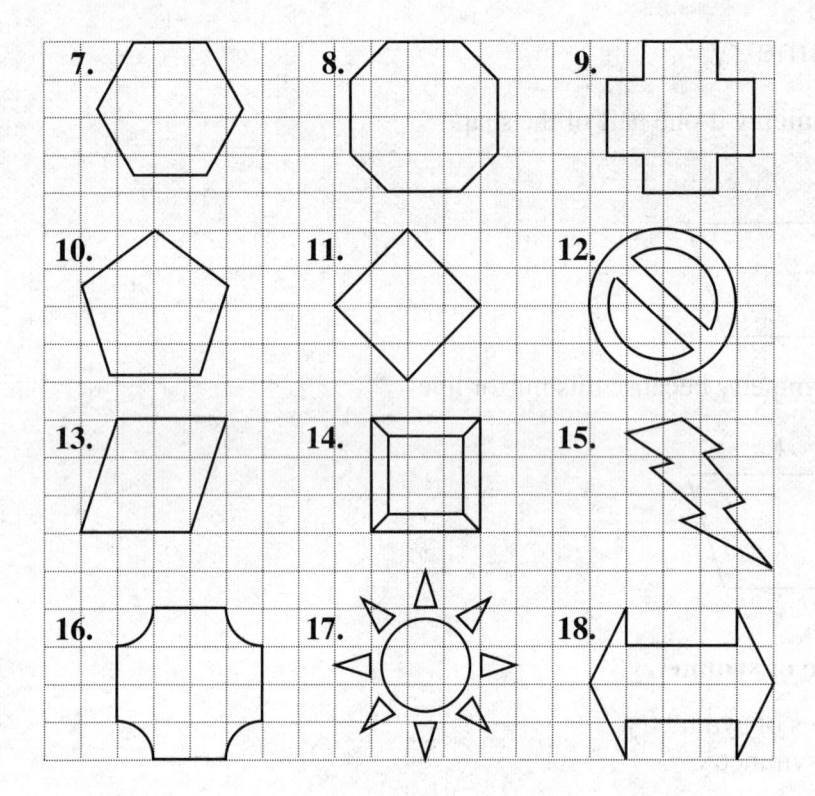

7.
8.
9.
10.
11.
12.
13.
14.
15.
16.
17.
18.

14.5 Rotational symmetry

The **order of rotational symmetry** of a shape is the number of times it fits back into its original position when it is rotated through 360°.

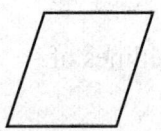

This shape has **rotational symmetry of order 2** because it fits back into its original position twice when it is rotated through 360°.

Start — After rotating 180° — After rotating 360°

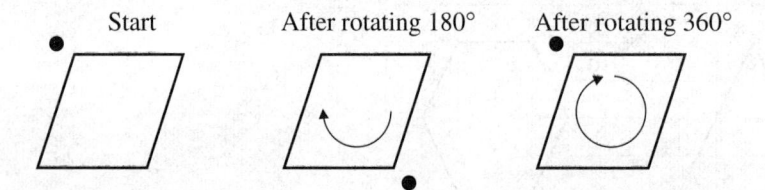

This shape has **rotational symmetry of order 4** because it fits back into its original position 4 times when it is rotated through 360°.

Exercise 14E

1. State the order of rotational symmetry of each shape.

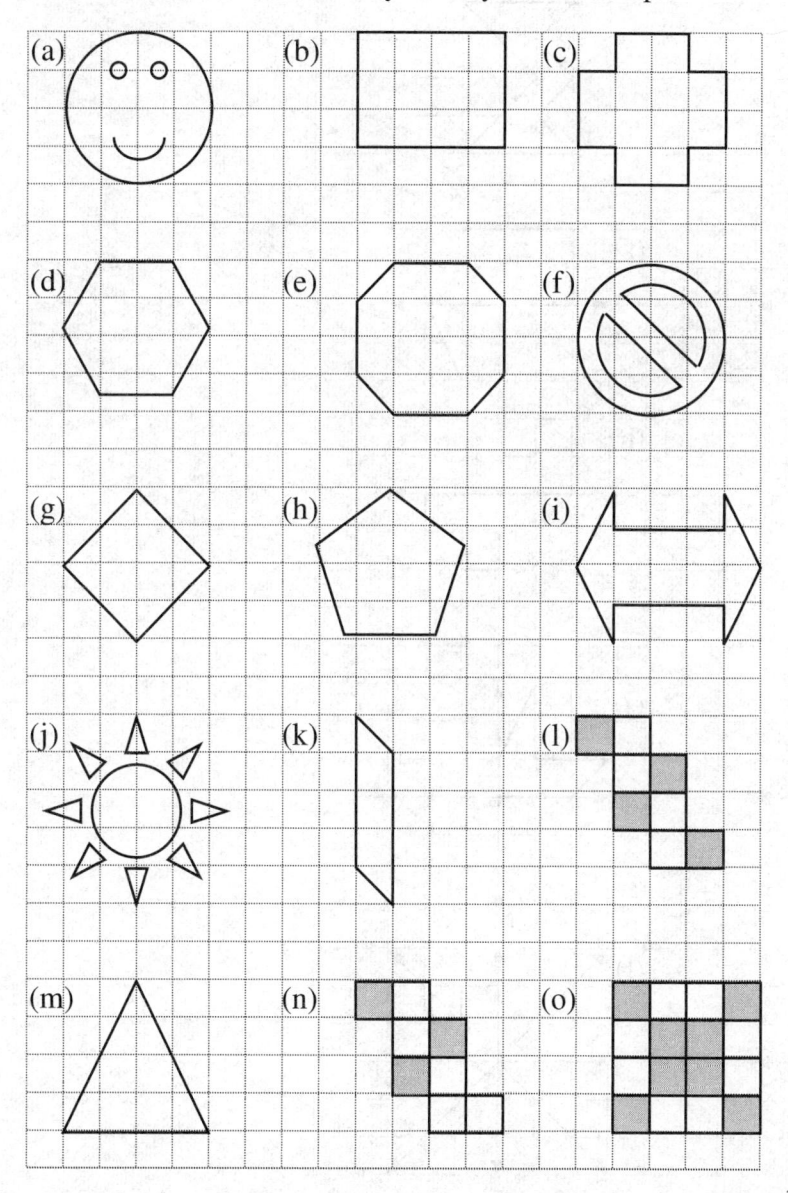

Hint:

If a shape only fits back after a full turn, it has order of rotational symmetry 1.

2. (i) Copy and complete each shape so that the arrow lines are lines of symmetry.
   (ii) State the order of rotational symmetry of each completed shape.

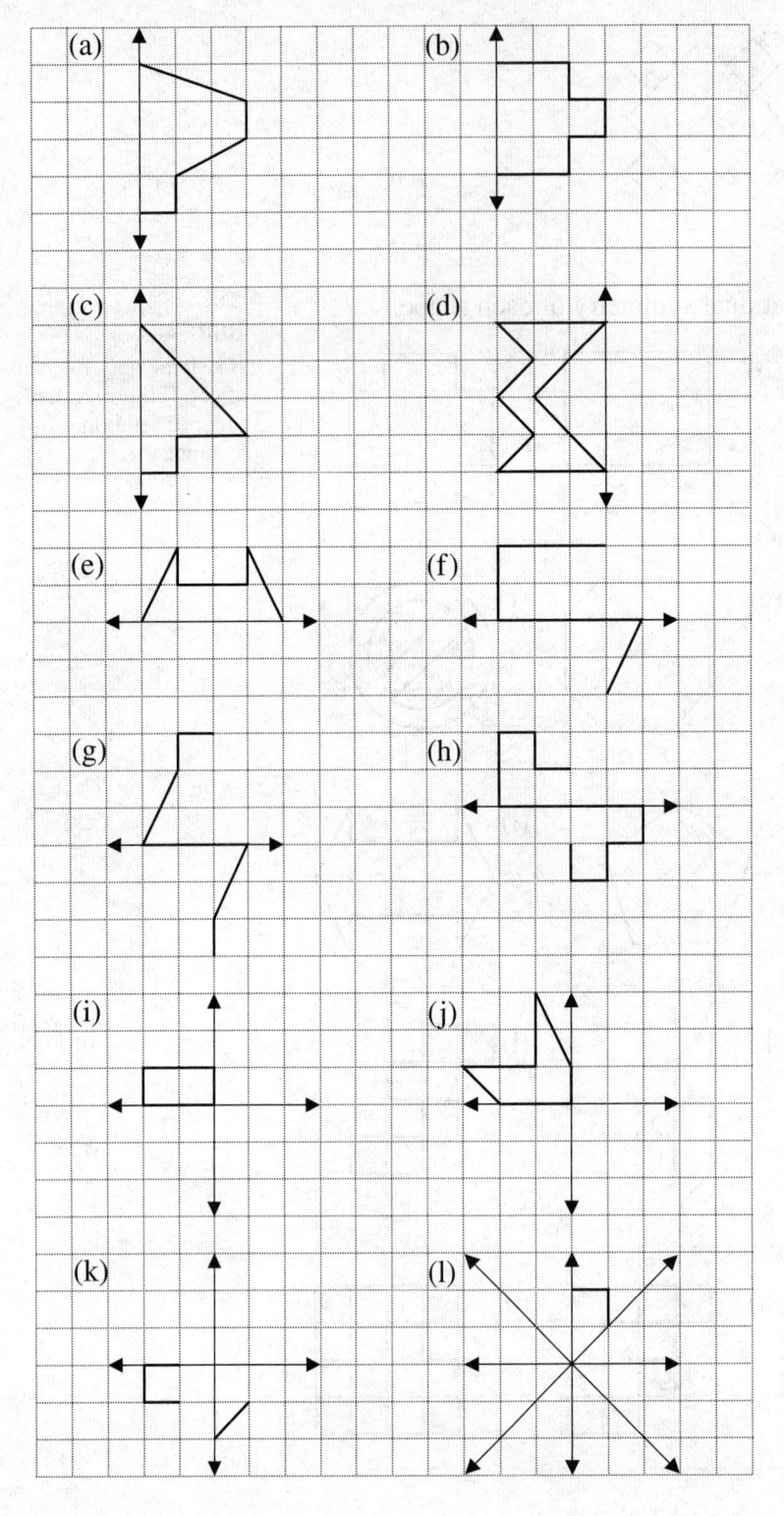

(a)

(b)

(c)

(d)

(e)

(f)

(g)

(h)

(i)

(j)

(k)

(l)

14.6 Enlargements

An **enlargement** changes the size of a shape. Enlargements are usually completed on square grids.

This shape is drawn on a 1 cm grid.

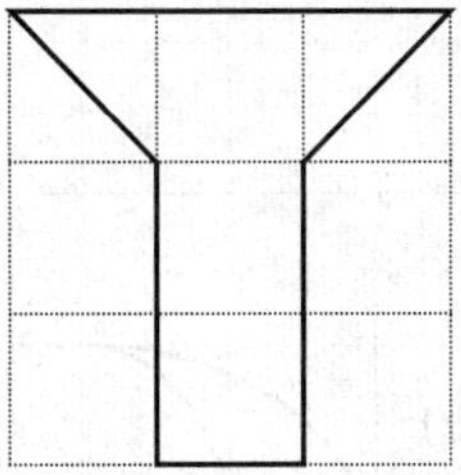

This is the shape drawn on a 2 cm grid.

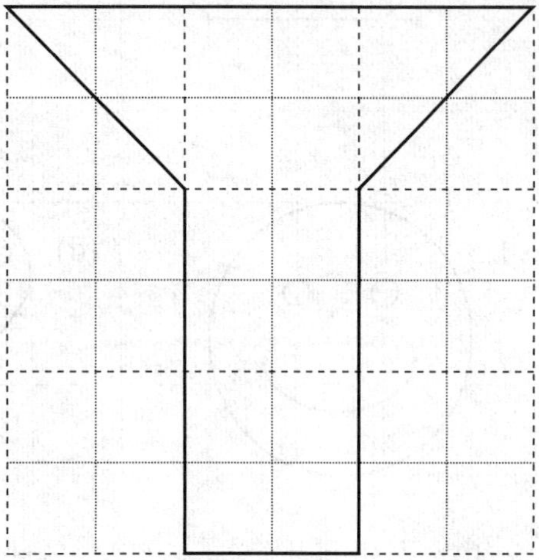

Note: These two shapes are **not** congruent. One is larger than the other.

The shape has been **enlarged with a scale factor of 2**.

Exercise 14F

1. Draw a 2 cm grid on squared paper. Use the grid to enlarge each of these shapes with a scale factor of 2.

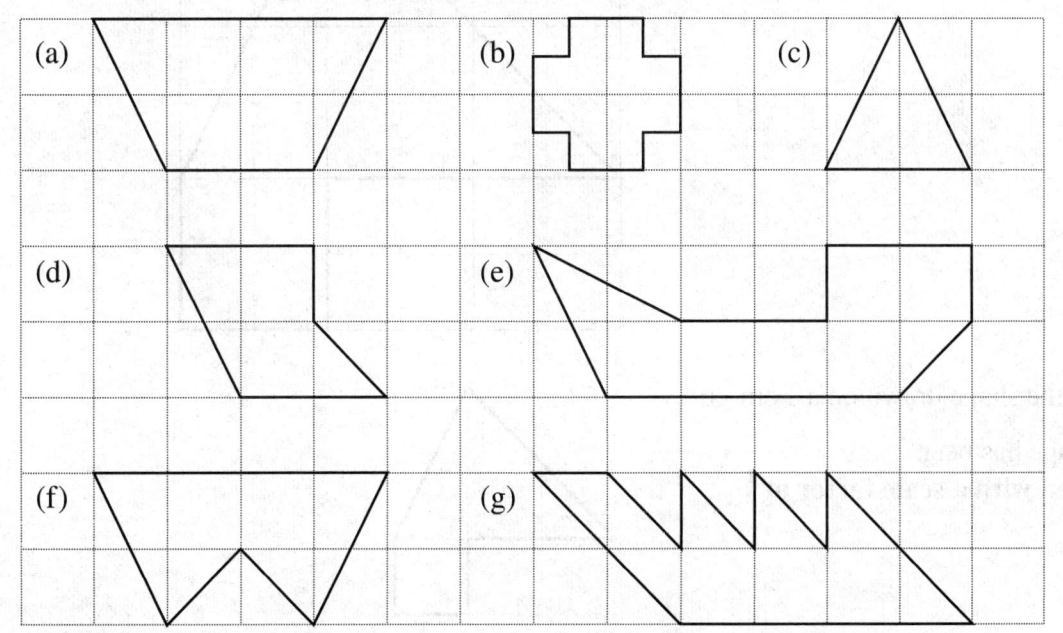

(a) (b) (c)

(d) (e)

(f) (g)

2. Draw a 3 cm grid on squared paper. Use the grid to enlarge each of these shapes with a scale factor of 3.

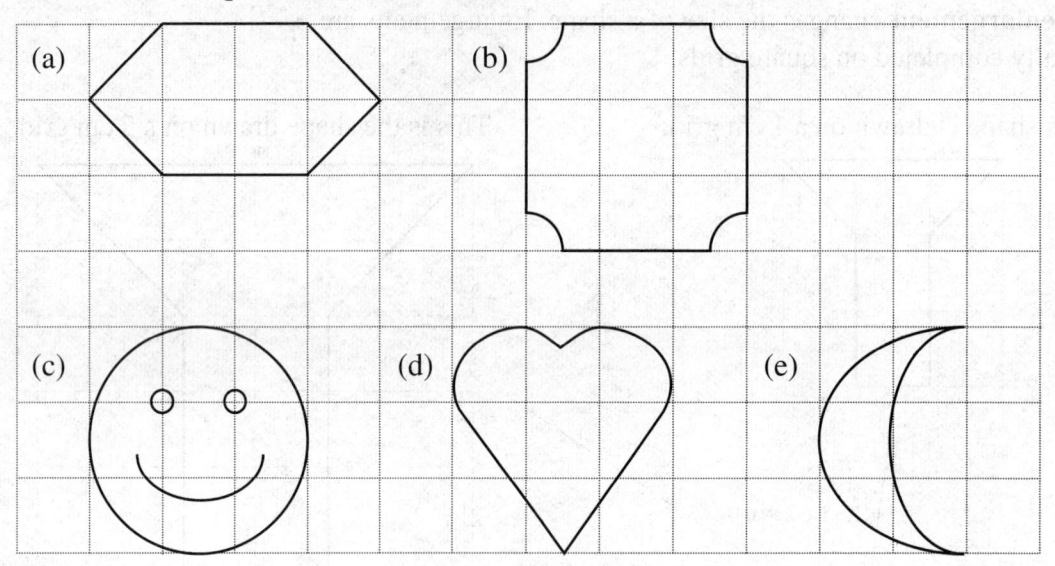

(a)

(b)

(c)

(d)

(e)

14.7 Fractional enlargements

A **fractional enlargement** makes a shape smaller.

This shape is drawn on a 2 cm grid.

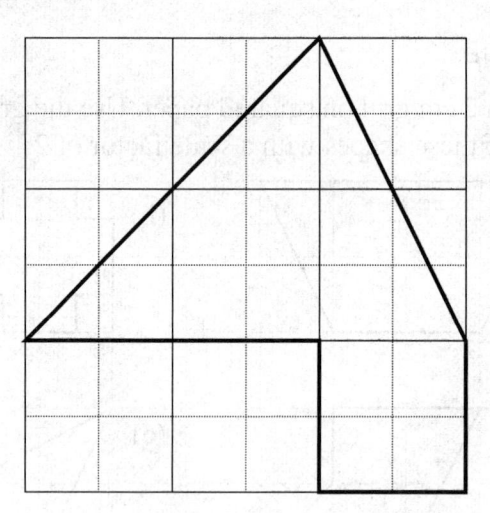

This is the shape drawn on a 1 cm grid.

The shape has been **enlarged with a scale factor of $\frac{1}{2}$.**

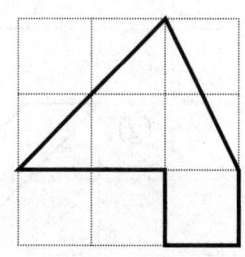

Fractional enlargements **323**

Exercise 14G

1. The shapes below are drawn on a 2 cm grid. Use a 1 cm grid to enlarge each of these shapes with a scale factor of $\frac{1}{2}$.

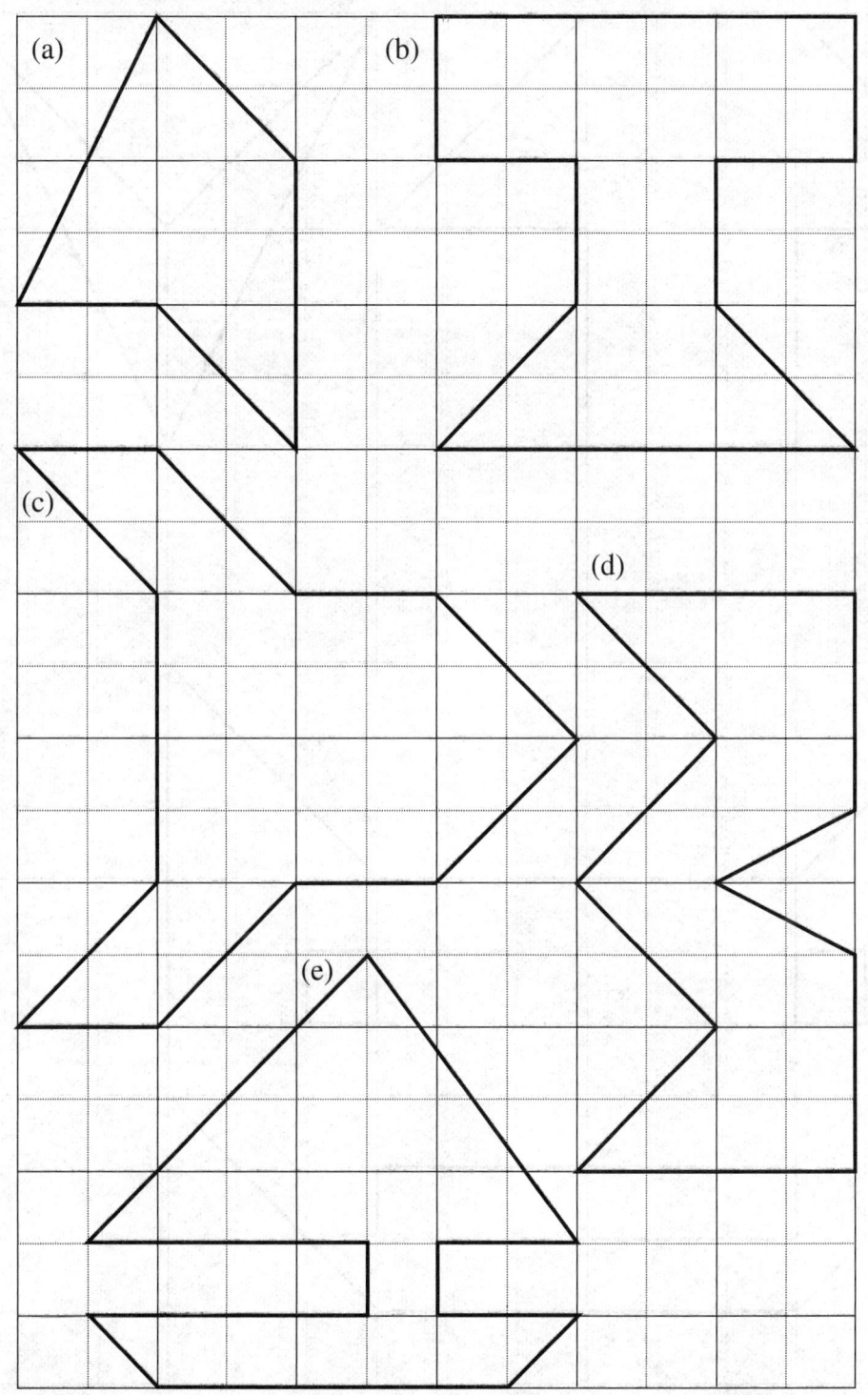

(a)

(b)

(c)

(d)

(e)

324 Shape and Space 4

2. The shapes below are drawn on a 3 cm grid. Use a 1 cm grid to enlarge each of these shapes with a scale factor of $\frac{1}{3}$.

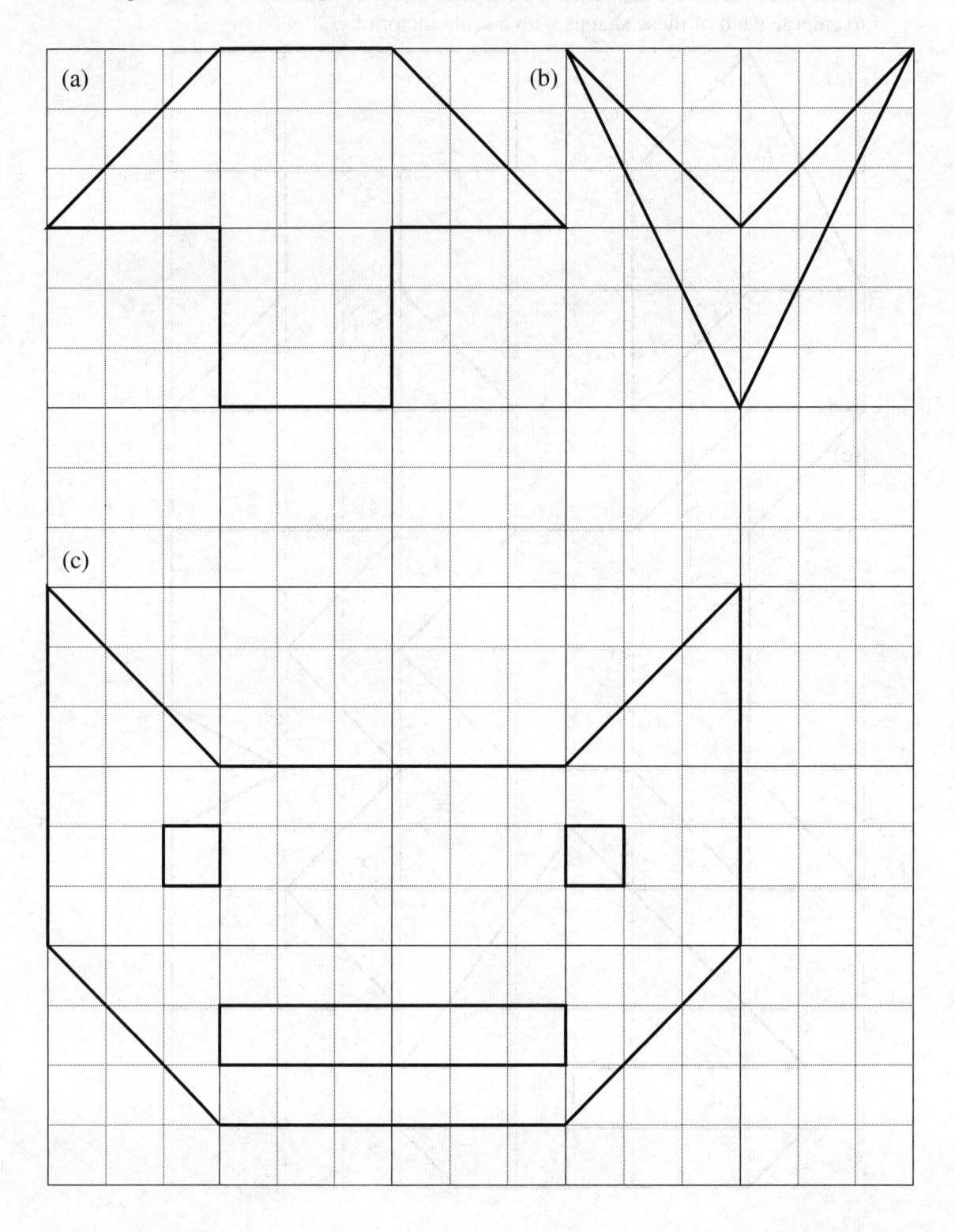

(a)

(b)

(c)

Summary

1. A translation slides a shape from one position to another without turning it.

   Translations are often written in a vertical bracket.

   The horizontal movement is always put at the top of the bracket.

   A plus sign shows that the movement is to the **right** or **up**.

   A minus sign shows that the movement is to the **left** or **down**.

2. A **reflection** makes an image of a shape in a mirror line.

Checkout 14

1. Use vertical brackets to write down the translations which move the shaded moon to each new position.

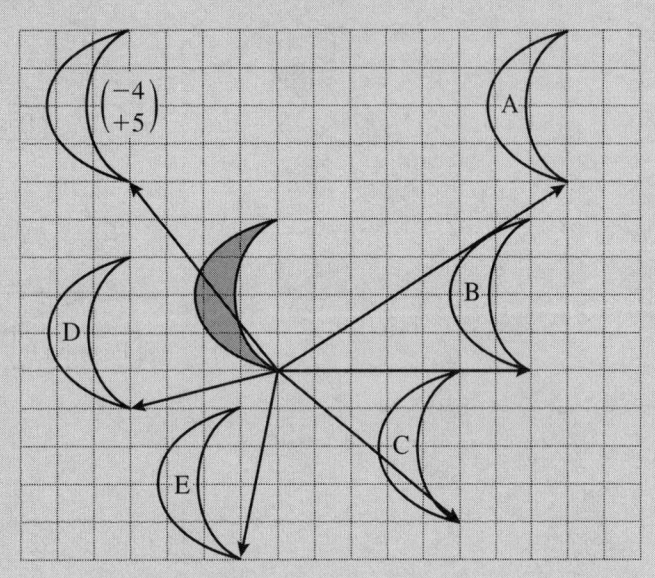

2. Copy this diagram and draw the image of each object.

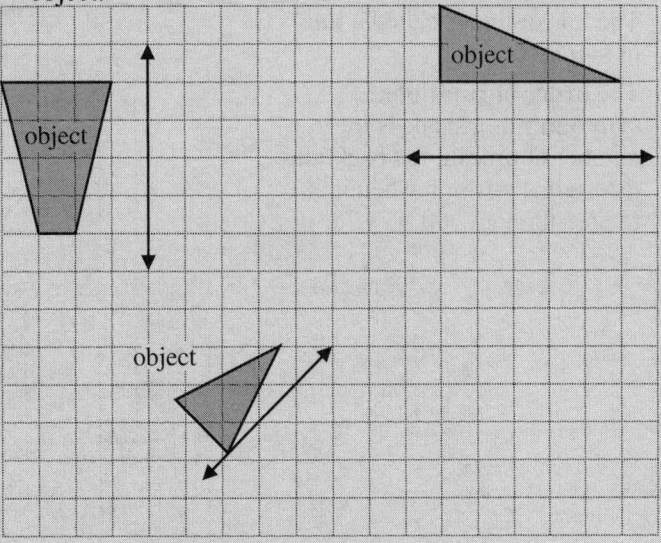

326 Shape and Space 4

3. A **rotation** moves a shape by turning it about a point called the centre of rotation.

3. (a) Write down the anticlockwise rotations about M which move the shaded triangle to positions A, B and C.
(b) Write down the clockwise rotations about M which move the shaded triangle to positions A, B and C.

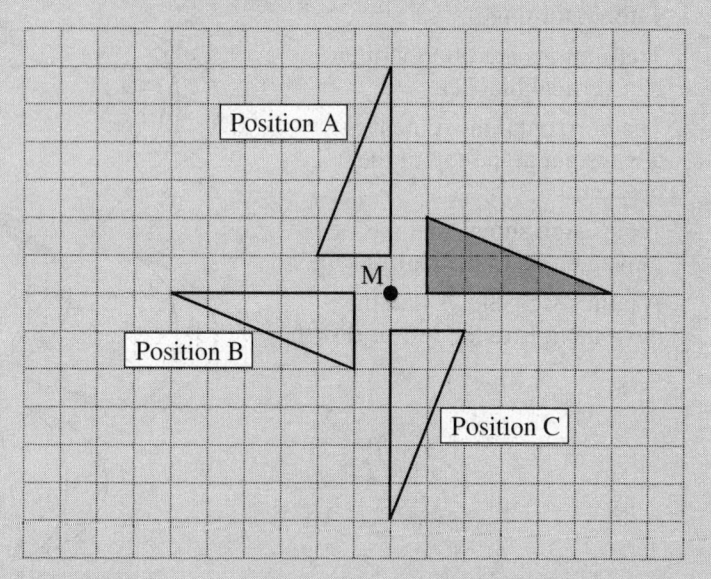

4. A shape has **reflectional symmetry** if a mirror line can be drawn which reflects one half of the shape onto the other. The mirror line is called a **line of symmetry**.

The **order of rotational symmetry** of a shape is the number of times it fits back into its original position when it is rotated through 360°.

4. (a) Copy and complete each shape so that the arrow lines are lines of symmetry.
(b) State the order of rotational symmetry of each completed shape.

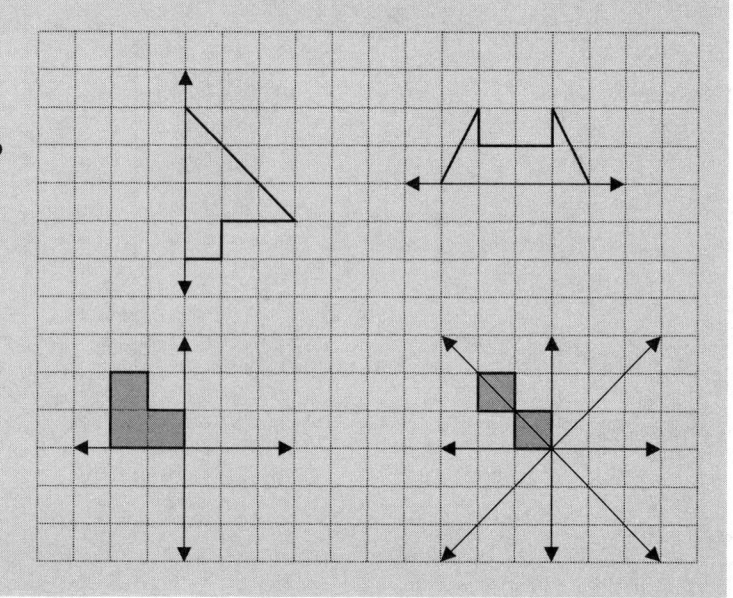

5. An **enlargement** changes the size of a shape.

   This means the image is not congruent to the original shape.

5. Draw a 2 cm grid on squared paper. Use the grid to enlarge this shape with a scale factor of 2.

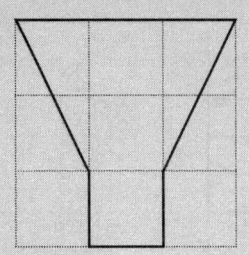

6. A **fractional enlargement** makes a shape smaller.

6. The shape below is drawn on a 2 cm grid. Use a 1 cm grid to enlarge the shape with a scale factor of $\frac{1}{2}$.

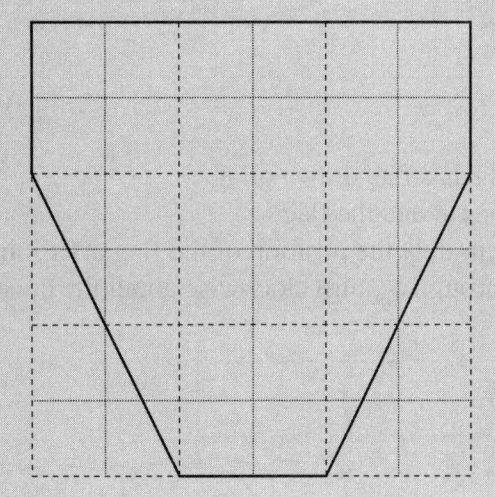

Revision exercise 14

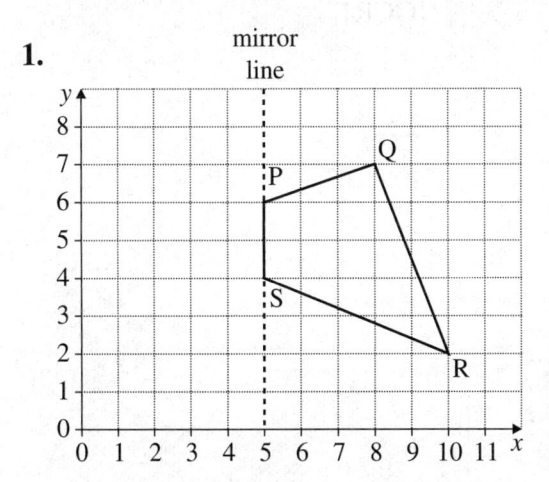

1.
   (a) Write down the coordinates of the point labelled Q.
   (b) Copy the diagram and reflect the shape PQRS in the mirror line.
   (c) Look at the reflection of the point R. Write down its coordinates.

   [OCR]

2. The diagram shows a logo and a mirror line.
   Copy the diagram.
   Draw the reflection of the logo in the mirror line.

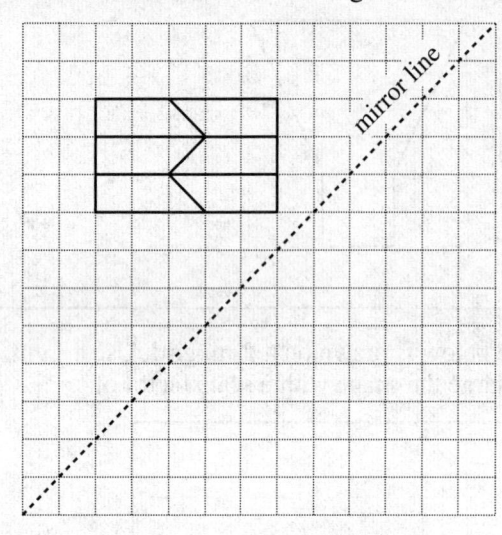

   [AQA/NEAB]

3. This grid has a flag drawn on it.
   Copy the grid and the flag.
   Draw accurately the position of the flag after it has been rotated through a $\frac{1}{4}$-turn clockwise about the cross on the grid.

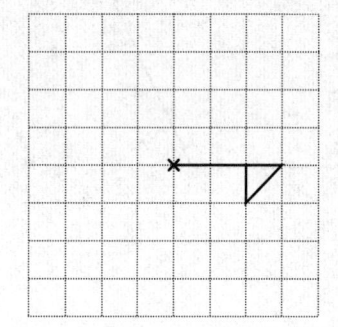

   [OCR]

4.

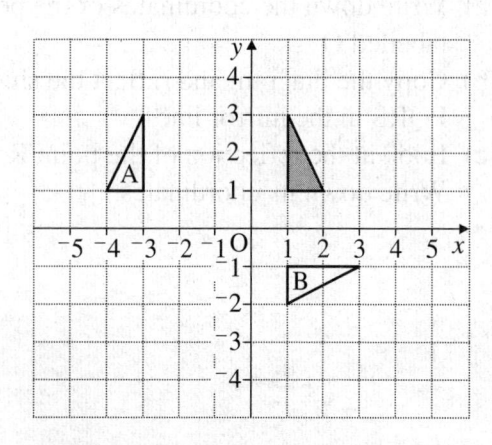

(a) Triangle A is a reflection of the shaded triangle.
    Draw the mirror line for this reflection on a copy of the diagram.

(b) Describe fully the transformation that maps the shaded
    triangle onto triangle B.   [AQA/NEAB]

5. (a) Copy the grid and reflect the 'L' shape in the x-axis.

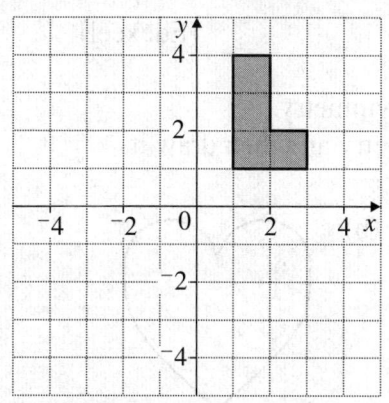

(b) Copy the grid and rotate the 'L' shape 90°
    anticlockwise, centre (0, 0).

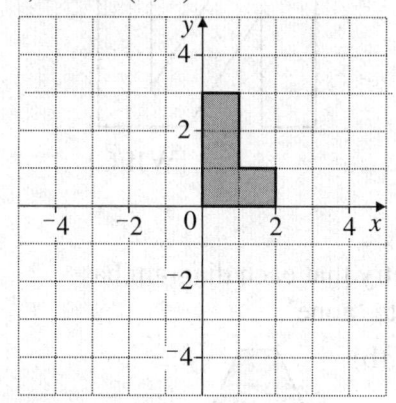

(c) Copy the grid and translate the 'L' shape 3 units to the
    right and 2 units up.

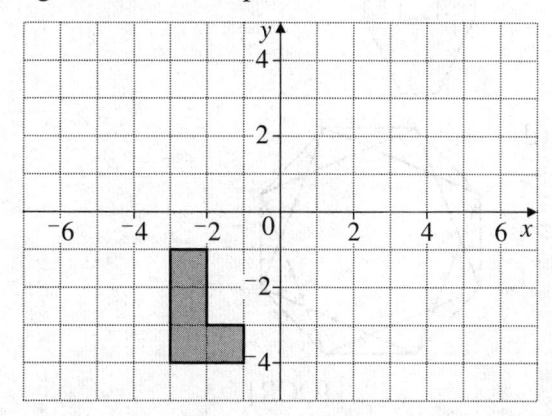

[OCR]

6. Copy each of the shapes that have rotational symmetry.

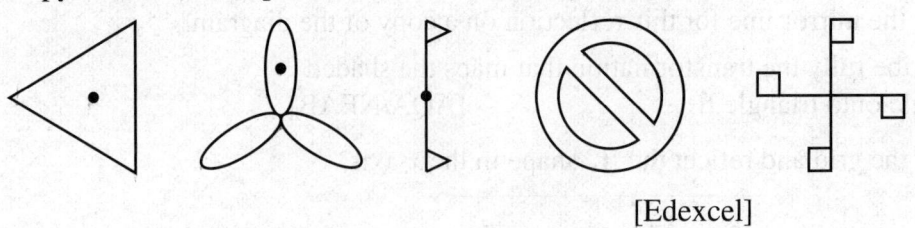

[Edexcel]

7. Some of these shapes have mirror symmetry.
Copy each shape with mirror symmetry and then draw its mirror line.

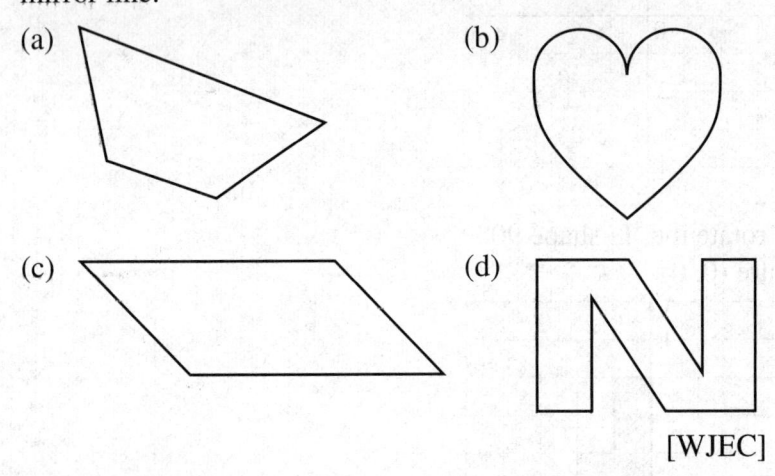

(a)

(b)

(c)

(d)

[WJEC]

8. Here are some diagrams.
Write the order of rotational symmetry that each diagram has.
If it has no rotational symmetry write 'none'.

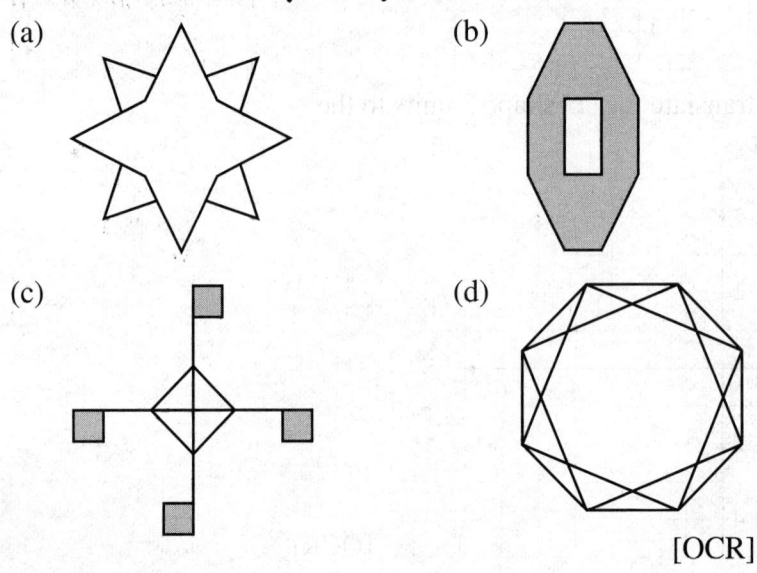

(a)

(b)

(c)

(d)

[OCR]

9. Which of these signs have line symmetry?
   (a)   (b)    (c)    (d) 
   (e)    (f)    (g)    (h)

   [Edexcel]

10. Draw in all the lines of symmetry on a copy of each of these shapes.
    (a)   (b)

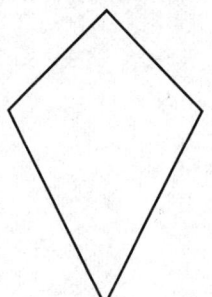

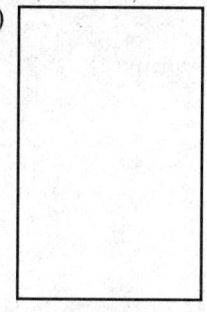

    [Edexcel]

11. Draw an enlargement of the shape shown below using a scale factor of two.

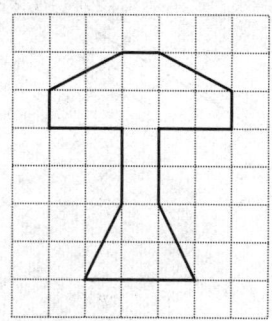

    [AQA/NEAB]

12. Draw an enlargement of the shape below. Use a scale factor of two.

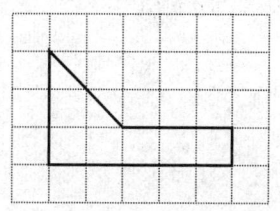

    [OCR]

15 DATA HANDLING 3

Statistics are all around us:

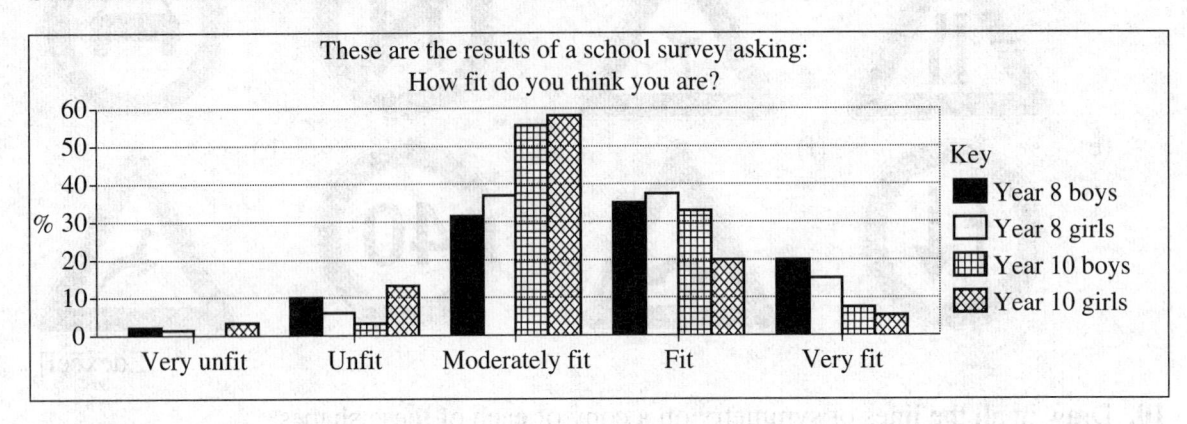

These are the results of a school survey asking:
How fit do you think you are?

Key:
- Year 8 boys
- Year 8 girls
- Year 10 boys
- Year 10 girls

This unit is about:

- Grouped data, bar charts and frequency polygons
- Pie charts drawn with a protractor
- Pie charts drawn with a pie chart scale
- Reading information from pie charts

You need to remember:

Check in 15

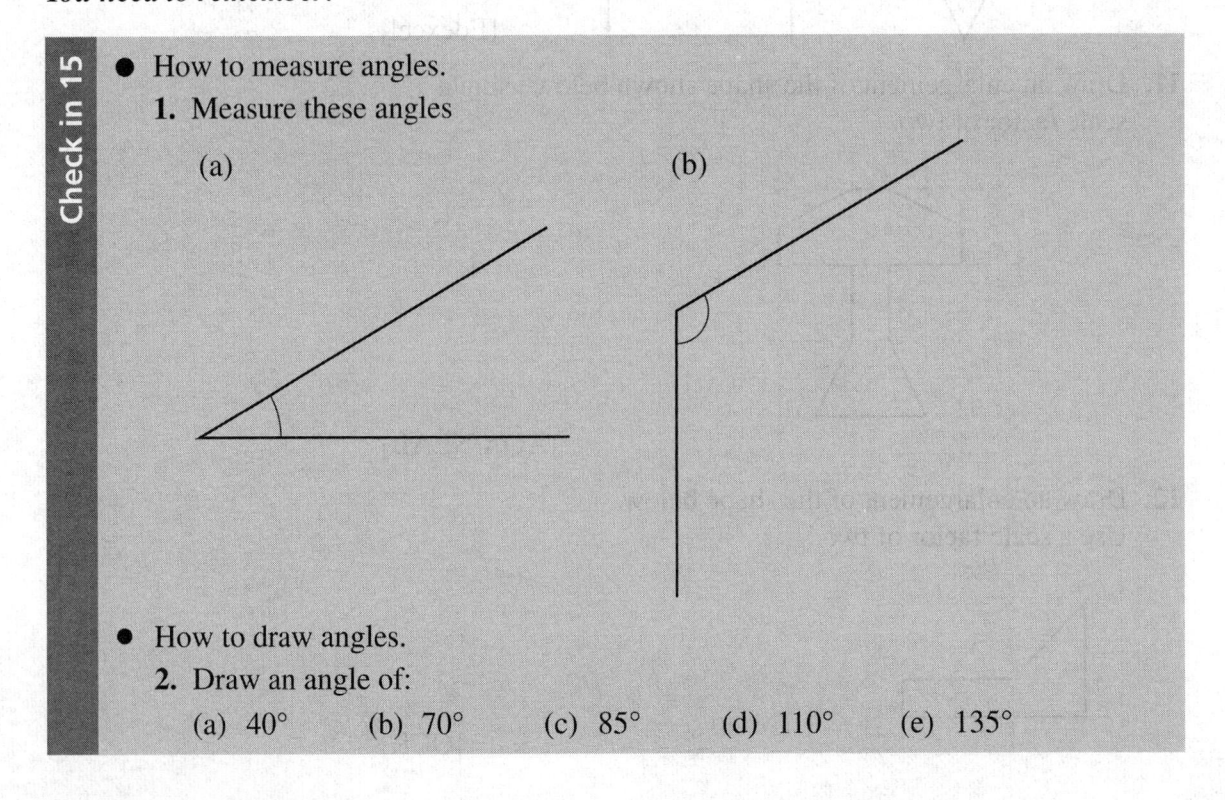

- How to measure angles.
  1. Measure these angles
     (a)
     (b)

- How to draw angles.
  2. Draw an angle of:
     (a) 40°   (b) 70°   (c) 85°   (d) 110°   (e) 135°

15.1 Grouped data, bar charts and frequency polygons

These are the marks of thirty students in a maths examination marked out of 50.

22 32 29 7 13 41 34 28 27 39
18 33 45 28 39 31 17 41 35 28
15 8 33 47 21 27 34 36 33 29

Data with lots of different values is usually organised into a **frequency table**. The data could be organised into this frequency table.

Mark	Frequency
1 to 10	2
11 to 20	4
21 to 30	9
31 to 40	11
41 to 50	4

Hint:
Frequency means total.

The table can be illustrated with a bar chart like this:

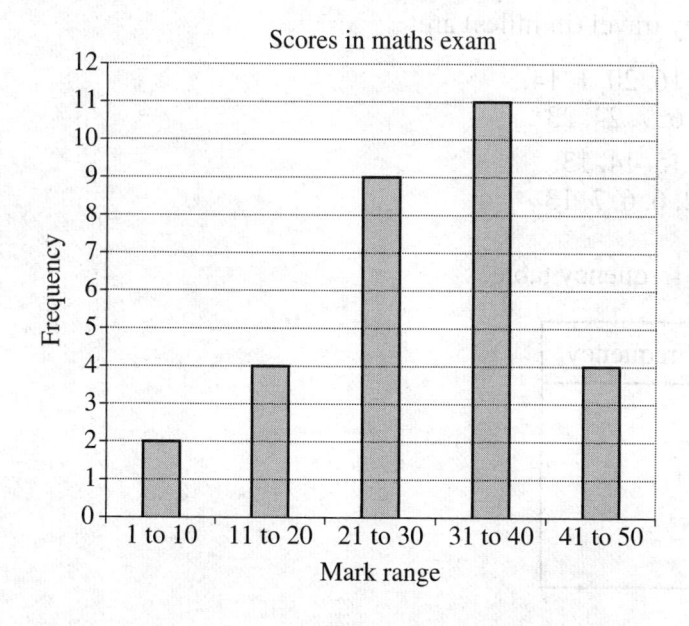

Scores in maths exam

Or with a **frequency polygon** like this:

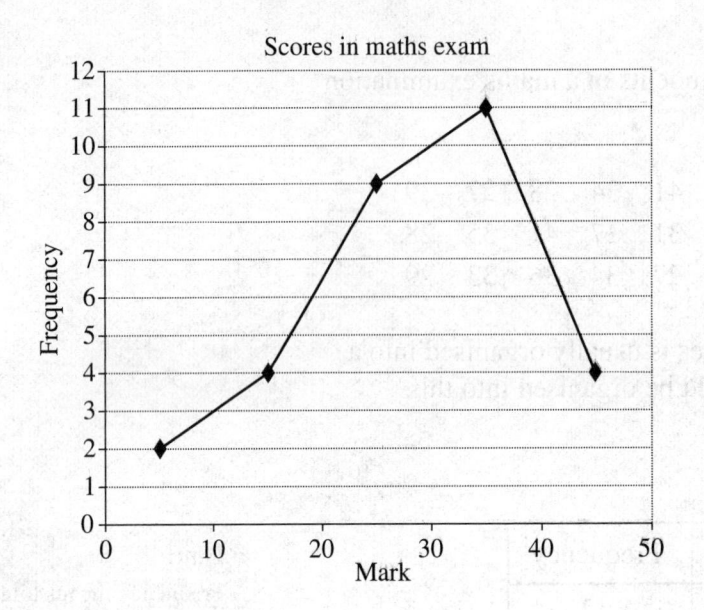

Scores in maths exam

(Frequency polygon plotted with points at Mark 5→2, 15→4, 25→9, 35→11, 45→4)

You draw a frequency polygon by:

- plotting points over the **middle** of each group
- joining the points with straight lines.

Exercise 15A

1. Lisa Jones and Orla Carli both make twenty car journeys in one week. The distances they travel (in miles) are:

    Lisa: 7, 8, 10, 15, 11, 17, 16, 20, 1, 14,
            13, 13, 12, 11, 3, 2, 6, 7, 24, 23

    Orla: 3, 6, 7, 8, 9, 10, 11, 15, 14, 13,
            18, 16, 20, 23, 7, 12, 6, 6, 7, 13

    (a) Copy and complete the frequency table.

Distance (miles)	Frequency
1 to 5	
6 to 10	
11 to 15	
16 to 20	
21 to 25	

(b) Draw two bar charts to illustrate the data. Use axes like these:

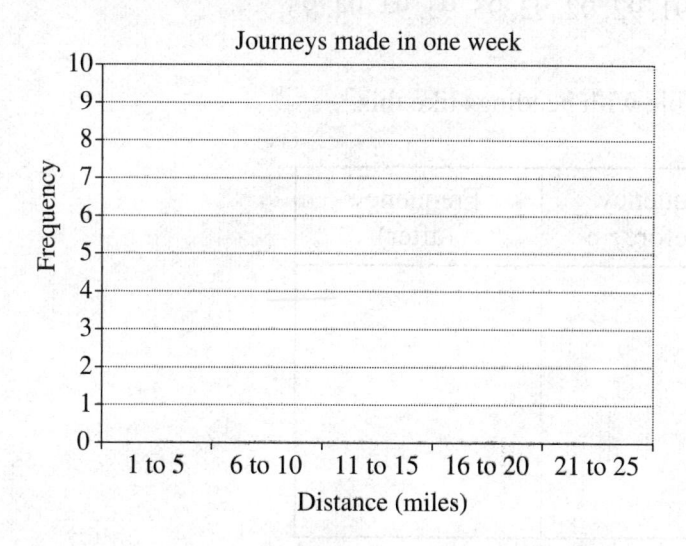

Journeys made in one week

[Bar chart axes: Frequency (0 to 10) vs Distance (miles) with categories 1 to 5, 6 to 10, 11 to 15, 16 to 20, 21 to 25]

(c) Draw two frequency polygons to illustrate the data. Draw **both** frequency polygons on **one** set of axes like these. Remember to plot points above the **middle** of each group.

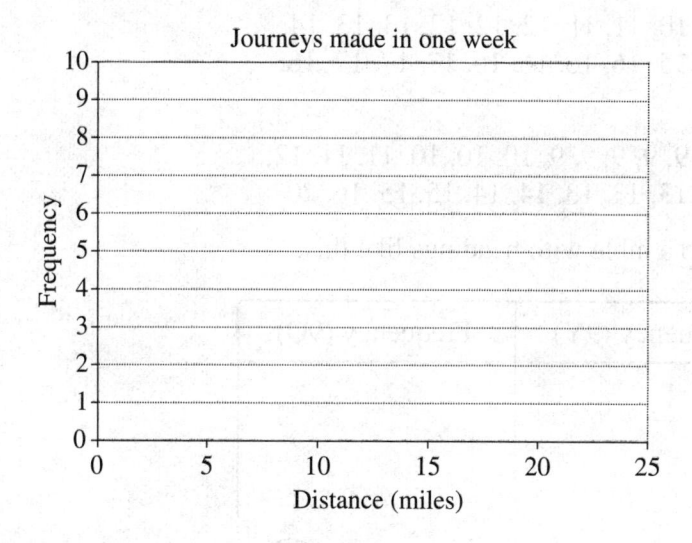

Journeys made in one week

[Axes: Frequency (0 to 10) vs Distance (miles) (0 to 25)]

2. Thirty members of a health club are weighed, to the nearest kilogram, before and after a three-month healthy eating scheme. These are the results.

Before: 77, 81, 82, 84, 84, 86, 86, 88, 88, 88, 90, 91, 92, 93, 93, 94, 95, 95, 96, 96, 97, 97, 97, 98, 99, 100, 101, 101, 104, 105

After: 77, 78, 78, 80, 82, 83, 84, 85, 86, 86, 87, 87, 88, 90, 90, 91, 91, 91, 92, 92, 93, 93, 93, 94, 94, 95, 95, 96, 96, 98

Organise the data into a table with headings like this:

Weight (kilograms)	Frequency (before)	Frequency (after)
76 to 80		
81 to 85		
86 to 90		
91 to 95		
96 to 100		
101 to 105		

3. A history test is marked out of 20. These are the marks for two different classes who take the test.

Class 9Y 1, 3, 4, 7, 9, 9, 10, 11, 11, 12, 12, 12, 13, 13, 14, 15, 15, 15, 15, 15, 16, 16, 16, 16, 17, 17, 17, 18, 19, 20

Class 9Q 7, 7, 8, 8, 9, 9, 9, 9, 9, 9, 9, 10, 10, 10, 11, 11, 12, 12, 12, 12, 13, 13, 13, 13, 14, 14, 15, 15, 16, 20

(a) Organise the data into a table with headings like this:

Mark	Frequency (9Y)	Frequency (9Q)
0 to 2		
3 to 5		
6 to 8		
9 to 11		

(b) Draw two bar charts to illustrate the data.

(c) Draw two frequency polygons to illustrate the data. Draw **both** frequency polygons on **one** set of axes. Remember to plot points above the **middle** of each group.

4. A bus company uses a 20-seat mini-bus to run excursions to a theme park. On two different days the ages of the passengers in the mini-bus were:

Day 1   4, 13, 23, 2, 3, 14, 4, 9, 17, 5, 6, 6, 6, 7, 8, 17, 4, 27, 4, 9
Day 2   24, 28, 35, 36, 31, 29, 13, 16, 16, 28, 38, 34, 17, 18, 23, 32, 36, 28, 4, 7

(a) Organise the data into a table with headings like this:

Age	Frequency (Day 1)	Frequency (Day 2)
0 to 4		
5 to 9		
10 to 14		
15 to 19		

(b) Draw two bar charts to illustrate the data.
(c) Draw two frequency polygons to illustrate the data. Draw **both** frequency polygons on **one** set of axes. Remember to plot points above the **middle** of each group.

15.2 Pie charts drawn with a protractor

A **pie chart** is a good way to show how something is shared out. This pie chart shows how Bill spent a day. It shows how 24 hours are shared out between different activities.

To draw a pie chart with a protractor, you need to find the angle for each sector. The pie chart for Bill's day was drawn from this table.

Bill's day
Other (1)
Playing with friends (4)
Sleeping (8)
School (7)
Watching TV (4)

Activity	Time (hours)
School	7
Sleeping	8
Playing with friends	4
Watching TV	4
Other	1
Total	24

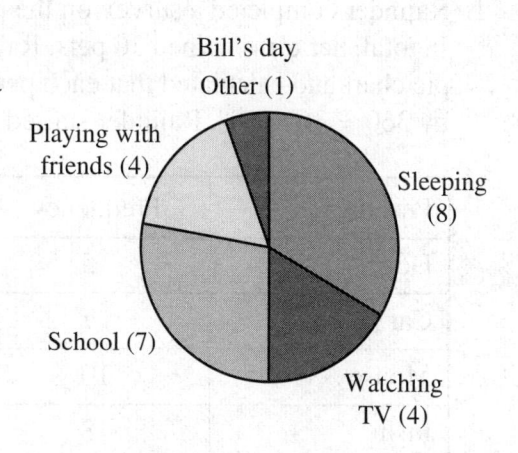

There are 360° in a circle. This means that each hour is represented by 360 ÷ 24 = 15°. A column for angles was added to the table.

Activity	Time (hours)	Angle
School	7	7 × 15° = 105°
Sleeping	8	8 × 15° = 120°
Playing with friends	4	4 × 15° = 60°
Watching TV	4	4 × 15° = 60°
Other	1	1 × 15° = 15°
Total	24	360°

To draw a pie chart follow these steps:

- Draw a suitable sized circle
- Draw one line from the centre to the edge of the circle
- From this starting line, use a protractor to measure the first sector
- Add each sector in turn until the pie chart is complete
- Label the pie chart clearly.

Exercise 15B

1. Rajinder completed a survey on the pets owned by her class. In total, her class owned 36 pets. Rajinder wanted to draw a pie chart and calculated that each pet would be represented by 360 ÷ 36 = 10°. Rajinder started to complete this table.

Pets owned	Frequency	Angle
Dog	5	5 × 10° = 50°
Cat	7	
Mouse	10	
Fish	8	
Hamster	6	
Totals	36	360°

(a) Copy and complete the table.
(b) Draw the pie chart.

2. A junior school class of 30 pupils completed a survey on how each pupil came to school. To draw a pie chart they calculated that each pupil would be represented by 360 ÷ 30 = 12°. They started to complete this table.

Ways of coming to school	Number of pupils	Angle
Parent's car	10	10 × 12° = 120°
Friend's car	4	
Bus	2	
Walk	8	
Cycle	6	
Totals	30	360°

(a) Copy and complete the table.
(b) Draw the pie chart.

3. Every householder in a district has to pay a tax to the local council. The council wants to prepare a pie chart to show how the tax is spent. This table shows how every £180 of spending is made up.

Type of spending	Amount	Angle
Highways and planning	£14	14 × 2 = 28°
Sports and recreation	£28	
Environmental health	£32	
Housing	£27	
Administration	£47	
Emergencies	£32	
Totals	£180	360°

(a) Why has £14 been multiplied by 2 to calculate the pie chart angle?
(b) Copy and complete the table.
(c) Draw the pie chart.

4. A plastic moulding company owns two factories. A manager wishes to prepare two pie charts to compare the running costs of the two factories. He starts to draw up these tables which show how every £90 spent in the two factories is accounted for.

Expenditure	Factory A	Angle
Wages	£30	30 × 4 = 120°
Raw materials	£40	
Overheads	£20	
Totals	£90	360°

Expenditure	Factory B	Angle
Wages	£25	25 × 4 = 100°
Raw materials	£35	
Overheads	£30	
Totals	£90	360°

(a) Why has £30 been multiplied by 4 in the first table to calculate the pie chart angle?
(b) Copy and complete the tables.
(c) Draw the two pie charts.

5. A museum is open all year. A manager wants to compare the number of visitors in two different years. She starts to draw up these tables which show the numbers of visitors in spring, summer, autumn and winter.

Season	Visitors 1999 (thousands)	Angle
Spring	7	7 × 9 = 63°
Summer	18	
Autumn	9	
Winter	6	
Totals	40	360°

Season	Visitors 2000 (thousands)	Angle
Spring	8	8 × 6 = 48°
Summer	31	
Autumn	14	
Winter	7	
Totals	60	360°

(a) Why has 7 been multiplied by 9 in the first table to calculate the pie chart angle?
(b) Why has 8 been multiplied by 6 in the second table to calculate the pie chart angle?
(b) Copy and complete the tables.
(c) Draw the two pie charts.

6. Sunshine Desserts is developing a new range of sponge puddings. These are the results of taste tests with two different groups of people. The results will be illustrated with two pie charts.

Flavour	Number of first choices (Test 1)	Angle
Strawberry	54	
Raspberry	47	
Orange	21	
Apple	23	
Pear	35	
Totals		

Flavour	Number of first choices (Test 2)	Angle
Strawberry	32	
Raspberry	44	
Orange	34	
Apple	40	
Pear	30	
Totals		

(a) Copy and complete the tables.
(b) Draw the two pie charts.

15.3 Pie charts drawn with a pie chart scale

If the data for a pie chart is presented as percentages, it is easier to draw the pie chart using a **pie chart scale**. A pie chart scale is a circular measure divided up from 0% to 100%.

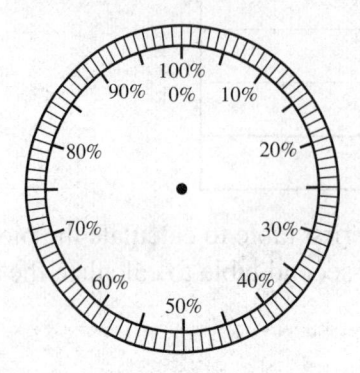

Stacey asked 50 pupils how they travelled to school.
This table shows her results.

Type of transport	Number	Percentage
Bus	23	46%
Walk	14	28%
Car	8	16%
Bike	5	10%
Totals	50	100%

Using a pie chart scale, this pie chart can be drawn to illustrate the table.

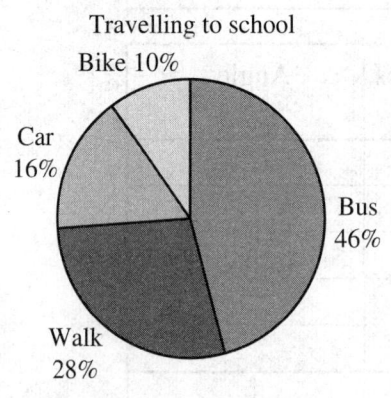

You work out percentages by:
- Dividing each frequency by the total of the frequencies
- Multiplying the answer by 100.

Exercise 15C

1. The BBC estimates that the money collected from licence fees is spent in this way:

   Capital costs 25%
   BBC1   35%
   BBC2   20%
   Radio   20%

   Draw a pie chart to illustrate this data.

2. This table shows results from the General Household Survey of 1994.

Type of dwelling	Frequency
Detached house	20%
Semi-detached house	31%
Terraced house	28%
Flat or maisonette (purpose built)	15%
Flat or maisonette (converted)	5%
With business or shop	1%
Totals	100%

   Draw a pie chart to illustrate the data in the table

3. In a taste test in a GCSE Food class, students were asked to vote for their favourite sausage. Four brands were compared. Sammy-Jo Afford started to draw up this table of results.

Brand	Votes	Percentage
Pork	5	5 ÷ 25 × 100 = 20%
Pork with apple	10	10 ÷ 25 × 100 = 40%
Pork with herbs	6	
Vegetarian	4	
Totals	25	100%

   (a) Copy and complete the table.
   (b) Draw a pie chart to illustrate the data in the table.

4. A youth club offers four different activities: football, snooker, table tennis and aerobics. All the club members are asked which is their favourite activity. The results are shown in this table.

Activity	Number of first choices	Percentage
Football	30	30 ÷ 150 × 100 = 20%
Snooker	15	
Table tennis	45	
Aerobics	60	
Totals	150	100%

(a) Copy and complete the table.
(b) Draw a pie chart to illustrate the data in the table.

5. A group of Year 7 pupils and a group of Year 11 pupils are asked how they think a £1 000 donation to the school should be spent. These tables show the results.

Spending idea	Votes from Year 7	Percentage
Computer for the library	48	48 ÷ 200 × 100 = 24%
Sports equipment	84	
Staging for school productions	46	
Display boards in the school entrance	22	
Totals	200	100%

Spending idea	Votes from Year 11	Percentage
Computer for the library	45	45 ÷ 180 × 100 = 25%
Sports equipment	63	
Staging for school productions	54	
Display boards in the school entrance	18	
Totals	180	100%

(a) Copy and complete the tables.
(b) Draw two pie charts to illustrate the data in the tables.

6. Shaun is designing a CD holder for his GCSE Technology examination. Before he completes a final design he uses a questionnaire to test his ideas. One question Shaun uses is:

   What finish would you prefer for the product?

   Polished wood ☐   Stained wood ☐   Painted ☐

   These tables show the responses to the question from a group of pupils and a group of adults.

Finish	Choices (pupils)	Percentage
Polished wood	6	
Stained wood	36	
Painted	18	
Totals		

Finish	Choices (adults)	Percentage
Polished wood	15	
Stained wood	24	
Painted	21	
Totals		

   (a) Copy and complete the tables.
   (b) Draw two pie charts to illustrate the data in the tables.

15.4 Reading information from pie charts

Pie charts are used to show information. You need to be able to understand this information.

Exercise 15D

1. A shop sells a sweatshirt in four sizes: small, medium, large and extra large. This pie chart shows the weekly sales of different sizes.
   (a) What percentage of the sweatshirts sold were small?
   (b) Which was the most popular size?
   (c) The shop sold a total of 25 sweatshirts. How many of these were large?

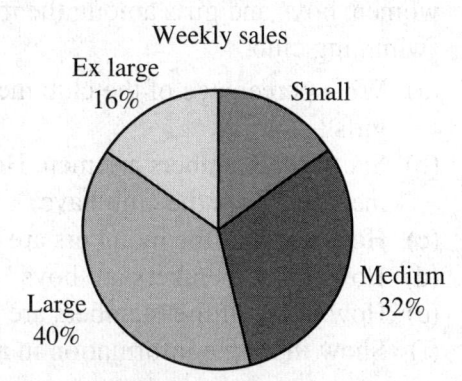

(d) How many medium sweatshirts were sold?
(e) Show the same information in a bar chart.

2. An office manager calculates that her average working day is divided up in the way shown in this pie chart.

   Division of the day: Leisure 45°, Eating 45°, Travel 45°, Sleeping 90°, Working

   (a) What is the size of the angle which represents working?
   (b) There are 24 hours in the manager's day. How many hours does she spend sleeping?
   (c) How many hours does the manager spend travelling?
   (d) How many hours does the manager spend working?
   (e) Show the same information in a bar chart.

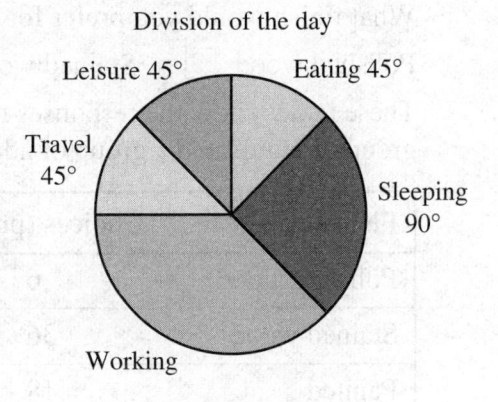

3. This pie chart shows the monthly rainfall for a seaside town during the tourist season.

   Monthly rainfall: September, April, August 56°, May 60°, July 40°, June 48°

   (a) Equal amounts of rain fell during September and April. What is the size of the angle which represents the rainfall in April?
   (b) A total of 90 mm of rain fell during the whole tourist season. What angle in the pie chart would represent a rainfall of 1 mm?
   (c) What was the rainfall in May?
   (d) What was the rainfall in September?
   (e) Show the same information in a bar chart.

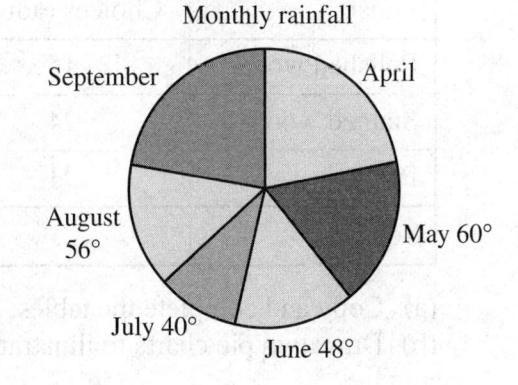

4. This pie chart shows the distribution of men, women, boys and girls among the members of a swimming club.

   Membership of a swimming club: Men 10%, Women 35%, Boys 30%, Girls

   (a) What percentage of the club members are girls?
   (b) Six of the members are men. How many members does the club have?
   (c) How many of the members are girls?
   (d) How many members are boys?
   (e) How many of the members are women?
   (f) Show the same information in a bar chart.

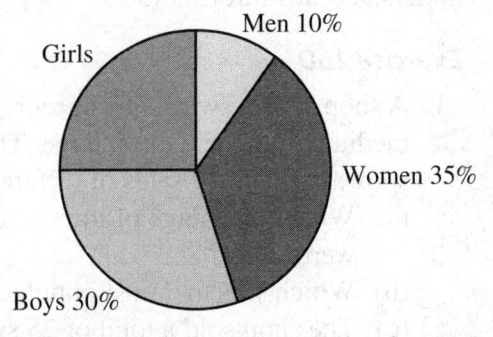

5. This pie chart shows the results of a class survey on pet ownership.
   (a) What is the size of the angle which represents cats?
   (b) The survey found that 1 person owned a fish. How many pupils owned snakes?
   (c) How many pupils owned dogs?
   (d) How many pupils owned birds?
   (e) Show the same information in a bar chart.

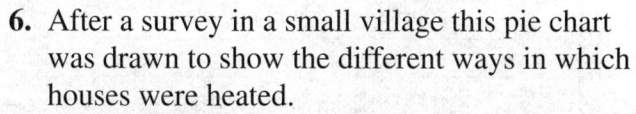

   Pet ownership
   Snakes 40°, Cats, Dogs 60°, Fish 20°, Birds 160°

6. After a survey in a small village this pie chart was drawn to show the different ways in which houses were heated.
   (a) What percentage of the houses are heated by coal?
   (b) 20 houses are heated by gas. How many houses are heated by coal?
   (c) How many of the houses are heated by electricity?
   (d) How many of the houses are heated by oil?
   (e) How many houses are there in the village?
   (f) Show the same information in a bar chart.

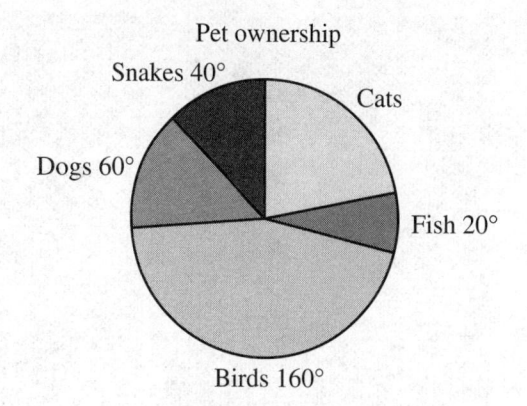

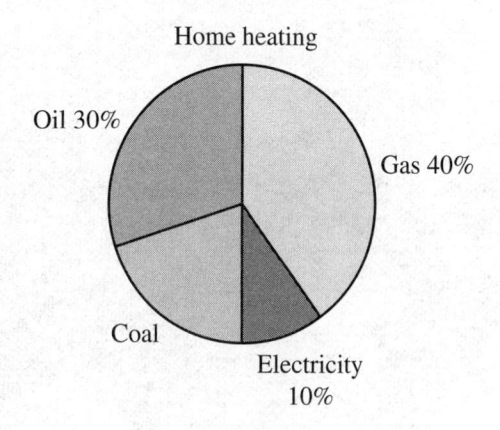

   Home heating
   Oil 30%, Gas 40%, Coal, Electricity 10%

Summary

1. Data with lots of different values is usually organised into a **frequency table**. The tables can be illustrated with **bar charts** or **frequency polygons**.

Checkout 15

1. Lisa Jones and Orla Carli both make twenty car journeys in one week. The distances they travel (in miles) are:
   Lisa: 3, 4, 7, 15, 6, 7, 8, 9, 4, 11, 5, 16, 7, 8, 11, 12, 4, 4, 17, 3
   Orla: 2, 4, 15, 22, 2, 1, 5, 7, 8, 9, 13, 14, 15, 23, 14, 18, 22, 7, 6, 24

(a) Organise the data into two tables with headings like this:

Distance (miles)	Frequency
1 to 5 6 to 10 11 to 15 16 to 20 21 to 25	

(b) Draw two bar charts to illustrate the data. Use axes like these:

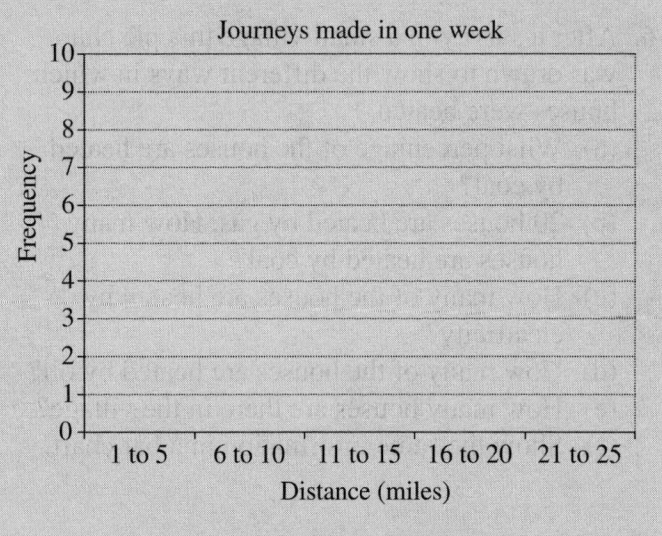

Journeys made in one week

(c) Draw two frequency polygons to illustrate the data. Draw **both** frequency polygons on **one** set of axes like these. Remember to plot points above the **middle** of each group.

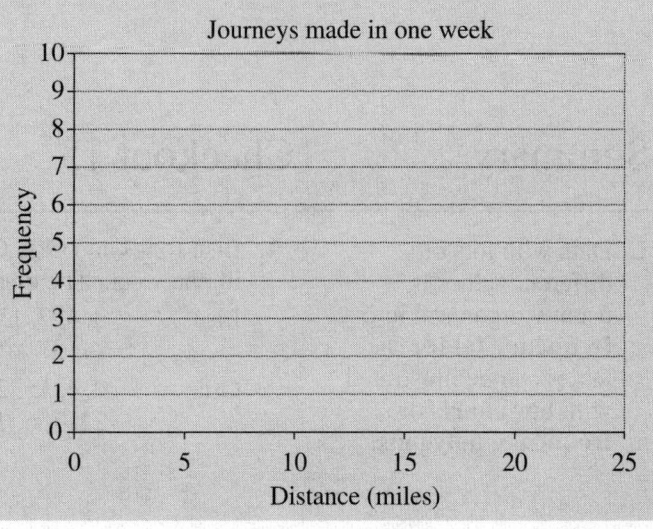

Journeys made in one week

2. A **pie chart** is a good way to show how something is shared out.
To draw a pie chart with a protractor, first calculate the angle for each sector.

2. A heritage park is open all year. This table shows the numbers of visitors in spring, summer, autumn and winter.

Season	Visitors (thousands)	Angle
Spring	10	10 × 6 = 60°
Summer	25	
Autumn	16	
Winter	9	
Totals	60	360°

(a) Why has 10 been multiplied by 6 in the table to calculate the pie chart angle?
(b) Copy and complete the table.
(c) Draw the pie chart.

3. If the data for a pie chart is presented as percentages, it is easier to draw the pie chart with a **pie chart scale**. A pie chart scale is a circular measure divided up from 0% to 100%.

3. In a taste test in a GCSE Food class, students were asked to vote for their favourite pizza. Four toppings were compared. Carla started to draw up this table of results.

Topping	Votes	Percentage
Cheese and tomato	4	4 ÷ 25 × 100 = 16%
Pepperoni and ham	12	12 ÷ 25 × 100 = 48%
Garlic and mushroom	3	
Roast vegetable	6	
Totals	25	100%

(a) Copy and complete the table.
(b) Draw a pie chart to illustrate the data in the table.

4. Sometimes you will be asked to read information from a pie chart.

4. (a) This pie chart shows the results of a survey into school transport.

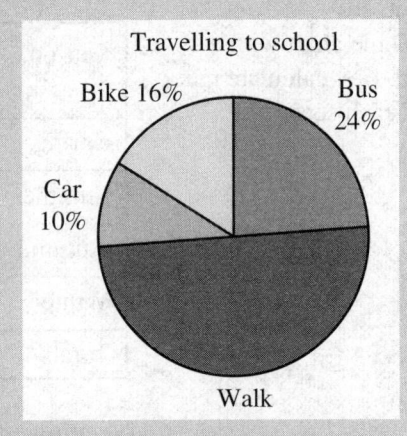

Travelling to school
Bike 16%
Bus 24%
Car 10%
Walk

(i) What percentage of children walked to school?
(ii) 20 children came by car, how many came by bus?
(iii) Show the same information with a bar chart.

(b) This pie chart shows the results of a survey into the sporting activities a group of Year 10 boys took part in each week.

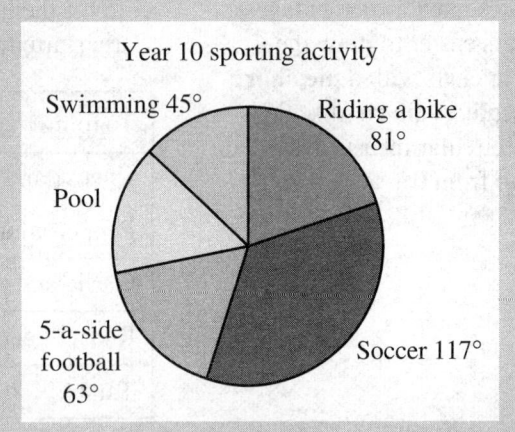

Year 10 sporting activity
Swimming 45°
Riding a bike 81°
Pool
5-a-side football 63°
Soccer 117°

(i) What is the pie chart angle that represents pool?
(ii) 5 boys went swimming. How many degrees represent each boy in the pie chart?
(iii) How many boys played soccer?
(iv) How many boys played five-a-side football?
(v) How many boys went for a bike ride?
(vi) Show the same information with a bar chart.

Revision exercise 15

1. Karen's local shop sells newspapers.
   Both of these diagrams show the papers sold last Monday.

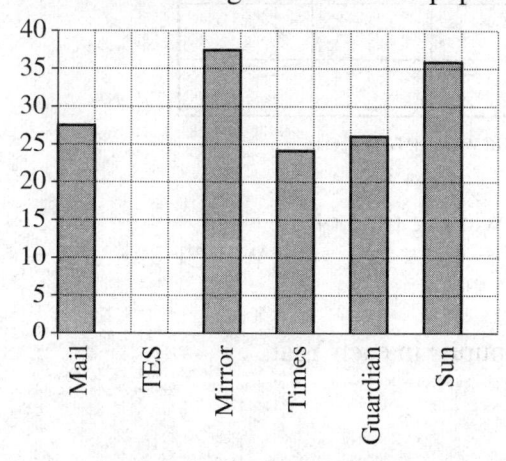

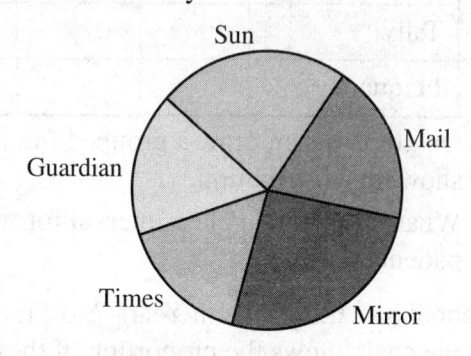

   (a) (i) How many copies of the TES were sold?
       (ii) Which newspaper sold the most copies on Monday?

   (b) Why does the pie chart have only 5 sectors?

   This graph shows the total number of newspapers sold by the shop last week.

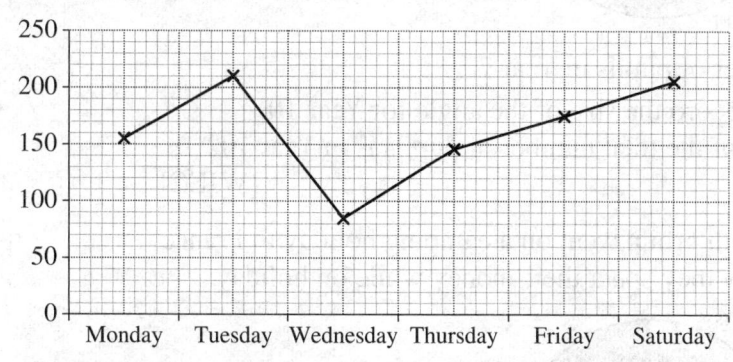

   (c) (i) How many newspapers were sold on Tuesday?
       (ii) On which days were fewer than 150 newspapers sold?
   [OCR]

2. The following numbers show the times in minutes, correct to the nearest minute, which patients at a surgery had to wait before seeing the doctor.

4	12	15	25	32	7	45	23	27	13
28	8	21	13	45	26	16	17	28	24
26	45	13	17	42	24	25	14	31	20
5	30	29	9	10	10	22	27	13	10

(a) Complete the following table to show a grouped frequency distribution of the waiting times of the patients.

Time (minutes)	1 to 10	11 to 20	21 to 30	31 to 40	41 to 50
Tally					
Frequency					

(b) On graph paper, draw a grouped frequency diagram to show this distribution.

(c) What is the modal class interval for the waiting time of the patients? [WJEC]

3. A school has 720 pupils in Years 7 to 11.
The pie chart shows the proportion of these pupils in each Year.

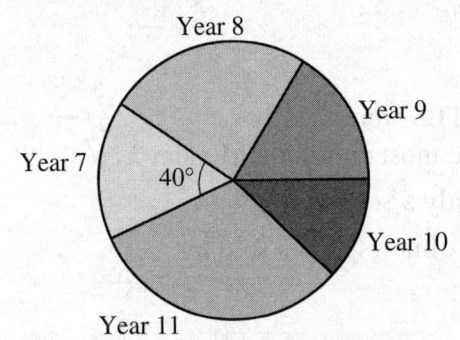

(a) Calculate the number of pupils in Year 7.
(b) (i) Measure and record the size of the angle for Year 10.
    (ii) What fraction of the total number of pupils is in Year 10?
    [WJEC]

4. Some members of a youth group went on a camping holiday to France. The pie chart shows how they spent their money while on holiday.

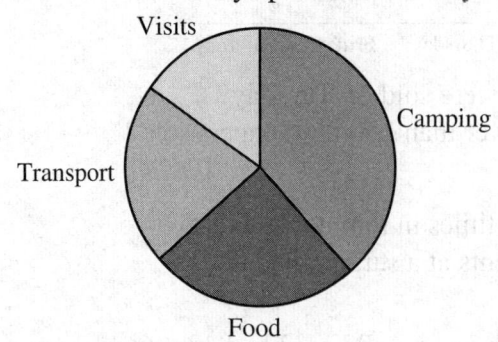

The cost of the food was £240.
(a) What was the total cost of the holiday?
(b) How much did they spend on transport? [OCR]

5. The pie chart shows information from a survey about the holiday destinations of a number of people.

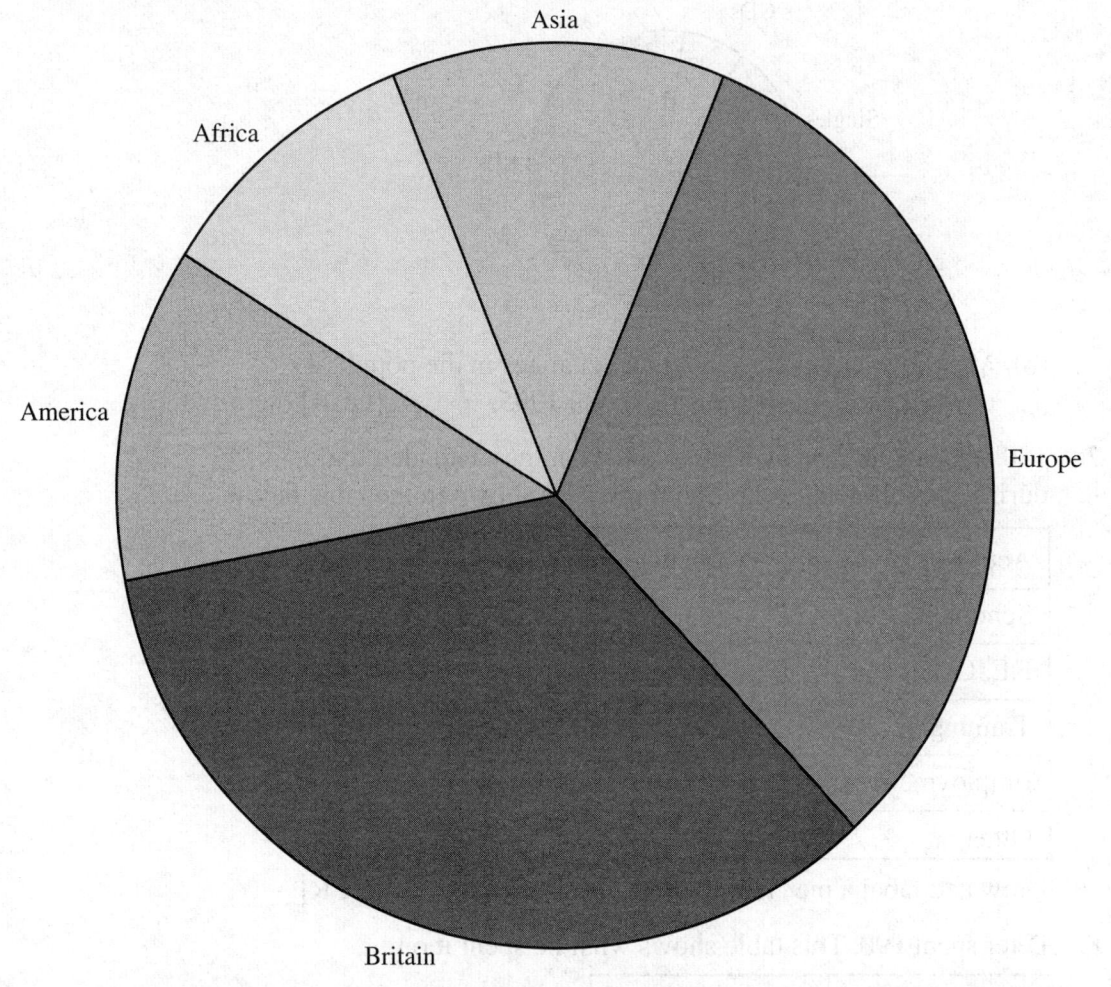

(a) (i) Which holiday destination is the mode?
 (ii) America is the holiday destination of 21 people. How many people go to Africa?

In another survey, it was found that America is the holiday destination of 25 people out of 180 people asked.

(b) What percentage of all the people asked in these two surveys gave America as their holiday destination? [AQA/SEG]

6. Recorded music is sold in 5 different formats. This table shows the percentage of total sales for each format for the UK in 1995.

Format	LPs	Cassettes	Singles	CDs	Music video
Percentage	1	18	11	67	3

(a) Draw and label a pie chart to show this information.

This pie chart shows the sales for 1985.

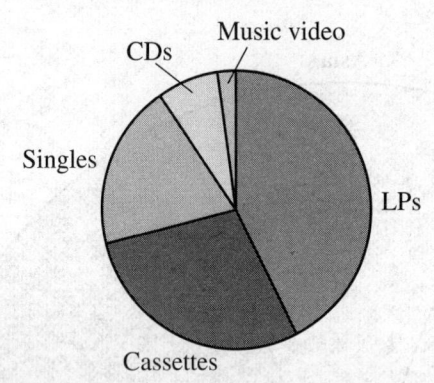

(b) Make two comments about any changes in the popularity of the 5 formats between 1985 and 1995. [OCR]

7. 180 students in Year 11 were asked what they intended to do during the following year. The results are shown in the table below.

Activity	Frequency
School 6th Form	81
F.E. College	40
Training	28
Employment	12
Other	19

Draw and label a pie chart to show these choices. [OCR]

8. Peter spent £90. This table shows what he spent it on.

Items	Amount spent
Bus fares	£13
Going out	£24
Clothes	£30
CDs	£15
Other	£8
Total spending	£90

(a) Show this information on a pie chart.
   Label each section clearly with the angle or percentage.
(b) What fraction did Peter spend on clothes? [OCR]

16 Shape and Space 5

This unit is about:

- Perimeters
- Area by counting squares
- Area of a rectangle by calculation
- Areas of shapes made from rectangles
- Area of a parallelogram
- Area of a triangle
- Area of a compound shape

You need to remember:

> **Check in 16**
>
> - How to multiply decimals.
>   1. Work out:
>   (a) 2×3.5 (b) 3×4.1 (c) 5×6.2 (d) 3.6×10
>   (e) 4×3.8 (f) 9.3×10 (g) 3.4×1.2 (h) 8.4×9.5
> - How to divide by 2 in your head.
>   2. Write down the answer to:
>   (a) $17 \div 2$ (b) $28 \div 2$ (c) $17.4 \div 2$ (d) $35 \div 2$
>   (e) $41 \div 2$ (f) $27.4 \div 2$ (g) $87.3 \div 2$ (h) $56.7 \div 2$

16.1 Perimeters

The distance round the outside of a shape is called its **perimeter**.

The perimeter of this rectangle is 16 cm.

You just add up the lengths: 6 + 2 + 6 + 2 = 16

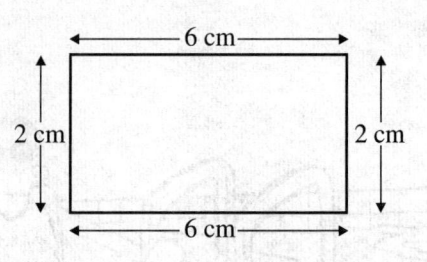

Example

Find the perimeter of this shape drawn on a 1 centimetre grid.

The diagonal of a 1 cm square is approximately 1·4 cm long.

The perimeter of the shape = 4 + 1·4 + 1·4 + 1 + 2 + 3 = 12·8 cm.

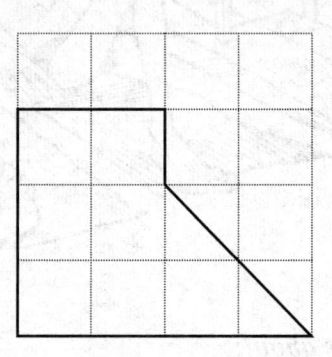

Exercise 16A

Find the perimeter of each of these shapes drawn on a 1 cm grid.

1.

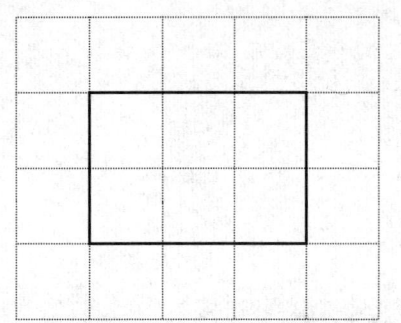

2.

3.

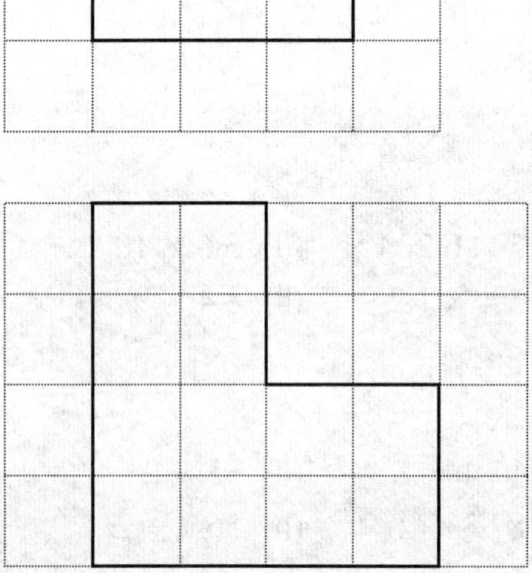

4.

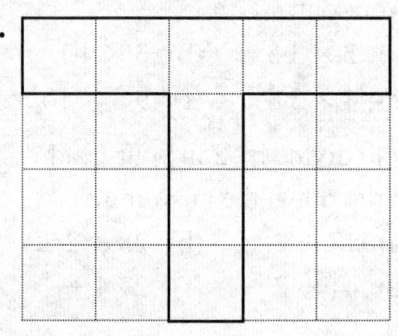

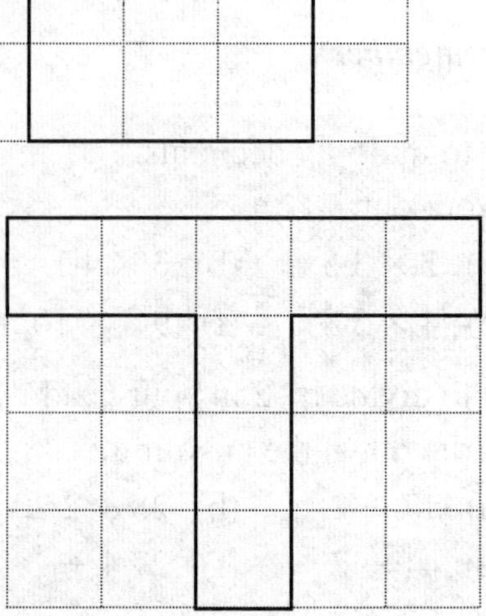

Perimeters 357

5. 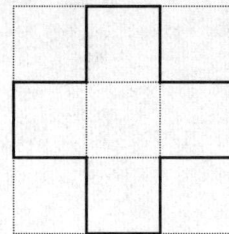
6. 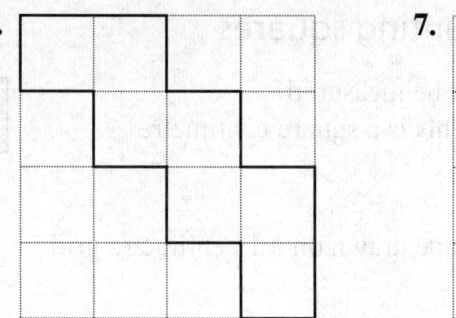
7. 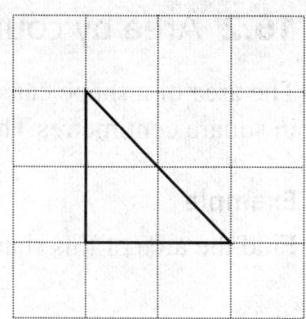
8. 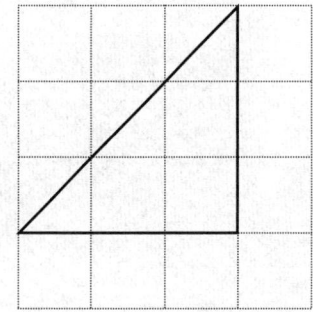
9. 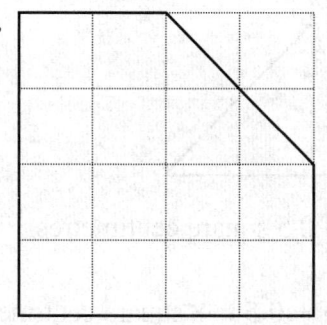
10. 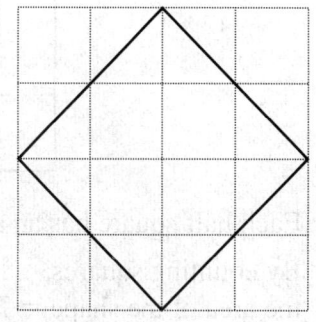
11. 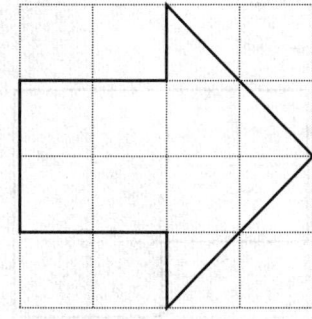
12. 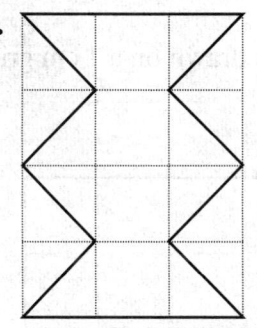
13. 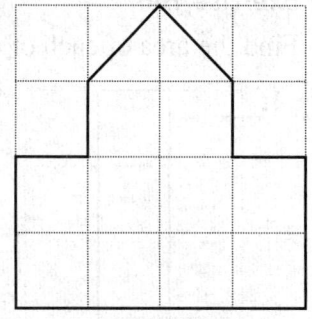
14. 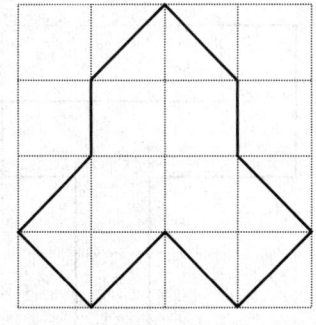
15.

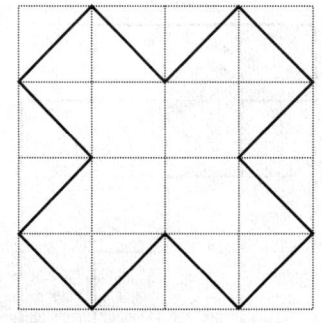

16.2 Area by counting squares

The area of a shape can be measured in square centimetres. This is a square centimetre.

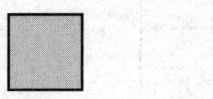

Example

Find the area of this shape drawn on a 1 centimetre grid.

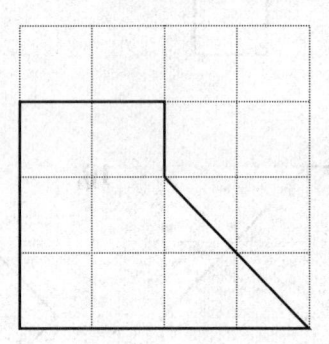

Each half square has an area of 0·5 square centimetres.

By counting squares,
the area of the shape = 7 + 0·5 + 0·5 = 8 square centimetres.

The answer is normally shortened to 8 cm².

Exercise 16B

Find the area of each of these shapes drawn on a 1 cm grid.

1.

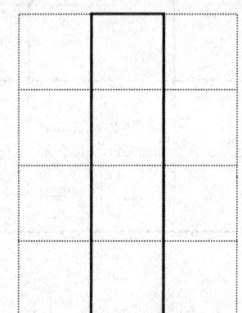

2.

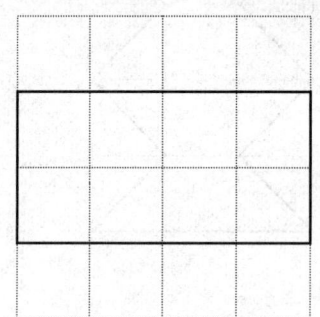

3.

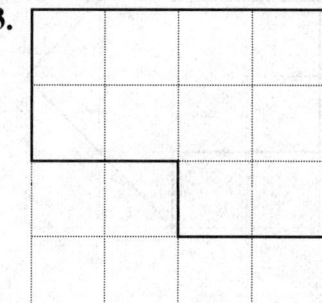

4.

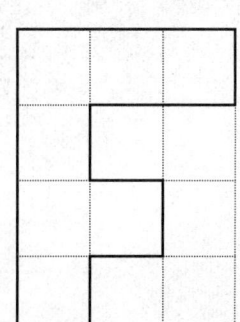

5.

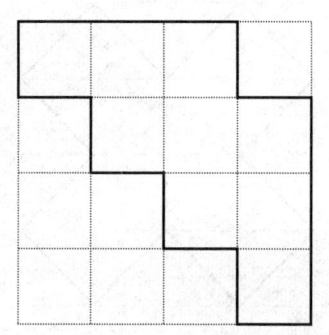

6.

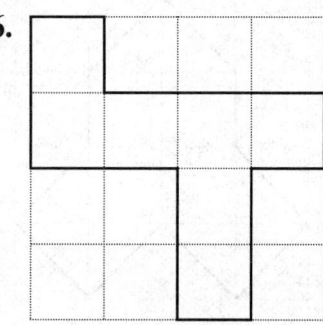

Area by counting squares 359

7.

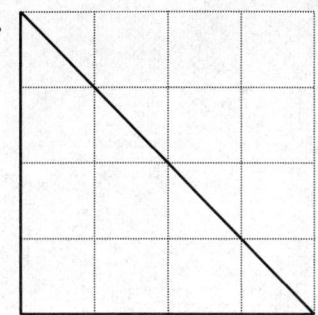

8.

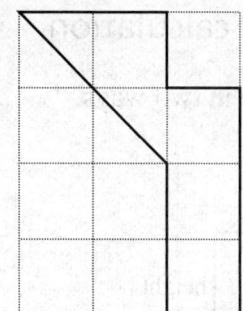

9.

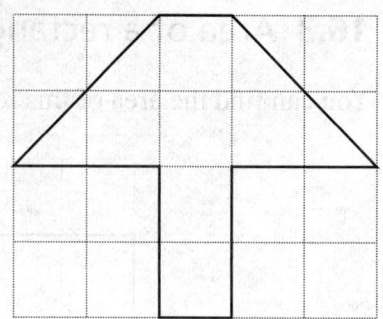

10.

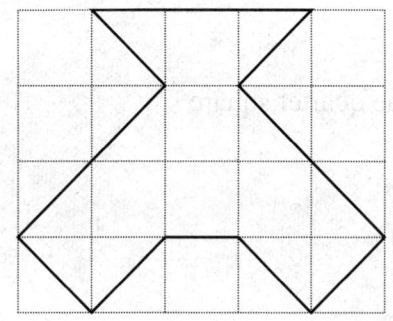

11.

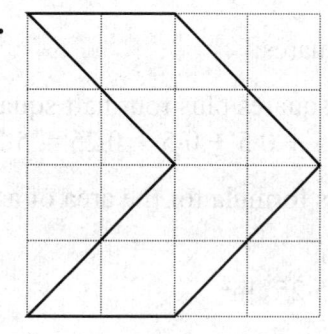

12.

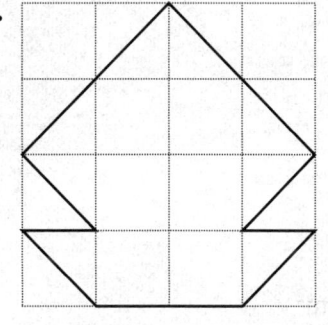

13.

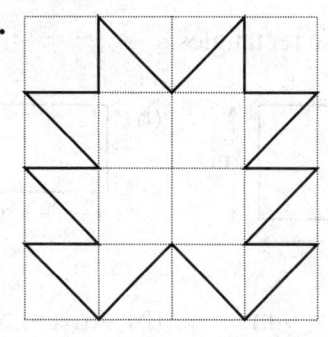

14.

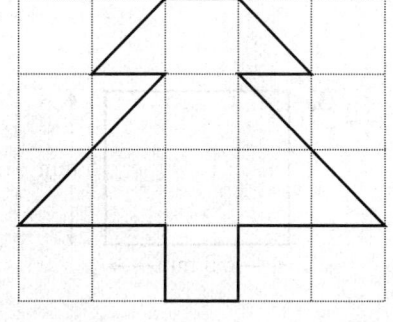

15.

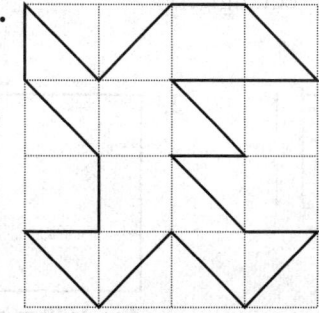

16.3 Area of a rectangle by calculation

You can find the area of this rectangle in two ways.

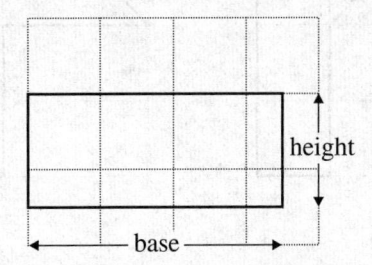

First, by counting squares:

Area = three whole squares plus four half squares plus one quarter square
= 3 + 0·5 + 0·5 + 0·5 + 0·5 + 0·25 = 5·25 cm²

Second, by using this formula for the area of a rectangle:

Area = base × height
= 3·5 × 1·5 = 5·25 cm²

Areas may also be calculated in square metres (m²) or square millimetres (mm²).

Examples

Find the area of these rectangles.

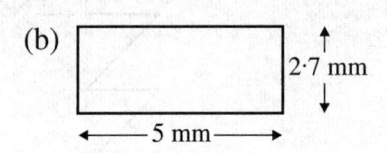

(a) 4·5 m by 2 m

(b) 5 mm by 2·7 mm

(a) Area = 2 × 4·5 = 9 m²   (b) Area = 5 × 2·7 = 13·5 mm²

Exercise 16C

Find the area of each rectangle.

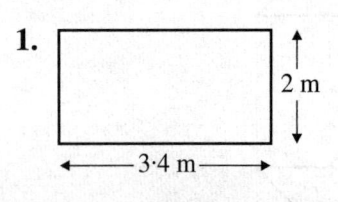

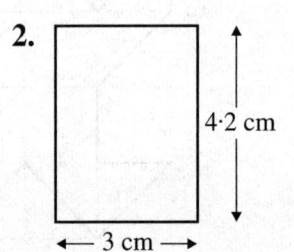

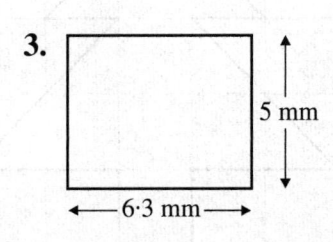

1. 3·4 m by 2 m

2. 3 cm by 4·2 cm

3. 6·3 mm by 5 mm

4. [square: 5 m × 5 m]

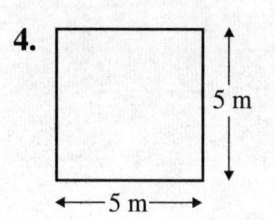

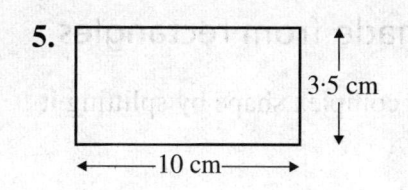

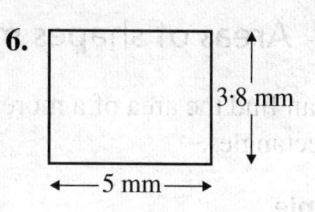

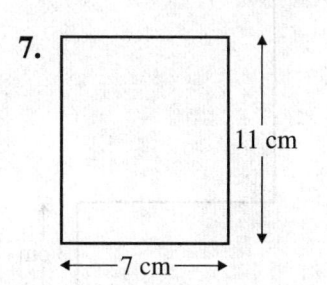

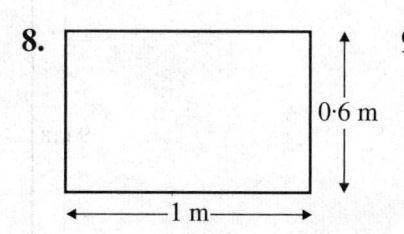

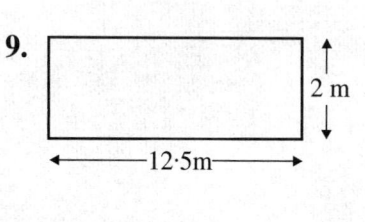

5. [rectangle: 10 cm × 3·5 cm]

6. [rectangle: 5 mm × 3·8 mm]

7. [rectangle: 7 cm × 11 cm]

8. [rectangle: 1 m × 0·6 m]

9. [rectangle: 12·5 m × 2 m]

10. Copy and complete the table for each square:

Square	Base	Height	Area
(a)	1 cm	1 cm	
(b)	10 mm	10 mm	

Remember: 1 cm = 10 mm

11. Look at your table in Question 10.
    Now copy and complete:

    $1 \text{ cm}^2 = \square \text{ mm}^2$

12. Copy and complete the table for each square:

Square	Base	Height	Area
(a)	1 m	1 m	
(b)	100 cm	100 cm	

Remember: 1 m = 100 cm

13. Look at your table in Question 12.
    Now copy and complete:

    $1 \text{ m}^2 = \square \text{ cm}^2$

16.4 Areas of shapes made from rectangles

You can find the area of a more complex shape by splitting it into rectangles.

Example

Find the area of this shape.

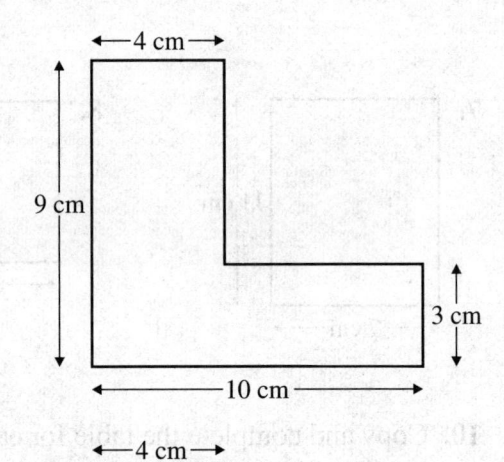

Split the shape into rectangles.

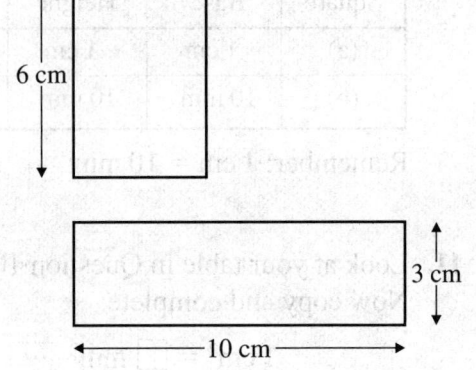

Area = (4 × 6) + (10 × 3) = 24 + 30 = 54 cm²

Exercise 16D

Find the area of each shape.

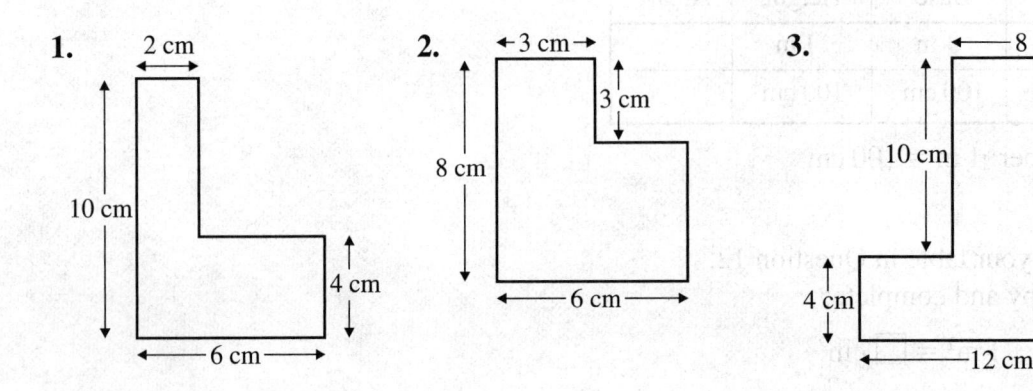

1.
2.
3.

4. 10 mm, 20 mm, 8 mm, 6 mm

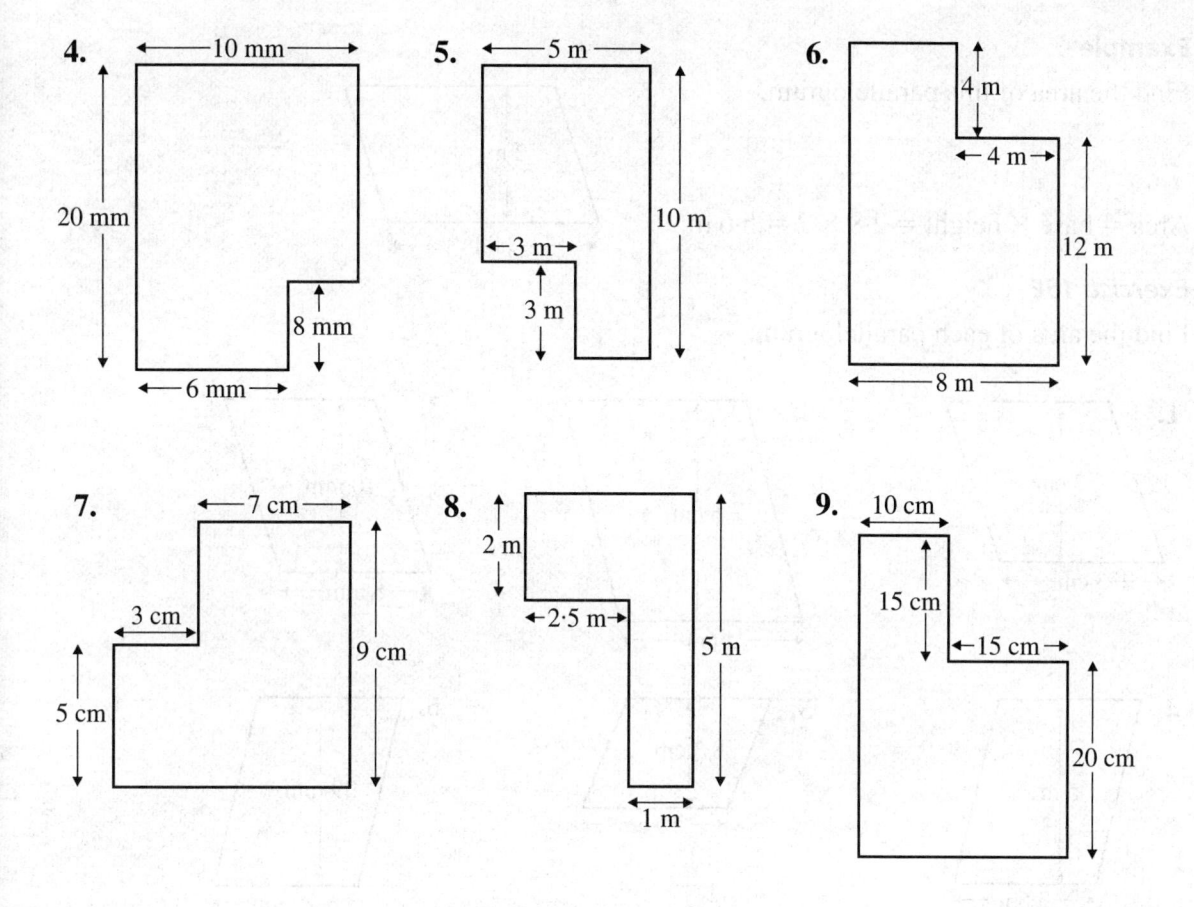

5. 5 m, 10 m, 3 m, 3 m

6. 4 m, 4 m, 12 m, 8 m

7. 7 cm, 3 cm, 9 cm, 5 cm

8. 2 m, 2·5 m, 5 m, 1 m

9. 10 cm, 15 cm, 15 cm, 20 cm

16.5 Area of a parallelogram

Any parallelogram can be changed into a rectangle with the same height and base length.

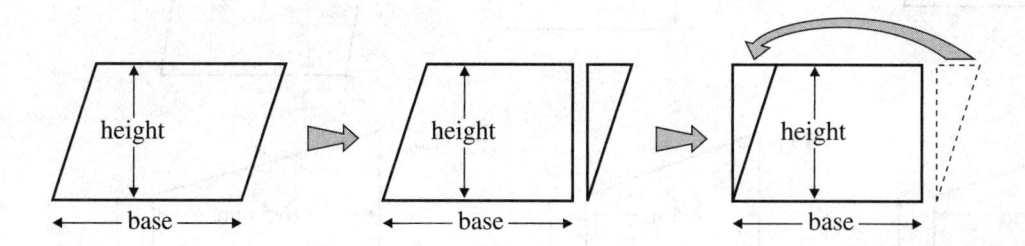

Rectangles and parallelograms have the same area formula:

Area = base × height

Remember:
It is the perpendicular height, not the slant height.

Example

Find the area of this parallelogram.

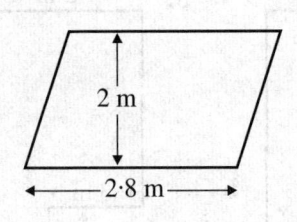

Area = base × height = 2·8 × 2 = 5·6 m²

Exercise 16E

Find the area of each parallelogram.

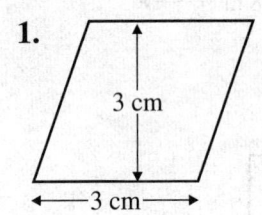

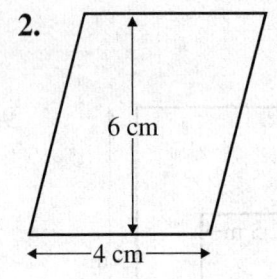

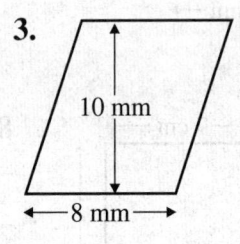

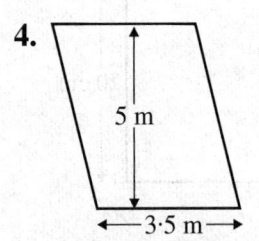

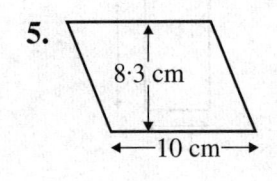

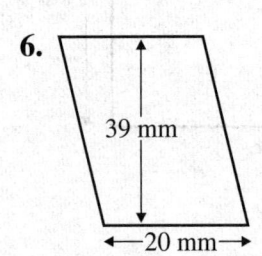

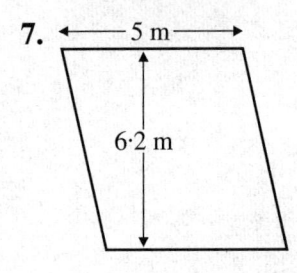

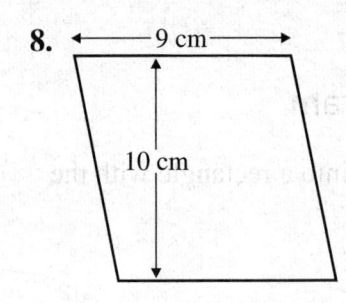

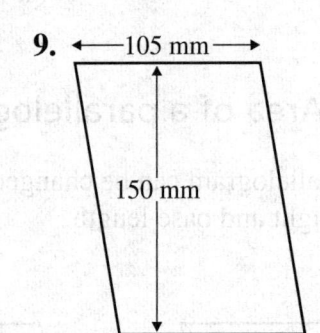

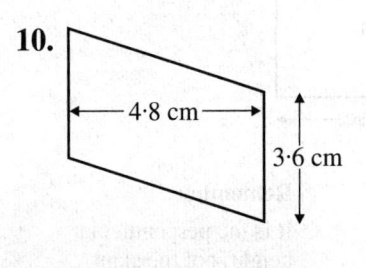

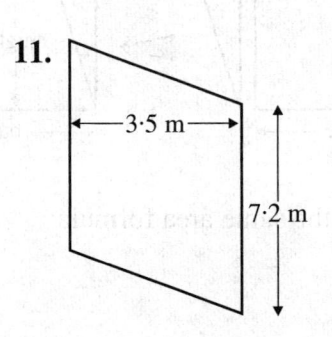

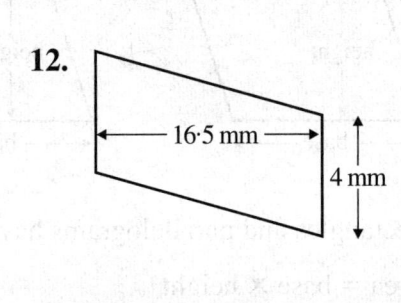

1. 3 cm (height), 3 cm (base)
2. 6 cm (height), 4 cm (base)
3. 10 mm (height), 8 mm (base)
4. 5 m (height), 3·5 m (base)
5. 8·3 cm (height), 10 cm (base)
6. 39 mm (height), 20 mm (base)
7. 5 m (base), 6·2 m (height)
8. 9 cm (base), 10 cm (height)
9. 105 mm (base), 150 mm (height)
10. 4·8 cm (base), 3·6 cm (height)
11. 3·5 m (base), 7·2 m (height)
12. 16·5 mm (base), 4 mm (height)

13.

8·5 m
9·4 m

14.

22·5 cm
12 cm

15.

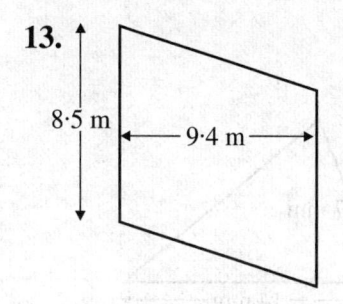

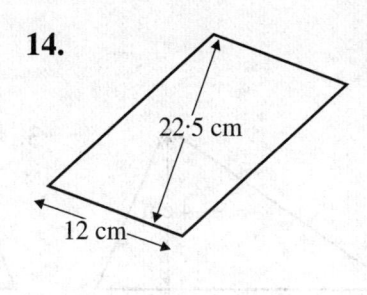

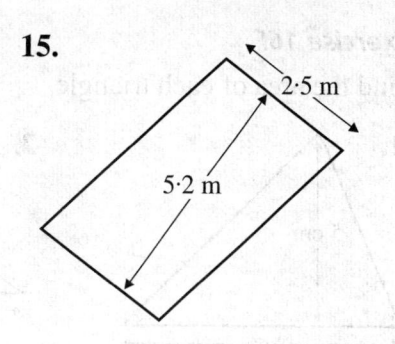

2·5 m
5·2 m

16.6 Area of a triangle

Any triangle is half of a parallelogram with the same base and height.

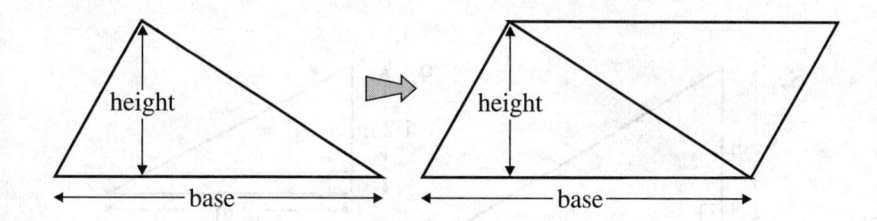

Remember:
The height is the perpendicular height.

The formula for the area of a triangle is therefore:

Area = $\frac{1}{2}$ of (base × height)

= $\frac{1}{2}$ × base × height

Example
Find the area of this triangle.

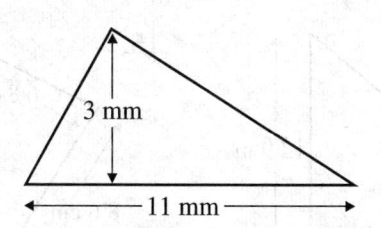

3 mm
11 mm

Area = $\frac{1}{2}$ × base × height = $\frac{1}{2}$ × 11 × 3 = $\frac{1}{2}$ × 33 = 16·5 mm²

Exercise 16F

Find the area of each triangle.

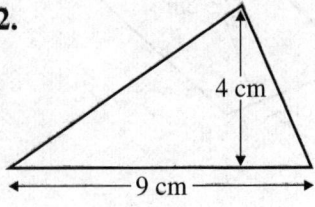

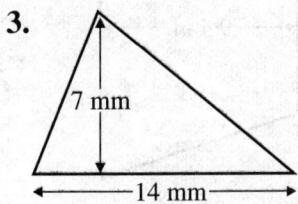

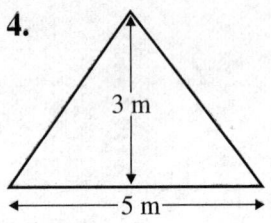

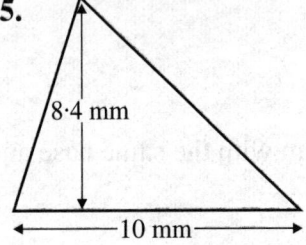

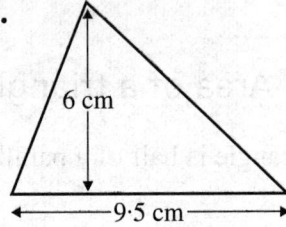

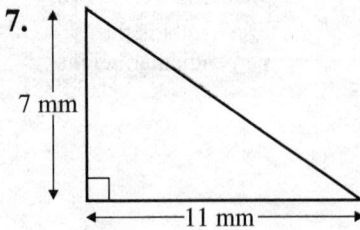

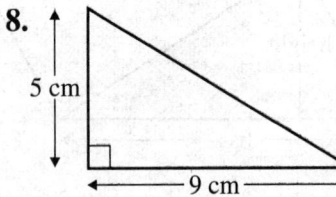

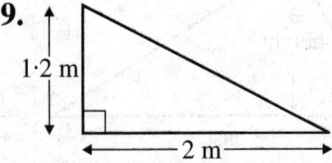

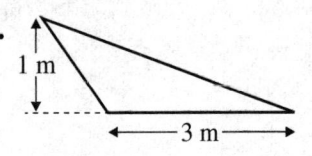

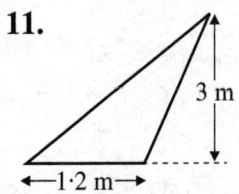

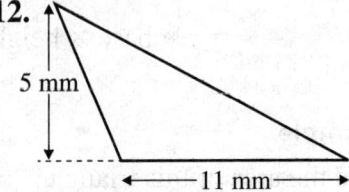

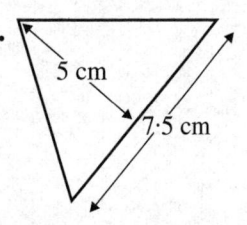

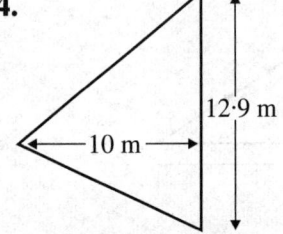

1. Triangle with height 5 cm and base 8 cm.
2. Triangle with height 4 cm and base 9 cm.
3. Triangle with height 7 mm and base 14 mm.
4. Triangle with height 3 m and base 5 m.
5. Triangle with height 8·4 mm and base 10 mm.
6. Triangle with height 6 cm and base 9·5 cm.
7. Right triangle with height 7 mm and base 11 mm.
8. Right triangle with height 5 cm and base 9 cm.
9. Right triangle with height 1·2 m and base 2 m.
10. Triangle with height 1 m and base 3 m.
11. Triangle with height 3 m and base 1·2 m.
12. Triangle with height 5 mm and base 11 mm.
13. Triangle with sides 5 cm and 7·5 cm.
14. Triangle with base 10 m and height 12·9 m.
15. Triangle with sides 6·8 cm and 8·6 cm.

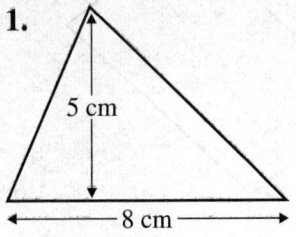

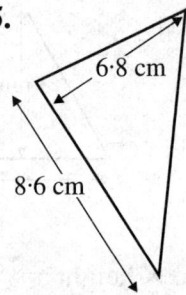

16.7 Area of a compound shape

A compound shape is made from two or more basic shapes.
To find the area you need to split it up into shapes you know.

Example

Find the area of this shape.

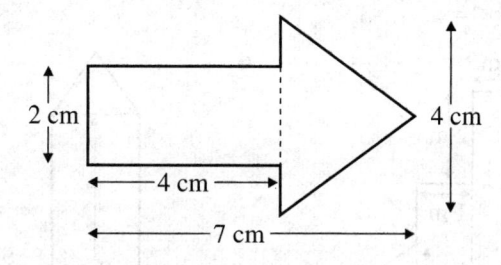

Split the shape up.

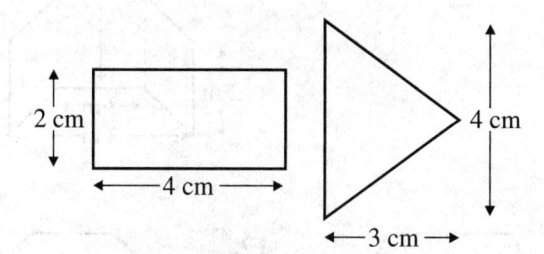

Area = $(2 \times 4) + \frac{1}{2}$ of $(3 \times 4) = 8 + 6 = 14 \text{ cm}^2$

Exercise 16G

Find the area of each shape.

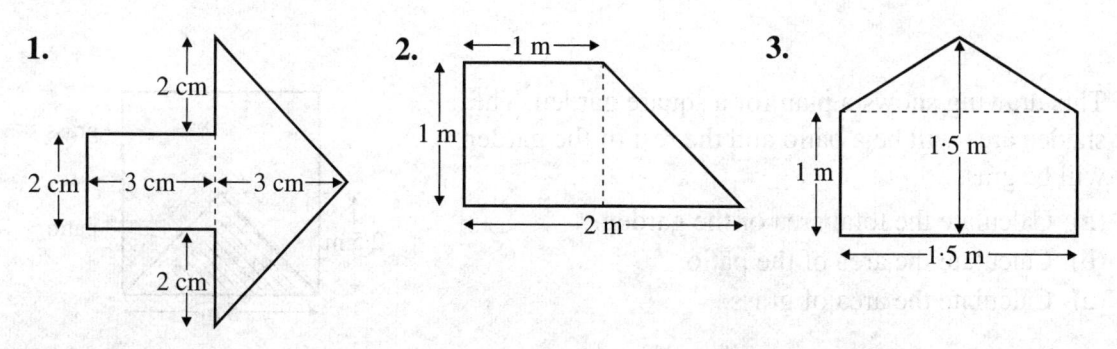

1.
2.
3.

368 Shape and Space 5

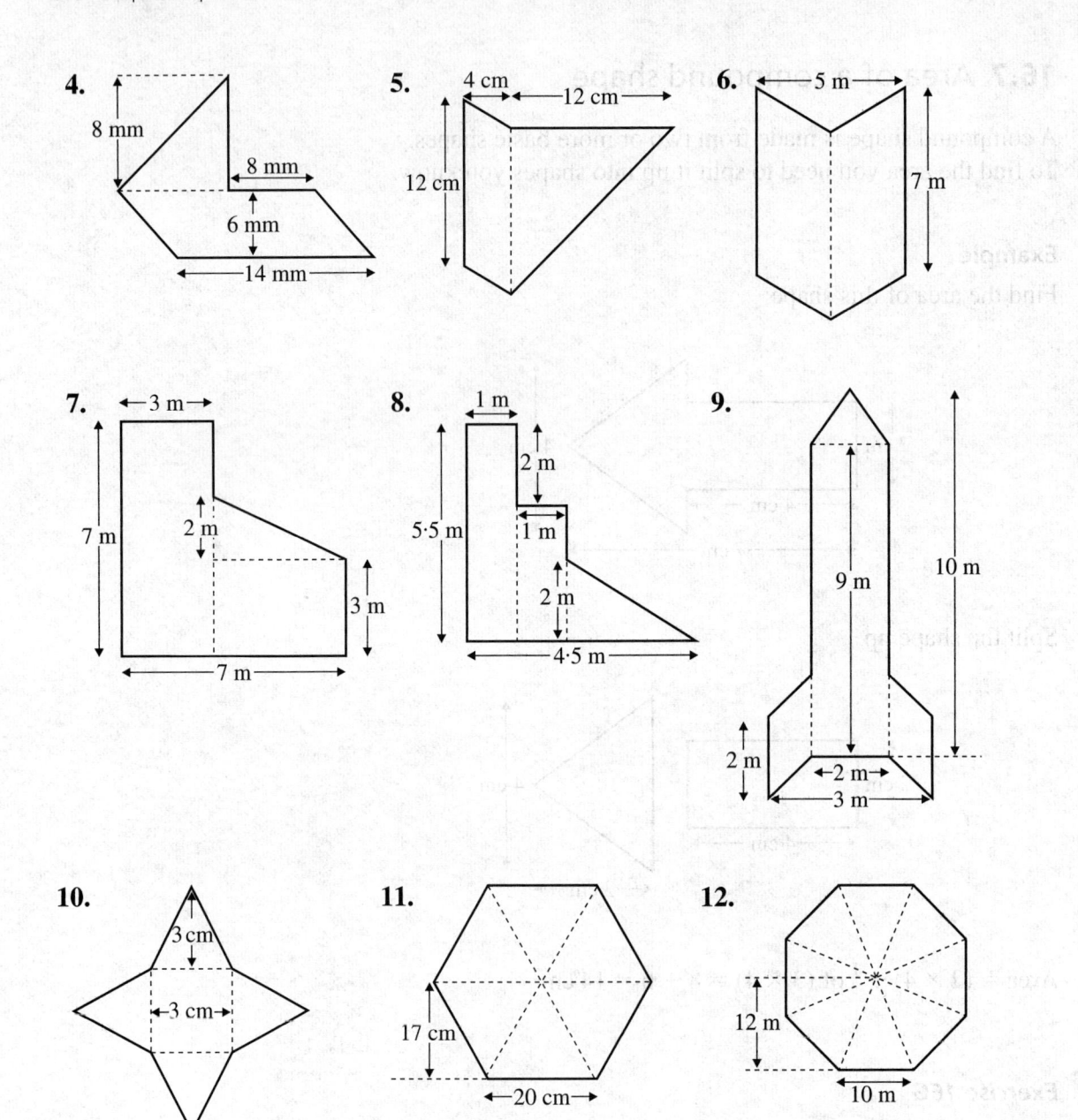

4. 8 mm, 8 mm, 6 mm, 14 mm

5. 4 cm, 12 cm, 12 cm

6. 5 m, 7 m

7. 3 m, 7 m, 2 m, 3 m, 7 m

8. 1 m, 2 m, 5·5 m, 1 m, 2 m, 4·5 m

9. 9 m, 10 m, 2 m, 2 m, 3 m

10. 3 cm, 3 cm

11. 17 cm, 20 cm

12. 12 m, 10 m

13. This drawing shows a plan for a square garden. The shaded area will be a patio and the rest of the garden will be grass.

   (a) Calculate the total area of the garden.
   (b) Calculate the area of the patio.
   (c) Calculate the area of grass.

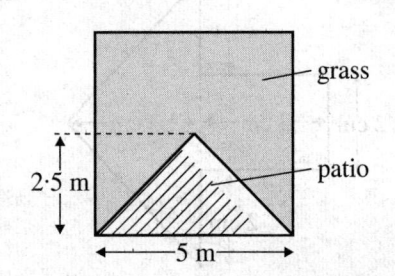

   2·5 m, 5 m
   grass, patio

14. This drawing shows a patio door with three glass windows.
    The glass in each window is 2 metres by 1·4 metres.

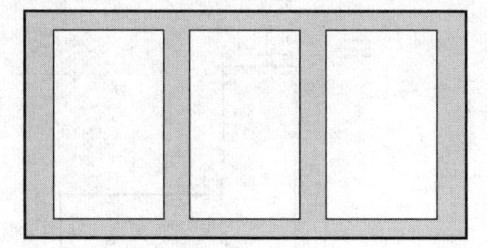

    (a) Calculate the area of glass in one window.
    (b) Calculate the area of glass in the door.
    (c) Glass costs £2·50 a square metre. Calculate the cost of the glass in the door.

15. Use 1 centimetre squared paper to answer this question.
    (a) Rectangle A is 8 cm high. It has a perimeter of 24 cm. Draw rectangle A.
    (b) Rectangle B is 5 cm wide. It has an area of 30 cm². Draw rectangle B.
    (c) Rectangle C is 9 cm high. It has the same area as a 6 cm square. Draw rectangle C.

Summary

Checkout 16

1. The distance round the outside of a shape is called its **perimeter**.
   The area of a shape is measured in square centimetres (cm²), square metres (m²) or square millimetres (mm²).

1. (a) Find the perimeter of this shape drawn on a 1 centimetre grid.

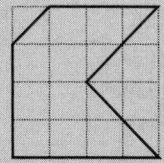

   (b) Find the area of the shape.

2. The area of a rectangle can be found with the formula
   Area = base × height

2. Find the area of these rectangles.
   (a) 10 cm × 3 cm
   (b) 2·5 m × 2 m

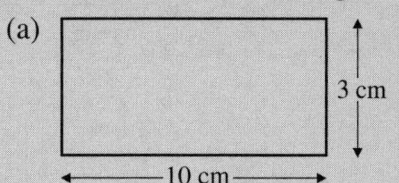

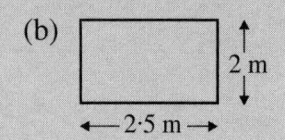

3. The area of some shapes can be found by dividing them into rectangles.

3. Find the area of this shape.

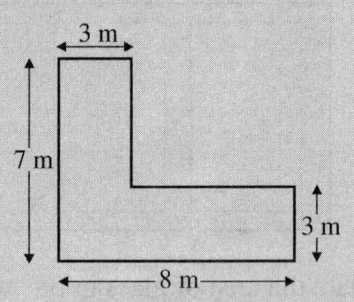

4. The area of a parallelogram can also be found with the formula
   Area = base × height

4. Find the area of this parallelogram.

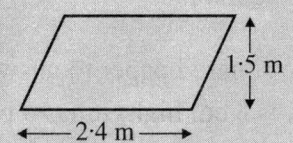

5. The area of a triangle can be found with this formula
   Area = $\frac{1}{2}$ × base × height

5. Find the area of these triangles.

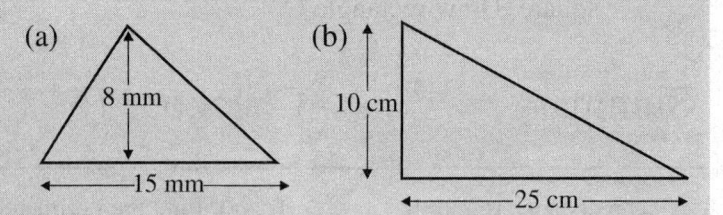

   (a)

   (b)

6. The area of a compound shape can be found by splitting it into basic shapes.

6. Find the area of this shape.

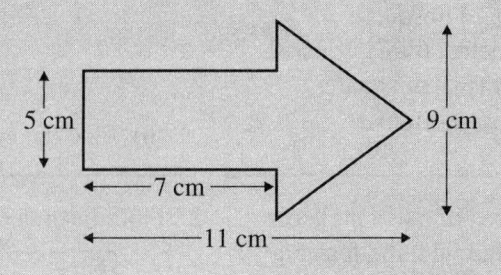

Revision exercise 16

1.

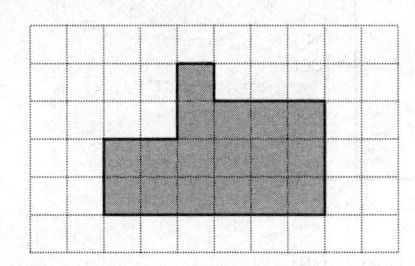

This shape is drawn on a 1 cm grid.
- (a) Find the area, in cm², of the shape.
- (b) Find the perimeter, in cm, of the shape. [Edexcel]

2. Find the area of these floors.
Each square represents a square metre.

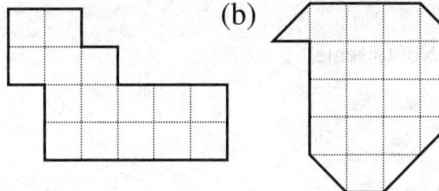

(a)   (b)   (c)

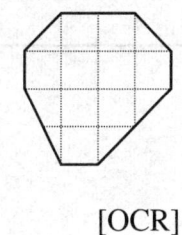

[OCR]

3.

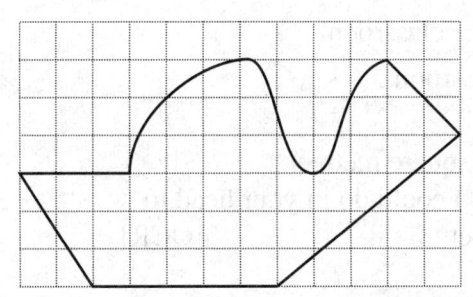

By counting squares, estimate the area of the above shape.
[WJEC]

4. A children's playground is a rectangle 9 m by 7 m. 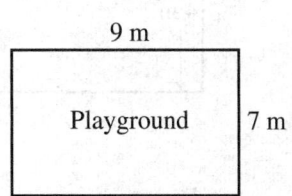
- (a) What is the perimeter of this playground?
- (b) What is the area of this playground?
State clearly the units of your answer. [OCR]

5.

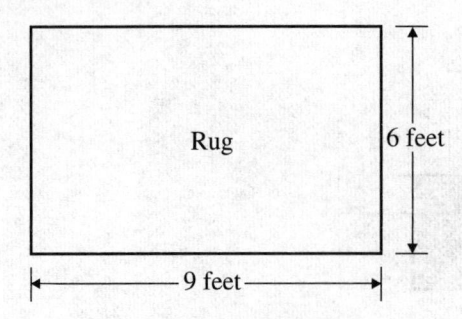

A rectangular rug is 9 feet long and 6 feet wide.
   (a) Calculate its area in square yards.
       [1 yard = 3 feet]
   (b) The rug costs £495.
       Calculate the price per square yard.   [AQA/NEAB]

6. This is the floor plan of a classroom.

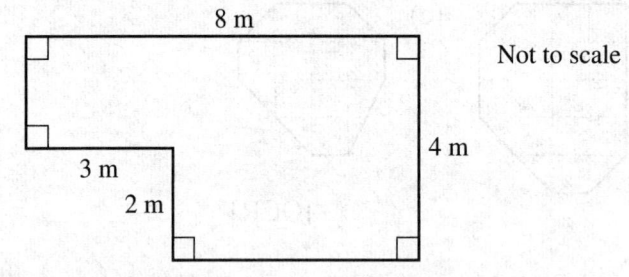

   (a) Work out the perimeter of the classroom.
   (b) Work out the area of the classroom.
   (c) The room is to be carpeted.
       The carpet costs £18·75 per square metre.
       Write down a calculation you could do in your head to
       estimate the cost of the carpet.   [OCR]

7.

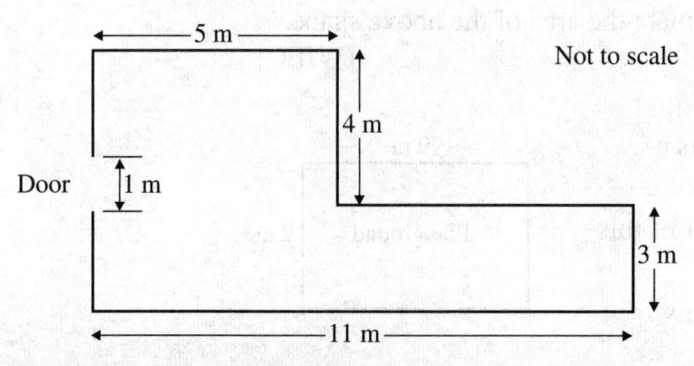

The diagram shows the plan of the floor of a room.

(a) Calculate the perimeter of the room.

(b) Wooden skirting board is fitted around the perimeter, but not across the doorway.
It costs 83p per metre.
Calculate the cost of the skirting board needed for this room.

(c) Calculate the area of the floor of the room.

(d) Carpet tiles measure 1 m by 1 m.
They are sold in boxes each containing 12 tiles.
Each box costs £103·50.
  (i) How many boxes are needed to carpet this floor area?
  (ii) What is their total cost? [AQA/NEAB]

8. The diagram shows a triangular prism.

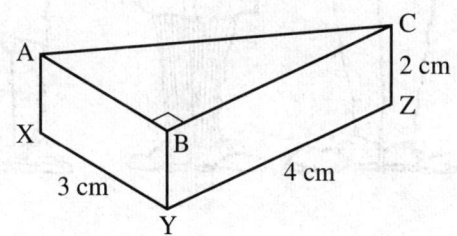

Angle ABC = 90°.
XY = 3 cm,
YZ = 4 cm and
CZ = 2 cm.

(a) Calculate the area of the triangle ABC.

(b) Draw an accurate net of the prism. [AQA/SEG]

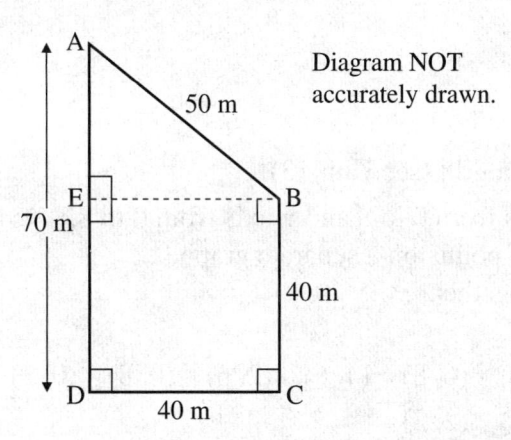

9. Diagram NOT accurately drawn.

(a) Work out the perimeter of the whole shape ABCD.

In part (b) you must write down the units with your answers.

(b) Work out the area of
  (i) the square EBCD
  (ii) the triangle ABE [Edexcel]

17 Data Handling 4

People are different shapes and sizes.

This unit is about:

- Variables
- Correlation
- Scatter diagrams

You need to remember:

- How to plot coordinates on a grid (see Unit 13).

  1. Draw a graph with *x*-axis from 0 to 8 and *y*-axis from 0 to 8.
     Plot each of these sets of points on a separate graph.
     Join each set of points together.
     What shapes do you get?

     (a) (2, 1) (4, 1) (6, 3) (6, 8) (4, 6) (2, 6) (0, 8) (0, 3)
     (b) (2, 2) (4, 2) (4, 3) (2, 3)
     (c) (1, 5) (1, 4) (2, 4) (2, 5)
     (d) (4, 4) (4, 5) (5, 5) (5, 4)

17.1 Variables

Variables are properties which can change. For example, look at this car.

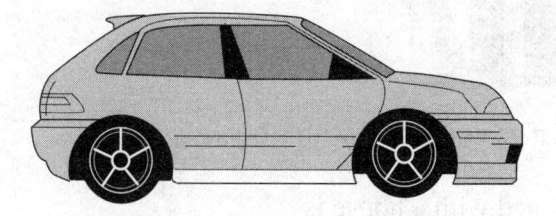

Some of the variables which can be associated with a car are:

- make
- model
- price
- top speed
- colour
- engine size
- weight
- number of gears
- number of seats

Exercise 17A

1. One variable which could be associated with a dog is 'breed'.

   List five more variables which can be associated with a dog.

2. One variable which could be associated with a person is 'shoe size'.

   Of course, she's not like us...

   List five more variables which can be associated with a person.

3. One variable which can be associated with a book is 'number of pages'.

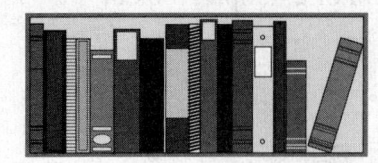

List five more variables which can be associated with a book.

4. One variable which can be associated with a house is 'number of bedrooms'.

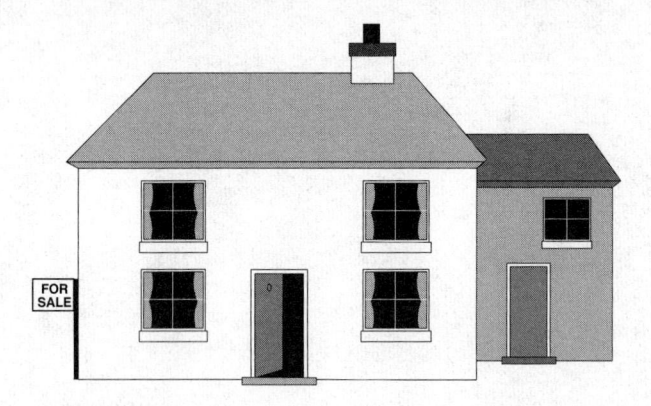

List five more variables which can be associated with a house.

17.2 Correlation

Two variables are **positively correlated** if, as one increases, the other tends to increase.

Two variables are **negatively correlated** if, as one increases, the other tends to decrease.

Two variables are **not correlated** if, as one increases, it tends to have no effect on the other.

Example 1
Do tall men tend to have bigger feet than short men?

If your answer to this question is, 'yes they do', you are saying:

> In men, height and shoe size are **positively correlated**.
> As height increases, shoe size will also tend to increase.

Example 2

I want to buy a Ford Escort. Will older cars tend to cost less than newer cars?

If your answer to this question is, 'yes they will', you are saying:

> In Ford Escorts, age and price are **negatively correlated**. As the age of a car increases, its value tends to decrease.

Example 3

Is there a link between being good at mathematics and being a good dancer?

If your answer to this question is, 'no there is not', you are saying:

> Skills in mathematics and dancing are **not correlated**. There is no connection between the two skills.

Exercise 17B

In each of the following examples, say whether you think the two variables are:

- positively correlated
- negatively correlated
- not correlated

1. The number of bedrooms in a house and its market value.
2. The age of a used motorbike and its value.
3. The height of a man and his weight.
4. The length of a woman's hair and her shoe size.
5. The age of a child and the time they take to run 50 metres.
6. The age of an adult and the time they take to run 50 metres.
7. The age of an adult and the colour of their car.
8. The value of a centre forward and the number of goals he scores each season.
9. The value of a goalkeeper and the number of goals he lets in each season.
10. The annual winnings of a tennis star and her shoe size.

17.3 Scatter diagrams

These are the test scores for 10 students in mathematics and science.

Student	A	B	C	D	E	F	G	H	I	J
Maths	3	7	6	8	9	2	4	7	9	8
Science	2	6	7	9	7	3	6	8	8	7

Looking at the table, you might decide that marks in mathematics and science seem to be positively correlated. One way to show the correlation is to draw a graph like this, called a **scatter diagram**.

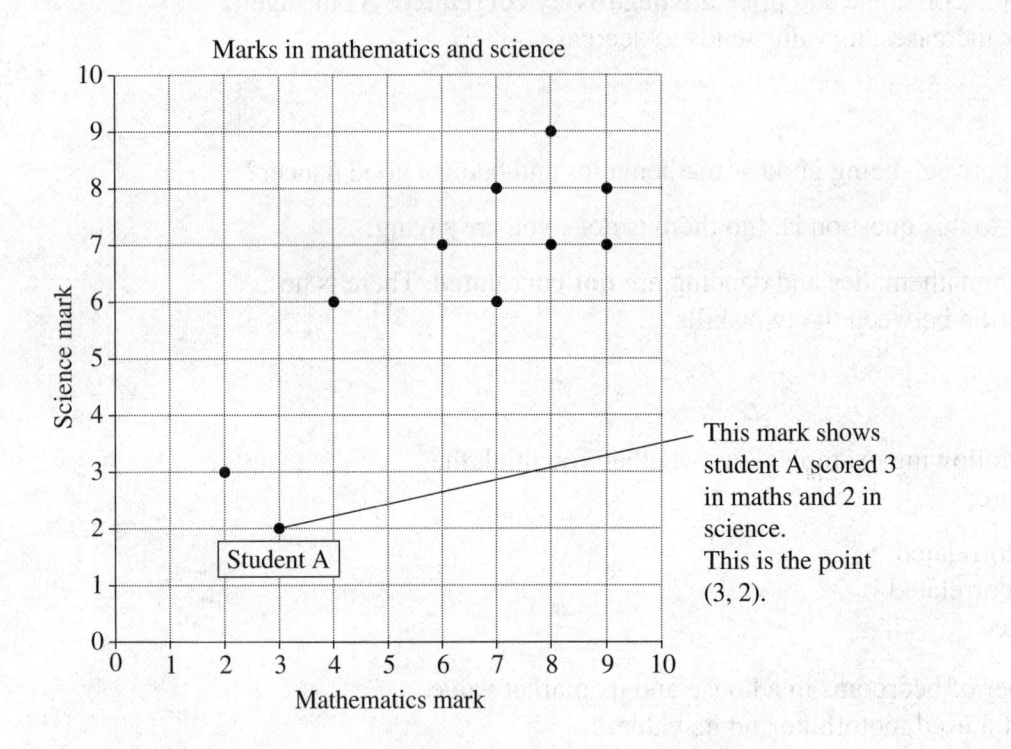

Marks in mathematics and science

This mark shows student A scored 3 in maths and 2 in science.
This is the point (3, 2).

The scatter diagram shows a positive correlation because the points are in a 'sausage shaped' area, going upwards from left to right. These scatter diagrams show positive, negative and no correlation.

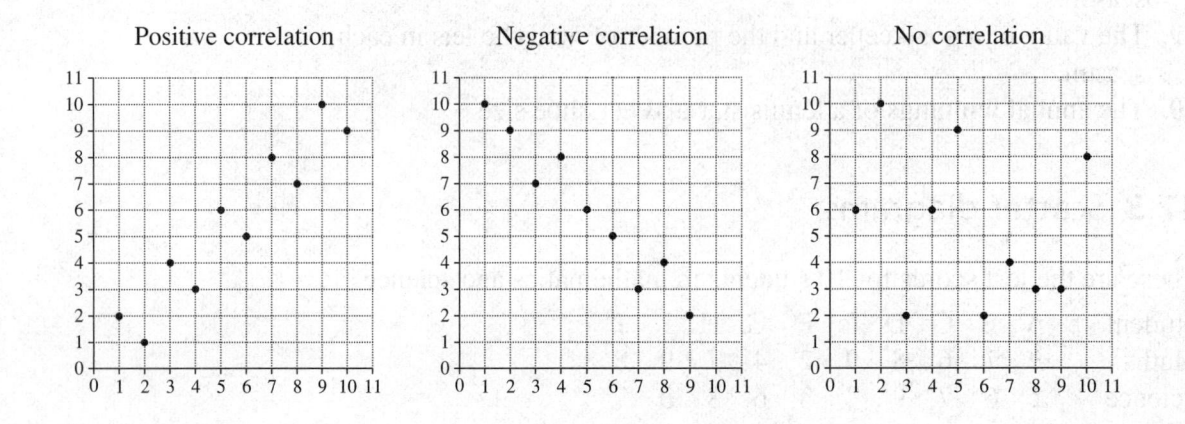

Positive correlation   Negative correlation   No correlation

Exercise 17C

1. This table records the year group of 10 students and the number of days they were absent from school in one year.

Year	7	7	8	8	9	9	10	10	11	11
Absence	0	2	3	2	3	4	6	2	5	8

   (a) Copy and complete this scatter diagram to show the data in the table.

   (b) What correlation does your completed scatter diagram show?

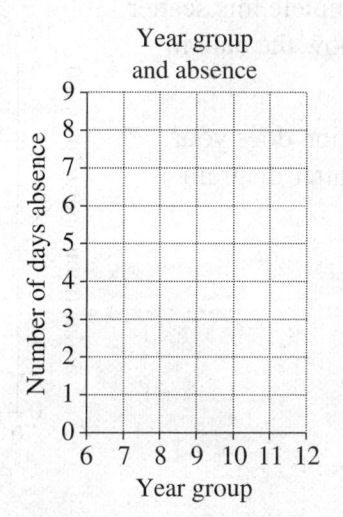

2. A food stall owner recorded the average temperature for ten weeks and the number of cans of soup powder she used during each week. These are her results.

Temp	1°C	1°C	3°C	3°C	4°C	4°C	6°C	7°C	10°C	12°C
Cans	10	6	8	6	5	6	4	2	2	1

   (a) Copy and complete this scatter diagram to show the data in the table.

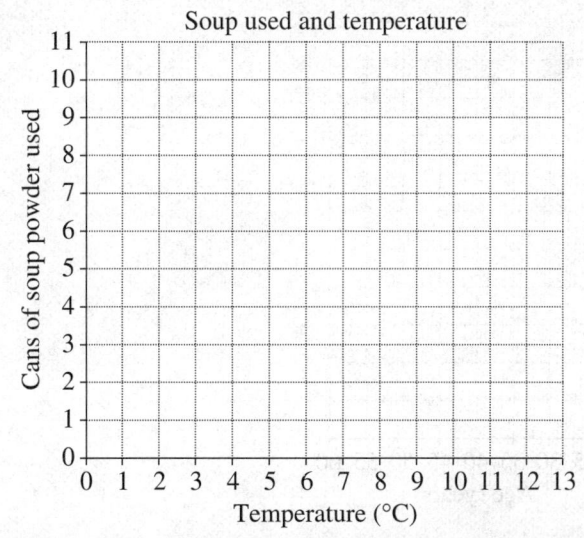

   (b) What correlation does your completed scatter diagram show?

3. Lucy did a survey on the age and value of a certain type of used car. She collected this data.

Age (years)	1	1	2	2	3	4	4	5	6	7
Value (nearest thousand pounds)	9	8	7	5	6	3	4	4	2	2

(a) Copy and complete this scatter diagram to show the data in the table.

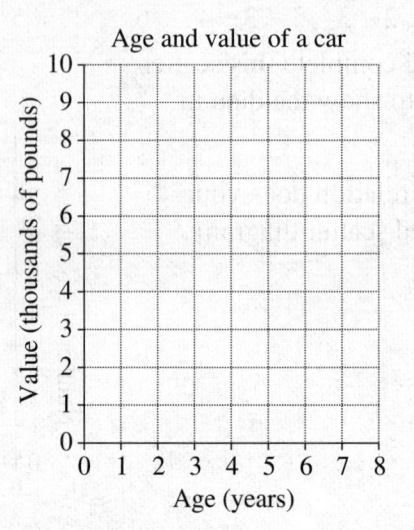

(b) What correlation does your completed scatter diagram show?

4. Ten teachers take part in a 100-metre race on Sports Day.
This table shows the age of the teachers (in years) and their time (in seconds) to run the race.

Age	24	25	31	33	35	42	46	48	51	56
Time	14	12	18	16	12	20	22	24	26	30

(a) Copy and complete this scatter diagram to show the data in the table.

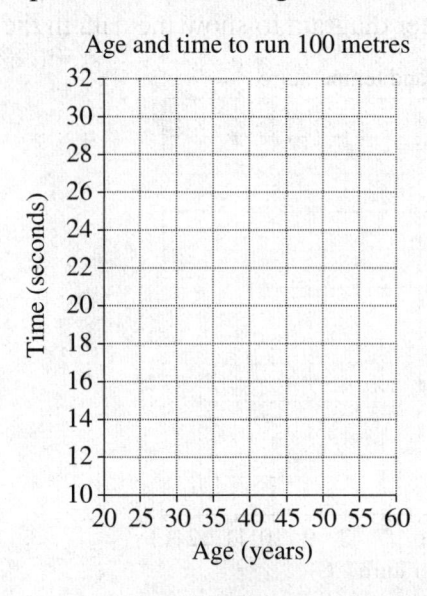

(b) What correlation does your completed scatter diagram show?

5. Adrian collects this data on car engine sizes in litres and average fuel consumption in kilometres per litre.

Engine size	1	1	1·5	1·5	2	2	2	2·5	3	3·5
Fuel consumption	15	14	12	13	15	11	10	9	9	8

(a) Copy and complete this scatter diagram to show the data in the table.

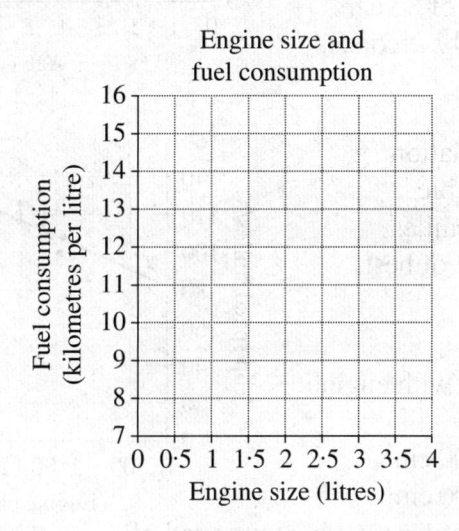

Engine size and fuel consumption

(b) What correlation does your completed scatter diagram show?

17.4 Line of best fit

When a scatter diagram shows two variables are highly correlated, you can draw a **line of best fit**.

This is the straight line which goes through the point representing the mean of each set of data, passing close to as many points as possible.

Example
This table shows the ages of 10 children and their times to run 100 m.

Child	A	B	C	D	E	F	G	H	I	J
Age	8	4	11	8	6	7	5	4	9	10
Time (seconds)	17	23	14	15	20	20	22	26	15	16

(a) Draw a scatter diagram and add the line of best fit.
(b) Estimate the time a child of 8 years and 6 months would take to run 100 m.

(a) You draw the scatter diagram and then position the line of best fit, balancing points above the line with points below the line.

(b) Draw a line up from the age axis to the line of best fit and then across to the time axis. You can estimate that a child of 8 years 6 months will run 100 m in about 17 seconds.

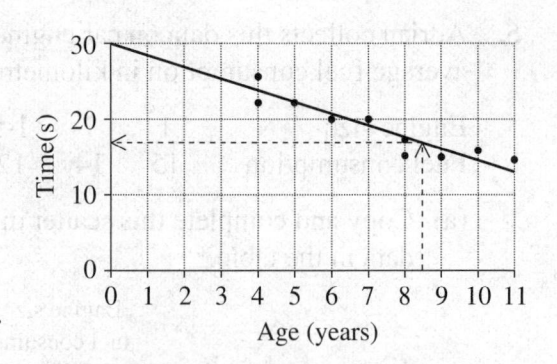

Exercise 17D

1. This scatter graph shows the correlation between the engine capacity (in cubic centimetres) and the top speed (in miles per hour) of a group of cars. A line of best fit has been added.

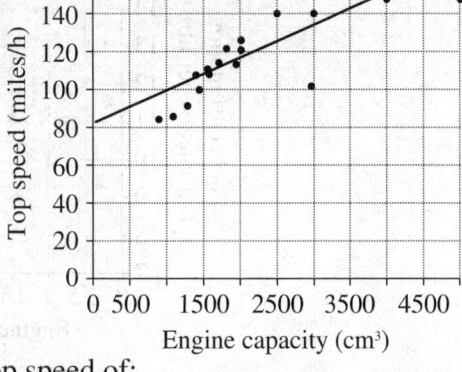

   (a) Comment on any correlation.
   (b) Estimate the top speed of cars with engine capacities of:

   (i) 2 000 cm²   (ii) 3 500 cm³
   (iii) 4 500 cm³   (iv) 1 000 cm³

   (c) Estimate the engine capacity of a car with a top speed of:

   (i) 100 miles/h   (ii) 130 miles/h   (iii) 90 miles/h   (iv) 110 miles/h

2. Draw the line of best fit for the graphs you drew in Exercise 17C if such a line is appropriate.

Summary

1. **Variables** are properties which can change.

2. Two variables are **positively correlated** if, as one increases, the other tends to increase.
Two variables are **negatively correlated** if, as one increases, the other tends to decrease.
Two variables are **not correlated** if, as one increases, it tends to have no effect on the other.

Checkout 17

1. One variable which could be associated with a wild bird is 'wingspan'. List five more variables which could be associated with a wild bird.

2. In each of the following examples, say whether you think the two variables are:
   - positively correlated
   - negatively correlated
   - not correlated

   (a) The average daily temperature and the number of ice creams a shop sells.
   (b) The average daily temperature and the number of overcoats a shop sells.
   (c) The average daily temperature and the number of computers a shop sells.

3. One way to show correlation is to draw a graph called **a scatter diagram**.

3. This table shows the ages (in years) of a group of 10 children and the time (in seconds) they take to run 100 metres.

Age	4	4	5	6	6	7	8	9	10	11
Time	24	22	20	18	20	17	19	15	16	14

(a) Copy and complete this scatter diagram to show the data in the table.

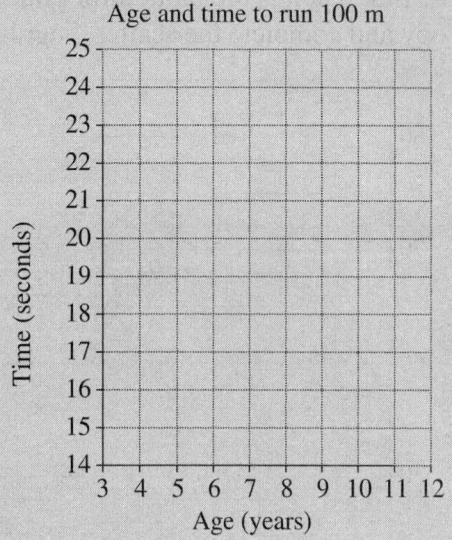

Age and time to run 100 m

(b) What correlation does your scatter diagram show?

Revision exercise 17

1. The table shows the scores of six pupils in Paper 1 and Paper 2 of a mathematics examination.

Score in Paper 1	20	32	15	6	25	16
Score in Paper 2	14	21	11	4	15	13

(a) On a copy of the graph, draw a scatter diagram to show these scores.

(b) What kind of correlation does your scatter diagram show?

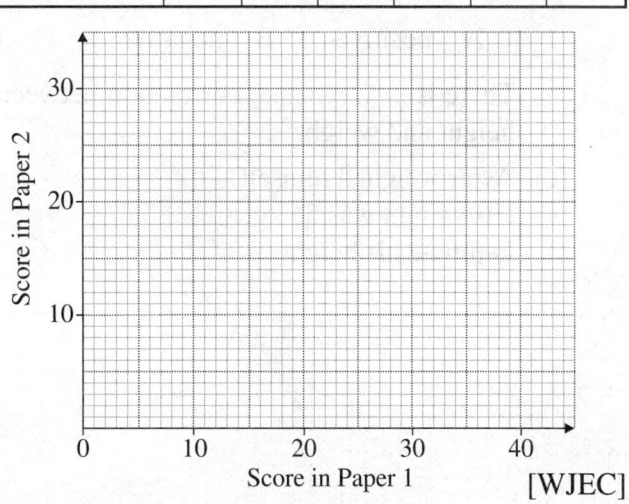

[WJEC]

2. Levinna collected the following data about the height and weight of students in her class.

Height (cm)	172	168	149	164	160	176	169	180	172	162	171	153	162
Weight (kg)	56	58	44	63	57	74	68	71	58	60	68	46	49

(a) The first 5 points are plotted for you.
Copy and complete the scatter diagram for these results.

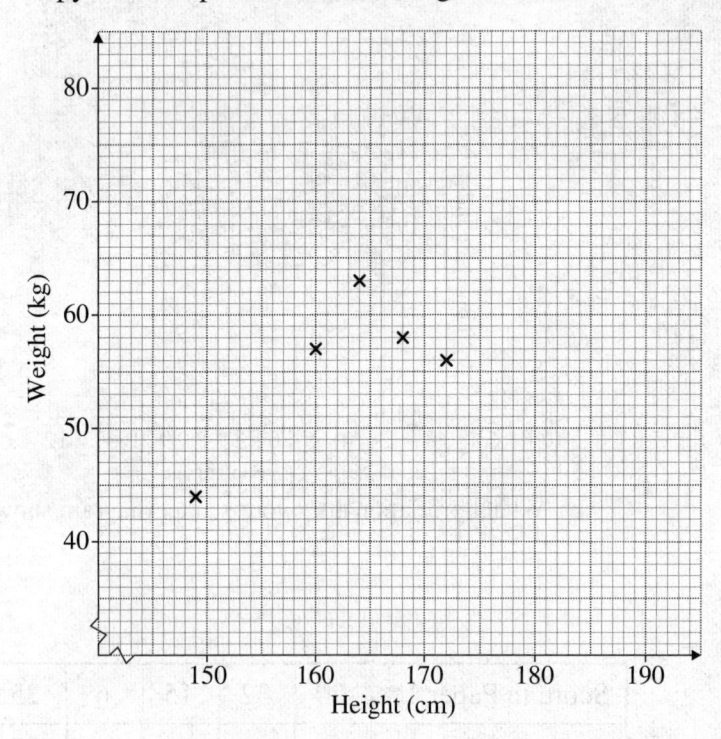

(b) Which of the following words completes the sentence below.

    A positive   B negative   C no

There is .... correlation between a student's height and weight.

(c) Avtar weighed himself.
His weight was 55 kg.
Estimate his height.   [OCR]

3. Barrie recorded the heights of 8 competitors in a race and the times they took to run 200 metres.
   These are the results.

Height (cm)	180	190	178	160	174	182	174	186
Time (seconds)	33	30	33	35	36	32	34	28

(a) Show these results on a copy of the scatter diagram below.

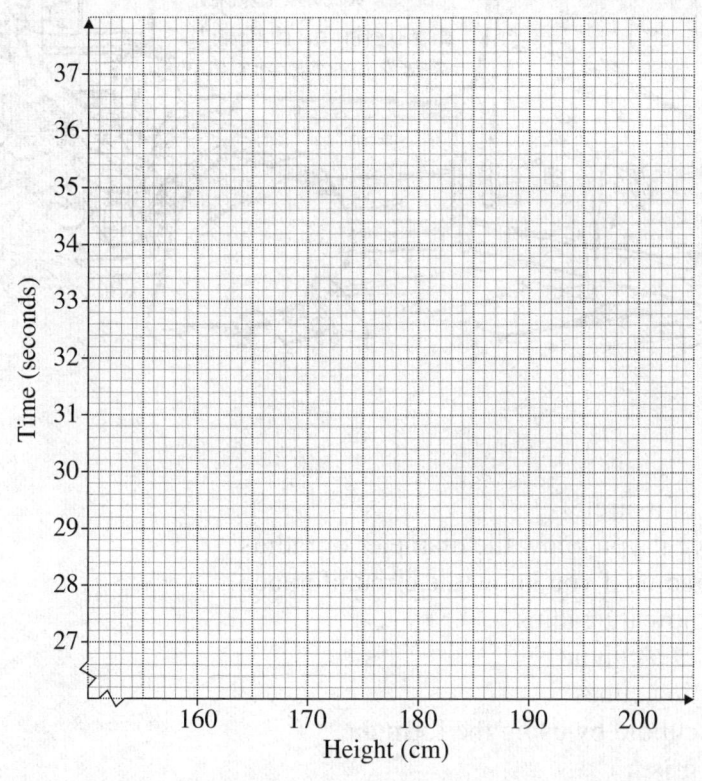

(b) Comment on the relationship between the height of the eight competitors and the time they took to run 200 metres.   [OCR]

18 SHAPE AND SPACE 6

This unit is about:

- The radius and diameter of a circle
- Finding the circumference if you know the diameter or radius
- Finding the diameter or radius if you know the circumference
- Finding the area if you know the radius
- Finding the surface area of a cuboid
- Finding volume by counting cubes
- Finding the volume of a cuboid by using the formula
- Finding the volume of a prism

You need to remember:

Check in 18

- How to multiply decimals.
  1. Find:
     (a) $3·1 \times 6$ (b) $3·1 \times 14$ (c) $3·1 \times 4·5$
     (d) $3·14 \times 10$ (e) $3·14 \times 12$ (f) $3·14 \times 5·2$
     (g) $3·14 \times 5 \times 5$ (h) $3·14 \times 8 \times 8$ (i) $3·14 \times 2 \times 2$
- How to sketch a net of a cuboid.
  2. Sketch the net of a cuboid measuring:
     (a) 2 cm by 2 cm by 5 cm   (b) 3 cm by 1 cm by 6 cm

18.1 The radius and diameter of a circle

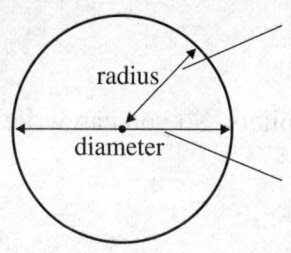

The **radius** is a line from the centre to a point on the circle.

The **diameter** is a line joining two points on the circle and passing through the centre. The diameter is twice as long as the radius.

You draw circles with a pair of compasses.

Exercise 18A
1. Draw circles with a radius of:
   (a) 5 cm (b) 3 cm (c) 6 cm (d) 20 mm (e) 45 mm
2. Draw circles with a diameter of:
   (a) 8 cm (b) 6 cm (c) 5 cm (d) 110 mm (e) 70 mm
3. Find the diameter of a circle with a radius of:
   (a) 5 cm (b) 7 cm (c) 2·5 cm (d) 6·4 m (e) 9·3 mm
4. Find the radius of a circle with a diameter of:
   (a) 20 cm (b) 32 cm (c) 7 cm (d) 15 m (e) 16·6 mm

18.2 Finding the circumference if you know the diameter or radius

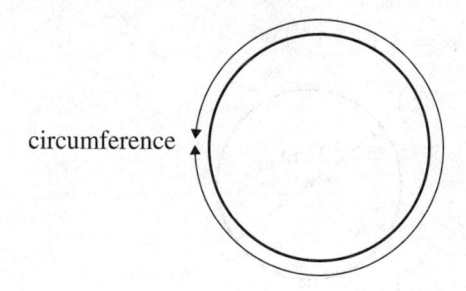

The **circumference** of a circle is the distance round the circle. It is a special name for the perimeter of a circle.

The circumference is difficult to measure accurately.
If you know the radius or diameter then you can calculate the circumference.

To find the circumference, the diameter is multiplied by a number close to 3.

The number 3·1 gives an approximate answer.
The number 3·14 gives a more accurate answer.
The number 3·142 gives an even more accurate answer.

The Greek letter π (pi) is used to represent all these possible multipliers. So you can write:

Circumference = π × diameter

or

$C = \pi d$

You will usually be told which approximation to use for π.

Example 1

Find the circumference of this circle if $\pi = 3·1$.

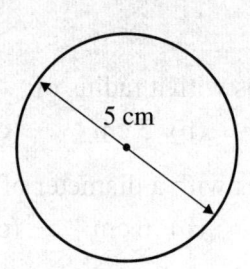

$C = \pi d = 3·1 \times 5 = 15·5$ cm

5 cm

Example 2

Find the circumference of this circle if $\pi = 3·14$.

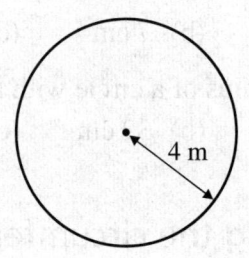

The radius is 4 m, so the diameter = 2 × 4 = 8 m
$C = \pi d = 3·14 \times 8 = 25·12$ m

4 m

Exercise 18B

1. Find the circumference of each circle if $\pi = 3·1$.

   (a) 4 cm
   (b) 6 cm
   (c) 2 cm
   (d) 8 mm
   (e) 3 m
   (f) 2·5 cm

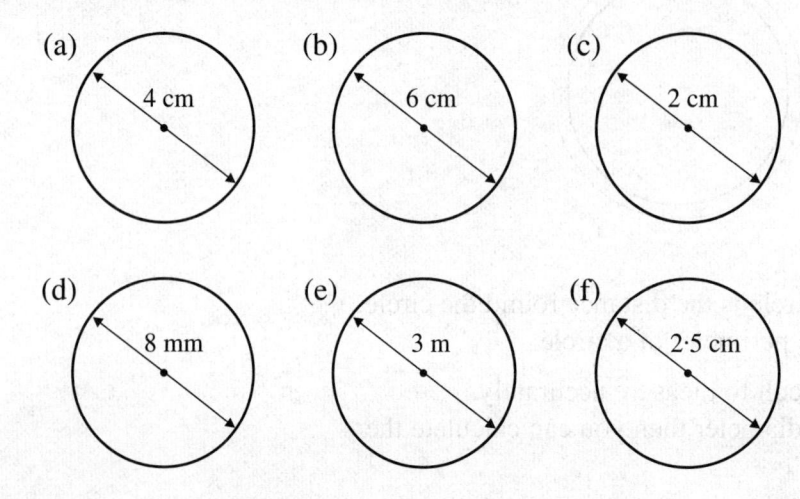

2. Find the circumference of each circle if $\pi = 3.14$.

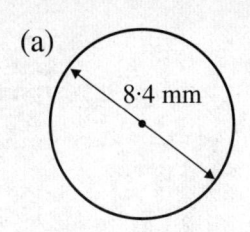

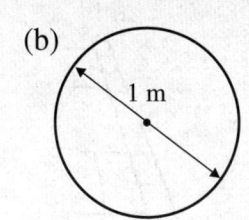

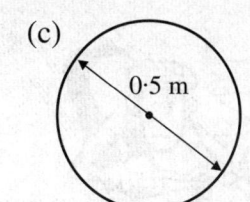

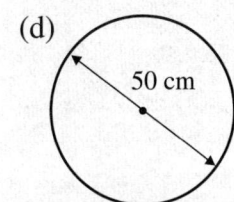

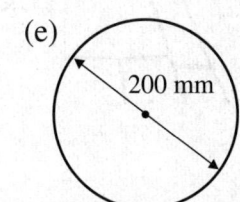

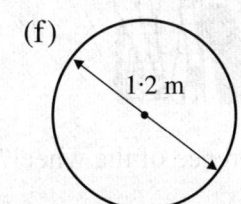

(a) 8·4 mm
(b) 1 m
(c) 0·5 m
(d) 50 cm
(e) 200 mm
(f) 1·2 m

3. Find the circumference of each circle if $\pi = 3.1$.

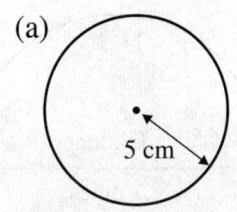

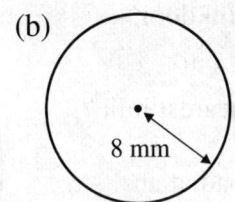

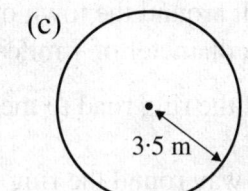

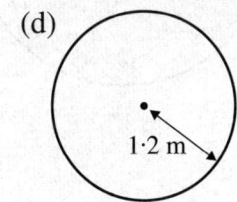

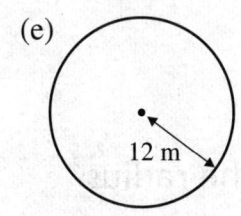

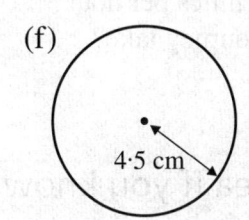

(a) 5 cm
(b) 8 mm
(c) 3·5 m
(d) 1·2 m
(e) 12 m
(f) 4·5 cm

4. Find the circumference of each circle if $\pi = 3.14$.

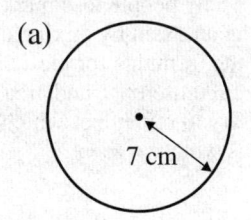

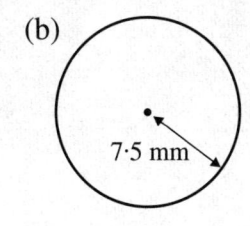

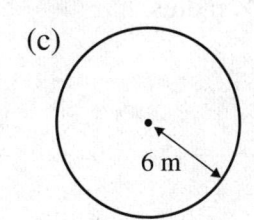

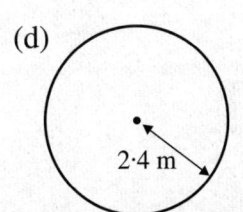

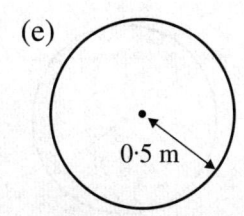

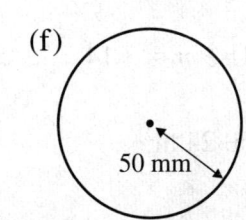

(a) 7 cm
(b) 7·5 mm
(c) 6 m
(d) 2·4 m
(e) 0·5 m
(f) 50 mm

5. The front wheel on John's bike has a diameter of 70 cm.

   (a) What is the circumference of the wheel?
       Take π to be 3·14.
   (b) John cycles along the road. How far will he travel each time the front wheel turns 10 times?

6. A ring road is to be built around the town of Inkdoor.
   It will be a circle with a diameter of 7 miles.

   (a) What is the length of the ring road to the nearest mile?
       Take π to be 3·14.
   (b) Salina travels all the way round the ring road at an average speed of 66 miles per hour.
       How long will this journey take?

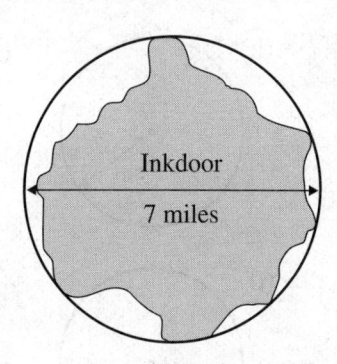

18.3 Finding the area if you know the radius

The area of a circle is found using the formula:

$$\text{Area} = \pi \times \text{radius} \times \text{radius}$$

or

$$A = \pi r^2$$

Hint:
Many people lose marks in an exam by mixing up the formulae for the circumference and area. Try to remember which is which.

Example

Find the area of this circle. Use $\pi = 3\cdot14$.

$A = \pi r^2 = 3\cdot14 \times 4 \times 4 = 50\cdot24 \text{ m}^2$

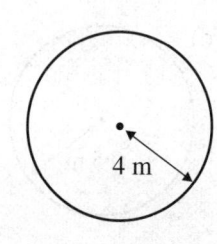

Exercise 18C

1. Find the area of each circle if $\pi = 3{\cdot}1$.

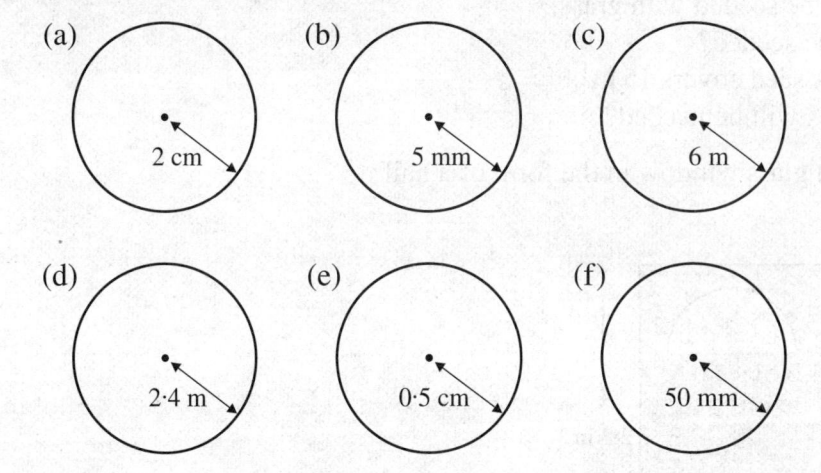

(a) 2 cm

(b) 5 mm

(c) 6 m

(d) 2·4 m

(e) 0·5 cm

(f) 50 mm

2. Find the area of each circle if $\pi = 3{\cdot}14$.

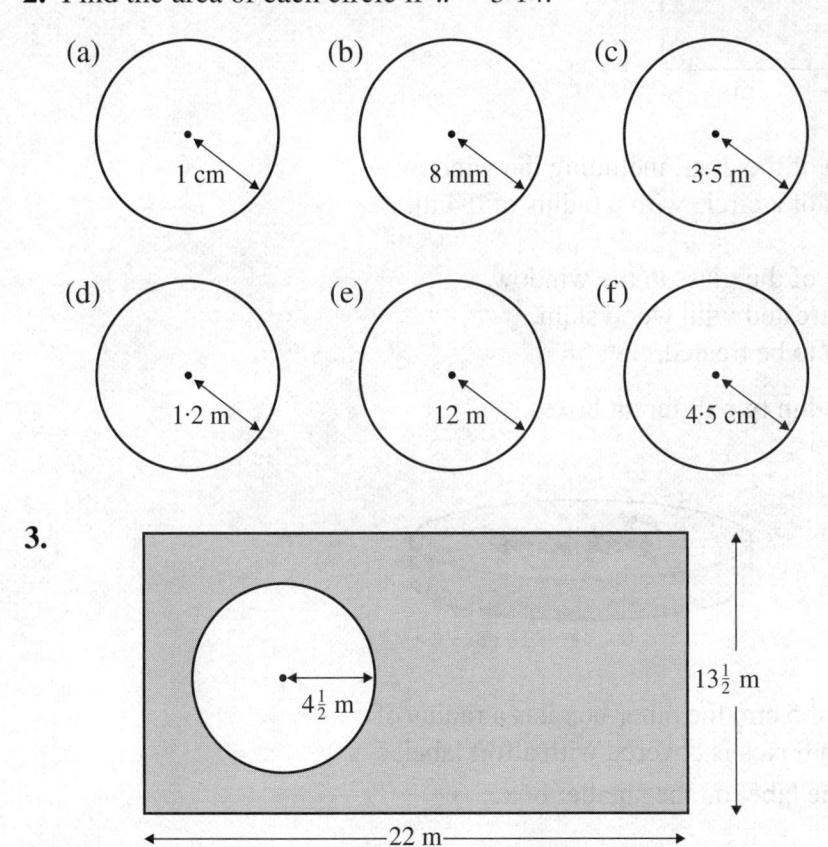

(a) 1 cm

(b) 8 mm

(c) 3·5 m

(d) 1·2 m

(e) 12 m

(f) 4·5 cm

3.

$13\frac{1}{2}$ m

$4\frac{1}{2}$ m

22 m

The diagram shows a rectangular garden measuring 22 m by $13\frac{1}{2}$ m.
There is a circular pond in the garden with a radius of $4\frac{1}{2}$ m.

(a) What is the total area of the garden?
(b) What is the area of the pond? Take π to be 3·14.
(c) The garden is to be seeded with grass.
What area will be seeded?
(d) One box of grass seed covers 15 m^2.
How many boxes will be needed?

4. A wooden door has a glass window in the form of a half circle.

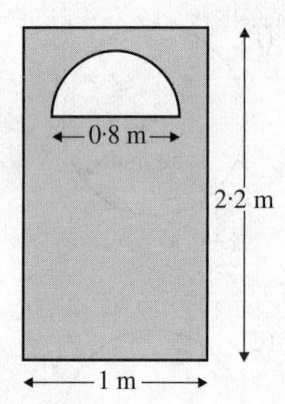

←0·8 m→

2·2 m

←1 m→

(a) Calculate the area of the door, including the window.
(b) Calculate the area of a circle with a radius of 0·4 m.
Use π = 3·14.
(c) Calculate the area of the glass in the window.
(d) The door is to be treated with wood stain.
Calculate the area to be treated.

5. A French cheese is sold in two different boxes.
Both boxes are cylinders.

Fromage   *Fromage*

←5 cm→   ←10 cm→

One box has a radius of 5 cm, the other box has a radius of 10 cm. The top of both boxes is covered with a foil label.
(a) Find the area of the label on the smaller box.
Use π = 3·14.
(b) Find the area of the label on the big box. Use π = 3·14.
(c) Divide the area of the big box label by the area of the small box label. What do you notice?

18.4 Finding the surface area of a cuboid

This net of this cuboid shows that it has six faces.

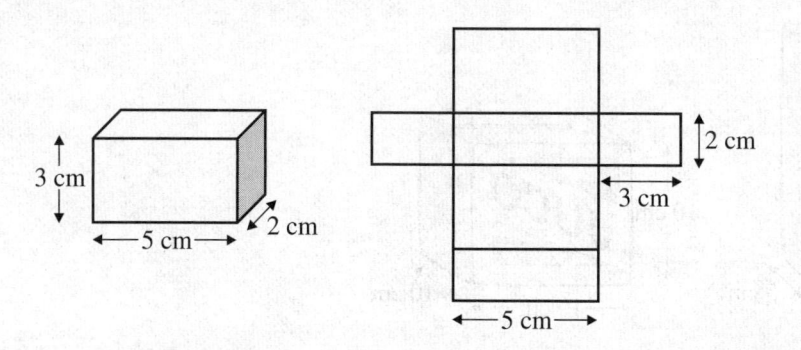

> There is more about nets on page 127.

Total surface area = (2 × 3) + (2 × 3) + (3 × 5) + (3 × 5) + (2 × 5) + (2 × 5)
= 6 + 6 + 15 + 15 + 10 + 10 = 62 cm²

Exercise 18D

1. Sketch the net of each cuboid and calculate the total surface area.

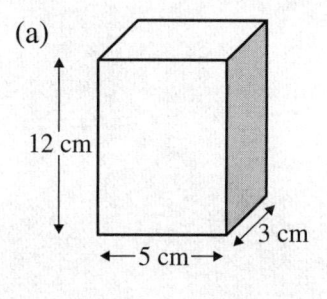

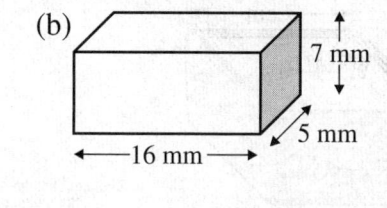

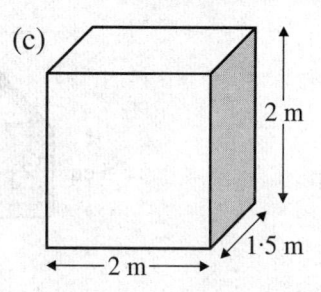

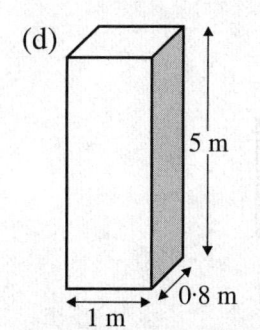

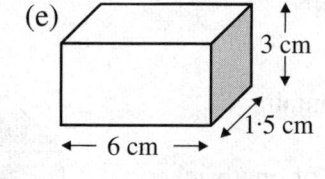

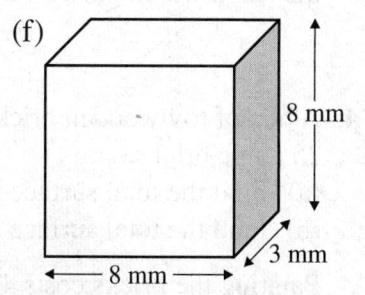

(a) 12 cm, 5 cm, 3 cm

(b) 7 mm, 16 mm, 5 mm

(c) 2 m, 2 m, 1·5 m

(d) 5 m, 1 m, 0·8 m

(e) 3 cm, 6 cm, 1·5 cm

(f) 8 mm, 8 mm, 3 mm

2. A drinks manufacturer is considering two different cuboid-shaped containers for a new fruit juice. Both containers hold the same amount of juice.

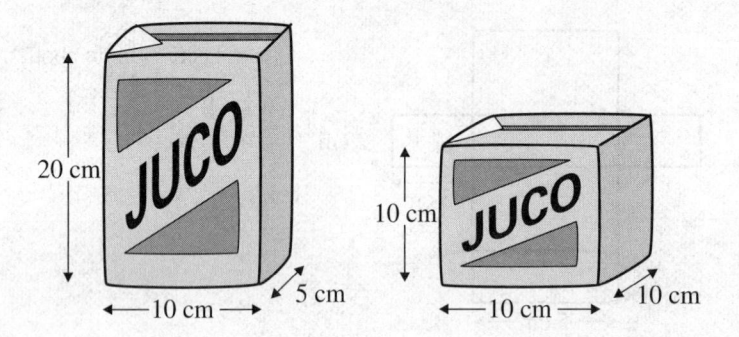

   (a) Find the total surface area of the 20 cm by 10 cm by 5 cm container.
   (b) Find the total surface area of the 10 cm by 10 cm by 10 cm container.

   The containers are made from a special foil-covered card. 50 cm² of the card costs 1p.

   (c) Find the cost of the card used in each container.

3. DJ's cat food is sold in tins like this:

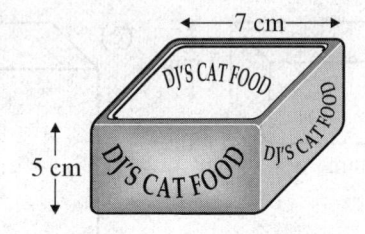

   The area of the top of the tin is 56 cm². Work out the area of the label, which goes all the way round the sides of the tin.

4. A box of toy wooden bricks contains 25 cubic bricks.
   (a) Find the total surface area of one brick.
   (b) Find the total surface area of 25 bricks.

   Painting the bricks costs 4p per 100 cm².

   (c) Find the cost of painting 25 bricks.

18.5 Finding volume by counting cubes

The volume of a solid is the amount of space it fills. Volume is measured in cubes. The common units are:

cubic millimetre   (mm^3)
cubic centimetre   (cm^3)
cubic metre   (m^3)

Example

Find the volume of these solids if each cube has a volume of 1 cm^3.

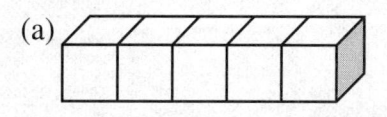

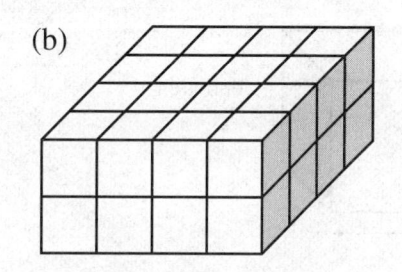

(a)   (b)

(a) Volume = 5 cm^3 (b) Volume = 32 cm^3

Exercise 18E

Find the volume of each solid if each cube has a volume of 1 cm^3.

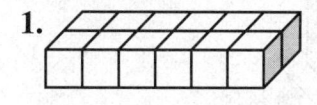

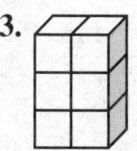

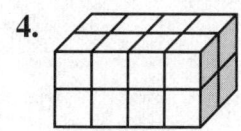

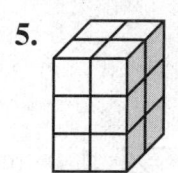

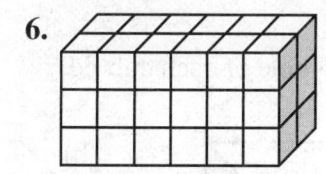

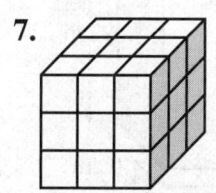

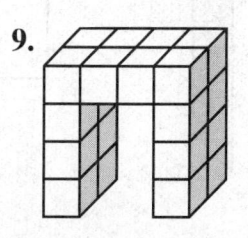

1.
2.
3.
4.
5.
6.
7.
8.
9.

10.

11.

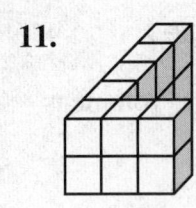

12.

18.6 Finding the volume of a cuboid by using the formula

The volume of a cuboid can be found by using the formula:

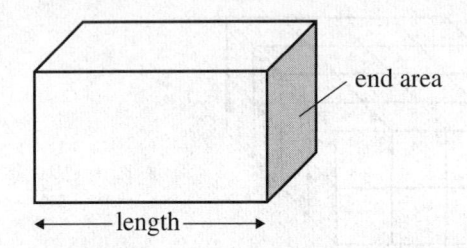

Volume = end area × length

Example
Find the volume of this cuboid.

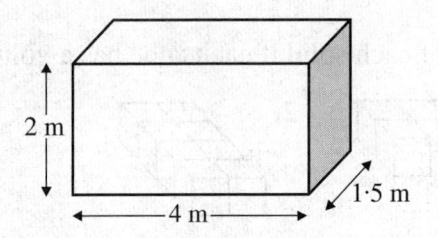

end area = 2 × 1·5 = 3 m²
volume = 3 × 4 = 12 m³

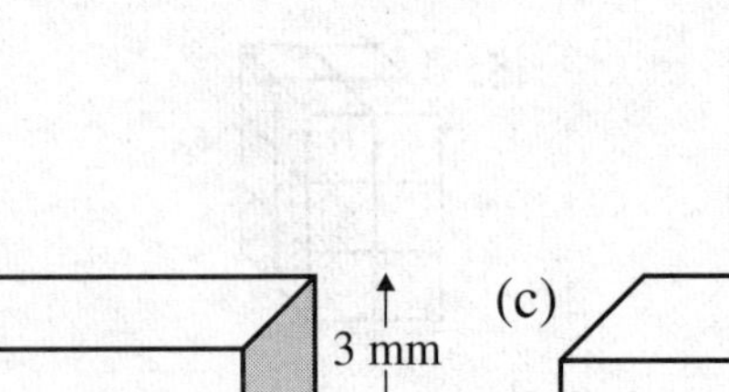

Exercise 18F
1. Find the volume of each cuboid.

(a) 10 cm, 3 cm, 2 cm

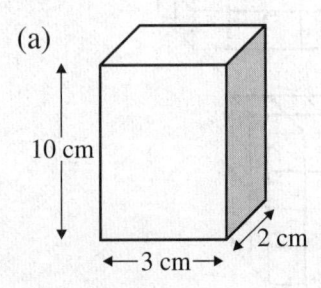

(b) 12 mm, 3 mm, 2 mm

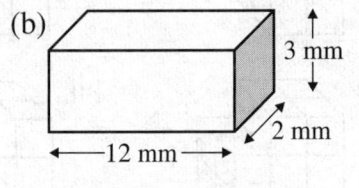

(c) 9 cm, 9 cm, 6 cm

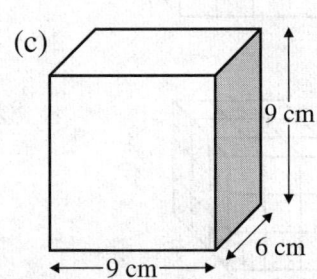

(d) 6 m, 1.5 m, 1 m

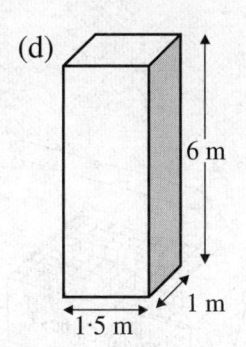

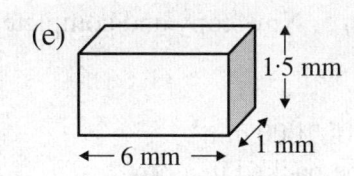

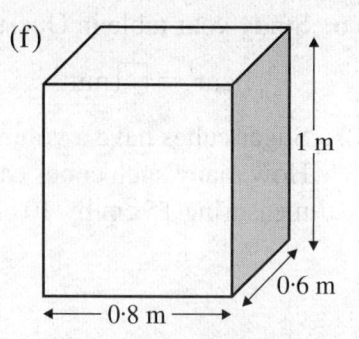

(e) 1.5 mm, 6 mm, 1 mm

(f) 1 m, 0.8 m, 0.6 m

2. The diagram shows a matchbox measuring 5 cm by 4 cm by 2 cm.
   (a) Find the volume of the matchbox.

   12 of these matchboxes are packed in a carton with a base 10 cm by 8 cm.

   Find:
   (b) The volume of the carton.
   (c) The height of the carton.

3. The fuel tank of a car is a cuboid 50 cm by 40 cm by 20 cm.
   (a) Find the volume of the fuel tank.

   One litre of fuel has a volume of 1 000 cm³.

   (b) How many litres of fuel will the tank hold?
   (c) If petrol costs 75p per litre, how much will it cost to fill the fuel tank?

4. A packet of icing sugar is 9 cm by 6 cm by 16 cm.
   (a) Find the volume of the box.
   (b) The sugar in a new packet fills the box to within 1 cm of the top. Find the volume of sugar in a new packet.
   (c) Some of the sugar in a packet has been used. The sugar in the box is now 9 cm deep. What volume of sugar has been used?

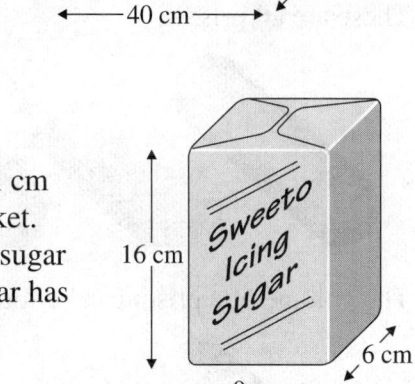

5. (a) What is the name of the cuboid with all edges the same?
   (b) Copy and complete, for these cuboids:

   Remember: 1 cm = 10 mm

Length	Width	Height	Volume
1 cm	1 cm	1 cm	
10 mm	10 mm	10 mm	

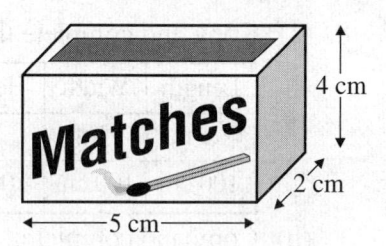

6. Study your table in Question 5. Now copy and complete:

    $1 \text{ cm}^3 = \Box \text{ mm}^3$

7. Sugar cubes have a volume of 1000 mm³.
   How many such cubes can be packed in a box measuring 15 cm by 10 cm by 5 cm?

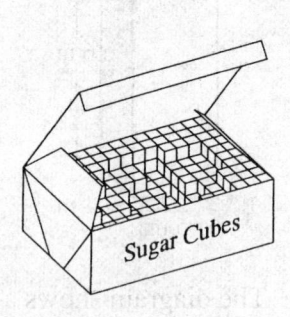

8. (a) Copy and complete the table.

Length	Width	Height	Volume
1 m	1 m	1 m	
100 cm	100 cm	100 cm	

   (b) Copy and complete:

    $1 \text{ m}^3 = \Box \text{ cm}^3$

9. How many cubic millimetres make 1 m³?

   Remember: 1 m = 100 cm = 1 000 mm.

18.7 Finding the volume of a prism

A **prism** is a solid with the same shape along its length.
These are all prisms:

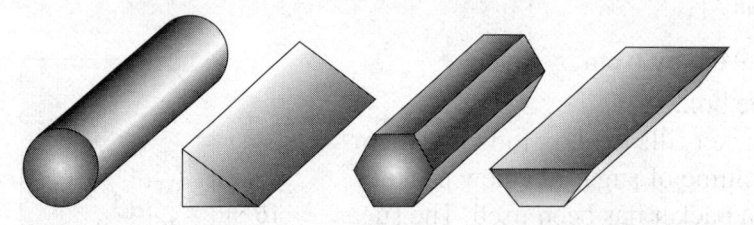

The volume of a prism can be found by using the formula:

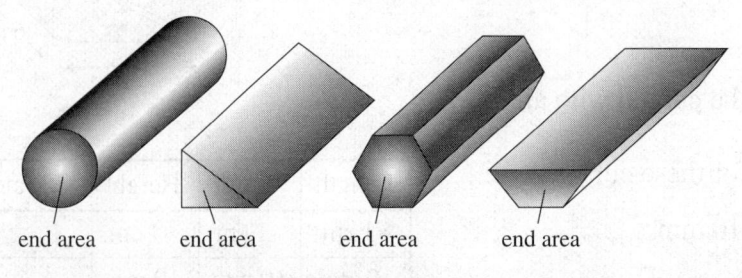

end area   end area   end area   end area

Volume = end area × length

Example

Find the volume of each prism. Use $\pi = 3{\cdot}14$.

(a) 10 cm, 4 cm

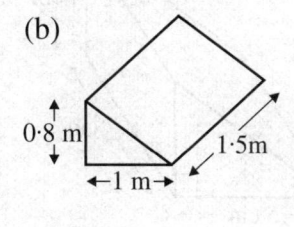

(b) 0·8 m, 1 m, 1·5 m

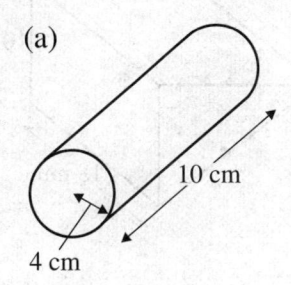

(a) Volume = end area × length
    = 3·14 × 4 × 4 × 10
    = 502·4 cm³

(b) Volume = end area × length
    = ½ of (0·8 × 1) × 1·5
    = 0·4 × 1·5
    = 0·6 m³

Exercise 18G

1. Find the volume of each prism. Use $\pi = 3{\cdot}14$.

(a) 2 m, 6 m

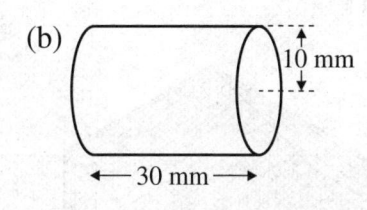

(b) 10 mm, 30 mm

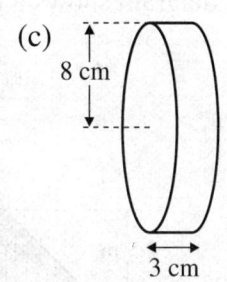

(c) 8 cm, 3 cm

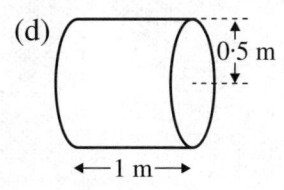

(d) 0·5 m, 1 m

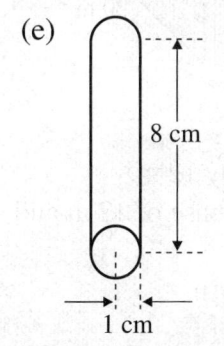

(e) 8 cm, 1 cm

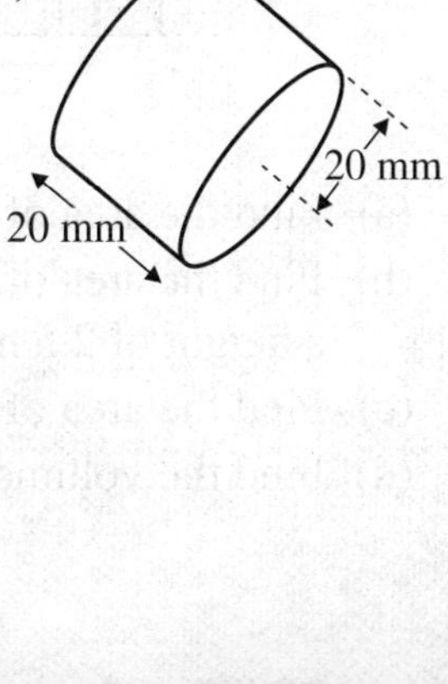

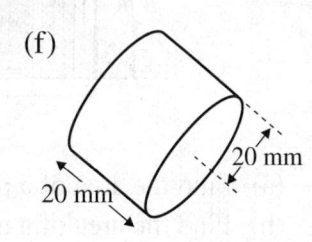

(f) 20 mm, 20 mm

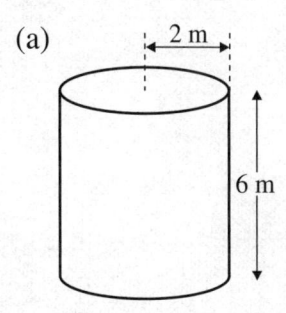

2. Find the volume of each prism.

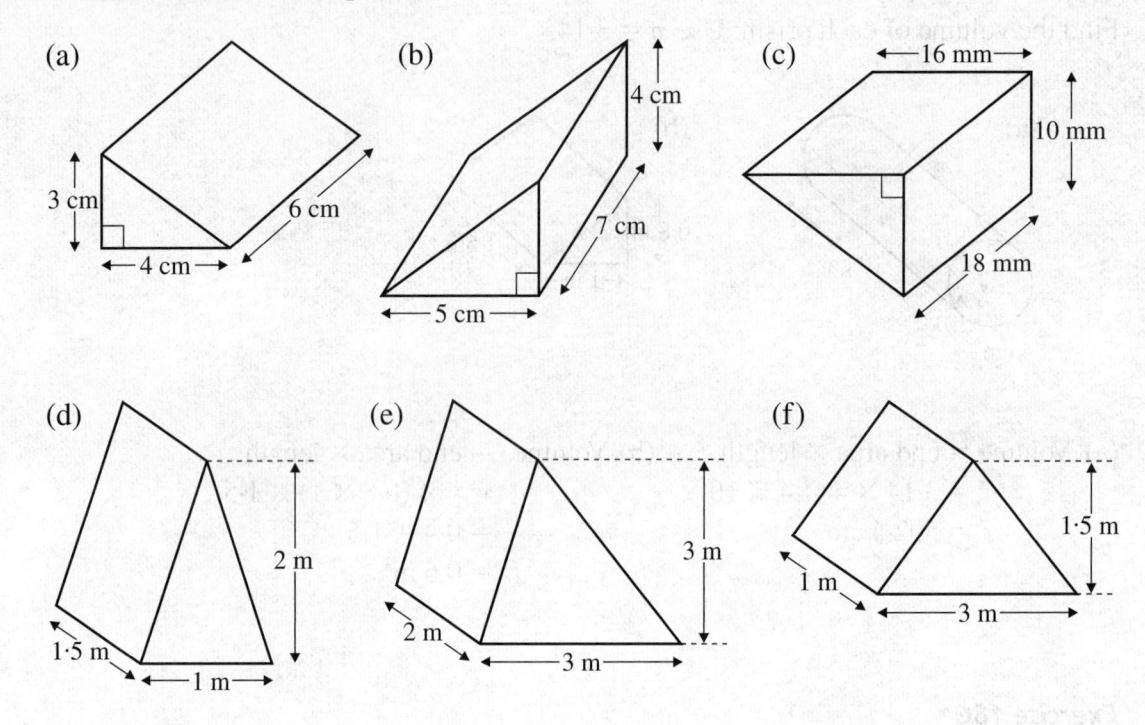

(a) 3 cm, 4 cm, 6 cm

(b) 4 cm, 5 cm, 7 cm

(c) 16 mm, 10 mm, 18 mm

(d) 2 m, 1.5 m, 1 m

(e) 2 m, 3 m, 3 m

(f) 1 m, 1.5 m, 3 m

3. This diagram shows a barn.

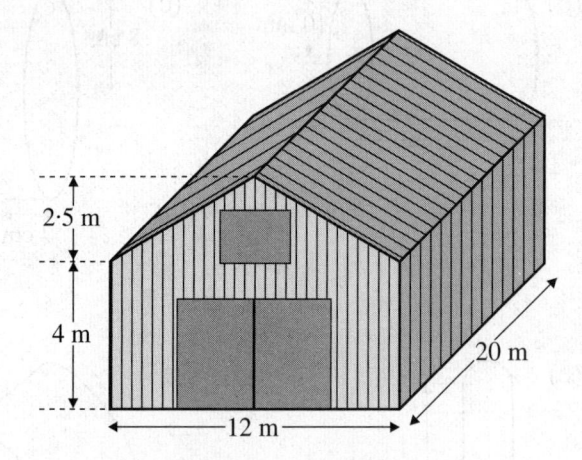

2.5 m, 4 m, 12 m, 20 m

(a) Find the area of a rectangle 4 m by 12 m.
(b) Find the area of a triangle with a base of 12 m and a height of 2·5 m.
(c) Find the area of one end of the barn.
(d) Find the volume of the barn.

4. A swimming pool is in the shape of a prism like this:

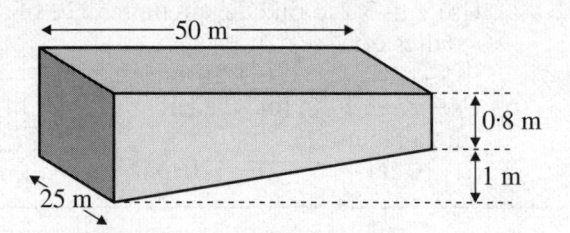

   (a) Find the area of a rectangle 50 m by 0·8 m.
   (b) Find the area of a triangle with a base of 50 m and a height of 1 m.
   (c) The pool is filled with water to a greatest depth of 1·8 m. Find the volume of water in the pool.

5. The coffee urn in a café is a cylinder with a radius of 20 cm and a height of 50 cm.
   (a) Find the volume of coffee in the urn when it is full.
   (b) Each cup of coffee served has a volume of 125 cm³. How many cups of coffee can be served from a full urn?

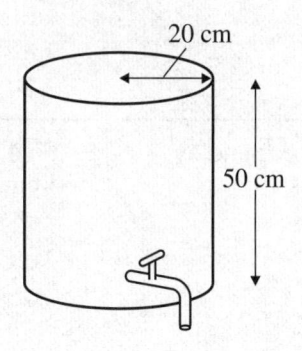

Summary

1. These words are used to describe circles.

   circumference, radius, diameter

Checkout 18

1. (a) Draw circles with a radius of:
      (i) 4 cm (ii) 25 mm
   (b) Draw circles with a diameter of:
      (i) 10 cm (ii) 120 mm

2. The circumference of a circle can be found with the formula
   $C = \pi d$

2. (a) Use $\pi = 3\cdot 1$ to find the circumference of a circle with a radius of:
   (i) 4 cm (ii) 25 mm
   (b) Use $\pi = 3\cdot 14$ to find the circumference of a circle with a radius of:
   (i) 10 cm (ii) 120 mm

3. The area of a circle can be found with the formula:
   $A = \pi r^2$

3. Use $\pi = 3\cdot 14$ to find the area of a circle with a radius of:
   (a) 8 cm (b) 20 mm

4. The total surface area of a cuboid can be found by sketching its net.

4. Sketch the net of this cuboid and calculate its total surface area.

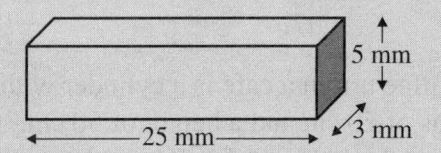

   5 mm, 25 mm, 3 mm

5. Volumes can be found by counting cubes.

5. Find the volume of this solid if each cube has a volume of 1 cm³.

6. The volume of a cuboid can be found using the formula
   Volume = end area × length

6. Find the volume of this cuboid.

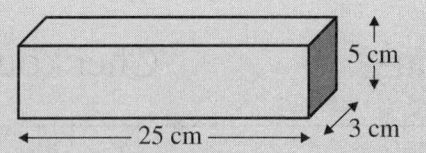

   5 cm, 25 cm, 3 cm

7. The volume of a prism can also be found using the formula
   Volume = end area × length

7. Find the volume of each prism. Use $\pi = 3\cdot 14$.

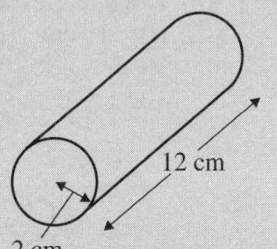

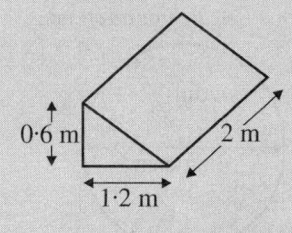

   12 cm, 2 cm

   0·6 m, 2 m, 1·2 m

Revision exercise 18

1. Some oil is spilt. The spilt oil is in the shape of a circle.
   The circle has a diameter of 12 centimetres.

   (a) Work out the circumference, in cm, of the spilt oil.
   Give your answer correct to 1 decimal place.

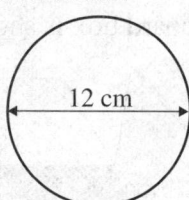

   The diameter of the spilt oil increases by 30%.

   (b) Work out the new diameter, in centimetres, of the spilt oil. [Edexcel]

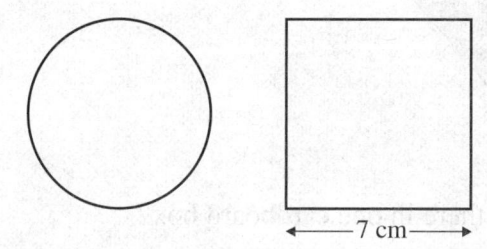

2. The circumference of the circle and the perimeter of the square are equal.
   Calculate the radius of the circle. [AQA/NEAB]

3. The diagram shows part of a garden, in the form of a square, with a circular pond, of radius 3 m, surrounded by a lawn.

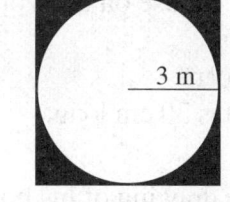

   (a) Calculate the circumference of the pond, giving your answer to an appropriate degree of accuracy.

   (b) Calculate the area of the lawn. [WJEC]

4. Penny is stacking crates.
   Each crate is a cube of side 1 m.
   Find the volume of this stack of crates.
   State the units of your answer. [OCR]

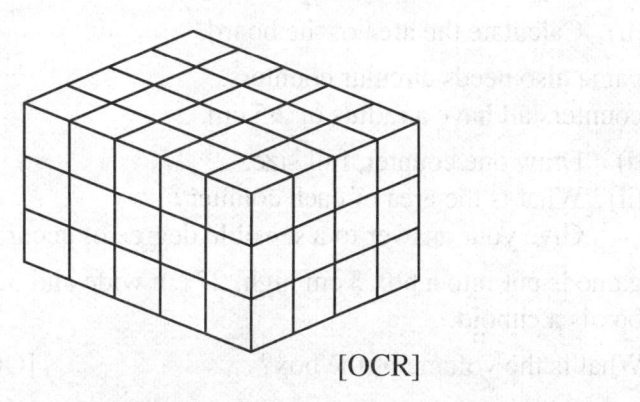

5. A factory produces packets of tea.
These packets are put into cardboard boxes to be delivered to shops.
A drawing of one cardboard box is shown below.

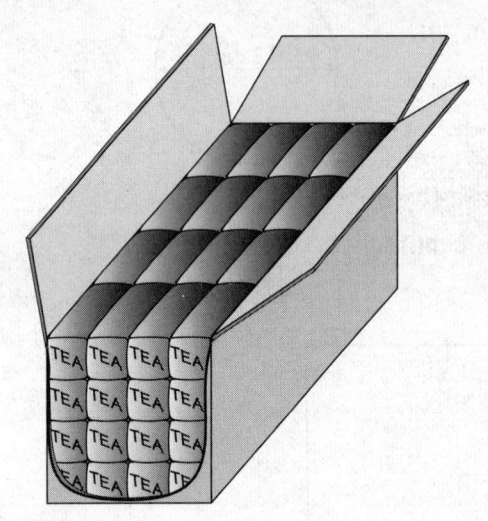

(a) How many packets of tea are there in one cardboard box?

(b) Each packet of tea measures 12 cm by 8 cm by 8 cm.
Calculate the volume of one packet of tea.

[AQA/NEAB]

6. James designs a game for use on his work experience at a nursery school.
It needs a triangular board.
Each side of the board is 30 cm long.
Each angle is 60°.

(a) (i) Make a scale drawing of his board.
Use a scale of 1 cm to 5 cm.

The height of the board for James' game is 26 cm.

(ii) Calculate the area of the board.

The game also needs circular counters.
The counters all have a radius of 2·5 cm.

(b) (i) Draw one counter, full size.
(ii) What is the area of each counter?
Give your answer to a sensible degree of accuracy.

The game is put into a box 3 cm high, 27 cm wide and 32 cm long.
The box is a cuboid.

(c) What is the volume of the box? [OCR]

7. An ingot of metal is in the form of a cuboid 64 cm long, 49 cm wide and 27 cm thick.

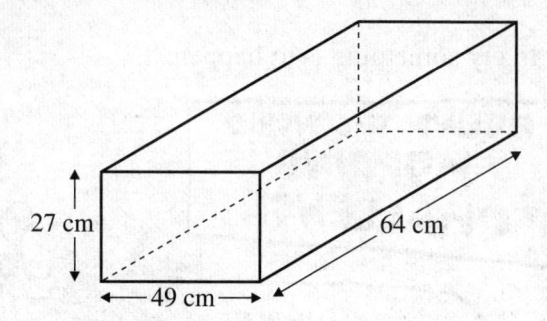

(a) Calculate the volume, in cm³, of the ingot.

The ingot of metal is melted and re-cast into the shape of a cube.
One-eighth of the metal is lost during this process.

(b) How much metal is in the new ingot?

(c) The new ingot has a side of length x cm.
Explain why $x = 42$. [AQA/NEAB]

19 Data Handling 5

You use probability to describe how likely something is to happen.

This unit is about:

- Simple probability
- Probabilities of 0 and 1
- Probability scales
- Probabilities when two things happen

You need to remember:

- How to simplify fractions (see Unit 12).
  1. Simplify:
     (a) $\frac{4}{6}$ (b) $\frac{3}{6}$ (c) $\frac{8}{10}$ (d) $\frac{10}{12}$ (e) $\frac{3}{15}$
     (f) $\frac{5}{15}$ (g) $\frac{12}{18}$ (h) $\frac{24}{30}$ (i) $\frac{2}{14}$ (j) $\frac{9}{12}$
- How to change a fraction to a decimal.
  2. Change into decimals:
     (a) $\frac{1}{2}$ (b) $\frac{1}{4}$ (c) $\frac{2}{5}$ (d) $\frac{3}{4}$ (e) $\frac{5}{8}$
     (f) $\frac{7}{10}$ (g) $\frac{1}{3}$ (h) $\frac{2}{3}$ (i) $\frac{5}{9}$ (j) $\frac{4}{7}$
- How to change a decimal into a percentage.
  3. Change into percentages:
     (a) 0.25 (b) 0.75 (c) 0.5 (d) 0.125 (e) 0.333
     (f) 0.147 (g) 0.9 (h) 0.05 (i) 0.45 (j) 0.09

19.1 Simple probability

Elizabeth, Daniel and Steve are going to roll a dice to see who will go first in a game. The highest score goes first.

Elizabeth rolls the dice first and scores a 3.

Before he rolls the dice, Daniel wants to know what is the **probability** that he will beat Elizabeth.

There are six possible results when you roll a dice: 1, 2, 3, 4, 5 and 6. Three of these, 4, 5 and 6, will allow Daniel to beat Elizabeth.

The probability that Daniel will beat Elizabeth $= \frac{3}{6} = \frac{1}{2}$

Daniel rolls a 4. Steve will start first if he rolls a 5 or a 6.
The probability that Steve starts first $= \frac{2}{6} = \frac{1}{3}$

Probabilities can be written as fractions, decimals or percentages.
The probability that Daniel beats Elizabeth $= \frac{1}{2} = 0.5 = 50\%$
The probability that Steve starts first $= \frac{1}{3}$
$= 0.333$ (to 3 decimal places) $= 33.3\%$

Example 1
What is the probability of selecting a letter at random from the word TEACHER and getting a vowel?

There are three vowels (e, a, e) out of seven letters.

The probability $= \frac{3}{7} = 0.428 = 42.8\%$

Example 2
What is the probability of cutting a deck of cards and getting a red king or a black ace?

There are two red kings and two black aces out of 52 cards.

The probability $= \frac{4}{52} = 0.076 = 7.6\%$

Exercise 19A

In this exercise, give every answer first as a fraction, then as a decimal correct to 3 decimal places and finally as a percentage.

1. Bob tossed a one pound coin. What is the probability that he gets:
   (a) a head   (b) a tail?

2. Toni rolls a dice. What is the probability that she gets:
   (a) a six
   (b) an even number
   (c) less than five
   (d) a one or a two?

3. A bag contains 2 mints, 3 toffees and 5 fruit chews. If one sweet is selected at random, what is the probability of getting:
   (a) a mint
   (b) a toffee
   (c) a fruit chew
   (d) a mint or a toffee?

4. One letter is selected at random from the word SUCCESSFUL. What is the probability that the letter is:
   (a) an S
   (b) an E
   (c) a C or a U
   (d) a vowel
   (e) neither a C nor an S?

5. On a supermarket shelf there are 20 jars of Tom's favourite coffee. Tom does not notice that 5 of these are decaffeinated. If Tom picks a jar at random, what is the probability that the coffee is:
   (a) decaffeinated
   (b) not decaffeinated?

6. In a class there are 14 girls and 16 boys. 3 of the girls and 2 of the boys wear glasses. If a pupil is selected at random from the class, what is the probability that the pupil is:
   (a) a girl
   (b) a boy
   (c) a girl who wears glasses
   (d) a pupil who wears glasses?

7. In a cupboard a family has a box filled with packets of crisps. There are 5 cheese and onion flavour, 8 plain and 7 salt and vinegar flavour. If a bag is selected at random, what is the probability that the flavour will be:
   (a) cheese and onion
   (b) plain
   (c) salt and vinegar
   (d) not plain?

8. A pencil case contains 15 felt tips, 9 crayons and 1 pencil. In a hurry, Mrs Smith grabs one item from the case at random to write down a phone message. What is the probability that the phone message is written down with:
   (a) a felt tip
   (b) a crayon
   (c) a pencil
   (d) a felt tip or a pencil?

9. A pack of 52 cards is cut. What is the probability that the cut card is:
   (a) red
   (b) a two
   (c) a red queen
   (d) a club
   (e) the ace of hearts?

10. This pie chart shows the ways that 50 houses in a small village are heated.
    If a house is selected at random, what is the probability that it is heated by:
    (a) coal
    (b) oil
    (c) electricity
    (d) gas?

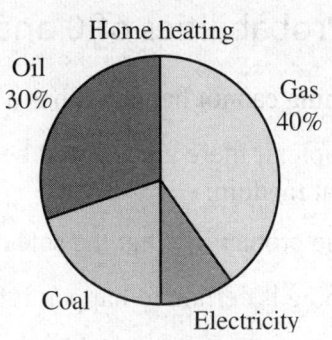

    Home heating
    Oil 30%
    Gas 40%
    Coal
    Electricity

11. A class completed a survey on how each pupil came to school. This table shows their results.

Ways of coming to school	Number of pupils
Parent's car	10
Friend's car	4
Bus	2
Walk	8
Cycle	6

    If a pupil is selected at random, what is the probability that their way of coming to school is:
    (a) by bus   (b) by parent's car   (c) by cycle   (d) not by walking?

12. This bar chart shows the marks that a group of students scored in a test.

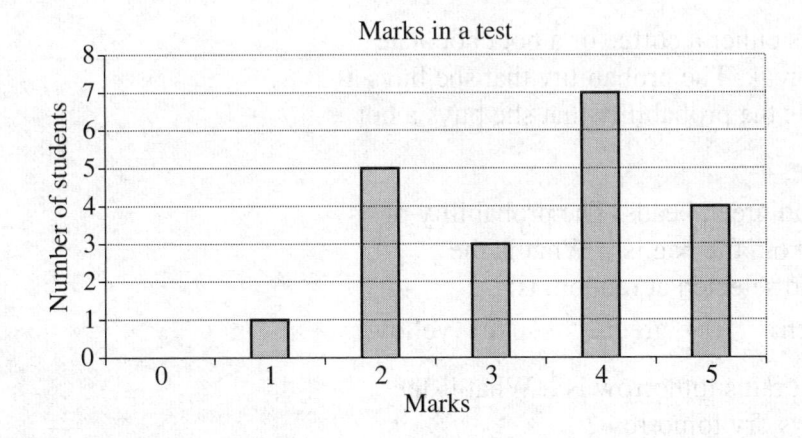

    Marks in a test

    If a student is selected from the group at random, what is the probability that their test mark was:
    (a) 2   (b) 1   (c) more than 3   (d) less than 5?

19.2 Probabilities of 0 and 1

If something cannot happen it has a probability of 0 or 0%.

For example, if there are five red beads in a bag and one is selected at random,

> the probability that the selected bead is green $= \frac{0}{5} = 0 = 0\%$

If something is certain to happen it has a probability of 1 or 100%.

For example, if there are five red beads in a bag and one is selected at random,

> the probability that the selected bead is red $= \frac{5}{5} = 1 = 100\%$

Example

Vicky Jones is driving in a strange town looking for a friend's new house. She gets lost and decides to stop and ask the next person she sees for directions. If the probability that the person is female is 0·6, what is the probability that the person is male?

The probability that the person is either male or female $= 1$
The probability that the person is male $= 1 - 0·6 = 0·4$

Exercise 19B

1. The probability that Nicola wins a race is $\frac{1}{5}$. What is the probability that she does not win the race?

2. Every day, Carla buys either a coffee or a hot chocolate during her morning break. The probability that she buys a coffee is 0·65. What is the probability that she buys a hot chocolate?

3. A bag contains red and green beads. The probability of selecting a red bead from the bag is $\frac{1}{4}$. What is the probability that a bead selected at random is:
   (a) either red or green   (b) green   (c) yellow?

4. The probability that it rains tomorrow is $\frac{1}{8}$. What is the probability that it stays dry tomorrow?

5. If a sweet is selected at random from a bag, the probability that it is not a mint is 75%. What is the probability that the sweet is a mint?

6. The probability that a milling machine breaks down during a night shift is 12%. What is the probability that the machine does not break down during a night shift?

7. A machine makes compact discs. The probability that the machine makes a perfect disc is 0·98. What is the probability that the machine makes a faulty disc?

8. The probability that Janet is late for school tomorrow is 22%. What is the probability that Janet is not late for school tomorrow?

9. A bag contains red and green beads. The probability that a bead selected at random is red is 45%. What is the probability that a bead selected at random is:
   (a) either red or green   (b) green   (c) yellow?

10. In a seaside town, the probability of a wet day during June is $\frac{7}{30}$. What is the probability of a dry day during June?

11. A bag contains blue and green beads. If two beads are selected from the bag, the probability that they are the same colour is $\frac{5}{9}$. What is the probability that the beads are different colours?

12. The probability that Mr Jones is delayed by a level crossing on his way to work is 60%. What is the probability that Mr Jones is not delayed by the level crossing?

13. If a sweet is selected at random from a bag, the probability that it is a fruit chew is 0·3. The probability that it is a toffee is 0·25. What is the probability that it is neither a fruit chew nor a toffee?

14. Every day, Malcolm either wears black, grey or brown socks. The probability that he wears black socks is 0·5. The probability that he does not wear grey socks is 0·7. What is the probability that he wears brown socks?

15. A box of crisps has a mixture of cheese and onion flavour, plain and salt and vinegar flavour. The probability of selecting a bag at random and getting cheese and onion flavour is 0·2. The probability of selecting a bag at random and getting salt and vinegar flavour is 0·5. What is the probability of selecting a bag at random and getting plain crisps?

19.3 Probability scales

Probabilities are sometimes shown on a **probability scale**. This is a number line from 0 to 1.

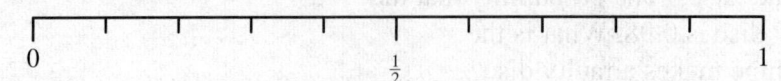

```
├──┬──┬──┬──┬──┬──┬──┬──┬──┬──┤
0              ½                1
```

Example

The probability that it will rain tomorrow is 0·4. Mark the probabilities that it will rain or stay dry tomorrow on a probability scale.

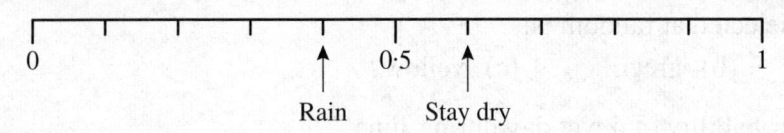

```
├──┬──┬──┬──┬──┬──┬──┬──┬──┬──┤
0         ↑    0·5  ↑            1
         Rain     Stay dry
```

Exercise 19C

1. A bag contains 3 red beads and 7 green beads. One bead is selected at random from the bag.
   (a) What is the probability that the bead is red?
   (b) What is the probability that the bead is green?
   (c) Copy this probability scale and mark both probabilities on it.

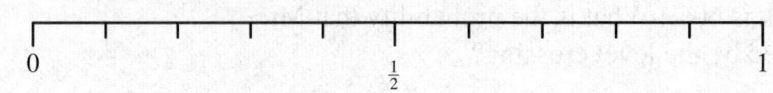

   ```
   ├──┬──┬──┬──┬──┬──┬──┬──┬──┬──┤
   0              ½                1
   ```

2. There are 1 000 combinations on a bike lock.
   (a) If somebody tries 100 combinations, what is the probability that they will open the lock?
   (b) Copy this probability scale and mark this probability on it.

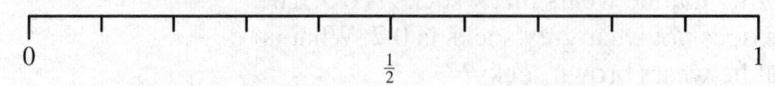

   ```
   ├──┬──┬──┬──┬──┬──┬──┬──┬──┬──┤
   0              ½                1
   ```

3. Juanita has eight pairs of earrings, three silver, one gold and four jewelled. She cannot decide which pair to wear so she chooses a pair at random.
   (a) What is the probability that she picks a silver pair of earrings?
   (b) What is the probability that she picks the gold pair of earrings?

(c) What is the probability that she picks a jewelled pair of earrings?
(d) Copy this probability scale and mark all three probabilities on it.

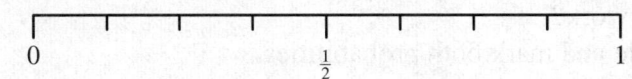

```
├───┬───┬───┬───┬───┬───┬───┬───┬───┬───┤
0              $\frac{1}{2}$              1
```

4. Carlos was late for school on 38 days out of 190 last year.
   (a) On any school day last year, what was the probability that Carlos was late?
   (b) On any school day last year, what was the probability that Carlos was not late?
   (c) Copy this probability scale and mark both probabilities on it.

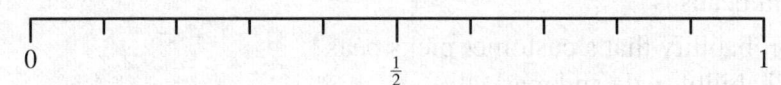

```
├───┬───┬───┬───┬───┬───┬───┬───┬───┬───┤
0              $\frac{1}{2}$              1
```

5. There are 100 red, yellow and green beads in a bag. If a bead is selected at random, the probability that it is red is 0·6 and the probability that it is green is 0·3.
   (a) What is the probability that a bead selected at random from the bag is yellow?
   (b) Copy this probability scale and mark all three probabilities on it.

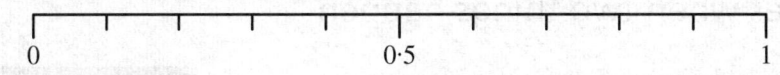

```
├───┬───┬───┬───┬───┬───┬───┬───┬───┬───┤
0              0·5              1
```

6. Amit walked to school with Callum on 48 days out of 60 last term.
   (a) On any day last term, what was the probability that Amit walked to school with Callum? Give your answer as a decimal.
   (b) On any day last term, what was the probability that Amit did not walk to school with Callum? Give your answer as a decimal.
   (c) Copy this probability scale and mark both probabilities on it.

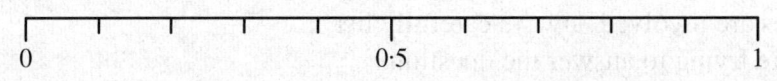

```
├───┬───┬───┬───┬───┬───┬───┬───┬───┬───┤
0              0·5              1
```

7. The probability that Mrs Jones buys a newspaper on her way to work is 30%.
   (a) What is the probability that Mrs Jones does not buy a newspaper on her way to work?
   (b) Copy this probability scale and mark both probabilities on it.

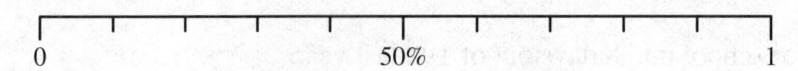

   ```
   |---|---|---|---|---|---|---|---|---|---|
   0                   50%                  1
   ```

8. A restaurant offers a choice of one vegetable from peas, carrots, broccoli and green beans. Experience has shown that the probability that a customer picks broccoli is 10%. A customer is twice as likely to pick carrots and three times as likely to pick green beans.
   (a) What is the probability that a customer picks peas?
   (b) Copy this probability scale and mark all four probabilities on it.

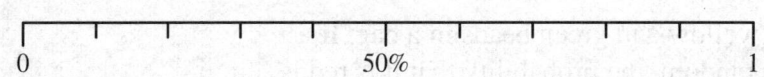

   ```
   |---|---|---|---|---|---|---|---|---|---|
   0                   50%                  1
   ```

19.4 Probabilities when two things happen

A school canteen offers a choice of fish pie, sausages or chilli, served with either a baked potato or chips. If William picks a meal at random, what is the probability that he picks sausages and chips?

Today's Specials

Fish Pie
Sausages
Chilli

All served with Chips
or
Baked potatoes

There are six possible meal combinations:

fish pie with chips   fish pie with baked potato
sausages with chips   sausages with baked potato
chilli with chips   chilli with baked potato

The probability that William picks sausages and chips
= $\frac{1}{6}$ = 0.167 = 16.7%

If two separate choices are involved, always carefully list all the outcomes before trying to answer the question.

A tree diagram can help you identify all the outcomes:

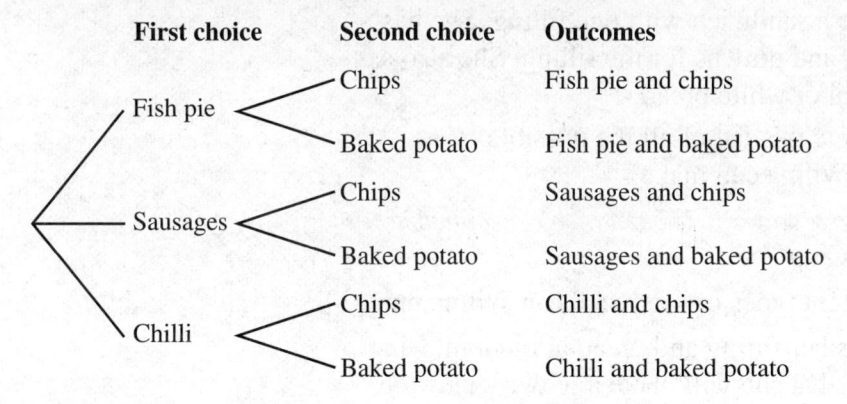

First choice	Second choice	Outcomes
Fish pie	Chips	Fish pie and chips
Fish pie	Baked potato	Fish pie and baked potato
Sausages	Chips	Sausages and chips
Sausages	Baked potato	Sausages and baked potato
Chilli	Chips	Chilli and chips
Chilli	Baked potato	Chilli and baked potato

Example

Susan flips two coins.

(a) Copy and complete this table to show all the possible outcomes.

	Second coin head	Second coin tail
First coin head	head head	
First coin tail		

(b) What is the probability that the result is a head and a tail?

(a) This is the completed table:

	Second coin head	Second coin tail
First coin head	head head	head tail
First coin tail	tail head	tail tail

A tree diagram can be used instead of the table:

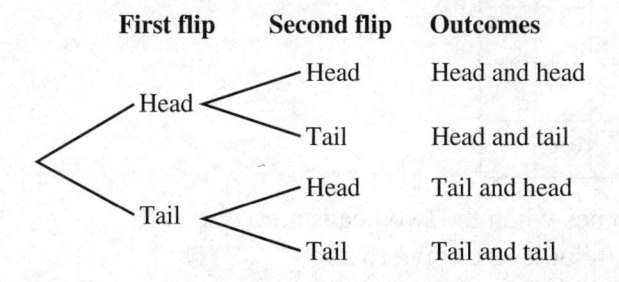

First flip	Second flip	Outcomes
Head	Head	Head and head
Head	Tail	Head and tail
Tail	Head	Tail and head
Tail	Tail	Tail and tail

(b) There are two results out of four which give a head and a tail.

The probability that the result is a head and a tail $= \frac{2}{4} = \frac{1}{2} = 0 \cdot 5 = 50\%$

Exercise 19D

1. Wilma wants to make a sandwich with one filling. She has cheese, ham, chicken and prawns for the filling. She also as a choice of wholemeal or white bread.
   (a) Copy and complete this list of all the possible sandwiches that Wilma can make.

   cheese with white bread   cheese with wholemeal bread
   ham with white bread

   (b) How many different types of sandwich can Wilma make?
   (c) If Wilma chooses her filling and bread at random, what is the probability that she will make a prawn sandwich with wholemeal bread?

2. Shaina is choosing her outfit to wear to a school disco. She has four tops, one red, one blue, one black and one silver. She also has three skirts, one red, one white and one gold.
   (a) Copy and complete this list of all the outfits that Shaina could wear:

   red top with red skirt   red top with white skirt   red top with gold skirt
   blue top with red skirt   blue top with white skirt

   (b) How many diferent outfits can Shaina wear?
   (c) If Shaina chooses her top and skirt at random, what is the probability that she will wear a silver top with a white or gold skirt?

3. A bag contains two red beads and one white bead. A bead is selected at random from the bag, replaced, and then another bead is selected.
   (a) Copy and complete this table showing all the possible pairs of beads.

	R	R	W
R	RR		
R			RW
W		WR	

   (b) There are 9 possible outcomes when the two beads are selected. How many of these outcomes give two red beads?
   (c) What is the probability that the two beads selected will be:
       (i) both red   (ii) both white   (iii) different colours?

4. One bag contains 2 yellow beads and 1 green bead. Another bag contains 1 yellow bead, 1 green bead and 1 blue bead. A bead is selected at random from both bags.
   (a) Copy and complete this table showing all possible pairs of beads.

	Y	Y	G
Y			YG
G		GY	
B	BY		

   (b) There are 9 possible outcomes when the two beads are selected. How many of these outcomes give two yellow beads?
   (c) What is the probability that the two beads selected will be:
      (i) both yellow   (ii) both green   (iii) one blue and one green
      (iv) one yellow and one blue   (v) different colours?

5. Jorina has two spinners, each marked with the numbers from 1 to 4.

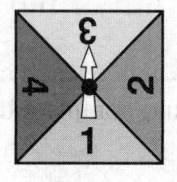

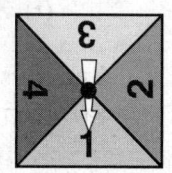

   The spinners are used for a board game. Both arrows are spun and the score is the sum of the two numbers pointed to. The score shown is 3 + 1 = 4.
   (a) Copy and complete this table showing all the possible scores.

+	1	2	3	4
1			4	
2	3			
3		5		
4				8

   (b) There are 16 possible outcomes when the spinners are spun. How many of these give a score of 5?
   (c) What is the probability of scoring 5?
   (d) What is the probability of scoring:
      (i) 2   (ii) 3   (iii) 4   (iv) 6   (v) 7   (vi) 8?

6. Jorina has another game with two different spinners marked with numbers like this:

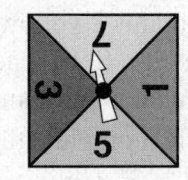

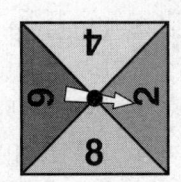

   Both arrows are spun and the score is the sum of the two numbers pointed to. The score shown is 7 + 2 = 9.

   (a) Copy and complete this table showing all the possible scores.

+	1	3	5	7
2	3			
4			9	
6		9		
8				15

   (b) There are 16 possible outcomes when the spinners are spun. How many of these give a score of 5?
   (c) What is the probability of scoring 5?
   (d) What is the probability of scoring:
       (i) 3   (ii) 7   (iii) 9   (iv) 11   (v) an odd number   (vi) an even number?

7. Lee rolls two dice, each numbered from 1 to 6.
   (a) Copy and complete this table showing all the possible scores.

+	1	2	3	4	5	6
1	2					
2						8
3		5				
4				8		
5			8			
6						11

   (b) There are 36 possible outcomes when the dice are rolled. How many of these give a score of 7?
   (c) What is the probability of scoring 7?
   (d) What is the probability of scoring:
       (i) 3   (ii) 8   (iii) 5   (iv) 9   (v) 1   (vi) an even number?

Summary

1. Probabilities can be written as fractions, decimals or percentages. If a single coin is flipped the probability that it comes down heads is:
$\frac{1}{2} = 0.5 = 50\%$

2. If something cannot happen it has a probability of 0 or 0%. If something is certain to happen it has a probability of 1 or 100%.

3. Probabilities are sometimes shown on a **probability scale**. This is a number line from 0 to 1.

4. If two separate choices are involved, always carefully list all the outcomes before trying to answer the question.

Checkout 19

1. A single letter is selected from the word SURREALISM. What is the probability that the letter is:
   (a) an S   (b) an M   (c) a vowel   (d) not a vowel?

2. Melissa will pick either potato chips or a baked potato to go with her cheese salad. The probability that she will pick a baked potato is 0·6. What is the probability that Melissa picks:
   (a) chips   (b) cabbage   (c) cooked potatoes?

3. A bag contains 2 red beads and 8 green beads. One bead is selected at random from the bag.
   (a) What is the probability that the bead is red?
   (b) What is the probability that the bead is green?
   (c) Copy this probability scale and mark both probabilities on it.

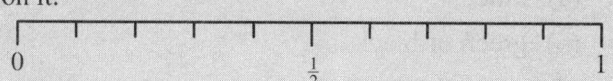

   0 — — — — $\frac{1}{2}$ — — — — 1

4. One bag contains 2 purple beads and 1 red bead. Another bag contains 1 purple bead and 2 red beads. A bead is selected at random from both bags.
   (a) Copy and complete this table showing all possible pairs of beads.

	P	P	R
P			PR
R		RP	
R	RP		

   (b) There are 9 possible outcomes when the two beads are selected. How many of these outcomes give two red beads?
   (c) What is the probability that the two beads selected will be:
   (i) both red   (ii) both purple
   (iii) one purple and one red?

Revision exercise 19

1. This multipack of crisps contains 20 packets.
   Josie takes out a packet without looking.
   What is the probability that it is
   (a) salt and vinegar
   (b) plain or smokey bacon?

   CRISPS
   SAVE WITH MULTIPACK
   5 Salt & Vinegar
   3 Plain
   4 Smokey Bacon
   6 Cheese & Onion
   2 Prawn Cocktail

   [OCR]

2. A bag contains 4 green balls, 8 blue balls, 15 yellow balls and 6 black balls.
   A ball is taken at random from the bag.
   Find the probability that it is
   (a) blue
   (b) green or black
   (c) not yellow [OCR]

3. Anil is playing dominoes.
   There are seven dominoes face down on the table.
   One of them is the 'double six'. It is Anil's turn to pick up.
   (a) What is the probability that he will pick the 'double six'?
   (b) What is the probability that he will **not** pick the 'double six'? [OCR]

4. A game in an amusement arcade can show the following pictures. The fraction under each picture shows the probability of the picture being shown at the first window.

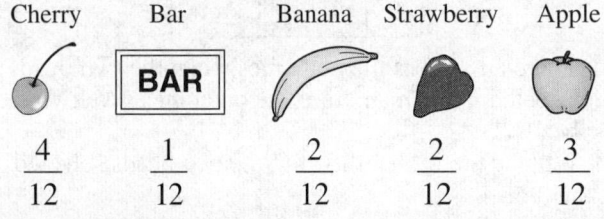

Cherry	Bar	Banana	Strawberry	Apple
$\frac{4}{12}$	$\frac{1}{12}$	$\frac{2}{12}$	$\frac{2}{12}$	$\frac{3}{12}$

   Calculate the probability of the game **not** showing a Bar at the first window. [Edexcel]

5. Polly has kept records of the weather for five years. She works out that the probability that it will rain on any day in September is 0·2.
   (a) What is the probability that it will **not** rain on September 15th?
   (b) On how many September days could it be expected to rain? [OCR]

6. Alison, Brenda, Claire and Donna are the only runners in a race.
   The probabilities of Alison, Brenda and Claire winning the race are shown below.

Alison	Brenda	Claire	Donna
0·31	0·28	0·24	

   Work out the probability that Donna will win the race. [Edexcel]

7. (a) Graham estimated that the probability of a girl having blue eyes is 0·2 and that the probability of a boy having blue eyes is 0·24.
       (i) What is Graham's estimate of the probability of a girl not having blue eyes?
       (ii) In a school of 800 children, 350 are girls. About how many of these children would Graham expect to have blue eyes?
   (b) A bag contains 4 toffees, 6 mints and 5 chocolates. Jill takes a sweet at random from the bag. What is the probability that the sweet she takes out is **not** a mint?
   (c) The events A and B are described below.

       A   One red sweet is picked at random from a bag containing 3 red and 7 white sweets.
       B   Water will overflow when 2 litres of water are poured into a litre container.

   Write A and B at approximate positions of their probabilities on a probability scale. [WJEC]

8. The table shows the bus fares paid by some pupils to travel to school.

Name	Neil	Daksha	Tarik	Sarah	Marc	Tom	Rob	Sita
Bus fare to school in pence	45	60	35	35	60	35	35	40

   (a) Write down the range of these bus fares.

   One of these pupils is to be chosen at random.

   (b) What is the most likely bus fare of the chosen pupil?

   (c) Mark with an X on a number line the probability that the chosen pupil pays a 40 pence bus fare.
   [Edexcel]

9. Here is a fair spinner used in a game. The score is the number where the arrow stops.
   Helen spins the spinner once.

   (a) What score is she most likely to get?

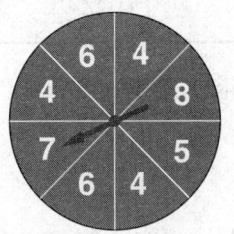

   (b) Mark with a cross (X), on a probability scale, the probability that she gets a score of less than four. Explain your answer.

   (c) Mark with a cross (X), on a probability scale, the probability that she gets an even number score. Explain your answer. [OCR]

10. Here are the numbers of people living in the different houses in a short road.

    4, 2, 3, 4, 5, 1, 3, 2

    (a) Work out the mean number of people per house.

    (b) Work out the range of the number of people living in a house.

    One of the houses is to be chosen at random.

    (c) On a probability line, mark with an X the probability that the house chosen will be the one with 5 people. [Edexcel]

11.

Group A	
Geography	(G)
History	(H)
Sociology	(S)
Economics	(E)

Group B	
Physics	(P)
Chemistry	(C)
Biology	(B)

Havva must choose one subject from each group of subjects above.
Write down all the possible combinations.
The first two have been done for you.

    GP, GC, ...   [OCR]

12. A packet contains only yellow counters and green counters.
There are 8 yellow counters and 5 green counters.
A counter is to be taken from the packet at random.

  (a) Write down the probability that
      (i) a yellow counter will be taken
      (ii) a yellow counter will **not** be taken

A second counter is to be taken from the packet.

  (b) Write down all the possible outcomes of taking two counters from the packet.   [Edexcel]

13. (a) Three coins are tossed in the air.
When they land Andrew records the heads (H) and the tails (T) obtained in the following way.

    HHH   HHT   HTH   ...

List all the other possible results.
Hence write down the probability of obtaining two tails and a head, in any order.

  (b) In one turn of a game at a fête, a contestant spins two spinners.
Each spinner is numbered 1 to 5 and these numbers are equally likely to occur.
A contestant's score is the sum of the two numbers shown on the spinners.
    (i) Copy and complete the following table to show the possible outcomes of a contestant's score on one turn.

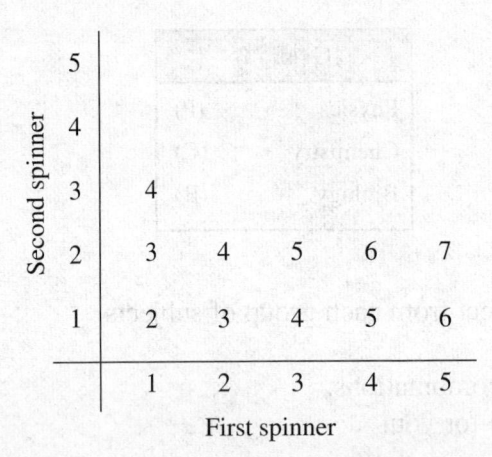

	5					
Second spinner	4					
	3	4				
	2	3	4	5	6	7
	1	2	3	4	5	6
		1	2	3	4	5
			First spinner

(ii) What is the probability of scoring 2 on one turn?

(iii) Contestants win a prize if they score 8 or more.
Jennifer has one turn at the game.
What is the probability that she wins a prize?

(iv) At the fête, 200 people each have one turn at the game.
Approximately how many of them will win a prize?

[WJEC]

14. Two fair spinners are used for a game.
The scores from each spinner are added together.

For example: The total score from these two spinners is $4 + 5 = 9$

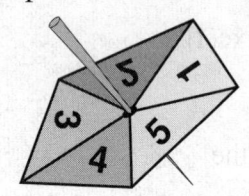

(a) Copy and complete this table to show all the possible totals for the two spinners.

	1	2	3	4	5
2	3	4			
3	4	5			
4					
5					
6					

(b) What is the probability of scoring
(i) a total of 3
(ii) a total of more than 8?   [AQA/NEAB]

20 Coursework Advice

Coursework is very important because the marks count towards your final GCSE grade. This section offers some advice about how to tackle coursework tasks. The two sections offer separate advice on:

- General mathematical investigations
- Data handling tasks

20.1 Mathematical investigations

This is a typical problem.

> Boxes are stacked in a supermarket to make a display like this: 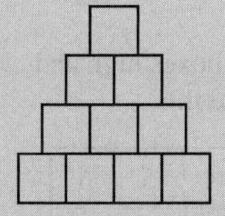
>
> - Investigate how many boxes would be needed to make displays like this of different heights.
> - Investigate how many boxes would be needed to make different types of displays.

Getting started

Always start an investigation by trying out several different cases of the problem. Often drawing sketches will help.

To get started on this problem, draw sketches of stacks like these:

Two boxes high
Three boxes used

Five boxes high
Fifteen boxes used

One box high
One box used

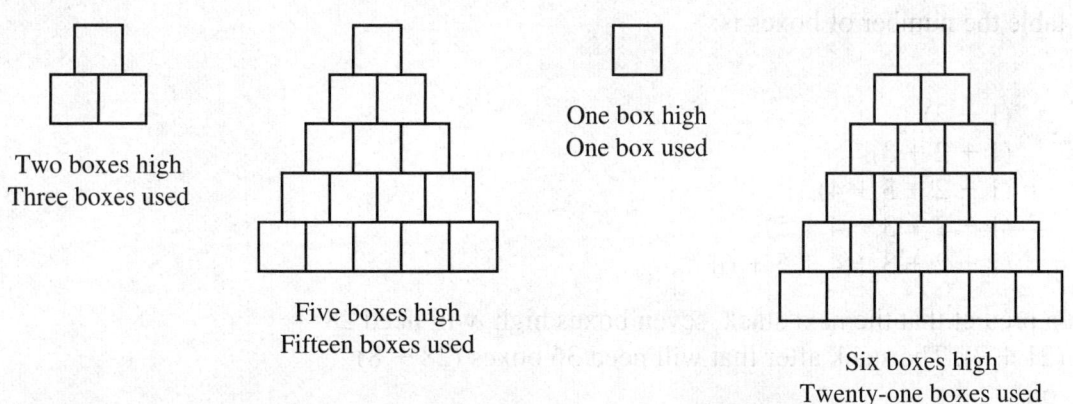

Six boxes high
Twenty-one boxes used

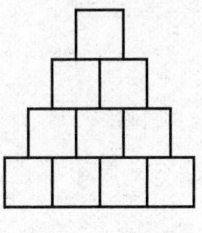

Four boxes high
Ten boxes used

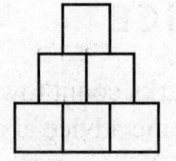

Three boxes high
Six boxes used

Organising results

As you start to collect information on several different cases, try to organise your results. Usually the best way to do this is in a table, starting with the simplest case.

The simplest stack is one box high, the next is two boxes high and so on. You can organise your results into a table like this.

Number of boxes high	1	2	3	4	5	6
Number of boxes in the stack	1	3	6	10	15	21

Describing the problem and making simple predictions

By now you should be starting to understand the problem and be able to describe it in words. You may be able to make some simple predictions. **After** you have made predictions, you should show they are correct.

Each row in a stack has one more box than the row above.
In the table the number of boxes is:

- 1
- 3   (1 + 2)
- 6   (1 + 2 + 3)
- 10   (1 + 2 + 3 + 4)
- 15   (1 + 2 + 3 + 4 + 5)
- 21   (1 + 2 + 3 + 4 + 5 + 6)

You can predict that the next stack, seven boxes high, will need 28 boxes (21 + 7). The stack after that will need 36 boxes (28 + 8) and so on.

These diagrams show that your predictions are correct.

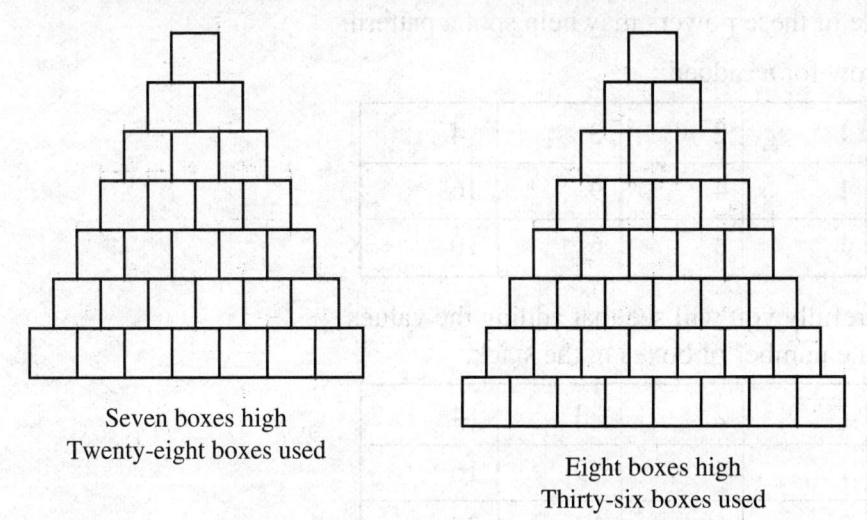

Seven boxes high
Twenty-eight boxes used

Eight boxes high
Thirty-six boxes used

Searching for a formula and checking it

This is often the most difficult part of a coursework task. You are trying to find a formula to predict the result in the *n*th case.

You know how to find a formula for the *n*th term when there is a constant difference between each term. For example:

Term number	1	2	3	4
Term	4	7	10	13

Because there is a constant difference of 3, this series is based on the three times table.

Three times table	3	6	9	12
Term	4	7	10	13

The formula for the *n*th term is:

nth term $= 3n + 1$

However, in this investigation there is not a constant difference between the terms.

Stack height (n)	1	2	3	4
Boxes	1	3	6	10

Hint:
There is more about finding the *n*th term on page 270.

Formulae in cases like this will often involve powers of n like n^2. Adding a row to the table of these powers may help spot a pattern.

This is the table with a row for n^2 added:

Stack height (n)	1	2	3	4
n^2	1	4	9	16
Boxes	1	3	6	10

If you study the table carefully you will see that adding the values of n and n^2 gives twice the number of boxes in the stack.

Stack height (n)	1	2	3	4
n^2	1	4	9	16
$n^2 + n$	2	6	12	20
Boxes	1	3	6	10

At this stage, there are no short cuts. You simply have to search and search until you discover the formula.

The formula is:

Number of boxes in a stack n boxes high $= \dfrac{(n^2 + n)}{2}$

To check the formula you need to test out a prediction.

The formula predicts that a stack ten boxes high needs 55 boxes: $\left(\dfrac{10^2 + 10}{2}\right)$.

You check this by drawing the stack.

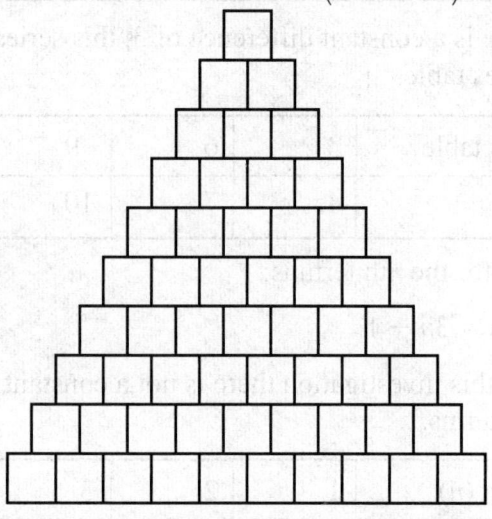

Ten boxes high
Fifty-five boxes used

Extending the problem

The next stage is to think about changes to the basic coursework problem.

For example, investigating stacks like these could extend this coursework.

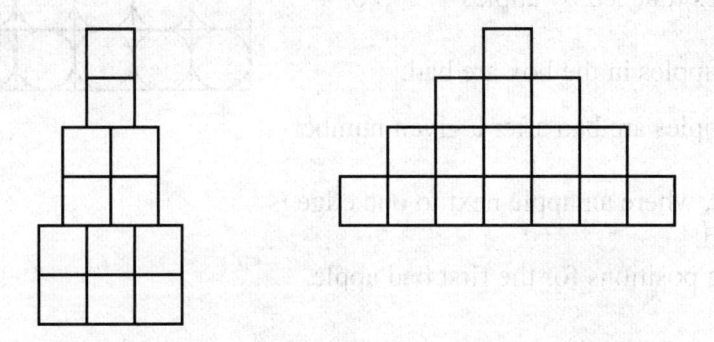

You now need to repeat all the previous stages until you have found and checked a formula for your new type of stack.

Exercise 20A: Coursework tasks for practice

1. This square has been drawn on dotty paper.

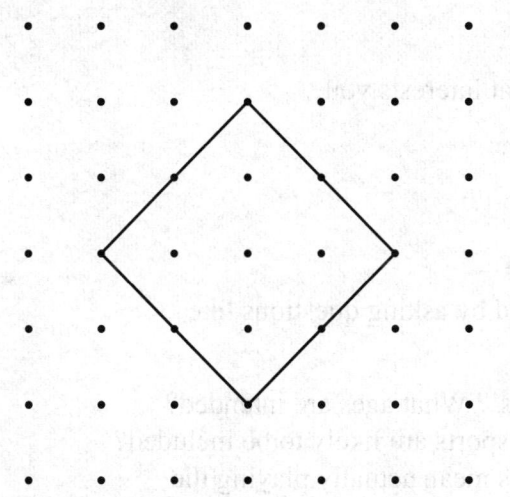

   It was drawn at 45° and each corner is on a dot.
   There are four dots inside the square.

   - Investigate the number of dots inside different size squares drawn in the same way.
   - Investigate the number of dots inside rectangles drawn in the same way.

2. Apples are stored for the winter in a square box like this:

   Each apple just touches the apples next to it.
   After one day, apple number 1 goes bad.
   After another day, all the apples touched by apple number 1 go bad (apples 2, 3 and 4).
   After another day, any apples touched by apples 1, 2, 3 or 4 go bad.
   This continues until all the apples in the box are bad.

   - Investigate how many apples are bad after a given number of days.
   - Investigate bigger boxes, where an apple next to one edge is always the first to go bad.
   - Investigate other starting positions for the first bad apple.

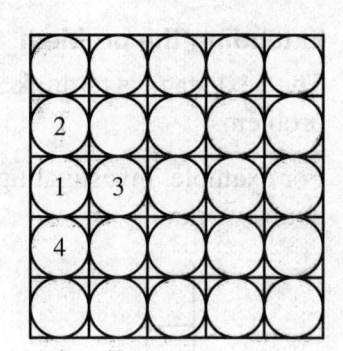

20.2 Data handling tasks

You may be provided with data to analyse or you may be asked to collect your own data.

If you are collecting your own data it is important to think carefully about what you want to find out.

Starting points

A good starting point is a question that interests you.

For example, a starting point might be:

> Do more boys than girls like sport?

Developing a survey questionnaire

A starting point needs to be developed by asking questions like these:

- What is meant by 'boys' and 'girls'? What ages are intended?
- What is meant by 'sport'? Which sports are likely to be included?
- What is meant by 'like'? Does this mean actually playing the sport or simply being interested in it?
- If 'being interested' is included, what does this actually mean?

The answers might be:

- The intended age group is Year 11: 15 to 16 year olds.
- The sports will be: football; netball; rugby; hockey; basketball; athletics.

- Liking the sport can mean either playing or being interested or both. Because some of the sports may be compulsory for Year 11 students, one question will ask whether the sports are enjoyable and another will ask if students will continue playing after they leave school.
- Being interested can mean: watching the sport on TV; watching the sport live; reading about the sport in newspapers; listening to the sport on the radio.

You can now develop some possible questions for a survey.

Try to make all your questions multi-choice with boxes to tick. It is much easier to analyse data collected from questions with tick box answers.

Possible questions for a survey might be:

1. Please tick one box.
   - ☐ Male
   - ☐ Female

2. Which of these sports do you enjoy playing?
   - ☐ Football
   - ☐ Netball
   - ☐ Rugby
   - ☐ Hockey
   - ☐ Basketball
   - ☐ Athletics
   - ☐ None of these

3. Which of these sports will you continue playing when you leave school?
   - ☐ Football
   - ☐ Netball
   - ☐ Rugby
   - ☐ Hockey
   - ☐ Basketball
   - ☐ Athletics
   - ☐ None of these

4. Do you take an interest in a sport?
   - ☐ Yes
   - ☐ No

If your answer to Question 4 was no, do not answer Questions 5 and 6.

5. How would you rate your interest on a scale from 1 to 10?
   - ☐ 10 Committed fan
   - ☐ 9
   - ☐ 8   Very interested
   - ☐ 7
   - ☐ 6   Quite interested
   - ☐ 5
   - ☐ 4   Fairly interested
   - ☐ 3
   - ☐ 2   Vaguely interested
   - ☐ 1

6. If you do take an interest in a sport, do you?
- [ ] Watch the sport on TV
- [ ] Watch the sport live
- [ ] Read newspaper articles about the sport
- [ ] Listen to the sport on the radio

Testing a survey questionnaire

When you have developed your questionnaire it should be tested on a small sample.

This questionnaire could be tested on eight students (four girls, four boys).

There may be problems:

- Are any questions confusing?
- Is it clear whether one box only should be ticked for a question or whether several boxes can be ticked?
- Will you be able to organise the data from the survey easily?

For example, you may need to add 'please tick one box only' to Question 5.

The last question is very important. Think about how you can organise the data from the eight responses. You may use tables like this:

Which of these sports do you enjoy playing?

	Male	Female
Football		
Netball		
Rugby		
Hockey		
Basketball		
Athletics		
None of these		

Try these tables out with your small sample data to make sure there will not be any problems.

If you do discover problems, change your questionnaire.

Organise your data

You should try to collect at least 50 completed questionnaires. You should try to collect roughly the same number from boys as from girls.

When you have your data the responses to each question must be organised into tables. One table was shown in the previous section, here is another one with some responses.

Do you take an interest in a sport?

	Male	Female
Yes	21	17
No	4	8

Presenting your data

Each question should be illustrated with graphs and a conclusion should be drawn.
For example, the table in the last section can be illustrated with these graphs.

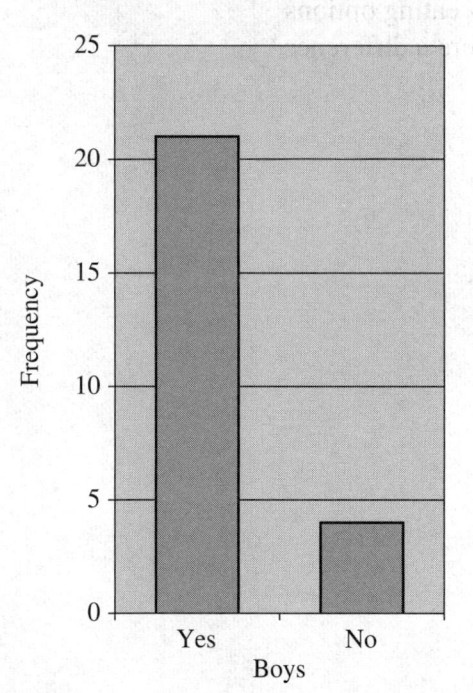

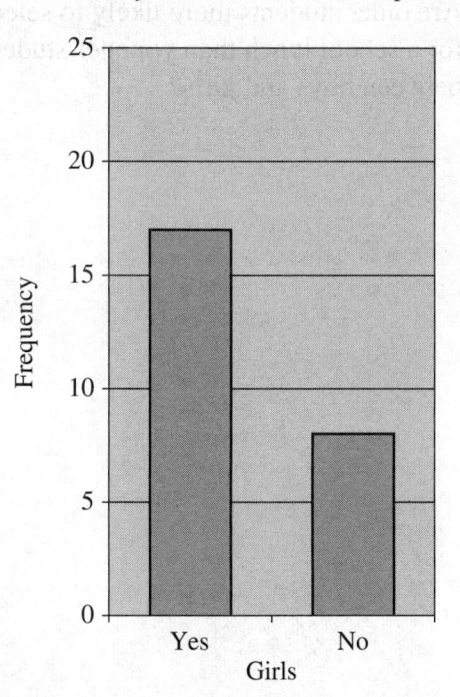

From the graphs you can say: **More boys take an interest in sport than girls.**

Numerical analysis

Try to include some questions which will have a number as an answer. This will allow you to work out averages and ranges. For example, Question 5 was included because it will allow an analysis like this:

How would you rate your interest on a scale from 1 to 10?

	Male	Female
Mean	7·4	4·3
Range	7	9

Exercise 20B: Data handling tasks for practice

Printing questionnaires is very time consuming and expensive. You should practise developing questionnaires so you are ready when it comes to the real thing. Here are some starting points.

- Are children more likely to smoke if their parents smoke? Is there a difference between boys and girls?
- Is there a difference between the music liked by students in different year groups? Is there a difference between boys and girls?
- Are older students more likely to select healthy eating options for a school lunch than younger students? Is there a difference between boys and girls?

Answers

1 Number 1

Exercise 1A

1. (a) 40 (b) 5 (c) 800 (d) 3 (e) 0 (f) 200 (g) 3 000
   (h) 20 (i) 4 (j) 6 000 (k) 0 (l) 8 (m) 300 (n) 70
   (o) 2 000 (p) 1 (q) 60 (r) 900 (s) 3 000 (t) 0
2. 300, 40, 8
3. 900, 0, 3
4. 2 000, 600, 50, 8
5. 7 000, 100, 90, 0
6. 3 000, 500, 20, 7
7. 1 000, 400, 10, 1
8. 8 000, 0, 0, 6
9. 10 000, 2 000, 400, 60, 7
10. (a) 258, 285, 528, 582, 825, 852 (b) 258, 285, 528, 582, 825, 852
11. (a) 379, 397, 739, 793, 937, 973 (b) 379, 397, 739, 793, 937, 973
12. (a) 1 046, 1 064, 1 406, 1 460, 1 604, 1 640, 4 016, 4 061, 4 106, 4 160, 4 601, 4 610, 6 014, 6 041, 6 104, 6 140, 6 401, 6 410
    (b) 1 046, 1 064, 1 406, 1 460, 1 604, 1 640, 4 016, 4 061, 4 106, 4 160, 4 601, 4 610, 6 014, 6 041, 6 104, 6 140, 6 401, 6 410

Exercise 1B

1. (a) 374 (b) 211 (c) 548 (d) 609 (e) 760 (f) 125 (g) 3 715
   (h) 6 419 (i) 14 990 (j) 17 845 (k) 24 519 (l) 48 660 (m) 86 886 (n) 68 068
   (o) 92 003 (p) 212 113 (q) 318 716 (r) 608 339 (s) 580 297 (t) 600 404
2. (a) three hundred and fifty-eight (b) two hundred and seventeen
   (c) six hundred and seventy-seven (d) four hundred and sixty-nine
   (e) one hundred and eleven (f) two thousand five hundred and nineteen
   (g) six thousand and eighty-five (h) nine thousand eight hundred and one
   (i) seven thousand four hundred and forty-two (j) five thousand six hundred and thirteen
   (k) fifteen thousand seven hundred and twenty-three (l) eighteen thousand four hundred and fifty-nine
   (m) thirty-four thousand and ninety-eight (n) sixty-seven thousand one hundred and twelve
   (o) ten thousand one hundred and eleven
   (p) two hundred and thirty-one thousand two hundred and fourteen
   (q) six hundred and sixteen thousand two hundred and seventy
   (r) one hundred and nine thousand seven hundred and ten
   (s) one hundred thousand
   (t) eight hundred and fifty-seven thousand two hundred and forty-three
3. Californian Redwood: three hundred and sixty-six feet
   Douglas Fir: three hundred and two feet
   Noble Fir: two hundred and seventy-eight feet
   Giant Sequoia: two hundred and seventy-two feet
   Ponderosa Pine: two hundred and twenty-three feet
   Cedar: two hundred and nineteen feet
   Sitka Spruce: two hundred and sixteen feet
   Western Larch: one hundred and seventy-seven feet
   Hemlock: one hundred and sixty-three feet
   Beech: one hundred and sixty-one feet
   Black Cottonwood: one hundred and forty-seven feet
4. Mercury: three thousand and thirty-two miles
   Pluto: three thousand seven hundred miles
   Mars: four thousand two hundred and seventeen miles
   Venus: seven thousand five hundred and twenty-one miles
   Earth: seven thousand nine hundred and sixty-two miles
   Neptune: thirty thousand eight hundred miles
   Uranus: thirty-two thousand two hundred miles
   Saturn: seventy-four thousand six hundred miles
   Jupiter: eighty-eight thousand seven hundred miles
   Sun: eight hundred and sixty-five thousand five hundred miles

Exercise 1C

1. (a) 10 (b) 20 (c) 10 (d) 30 (e) 30 (f) 20 (g) 40
   (h) 50 (i) 50 (j) 60 (k) 50 (l) 60 (m) 80 (n) 70
   (o) 80 (p) 90 (q) 100 (r) 100 (s) 60 (t) 90
2. (a) 260 (b) 250 (c) 260 (d) 320 (e) 490 (f) 140 (g) 140
   (h) 130 (i) 800 (j) 970 (k) 310 (l) 310 (m) 300 (n) 210
   (o) 220 (p) 590 (q) 600 (r) 790 (s) 900 (t) 1 000
3. 54, 52, 65, 69
4. (a) 75, 76, 77, 78, 79, 80, 81, 82, 83, 84   (b) 125, 126, 127, 128, 129, 130, 131, 132, 133, 134
   (c) 295, 296, 297, 298, 299, 300, 301, 302, 303, 304   (d) 355, 356, 357, 358, 359, 360, 361, 362, 363, 364
   (e) 995, 996, 997, 998, 999, 1 000, 1 001, 1 002, 1 003, 1 004

Exercise 1D

1. (a) 300 (b) 600 (c) 900 (d) 500 (e) 400 (f) 500 (g) 800
   (h) 700 (i) 800 (j) 600 (k) 200 (l) 300 (m) 300 (n) 800
   (o) 700 (p) 700 (q) 500 (r) 600 (s) 900 (t) 1 000
2. (a) 1 000 (b) 1 400 (c) 1 400 (d) 1 300 (e) 1 300 (f) 1 600 (g) 3 400
   (h) 4 300 (i) 4 400 (j) 8 100 (k) 5 000 (l) 5 100 (m) 5 100 (n) 3 800
   (o) 3 900 (p) 3 000 (q) 8 000 (r) 9 000 (s) 8 900 (t) 13 000
3. 518, 549, 650, 660
4. (a) 150 to 249 (b) 450 to 549 (c) 750 to 849
   (d) 2 850 to 2 949 (e) 55 550 to 55 649
5. Greenland 840 000 square miles   New Guinea 316 900 square miles
   Borneo 287 000 square miles   Madagascar 227 000 square miles
   Baffin (Canada) 183 800 square miles Sumatra 182 900 square miles
   Honshu (Japan) 88 900 square miles   Great Britain 88 800 square miles
   Victoria (Canada) 82 100 square miles Ellesmere (Canada) 81 900 square miles

Exercise 1E

1. (a) 4 000 (b) 2 000 (c) 2 000 (d) 1 000 (e) 2 000 (f) 6 000 (g) 6 000
   (h) 6 000 (i) 5 000 (j) 8 000 (k) 8 000 (l) 6 000 (m) 3 000 (n) 8 000
   (o) 7 000 (p) 7 000 (q) 9 000 (r) 10 000 (s) 10 000 (t) 10 000
2. (a) 11 000 (b) 18 000 (c) 20 000 (d) 12 000 (e) 16 000 (f) 25 000 (g) 60 000
   (h) 24 000 (i) 32 000 (j) 22 000 (k) 45 000 (l) 26 000 (m) 501 000 (n) 235 000
   (o) 568 000 (p) 234 000 (q) 350 000 (r) 500 000 (s) 1 000 000 (t) 950 000
3. (a) 5 500 to 6 499 (b) 4 500 to 5 499
   (c) 18 500 to 19 499 (d) 54 500 to 55 499
4. Wimbledon 10 000   Southampton 15 000   Coventry 23 000   Blackburn 28 000
   Sheffield Wednesday 34 000 Middlesbrough 35 000   Newcastle 37 000   Arsenal 38 000
   Everton 39 000   Manchester United 55 000

Exercise 1F

1. 20   2. 20   3. 40   4. 40   5. 60   6. 80   7. 70
8. 90   9. 90   10. 100   11. 100   12. 200   13. 200   14. 300
15. 300   16. 400   17. 500   18. 400   19. 700   20. 700   21. 1 000
22. 2 000   23. 4 000   24. 5 000   25. 7 000   26. 8 000   27. 8 000   28. 6 000
29. 20 000   30. 10 000

Exercise 1G

1. (a) 10 (b) 8 (c) 8 (d) 15 (e) 9 (f) 11 (g) 7
   (h) 15 (i) 10 (j) 13 (k) 12 (l) 12 (m) 16 (n) 13
   (o) 10 (p) 13 (q) 18 (r) 16 (s) 17 (t) 14 (u) 10
   (v) 12 (w) 14 (x) 11 (y) 14
2. (a) 13 (b) 17 (c) 15 (d) 19 (e) 14 (f) 18 (g) 16
   (h) 20 (i) 12 (j) 15 (k) 19 (l) 17 (m) 19 (n) 17
   (o) 18 (p) 16 (q) 18 (r) 18 (s) 19 (t) 20 (u) 15
   (v) 14 (w) 13 (x) 17 (y) 14

3. (a) 30   (b) 40   (c) 50   (d) 70   (e) 80   (f) 60   (g) 50
   (h) 80   (i) 90   (j) 110 (k) 110 (l) 140 (m) 130 (n) 130
   (o) 100 (p) 110 (q) 150 (r) 170 (s) 140 (t) 130 (u) 160
   (v) 120 (w) 90   (x) 150 (y) 120
4. (a) 57   (b) 55   (c) 48   (d) 99   (e) 105 (f) 93   (g) 121
   (h) 106 (i) 158 (j) 117 (k) 87   (l) 132 (m) 136 (n) 106
   (o) 165 (p) 83   (q) 88   (r) 115 (s) 116 (t) 123 (u) 119
   (v) 187 (w) 74   (x) 111
5. (a) 31   (b) 46   (c) 29   (d) 33   (e) 69   (f) 52   (g) 47
   (h) 95   (i) 76   (j) 89   (k) 101 (l) 106 (m) 107 (n) 115
   (o) 133 (p) 138 (q) 162 (r) 124 (s) 121 (t) 198 (u) 187
   (v) 175 (w) 193 (x) 207 (y) 201
6. (a) 137 (b) 143 (c) 166 (d) 126 (e) 177 (f) 128 (g) 98
   (h) 159 (i) 148 (j) 139 (k) 139 (l) 108 (m) 60   (n) 63
   (o) 103 (p) 75   (q) 71   (r) 97   (s) 134 (t) 136 (u) 132
   (v) 164 (w) 127 (x) 198

Exercise 1H

1. (a) 29   (b) 37   (c) 78   (d) 78   (e) 100 (f) 63   (g) 73
   (h) 82   (i) 56   (j) 64   (k) 28   (l) 34   (m) 44   (n) 85
   (o) 90   (p) 82   (q) 38   (r) 34   (s) 63   (t) 75   (u) 118
   (v) 123 (w) 161 (x) 147 (y) 165
2. (a) 132p (b) 103p (c) 123p (d) 145p (e) 142p (f) 160p (g) 155p
   (h) 90p (i) 110p (j) 220p (k) 285p (l) 310p (m) 200p (n) 210p
   (o) 195p (p) 420p

3.

Saved this week	Total so far
£12	£12
£17	£29
£9	£38
£22	£60
£35	£95
£5	£100
£16	£116
£17	£133
£24	£157
£18	£175
£6	£181
£11	£192
£23	£215

4.

By end of month	Days passed
January	31
February	59
March	90
April	120
May	151
June	181
July	212
August	243
September	273
October	304
November	334
December	365

Exercise 1I

1. (a) 3   (b) 6   (c) 3   (d) 6   (e) 5   (f) 9   (g) 9
   (h) 8   (i) 6   (j) 7   (k) 5   (l) 7   (m) 2   (n) 6
   (o) 8   (p) 9   (q) 8   (r) 8   (s) 7   (t) 7   (u) 9
   (v) 6   (w) 9   (x) 6   (y) 7
2. (a) 22   (b) 42   (c) 63   (d) 82   (e) 41   (f) 40   (g) 22
   (h) 84   (i) 31   (j) 54   (k) 55   (l) 43   (m) 121 (n) 152
   (o) 183 (p) 233 (q) 60   (r) 83   (s) 80   (t) 21   (u) 44
   (v) 51   (w) 72   (x) 73   (y) 90
3. (a) 25   (b) 17   (c) 36   (d) 29   (e) 48   (f) 36   (g) 53
   (h) 12   (i) 14   (j) 45   (k) 57   (l) 47   (m) 19   (n) 17
   (o) 24   (p) 23   (q) 27   (r) 15   (s) 45   (t) 15   (u) 39
   (v) 61   (w) 16   (x) 63   (y) 38

4. (a) 33 (b) 13 (c) 52 (d) 24 (e) 33 (f) 21 (g) 41
   (h) 22 (i) 31 (j) 61 (k) 41 (l) 40 (m) 12 (n) 27
   (o) 41 (p) 20 (q) 31 (r) 11 (s) 34 (t) 46 (u) 42
   (v) 44 (w) 64 (x) 55 (y) 45
5. (a) 17 (b) 39 (c) 19 (d) 26 (e) 78 (f) 58 (g) 78
   (h) 68 (i) 47 (j) 39 (k) 29 (l) 79 (m) 27 (n) 68
   (o) 67 (p) 28 (q) 39 (r) 27 (s) 46 (t) 55 (u) 85
   (v) 55 (w) 25 (x) 74 (y) 52
6. (a) 19 (b) 59 (c) 28 (d) 69 (e) 27 (f) 28 (g) 29
   (h) 47 (i) 78 (j) 6   (k) 7   (l) 59 (m) 78 (n) 38
   (o) 35 (p) 25 (q) 29 (r) 37 (s) 67 (t) 27 (u) 25
   (v) 54 (w) 36 (x) 29 (y) 56

7.

Time passed between checks	Time left
18 mins	222 mins
25 mins	197 mins
23 mins	174 mins
31 mins	143 mins
42 mins	101 mins
17 mins	84 mins
56 mins	28 mins
28 mins	0 mins

8.

Time (mins)	Temp (°C)	Temp fall (°C)
0	176	–
5	155	21
10	138	17
15	124	14
20	112	12
25	98	14
30	96	2
35	95	1
40	81	14
45	64	17
50	43	21
55	31	12
60	29	2

Exercise 1J

1. (a) 79   (b) 99   (c) 99   (d) 97   (e) 196 (f) 687 (g) 779
   (h) 877 (i) 956 (j) 777 (k) 549 (l) 339 (m) 888 (n) 289
   (o) 938 (p) 845 (q) 398 (r) 888 (s) 799 (t) 979 (u) 899
   (v) 989 (w) 159 (x) 388 (y) 189
2. (a) 70   (b) 94   (c) 65   (d) 54   (e) 80   (f) 380 (g) 683
   (h) 860 (i) 691 (j) 225 (k) 328 (l) 507 (m) 449 (n) 510
   (o) 469 (p) 529 (q) 817 (r) 919 (s) 1 012 (t) 439 (u) 365
   (v) 876 (w) 655 (x) 439 (y) 919
3. (a) 112 (b) 122 (c) 100 (d) 120 (e) 123 (f) 205 (g) 311
   (h) 607 (i) 265 (j) 325 (k) 1 222 (l) 432 (m) 471 (n) 330
   (o) 531 (p) 731 (q) 932 (r) 901 (s) 903 (t) 920 (u) 1 245
   (v) 1 285 (w) 1 676 (x) 1 150 (y) 1 000
4. (a) 170 (b) 112 (c) 579 (d) 215 (e) 965
5. (a) £105 (b) £113 (c) £198 (d) £145 (e) £212

Exercise 1K

1. (a) 31   (b) 24   (c) 24   (d) 52   (e) 44   (f) 111 (g) 114
   (h) 222 (i) 511 (j) 322 (k) 220 (l) 122 (m) 311 (n) 336
   (o) 321 (p) 320 (q) 202 (r) 543 (s) 402 (t) 320 (u) 105
   (v) 236 (w) 542 (x) 636 (y) 111
2. (a) 317 (b) 236 (c) 158 (d) 119 (e) 108 (f) 428 (g) 333
   (h) 218 (i) 514 (j) 444 (k) 208 (l) 118 (m) 706 (n) 308
   (o) 113 (p) 145 (q) 73   (r) 571 (s) 281 (t) 50   (u) 420
   (v) 11   (w) 94   (x) 178 (y) 265

3. (a) 155 (b) 327 (c) 179 (d) 263 (e) 263 (f) 465 (g) 167
   (h) 255 (i) 169 (j) 89 (k) 275 (l) 89 (m) 137 (n) 198
   (o) 388 (p) 199 (q) 147 (r) 479 (s) 199 (t) 98 (u) 619
   (v) 178 (w) 339 (x) 329 (y) 541

4.

Runner	Time behind winner
1st	–
2nd	+8 mins
3rd	+14 mins
4th	+18 mins
5th	+20 mins
6th	+23 mins
7th	+25 mins
8th	+28 mins
9th	+31 mins
10th	+36 mins
11th	+39 mins
12th	+42 mins
13th	+46 mins
14th	+50 mins
15th	+57 mins
16th	+63 mins
17th	+70 mins
18th	+74 mins
19th	+76 mins
20th	+79 mins

Exercise 1L

1. (a) ⁻8°C, ⁻7°C, ⁻6°C, 2°C, 5°C, 7°C
   (b) ⁻7°C, ⁻3°C, ⁻2°C, ⁻1°C, 0°C, 1°C, 5°C, 6°C
   (c) 0°C, 3°C, 4°C, 4°C, 5°C, 6°C, 7°C, 8°C, 9°C, 9°C
   (d) ⁻4°C, ⁻3°C, ⁻2°C, ⁻1°C, 0°C, 1°C, 2°C, 3°C, 4°C, 5°C
   (e) ⁻50°C, ⁻40°C, ⁻30°C, ⁻20°C, ⁻10°C, 0°C, 10°C, 30°C, 40°C, 50°C
   (f) ⁻20°C, ⁻19°C, ⁻17°C, ⁻13°C, ⁻9°C, ⁻7°C, ⁻6°C, 8°C, 11°C, 11°C
   (g) ⁻73°C, ⁻56°C, ⁻29°C, ⁻17°C, ⁻16°C, 21°C, 32°C, 43°C, 65°C, 81°C
   (h) 0°C, 34°C, 39°C, 55°C, 65°C, 67°C, 76°C, 82°C, 90°C, 93°C
2. 58°C, 56·7°C, 53·1°C, 46°C, ⁻45°C, ⁻58·3°C, ⁻68°C, ⁻88·3°C

Exercise 1M

1. (a) 13°C (b) ⁻3°C (c) 3°C (d) ⁻13°C
2. (a) 5°C (b) ⁻1°C (c) 1°C (d) ⁻5°C
3. (a) 11°C (b) ⁻3°C (c) 3°C (d) ⁻11°C
4. (a) 11°C (b) 7°C (c) ⁻7°C (d) ⁻11°C
5. (a) 11°C (b) ⁻9°C (c) 9°C (d) ⁻11°C
6. (a) 11°C (b) ⁻1°C (c) 1°C (d) ⁻11°C
7. (a) 17°C (b) 5°C (c) ⁻5°C (d) ⁻17°C
8. (a) 21°C (b) 5°C (c) ⁻5°C (d) ⁻21°C
9. (a) 12°C (b) 6°C (c) ⁻6°C (d) ⁻12°C
10. (a) 20°C (b) 10°C (c) ⁻10°C (d) ⁻20°C
11. (a) 19°C (b) ⁻5°C (c) 5°C (d) ⁻19°C
12. (a) 20°C (b) 0°C (c) 0°C (d) ⁻20°C
13. (a) 14°C (b) 0°C (c) 0°C (d) ⁻14°C
14. (a) 18°C (b) 10°C (c) ⁻10°C (d) ⁻18°C

440 Answers

15.	(a)	30°C	(b)	⁻10°C	(c)	10°C	(d)	⁻30°C
16.	(a)	30°C	(b)	10°C	(c)	⁻10°C	(d)	⁻30°C
17.	(a)	27°C	(b)	9°C	(c)	⁻9°C	(d)	⁻27°C
18.	(a)	40°C	(b)	⁻10°C	(c)	10°C	(d)	⁻40°C
19.	(a)	20°C	(b)	6°C	(c)	⁻6°C	(d)	⁻20°C
20.	(a)	54°C	(b)	8°C	(c)	⁻8°C	(d)	⁻54°C

Exercise 1N

1.	(a)	9	(b)	⁻1	(c)	⁻1	(d)	1	(e)	⁻9	(f)	⁻9
2.	(a)	12	(b)	⁻2	(c)	⁻2	(d)	2	(e)	⁻12	(f)	⁻12
3.	(a)	10	(b)	6	(c)	6	(d)	⁻6	(e)	⁻10	(f)	⁻10
4.	(a)	12	(b)	⁻6	(c)	⁻6	(d)	6	(e)	⁻12	(f)	⁻12
5.	(a)	15	(b)	⁻3	(c)	⁻3	(d)	3	(e)	⁻15	(f)	⁻15
6.	(a)	16	(b)	4	(c)	4	(d)	⁻4	(e)	⁻16	(f)	⁻16
7.	(a)	8	(b)	2	(c)	2	(d)	⁻2	(e)	⁻8	(f)	⁻8
8.	(a)	7	(b)	5	(c)	5	(d)	⁻5	(e)	⁻7	(f)	⁻7
9.	(a)	17	(b)	⁻3	(c)	⁻3	(d)	3	(e)	⁻17	(f)	⁻17
10.	(a)	7	(b)	3	(c)	3	(d)	⁻3	(e)	⁻7	(f)	⁻7
11.	(a)	14	(b)	8	(c)	8	(d)	⁻8	(e)	⁻14	(f)	⁻14
12.	(a)	21	(b)	⁻7	(c)	⁻7	(d)	7	(e)	⁻21	(f)	⁻21

Exercise 1O

1.	(a)	15	(b)	5	(c)	5	(d)	15	(e)	⁻5	(f)	⁻15	(g)	⁻15	(h)	⁻5
2.	(a)	1	(b)	⁻1	(c)	1	(d)	⁻1	(e)	⁻13	(f)	13	(g)	13	(h)	⁻13
3.	(a)	⁻7	(b)	7	(c)	7	(d)	⁻1	(e)	⁻1	(f)	1	(g)	⁻7	(h)	1
4.	(a)	12	(b)	0	(c)	0	(d)	⁻12	(e)	0	(f)	⁻12	(g)	12	(h)	0
5.	(a)	12	(b)	8	(c)	8	(d)	12	(e)	⁻8	(f)	⁻12	(g)	⁻12	(h)	⁻8
6.	(a)	⁻7	(b)	7	(c)	⁻7	(d)	7	(e)	⁻9	(f)	9	(g)	9	(h)	⁻9
7.	(a)	⁻10	(b)	10	(c)	10	(d)	⁻4	(e)	⁻4	(f)	4	(g)	⁻10	(h)	4
8.	(a)	19	(b)	⁻1	(c)	1	(d)	⁻19	(e)	1	(f)	⁻19	(g)	19	(h)	⁻1
9.	(a)	13	(b)	5	(c)	5	(d)	13	(e)	⁻5	(f)	⁻13	(g)	⁻13	(h)	⁻5
10.	(a)	1	(b)	⁻1	(c)	1	(d)	⁻1	(e)	⁻3	(f)	3	(g)	3	(h)	⁻3
11.	(a)	⁻19	(b)	19	(c)	19	(d)	⁻13	(e)	⁻13	(f)	13	(g)	⁻19	(h)	13
12.	(a)	18	(b)	0	(c)	0	(d)	⁻18	(e)	0	(f)	⁻18	(g)	18	(h)	0

Exercise 1P

1.	£740	**2.**	£1 910	**3.**	£39	**4.**	£1 040	**5.**	£675	**6.**	0	**7.**	£100
8.	£17	**9.**	£200	**10.**	£370	**11.**	⁻£150	**12.**	⁻£1	**13.**	⁻£196	**14.**	⁻£100

Exercise 1Q

1. 10.30   **2.** (a) 11.45   (b) 2 hours 4 minutes   **3.** 1 hour 39 minutes   **4.** (a) 29 minutes   (b) 16.23

Checkout 1

1. (a) 70   (b) 800
2. (a) 3 994   (b) seven thousand eight hundred and forty-three
3. (a) (i) 80   (ii) 100   (iii) 230
   (b) (i) 700   (ii) 400   (iii) 2 500
   (c) (i) 4 000   (ii) 23 000   (iii) 45 000
4. (a) 40   (b) 40   (c) 300   (d) 600   (e) 2 000   (f) 2 000
5. (a) 14   (b) 17   (c) 110   (d) 95   (e) 56   (f) 62   (g) 38
   (h) 62   (i) 6   (j) 43   (k) 15   (l) 41   (m) 28   (n) 17
6. (a) 658   (b) 397   (c) 123   (d) 1 000   (e) 32
   (f) 311   (g) 317   (h) 571   (i) 275   (j) 199
7. ⁻4°C, ⁻3°C, ⁻2°C, ⁻1°C, 0°C, 1°C, 2°C, 3°C, 4°C, 7°C
8. (a) 23°C   (b) 7°C   (c) ⁻7°C   (d) ⁻23°C
9. (a) 17   (b) ⁻5   (c) ⁻5   (d) 5   (e) ⁻17   (f) ⁻17
10. (a) ⁻10   (b) 10   (c) 10   (d) ⁻4
   (e) ⁻4   (f) 4   (g) ⁻10   (h) 4

Revision exercise 1

1. (a) 6 tens (60) (b) seven thousands (7 000)
   (c) four hundred and sixty thousand five hundred
2. 2 014
3. 7, 23, 36, 39, 46, 49
4. (a) eight hundred and seven (b) 100 057 (c) 483, 712, 2 104, 2 901, 5 342
5. (a) (i) 941 (ii) 149 (b) 0 to make 6 190
6. (a) 5 607 (b) 2 370
7. 36 100
8. (a) thirty thousand five hundred and twenty (b) (i) 30 500 (ii) 31 000
9. England's score was higher by 6 runs.
10.

Input	Output
6	2
9	5
18	14
33	29

11. 147 cm
12. (a) three thousand and ten metres (b) 205 m
13. York, Leeds, Newcastle, Scarborough, Hull, York or York, Hull, Scarborough, Newcastle, Leeds, York.
14. (a) Thursday (b) Tuesday
15. (a) 9 feet (b) ⁻4, ⁻2, ⁻1, 0, 1, 5
16. (a) 10°C (b) ⁻19°C
17. 3 454 m
18. 25°C
19. (a) Bournemouth (b) Aviemore (c) 13°C (d) 14°C

2 Shape and space 1

Check in 2

1. (a) $\frac{3}{8}$ (b) $\frac{5}{8}$ (c) $\frac{1}{4}$ (d) $\frac{7}{8}$
2. (a) clockwise (b) anticlockwise (c) anticlockwise (d) clockwise

Exercise 2A

1. (a) $\frac{1}{2}$ turn (b) $\frac{1}{2}$ turn (c) $\frac{1}{4}$ turn (d) $\frac{1}{4}$ turn (e) $\frac{1}{2}$ turn (f) $\frac{1}{8}$ turn (g) $\frac{3}{8}$ turn (h) $\frac{3}{4}$ turn
   (i) $\frac{3}{4}$ turn (j) $\frac{3}{4}$ turn (k) $\frac{1}{8}$ turn (l) $\frac{3}{8}$ turn (m) $\frac{7}{8}$ turn (n) $\frac{5}{8}$ turn (o) $\frac{3}{4}$ turn (p) $\frac{5}{8}$ turn
2. (a) $\frac{1}{2}$ turn (b) $\frac{1}{2}$ turn (c) $\frac{3}{4}$ turn (d) $\frac{3}{4}$ turn (e) $\frac{1}{2}$ turn (f) $\frac{7}{8}$ turn (g) $\frac{5}{8}$ turn (h) $\frac{1}{4}$ turn
   (i) $\frac{1}{4}$ turn (j) $\frac{1}{4}$ turn (k) $\frac{7}{8}$ turn (l) $\frac{5}{8}$ turn (m) $\frac{1}{8}$ turn (n) $\frac{3}{8}$ turn (o) $\frac{1}{4}$ turn (p) $\frac{3}{8}$ turn

Exercise 2B

1. (a) 90° (b) 90° (c) 180° (d) 270° (e) 180° (f) 90° (g) 270° (h) 180°
   (i) 270° (j) 90° (k) 180° (l) 270° (m) 45° (n) 45° (o) 45° (p) 45°
2. (a) 270° (b) 270° (c) 180° (d) 90° (e) 180° (f) 270° (g) 90° (h) 180
   (i) 90° (j) 270° (k) 180° (l) 90° (m) 315° (n) 315° (o) 315° (p) 315°

Exercise 2C

1. A 20° B 70° C 170° D 120° E 105° F 35° G 135°
   H 155° I 94° J 58° K 141° L 87°
2. A 30° B 80° C 160° D 100° E 115° F 5° G 145°
   H 55° I 62° J 139° K 146° L 153°

Exercise 2D

1. a 30° acute b 50° acute c 80° acute d 160° obtuse e 120° obtuse
   f 35° acute g 75° acute h 135° obtuse i 95° obtuse j 48° acute
   k 20° acute l 70° acute m 110° obtuse n 150° obtuse o 25° acute
   p 45° acute q 145° obtuse r 62° acute s 88° acute t 162° obtuse

Exercise 2F

1. Angle x can be called angle RQP or angle PQR. Angle y can be called angle QPR or angle RPQ. Angle z can be called angle PRQ or angle QRP.
2. Angle x can be called angle GEF or angle FEG. Angle y can be called angle EFG or angle GFE. Angle z can be called angle EGF or angle FGE.
3. Angle x can be called angle ACB or angle BCA. Angle y can be called angle BAC or angle CAB. Angle z can be called angle ABC or angle CBA.
4. Angle x can be called angle RTS or angle STR. Angle y can be called angle SRT or angle TRS. Angle z can be called angle RST or angle TSR.
5. Angle x can be called angle JKL or angle LKJ. Angle y can be called angle KJL or angle LJK. Angle z can be called angle JLK or angle KLJ.
6. Angle x can be called angle MON or angle NOM. Angle y can be called angle OMN or angle NMO. Angle z can be called angle MNO or angle ONM.

Exercise 2H

1. (c) 86 m   2. (b) 5·4 m   4. (b) 35 m   5. (b) 43 km   6. (b) 45 km   8. (c) 34 km

Exercise 2I

7. (b) 045°   8. (d) 163°

Checkout 2

1. (a) $\frac{3}{4}$ turn   (b) $\frac{5}{8}$ turn
2. (a) 45°   (b) 270°
3. (a) acute   (b) obtuse
4. A 60°   B 130°
6. Angle x can be called angle BAC or angle CAB. Angle y can be called angle ABC or angle CBA. Angle z can be called angle ACB and or BCA.
8. (b) 120 m

Revision exercise 2

1. (a) West   (b) NW
2. (a) Garage   (b) (i) East   (ii) SW   (iii) SE
3. (a) $x = 39°, y = 105°$ (b) 9 cm
4. 145°
7. (b) 8 km   (c) 136°
8. (a) Cardiff   (b) NE   (c) 305°

3 Data handling 1

Check in 3

1. (a) 3   (b) 8   (c) 16   (d) 13
2. (a) |||| |||| |||| (b) |||| | (c) |||| |||| |||| |||| | (d) |||| |||| |||| ||

Exercise 3A

1. Suitable questions might be:
   Tick one box for your gender.
   ☐ Boy   ☐ Girl
   Tick one box for your year group.
   ☐ 7 ☐ 8   ☐ 9   ☐ 10   ☐ 11   ☐ Sixth Form
   Do you consider your health before deciding what to eat for lunch?
   ☐ Yes   ☐ No
2. Suitable questions might be:
   Tick one box for your gender.
   ☐ Male   ☐ Female
   Tick one box for your age.
   ☐ 21–30   ☐ 31–40   ☐ 41–50   ☐ 51–60   ☐ over 60
   Tick one box for the number of hours of television you watch during an average day.
   ☐ less than 1   ☐ 1 to 2   ☐ 2 to 3   ☐ 3 to 4   ☐ 4 to 5   ☐ more than 5

4. Suitable questions might be:
   Do you smoke cigarettes?
   ☐ Yes   ☐ No
   If you do smoke, how many cigarettes do you smoke each day?
   ☐ 1 to 5   ☐ 6 to 10   ☐ 11 to 15   ☐ 16 to 20   ☐ more than 20
   Tick one box in each line.
   Does your mother smoke?   ☐ Yes   ☐ No
   Does your father smoke?   ☐ Yes   ☐ No

Exercise 3B

1. (a)

Number of eggs	Tally	Frequency
0							5
1				2
2								6
3						4
4								6
5				2

   (b) bars with heights: 5, 2, 6, 4, 6, 2

2. (a)

Girls	Tally	Frequency
Yes	||||| ||||| ||	12
No	||||| |||	8

Boys	Tally	Frequency
Yes	||||| ||||	9
No	||||| |||||		11

   (b) Girls: bars with heights 12 and 8.   Boys: bars with heights 8 and 11.

3. (a)

Type of sausage	Tally	Frequency
Porkers	||||| ||||	9
Sizzlers	|||	3
Yumbos	||||| ||	7
Bangers	||||| |||||		11

   (b) bars with heights 9, 3, 7 and 11.

4. (a)

Score (Kathy)	Tally	Frequency
1				2
2				2
3				2
4										8
5							5
6								6

Score (Kyle)	Tally	Frequency
1				2
2				2
3						4
4									7
5								6
6						4

   (b) Kathy: bars with heights 2, 2, 2, 8, 5 and 6.   Kyle: bars with heights 2, 2, 4, 7, 6 and 4.

5. (a)

Number of hours watched (Men)	Tally	Frequency
less than one hour	||||	4
one to two hours	||	2
two to three hours	||||| |||	8
three to four hours	||||	4
more than four hours	||	2

Number of hours watched (Women)	Tally	Frequency
less than one hour	|||	3
one to two hours	||||	4
two to three hours	||||| ||	7
three to four hours	||||	4
more than four hours	||	2

   (b) Men: bars with heights 4, 2, 8, 4, 2.   Women: bars with heights 3, 4, 7, 4, 2.

Checkout 3

1. Possible questions might be:
   How long does it take you to travel to this supermarket?
   ☐ less than 5 minutes ☐ 5 to 10 minutes ☐ 10 to 15 minutes
   ☐ 15 to 20 minutes ☐ more than 20 minutes
   How often do you visit this supermarket?
   ☐ once a day ☐ twice a week ☐ once a week
   ☐ once every two weeks ☐ once a month ☐ less than once a month
   How much do you spend each time you visit this supermarket?
   ☐ less than £10 ☐ between £10 and £20 ☐ between £20 and £50
   ☐ between £50 and £100 ☐ more than £100

2. (a)

Colour of car	Tally	Frequency
white	ⵏⵏⵏ ⵏⵏⵏ	10
blue	ⵏⵏⵏ	5
red	ⵏⵏⵏ IIII	9
green	ⵏⵏⵏ I	6

(b) bars with heights 10, 5, 9, 6.

Revision exercise 3

4.

Number of books	Frequency
0 to 2	11
3 to 5	15
6 to 8	13
more than 8	6

5. (a) Saturday
   (b) 17 hours
6. (a) Friday
   (b) more people shopped on Sundays
   (c) true
7. bars with heights 14, 17, 8, 9, 6.
8. (a) bars with heights 40, 40, 20, 15, 35, 50.
   (c) pictogram showing 60, 80, 50, 35
10. (a) 80 (b) 50
11. (a) 450 (c) pictogram showing 500, 450, 200, 400, 300

4 Number 2

Check in 4

1. (a) 6 (b) 60 (c) 600 (d) 7 000 (e) 700 (f) 70 (g) 40
   (h) 400 (i) 4 000 (j) 10

Exercise 4A

1. (a) 60 (b) 70 (c) 110 (d) 230 (e) 320 (f) 450 (g) 800
   (h) 610 (i) 560 (j) 980 (k) 1 120 (l) 1 720 (m) 4 510 (n) 3 900
   (o) 9 160 (p) 2 060 (q) 1 010 (r) 9 030 (s) 7 000 (t) 3 410
2. (a) 80 (b) 240 (c) 330 (d) 720 (e) 1 000 (f) 1 440
3. (a) 50 (b) 130 (c) 220 (d) 350 (e) 700 (f) 1 000

Exercise 4B

1. (a) 600 (b) 700 (c) 1 100 (d) 2 300 (e) 3 200 (f) 4 500 (g) 8 000
   (h) 6 100 (i) 5 600 (j) 9 800 (k) 11 200 (l) 17 200 (m) 45 100 (n) 39 000
   (o) 91 600 (p) 20 600 (q) 10 100 (r) 90 300 (s) 70 000 (t) 34 100
2. (a) 300 (b) 900 (c) 2 000 (d) 4 500 (e) 60 000 (f) 49 900
3. (a) 200 (b) 3 800 (c) 2 700 (d) 8 000 (e) 7 600 (f) 10 000

Exercise 4C

1. (a) 6 000 (b) 7 000 (c) 11 000 (d) 23 000 (e) 32 000 (f) 45 000 (g) 80 000
   (h) 61 000 (i) 56 000 (j) 98 000 (k) 112 000 (l) 172 000 (m) 451 000 (n) 390 000
   (o) 916 000 (p) 206 000 (q) 101 000 (r) 903 000 (s) 700 000 (t) 341 000
2. (a) 4 000 (b) 19 000 (c) 27 000 (d) 83 000 (e) 100 000 (f) 153 000
3. (a) 5 000 (b) 13 000 (c) 22 000 (d) 35 000 (e) 70 000 (f) 100 000

Exercise 4D

1. (a) 7 (b) 8 (c) 12 (d) 32 (e) 21 (f) 61 (g) 80
   (h) 51 (i) 65 (j) 89 (k) 125 (l) 127 (m) 451 (n) 290
   (o) 903 (p) 120 (q) 303 (r) 200 (s) 500 (t) 410
2. (a) £1 (b) £90 (c) £1 000 (d) £4 500 (e) £26 780 (f) £187 834
3. (a) 6 centimetres (b) 17 centimetres (c) 23 centimetres
   (d) 30 centimetres (e) 50 centimetres (f) 75 centimetres

Exercise 4E

1. (a) 7 (b) 6 (c) 12 (d) 13 (e) 25 (f) 26 (g) 8
   (h) 31 (i) 75 (j) 18 (k) 12 (l) 127 (m) 87 (n) 29
   (o) 193 (p) 128 (q) 133 (r) 200 (s) 550 (t) 2 419
2. (a) 3 metres (b) 9 metres (c) 6 metres
   (d) 45 metres (e) 78 metres (f) 67 metres
3. (a) £2 (b) £4 (c) £10 (d) £30 (e) £25 (f) £87
4. (a) 466p (b) 580p (c) 166p (d) 477p (e) 584p (f) 294p (g) 191p
   (h) 36p (i) 306p (j) 382p (k) 362p (l) 14p

Exercise 4F

1. (a) 7 (b) 4 (c) 12 (d) 32 (e) 21 (f) 49 (g) 18
   (h) 512 (i) 165 (j) 890 (k) 125 (l) 270 (m) 1 450 (n) 2 900
   (o) 5 030 (p) 6 200 (q) 3 435 (r) 52 430 (s) 5 367 (t) 41 321
2. (a) 1 litre (b) 9 litres (c) 10 litres
   (d) 5 litres (e) 27 litres (f) 78 litres
3. (a) 6 kilometres (b) 8 kilometres (c) 10 kilometres
   (d) 31 kilometres (e) 55 kilometres (f) 170 kilometres

Exercise 4G

1. (a) 6 (b) 12 (c) 20 (d) 12 (e) 9 (f) 16 (g) 15
   (h) 10 (i) 24 (j) 21 (k) 16 (l) 30 (m) 28 (n) 24
   (o) 40 (p) 32 (q) 14 (r) 8 (s) 30 (t) 20 (u) 40
   (v) 45 (w) 18 (x) 4 (y) 50
2. (a) 45 (b) 49 (c) 36 (d) 54 (e) 80 (f) 63 (g) 64
   (h) 81 (i) 70 (j) 100 (k) 48 (l) 72 (m) 90 (n) 63
   (o) 72 (p) 60 (q) 56 (r) 42 (s) 18 (t) 27 (u) 35
   (v) 36 (w) 56 (x) 42 (y) 25
3. (a) 150 (b) 160 (c) 180 (d) 200 (e) 180 (f) 240 (g) 270
   (h) 360 (i) 210 (j) 250 (k) 180 (l) 480 (m) 300 (n) 320
   (o) 400 (p) 120 (q) 240 (r) 240 (s) 350 (t) 490 (u) 540
   (v) 160 (w) 90 (x) 80
4. (a) 3 600 (b) 3 000 (c) 3 600 (d) 4 500 (e) 4 200 (f) 1 400 (g) 1 200
   (h) 1 500 (i) 2 100 (j) 1 800 (k) 1 000 (l) 2 700 (m) 2 800 (n) 4 800
   (o) 3 200 (p) 5 400 (q) 3 600 (r) 3 500 (s) 6 300 (t) 6 400 (u) 7 200
   (v) 8 100 (w) 5 600 (x) 4 200 (y) 1 800
5. (a) 27 000 (b) 24 000 (c) 20 000 (d) 18 000 (e) 8 000 (f) 35 000 (g) 36 000
   (h) 49 000 (i) 32 000 (j) 45 000 (k) 25 000 (l) 36 000 (m) 56 000 (n) 35 000
   (o) 54 000 (p) 9 000 (q) 16 000 (r) 10 000 (s) 63 000 (t) 42 000 (u) 40 000
   (v) 12 000 (w) 64 000 (x) 56 000 (y) 72 000
6. (a) 1 200 (b) 1 600 (c) 3 000 (d) 2 800 (e) 2 400 (f) 1 200 (g) 1 800
   (h) 1 800 (i) 800 (j) 1 400 (k) 3 000 (l) 2 800 (m) 4 200 (n) 4 000
   (o) 4 800 (p) 21 000 (q) 6 000 (r) 24 000 (s) 48 000 (t) 63 000 (u) 20 000
   (v) 15 000 (w) 36 000 (x) 36 000 (y) 72 000

Exercise 4H

1. (a) 60 (b) 42 (c) 78 (d) 32 (e) 51 (f) 56 (g) 96
   (h) 72 (i) 64 (j) 75 (k) 100 (l) 120 (m) 156 (n) 54
   (o) 280 (p) 112 (q) 279 (r) 336 (s) 294 (t) 264 (u) 216
   (v) 234 (w) 602 (x) 330 (y) 315
2. (a) £108 (b) £180 (c) £207 (d) £270 (e) £324

446 Answers

3. (a) 600 kg (b) 800 kg (c) 14 000 kg (d) 2 400 kg (e) 5 600 kg
4. (a) £80 (b) £96 (c) £160 (d) £216 (e) £408

Exercise 4I

1. (a) 7 (b) 4 (c) 6 (d) 9 (e) 7 (f) 3 (g) 3
   (h) 2 (i) 4 (j) 9 (k) 10 (l) 7 (m) 7 (n) 9
   (o) 5 (p) 9 (q) 6 (r) 6 (s) 6 (t) 7 (u) 7
   (v) 8 (w) 6 (x) 5 (y) 9
2. (a) 5 r 1 (b) 4 r 2 (c) 5 r 3 (d) 4 r 1 (e) 5 r 3 (f) 5 r 1 (g) 5 r 3
   (h) 2 r 5 (i) 1 r 6 (j) 1 r 2 (k) 10 r 1 (l) 8 r 2 (m) 8 r 2 (n) 8 r 3
   (o) 4 r 5 (p) 9 r 2 (q) 3 r 4 (r) 8 r 1 (s) 9 r 3 (t) 6 r 2 (u) 4 r 6
   (v) 9 r 3 (w) 9 r 3 (x) 8 r 3 (y) 10 r 8
3. (a) 9 (b) 10 (c) 8 (d) 10 (e) 11
4. (a) 4 (b) 6 (c) 6 (d) 9 (e) 10

Exercise 4J

1. (a) 8 (b) 2 (c) 6 (d) 4 (e) 3 (f) 10 (g) 2
   (h) 3 (i) 8 (j) 5 (k) 5 (l) 2 (m) 6 (n) 7
   (o) 5 (p) 4 (q) 5 (r) 9 (s) 7 (t) 3 (u) 2
   (v) 5 (w) 7 (x) 8 (y) 6
2. (a) 2 (b) 3 (c) 6 (d) 5 (e) 4 (f) 9 (g) 2
   (h) 3 (i) 4 (j) 8 (k) 8 (l) 6 (m) 8 (n) 3
   (o) 4 (p) 7 (q) 7 (r) 3 (s) 7 (t) 9 (u) 9
   (v) 6 (w) 9 (x) 6
3. (a) 5 (b) 4 (c) 6 (d) 9 (e) 2 (f) 4 (g) 8
   (h) 8 (i) 6 (j) 3 (k) 8 (l) 7 (m) 2 (n) 9
   (o) 7 (p) 5 (q) 6 (r) 4 (s) 9 (t) 5 (u) 6
4. (a) 30 (b) 60 (c) 70 (d) 120 (e) 40 (f) 80 (g) 600
   (h) 700 (i) 400 (j) 400 (k) 500 (l) 500 (m) 400 (n) 700
   (o) 900 (p) 400 (q) 6 000 (r) 600 (s) 7 000 (t) 50 (u) 90
   (v) 90 (w) 80 (x) 600 (y) 8 000

Exercise 4K

1. (a) 468 (b) 696 (c) 8 048 (d) 69 (e) 8 604 (f) 225 (g) 144
   (h) 310 (i) 141 (j) 336 (k) 512 (l) 235 (m) 588 (n) 783
   (o) 344 (p) 726 (q) 1 705 (r) 1 242 (s) 924 (t) 4 581 (u) 2 070
   (v) 4 504 (w) 3 282 (x) 2 916 (y) 5 192
2. (a) 1 300 (b) 2 040 (c) 1 800 (d) 2 280 (e) 1 760 (f) 2 880 (g) 2 010
   (h) 3 650 (i) 7 040 (j) 1 560 (k) 2 240 (l) 3 180 (m) 4 270 (n) 7 470
   (o) 2 800 (p) 1 710 (q) 9 240 (r) 28 350 (s) 20 640 (t) 18 180 (u) 18 600
   (v) 32 200 (w) 20 790 (x) 62 720 (y) 41 130
3. (a) 84 (b) 161 (c) 280 (d) 266 (e) 364
4. (a) £1 530 (b) £2 070 (c) £3 420 (d) £6 480 (e) £8 820

Exercise 4L

1. (a) 884 (b) 2 880 (c) 1 272 (d) 1 504 (e) 2 408 (f) 1 932 (g) 1 288
   (h) 2 268 (i) 1 044 (j) 3 230 (k) 1 357 (l) 1 672 (m) 1 904 (n) 4 675
   (o) 3 042 (p) 2 025 (q) 2 916 (r) 4 992 (s) 5 568 (t) 2 295 (u) 2 613
   (v) 2 052 (w) 4 930 (x) 7 200 (y) 3 770
2. (a) 9 594 (b) 12 386 (c) 39 831 (d) 27 315 (e) 26 280 (f) 14 835 (g) 14 944
   (h) 47 806 (i) 35 478 (j) 39 566 (k) 60 265 (l) 41 440 (m) 23 785 (n) 49 610
   (o) 23 592 (p) 59 508 (q) 30 282 (r) 19 125 (s) 27 775 (t) 49 166 (u) 48 068
   (v) 27 824 (w) 65 100 (x) 82 302 (y) 53 976
3. (a) £1 476 (b) £1 722 (c) £2 091 (d) £2 583 (e) £3 198
4. (a) 2 025 kg (b) 3 600 kg (c) 6 480 kg (d) 26 370 kg (e) 38 475 kg

Exercise 4M

1. (a) 51 (b) 72 (c) 46 (d) 52 (e) 57 (f) 73 (g) 88
   (h) 58 (i) 40 (j) 24 (k) 94 (l) 99 (m) 42 (n) 76
   (o) 44 (p) 87 (q) 87 (r) 96 (s) 65 (t) 25 (u) 29
   (v) 82 (w) 77 (x) 65 (y) 64
2. (a) 68 r 1 (b) 66 r 2 (c) 30 r 4 (d) 29 r 3 (e) 61 r 1 (f) 17 r 1 (g) 39 r 1
   (h) 28 r 2 (i) 17 r 5 (j) 19 r 5 (k) 15 r 5 (l) 18 r 3 (m) 20 r 5 (n) 32 r 3
   (o) 23 r 3 (p) 50 r 2 (q) 97 r 1 (r) 92 r 1 (s) 39 r 2 (t) 80 r 2 (u) 55 r 5
   (v) 41 r 2 (w) 46 r 2 (x) 60 r 3 (y) 46 r 7
3. (a) 13 (b) 18 (c) 25 (d) 43 (e) 52
4. (a) 45 boxes, 1 left over (b) 73 boxes, 2 left over (c) 50 boxes, 5 left over
   (d) 79 boxes, 1 left over (e) 83 boxes, 4 left over

Exercise 4N

1. (a) 15 (b) 26 (c) 15 (d) 24 (e) 64 (f) 25 (g) 16
   (h) 15 (i) 16 (j) 42 (k) 22 (l) 32 (m) 20 (n) 15
   (o) 26 (p) 21 (q) 24 (r) 15 (s) 14 (t) 22 (u) 23
   (v) 12 (w) 21 (x) 25 (y) 13
2. (a) 11 r 3 (b) 14 r 5 (c) 15 r 5 (d) 22 r 6 (e) 17 r 1 (f) 12 r 2 (g) 24 r 5
   (h) 22 r 3 (i) 16 r 1 (j) 20 r 5 (k) 16 r 16 (l) 17 r 5 (m) 15 r 5 (n) 22 r 10
   (o) 31 r 11 (p) 12 r 6 (q) 16 r 9 (r) 40 r 3 (s) 30 r 10 (t) 41 r 5 (u) 21 r 8
   (v) 23 r 20 (w) 32 r 18 (x) 43 r 10 (y) 14 r 31
3. (a) 32 (b) 33 (c) 41 (d) 73 (e) 81
4. (a) 2 bars, 2p change (b) 5 bars, 5p change (c) 6 bars, 48p change
   (d) 9 bars, 9p change (e) 16 bars, 6p change

Exercise 4O

1. (a) 1, 2, 4, 8 (b) 1, 2, 3, 6, 18, 9 (c) 1, 2, 5, 10
   (d) 1, 2, 3, 4, 6, 12 (e) 1, 3, 9, 27 (f) 1, 2, 4, 7, 14, 28
   (g) 1, 23 (h) 1, 2, 3, 4, 6, 9, 12, 18, 36 (i) 1, 5, 7, 35
   (j) 1, 31 (k) 1, 2, 4, 5, 8, 10, 20, 40 (l) 1, 2, 3, 4, 6, 8, 12, 16, 24, 48
   (m) 1, 2, 5, 10, 25, 50 (n) 1, 3, 17, 51 (o) 1, 2, 4, 8, 16, 32, 64
2. (a) 16, 18, 20, 22, 24 (b) 24, 26, 28, 30, 32 (c) 38, 40, 42, 44, 46
   (d) 110, 112, 114, 116, 118 (e) 202, 204, 206, 208, 210
3. (a) 19, 21, 23, 25, 27 (b) 23, 25, 27, 29, 31 (c) 55, 57, 59, 61, 63
   (d) 73, 75, 77, 79, 81 (e) 313, 315, 317, 319, 321
4. (a) 3 is a factor (b) 3 is a factor
   (c) 2, 3, 5, 7, 11, 13, 17, 19, 23, 29, 31, 37, 41, 43, 47
5. (a) 4, 8, 12, 16, 20, 24 (b) 5, 10, 15, 20, 25, 30 (c) 6, 12, 18, 24, 30, 36
   (d) 7, 14, 21, 28, 35, 42 (e) 8, 16, 24, 32, 40, 48 (f) 10, 20, 30, 40, 50, 60
   (g) 12, 24, 36, 48, 60, 72 (h) 15, 30, 45, 60, 75, 90 (i) 20, 40, 60, 80, 100, 120
   (j) 50, 100, 150, 200, 250, 300
6. (a) 18 (b) 9 (c) 15 (d) 12 (e) 17
7. (a) 14 (b) 5 (c) 9 (d) 1 (e) 2
8. (a) 24 (b) 25 (c) 20 (d) 3 (e) 11
9. (a) 1, 5 (b) 1, 7 (c) 1, 2, 3, 4, 6, 12
   (d) 1, 2, 3, 6 (e) 1, 5 (f) 1, 2, 4, 8

Exercise 4P

1. (a) 8 (b) 25 (c) 9 (d) 7 (e) 15 (f) 11 (g) 12
   (h) 10 (i) 50 (j) 30 (k) 22 (l) 72
2. (a) 12 (b) 15 (c) 7 (d) 13 (e) 14 (f) 1 (g) 25
   (h) 1 (i) 14 (j) 6 (k) 4 (l) 36

Exercise 4Q

1. (a) 30 (b) 60 (c) 210 (d) 140 (e) 315 (f) 70 (g) 210
   (h) 30 (i) 40
2. (a) 120 (b) 126 (c) 168 (d) 280 (e) 168 (f) 315 (g) 770
   (h) 90 (i) 120

Exercise 4R

1. (a) 3:1   (b) 3:4   (c) 5:3   (d) 5:4   (e) 7:8   (f) 7:3
2. (a) 1:5   (b) 2:3   (c) 1:7   (d) 3:5   (e) 1:9   (f) 2:7   (g) 3:10
   (h) 1:3   (i) 5:7   (j) 4:5   (k) 1:6   (l) 5:9   (m) 6:7   (n) 3:8
   (o) 2:5   (p) 1:4   (q) 2:9   (r) 3:4   (s) 3:5   (t) 4:7   (u) 1:4:6
   (v) 5:6:7   (w) 5:8:2   (x) 7:8:5   (y) 2:3:4
3. (a) 1:4   (b) 2:5   (c) 4:5   (d) 1:20   (e) 9:20   (f) 8:25   (g) 9:50
   (h) 3:4   (i) 33:50   (j) 99:100
4. (a) 1:2   (b) 13:20   (c) 2:3   (d) 1:2   (e) 2:3   (f) 2:5   (g) 3:4
   (h) 3:7   (i) 1:5   (j) 2:5
5. 1:4   6. 1:7   7. 1:2   8. 3:5   9. 4:5   10. 20:17

Exercise 4S

1. (a) 400 g, 300 g, 320 g   (b) 600 g, 450 g, 480 g   (c) 800 g, 600 g, 640 g
   (d) 100 g, 75 g, 80 g   (e) 300 g, 225 g, 240 g
2. (a) 6 litres, 4 litres   (b) 12 litres, 8 litres   (c) 15 litres, 10 litres
   (d) 30 litres, 20 litres   (e) 21 litres, 14 litres
3. (a) 200   (b) 240   (c) 100   (d) 380   (e) 268
4. (a) £24   (b) £48   (c) £36   (d) £2·40   (e) £7·20
5. (a) 240 miles   (b) 360 miles   (c) 6 miles   (d) 90 miles   (e) 72 miles
6. (a) 24 cm   (b) 36 cm   (c) 18 cm   (d) 0·5 cm   (e) 5 cm
7. (a) 1 600   (b) 2 400   (c) 160   (d) 480   (e) 2 240
8. (a) 16, 24, 800 g   (b) 24, 36, 1 200 g   (c) 2, 3, 100 g
   (d) 6, 9, 300 g   (e) 14, 21, 700 g
9. (a) 32, 1 600 g   (b) 2, 100 g   (c) 4, 200 g
   (d) 16, 800 g   (e) 12, 600 g
10. (a) £96, £24   (b) £8, £2   (c) £24, £6   (d) £48, £12   (e) £72, £18

Exercise 4T

1. (a) 3, 21   (b) 9, 15   (c) 18, 6   (d) 4, 20   (e) 10, 14
2. (a) 48, 24   (b) 18, 54   (c) 45, 27   (d) 56, 16   (e) 32, 40
3. (a) 63, 7   (b) 42, 28   (c) 10, 60   (d) 30, 40   (e) 21, 49
4. (a) 80, 40   (b) 72, 48   (c) 20, 100   (d) 84, 36   (e) 108, 12
5. (a) 88, 11   (b) 77, 22   (c) 90, 9   (d) 45, 54   (e) 33, 66
6. (a) 35, 7   (b) 36, 6   (c) 31·5, 10·5   (d) 30, 12   (e) 24, 18
7. (a) 112, 16   (b) 40, 88   (c) 60, 68   (d) 48, 80   (e) 62, 66
8. (a) 5, 10, 25   (b) 8, 16, 16   (c) 8, 12, 20   (d) 4, 8, 28   (e) 10, 10, 20
9. (a) 72, 120, 168   (b) 40, 140, 180   (c) 40, 120, 200
   (d) 300, 45, 15   (e) 72, 90, 198
10. (a) 84, 210, 336   (b) 35, 280, 315   (c) 30, 60, 540
    (d) 147, 168, 315   (e) 270, 216, 144
11. 48 g   12. £200, £250   13. £9
14. 600 g, 150 g, 150 g   15. 150 litres, 90 litres, 60 litres

Exercise 4U

1. (a) 5   (b) 3   (c) 9   (d) 7   (e) 10
2. (a) 17   (b) 43   (c) 284
3. 22

Checkout 4

1. (a) 230   (b) 360
2. (a) 1 700   (b) 3 000
3. (a) 7 000   (b) 49 000
4. (a) 5   (b) 56
5. (a) 4   (b) 35
6. (a) 3   (b) 78
7. (a) 42   (b) 72   (c) 200   (d) 63 000
   (e) 115   (f) 336   (g) 6   (h) 7

8. (a) 5 r 1 (b) 9 r 2 (c) 8 (d) 9 (e) 750 (f) 900
   (g) 1 185 (h) 41 454 (i) 125 (j) 81 r 2 (k) 27 (l) 45 r 6
9. (a) 1, 2, 4, 8, 16, 32 (b) 1, 2, 3, 4, 5, 6, 10, 12, 15, 20, 30, 60
10. (a) 44, 46, 48, 50, 52 (b) 266, 268, 270, 272, 274
11. (a) 53, 55, 57, 59, 61 (b) 379, 381, 383, 385, 387
12. 7, 2, 23, 31, 37, 53
13. (a) 4, 8, 12, 16, 20 (b) 12, 24, 36, 48, 60
14. (a) 1 : 4 (b) 5 : 4 : 3
15. 14 litres
16. (a) £4, £20 (b) £10, £12, £2

Revision exercise 4

1. (a) 40 (b) 5 000 (c) 60
2. (a) (i) 4 (ii) 8 (b) (i) 600 (ii) 6 000
3. (a) 1 600 m (b) 1·6 km
4. 5   5. £21·94
6. (a) £7 488 (b) £2 488
7. (a) (i) 5 (ii) £102·44 (b) 44 mph
8. $34 \times 8 = 272$, $68 \times 4 = 272$, $136 \times 2 = 272$ 9. £7·44
10. (a) 12, 20, 24, 30, 100 (b) 20, 30, 100 (c) 24
11. 1, 24 or 2, 12 or 3, 8 or 4, 6   12. £14
13. 21 packs, 19 left
14. (a) 32 (b) 6 894 g
15. (a) 5 km per hour (b) 8 hours 45 minutes
16. (a) 15 (b) 25p
17. (a) 6 (b) 4
18. (a) 1, 2, 3, 6, 9, 18 (b) 2, 3
19. 17, 19
20. (a) 26 and 74 (b) 23 and 73 (c) $73 \times 74 = 5\,402$
    (d) 56 (e) 23 or 73
21. (a) 35 g (b) 14 g
22. £76·80
23. (a) 875 g (b) 375 g, brown rice, 750 g carrots, juice of $1\frac{1}{2}$ oranges, 3 tablespoons olive oil, 150 g walnuts

5 Algebra 1

Check in 5

1. 11   2. 5   3. $^-5$ 4. $^-11$ 5. 5   6. $^-11$ 7. 11   8. $^-5$
9. 18   10. $^-4$ 11. 4   12. $^-18$ 13. $^-4$ 14. $^-18$ 15. 18   16. 4
17. 10   18. 0   19. 0   20. $^-10$ 21. 0   22. $^-10$ 23. 10   24. 0

Exercise 5A

1. (a) $m - 15$ (b) $m + 2$ (c) $m - 6$ (d) $m + 8$ (e) $m + 1$ (f) $m - 10$
2. (a) $y + 2$ (b) $y - 4$ (c) $y + 7$ (d) $y + 1$ (e) $y - 9$ (f) $y - 2$
3. (a) $h + 15$ (b) $h - 12$ (c) $h + 10$ (d) $h - 4$ (e) $h + 1$ (f) $h - 11$
4. (a) $c + 5$ (b) $c - 16$ (c) $c + 3$ (d) $c - 1$ (e) $c + 6$ (f) $c - 2$

Exercise 5B

1. (a) $2a$ (b) $\frac{a}{3}$ (c) $3a$ (d) $\frac{a}{4}$ (e) $5a$ (f) $\frac{a}{20}$
2. (a) $4m$ (b) $\frac{m}{7}$ (c) $\frac{m}{9}$ (d) $3m$ (e) $6m$ (f) $\frac{m}{2}$
3. (a) $4d$ (b) $2d$ (c) $16d$ (d) d (e) $5d$ metres (f) $\frac{d}{2}$ litres
4. (a) $\frac{b}{4}$ (b) $\frac{b}{6}$ (c) $\frac{b}{8}$ (d) $\frac{b}{12}$ (e) $\frac{b}{16}$ (f) $\frac{b}{15}$

Exercise 5C

1. (a) (i) £55 (ii) £75 (iii) £105 (iv) £215 (b) $b = r + 25$
2. (a) (i) £22·50 (ii) £45 (iii) £90 (iv) £67·50 (b) $w = 4·5n$

450 Answers

3. (a) (i) £5 800 (ii) £3 400 (iii) £8 200 (iv) £4 600 (b) $T = 24M + 1\,000$
4. (a) (i) 90°F (ii) 110°F (iii) 130°F (iv) 230°F (b) $F = 2C + 30$
5. (a) (i) 540p (ii) 790p (iii) 440p (iv) 1 290p (b) $C = 25w + 40$
6. (a) (i) £4 (ii) £2 (iii) £2·50 (iv) £1·25 (b) $c = \frac{20}{p}$
7. (a) (i) 5 (ii) 11 (iii) 8 (iv) 2 (b) $S = 3L - 25$
8. (a) (i) £18 (ii) £13 (iii) £12 (iv) £11 (b) $c = \frac{120}{n} + 8$

Exercise 5D

1. (a) 10 (b) 11 (c) 16 (d) 4 (e) 1 (f) 21 (g) 26
   (h) 18 (i) 15 (j) 13
2. (a) 12 (b) 21 (c) 2 (d) 6 (e) 0 (f) 18 (g) 14
   (h) 17 (i) 4 (j) 6
3. (a) 15 (b) 17 (c) 3 (d) 2 (e) 0 (f) 15 (g) 19
   (h) 5 (i) 15 (j) 5
4. (a) 21 (b) 31 (c) 10 (d) 10 (e) 40 (f) 40 (g) 60
   (h) 60 (i) 37 (j) 37
5. (a) 32 (b) 32 (c) 32 (d) 2 (e) 10 (f) 48 (g) 48
   (h) 48 (i) 8 (j) 2
6. (a) 10 (b) 20 (c) 9 (d) 8 (e) 17 (f) 11 (g) 5
   (h) 5 (i) 14 (j) 19
7. (a) 5 (b) 9 (c) 9 (d) 7 (e) 2 (f) 16 (g) 9
   (h) 3 (i) 6 (j) 0
8. (a) 11 (b) 15 (c) 15 (d) 21 (e) 21 (f) 16 (g) 16
   (h) 29 (i) 2 (j) 1
9. (a) 30 (b) 30 (c) 60 (d) 0 (e) 65 (f) 65 (g) 0
   (h) 15 (i) 0 (j) 0
10. (a) 24 (b) 36 (c) 36 (d) 0 (e) 10 (f) 30 (g) 60
    (h) 90 (i) 6 (j) 12

Exercise 5E

1. (a) 12 (b) 60 (c) 16 (d) 15 (e) 24 (f) 24 (g) 8
   (h) 14 (i) 21 (j) 35
2. (a) 2 (b) 6 (c) 4 (d) 3 (e) 9 (f) 6 (g) 6
   (h) 9 (i) 9 (j) 2
3. (a) 20 (b) 40 (c) 40 (d) 8 (e) 10 (f) 3 (g) 3
   (h) 45 (i) 45 (j) 45
4. (a) 50 (b) 50 (c) 6 (d) 3 (e) 2 (f) 30 (g) 30
   (h) 15 (i) 15 (j) 10
5. (a) 21 (b) 21 (c) 10 (d) 4 (e) 4 (f) 400 (g) 400
   (h) 24 (i) 24 (j) 28
6. (a) 50 (b) 10 (c) 20 (d) 52 (e) 100 (f) 45 (g) 30
   (h) 30 (i) 40 (j) 25
7. (a) 6 (b) 8 (c) 12 (d) 12 (e) 4 (f) 10 (g) 20
   (h) 20 (i) 6 (j) 5·5
8. (a) 6 (b) 6 (c) 12 (d) 12 (e) 4 (f) 5 (g) 15
   (h) 15 (i) 9 (j) 9
9. (a) 12 (b) 23 (c) 20 (d) 60 (e) 23 (f) 32 (g) 32
   (h) 54 (i) 54 (j) 65
10. (a) ⁻1 (b) 12 (c) 0 (d) 21 (e) 21 (f) 45 (g) 45
    (h) 9 (i) 9 (j) 6

Exercise 5F

1. (a) 1 (b) 4 (c) 9 (d) 1 (e) 8 (f) 27 (g) 1
   (h) 16 (i) 81 (j) 1 (k) 1
2. (a) 25 (b) 36 (c) 49 (d) 125 (e) 216 (f) 343 (g) 625
   (h) 1 296 (i) 2 401 (j) 3 125 (k) 2·2
3. (a) 64 (b) 61 (c) 100 (d) 512 (e) 729 (f) 1 000 (g) 4 096
   (h) 6 561 (i) 10 000 (j) 32 768 (k) 3 (l) 3·2

Algebra 1 **451**

4. (a) 50 (b) 72 (c) 98 (d) 180 (e) 150 (f) 294 (g) 252
   (h) 245 (i) 175 (j) 121 (k) 4
5. (a) 8 (b) 54 (c) 48 (d) 18 (e) 32 (f) 64 (g) 6
   (h) 12 (i) 18 (j) 13
6. (a) 1 (b) 8 (c) 5 (d) 1 (e) 1 (f) 2 (g) 2
   (h) 4 (i) 8 (j) 16
7. (a) 16 (b) 41 (c) 189 (d) 50 (e) 32 (f) 82 (g) 82
   (h) 9 (i) 9 (j) 48
8. (a) 12 (b) 36 (c) 24 (d) 12 (e) 216 (f) 49 (g) 60
   (h) 60 (i) 12 (j) 12
9. (a) 5 (b) 4 (c) 29 (d) 30 (e) 12 (f) 36 (g) 512
   (h) 128 (i) 256 (j) 343
10. (a) 15 (b) 5 (c) 18 (d) 50 (e) 101 (f) 2 (g) 5 000
    (h) 1 250 (i) 1 125 (j) 225

Exercise 5G

1. (a) $^-4$ (b) $^-3$ (c) 2 (d) $^-10$ (e) 15 (f) $^-21$ (g) $^-16$
   (h) $^-24$ (i) $^-13$ (j) $^-15$
2. (a) 0 (b) 9 (c) $^-10$ (d) 18 (e) $^-12$ (f) $^-18$ (g) $^-22$
   (h) $^-7$ (i) $^-44$ (j) 30
3. (a) 5 (b) 7 (c) 13 (d) $^-8$ (e) 10 (f) $^-15$ (g) $^-11$
   (h) $^-15$ (i) $^-5$ (j) 45
4. (a) $^-19$ (b) $^-9$ (c) $^-30$ (d) 50 (e) $^-40$ (f) $^-40$ (g) $^-60$
   (h) $^-60$ (i) $^-43$ (j) $^-43$
5. (a) 0 (b) $^-32$ (c) $^-32$ (d) 34 (e) $^-22$ (f) $^-48$ (g) $^-48$
   (h) $^-16$ (i) $^-88$ (j) 98
6. (a) 9 (b) 12 (c) 6 (d) $^-8$ (e) $^-2$ (f) $^-6$ (g) 10
   (h) $^-10$ (i) 5 (j) $^-7$
7. (a) 0 (b) $^-4$ (c) $^-4$ (d) $^-12$ (e) $^-12$ (f) 4 (g) 16
   (h) $^-28$ (i) $^-10$ (j) 6
8. (a) 1 (b) $^-3$ (c) $^-3$ (d) 15 (e) 15 (f) $^-16$ (g) $^-16$
   (h) 7 (i) 22 (j) $^-9$
9. (a) $^-30$ (b) 10 (c) $^-20$ (d) $^-40$ (e) $^-5$ (f) 25 (g) 20
   (h) 45 (i) $^-120$ (j) 80
10. (a) $^-24$ (b) $^-36$ (c) $^-36$ (d) 0 (e) $^-110$ (f) $^-30$ (g) $^-60$
    (h) $^-90$ (i) $^-6$ (j) $^-12$

Exercise 5H

1. (a) 4 (b) 6 (c) 9 (d) 26 (e) 51 (f) 32
2. (a) 12 (b) 9 (c) 6 (d) 3 (e) 4·5 (f) 6·3
3. (a) 16 cm (b) 26 cm (c) 6 cm (d) 36 cm (e) 15 cm (f) 12 cm
4. (a) 200 (b) 150 (c) 240 (d) 250 (e) 240 (f) 175
5. (a) 4 (b) 10 (c) 5 (d) 0 (e) 10·5 (f) $^-2$
6. (a) 6 (b) 16 (c) 10 (d) 20 (e) 20 (f) 3
7. (a) 34 (b) 36 (c) 38 (d) 32 (e) 30 (f) 28
8. (a) 3 (b) 4 (c) 7 (d) 10 (e) 24 (f) 1·5
9. (a) 12 (b) 27 (c) 3 (d) 48 (e) 75 (f) 6·75
10. (a) 10 (b) 2 (c) 19·5 (d) 8 (e) 4·5 (f) 17·5

Exercise 5I

1. $11a$ 2. $10y$ 3. $3w$ 4. $6x$ 5. $13m$ 6. $4q$ 7. $2v$ 8. $11r$ 9. $20b$ 10. $10g$
11. $5w$ 12. $3x$ 13. t 14. $3e$ 15. $6u$ 16. u 17. $3y$ 18. $6i$ 19. r 20. x
21. $14x$ 22. $12y$ 23. $9t$ 24. $19a$ 25. $9b$ 26. $4x$ 27. $8w$ 28. $6d$ 29. $11e$ 30. $18r$
31. $8x$ 32. $3a$ 33. $4q$ 34. $2b$ 35. x 36. x 37. $3x$ 38. z 39. $2e$ 40. $7a$
41. $3x$ 42. $2y$ 43. $4m$ 44. $3u$ 45. y 46. $6z$ 47. b 48. $3d$ 49. $3h$ 50. $4a$

Exercise 5J

1. $7x + 3y$ 2. $9t + 6s$ 3. $9m + 3n$ 4. $4a + 4b$ 5. $9y + 3z$ 6. $11r + 5s$
7. $10y + 4$ 8. $7u + 4v$ 9. $6n + 11$ 10. $5e + 6f$ 11. $4x + 3y$ 12. $a + 8b$

13. $2x + y$
14. $5f + 1$
15. $m + 3n$
16. $2x + 2y$
17. $4v + 5$
18. $3p + 2q$
19. $2r + 3s$
20. $a + 4b$
21. $3x + 4y$
22. $a + 1$
23. $e + 2f$
24. $s + 1$
25. $3x + 2y$
26. $3r + 2s$
27. $5x + y$
28. $4u + 2$
29. $3a + b$
30. $y + z$
31. $4a - 2b$
32. $7x - 2y$
33. $7e - 3f$
34. $15u - 5t$
35. $8y - z$
36. $2a - 3b$
37. $2m - n$
38. $2a - 1$
39. $7y - 20$
40. $3x - 5y$

Exercise 5K
1. $6a$
2. $3b$
3. $4x + 2y$
4. $12a$
5. $5x + 4y$
6. $8m$
7. $15a$
8. $4a + 8$
9. $8x + 4y$
10. $4m + 6n$
11. $12e + 10$
12. $6e + 4f$

Checkout 5
1. (a) $s + 3$ (b) $s - 3$ (c) $3s$ (d) $\frac{s}{2}$
2. (a) (i) £110 (ii) £185 (b) $C = 20H + P$
3. (a) 3 (b) 2 (c) 12 (d) 16 (e) 11 (f) 2 (g) 6
   (h) 60 (i) 14 (j) 20 (k) 2 (l) 30 (m) 4 (n) 64
   (o) 18
4. (a) $^-1$ (b) 5 (c) 6 (d) $^-12$ (e) 4 (f) 21 (g) 5
   (h) $^-4$ (i) 0 (j) 6 (k) $^-3$ (l) $^-9$
5. (a) (i) 22 (ii) 10 (iii) 4 (b) (i) 7 (ii) 1
6. (a) (i) $12t$ (ii) $12y$ (iii) $6a$ (iv) $6a + 7b$ (v) $2x + 8y$ (vi) $5d + e$
   (vii) $7x - y$ (viii) $5a - 2b$ (ix) $7p - 6q$ (x) $3u - 5v$ (b) $2x + 2y + 8$

Revision exercise 5
1. (a) £19·20 (b) £54·20
2. (a) 3·6 m (b) multiply by 10 then divide by 3
3. (a) £14 (b) $C = 4h + 6$ (c) 5 metres
4. (a) $y = 3k - 1$ (b) 5
5. (a) 68°F (b) 24°F
6. (a) 50, 23 (b) $f = \frac{9c}{5} + 32$
7. (a) $x + y$ (b) £$5(x + y)$
8. (a) $8x$ (b) $2x$ (c) $12x$ (d) $20x$
9. 20
10. (a) $4x + 11$ (b) 54
11. (a) 30p (b) D

6 Shape and space 2

Exercise 6A

Name	Plane faces	Curved surfaces	Vertices	Edges
Cube	6	0	8	12
Cuboid	6	0	8	12
Cylinder	2	1	0	2
Triangular prism	5	0	6	9
Cone	1	1	1	1
Sphere	0	1	0	0
Square pyramid	5	0	5	8
Triangular pyramid	4	0	4	6

Exercise 6B
1. (a), (b), (d), (e), (f), (g) and (i) are nets for a cube

Exercise 6D

1. plan / front / side
2. plan / front / side
3. plan / front / side
4. plan / front / side
5. plan / front / side
6. plan / front / side
7. plan / front / side
8. plan / front / side
9. plan / front / side

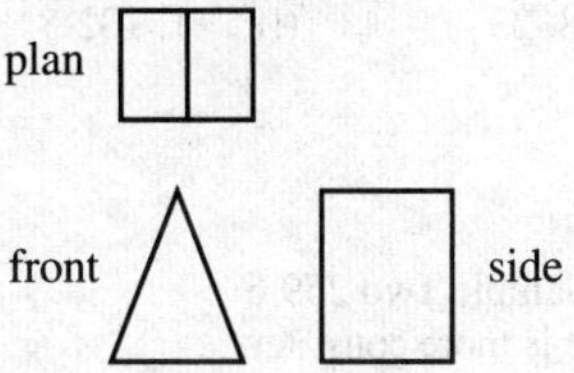

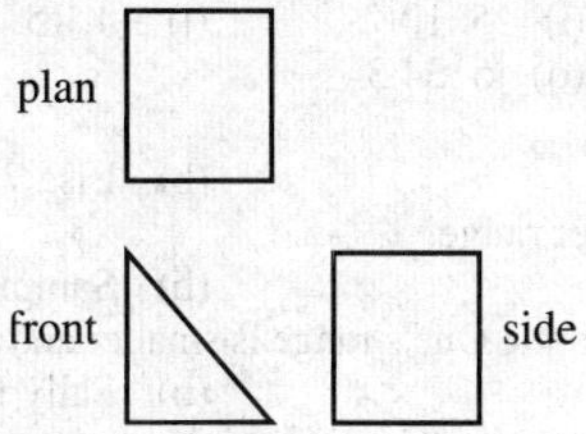

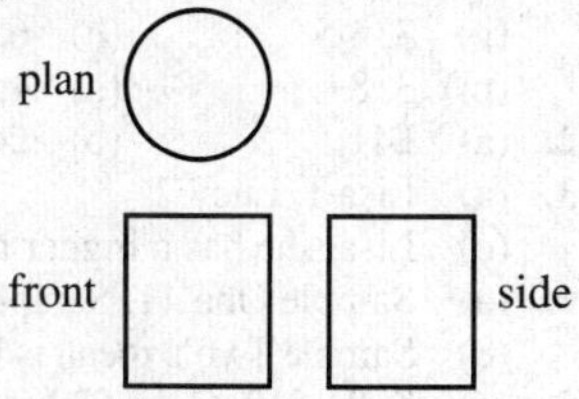

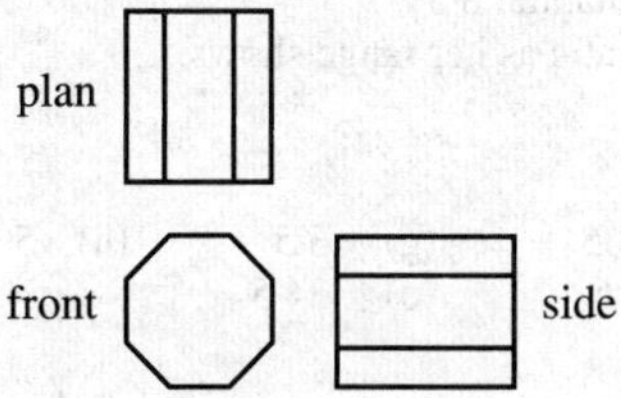

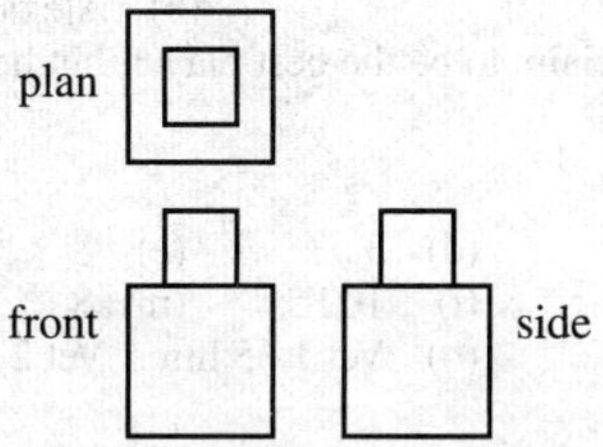

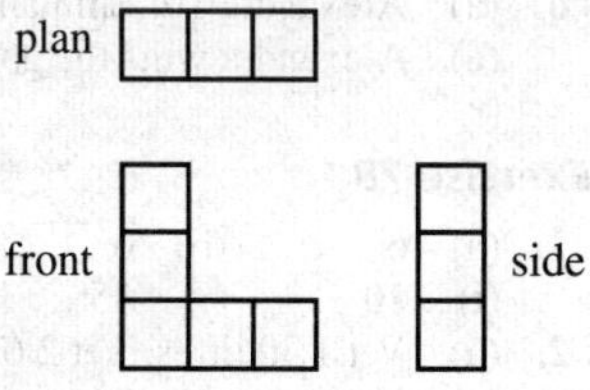

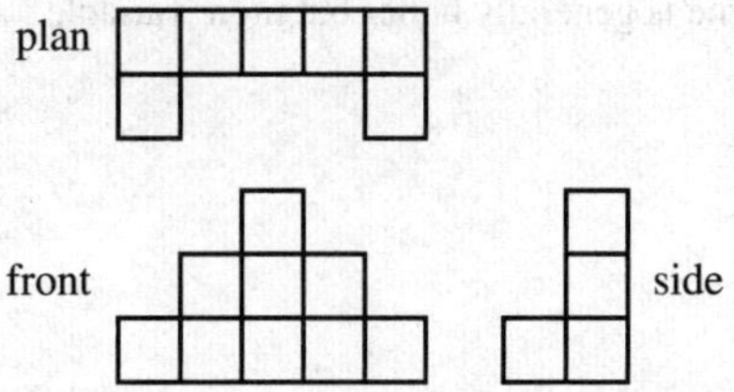

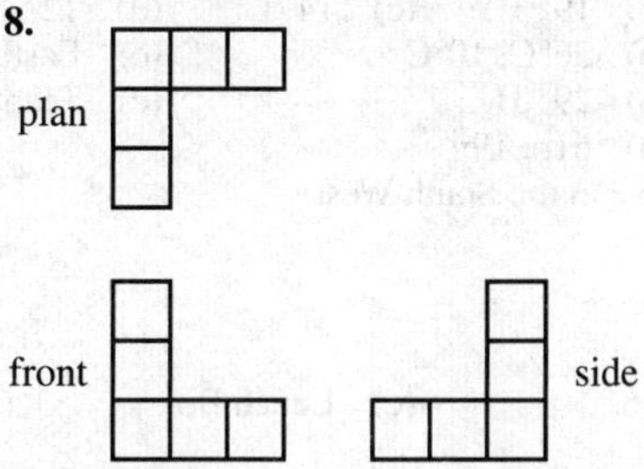

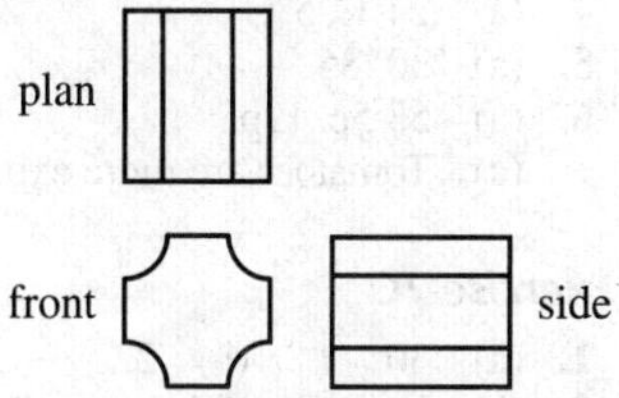

Checkout 6

1. (a) 0 curved surfaces, 6 plane faces, 12 edges, 8 vertices
   (b) 1 curved surface, 2 plane faces, 2 edges, 0 vertices
4. (a) plan / front / side

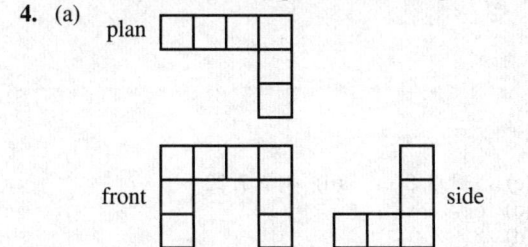

Revision exercise 6

1. (a) (i) cylinder (ii) cone (b) 8 (c) 6
3. 
4. (a) 9 (b)

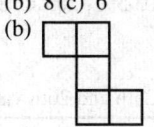

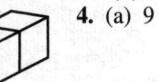

7 Data handling 2

Check in 7

1. (a) 22 (b) 30 (c) 43 (d) 48 (e) 81 (f) 140 (g) 269
2. (a) 30 (b) 21 (c) 72 (d) 42 (e) 90 (f) 12 (g) 24 r 2
   (h) 40 (i) 30 (j) 24
3. (a) 2, 5, 6, 7, 9, 23 (b) 47, 63, 89, 105, 121 (c) 1, 2, 2, 5, 6, 6, 7, 7, 9 (d) 9, 12, 12, 15, 17, 17, 19, 21

Exercise 7A

1. (a) 4, 6 (b) 2, 6 (c) 7, 4 (d) 4, 3 (e) 4, 8 (f) 3, 3·5
   (g) 3, 3·5 (h) 6, 5·25 (i) 5, 10·7 (j) 4, 15 (k) 8, 23 (l) 1, 102·5
   (m) 3, 8 (n) 4, 16 (o) 5, 34·3
2. (a) £41 (b) £4·10
3. (a) Lisa 1, Lucy 7 (b) Lisa 7·5, Lucy 7·3
   (c) Lisa, she has a higher mean and lower range.
4. (a) Sample One 41, Sample Two 84 (b) Sample One 251·9, Sample Two 259·6
   (c) Sample Two's mean is higher, but Sample One's range is smaller and so Sample One is more consistent.
5. (a) Sally £10, Greg £20 (b) Sally £10·50, Greg £10·50
   (c) On average, they save the same amount, but Greg's savings show much more variation with a greater range.
6. (a) Alexandra 10, Emmanuel 5 (b) Alexandra 8, Emmanuel 8·5
   (c) Alexandra wins the game and can claim to be the best player, but her play is erratic as her range shows.

Exercise 7B

1. (a) 6 (b) 6 (c) 4 (d) 3 (e) 8 (f) 3·5 (g) 3·5 (h) 5
   (i) 10 (j) 15 (k) 22 (l) 102·5 (m) 8 (n) 16 (o) 34·5
2. (a) Vet 1 30 litres, Vet 2 6 litres (b) Vet 1 35 litres, Vet 2 23 litres
   (c) Vet is more consistent.
3. (a) 20 (b) 19 (c) 14 (d) 12
4. (a) 24°C, 5°C (b) 26°C, 10°C (c) Eastbourne is generally hotter but more variable.
5. (a) 30, 85 (b) 29, 31 (c) Team 2
6. (a) 53·5p, 19p (b) 61p, 19p
   (c) Tomatoes are more expensive in the South West.

Exercise 7C

1. (a) 30 (b) 22
2. (b) Kwik Bite 35, Lunch Box 46 (c) Lunch Box

Exercise 7D

1. 11
2. 2
3. (a) 8 and 9 (biomodal), 4 (b) 7, 2
4. (a) 5, 5 (b) 6, 4
5. (a) 36 000 (b) Summer
6. Vanilla

Exercise 7E

1. (a) 5, 4, 3, 8 (b) 25, 25, 23, 5 (c) 3, 3, 3, 3 (d) 8, 7, 7, 22
2. (a) 3 (b) 2 (c) 6 (d) 6
3. (a) ⁻1 (b) 0 (c) 1 (d) 5
4. (a) £2·25, £2·25, £2, £2·50 (b) £2·45, £1, £1, £5·75
5. (a) 126 mm, 125 mm, 125 mm, 14 mm (b) 143·8 mm, 144·5 mm, 145 mm, 11 mm
6. (a) 197°C, 197°C, 195°C, 14°C (b) 203°C, 203·5°C, 205°C, 8°C

Exercise 7F

1. (a) 2 (b) 3 (c) between 25th and 26th values (d) 1
   (e)

Number of children	Number of houses	Number of children × Number of houses
0	14	0
1	15	15
2	18	36
3	3	9
4	0	0
Totals	50	60

   (f) 1·2 children

Data handling 2 455

2. (a) 2 (b) 9 (c) between 15th and 16th values (d) 3
   (e)
   (f) 3·5

Number of eggs	Frequency	Number of eggs × Frequency
0	4	0
1	1	1
2	7	14
3	4	12
4	4	16
5	4	20
6	3	18
7	1	7
8	1	8
9	1	9
Totals	30	105

3. (a) 8 (b) 7 (c) between 10th and 11th values (d) 7
   (e)
   (f) 7

Number correct	Frequency	Number correct × Frequency
0	0	0
1	0	0
2	0	0
3	1	3
4	1	4
5	2	10
6	3	18
7	4	28
8	5	40
9	3	27
10	1	10
Totals	20	140

4. (a) 1 (b) 5 (c) between 50th and 51st values (d) 2
   (e)
   (f) 1·96

Number of tests taken	Frequency	Number of tests taken × Frequency
1	43	43
2	31	62
3	17	51
4	6	24
5	2	10
6	1	6
Totals	100	196

5. (a) 34 (b) 6 (c) 13th value (d) 34
   (e)

Number of sweets	Number of packets	Number of sweets × Number of packets
30	4	120
31	1	31
32	2	64
33	4	132
34	8	272
35	3	105
36	3	108
Totals	25	832

   (f) 33·28 (g) Yes, they can use the median or mode.

Checkout 7

1. (a) 4, 3 (b) 2·25, 5 (c) 11, 5 (d) 14·6, 4
2. (a) 3 (b) 1·5 (c) 10·5 (d) 14·5
3. (a) 3 (b) 1 (c) 10 (d) 16

456 Answers

4. (a) 3 (b) 2 (c) 0 (d) 9
5. (a) 1 (b) 4 (c) between 25th and 26th values (d) 2 (f) 1·66
   (e)

Number of children	Number of houses	Number of children × Number of houses
0	1	0
1	23	23
2	19	38
3	6	18
4	1	4
Totals	50	83

Revision exercise 7
1. 14
2. 24
3. (a) (i) 4 (ii) 13·9 cm (b) There is less variation in the handspans of the first group.
4. (a) (i) 2 (ii) 15·2
   (b) The shopkeeper should stock Grade B eggs as less were broken during the week.
5. (a) 10 mm (b) 0 mm (c) 1 mm (d) 2·8 mm (e) mean
6. (a) 56 (b) 53 (c) 25
7. (a) (i) Tuesday (ii) 15 (iii) 6 (b) 12·2
   (c) (i) bars with heights 12, 14, 8, 18, 23 (ii) 15
   (iii) The week in April, it had a lower mean.
8. (a)

Number of colonies	Frequency	Number of colonies × Frequency
0	7	0
1	10	10
2	5	10
3	2	6
4	1	4
Totals	25	30

(b) 1·2 (c) 1

   (d) (i) Both have a mode of 1, mean of 1·2, median of 1 and a range of 4.
   (ii) More squares were counted in the second sample.
9. (a) 26 (b) 2 (c) 2·1
10. (a) 9 (b) 8 (c) 7·72

8 Number 3

Check in 8
1. 132 2. 332 3. 612 4. 656 5. 365 6. 41 7. ⁻19
8. 124 9. 167 10. 729

Exercise 8A
1. (a) 2·1 (b) 3·1 (c) 5·7 (d) 1·8 (e) 4·6 (f) 3·2
   (g) 6·5 (h) 7·1 (i) 9·8 (j) 8·9
3. (a) 5·8 cm (b) 6·3 cm (c) 2·9 cm (d) 4·4 cm (e) 8·1 cm (f) 9·7 cm
   (g) 7·9 cm (h) 5·2 cm (i) 10·5 cm (j) 12·6 cm (k) 4 cm 9 mm (l) 9 cm 5 mm
   (m) 10 cm 3 mm (n) 8 cm 3 mm (o) 9 cm 1 mm (p) 1 cm 9 mm (q) 3 cm 8 mm
   (r) 8 cm 6 mm (s) 12 cm 4 mm (t) 13 cm 3 mm

Exercise 8B
1. 1·1, 1·7, 1·9, 2·3, 2·4   2. 2·7, 3·1, 3·8, 4·0, 4·3
3. 2·6, 4·5, 5·4, 6·2, 6·8, 8·6   4. 1·9, 3·5, 5·3, 6·7, 7·6, 9·1
5. 12·0, 12·0, 12·2, 12·4, 12·8, 13·3, 13·5, 13·7   6. 1·1, 1·7, 2·5, 2·6, 2·9, 3·0, 3·6, 4·3, 4·4, 6·2
7. 2·6, 4·6, 4·9, 5·6, 7·3, 7·3, 8·0, 8·1, 8·2, 9·1   8. 0·7, 0·9, 1·5, 1·7, 2·1, 2·2, 2·6, 3·0, 3·4, 3·5
9. 0·3, 1·5, 2·9, 3·0, 3·8, 5·1, 6·7, 7·6, 8·3, 9·2   10. 13·0, 13·2, 13·3, 14·3, 14·5, 14·6, 15·0, 15·1, 15·6, 18·0, 18·2, 19·4
11. 22·0, 22·1, 22·4, 22·5, 22·8, 22·9, 23·0, 23·0, 23·6, 23·6, 23·8, 23·8
12. 40·1, 41·0, 42·6, 43·4, 43·5, 43·8, 44·3, 44·7, 45·3, 46·2, 47·4, 48·3

Number 3 **457**

Exercise 8C

1. (a) 2·48 (b) 3·56 (c) 3·73 (d) 4·19 (e) 7·01 (f) 6·19
   (g) 4·07 (h) 8·55 (i) 9·83 (j) 3·08
3. (a) 3·38 m (b) 2·30 m (c) 2·03 m (d) 2·09 m (e) 4·01 m (f) 4·87 m
   (g) 5·06 m (h) 3·50 m (i) 1·05 m (j) 4·96 m (k) 4 m 92 cm (l) 3 m 51 cm
   (m) 1 m 99 cm (n) 2 m 60 cm (o) 2 m 6 cm (p) 2 m 45 cm (q) 4 m 9 cm (r) 3 m 10 cm
   (s) 3 m 1 cm (t) 2 m 11 cm

Exercise 8D

1. 2·23, 2·32, 3·02, 3·14, 3·20, 3·41
2. 1·21, 1·34, 1·43, 1·55, 1·84, 1·91
3. 4·04, 4·12, 4·13, 4·22, 4·31, 4·44
4. 5·02, 5·06, 5·12, 5·21, 5·63, 5·82
5. 4·02, 4·52, 5·50, 6·03, 6·21, 7·25
6. 9·01, 9·03, 9·03, 9·04, 9·10, 9·33
7. 10·09, 10·68, 10·99, 11·99, 12·21, 12·34, 12·35, 13·52
8. 3·05, 4·5, 5·16, 5·2, 6·34, 6·7
9. 0·01, 0·09, 0·1, 0·13, 0·3, 0·9
10. 9·0, 9·03, 9·19, 9·2, 9·29, 9·3
11. 12·37, 12·37, 12·4, 12·4, 12·45, 12·5, 12·8, 12·89, 12·9, 12·98
12. 32·05, 32·06, 32·2, 32·27, 32·5, 32·56, 32·6, 32·65, 32·7, 32·72

Exercise 8E

1. (a) $5 + \frac{3}{10}$ (b) $4 + \frac{8}{10} + \frac{5}{100}$ (c) $2 + \frac{7}{10} + \frac{9}{100}$
   (d) $6 + \frac{6}{10} + \frac{1}{100}$ (e) $6 + \frac{1}{10} + \frac{6}{100}$ (f) $1 + \frac{6}{10} + \frac{6}{100} + \frac{4}{1000}$
   (g) $\frac{9}{10} + \frac{3}{100} + \frac{2}{1000}$ (h) $9 + \frac{3}{1000}$ (i) $8 + \frac{7}{100} + \frac{2}{1000}$
   (j) $5 + \frac{3}{10} + \frac{2}{1000}$ (k) $20 + 6 + \frac{2}{10} + \frac{5}{100}$ (l) $30 + 1 + \frac{3}{10} + \frac{2}{100} + \frac{5}{1000}$
   (m) $200 + 30 + 1 + \frac{4}{10}$ (n) $300 + 40 + 5 + \frac{6}{10} + \frac{7}{100}$ (o) $30 + 4 + \frac{7}{100} + \frac{5}{1000}$
   (p) $10 + 2 + \frac{3}{10} + \frac{4}{100} + \frac{6}{1000}$ (q) $20 + 3 + \frac{7}{10} + \frac{6}{100} + \frac{1}{1000}$ (r) $90 + 7 + \frac{3}{100} + \frac{5}{1000}$
   (s) $30 + 9 + \frac{1}{100} + \frac{2}{1000}$ (t) $9 + \frac{2}{1000}$ (u) $9 + \frac{2}{10} + \frac{1}{1000}$
   (v) $10 + 9 + \frac{4}{10} + \frac{5}{100} + \frac{7}{1000}$ (w) $20 + 5 + \frac{6}{10} + \frac{5}{100} + \frac{8}{1000}$ (x) $60 + 7 + \frac{5}{100} + \frac{4}{1000}$
   (y) $30 + 3 + \frac{3}{10} + \frac{3}{100} + \frac{3}{1000}$
2. (a) 3·7 (b) 7·3 (c) 6·35 (d) 7·06 (e) 27·316 (f) 31·501
   (g) 40·368 (h) 45·079 (i) 60·007 (j) 75·403 (k) 148·657 (l) 305·07
   (m) 580·501 (n) 111·111 (o) 37·203 (p) 657·036 (q) 7 257·863 (r) 5 203·506
   (s) 6 000·006 (t) 500·302 (u) 189·067 (v) 2 220·222 (w) 3 105·062 (x) 7 206·755

Exercise 8F

1. (a) 1, 2, 2, 2, 2 (b) 3, 4, 4, 4, 3 (c) 7, 9, 5, 5, 6, 3 (d) 4, 5, 2, 9, 8, 7
   (e) 12, 13, 12, 14, 12, 13, 12, 14 (f) 16, 12, 18, 15, 15, 13, 13, 15, 19, 18, 15, 13
   (g) 22, 24, 23, 24, 22, 23, 23, 24, 23, 22, 24 (h) 45, 44, 43, 46, 41, 40, 44, 48, 45, 47, 44, 43
2. A, D, F, G, H or J

Exercise 8G

1. (a) 2·3, 2·3, 3·4, 3·1, 3·3, 3·1 (b) 1·6, 1·2, 1·3, 1·4, 2·0, 1·9 (c) 4·2, 5·0, 4·4, 4·1, 4·4, 4·1
   (d) 5·1, 5·6, 5·8, 6·0, 5·2, 5·2 (e) 6·1, 7·3, 4·5, 4·2, 5·6, 7·0 (f) 9·0, 9·8, 9·1, 9·1, 9·1, 9·4
   (g) 12·2, 12·4, 12·0, 10·7, 12·3, 13·5, 11·0, 10·1 (h) 3·1, 4·5, 6·7, 6·3, 5·2, 6·0
2. A, C, D, F, G, H, I or J

Exercise 8H

1. (a) 2·33, 2·24, 3·40, 3·10, 3·24, 3·50 (b) 1·51, 1·28, 1·33, 1·49, 1·92, 1·85
   (c) 4·23, 4·13, 4·37, 4·15, 4·35, 4·40 (d) 5·02, 5·16, 5·20, 5·11, 6·00, 5·12
   (e) 6·40, 7·53, 4·66, 4·60, 5·55, 6·53 (f) 9·94, 9·40, 9·10, 10·00, 9·31, 9·14
   (g) 12·01, 12·32, 11·90, 10·61, 12·31, 13·06, 10·93, 10·39 (h) 3·06, 4·52, 7·00, 6·99, 5·11, 5·22, 8·00, 4·46
2. A, B, D, G, I or J

Exercise 8I

1. (a) 0·7 (b) 0·8 (c) 0·9 (d) 0·8 (e) 0·7 (f) 0·6 (g) 0·6 (h) 0·6 (i) 0·4
   (j) 0·9 (k) 0·9 (l) 0·8 (m) 1·0 (n) 1·0 (o) 0·8 (p) 1·3 (q) 1·5 (r) 2·5
   (s) 2·4 (t) 3·9 (u) 2·7 (v) 4·0 (w) 2·0 (x) 6·0 (y) 3·2

458 Answers

2. (a) 1·1 (b) 1·3 (c) 1·6 (d) 1·3 (e) 1·1 (f) 1·2 (g) 1·2 (h) 1·4 (i) 1·1
   (j) 1·1 (k) 1·3 (l) 1·6 (m) 1·8 (n) 1·5 (o) 1·6 (p) 2·2 (q) 3·4 (r) 2·2
   (s) 4·4 (t) 5·7 (u) 3·0 (v) 7·0 (w) 3·1 (x) 4·7 (y) 5·2
3. (a) 8·2 (b) 10·6 (c) 3·9 (d) 13·5 (e) 3·6 (f) 6·9 (g) 3·8 (h) 4·8 (i) 10·4
   (j) 12·6 (k) 10·0 (l) 9·7 (m) 7·7 (n) 14·4 (o) 13·5 (p) 12·5 (q) 6·3 (r) 16·2
   (s) 6·0 (t) 8·0 (u) 15·9 (v) 11·7 (w) 8·8 (x) 18·0 (y) 15·9
4. (a) 11·0 (b) 14·2 (c) 8·3 (d) 9·1 (e) 6·2 (f) 3·3 (g) 11·1 (h) 3·5 (i) 6·3
   (j) 7·2 (k) 5·5 (l) 6·1 (m) 8·1 (n) 8·4 (o) 5·7 (p) 6·4 (q) 6·0 (r) 10·6
   (s) 9·6 (t) 14·8 (u) 9·4 (v) 15·4 (w) 11·6 (x) 18·1 (y) 17·1
5. (a) 0·34 (b) 2·65 (c) 1·76 (d) 1·94 (e) 3·82 (f) 0·94 (g) 1·85 (h) 5·85 (i) 7·76
   (j) 3·94 (k) 1·65 (l) 2·59 (m) 1·89 (n) 3·79 (o) 2·99 (p) 1·51 (q) 3·64 (r) 5·84
   (s) 4·82 (t) 8·96 (u) 1·38 (v) 2·04 (w) 4·56 (x) 9·00 (y) 5·08

Exercise 8J

1. (a) 10·9 (b) 20·1 (c) 15·1 (d) 21·3 (e) 17·5 (f) 24·1 (g) 17·3
   (h) 10·3 (i) 12·5 (j) 18·8 (k) 22·5 (l) 9·5 (m) 13·3 (n) 24·4
   (o) 10·3 (p) 11·2 (q) 11·5 (r) 11·3 (s) 19·8 (t) 7·7 (u) 12·0
   (v) 10·5 (w) 56·1 (x) 29·2 (y) 28·2
2. (a) 7·99 (b) 13·57 (c) 17·79 (d) 4·99 (e) 17·89 (f) 10·91 (g) 14·73
   (h) 8·85 (i) 10·85 (j) 11·82 (k) 14·07 (l) 9·68 (m) 18·07 (n) 21·08
   (o) 23·18 (p) 3·1 (q) 7·23 (r) 6·56 (s) 6·6 (t) 10·07 (u) 20·32
   (v) 26 (w) 26·5 (x) 91·11 (y) 165·83
3. (a) 11·5 (b) 25·1 (c) 25 (d) 27·8 (e) 31·2 (f) 37 (g) 27·7
   (h) 18·6 (i) 10·59 (j) 14·68 (k) 12·55 (l) 18·87 (m) 17·78 (n) 14·54
   (o) 24·64 (p) 110·415 (q) 64·037 (r) 9 (s) 37·74 (t) 70·05 (u) 29·89
   (v) 87·246 (w) 89·86 (x) 45·447 (y) 139·812
4. £3·75, £2·89 and £2·86

Exercise 8K

1. (a) 0·7 (b) 0·7 (c) 0·1 (d) 0 (e) 0·2 (f) 0·4 (g) 0·1 (h) 0·1 (i) 0·3
   (j) 0·4 (k) 2·5 (l) 4·1 (m) 3·2 (n) 2·3 (o) 5·4 (p) 1·2 (q) 3·4 (r) 4·2
   (s) 4·0 (t) 5·2 (u) 5·3 (v) 3·2 (w) 3·6 (x) 2·0 (y) 4·8
2. (a) 0·9 (b) 0·8 (c) 0·8 (d) 0·8 (e) 0·8 (f) 0·8 (g) 0·7 (h) 0·7 (i) 0·7
   (j) 0·6 (k) 0·6 (l) 0·5 (m) 0·9 (n) 0·5 (o) 0·7 (p) 0·9 (q) 0·7 (r) 0·6
   (s) 0·3 (t) 0·7 (u) 0·4 (v) 0·6 (w) 0·2 (x) 0·4 (y) 0·8
3. (a) 6·6 (b) 4·6 (c) 0·5 (d) 5·4 (e) −2·2 (f) 4 (g) 6·4 (h) 0·8 (i) 2·1
   (j) 3·6 (k) 3·7 (l) 1·9 (m) 1·5 (n) 1·7 (o) 1·7 (p) 3·9 (q) 1·6 (r) 2·4
   (s) 1·9 (t) 4·8 (u) 2·7 (v) 1·8 (w) 1·4 (x) 0·9 (y) 0·8

Exercise 8L

1. (a) 11·1 (b) 23·1 (c) 22·7 (d) 24·2 (e) 14 (f) 20·9 (g) 42·7 (h) 34·9 (i) 10·8
   (j) 62·6 (k) 29·2 (l) 15·5 (m) 36·2 (n) 35·1 (o) 8·2 (p) 3·9 (q) 26·8 (r) 48·9
   (s) 57·6 (t) 18·8 (u) 26·9 (v) 64·8 (w) 66·7 (x) 27·8 (y) 49·8
2. (a) 21·22 (b) 45·42 (c) 35·24 (d) 33·02 (e) 22·22 (f) 23·17 (g) 11·05 (h) 12·27 (i) 51·05
   (j) 12·18 (k) 12·51 (l) 42·81 (m) 46·28 (n) 20·91 (o) 72·51 (p) 5·35 (q) 8·72 (r) 5·22
   (s) 16·31 (t) 6·24 (u) 48·62 (v) 2·83 (w) 32·66 (x) 28·25 (y) 48·47
3. (a) 62·62 (b) 57·75 (c) 24·79 (d) 66·81 (e) 41·91 (f) 13·25 (g) 25·54 (h) 34·05 (i) 72·13
   (j) 11·13 (k) 0·78 (l) 6·75 (m) 10·83 (n) 46·27 (o) 13·88 (p) 35·85 (q) 25·64 (r) 8·38
   (s) 38·76 (t) 15·76 (u) 7·47 (v) 8·19 (w) 66·44 (x) 85·33 (y) 28·53
4. £21·49, £12·70, £32·01, £12·66, £10·51, £23·01, £10·61, £13·91, £20·01, £14·31

Checkout 8

1. (a) (i) 7 tenths (ii) 4 units (c) 3 tenths
   (b) (i) 3·5 cm (ii) 6·8 cm
   (c) (i) 4 cm 3 mm (ii) 9 cm 9 mm (d) 2·4, 2·9, 3·0, 3·2, 3·4, 3·5, 3·8, 4·2
2. (a) (i) 9 hundredths (ii) 8 tenths (iii) 7 hundredths
   (b) (i) 3·54 m (ii) 6·83 m
   (c) (i) 4 m 78 cm (ii) 13 m 65 cm

3. (a) 6·08, 6·09, 6·25, 6·28, 6·30, 6·31, 6·42, 6·80 (b) 5·04, 5·05, 5·4, 5·5, 5·55, 5·6, 5·65, 5·7
4. (a) (i) 2 thousandths (ii) 6 thousandths (iii) 7 hundredths
   (b) (i) 3·237 (ii) 25·736
5. (a) 7·048, 7·401, 7·421, 7·423, 7·427, 7·435
   (b) 8·049, 8·059, 8·488, 8·5, 8·55, 8·63, 8·653, 8·76
6. (a) 13 (b) 14 (c) 4
7. (a) 5·6 (b) 8·8 (c) 7·0
8. (a) 6·78 (b) 7·05 (c) 13·00
9. (a) 1·1 (b) 3·9 (c) 1·15 (d) 0·79 (e) 7·9 (f) 4·38 (g) 0·6
   (h) 1·1 (i) 4·5 (j) 0·8
10. (a) 12·4 (b) 23·36 (c) 84·34 (d) 53·16 (e) 11·2 (f) 28·8 (g) 65·65 (h) 53·55

Revision exercise 8

1. (a) 7 531 (b) 1 357 (c) 1·357
2. 1·9 kg
3. (a) (i) 1·8 kg (ii) 1 800 g (b) 3·1 kg
4. (a) (i) £18·85 (ii) £1·15 (b) (i) 108 (ii) £13
5. Mum £1·85, Dad £1·95, Sharon £1·20, Me £1·65, Total £6·65

9 Shape and space 3

Check in 9

1. (a) 180° (b) 180° (c) 90° (d) 90° (e) 270° (f) 270° (g) 45°
   (h) 45° (i) 135°
2. (a) 180° (b) 180° (c) 90° (d) 90° (e) 45° (f) 90° (g) 315°
   (h) 315° (i) 225°

Exercise 9A

1. 50° 2. 10° 3. 45° 4. 65° 5. 85° 6. 28° 7. 56° 8. 33°
9. 35° 10. 35° 11. 45° 12. 40° 13. 115° 14. 148° 15. 69° 16. 96°
17. 47° 18. 152° 19. 35° 20. 50° 21. 60° 22. 160° 23. 295° 24. 198°
25. 237° 26. 90° 27. 45° 28. 286° 29. 50° 30. 40°

Exercise 9B

1. $a = 100°, b = 80°, c = 100°$
2. $d = 145°, e = 35°, f = 35°$
3. $g = 85°, h = 85°, i = 95°$
4. $j = 76°, k = 104°, l = 104°$
5. $m = 122°, n = 58°, o = 58°$
6. $p = 139°, q = 41°, r = 41°$
7. $s = 100°, t = 60°, u = 100°$
8. $v = 60°, w = 60°, x = 90°$
9. $y = 50°, z = 130°, a = 50°$

Exercise 9C

1. $a = 60°, b = 60°, c = 120°, d = 120°, e = 60°, f = 60°, g = 120°$
2. $h = 100°, i = 100°, f = 80°, k = 100°, l = 80°, m = 100°, n = 80°$
3. $o = 115°, p = 65°, q = 65°, r = 115°, s = 65°, t = 115°, u = 65°$
4. $v = 135°, w = 45°, x = 135°, y = 45°, z = 45°, a = 135°, b = 135°$
5. $c = 288°$
6. $d = 55°, e = 125°$
7. $f = 60°, g = 60°, h = 60°, i = 240°, j = 120°, k = 240°$
8. $l = 125°, m = 235°$

Exercise 9D

1. 30° 2. 78° 3. 55° 4. 25° 5. 78° 6. 140° 7. 100° 8. 63°
9. 133° 10. 90° 11. 79° 12. 111°

Exercise 9E

1. $a = 70°$ 2. $b = 62°$ 3. $c = 78°$ 4. $d = 35°$
5. $e = 26°$ 6. $f = 78°, g = 24°$ 7. $h = 116°, i = 32°$ 8. $y = 82°, k = 16°$
9. $l = 45°, m = 90°$ 10. $n = 75°, o = 30°$

Exercise 9G
1. $p = 45°, q = 135°$ 2. $m = 40°, n = 140°$ 3. $c = 36°, d = 144°$ 4. $a = 30°, b = 150°$

Exercise 9H
1. $x = 130°$
2. (a) 360° (b) 110°
3. (a) 720° (b) 115°
4. (a) 1 080° (b) 110°

Checkout 9
1. $a = 20°, b = 58°, c = 85°$ 2. $e = 140°, f = 40°, g = 140°$
3. $e = 68°, f = 68°, g = 112°, h = 112°, i = 68°, j = 68°, k = 112°$
4. $a = 16°$ 5. $a = 74°, b = 48°, c = 84°$ 7. $p = 60°, q = 120°$
8. (a) 720° (b) 115°

Revision exercise 9
1. $p = 125°, q = 55°, r = 55°, s = 52°, t = 50°$ 2. $x = 65°$
3. (a) (i) obtuse (ii) isosceles (b) 35° (c) 35°
4. $a = 60°, b = 120°, c = 120°$
5. (a) All sides are the same length. (b) Angles are not all the same in a rhombus.
6. (a) 62° (b) 60° (c) 135°
7. (a) (i) pentagon
   (ii) Its angles are not all the same size, or its sides are not all the same length.
   (b) (ii) $d = 147°$
8. (a) (i) 33° (ii) 95° (b) (i) 36° (ii) 36°
9. (a) 45° (b) 135°
10. (a) 72° (b) isosceles

10 Number 4

Check in 10
1. (a) 238 (b) 115 (c) 816 (d) 6 084 (e) 24 840
2. (a) 24 (b) 87 (c) 72 (d) 25 (e) 51

Exercise 10A
1. (a) 560 (b) 4 530 (c) 2 730 (d) 7 030 (e) 1 020 (f) 45 (g) 87
   (h) 193 (i) 541 (j) 789 (k) 72·3 (l) 52·7 (m) 232·1 (n) 305·6
   (o) 216·7 (p) 6·7 (q) 3·45 (r) 2·05 (s) 5·28 (t) 2·23 (u) 0·2
   (v) 0·345 (w) 0·52 (x) 0·674 (y) 0·054 2
2. (a) 20 mm (b) 60 mm (c) 80 mm (d) 10 mm (e) 20 mm (f) 26 mm (g) 74 mm
   (h) 59 mm (i) 43 mm (j) 35 mm (k) 158 mm (l) 249 mm (m) 355 mm (n) 896 mm
   (o) 289 mm (p) 25·6 mm (q) 53·7 mm (r) 70·5 mm (s) 90·8 mm (t) 67·5 mm (u) 9 mm
   (v) 7 mm (w) 1 mm (x) 2 mm (y) 3·5 mm

Exercise 10B
1. (a) 700 (b) 600 (c) 5 700 (d) 12 300 (e) 34 700 (f) 450 (g) 780
   (h) 340 (i) 1 870 (j) 2 730 (k) 567 (l) 731 (m) 1 956 (n) 83
   (o) 3 451 (p) 53·7 (q) 34·7 (r) 52·4 (s) 56·4 (t) 23·1 (u) 3·2
   (v) 7·61 (w) 9·32 (x) 7·25 (y) 0·15
2. (a) 200 cm (b) 500 cm (c) 300 cm (d) 400 cm (e) 100 cm (f) 150 cm (g) 170 cm
   (h) 250 cm (i) 890 cm (j) 760 cm (k) 1 530 cm (l) 2 950 cm (m) 3 280 cm (n) 2 750 cm
   (o) 3 410 cm (p) 564 cm (q) 925 cm (r) 863 cm (s) 934 cm (t) 731 cm (u) 25 cm
   (v) 37 cm (w) 83 cm (x) 62 cm (y) 77 cm

Exercise 10C

1. (a) 5 000 (b) 9 000 (c) 67 000 (d) 453 000 (e) 217 000 (f) 3 500
   (g) 9 800 (h) 5 400 (i) 17 700 (j) 47 300 (k) 5 680 (l) 7 510
   (m) 19 760 (n) 930 (o) 38 510 (p) 437 (q) 347 (r) 724
   (s) 594 (t) 271 (u) 52·3 (v) 96·1 (w) 97·2 (x) 81·5
   (y) 0·5
2. (a) 4 000 ml (b) 1 500 ml (c) 1 700 ml (d) 15 300 ml (e) 27 500 ml (f) 9 340 ml
   (g) 7 310 ml (h) 250 ml (i) 373 ml (j) 6 258 ml
3. (a) 5 000 m (b) 2 400 m (c) 4 500 m (d) 12 500 m (e) 18 400 m (f) 45 900 m
   (g) 7 450 m (h) 526 m (i) 573 m (j) 9 456 m
4. (a) 9 000 g (b) 6 400 g (c) 3 200 g (d) 14 700 g (e) 14 800 g (f) 32 800 g
   (g) 6 330 g (h) 585 g (i) 843 g (j) 7 540 g

Exercise 10D

1. (a) 7 (b) 25 (c) 34 (d) 25 (e) 456 (f) 2·3 (g) 6·7
   (h) 12·3 (i) 45·6 (j) 27·1 (k) 4·56 (l) 3·47 (m) 6·59 (n) 9·99
   (o) 5·62 (p) 0·47 (q) 0·903 (r) 0·617 (s) 0·81 (t) 0·76
   (u) 0·032 (v) 0·09 (w) 0·009 (x) 0·053 (y) 0·005 3
2. (a) 20 cm (b) 60 cm (c) 50 cm (d) 10 cm (e) 6 cm (f) 26 cm (g) 74 cm
   (h) 59 cm (i) 43 cm (j) 35 cm (k) 15·8 cm (l) 24·9 cm (m) 35·5 cm (n) 89·6 cm
   (o) 28·9 cm (p) 2·56 cm (q) 5·37 cm (r) 7·05 cm (s) 9·08 cm (t) 6·75 cm

Exercise 10E

1. (a) 7 (b) 25 (c) 34 (d) 25 (e) 456 (f) 2·3 (g) 6·7
   (h) 12·3 (i) 45·6 (j) 27·1 (k) 4·56 (l) 3·47 (m) 6·59 (n) 9·99
   (o) 5·62 (p) 0·247 (q) 0·193 (r) 0·261 7 (s) 0·081 (t) 0·076 (u) 0·003 2
   (v) 0·009 (w) 0·000 9 (x) 0·005 3 (y) 0·000 53
2. (a) 2 m (b) 6 m (c) 5 m (d) 1 m (e) 0·6 m (f) 2·6 m (g) 7·4 m
   (h) 5·9 m (i) 4·3 m (j) 3·5 m (k) 1·58 m (l) 2·49 m (m) 3·55 m (n) 8·96 m
   (o) 2·89 m (p) 0·256 m (q) 0·537 m (r) 0·705 m (s) 0·908 m (t) 0·675 m

Exercise 10F

1. (a) 5 (b) 9 (c) 3·5 (d) 9·8 (e) 5·4 (f) 17·7
   (g) 47·3 (h) 5·68 (i) 7·55 (j) 9·374 (k) 3·856 (l) 0·437
   (m) 0·271 (n) 0·052 3 (o) 0·096 1 (p) 0·009 72 (q) 0·008 1 (r) 0·005 7
   (s) 0·009 (t) 0·011 (u) 0·000 5 (v) 0·001 9 (w) 0·000 17 (x) 0·000 05
   (y) 0·003 142
2. (a) 0·4 litres (b) 0·15 litres (c) 0·17 litres (d) 0·053 litres (e) 0·025 litres
   (f) 0·075 litres (g) 0·75 litres (h) 0·25 litres (i) 0·5 litres (j) 1·25 litres
3. (a) 0·5 km (b) 0·24 km (c) 3·5 km (d) 12·7 km (e) 18·45 km (f) 45·9 km
   (g) 7·457 km (h) 5·269 km (i) 0·573 5 km (j) 1·456 8 km
4. (a) 0·9 kg (b) 0·64 kg (c) 0·32 kg (d) 0·147 kg (e) 0·148 kg (f) 1·328 kg
   (g) 1·633 kg (h) 2·585 kg (i) 3·843 kg (j) 7·5 kg

Exercise 10G

1. (a) 1 (b) 0·8 (c) 0·9 (d) 3 (e) 1·4 (f) 4 (g) 1·8
   (h) 1·2 (i) 1 (j) 0·6 (k) 3·2 (l) 1·6 (m) 4·5 (n) 4·8
   (o) 2·4 (p) 6·3 (q) 0·8 (r) 0·1 (s) 0·9 (t) 1·5
2. (a) 0·18 (b) 0·05 (c) 0·42 (d) 0·24 (e) 0·36 (f) 0·35 (g) 0·27
   (h) 0·64 (i) 0·49 (j) 0·04 (k) 0·03 (l) 0·36 (m) 0·72 (n) 0·28
   (o) 0·56 (p) 0·81 (q) 0·02 (r) 0·06 (s) 0·54 (t) 0·07
3. (a) 0·25 (b) 0·12 (c) 0·24 (d) 0·16 (e) 0·18 (f) 0·27 (g) 0·28
   (h) 0·4 (i) 0·14 (j) 0·15 (k) 0·12 (l) 0·09 (m) 0·04 (n) 0·05
   (o) 0·06 (p) 0·3 (q) 0·07 (r) 0·08 (s) 0·08 (t) 0·2
4. (a) 0·016 (b) 0·018 (c) 0·004 (d) 0·032 (e) 0·036 (f) 0·003 (g) 0·006
   (h) 0·42 (i) 0·064 (j) 0·054 (k) 0·056 (l) 0·009 (m) 0·048 (n) 0·01
   (o) 0·045 (p) 0·063 (q) 0·072 (r) 0·049 (s) 0·021 (t) 0·024

5. (a) 3·6 (b) 4·4 (c) 4·4 (d) 4·5 (e) 3·9 (f) 0·24 (g) 0·55
   (h) 0·64 (i) 0·63 (j) 0·82 (k) 0·64 (l) 0·88 (m) 0·55 (n) 0·84
   (o) 0·99 (p) 0·024 (q) 0·055 (r) 0·186 (s) 0·168 (t) 0·06
6. (a) £3·60 (b) £6 (c) £3·60 (d) £4·80 (e) £8·80 (f) £3·75

Exercise 10H

1. (a) 31·5 (b) 44·8 (c) 19·5 (d) 41 (e) 28·2 (f) 99 (g) 65·2
   (h) 203·7 (i) 207 (j) 195·6
2. (a) 26 (b) 35·15 (c) 63·42 (d) 25·5 (e) 42·88 (f) 42·48 (g) 31·2
   (h) 26·31 (i) 41·85 (j) 14·7
3. (a) 228 (b) 576 (c) 486 (d) 135 (e) 342 (f) 144·4 (g) 258
   (h) 280·2 (i) 604·8 (j) 365·5
4. (a) 2·72 (b) 2·25 (c) 3·96 (d) 5·85 (e) 9·5 (f) 34·276 (g) 8·442
   (h) 14·025 (i) 2·25 (j) 30·672
5. (a) £25·68 (b) £42·80 (c) £171·20 (d) £66·77 (e) £121·55
6. (a) £130·20 (b) £4 947·60
7. (a) 305·4 hours (b) £158·81
8. (a) £34·80 (b) £8·52 (c) £208·80 (d) £18·18 (e) £57·70

Exercise 10I

1. (a) 3·2 (b) 1·3 (c) 2·7 (d) 8·1 (e) 1·6 (f) 2·7 (g) 5·8
   (h) 5·3 (i) 5·7 (j) 4·8 (k) 0·56 (l) 0·58 (m) 1·24 (n) 0·15
   (o) 0·84 (p) 1·25 (q) 5·41 (r) 3·05 (s) 2·24 (t) 1·37
2. (a) 3·5 (b) 3·75 (c) 3·25 (d) 4·4 (e) 10·5 (f) 16·75 (g) 3·6
   (h) 18·5 (i) 8·25 (j) 4·5 (k) 34·5 (l) 25·2 (m) 56·5 (n) 0·75
   (o) 0·8 (p) 0·5 (q) 0·25 (r) 1·125 (s) 0·875 (t) 1·625
3. (a) £3 091·75 (b) £1 545·88 (c) £2 473·40 (d) £6 183·50 (e) £1 236·70

Exercise 10J

1. (a) 5·$\dot{3}$ (b) 2·$\dot{3}$ (c) 2·$\dot{7}$ (d) 45·$\dot{3}$ (e) 45·$\dot{6}$ (f) 3·8$\dot{3}$ (g) 4·1$\dot{6}$
   (h) 13·$\dot{6}$ (i) 1·$\dot{3}$ (j) 3·$\dot{4}$ (k) 0·5$\dot{4}$ (l) 0·7$\dot{8}$ (m) 4·1$\dot{6}$ (n) 1·0$\dot{3}$
   (o) 0·40$\dot{3}$ (p) 0·11$\dot{6}$ (q) 0·07$\dot{3}$ (r) 0·03$\dot{1}$ (s) 0·0$\dot{6}$ (t) 0·1$\dot{3}$
2. (a) £4·67 (b) £5·67 (c) £6·17 (d) £5·13 (e) £4·93

Exercise 10K

1. (a) 5·55, 5·6 (b) 1 363·23, 1 363·2 (c) 98·61, 98·6 (d) 1·295, 1·3
   (e) 254·4, 254·4 (f) 68·25, 68·3 (g) 1 628·66, 1 628·7 (h) 41·134, 41·1
   (i) 222·08, 222·1 (j) 1 214·35, 1 214·4 (k) 282·44, 282·4 (l) 443·94, 443·9
   (m) 108·36, 108·4 (n) 26·124 8, 26·1 (o) 447·372, 447·4 (p) 42·704, 42·7
   (q) 422·475, 422·5 (r) 1 294·98, 1 295·0 (s) 3 441·62, 3 441·6 (t) 5 068·413, 5 068·4
2. (a) £5·82 (b) £3·67 (c) £2·71 (d) £7·02 (e) £3·14 (f) £1·36 (g) £1·91
   (h) £5·74 (i) £2·44 (j) £2·30 (k) £1·25 (l) £2·48
3. (a) £297 (b) £63
4. (a) £22·90 (b) £17·40 (c) £11·45 (d) £4·12 (e) £21·53

Exercise 10L

1. (a) 3·2 (b) 5·6 (c) 15·2 (d) 38·2 (e) 20·7 (f) 1·9 (g) 0·5
   (h) 3·5 (i) 1·5 (j) 4·4 (k) 16·7 (l) 58·2 (m) 27·2 (n) 62·8
   (o) 76·9 (p) 1·9 (q) 0·2 (r) 7·2 (s) 10·7 (t) 0·2
2. (a) £14·49 (b) £12·21 (c) £10·79 (d) £11·31 (e) £9·87
3. (a) £4·67 (b) £8
4. (a) 95 000 m (b) 1583·$\dot{3}$ m (c) 26·3$\dot{8}$ m

Exercise 10M

1. (a) 16·1 km (b) 6·44 km (c) 40·3 km (d) 13·7 km
2. 191 kg 3. 13·7 litres 4. (a) 142 cm (b) 1·42 m
5. (a) 846 gallons (b) Bad estimate
6. 76·3 kg

Checkout 10

1. (a) 134·5 (b) 2·5 (c) 10·34
2. (a) 34 mm (b) 138 mm (c) 96 mm
3. (a) 1 345 (b) 25·3 (c) 103·4
4. (a) 342 cm (b) 1 308 cm (c) 967 cm
5. (a) 13 450 (b) 253 (c) 1 532·4
6. (a) 3 420 ml (b) 3 108 ml (c) 350 ml
7. (a) (i) 1·34 (ii) 2·5 (iii) 0·134
   (b) (i) 4·5 cm (ii) 12·7 cm (iii) 0·6 cm
8. (a) (i) 1·348 (ii) 0·253 (iii) 0·014
   (b) (i) 3·42 m (ii) 0·35 m (iii) 1·96 m
9. (a) (i) 1·345 (ii) 0·253 (iii) 0·001 5
   (b) (i) 1·342 litres (ii) 0·31 litres (iii) 0·035 litres
10. (a) (i) 1·5 (ii) 1·2 (iii) 0·12 (iv) 0·03
    (v) 4·8 (vi) 9·9 (vii) 0·36 (viii) 0·096
    (b) (i) 33·6 (ii) 21·15 (iii) 2·25 (iv) 13·632
11. (a) 0·9 (b) 0·84 (c) 3·06 (d) 0·16
    (e) 5·75 (f) 1·875
12. (a) 5·6̇ (b) 0·0̇6̇ (c) 1·3̇8̇ (d) 0·20̇16̇
13. (a) (i) 219·6 (ii) 2·8 (iii) 1 484·2 (iv) 73·3
    (v) 0·8 (vi) 2·6 (vii) 4·9 (viii) 0·3
    (b) (i) 4·52 (ii) 54·52 (iii) 8·20 (iv) 10·78
    (v) 2·63 (vi) 0·19 (vii) 5·69 (viii) 1·14

Revision exercise 10

1. (a) £470 (b) £14·10
2. 1 250 g
3. centimetres
4. 2·5 years
5. (a) £2·24 (b) 74p
6. (a) 936 (b) £25·16
7. (a) £3·25 (b) 14 (c) 20
8. (a) 75 000, 60 000 (b) £8·02
9. (a) 3·141 6 (b) the two kilogram bar (c) millilitres
10. (a) 6·25 ml (b) 330 ml
11. (a)

Item	Cost
1 jar of honey	£ 1·76
2·5 kilograms of new potatoes at 36p/kg	£ 0·90
2 jars of tea at £1·98 per jar	£ 3·96
Topside of beef	£11·45
3 packets of Weetabix at £1·54 per packet	£ 4·62
Total	£22·69

(b) 4

12. (a) £36·00 should be £3·60 (b) £17·24
13. £29·98, £16·98, £46·96
14. £10·55

11 Algebra 2

Check in 11

1. (a) 11 (b) 3 (c) ⁻3 (d) ⁻11 (e) 3 (f) ⁻11 (g) 11 (h) ⁻3
   (i) 15 (j) ⁻9 (k) 9 (l) ⁻15 (m) ⁻9 (n) ⁻15 (o) 15 (p) 9
2. (a) 9 (b) 12 (c) 25 (d) ⁻14 (e) 43 (f) 12 (g) 20 (h) 80
   (i) 16 (j) 125

Answers

Exercise 11A
1. ⁻8   2. ⁻15   3. ⁻6   4. ⁻6   5. ⁻16   6. ⁻18   7. ⁻16   8. ⁻27
9. ⁻20   10. ⁻6   11. ⁻24 12. ⁻12 13. ⁻28 14. ⁻40 15. ⁻9   16. ⁻21
17. ⁻32 18. ⁻35 19. ⁻18 20. ⁻30 21. 9   22. 3   23. 7   24. 48
25. 45   26. 63   27. 36   28. 30   29. 5   30. 14   31. 54   32. 42
33. ⁻64 34. ⁻81 35. ⁻72 36. 8   37. ⁻24 38. ⁻36 39. ⁻4   40. 49

Exercise 11B
1. ⁻4   2. ⁻2   3. ⁻4   4. ⁻7   5. ⁻5   6. ⁻7   7. ⁻4   8. ⁻3
9. ⁻3   10. ⁻9   11. ⁻8   12. ⁻7   13. ⁻5   14. ⁻2   15. ⁻9   16. ⁻3
17. ⁻4   18. ⁻9   19. ⁻2   20. ⁻2   21. 2   22. 5   23. 5   24. 8
25. 7   26. 2   27. 2   28. 3   29. 2   30. 4   31. ⁻5   32. ⁻5
33. 5   34. ⁻2   35. ⁻2   36. 2   37. ⁻4   38. ⁻4   39. 6   40. 8

Exercise 11C
1. $8x$ 2. $18y$ 3. $14p$ 4. $25a$ 5. $36z$ 6. $24u$ 7. $20m$ 8. $21b$
9. $21q$ 10. $36w$ 11. $⁻12e$ 12. $⁻30t$ 13. $⁻6x$ 14. $⁻3y$ 15. $⁻4u$ 16. $⁻5x$
17. $⁻a$ 18. $⁻18d$ 19. $⁻40r$ 20. $⁻36y$ 21. $⁻6x$ 22. $⁻20c$ 23. $⁻42p$ 24. $⁻3x$
25. $⁻4y$ 26. $⁻2z$ 27. $⁻15t$ 28. $⁻t$ 29. $⁻x$ 30. $⁻16z$ 31. $4x$ 32. $15m$
33. $12p$ 34. $8x$ 35. $10y$ 36. $2t$ 37. t 38. $3e$ 39. e 40. $16x$

Exercise 11D
1. $4ab$ 2. $15st$ 3. $4ab$ 4. $49uv$ 5. $16cd$ 6. $6ab$ 7. $7xy$ 8. $30rs$
9. $24xy$ 10. $35pq$ 11. $6z^2$ 12. $7u^2$ 13. $5x^2$ 14. $6a^2$ 15. $4x^2$ 16. $9y^2$
17. $8r^2$ 18. $12e^2$ 19. $25t^2$ 20. $21w^2$ 21. $⁻6ab$ 22. $⁻10mn$ 23. $⁻3ab$ 24. $⁻2xy$
25. $⁻2xy$ 26. $⁻6z^2$ 27. $⁻6a^2$ 28. $⁻4r^2$ 29. $⁻3x^2$ 30. $⁻12b^2$ 31. $6ef$ 32. $8xy$
33. ef 34. rs 35. $12mn$ 36. $2x^2$ 37. $6y^2$ 38. $12a^2$ 39. x^2 40. $⁻y^3$

Exercise 11E
1. $3x + 6$ 2. $5y + 5$ 3. $8w + 24$ 4. $21 + 7e$ 5. $6a + 24$ 6. $4x - 4$
7. $5t - 15$ 8. $9e - 45$ 9. $12 - 3w$ 10. $5x - 20$ 11. $6a + 12$ 12. $20b + 12$
13. $30e + 18$ 14. $6x + 4$ 15. $30t + 20$ 16. $21r - 28$ 17. $16x - 24$ 18. $8 - 6m$
19. $5 - 5w$ 20. $24 - 12w$ 21. $10a + 15b$ 22. $6a + 24b$ 23. $14x + 14y$ 24. $18e + 24f$
25. $24t + 20u$ 26. $12x - 15y$ 27. $10a - 15b$ 28. $15b - 10a$ 29. $12w - 24x$ 30. $25m - 25n$

Exercise 11F
1. $7x + 18$ 2. $9y + 17$ 3. $14a + 27$ 4. $24z + 17$ 5. $30q + 24$ 6. $7x + 19$
7. $14w + 7$ 8. $13w + 20$ 9. $14w + 7$ 10. $9x$ 11. $7x + 5$ 12. $6a + 2$
13. $18w - 3$ 14. $15e - 1$ 15. $7x + 1$ 16. $7x - 5$ 17. $11y - 7$ 18. $8x - 10$
19. $13w - 16$ 20. $23z - 22$

Exercise 11G
1. $3b + 5ab$ 2. $5a - 3ab$ 3. $2y - 5xy$ 4. $x^2 + 2x$ 5. $y^2 + 7y$ 6. $2z^2 + z$
7. $2m^2 - m$ 8. $3d + 2d^2$ 9. $5a^2 - 3a$ 10. $2b^2 - 2b$ 11. $2b^2 - 2b$ 12. $3s^2 - 3s$
13. $10r^2 + 15r$ 14. $a + ab$ 15. $2x - xy$ 16. $a^2 + ab$ 17. $d^2 + 2de$ 18. $3m - 2mn$
19. $6a^2 + 8ab$ 20. $8xy + 12x^2$ 21. $6uv + 9u^2$ 22. $16r^2 + 8rs$ 23. $16r^2 - 8rs$ 24. $10x^2 - 6xy$
25. $12pq - 8p^2$

Exercise 11H
1. $⁻2a - 6$ 2. $⁻4x - 4$ 3. $⁻4b - 6$ 4. $⁻6 - 4z$ 5. $⁻20 - 30t$ 6. $⁻18w - 9$
7. $⁻10 - 10r$ 8. $⁻12b - 12$ 9. $⁻3x - 15$ 10. $⁻7x - 7x$ 11. $2 - 2x$ 12. $2x - 2$
13. $4 - 4s$ 14. $4s - 4$ 15. $3 - 6w$ 16. $8w - 4$ 17. $25 - 15x$ 18. $15x - 25$
19. $12 - 8p$ 20. $8p - 12$ 21. $⁻x - 2$ 22. $⁻y - 3$ 23. $⁻a - b$ 24. $⁻2a - 3b$
25. $⁻2x - y$ 26. $1 - x$ 27. $2x - y$ 28. $3b - 2a$ 29. $2y - 3x$ 30. $5q - 3p$
31. $⁻a^2 - ab$ 32. $⁻2x^2 - xy$ 33. $⁻3d - 2d^2$ 34. $⁻4v^2 - 2v$ 35. $⁻2s^2 - st$ 36. $st - t^2$
37. $6w - 4w^2$ 38. $8xy - 8x^2$ 39. $6ab - 6a^2$ 40. $20m^2 - 10mn$

Exercise 11I

1. $3(x+3)$
2. $5(x+3)$
3. $6(a+3)$
4. $4(m+3)$
5. $7(b+2)$
6. $4(r-4)$
7. $5(t-4)$
8. $9(w-2)$
9. $3(w-5)$
10. $4(y-6)$
11. $3(w+7)$
12. $6(m-6)$
13. $7(y+3)$
14. $11(a-2)$
15. $12(w+2)$
16. $3(2e+3)$
17. $4(2u+3)$
18. $5(3a+4)$
19. $6(2b+3)$
20. $3(4w+5)$
21. $4(3y-4)$
22. $5(4v-5)$
23. $6(3c-4)$
24. $3(2t-5)$
25. $7(2m-3)$
26. $3(5x+6)$
27. $8(2t-3)$
28. $5(6r+7)$
29. $6(5p-2)$
30. $7(4z+3)$

Exercise 11J

1. $a(1+b)$
2. $x(2+y)$
3. $p(3+5q)$
4. $t(3+2s)$
5. $a(5+7b)$
6. $x(6y+1)$
7. $t(4s+3)$
8. $e(5-4f)$
9. $u(7-5v)$
10. $b(3a-5)$
11. $3a(2b+3)$
12. $4u(2+3v)$
13. $5e(3+4f)$
14. $3x(3+4y)$
15. $4r(3+4s)$
16. $5y(4x-5)$
17. $6b(3a-2)$
18. $2y(2z-3)$
19. $3e(5-4f)$
20. $10q(2p-3)$
21. $x(x+y)$
22. $x(x^2+y)$
23. $a(2b+a)$
24. $t(5s+t)$
25. $5t(s+2t)$
26. $x(x+2y)$
27. $2x(x+y)$
28. $2x(x+2y)$
29. $7a(a^2+2b)$
30. $ab(2+3a)$

Exercise 11K

1. $x=4$
2. $y=3$
3. $a=7$
4. $s=1$
5. $x=1$
6. $y=0$
7. $c=8$
8. $z=12$
9. $f=45$
10. $m=8$
11. $x=^-1$
12. $y=^-4$
13. $a=^-5$
14. $e=^-6$
15. $t=^-5$
16. $x=^-6$
17. $d=^-4$
18. $z=^-7$
19. $y=^-4$
20. $d=^-8$

Exercise 11L

1. $x=20$
2. $e=17$
3. $a=11$
4. $z=5$
5. $t=10$
6. $u=10$
7. $d=8$
8. $r=21$
9. $x=7$
10. $d=22$
11. $d=4$
12. $x=4$
13. $t=2$
14. $y=0$
15. $u=6$
16. $x=0$
17. $b=^-6$
18. $z=^-1$
19. $p=^-5$
20. $g=^-3$

Exercise 11M

1. $x=4$
2. $r=5$
3. $w=9$
4. $y=6$
5. $m=6$
6. $a=8$
7. $u=3$
8. $y=3$
9. $t=8$
10. $c=3$
11. $y=^-5$
12. $x=^-3$
13. $t=^-5$
14. $x=^-9$
15. $u=^-4$
16. $y=^-3$
17. $r=^-8$
18. $y=^-5$
19. $z=^-10$
20. $t=^-1$
21. $x=2$
22. $x=9$
23. $f=8$
24. $v=2$
25. $x=4$
26. $x=7$
27. $a=21$
28. $s=^-7$
29. $r=^-10$
30. $m=20$

Exercise 11N

1. $x=16$
2. $c=15$
3. $a=12$
4. $t=7$
5. $y=9$
6. $m=35$
7. $x=48$
8. $z=10$
9. $t=24$
10. $h=45$
11. $j=^-20$
12. $y=^-15$
13. $z=^-42$
14. $d=^-3$
15. $r=^-18$
16. $d=^-8$
17. $y=^-30$
18. $u=^-30$
19. $x=^-30$
20. $t=^-12$
21. $x=18$
22. $z=24$
23. $r=45$
24. $m=45$
25. $s=20$
26. $e=56$
27. $e=^-56$
28. $e=^-56$
29. $e=56$
30. $a=^-48$

Exercise 11O

1. $x=6$
2. $x=4$
3. $a=7$
4. $e=2$
5. $m=1$
6. $s=2$
7. $p=6$
8. $x=3$
9. $s=8$
10. $y=1$
11. $y=4$
12. $x=3$
13. $a=4$
14. $z=6$
15. $x=2$
16. $x=10$
17. $p=6$
18. $m=5$
19. $t=1$
20. $x=2$
21. $x=8$
22. $x=2$
23. $a=6$
24. $x=2$
25. $z=1$
26. $q=^-1$
27. $y=^-2$
28. $z=3$
29. $m=12$
30. $y=^-3$
31. $a=8$
32. $z=9$
33. $p=20$
34. $q=12$
35. $x=5$
36. $y=15$
37. $a=^-4$
38. $x=^-14$
39. $x=9$
40. $x=12$

Exercise 11P

1. $x=5$
2. $a=4$
3. $z=1$
4. $m=2$
5. $p=0$
6. $z=8$
7. $t=7$
8. $x=5$
9. $t=5$
10. $q=4$
11. $x=4$
12. $a=3$
13. $z=1$
14. $s=2$
15. $x=4$
16. $x=6$
17. $x=3$
18. $a=3$
19. $y=1$
20. $z=2$
21. $x=2$
22. $x=4$
23. $y=6$
24. $y=4$
25. $y=2$
26. $y=^-2$
27. $x=1$
28. $a=4$
29. $y=^-1$
30. $y=^-3$

Exercise 11Q

1. $p=3$
2. $a=2$
3. $w=3$
4. $t=1$
5. $w=3$
6. $x=2$
7. $x=5.25$
8. $c=7$
9. $a=13$
10. $w=6$
11. $s=11$
12. $e=1$
13. $x=4$
14. $x=^-2$
15. $b=3.143$
16. $x=^-1$
17. $x=1$
18. $z=^-14$
19. $q=4$
20. $t=^-5$
21. $b=1.875$
22. $x=^-2$
23. $m=2$
24. $q=^-0.1$
25. $k=5$
26. $x=12$
27. $s=3$
28. $w=8$
29. $y=^-3$
30. $y=1.167$

Exercise 11R

1. (a) $y = 3x + 5$ (b) $y = \dfrac{3x-2}{3}$ (c) $y = 2 - 3x$ (d) $y = \dfrac{2x-5}{3}$
   (e) $y = \dfrac{2x-3}{2}$ (f) $y = \dfrac{a}{b} - \dfrac{1}{2}$

2. (a) $t = \dfrac{v-u}{f}$ (b) 10·59 (c) 46·7

3. (a) $s = \dfrac{v^2-u^2}{2f}$ (b) 14·4 (c) $v = \sqrt{u^2+2fs}$ (d) 57·68
   (e) $u = \sqrt{v^2-2fs}$ (f) 13·97

Checkout 11

1. (a) 20 (b) ⁻15 (c) ⁻8 (d) 24 (e) ⁻18 (f) ⁻16 (g) 36 (h) 14
   (i) ⁻9 (j) 4 (k) ⁻3 (l) 3 (m) ⁻3 (n) 5 (o) ⁻4 (p) 8
2. (a) $12d$ (b) $30x$ (c) $18w$ (d) $20y$ (e) ⁻$6e$ (f) ⁻$6y$ (g) ⁻$20r$ (h) $6x$
3. (a) $6xy$ (b) $20rs$ (c) $6wy$ (d) $5ab$ (e) ⁻$6ef$ (f) ⁻$6xy$ (g) $15st$ (h) $4r^2$
   (i) $6x^2$ (j) ⁻$2y^2$ (k) $15t^2$ (l) ⁻$7x^2$
4. (a) $4x + 8$ (b) $3x - 3$ (c) $12x + 18$ (d) $10t - 2$
   (e) $18 - 30j$ (f) $10a + 15c$ (g) $12x + 6y$ (h) $9u - 6v$
   (i) $x^2 + x$ (j) $d^2 + de$ (k) $2z^2 + 5z$ (l) $x^2 + xy$
   (m) $2s^2 + 3st$ (n) $2pq - 3p^2$ (o) $3c^2 + 6cd$ (p) $8xy - 12y^2$
5. (a) ⁻$2x - 2$ (b) ⁻$3z - 12$ (c) ⁻$8x - 12$ (d) ⁻$7x - 14$
   (e) $3 - 3x$ (f) $8 - 4x$ (g) $5x - 20$ (h) $30x - 12$
   (i) ⁻$y - 4$ (j) $6 - 2x$ (k) ⁻$a - b$ (l) $b - a$
   (m) ⁻$x^2 - 3x$ (n) $2y - y^2$ (o) $2s^2 - 2s$ (p) $12t^2 - 8pt$
6. (a) $3(x+3)$ (b) $5(t+3)$ (c) $4(m-5)$ (d) $7(t-2)$
   (e) $5(3x+8)$ (f) $3(3r+8)$ (g) $3(4x-5)$ (h) $10(2p-3)$
7. (a) $x(1+y)$ (b) $d(c+2)$ (c) $b(3a-2)$ (d) $2f(2-e)$
   (e) $x(2x+1)$ (f) $x(3x+2)$ (g) $a(2b-a)$ (h) $5x(1-2y)$
8. (a) $x = 25$ (b) $r = 0$ (c) $y = $ ⁻26
9. (a) $c = 10$ (b) $u = 7$ (c) $m = 4$
10. (a) $x = 12$ (b) $n = 10$ (c) $v = $ ⁻20
11. (a) $m = 10$ (b) $t = 2$ (c) $x = $ ⁻8
12. (a) $x = 3$ (b) $e = 10$ (c) $e = 3$
    (d) $x = 15$ (e) $m = 30$ (f) $c = 6$
13. (a) $x = 5$ (b) $x = 4$ (c) $y = 4$ (d) $e = $ ⁻1
14. (a) $x = 3$ (b) $y = 3$ (c) $t = 4$ (d) $x = 4$

Revision exercise 11

1. (a) (i) $3f + 2g$ (ii) $3ty$ (iii) r^2 (b) $6t + 15$
2. (a) $15x + 12$ (b) $63 - 18x$
3. 6
4. 24
5. (a) $A = 6$ (b) $B = 7$
6. (a) $5x + 9$ (b) (i) $5x + 9 = 34$ (ii) $x = 5$ cm
7. (a) $x + 4$ (b) $4x + 10$ (c) $x = 6$ m
8. (a) $(4x + 20)°$ (b) (i) $4x + 20 = 180$ (ii) smallest angle $= 44°$
9. (a) (i) 28 (ii) 8 (b) 13
10. (a) £290 (b) 31
11. (a) $x = 2$ (b) $x = \tfrac{1}{2}$
12. (a) $P = 60$ (b) $x = 2$
13. (a) $t = 3$ (b) $y = \tfrac{4}{7}$ (c) $x = 60$ (d) $p = 5$
14. (a) $x = 8$ (b) $y = $ ⁻3
15. (a) $x = 4$ (b) $x = \tfrac{1}{2}$
16. (a) $w = $ ⁻6 (b) $x = 8$ (c) $y = \tfrac{3}{2}$
17. (a) $x = 5$ (b) $x = \tfrac{1}{2}$
18. (a) $x = \tfrac{27}{4}$ (b) $y = 9$

12 Number 5

Check in 12

1. (a) 6 (b) 20 (c) 9 (d) 16 (e) 32 (f) 30 (g) 24 (h) 45 (i) 18
   (j) 49 (k) 54 (l) 63 (m) 56 (n) 81 (o) 42 (p) 35
2. (a) 7 (b) 6 (c) 7 (d) 3 (e) 7 (f) 5 (g) 6 (h) 6
   (i) 6 (j) 8 (k) 6 (l) 3 (m) 9 (n) 6 (o) 8 (p) 5

Exercise 12A

1. (a) $\frac{3}{4}$ (b) $\frac{1}{6}$ (c) $\frac{5}{8}$ (d) $\frac{1}{3}$ (e) $\frac{3}{7}$ (f) $\frac{4}{5}$
   (g) $\frac{5}{6}$ (h) $\frac{5}{9}$ (i) $\frac{7}{15}$ (j) $\frac{7}{10}$
2. (a) $\frac{13}{19}$ (b) $\frac{15}{19}$ (c) $\frac{6}{19}$ (d) $\frac{12}{19}$ (e) $\frac{3}{19}$ (f) $\frac{3}{19}$ (g) $\frac{4}{19}$
3. (a) $\frac{2}{7}$ (b) $\frac{1}{3}$ (c) $\frac{1}{4}$ (d) $\frac{3}{4}$ (e) $\frac{1}{2}$
4. (a) $\frac{3}{10}$ (b) $\frac{2}{5}$ (c) $\frac{2}{7}$ (d) $\frac{3}{8}$ (e) $\frac{3}{7}$

Exercise 12B

1. (a) $2\frac{2}{5}$ (b) $1\frac{3}{4}$ (c) $1\frac{4}{5}$ (d) $1\frac{1}{3}$ (e) $2\frac{1}{2}$ (f) 2 (g) $1\frac{1}{6}$ (h) $1\frac{1}{7}$ (i) $1\frac{2}{3}$
   (j) $1\frac{2}{7}$ (k) $1\frac{1}{12}$ (l) $6\frac{1}{3}$ (m) 3 (n) $7\frac{1}{4}$ (o) 9 (p) $6\frac{3}{5}$ (q) $5\frac{1}{2}$ (r) $2\frac{1}{4}$
   (s) $1\frac{2}{13}$ (t) $1\frac{1}{99}$ (u) $1\frac{1}{5}$ (v) $1\frac{4}{17}$ (w) $2\frac{3}{4}$ (x) $9\frac{1}{2}$ (y) $4\frac{1}{4}$
2. (a) $\frac{3}{2}$ (b) $\frac{7}{3}$ (c) $\frac{5}{4}$ (d) $\frac{7}{5}$ (e) $\frac{13}{6}$ (f) $\frac{11}{7}$ (g) $\frac{9}{8}$ (h) $\frac{17}{12}$ (i) $\frac{18}{13}$
   (j) $\frac{29}{4}$ (k) $\frac{13}{2}$ (l) $\frac{11}{3}$ (m) $\frac{11}{4}$ (n) $\frac{11}{5}$ (o) $\frac{17}{6}$ (p) $\frac{15}{7}$ (q) $\frac{13}{8}$ (r) $\frac{43}{12}$
   (s) $\frac{35}{17}$ (t) $\frac{26}{7}$ (u) $\frac{19}{2}$ (v) $\frac{22}{3}$ (w) $\frac{27}{4}$ (x) $\frac{9}{5}$ (y) $\frac{23}{6}$

Exercise 12C

1. $\frac{1}{3}$ 2. $\frac{1}{2}$ 3. $\frac{3}{4}$ 4. $\frac{2}{5}$ 5. $\frac{4}{5}$ 6. $\frac{1}{2}$ 7. $\frac{1}{2}$ 8. $\frac{2}{3}$

Exercise 12D

1. $\frac{9}{12}$ 2. $\frac{4}{6}$ 3. $\frac{20}{25}$ 4. $\frac{4}{8}$ 5. $\frac{6}{12}$ 6. $\frac{10}{15}$ 7. $\frac{9}{15}$ 8. $\frac{15}{20}$ 9. $\frac{16}{20}$
10. $\frac{7}{42}$ 11. $\frac{18}{42}$ 12. $\frac{7}{14}$ 13. $\frac{8}{14}$ 14. $\frac{15}{40}$ 15. $\frac{28}{40}$ 16. $\frac{3}{12}$ 17. $\frac{8}{12}$ 18. $\frac{21}{35}$
19. $\frac{30}{35}$ 20. $\frac{14}{24}$ 21. $\frac{15}{24}$ 22. $\frac{50}{90}$ 23. $\frac{18}{30}$ 24. $\frac{18}{45}$ 25. $\frac{9}{24}$

Exercise 12E

1. (a) $\frac{1}{2}$ (b) $\frac{1}{4}$ (c) $\frac{3}{4}$ (d) $\frac{2}{3}$ (e) $\frac{4}{5}$ (f) $\frac{3}{5}$ (g) $\frac{5}{7}$ (h) $\frac{8}{9}$ (i) $\frac{9}{10}$
   (j) $\frac{7}{11}$ (k) $\frac{1}{3}$ (l) $\frac{6}{7}$ (m) $\frac{1}{2}$ (n) 4 (o) $1\frac{1}{3}$ (p) $\frac{2}{3}$ (q) $1\frac{1}{4}$ (r) $\frac{3}{5}$
   (s) $1\frac{2}{5}$ (t) 1 (u) $\frac{9}{10}$ (v) $\frac{1}{3}$ (w) $\frac{6}{7}$ (x) $\frac{2}{3}$ (y) $\frac{22}{25}$
2. (a) $\frac{1}{2}$ (b) $\frac{1}{6}$ (c) $\frac{1}{4}$ (d) $\frac{1}{3}$ (e) $\frac{1}{12}$
3. (a) $\frac{5}{12}$ (b) $\frac{2}{3}$ (c) $\frac{3}{5}$ (d) $\frac{11}{12}$ (e) $\frac{2}{5}$
4. (a) $\frac{1}{4}$ (b) $\frac{1}{2}$ (c) $\frac{3}{4}$ (d) $\frac{4}{5}$ (e) $\frac{9}{20}$

Exercise 12F

1. (a) $\frac{4}{5}$ (b) 1 (c) $1\frac{1}{5}$ (d) $1\frac{2}{5}$ (e) $2\frac{2}{5}$
2. (a) 1 (b) $1\frac{1}{2}$ (c) 2 (d) $3\frac{1}{2}$ (e) 6
3. (a) $\frac{3}{7}$ (b) $\frac{5}{7}$ (c) 1 (d) $1\frac{1}{7}$ (e) 2
4. (a) 2 (b) $2\frac{1}{3}$ (c) 3 (d) $4\frac{1}{3}$ (e) 5
5. (a) $2\frac{1}{2}$ (b) 4 (c) $7\frac{1}{2}$ (d) $3\frac{1}{4}$ (e) $7\frac{1}{4}$
6. (a) $\frac{6}{11}$ (b) $\frac{8}{11}$ (c) $\frac{10}{11}$ (d) $11\frac{8}{11}$ (e) $5\frac{2}{11}$
7. (a) $2\frac{2}{3}$ (b) 2 (c) $3\frac{2}{3}$ (d) 7 (e) $13\frac{2}{3}$
8. (a) $4\frac{2}{3}$ (b) 4 (c) $4\frac{4}{9}$ (d) 11 (e) $4\frac{1}{3}$
9. (a) $2\frac{1}{4}$ (b) $2\frac{1}{2}$ (c) 3 (d) $6\frac{1}{2}$ (e) $6\frac{3}{4}$
10. (a) $3\frac{2}{3}$ (b) 4 (c) $3\frac{5}{6}$ (d) $4\frac{1}{3}$ (e) 7

Answers

Exercise 12G

1. (a) $\frac{2}{5}$ (b) $\frac{1}{5}$ (c) $3\frac{2}{5}$ (d) 6 (e) $1\frac{1}{5}$
2. (a) $\frac{1}{2}$ (b) $\frac{1}{4}$ (c) $3\frac{1}{2}$ (d) 8 (e) $9\frac{1}{4}$
3. (a) $\frac{1}{7}$ (b) $\frac{2}{7}$ (c) $1\frac{1}{7}$ (d) $4\frac{3}{7}$ (e) 7
4. (a) $3\frac{2}{9}$ (b) $1\frac{5}{9}$ (c) $\frac{1}{3}$ (d) $4\frac{2}{3}$ (e) $\frac{1}{9}$
5. (a) $1\frac{1}{2}$ (b) 3 (c) $5\frac{1}{2}$ (d) $1\frac{1}{4}$ (e) $\frac{1}{4}$
6. (a) $1\frac{1}{11}$ (b) $\frac{5}{11}$ (c) $3\frac{6}{11}$ (d) $5\frac{4}{11}$ (e) $\frac{8}{11}$
7. (a) $6\frac{1}{9}$ (b) 1 (c) $\frac{8}{9}$ (d) $\frac{7}{9}$ (e) $\frac{5}{9}$
8. (a) $4\frac{1}{4}$ (b) 4 (c) $3\frac{3}{4}$ (d) $3\frac{1}{2}$ (e) $3\frac{3}{8}$
9. (a) $1\frac{1}{2}$ (b) $2\frac{1}{2}$ (c) $3\frac{3}{4}$ (d) $10\frac{1}{4}$ (e) $-1\frac{1}{2}$
10. (a) $2\frac{3}{8}$ (b) $1\frac{3}{4}$ (c) $3\frac{1}{2}$ (d) $4\frac{3}{8}$ (e) $4\frac{7}{8}$

Exercise 12H

1. (a) $\frac{19}{20}$ (b) $1\frac{1}{4}$ (c) $\frac{13}{15}$ (d) $1\frac{1}{6}$ (e) $1\frac{13}{14}$ (f) $1\frac{7}{15}$ (g) $1\frac{13}{28}$ (h) $1\frac{29}{70}$ (i) $1\frac{13}{20}$
   (j) $1\frac{1}{4}$ (k) $2\frac{5}{6}$ (l) $3\frac{13}{20}$ (m) $2\frac{1}{3}$ (n) $3\frac{1}{10}$ (o) $3\frac{4}{5}$ (p) $4\frac{7}{12}$ (q) $4\frac{7}{15}$ (r) $6\frac{7}{20}$
   (s) $5\frac{11}{20}$ (t) $5\frac{1}{18}$ (u) $5\frac{1}{9}$ (v) $8\frac{3}{8}$ (w) $7\frac{21}{22}$ (x) $5\frac{3}{4}$ (y) $6\frac{1}{6}$
2. (a) $\frac{1}{10}$ (b) $\frac{1}{8}$ (c) $\frac{1}{4}$ (d) $\frac{1}{9}$ (e) $\frac{1}{16}$ (f) $\frac{1}{6}$ (g) $\frac{1}{3}$ (h) $\frac{7}{20}$ (i) $\frac{1}{20}$
   (j) $\frac{2}{3}$ (k) $3\frac{1}{3}$ (l) $2\frac{1}{6}$ (m) $3\frac{7}{20}$ (n) $2\frac{7}{15}$ (o) $3\frac{3}{20}$ (p) $1\frac{1}{10}$ (q) $4\frac{2}{3}$ (r) $4\frac{11}{21}$
   (s) $3\frac{1}{4}$ (t) $1\frac{7}{18}$ (u) $2\frac{7}{12}$ (v) $3\frac{11}{12}$ (w) $5\frac{3}{8}$ (x) $1\frac{13}{15}$ (y) $\frac{1}{2}$

Exercise 12I

1. (a) 2 (b) 5 (c) 25 (d) 50 (e) 200
2. (a) 5 (b) 11 (c) 16 (d) 25 (e) 150
3. (a) 6 (b) 2 (c) 1 (d) 12 (e) 100
4. (a) 25 (b) 9 (c) 22 (d) 36 (e) 48
5. (a) 2 (b) 1 (c) 10 (d) 100 (e) 200
6. (a) 7 (b) 9 (c) 8 (d) 11 (e) 12
7. (a) 2 (b) 3 (c) 8 (d) 9 (e) 100
8. (a) 5 (b) 7 (c) 21 (d) 45 (e) 60
9. (a) 12 (b) 27 (c) 15 (d) 90 (e) 1 200
10. (a) 18 (b) 30 (c) 15 (d) 66 (e) 375
11. (a) 8 (b) 14 (c) 20 (d) 32 (e) 100
12. (a) 24 (b) 6 (c) 18 (d) 28 (e) 40
13. (a) 3 (b) 9 (c) 240 (d) 93 (e) 135
14. (a) 30 (b) 55 (c) 40 (d) 200 (e) 150
15. (a) 16 (b) 20 (c) 40 (d) 48 (e) 480
16. (a) 14 (b) 28 (c) 245 (d) 350 (e) 700
17. 72
18. 9 000
19. (a) £20, £40 (b) £15, £30 (c) £10, £20 (d) £12, £24
    (e) £6, £12 (f) £16, £32 (g) £4, £8 (h) 80p, £1·60
20. Marianna 210, Barry 192

Exercise 12J

1. $\frac{3}{10}$
2. $\frac{1}{5}$
3. $\frac{3}{4}$
4. $\frac{9}{10}$
5. $\frac{4}{5}$
6. $\frac{1}{20}$
7. $\frac{9}{20}$
8. $\frac{1}{25}$
9. $\frac{3}{25}$
10. $\frac{6}{25}$
11. $\frac{3}{5}$
12. $\frac{1}{50}$
13. $\frac{11}{50}$
14. $\frac{49}{50}$
15. $\frac{7}{20}$
16. $\frac{18}{25}$
17. $\frac{19}{20}$
18. $\frac{13}{20}$
19. $\frac{17}{100}$
20. $\frac{21}{50}$
21. $\frac{3}{25}$
22. $\frac{7}{50}$
23. $\frac{4}{25}$
24. $\frac{99}{100}$
25. $\frac{3}{20}$

Exercise 12K

1. (a) 70 (b) 200 (c) 300 (d) 300 (e) 16 (f) 18 (g) 38 (h) 5 (i) 120
   (j) 18 (k) 27 (l) 140 (m) 180 (n) 18 (o) 102 (p) 156 (q) 4 (r) 4
   (s) 20 (t) 81 (u) 18 (v) 176 (w) 273 (x) 33 (y) 33
2. (a) 3·1 (b) 13·6 (c) 10·12 (d) 71·12 (e) 61·41 (f) 161·28 (g) 36
   (h) 6·65 (i) 228·6 (j) 568·4 (k) 120·6 (l) 1·35 (m) 14 (n) 42
   (o) 24·5 (p) 17·325 (q) 7 (r) 7·75 (s) 16·272 (t) 17·4 (u) 33·6
   (v) 12 (w) 3·6 (x) 2·1 (y) 4·890 6

3. (a) £12, £68 (b) £9, £51 (c) £4·50, £25·50 (d) £10·50, £59·50
   (e) £6·75, £38·25 (f) £7·20, £40·80 (g) £2·70, £15·30 (h) 72p, £4·08
4. (a) £112, £752 (b) £140, £940 (c) £210, £1 410 (d) £87·50, £587·50
   (e) £131·25, £881·25 (f) £56, £376 (g) £568·75, £3 818·75 (h) £68·25, £458·25

Exercise 12L

1. (a) 0·5, 50% (b) 0·25, 25% (c) 0·75, 75% (d) 0·6, 60% (e) 0·7, 70% (f) 0·55, 55%
   (g) 0·12, 12% (h) 0·54, 54% (i) 0·2, 20% (j) 0·9, 90% (k) 0·15, 15% (l) 0·72, 72%
   (m) 0·02, 2% (n) 0·4, 40% (o) 0·1, 10% (p) 0·45, 45% (q) 0·68, 68% (r) 0·86, 86%
   (s) 0·35, 35% (t) 0·84, 84% (u) 0·22, 22% (v) 0·65, 65% (w) 0·44, 44% (x) 0·98, 98%
   (y) 0·96, 96%
2. (a) £40 (b) £36 (c) £50 (d) 33·3% (e) 41·$\dot{6}$%

Exercise 12M

1. (a) 50% (b) 75% (c) 25% (d) 40% (e) 60% (f) 15% (g) 28% (h) 80%
   (i) 50% (j) 30% (k) 70% (l) 75% (m) 25% (n) 55% (o) 80% (p) 52%
   (q) 60% (r) 70% (s) 95% (t) 34% (u) 45% (v) 7% (w) 16% (x) 84%
   (y) 80%
2. 15%, 30%, 60%, 75%, 40%, 70%, 50%, 62·5%, 87·5%, 95%
3. (a) 25% (b) 50% (c) 20% (d) 45% (e) 60% (f) 75% (g) 80% (h) 85%
   (i) 65% (j) 95%
4.

Cash saving	% saving
£2·50	20%
£0·54	15%
£2·90	25%
£0·60	12·5%
£2·43	45%

5. (a) £1·80 (b) £0·18 (c) 10% (d) 18 (e) $\frac{1}{5}$

Exercise 12N

1. (a) £10·12 (b) £4·07 (c) £5·50 (d) £10·79 (e) £10·04
2. (a) £108·18 (b) £1·05 (c) £792·00 (d) £286 (e) £156·00 (f) £37·98
3. (a) £24·00 (b) £8·40 (c) £14·08 (d) 36p (e) £10·39
4. (a) £58·43 (b) £1·09 (c) £204·80 (d) £31·90 (e) £138·67 (f) £2·15

Checkout 12

1. (a) $\frac{3}{5}$ (b) $\frac{3}{4}$
2. (a) (i) $8\frac{1}{2}$ (ii) $5\frac{1}{3}$ (iii) $2\frac{1}{4}$ (b) (i) $\frac{7}{2}$ (ii) $\frac{11}{4}$ (iii) $\frac{23}{3}$
3. (a) $\frac{3}{4} = \frac{9}{12}$ (b) $\frac{1}{2} = \frac{12}{24}$ (c) $\frac{3}{8} = \frac{6}{16}$ (d) $\frac{4}{5} = \frac{20}{25}$
4. (a) $\frac{3}{4}$ (b) $\frac{2}{5}$ (c) $\frac{5}{8}$ (d) $\frac{1}{3}$
5. (a) $1\frac{1}{2}$ (b) $1\frac{2}{5}$ (c) $1\frac{3}{11}$ (d) $4\frac{1}{3}$ (e) $\frac{1}{2}$ (f) $\frac{2}{3}$
   (g) $\frac{1}{3}$ (h) $-\frac{1}{3}$ (i) $1\frac{7}{15}$ (j) $1\frac{7}{12}$ (k) $1\frac{8}{9}$ (l) $5\frac{3}{10}$
   (m) $\frac{2}{15}$ (n) $\frac{1}{8}$ (o) $1\frac{1}{2}$ (p) $2\frac{4}{9}$
6. (a) 5 (b) 8 (c) 50 (d) 120
7. (a) 12 (b) 48 (c) 75 (d) 225
8. (a) $\frac{1}{5}$ (b) $\frac{3}{4}$ (c) $\frac{9}{25}$
9. (a) 200 (b) 4 (c) 21 (d) 221 (e) £3·50 (f) £6·30
10. (a) 0·75, 75% (b) 0·8, 80% (c) 0·15, 15% (d) 0·92, 92%
11. (a) (i) 50% (ii) 48% (iii) 60% (b) 30%

Revision exercise 12

1. $4\frac{7}{8}$ inches 2. $1\frac{1}{2}$ inches
3. (a) 6 miles (b) $3\frac{1}{2}$ miles
4. (a) 10 : 20 (b) 90 miles

470 Answers

5. 780 grams   6. $\frac{3}{5}$
7. (a) $4\frac{3}{4}$ (b) $1\frac{1}{16}$
8. (a) £14·75   (b) 6   (c) £2·80
9. (a) (i) 40   (ii) 60   (b) $\frac{5}{8}$ (c) 25%   (d) 0·375
10. (a) (i) 0·25   (ii) $\frac{1}{5}$ (iii) 0·3   (iv) 0·2, $\frac{1}{4}$, 30%
    (b) £480   (c) £100 : £40
11. (a) 32   (b) £408
12. (a) 25%   (b) 12 squares should be shaded altogether.
13. (a) £29   (b) £484
14. £185 with $\frac{1}{5}$ off marked price   15. £36   16. £329·60   17. £1 860
18. (a) £130·23   (b) £136·74
19. (a) £155·63 per week   (b) £178·13   (c) £140
20. £235
21. (a) £4·20   (b) £28·20   (c) £4·23
    (d) More or less. In fact it is 3p less than the price before V.A.T.
22. (a) 11   (b) £252   (c) 22   (d) £7 840
23. 65%
24. (a) 11 million   (b) 20%
25. (a) 50%   (b) 1 : 1   (c) 210
26. (a) 75%   (b) Gladiators
27. (a) 57p   (b) Quickways   (c) The percentage reduction is bigger.   (d) 41%

13 Algebra 3

Check in 13

1. (a) 6   (b) 4   (c) −9   (d) 21   (e) 8   (f) 4   (g) 4
    (h) 14   (i) 11
2. (a) $x = 4$ (b) $y = 3$ (c) $y = 20$ (d) $t = 8$ (e) $t = 15$ (f) $r = 7$ (g) $x = 5$
    (h) $m = 4$ (i) $e = 2·5$ (j) $n = 14$

Exercise 13A

1. 2, 5, 8, 11, 14   2. 1, 3, 9, 27, 81   3. 5, 9, 13, 17, 21   4. 2, 6, 10, 14, 18
5. 100, 97, 94, 91, 88   6. 6, 11, 16, 21, 26   7. 1, 4, 16, 64, 256   8. 2, 7, 12, 17, 22
9. 3, 9, 15, 21, 27   10. 1, 8, 15, 22, 29   11. 100, 90, 80, 70, 60   12. 1, 1, 2, 3, 5

Exercise 13B

1. 32, 37   2. 60, 50   3. 3 125, 15 625   4. 25, 29   5. 29, 47
6. 19, 21   7. 32, 16   8. 16, 22   9. 243, 729   10. 23, 26
11. 40, 36   12. 78, 93   13. 0·01, 0·001   14. 67, 79   15. 43, 39
16. 13, 21   17. 21, 28   18. 56, 67   19. 200, 2 000   20. 0·25, 0·125

Exercise 13C

1. 2, 4, 6, 8, 10   2. 3, 6, 9, 12, 15   3. 4, 8, 12, 16, 20   4. 5, 10, 15, 20, 25
5. 6, 12, 18, 24, 30   6. 7, 14, 21, 28, 35   7. 8, 16, 24, 32, 40   8. 9, 18, 27, 36, 45
9. 10, 20, 30, 40, 50   10. 2, 3, 4, 5, 6   11. 4, 5, 6, 7, 8   12. 5, 6, 7, 8, 9
13. 3, 5, 7, 9, 11   14. 4, 7, 10, 13, 16   15. 5, 9, 13, 17, 21   16. 1, 3, 5, 7, 9
17. 2, 5, 8, 11, 14   18. 3, 7, 11, 15, 19   19. 7, 12, 17, 22, 27   20. 7, 10, 13, 16, 19
21. 1, 5, 9, 13, 17   22. 7, 9, 11, 13, 17   23. 1, 6, 11, 16, 21   24. 3, 9, 15, 21, 27
25. 9, 11, 13, 15, 17   26. 0, 3, 6, 9, 12   27. 9, 13, 17, 21, 25   28. 9, 14, 19, 24, 29
29. 11, 14, 17, 20, 23   30. 3, 13, 23, 33, 43

Exercise 13D

1. $2n + 3$, 103   2. $3n + 3$, 153   3. $4n + 3$, 203   4. $5n - 2$, 248   5. $6n + 2$, 302
6. $2n - 3$, 97   7. $3n - 2$, 148   8. $4n - 2$, 198   9. $5n - 1$, 249   10. $7n - 3$, 347
11. $2n + 5$, 105   12. $3n + 6$, 156   13. $4n + 7$, 207   14. $5n + 3$, 253   15. $10n + 4$, 504
16. $2n - 2$, 98   17. $3n + 2$, 152   18. $4n + 4$, 204   19. $5n + 8$, 258   20. $10n - 1$, 499

Exercise 13E

1. (a) 5
    (b)

Fences in metres	1	2	3	4
Metres of wood needed	5	9	13	17

    (c) $4n + 1$
    (d) 101 m
    (e) 10 m

2. (a)

Number of tables	1	2	3	4
Number of seats	4	6	8	10

    (b) $2n + 2$ (c) 42   (d) 15

3. (a) 14 cm
    (b)

Pattern number	1	2	3	4
Perimeter	8 cm	14 cm	20 cm	26 cm

    (c) $6n + 2$ (d) 362
    (e) 10th

4. (a) $3n + 4$ (b) 304   (c) 12th

5. (a)

Height of pyramid	1 can	2 cans	3 cans	4 cans
Number of cans in the bottom row	1	3	5	7

    (b) $2n - 1$ (c) 49
    (d) 30 cans high

Exercise 13F

1. A(1,5)   B(1,2)   C(2,1)   D(2,2)   E(3,3)   F(0,3)   G(2,4)
    H(4,4)   I(4,0)   J(5,3)

2. A(5,8)   B(5,4)   C(7,2)   D(8,0)   E(6,1)   F(4,3)   G(0,3)
    H(2,5)   I(1,2)   J(0,6)   K(2,8)   L(2,7)   M(3,6)

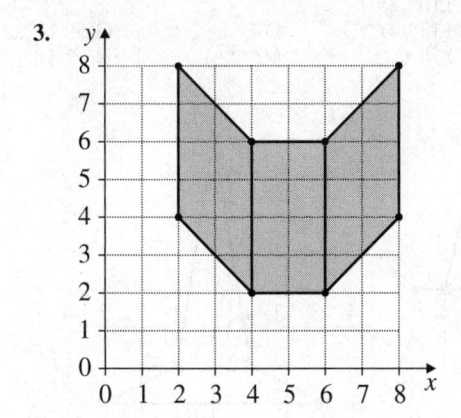

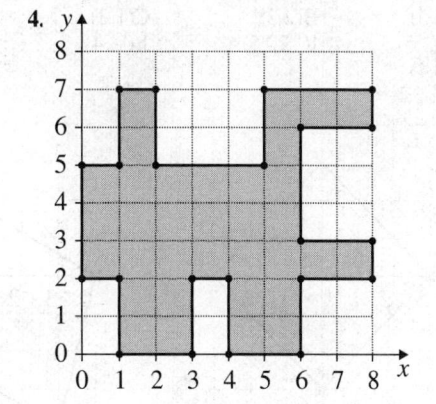

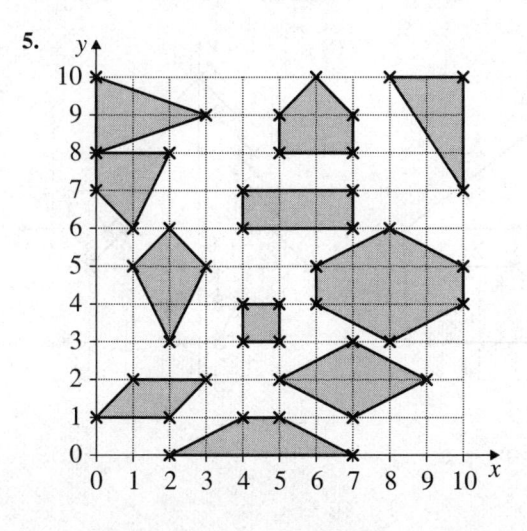

3.

4.

5.
    (a) isosceles triangle
    (b) quadrilateral
    (c) pentagon
    (d) parallelogram
    (e) square
    (f) kite
    (g) trapezium
    (h) right-angled triangle
    (i) rhombus
    (j) rectangle
    (k) hexagon

6.

Place	Location
Caves	(9,5)
Dead Person's Point	$(8\frac{1}{2},7\frac{1}{2})$
Stockade	(12,6)
Jack's Cabin	(11,5)
Treasure	(6,7)
More Treasure	$(11,2\frac{1}{2})$
Fresh Water Spring	$(6\frac{1}{2},4\frac{1}{2})$
Green Susan's Cabin	(8,2)
Swamp	(4,6)
Turtle Beach	(1,5)
First Landing	(2,4)
Gold Mine	(2,3)
Snake Pit	(3,1)

Exercise 13G

1. A(3,2) B(⁻3,2) C(0,1) D(⁻2,⁻2) E(2,3) F(⁻2,2) G(1,⁻1)
   H(1,1) I(⁻3,⁻3) J(2,⁻2) K(⁻2,0) L(0,⁻2)
2. A(2,5) B(2,3) C(1,2) D(3,0) E(3,⁻4) F(4,⁻1) G(5,⁻1)
   H(4,⁻5) I(⁻2,⁻5) J(0,⁻4) K(⁻1,⁻1) L(0,1) M(⁻2,3) N(⁻2,5)
   O(0,4)
3. (a) (b) 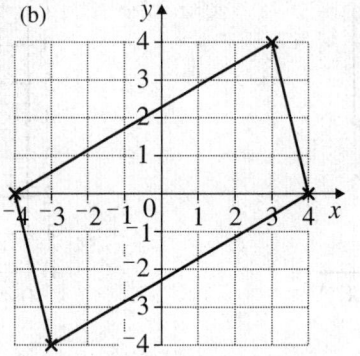 (c) 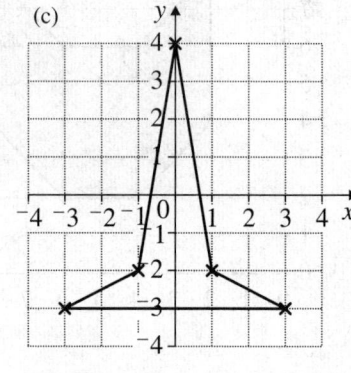 (d) 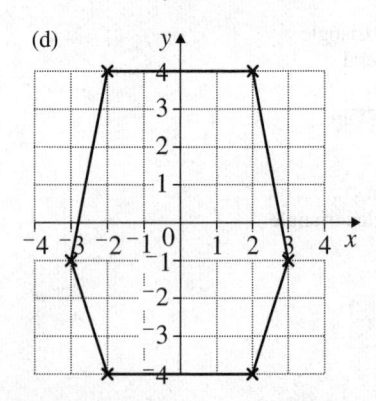 (e) 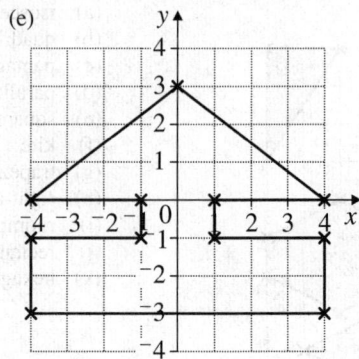 (f) 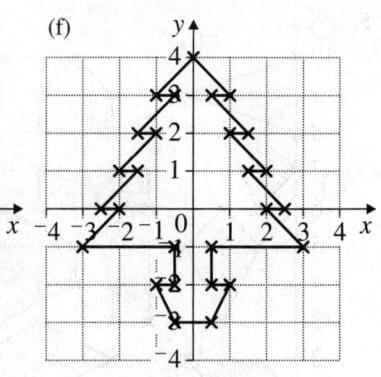
4. (b) (⁻2,⁻5) and (4,⁻5), or (⁻2,7) and (4,7)
5. (d) They all have a y-coordinate of 1.
6. (d) They all have an x-coordinate of 1.

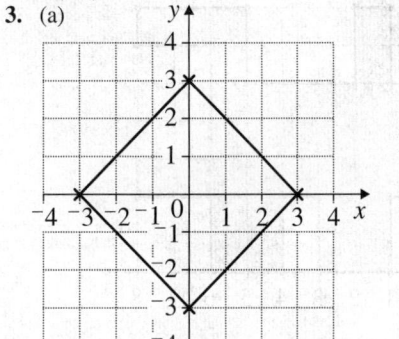

Exercise 13H

2. (a)

x	⁻2	⁻1	0	1	2
$y = x + 2$	0	1	2	3	4

(b)

x	⁻2	⁻1	0	1	2
$y = x + 3$	1	2	3	4	5

(c)

x	⁻2	⁻1	0	1	2
$y = x + 4$	2	3	4	5	6

(d)

x	⁻2	⁻1	0	1	2
$y = x - 1$	⁻3	⁻2	⁻1	0	1

(e)

x	⁻2	⁻1	0	1	2
$y = x - 2$	⁻4	⁻3	⁻2	⁻1	0

(f)

x	⁻2	⁻1	0	1	2
$y = x - 3$	⁻5	⁻4	⁻3	⁻2	⁻1

3. (a)

x	⁻2	⁻1	0	1	2
$y = x$	⁻2	⁻1	0	1	2

(b)

x	⁻2	⁻1	0	1	2
$y = 2x$	⁻4	⁻2	0	2	4

(c)

x	⁻2	⁻1	0	1	2
$y = 3x$	⁻6	⁻3	0	3	6

(d)

x	⁻2	⁻1	0	1	2
$y = {}^-2x$	4	2	0	⁻2	⁻4

(e)

x	⁻2	⁻1	0	1	2
$y = {}^-3x$	6	3	0	⁻3	⁻6

(f)

x	⁻2	⁻1	0	1	2
$y = {}^-x$	2	1	0	⁻1	⁻2

4. (a)

x	⁻2	⁻1	0	1	2
$y = 3 - x$	5	4	3	2	1

(b)

x	⁻2	⁻1	0	1	2
$y = 2 - x$	4	3	2	1	0

(c)

x	⁻2	⁻1	0	1	2
$y = 1 - x$	3	2	1	0	⁻1

(d)

x	⁻2	⁻1	0	1	2
$y = 4 - x$	6	5	4	3	2

(e)

x	⁻2	⁻1	0	1	2
$y = 8 - 2x$	12	10	8	6	4

6. (a)

x	⁻2	⁻1	0	1	2
$y = \frac{x}{2}$	⁻1	$-\frac{1}{2}$	0	$\frac{1}{2}$	1

(b)

x	⁻3	⁻1	0	1	3
$y = \frac{x}{3}$	⁻1	$-\frac{1}{3}$	0	$\frac{1}{3}$	1

(c)

x	⁻4	⁻1	0	1	4
$y = \frac{x}{4}$	⁻1	$-\frac{1}{4}$	0	$\frac{1}{4}$	1

(d)

x	⁻2	⁻1	0	1	2
$y = -\frac{x}{2}$	1	$\frac{1}{2}$	0	$-\frac{1}{2}$	⁻1

(e)

x	⁻3	⁻1	0	1	3
$y = -\frac{x}{3}$	1	$\frac{1}{3}$	0	$-\frac{1}{3}$	⁻1

(f)

x	⁻4	⁻1	0	1	4
$y = -\frac{x}{4}$	1	$\frac{1}{4}$	0	$-\frac{1}{4}$	⁻1

7. (a)

x	⁻2	⁻1	0	1	2
$y = 2x + 1$	⁻3	⁻1	1	3	5

(b)

x	⁻2	⁻1	0	1	2
$y = 3x - 1$	⁻7	⁻4	⁻1	2	5

(c)

x	⁻2	⁻1	0	1	2
$y = 2x - 3$	⁻7	⁻5	⁻3	⁻1	1

(d)

x	⁻2	⁻1	0	1	2
$y = \frac{x}{2} + 3$	2	$2\frac{1}{2}$	3	$3\frac{1}{2}$	4

(e)

x	⁻2	⁻1	0	1	2
$y = 3 - 2x$	7	5	3	1	⁻4

(f)

x	⁻2	⁻1	0	1	2
$y = 3x - 4$	⁻10	⁻7	⁻4	⁻1	2

Exercise 13I

2. (a)

x	⁻3	⁻2	⁻1	0	1	2	3
$y = x^2 + 2$	11	6	3	2	3	6	11

(b)

x	⁻3	⁻2	⁻1	0	1	2	3
$y = x^2 + 4$	13	8	5	4	5	8	13

2. (c)

x	-3	-2	-1	0	1	2	3
$y = x^2 + 6$	15	10	7	6	7	10	15

(d)

x	-3	-2	-1	0	1	2	3
$y = x^2 - 2$	7	2	-1	-2	-1	2	7

(e)

x	-3	-2	-1	0	1	2	3
$y = x^2 - 4$	5	0	-3	-4	-3	0	5

3. (a)

x	1	2	3	4	5	6	7	8	9	10	11	12
$y = \frac{12}{x}$	11	6	4	3	2.4	2	1.7	1.5	1.3	1.2	1.1	1

(b)

x	1	2	3	4
$y = \frac{4}{x}$	4	2	1.3	4

(c)

x	1	2	3	4	5	6
$y = \frac{6}{x}$	6	3	2	1.5	1.2	1

4. (a)

x	-3	-2	-1	0	1	2	3
x^2	9	4	1	0	1	4	9
$2x$	-6	-4	-2	0	2	4	6
$y = x^2 + 2x$	3	0	-1	0	3	8	15

5. (a)

x	-3	-2	-1	0	1	2	3
x^2	9	4	1	0	1	4	9
x	-3	-2	-1	0	1	2	3
$y = x^2 - x$	12	6	2	0	0	2	6

6. (a)

x	-3	-2	-1	0	1	2	3
8	8	8	8	8	8	8	8
x^2	9	4	1	0	1	4	9
$y = 8 - x^2$	-1	4	7	8	7	4	-1

7. (a)

x	-3	-2	-1	0	1	2
x^2	9	4	1	0	1	4
$3x$	-9	-6	-3	0	3	6
5	5	5	5	5	5	5
$y = x^2 - x$	5	3	3	5	9	15

Exercise 13J

1. (b) (i) 25 francs (ii) 75 francs (iii) 95 francs
(c) (i) 50p (ii) £3·50 (iii) £5·50
2. (b) (i) 0·5 ml (ii) 4 ml (iii) 5·5 ml
(c) (i) 4 months (ii) 20 months (iii) 10 months
3. (b) (i) 80p (ii) 240p (iii) 360p
(c) (i) 50 g (ii) 350 g (iii) 400 g
4. (a)

Number of people	10	30	50	70	90
Cost of disco (£)		25	35	45	55	65

(c) (i) £30 (ii) £37·50 (iii) £52·50
(d) (i) 80 (ii) 40 (iii) 60

Exercise 13K

1. (a) 9:00 (b) Dover (c) 1 hour (d) 310 km
(e) (i) 125 km (ii) 70 km (iii) 280 km
(f) 14:00 (g) 2 hours (h) 62·5 km/h

2. (a) 11 km (b) 30 minutes (c) 22 km/h (d) $2\frac{1}{2}$ hours (e) 30 minutes
   (f) 7 km (g) 14 km/h (h) 45 minutes (i) 45 minutes (j) 5·3 km/h
3. (a) 14:00 (b) 14:30 (c) 16:00 (d) 15:30 (e) 120 km
   (f) 60 km (g) 15:00 (h) 60 km/h (i) 120 km/h (j) 30 minutes
4. (a) 15 minutes (b) 6 km (c) 2 km (d) 3 km (e) 8 km
   (f) 10 minutes (g) 1 km (h) 15 minutes (i) 12 km/h (j) 24 km/h

Checkout 13

1. (a) 15, 18 (b) 10, 8 (c) 32, 64 (d) 25, 12·5
2. (a) 5, 10, 15, 20, 25 (b) 6, 7, 8, 9, 10 (c) 0, 1, 2, 3, 4 (d) 8, 11, 14, 17, 20
3. (a) $5n - 1$ (b) $3n + 8$ (c) $2n + 7$ (d) $4n + 3$
4. (b) $(^-1,1)$ and $(^-1,^-1)$, or $(3,1)$ and $(3,^-1)$
5. (a)

x	$^-2$	$^-1$	0	1	2
$y = x + 5$	3	4	5	6	7

(b)

x	$^-2$	$^-1$	0	1	2
$y = x - 5$	$^-7$	$^-6$	$^-5$	$^-4$	$^-3$

(c)

x	$^-2$	$^-1$	0	1	2
$y = 3x + 1$	$^-5$	$^-2$	1	4	7

(d)

x	$^-2$	$^-1$	0	1	2
$y = 2x - 4$	$^-8$	$^-6$	$^-4$	$^-2$	0

6. (a)

x	$^-3$	$^-2$	$^-1$	0	1	2	3
$y = x^2 + 3$	12	7	4	3	4	7	12

(b)

x	$^-3$	$^-2$	$^-1$	0	1	2	3
$y = x^2 - 5$	4	$^-1$	$^-4$	$^-5$	$^-4$	$^-1$	4

(c)

x	$^-3$	$^-2$	$^-1$	0	1	2	3
$y = 9 - x^2$	0	5	8	9	8	5	0

7. (b) (i) £80 (ii) £140 (c) (i) 7 hours (ii) 4 hours
8. (b) (i) 10.40 a.m. (ii) 10.30 a.m. (iii) 9.50 a.m. (iv) 50 km

Revision exercise 13

1. 40, add 9 each time
2. (a) 31, 37 (b) 25
3. (a) subtract 8 from previous term (b) 6 (c) $^-9$
4. (a) 31, 43 (b) add the next even number each time
5. (a) 24, 30 (b) add 6 each time
6. (a) 31 (b) $^-17$
7. (a) 19, 22 (b) add 3 each time (c) 61 (d) $3n + 1$
8. (a)

Input	Output
3	16
$^-2$	6

(b) 19, $4n - 1$

9. (a)

Posts	2	3	4	5	6
Rails	4	8	12	16	20

(b) 56. Subtract 1 from the number of posts and multiply by 4.

10. (a) (i) 31 (ii) add 5 each time (b) $m = 5p + 1$ (c) subtract 1 and divide by 5
11. (c) (0,7)
12. (b) 1 (c) kite (d) 18 square units
13. (a) (i) (7,4) (ii) (4,4) (b) $AC = 6, BD = 4$ (c) $x = 2·5$ (d) 12 square units
14. (a)

x	y
0	3
1	7
2	11
3	15
4	19

476 Answers

15. (a)

x	⁻2	⁻1	0	1	2	3
y	⁻7	⁻4	⁻1	2	5	8

(c) (i) 1·5 (ii) ⁻5·5

16. (a)

w	0	2	4	6	8	10
l	16	20	24	28	32	36

(d) 6·5 kg

17. (a)

x	⁻2	⁻1	0	1	2
$y = x^2 - 1$	3	0	⁻1	0	3

(c) 1·25

18. (a)

x	⁻2	⁻1	0	1	2	3	4
$x^2 + 2$	6	3	2	3	6	11	18

19. (a)

x	⁻3	⁻2	⁻1	0	1	2	3
x^2	9	4	1	0	1	4	9
$y = x^2 - 5$	4	⁻1	⁻4	⁻5	⁻4	⁻1	4

20. (a) DM21·60 (b) £3·50
21. (a) 19°C (b) 10·45
22. (a) 2·2 km (b) 7 minutes (c) He was stationary. (d) C to D
23. (a) He was stationary at the sports centre. (b) He slowed down.
    (c) He arrived home. (d) 12 km

14 Shape and space 4

Check in 14

1. A (2,1), B (5,2), C (1,0), D (3,⁻2), E (5,⁻1), F (0,⁻2), G (⁻1,2), H (0,3), I (⁻3,1), J (⁻4,2), K (⁻2,⁻1), L (⁻4,⁻3), M (⁻5,⁻1), N (⁻2,0)

Exercise 14A

1. A $\binom{+8}{+5}$ B $\binom{+10}{+2}$ C $\binom{+6}{0}$ D $\binom{+7}{-4}$ E $\binom{0}{-3}$
   F $\binom{-6}{-5}$ G $\binom{-6}{0}$ H $\binom{-6}{+4}$ I $\binom{0}{+3}$ J $\binom{-2}{+6}$

2. A $\binom{+7}{+5}$ B $\binom{-7}{+4}$ C $\binom{-1}{+5}$ D $\binom{+3}{+3}$ E $\binom{+7}{0}$
   F $\binom{+7}{-5}$ G $\binom{-5}{+1}$ H $\binom{-7}{-3}$ I $\binom{-1}{-4}$ J $\binom{+3}{-6}$

5. (a) $\binom{-14}{-1}$ (b) $\binom{-8}{0}$ (c) $\binom{-4}{-2}$ (d) $\binom{0}{-5}$ (e) $\binom{0}{-10}$
   (f) $\binom{+14}{+1}$ (g) $\binom{+10}{-1}$ (h) $\binom{+14}{-4}$ (i) $\binom{+14}{-4}$ (j) $\binom{+10}{-10}$
   (k) $\binom{-4}{-4}$ (l) $\binom{+8}{0}$ (m) $\binom{+8}{-5}$ (n) $\binom{-6}{-8}$ (o) $\binom{0}{-9}$
   (p) $\binom{-6}{+1}$ (q) $\binom{+6}{-1}$ (r) $\binom{+4}{+1}$ (s) $\binom{+12}{+4}$ (t) $\binom{-14}{+9}$

   All shapes are congruent to each other.

Exercise 14C

2. (a) 270° (b) 180° (c) 90° (d) 90° (e) 270° (f) 180° (g) 180° (h) 90°
   (i) 270° (j) 270° (k) 180° (l) 90°
3. (a) 90° (b) 270° (c) 180° (d) 270° (e) 180° (f) 90° (g) 90° (h) 180°
   (i) 270° (j) 180° (k) 270° (l) 90°

Data handling 3   477

Exercise 14D
1. There is one vertical line of symmetry.
2. There is one horizontal line of symmetry.
3. There is one vertical line of symmetry.
4. There is one vertical and one horizontal line of symmetry.
5. There is one vertical line of symmetry.
6. There is one vertical and one horizontal line of symmetry.
7. There are six lines of symmetry.
8. There is one vertical and one horizontal line of symmetry.
9. There are six lines of symmetry.
10. There are five lines of symmetry.
11. There are four lines of symmetry.
12. There are two lines of symmetry.
13. There are no lines of symmetry.
14. There are four lines of symmetry.
15. There are no lines of symmetry.
16. There are four lines of symmetry.
17. There are eight lines of symmetry.
18. There is one vertical and one horizontal line of symmetry.

Exercise 14E
1. (a) 1 (b) 2 (c) 4 (d) 6 (e) 4 (f) 2 (g) 4 (h) 5
   (i) 2 (j) 8 (k) 2 (l) 2 (m) 1 (n) 1 (o) 4
2. (a) 1 (b) 2 (c) 1 (d) 2 (e) 2 (f) 1 (g) 2 (h) 1
   (i) 2 (j) 2 (k) 2 (l) 4

Checkout 14
1. A $\begin{pmatrix}+8\\+5\end{pmatrix}$ B $\begin{pmatrix}+7\\0\end{pmatrix}$ C $\begin{pmatrix}+5\\-4\end{pmatrix}$ D $\begin{pmatrix}-4\\-4\end{pmatrix}$ E $\begin{pmatrix}-1\\-5\end{pmatrix}$
3. (a) A 90°, B 180°, C 270°   (b) A 270°, B 180°, C 90°
4. (b) 1, 2, 2, 4

Revision exercise 14
1. (a) (8,8)   (c) (0,2)
4. (a) y-axis   (b) clockwise rotation about (1,1) through 90°
5. (a) vertices at (1,⁻1), (3,⁻1), (3,⁻2), (2,⁻2), (2,⁻4) and (1,⁻4)
   (b) vertices at (0,0), (0,2), (⁻1,2), (⁻1,1), (⁻3,1) and (⁻3,0)
   (c) vertices at (⁻6,1), (⁻6,⁻2), (⁻4,⁻2), (⁻4,⁻1), (⁻5,⁻1) and (⁻5,1)
6. All except the third have rotational symmetry.
7. (b) has a vertical mirror line
8. (a) 4   (b) 2   (c) 4   (d) 8
9. (b), (d) and (f)
10. (a) one vertical line of symmetry   (b) one vertical and one horizontal line of symmetry

15 Data handling 3

Check in 15
1. (a) 30°   (b) 120°

Exercise 15A
1. (a) Lisa:

Distance (miles)	Frequency
1 to 5	3
6 to 10	5
11 to 15	7
16 to 20	3
21 to 25	2

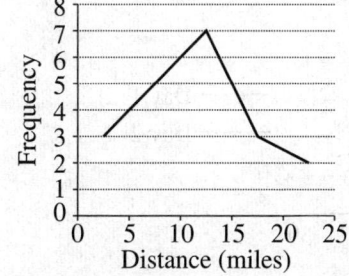

Orla:

Distance (miles)	Frequency
1 to 5	1
6 to 10	9
11 to 15	6
16 to 20	3
21 to 25	1

(b) Lisa: bars with heights 3, 5, 7, 3, 2   Orla: bars with heights 1, 9, 6, 3, 1
(c)

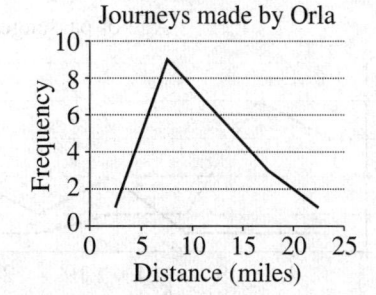

2.

Weight (kilograms)	Frequency (before)	Frequency (after)
76 to 80	1	4
81 to 85	4	4
86 to 90	6	7
91 to 95	7	12
96 to 100	8	3
101 to 105	4	0

3. (a)

Mark	Frequency (9Y)	Frequency (9Q)
0 to 2	1	0
3 to 5	2	0
6 to 8	1	4
9 to 11	5	12
12 to 14	6	10
15 to 17	12	3
18 to 20	3	1

(b) 9Y: bars with heights 1, 2, 1, 5, 6, 12, 3
9Q: bars with heights 0, 0, 4, 12, 10, 3, 1

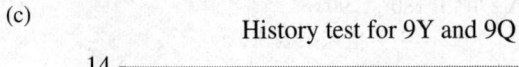

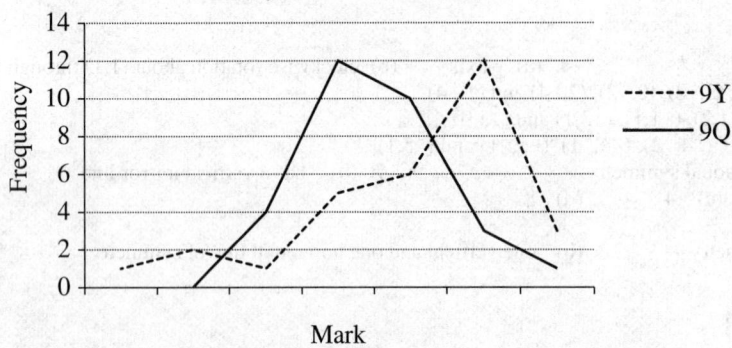

(c) History test for 9Y and 9Q

4. (a)

Age	Frequency (Day 1)	Frequency (Day 2)
0 to 4	6	1
5 to 9	8	1
10 to 14	2	1
15 to 19	2	4
20 to 24	1	2
25 to 29	1	4
30 to 34	0	4
35 to 39	0	3

(b) Day 1: bars with heights 6, 8, 2, 2, 1, 1, 0, 0
Day 2: bars with heights 1, 1, 1, 4, 2, 4, 4, 3

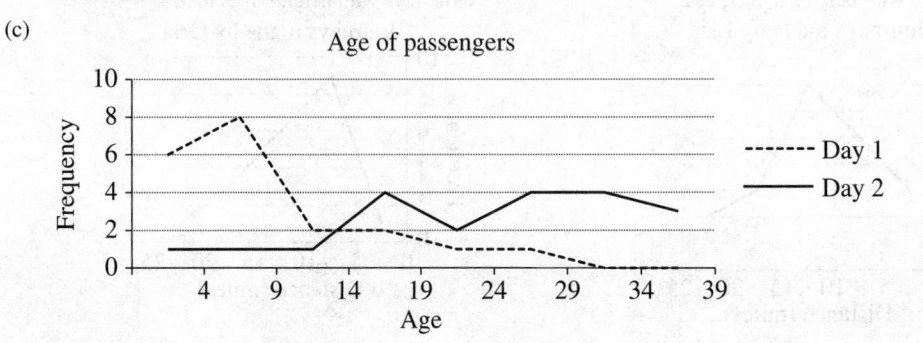

(c) Age of passengers

Exercise 15B

1. (a)

Pets owned	Frequency	Angle
Dog	5	50°
Cat	7	70°
Mouse	10	100°
Fish	8	80°
Hamster	6	60°
Totals	36	360°

2. (a)

Ways of coming to school	Number of pupils	Angle
Parent's car	10	120°
Friend's car	4	48°
Bus	2	24°
Walk	8	96°
Cycle	6	72°
Totals	30	360°

3. (b)

Type of spending	Frequency	Angle
Highways and planning	£14	28°
Sports and recreation	£28	56°
Environmental health	£32	64°
Housing	£27	54°
Administration	£47	94°
Emergencies	£32	64°
Totals	£180	360°

4. (b)

Expenditure	Factory A	Angle
Wages	£30	120°
Raw materials	£40	160°
Overheads	£20	80°
Totals	£90	360°

Expenditure	Factory B	Angle
Wages	£25	100°
Raw materials	£35	140°
Overheads	£30	120°
Totals	£90	360°

5. (c)

Season	Visitor 1999 (thousands)	Angle
Spring	7	63°
Summer	18	162°
Autumn	9	81°
Winter	6	54°
Totals	40	360°

Season	Visitor 2000 (thousands)	Angle
Spring	8	48°
Summer	31	186°
Autumn	14	84°
Winter	7	42°
Totals	60	360°

6. (a)

Flavour	Number of first choices (Test 1)	Angle
Strawberry	54	108°
Raspberry	47	94°
Orange	21	42°
Apple	23	46°
Pear	35	70°
Totals	180	360°

Flavour	Number of first choices (Test 2)	Angle
Strawberry	32	64°
Raspberry	44	88°
Orange	34	68°
Apple	40	80°
Pear	30	60°
Totals	180	360°

Exercise 15C

3. (a)

Brand	Votes	Percentage
Pork	5	20%
Pork with apple	10	40%
Pork with herbs	6	24%
Vegetarian	4	16%
Totals	25	100%

4. (a)

Activity	Number of first choices	Percentage
Football	30	20%
Snooker	15	10%
Table tennis	45	30%
Aerobics	60	40%
Totals	150	100%

5.

Spending idea	Votes from Year 7	Percentage
Computer for the library	48	24%
Sports equipment	84	42%
Staging for school productions	46	23%
Display boards in the school entrance	22	11%
Totals	200	100%

Spending idea	Votes from Year 7	Percentage
Computer for the library	45	25%
Sports equipment	63	35%
Staging for school productions	54	30%
Display boards in the school entrance	18	10%
Totals	180	100%

6.

Finish	Choices (pupils)	Percentage
Polished wood	6	10%
Stained wood	36	60%
Painted	18	30%
Totals	60	100%

Finish	Choices (adults)	Percentage
Polished wood	15	25%
Stained wood	24	40%
Painted	21	35%
Totals	60	100%

Exercise 15D

1. (a) 12%   (b) large   (c) 10   (d) 8   (e) bars with heights: 12, 32, 40, 16
2. (a) 135° (b) 6 hours (c) 3 hours (d) 9 hours (e) bars with heights: 6, 9, 3, 3, 3
3. (a) 78°   (b) 4°   (c) 15 mm (d) 19·5 mm (e) bars with heights: 20, 15, 12, 10, 14, 19·5
4. (a) 25%   (b) 60   (c) 15   (d) 18   (e) 21
   (f) bars with heights: 6, 21, 15, 18
5. (a) 80°   (b) 2   (c) 3   (d) 8   (e) bars with heights: 4, 8, 3, 2, 1
6. (a) 20%   (b) 10   (c) 5   (d) 15   (e) 50
   (f) bars with heights: 20, 5, 10, 15

Checkout 15

1. (a)

Distance miles	Frequency (Lisa)
1 to 5	7
6 to 10	7
11 to 15	4
16 to 20	2
21 to 25	0

Distance miles	Frequency (Orla)
1 to 5	5
6 to 10	5
11 to 15	5
16 to 20	1
21 to 25	4

(b) Lisa: bars with heights 7, 7, 4, 2, 0   Orla: bars with heights 5, 5, 5, 1, 4

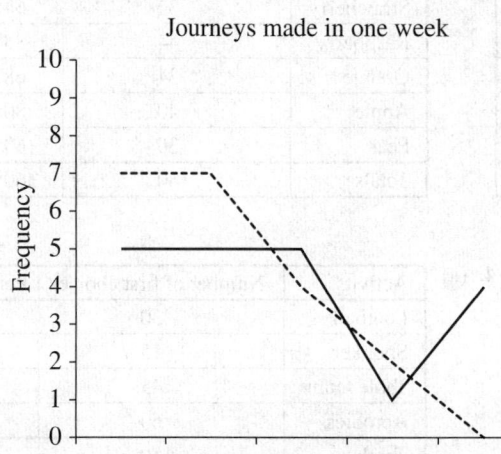

(c) Journeys made in one week

2.

Season	Visitors (thousands)	Angle
Spring	10	60°
Summer	25	150°
Autumn	16	96°
Winter	9	54°
Totals	60	360°

3.

Topping	Votes	Percentage
Cheese and tomato	4	16%
Pepperoni and ham	12	48%
Garlic and mushroom	3	12%
Roast vegetable	6	24%
Totals	25	100%

4. (a) (i) 50%   (ii) 48   (iii) bars with heights: 20, 32, 48, 100
  (b) (i) 54°   (ii) 9°   (iii) 13   (iv) 7   (v) 9   (vi) bars with heights: 6, 5, 9, 13, 7

Revision exercise 15

1. (a) (i) 0   (ii) Mirror   (b) TES has a sector angle of 0°.
  (c) (i) 210   (ii) Wednesday and Thursday

2. (a)

Time minutes	1 to 10	11 to 20	21 to 30	31 to 40	41 to 50
Frequency	8	11	15	2	4

(b) Patient waiting times (graph)   (c) 21 to 30 minutes

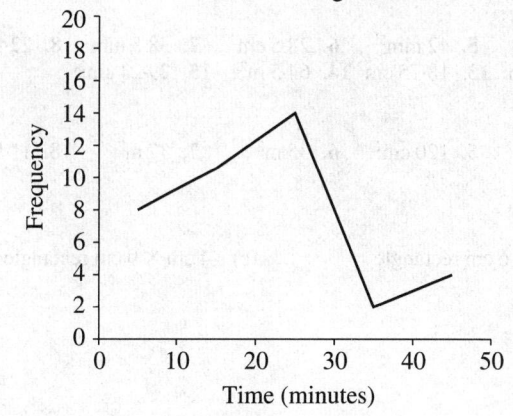

3. (a) 120   (b) (i) 40°   (ii) $\frac{1}{9}$
4. (a) £960   (b) £200
5. (a) (i) Britain   (ii) 18   (b) 12·8%
6. (a)

Format	LPs	Cassettes	Singles	CDs	Music video
Percentage	1	18	11	67	3
Angle	3·6	64·8	39·6	241·2	10·8

7.

Activity	Frequency	Angle
School 6th Form	81	162°
F.E. College	40	80°
Training	28	56°
Employment	12	24°
Other	19	38°

8. (a)

Items	Amount spent	Angle
Bus fares	£13	52°
Going out	£24	96°
Clothes	£30	120°
CDs	£15	60°
Other	£8	32°
Totals	£90	360°

(d) $\frac{1}{3}$

16 Shape and space 5

Check in 16

1. (a) 7   (b) 12·3   (c) 31   (d) 36   (e) 15·2   (f) 93   (g) 4·08   (h) 79·8
2. (a) 6   (b) 14   (c) 8·7   (d) 17·5   (e) 20·5   (f) 13·7   (g) 43·65   (h) 28·35

Exercise 16A
1. 10 cm 2. 14 cm 3. 16 cm 4. 18 cm 5. 12 cm 6. 16 cm 7. 6·8 cm 8. 10·2 cm
9. 14·8 cm 10. 11·2 cm 11. 13·6 cm 12. 17·2 cm 13. 14·8 cm 14. 13·2 cm 15. 16·8 cm

Exercise 16B
1. 4 cm^2 2. 8 cm^2 3. 10 cm^2 4. 7 cm^2 5. 9 cm^2 6. 7 cm^2 7. 8 cm^2 8. 5 cm^2
9. 8 cm^2 10. 10 cm^2 11. 8 cm^2 12. 10 cm^2 13. 9 cm^2 14. 9 cm^2 15. 8 cm^2

Exercise 16C
1. 6·8 m^2 2. 12·6 cm^2 3. 31·5 mm^2 4. 25 m^2 5. 35 cm^2 6. 19 mm^2 7. 77 cm^2 8. 0·6 m^2
9. 25 m^2 10. 1 cm^2, 100 mm^2 11. 100 12. 1 m^2, 10 000 cm^2 13. 10 000

Exercise 16D
1. 36 cm^2 2. 39 cm^2 3. 128 cm^2 4. 168 mm^2 5. 41 m^2 6. 112 m^2 7. 78 cm^2 8. 10 m^2 9. 650 cm^2

Exercise 16E
1. 9 cm^2 2. 24 cm^2 3. 80 mm^2 4. 17·5 m^2 5. 83 cm^2 6. 780 mm^2 7. 31 m^2 8. 90 cm^2
9. 15 750 mm^2 10. 17·28 cm^2 11. 25·2 m^2 12. 66 mm^2 13. 79·9 m^2 14. 270 cm^2 15. 13 m^2

Exercise 16F
1. 20 cm^2 2. 18 cm^2 3. 49 mm^2 4. 7·5 m^2 5. 42 mm^2 6. 28·5 cm^2 7. 38·5 mm^2 8. 22·5 cm^2
9. 1·2 m^2 10. 1·5 m^2 11. 1·8 m^2 12. 27·5 mm^2 13. 18·75 cm^2 14. 64·5 m^2 15. 29·24 cm^2

Exercise 16G
1. 15 cm^2 2. 1·5 m^2 3. 1·875 m^2 4. 108 mm^2 5. 120 cm^2 6. 35 m^2 7. 37 m^2 8. 11·5 m^2
9. 21 m^2 10. 27 cm^2 11. 1 020 cm^2 12. 480 m^2
13. (a) 25 m^2 (b) 6·25 m^2 (c) 18·75 m^2
14. (a) 2·8 m^2 (b) 8·4 m^2 (c) £21
15. (a) 4 cm × 8 cm rectangle (b) 5 cm × 6 cm rectangle (c) 4 cm × 9 cm rectangle

Checkout 16
1. (a) 17 cm^2 (b) 11·5 cm^2
2. (a) 30 cm^2 (b) 5 m^2
3. 36 m^2 4. 3·6 m^2
5. (a) 60 mm^2 (b) 125 cm^2
6. 53 cm^2

Revision exercise 16
1. (a) 17 cm^2 (b) 20 cm
2. (a) 15 m^2 (b) 17·5 m^2 (c) 12 m^2
3. about 40 cm^2
4. (a) 32 m (b) 63 m^2
5. (a) 6 square yards (b) £82·50
6. (a) 24 m^2 (b) 26 m^2 (c) 25 × 20
7. (a) 36 m^2 (b) £29·05 (c) 53 m^2 (d) (i) 5 (ii) £517·50
8. (a) 6 cm^2
9. (a) 200 m (b) (i) 1 600 m^2 (ii) 600 m^2

17 Data handling 4

Check in 17
1. (a) cat's face (b) rectangle (c) square (d) square

Exercise 17B
1. positively correlated 2. negatively correlated 3. positively correlated 4. not correlated
5. negatively correlated 6. positively correlated 7. not correlated 8. positively correlated
9. negatively correlated 10. not correlated

Exercise 17C
1. (a) coordinates at (7,0) (7,2) (8,3) (8,2) (9,3) (9,4) (10,6) (10,2) (11,5) (11,8)   (b) positive correlation
2. (a) coordinates at (1,10) (1,6) (3,8) (3,6) (4,5) (4,6) (6,4) (7,2) (10,2) (12,1)   (b) negative correlation
3. (a) coordinates at (1,9) (1,8) (2,7) (2,5) (3,6) (4,3) (4,4) (5,4) (6,2) (7,2)   (b) negative correlation
4. (a) coordinates at (24,14) (25,12) (31,18) (33,16) (35,12) (42,20) (46,22) (48,24) (51,26) (56,30)
    (b) positive correlation
5. (a) coordinates at (1,15) (1,14) (1·5,12) (1·5,13) (2,15) (2,11) (2,10) (2·5,9) (3,9) (3·5,8)   (b) negative correlation

Exercise 17D
1. (a) positive
    (b) (i) 118 miles/h   (ii) 145 miles/h   (iii) 160 miles/h   (iv) 100 miles/h
    (c) (i) 1 000 cm^3 (ii) 2 750 cm^3 (iii) 300 cm^3 (iv) 1 500 cm^3

Checkout 17
2. (a) positively correlated   (b) negatively correlated   (c) not correlated
3. (a) coordinates at (4,24) (4,22) (5,20) (6,18) (6,20) (7,17) (8,19) (9,15) (10,16) (11,14)   (b) negative correlation

Revision exercise 17
1. (a) coordinates at (20,14) (32,21) (15,11) (6,4) (25,15) (16,13)   (b) positive correlation
2. (a) coordinates at (172,56) (168,58) (149,44) (164,63) (160,57) (176,74) (169,68) (180,71) (172,58) (162,60) (171,68) (153,46) (162,49)   (b) A   (c) 165 cm
3. (a) coordinates at (180,33) (190,30) (178,33) (160,35) (174,36) (182,32) (174,34) (186,28)
    (b) The taller they were the quicker they ran.

18 Shape and space 6

Check in 18
1. (a) 18·6   (b) 43·4   (c) 13·95   (d) 31·4   (e) 37·68   (f) 16·328   (g) 78·5   (h) 200·96   (i) 12·56

Exercise 18A
3. (a) 10 cm   (b) 14 cm   (c) 5 cm   (d) 12·8 cm   (e) 18·6 cm
4. (a) 10 cm   (b) 16 cm   (c) 3·5 cm   (d) 7·5 cm   (e) 8·3 cm

Exercise 18B
1. (a) 12·4 cm   (b) 18·6 cm   (c) 6·2 cm   (d) 24·8 mm   (e) 9·3 m   (f) 7·75 cm
2. (a) 26·38 mm   (b) 3·14 m   (c) 1·57 m   (d) 157 cm   (e) 628 mm   (f) 3·77 m
3. (a) 31 cm   (b) 49·6 mm   (c) 21·7 m   (d) 7·4 m   (e) 74·4 m   (f) 27·9 cm
4. (a) 43·96 cm   (b) 47·1 mm   (c) 37·68 m   (d) 15·07 m   (e) 3·14 m   (f) 314 mm
5. (a) 219·8 cm   (b) 2 198 cm   6. (a) 22 miles   (b) 3 hours

Exercise 18C
1. (a) 12·4 cm^2 (b) 77·5 mm^2 (c) 111·6 m^2 (d) 17·9 m^2 (e) 0·78 cm^2 (f) 7 750 mm^2
2. (a) 3·14 cm^2 (b) 201 mm^2 (c) 38·5 m^2 (d) 4·5 m^2 (e) 452 m^2 (f) 63·6 cm^2
3. (a) 297 m^2 (b) 63·6 m^2 (c) 233 m^2 (d) 16
4. (a) 2·2 m^2 (b) 0·5 m^2 (c) 0·25 m^2 (d) 1·9 m^2
5. (a) 78·5 cm^2 (b) 314 cm^2 (c) The area of the big box label is four times the area of the small box label.

Exercise 18D
1. (a) 222 cm^2 (b) 454 mm^2 (c) 20 m^2
    (d) 19·6 m^2 (e) 63 cm^2 (f) 288 mm^2
2. (a) 700 cm^2 (b) 600 cm^2 (c) 14p, 12p
3. 150 cm^2
4. (a) 96 cm^2 (b) 2 400 cm^2 (c) 96p

Exercise 18E
1. 12 cm^3 2. 8 cm^3 3. 6 cm^3 4. 16 cm^3 5. 12 cm^3 6. 36 cm^3
7. 27 cm^3 8. 16 cm^3 9. 20 cm^3 10. 18 cm^3 11. 14 cm^3 12. 16 cm^3

Exercise 18F
1. (a) 60 cm³ (b) 72 cm³ (c) 486 cm³ (d) 9 m³ (e) 9 m³ (f) 0·48 m³
2. (a) 40 cm³ (b) 480 cm³ (c) 6 cm
3. (a) 40 000 cm³ (b) 40 litres (c) £30
4. (a) 864 cm³ (b) 810 cm³ (c) 324 cm³
5. (a) cube (b) 1 cm³, 1 000 mm³
6. 1 000   7. 750   8. 1 m³, 1 000 000 cm³   9. 1 000 000

Exercise 18G
1. (a) 75·3 m³ (b) 9 420 mm³ (c) 603 cm³
   (d) 0·785 m³ (e) 25·1 cm³ (f) 25 120 mm³
2. (a) 36 cm³ (b) 70 cm³ (c) 1 440 mm³
   (d) 1·5 m³ (e) 9 m³ (f) 2·25 m³
3. (a) 48 m² (b) 15 m² (c) 63 m² (d) 1 260 m³
4. (a) 40 m² (b) 25 m² (c) 1 625 m³
5. (a) 62 800 cm³ (b) 502

Checkout 18
2. (a) (i) 24·8 cm (ii) 155 mm (b) (i) 62·8 cm (ii) 753·6 mm
3. (a) 201 cm³ (b) 1 256 mm³
4. 430 mm³   5. 24 cm³   6. 375 m³   7. 151 cm³, 0·96 m³

Revision exercise 18
1. (a) 37·7 cm (b) 15·6 cm   2. 4·5 cm
3. (a) 18·8 m (b) 7·7 m²   4. 60 m³
5. (a) 64 (b) 768 cm³
6. (a) (ii) 390 cm² (b) (ii) 20 cm² (c) 2 592 cm³
7. (a) 84 672 cm³ (b) 74 088 cm³ (c) 42³ = 74 088

19 Data handling 5

Check in 19
1. (a) $\frac{2}{3}$ (b) $\frac{1}{2}$ (c) $\frac{4}{5}$ (d) $\frac{5}{6}$ (e) $\frac{1}{5}$
   (f) $\frac{1}{3}$ (g) $\frac{2}{3}$ (h) $\frac{4}{5}$ (i) $\frac{1}{7}$ (j) $\frac{3}{4}$
2. (a) 0·5 (b) 0·25 (c) 0·4 (d) 0·75 (e) 0·625
   (f) 0·7 (g) 0·333 (h) 0·667 (i) 0·5 (j) 0·571
3. (a) 25% (b) 75% (c) 50% (d) 12·5% (e) 33·3%
   (f) 14·7% (g) 90% (h) 5% (i) 45% (j) 9%

Exercise 19A
1. (a) $\frac{1}{2}$, 0·5, 50% (b) $\frac{1}{2}$, 0·5, 50%
2. (a) $\frac{1}{6}$, 0·167, 16·7% (b) $\frac{1}{2}$, 0·5, 50% (c) $\frac{2}{3}$, 0·667, 66·7% (d) $\frac{1}{3}$, 0·333, 33·3%
3. (a) $\frac{1}{5}$, 0·2, 20% (b) $\frac{3}{10}$, 0·3, 30% (c) $\frac{1}{2}$, 0·5, 50% (d) $\frac{1}{2}$, 0·5, 50%
4. (a) $\frac{3}{10}$, 0·3, 30% (b) $\frac{1}{10}$, 0·1, 10% (c) $\frac{2}{5}$, 0·4, 40% (d) $\frac{3}{10}$, 0·3, 30% (e) $\frac{1}{2}$, 0·5, 50%
5. (a) $\frac{1}{4}$, 0·25, 25% (b) $\frac{3}{4}$, 0·75, 75%
6. (a) $\frac{7}{15}$, 0·467, 46·7% (b) $\frac{8}{15}$, 0·533, 53·3% (c) $\frac{1}{10}$, 0·1, 10% (d) $\frac{1}{6}$, 0·167, 16·7%
7. (a) $\frac{1}{4}$, 0·25, 25% (b) $\frac{2}{5}$, 0·4, 40% (c) $\frac{7}{20}$, 0,35, 35% (d) $\frac{3}{5}$, 0·6, 60%
8. (a) $\frac{3}{5}$, 0·6, 60% (b) $\frac{9}{25}$, 0·36, 36% (c) $\frac{1}{25}$, 0·04, 4% (d) $\frac{16}{25}$, 0·64, 64%
9. (a) $\frac{1}{2}$, 0·5, 50% (b) $\frac{1}{13}$, 0·077, 7·7% (c) $\frac{1}{26}$, 0·038, 3·8% (d) $\frac{1}{4}$, 0·25, 25% (e) $\frac{1}{52}$, 0·019, 1·9%
10. (a) $\frac{1}{5}$, 0·2, 20% (b) $\frac{3}{10}$, 0·3, 30% (c) $\frac{1}{10}$, 0·1, 10% (d) $\frac{2}{5}$, 0·4, 40%
11. (a) $\frac{1}{15}$, 0·067, 6·7% (b) $\frac{1}{3}$, 0·333, 33·3% (c) $\frac{1}{5}$, 0·2, 20% (d) $\frac{11}{15}$, 0·733, 73·3%
12. (a) $\frac{1}{4}$, 0·25, 25% (b) $\frac{1}{20}$, 0·05, 5% (c) $\frac{3}{5}$, 0·6, 60% (d) $\frac{4}{5}$, 0·8, 80%

Exercise 19B
1. $\frac{4}{5}$ 2. 0·35   3. (a) 1 (b) $\frac{3}{4}$ (c) 0
4. $\frac{7}{8}$ 5. 25%   6. 88%   7. 0·02   8. 78%

9. (a) 1 (b) 55% (c) 0
10. $\frac{23}{30}$ 11. $\frac{4}{9}$ 12. 40% 13. 0·45 14. 0·2 15. 0·3

Exercise 19C

1. (a) $\frac{3}{10}$ (b) $\frac{7}{10}$ 2. (a) $\frac{1}{10}$
3. (a) $\frac{3}{8}$ (b) $\frac{3}{8}$ (c) $\frac{1}{2}$
4. (a) $\frac{1}{5}$ (b) $\frac{4}{5}$ 5. (a) 0·1
6. (a) 0·8 (b) 0·2
7. (a) 70% 8. (a) 40%

Exercise 19D

1. (a) cheese with white bread, cheese with wholemeal bread, ham with white bread, ham with wholemeal bread, chicken with white bread, chicken with wholemeal bread, prawns with white bread, prawns with wholemeal bread
   (b) 8 (c) $\frac{1}{8}$
2. (a) red top with red skirt, red top with white skirt, red top with gold skirt, blue top with red skirt, blue top with white skirt, blue top with gold skirt, black top with red skirt, black top with white skirt, black top with gold skirt, silver top with red skirt, silver top with white skirt, silver top with gold skirt
   (b) 12 (c) $\frac{1}{6}$
3. (a)

	R	R	W
R	RR	RR	RW
R	RR	RR	RW
R	WR	WR	WW

   (b) 4
   (c) (i) $\frac{4}{9}$ (ii) $\frac{1}{9}$ (iii) $\frac{4}{9}$

5. (a)

+	1	2	3	4
1	2	3	4	5
2	3	4	5	6
3	4	5	6	7
4	5	6	7	8

   (b) 4
   (c) $\frac{1}{4}$
   (d) (i) $\frac{1}{16}$ (ii) $\frac{1}{8}$ (iii) $\frac{3}{16}$ (iv) $\frac{3}{8}$ (v) $\frac{7}{16}$ (vi) $\frac{1}{2}$

6. (a)

+	1	3	5	7
2	3	5	7	9
4	5	7	9	11
6	7	9	11	13
8	9	11	13	15

   (b) 2
   (c) $\frac{1}{8}$
   (d) (i) $\frac{1}{16}$ (ii) $\frac{3}{16}$ (iii) $\frac{1}{4}$ (iv) $\frac{3}{16}$ (v) 1 (vi) 0

7. (a)

+	1	2	3	4	5	6
1	2	3	4	5	6	7
2	3	4	5	6	7	8
3	4	5	6	7	8	9
4	5	6	7	8	9	10
5	6	7	8	9	10	11
6	7	8	9	10	11	12

   (b) 6
   (c) $\frac{1}{6}$
   (d) (i) $\frac{1}{18}$ (ii) $\frac{5}{36}$ (iii) $\frac{1}{9}$ (iv) $\frac{1}{9}$ (v) 0 (vi) $\frac{1}{2}$

Checkout 19

1. (a) $\frac{1}{5}$ (b) $\frac{1}{10}$ (c) $\frac{2}{5}$ (d) $\frac{3}{5}$
2. (a) 0·4 (b) 0 (c) 1
3. (a) $\frac{1}{5}$ (b) $\frac{4}{5}$
4. (a)

	P	P	R
P	PP	PP	PR
R	RP	RP	RR
R	RP	RP	RR

   (b) 2 (c) (i) $\frac{2}{9}$ (ii) $\frac{2}{9}$ (iii) $\frac{5}{9}$

Revision exercise 19

1. (a) $\frac{1}{4}$ (b) $\frac{7}{20}$
2. (a) $\frac{8}{33}$ (b) $\frac{10}{33}$ (c) $\frac{6}{11}$
3. (a) $\frac{1}{7}$ (b) $\frac{6}{7}$
4. $\frac{11}{12}$
5. (a) 0·8 (b) 6
6. 0·17
7. (a) (i) 0·8 (ii) 70 (b) $\frac{3}{5}$ (c) positions: A at 0·3, B at 1
8. (a) 25p (b) 35p (c) $\frac{1}{8}$
9. (a) 4 (b) Cross at 0, it is impossible to get a score of less than four. (c) Cross at $\frac{3}{4}$.
10. (a) 3 (b) 4 (c) Cross showing probability of $\frac{1}{8}$.
11. GP, GC, GB, HP, HC, HB, SP, SC, SB, EP, EC, EB
12. (a) (i) $\frac{8}{13}$ (ii) $\frac{5}{13}$ (b) YY, YG, GY, GG
13. (a) THH, HTT, THT, TTG, TTT; $\frac{3}{8}$
    (b) (i)

5	6	7	8	9	10
4	5	6	7	8	9
3	4	5	6	7	8
2	3	4	5	6	7
1	2	3	4	5	6
	1	2	3	4	5

(ii) $\frac{1}{25}$ (iii) $\frac{6}{25}$ (iv) 48

14. (a)

	1	2	3	4	5
2	3	4	5	6	7
3	4	5	6	7	8
4	5	6	7	8	9
5	6	7	8	9	10
6	7	8	9	10	11

(b) (i) $\frac{1}{25}$ (ii) $\frac{6}{25}$

Index

acute angles, 38–40, 52
addition
   algebra, 104–5
   decimals, 166–9
   fractions, 247–8, 249, 259
   negative numbers, 23–4, 28
   tables, 11–12
   whole numbers, 12–14, 17–18, 28
algebra, 103–24, 220–39, 268–306
   addition, 104–5
   division, 105–6
   multiplication, 105–6
   rules, 220
   subtraction, 104–5
angles, 36, 177–82, 190–3
   drawing, 40–1
   measuring, 38–40, 52, 332
   naming, 41–2, 52
approximations, 5–10, 27–8
   decimals, 163–6, 173
area, 358–70

balance, 25
bank accounts, overdrawn, 25–6
bar charts, 59–62, 65, 333–7, 347–8
bearings, 48–51, 53
BoDMAS, 110–12
brackets
   equations, 232–3
   expanding, 223–5, 235–6

calculator operations, 211–13
centimetres, 199, 214
centre of rotation, 314, 326
circles, 387–92, 401–2
circumference, 387–90, 401–2
compound shapes, 367–9, 370
cones, 127
congruent shapes, 308
conversions, 213–14
coordinates, 276–82, 299, 307, 374
correlation, 376–83
coursework, 425–34
cubes, 126
   volume, 395–6, 402
cuboids, 126, 132, 386
   surface area, 393
   volume, 396–8, 402
cylinders, 126, 132

data
   collecting, 57–8
   grouped, 333–7
   handling, 56–69, 135–54, 332–54, 374–85, 406–24, 430–4
   tables, 145–8, 149
decagons, 188, 192
decimals
   adding, 166–9
   approximations, 163–6, 173
   dividing, 202–5, 209–10, 212–13, 214–15
   and fractions, 255, 260, 406
   multiplying, 199–202, 206–8, 211–12, 214–15, 355, 386
   ordering, 157–8, 160–1
   and percentages, 255, 260, 406
   place value, 156–7, 158–60, 161–2
   recurring, 210
   subtracting, 169–71
degrees, 176
denominator, 247
deposits, 25
diameter, 387–92, 401–2
distance–time graphs, 295–8, 300
distributions, 136–7, 148
division, 79–80, 84–7, 355
   algebra, 105–6
   decimals, 202–5, 209–10, 212–13, 214–15
   negative numbers, 221–2, 235
   ratios, 93–5, 97
   shortcuts, 74–6, 81–2, 96–7
dodecagons, 188, 192

elevations, 131–2, 133
enlargements, 321–4, 327
equations
   with brackets, 232–3
   curved, 287–90
   linear, 282–7
   operations, 231–2, 236
   solving, 226–35, 236, 268
equilateral triangles, 128, 183, 191
equivalent fractions, 243–5, 259
even numbers, 87–8, 97
expressions, 109
   factorising, 225–6, 236
   simplifying, 117–20, 121, 224
exterior angles, 187

factorisation, 225–6, 236
factors, 87–8, 97
formulae, 107–9, 121, 268
   changing subject of, 234–5
   finding, 427–8
   for sequences, 270–1, 299
   substitution, 115–17, 121
fractional enlargements, 322–4, 327
fractions, 240–52
   adding, 247–8, 249, 259
   and decimals, 255, 260, 406
   multiplying, 250–2, 260
   and percentages, 252
   simplifying, 246, 259, 406
   subtracting, 248–9
frequency polygons, 333–7, 347–8
frequency tables, 59, 333, 347–9
front elevation, 131–2, 133

graphs, 374
   of curved equations, 287–90, 299
   of linear equations, 282–7, 299
   of relationships, 291–4, 299
grouped data, 333–7

heptagons, 192
hexagons, 187, 192
highest common factor (HCF), 88–9
hundredths, 158–61, 165–6, 172

imperial units, 213–14
improper fractions, 243, 259
indices, substitution, 112–14
investigations, 425–30
isometric drawings, 129–30, 132–3
isosceles triangles, 183, 191

letters, as quantities, 103–6, 120
like terms, 117–18
linear equations, 282–7
lines, 177–8
lines of best fit, 381–2
lines of symmetry, 317, 326
litres, 201, 214
lowest common multiple (LCM), 89

mean, 136–7, 143–5, 148
median, 138–40, 143–5, 149
metric units, 213–14
millilitres, 201, 214

Index

millimetres, 199, 214
mixed numbers, 243, 259
mode, 141–5, 149
multiples, 87–8, 97
multiplication, 78–9, 82–4
    algebra, 105–6
    decimals, 199–202, 206–8, 211–12, 214–15, 355, 386
    fractions, 250–2, 260
    negative numbers, 221, 235
    shortcuts, 71–3, 96–7
    tables, 77–8, 240
    terms, 222–3

negative numbers
    adding, 23–4, 28
    dividing, 221–2, 235
    multiplying, 221, 235
    substitution, 114–15, 121
    subtracting, 24–5, 28
nets, 127–9, 132, 386, 393, 402
nonagons, 188, 192
numbers, 1–33, 70–101, 155–75, 198–219, 240–67
    rounding, 5–10, 27
    writing, 3–5
    see also negative numbers; whole numbers
numerator, 247

obtuse angles, 38–40, 52
octagons, 188, 192
odd numbers, 87–8, 97
opposite angles, 179, 190

parallel lines, 180–1, 191
parallelograms, 185, 192
    area, 363–5, 370
patterns, and sequences, 273–6
pentagons, 187, 192
percentages, 253–9
    and decimals, 255, 260, 406
    and fractions, 252
perimeters, 119–20, 356–7, 369
pi (π), 388, 402
pictograms, 63–4, 65
pie chart scales, 342–5, 349
pie charts, 241, 337–47, 349

place value, 2–3, 27
    decimals, 156–7, 158–60, 161–2
plans, 131–2, 133
polygons, 187–90, 192–3
powers, substitution, 112–14
prime numbers, 87–8, 97
prisms, 126
    volume, 398–401, 402
probability, 407–19
probability scales, 412–14, 419
problem solving, 425–30
protractors, 37, 52, 337–41
pyramids, 127

quadrilaterals, 184–6, 192
quantities, letters as, 103–6, 120
questionnaires, 430–4

radius, 387–92, 401–2
range, 136–7, 143–5, 148
ratios, 89–95, 97
    scaling, 91–3, 97
raw data, 59
rectangles, 119, 186, 192
    area, 360–3, 369–70
recurring decimals, 210, 215
reflectional symmetry, 317–18, 326
reflections, 311–13, 325
reflex angles, 38
relationships, graphs of, 291–4, 299
rhombuses, 185, 192
right angles, 190
rotational symmetry, 318–20, 326
rotations, 314–16, 326
rounding, 5–10, 27, 163–6, 173, 212, 216

scale drawings, 45–8, 53
scaling, 321–4
    ratios, 91–3, 97
scatter diagrams, 377–81, 383
sequences, 269–76, 298–9
shapes, 34–55, 125–34, 176–97, 307–31, 355–73, 386–405
    compound, 367–9, 370
    congruent, 308
    enlargements, 321–4, 327

reflections, 311–13, 325
rotations, 314–16, 326
translating, 308–11, 325
side elevation, 131–2, 133
spheres, 127
square roots, 95–6
squares, 95–6, 126, 186, 192
stem-and-leaf plots, 140–1
substitution, 109–17, 121
subtraction
    algebra, 104–5
    decimals, 169–71
    fractions, 248–9
    negative numbers, 24–5, 28
    whole numbers, 14–16, 19–20, 28
surface area, cuboids, 393
surveys, 57–8, 65, 430–4
symmetry, 317–20

tables, 145–8, 149
    addition, 11–12
tally marks, 59–62, 65
temperature, 20–3, 28
tenths, 156–8, 164–5, 172
terms, 117–18
    multiplying, 222–3
    in sequences, 269–76, 299
thousandths, 161–2, 172
three-dimensional shapes, 126–7, 132
translations, 308–11, 325
trapeziums, 185, 192
triangles, 181–4, 191, 192
    area, 365–6, 370
    drawing, 43–5, 52, 125
turns, 34–6, 52
two-dimensional shapes, 126–7, 132

units, 213–14

variables, 375–6, 382
volume, 395–401, 402

whole numbers
    adding, 12–14, 17–18, 28
    place value, 2–3, 27
    subtracting, 14–16, 19–20, 28
withdrawals, 25